lonely planet

Perth &
Western Australia

Terry Carter, Lara Dunston
Rebecca Chau, Virginia Jealous

On the Road

TERRY CARTER Coordinating author
During the gruelling road trip through the North we passed an untold number of brilliant surfing breaks, some well-known, some secret. However, the Margaret River area (p123), Western Australia's (WA's) spiritual home of surfing, is something else. The beauty of WA's wild coast with its fine wines and fab food is unmatched… Australia, you bloody beauty!

LARA DUNSTON Coordinating author
First day of research, we swept north through sunny Perth cruising an easy 270km through the Swan Valley to Cervantes. Nothing prepared me for the magic of the Pinnacles (p173) at sunset. Sublime, I thought. If the other landscapes and light are as spectacular as this, it will be bliss. And 13,000km later? They were.

VIRGINIA JEALOUS A cold, clear day and salty Lake Ballard (p161) morphed into a snowfield, crunching slightly underfoot and glary enough to make me squint behind sunglasses. In mid-horizon floated a mirage of salt shimmering into water, the horizontal planes of lake and sky broken by silhouettes of sculpted steel. Magic.

REBECCA CHAU The ferry to Rottnest (p91) is always full of promise. The trip back (pictured) is merely a chance to sleep, when pictures of the island's clownfish flutter beneath the eyelids. An author never nods on the job for long, though, so soon enough I was up in the best spot on the ferry: the back deck, for full sea-spray and sun.

See full author bios, page 282

Destination Perth & Western Australia

Western Australia (WA) is often labelled the last frontier, and with its immense dimensions, meagre population and Perth's distinction as the world's most isolated capital city, perhaps it's true. If it is, it certainly is a spectacular finale to what the planet has to offer. With brilliant sunshine, vivid landscapes, abundant and unique fauna and flora and remote rugged coastlines, WA is a delight for those who want to explore it at a leisurely pace.

Up north in the Kimberley, you'll encounter wide open spaces that shrewdly conceal striking gorges and waterfalls, ancient rock formations, and the enigmatic pearling town of Broome. At the other end of the state, the south is a playground of white-sand beaches, expanses of springtime wildflowers and lush green forests that teem with life.

At Margaret River, surfers carve world-class waves, while vignerons craft world-class wines, complemented by the inventive gourmet grub of the town's restaurants. Along the coast, wildlife-watching is extraordinary. Dive with the world's largest fish, interact with dolphins and seals, and enjoy the kangaroos, emus and reptiles that rule the russet red Outback.

However, it's not all animals and landscapes. Perth and neighbouring Fremantle are cosmopolitan cities, yet both retain a languorously laid-back feel, perhaps inspired by having so many fantastic beaches and parks at their doorstep.

And, to top it off, WA is big enough to really get lost in. You can wander along a beach for hours without seeing a footprint in the sand, be one of a handful of campers stargazing in a national park, or bushwalk for days without seeing a soul. Driving distances are mind-boggling, the terrain can be challenging and the elements often unforgiving, but the rewards are obvious. Jump in and see it before everyone else does.

JOHN BANAGAN

Camping & Caravanning

WAYNE WALTON

Rest your weary bones at one of the beautiful camp sites in Karijini National Park (p216)

Opposite:
Bathe in the light of the setting sun in the Gibson Desert (p162)
OLIVER STREWE

Ogle the coastline from your tent in stunning Leeuwin-Naturaliste National Park (p117)

ANDI

Off the Beaten Track

Discover breathtaking scenery near Twilight Cove (p148), Esperance

Negotiate the rocky road to exquisite Lennard River Gorge (p236)

Take your 4WD across rivers in the beautiful Kimberley (p222)

Indigenous Culture

Get to know the local littlies of the Kalumburu community (p237), Northern Kimberley

PETER PTSCHELINZEW

Watch local artists at work in the Kimberley (p222)

RICHARD I'ANSON

PETER PTSCHELINZEW

Observe indigenous cooking at a corroboree near Newman (p217), the Pilbara

Lifestyle, WA-style

Sink into Perth's laid-back café culture (p73)

Hit the surf at Cottesloe Beach (p64)

Sample the brews and devour fresh seafood at Little Creatures (p86), Fremantle

Contents

Regional Map Contents

The Kimberley pp224–5

Coral Coast & the Pilbara p202

Central West Coast p182

The Southern Outback p153

The Wheatbelt & the Midlands p171

Around Perth p90

Perth pp54–5

The Southwest p114

South Coast p134

Getting Started

First things first – Western Australia (WA) is huge. Decide what you *really* want to see and then plan just how you're going to manage visiting it. While it's an easy destination to travel through, underestimating the distances between highlights can leave you feeling as if you've driven a stage of a car rally every day, with ridiculously long road trains (semitrailer trucks towing several trailers) and errant wildlife thrown in for good measure. WA is a friendly state that ambles along at a relaxed pace – it's best to do the same.

WHEN TO GO

Deciding when to go to this mammoth state depends on where you want to go, and then seeing if the weather is agreeable at that time of year. During summer (December to February) the temperate southwest of WA attracts hordes of holidaymakers keen to hit the beaches by day and the beer gardens by night, with temperatures often topping 30°C and rarely dropping below 10°C. Around Perth it's magic, if a little hot, and in the outback it's hot as well. In the Kimberley it's the middle of the wet season (November to April), characterised by flash flooding and hot, sticky, oppressive conditions. While nature puts on a magnificent show at this time of year – with waterfalls and spectacular electrical storms – dodgy road access and the aforementioned conditions make it enjoyable for only the most adventurous travellers.

The northern part of WA is best visited in winter (June to August) or early spring (September to mid-October). After the Wet has finished, the river and creek crossings have subsided and the dirt roads opened, the conditions are dry and warm with summer-like averages of 30°C – allowing you to fully explore this magical area. While winter can be quite rainy in the south of the state, spring offers the best weather and opportunity to be dazzled by the fantastic wildflowers.

See Climate Charts (p248) for more information.

Along with the weather, keep a wary eye on the school-holiday calendar. At these times, every West Australian with kids decides to pack up and head off to their favourite holiday hot spot. Accommodation from caravan parks to condos is booked solid and seemingly sleepy coastal towns hum with holidaymakers. The Christmas crush is usually at its worst from late December to late January, with other holiday stints in the middle of April, July and October (see Holidays, p254). You've been warned!

COSTS

While Australia today is good value for overseas visitors from Europe and North America, it's no longer a bargain destination. Despite this, holidays

---

DON'T LEAVE HOME WITHOUT...

- sunscreen, sunglasses and a hat to deflect ultra-fierce UV rays (p279)
- a travel-insurance policy covering you for any planned high-risk activities (p254)
- extra-strength insect repellent to fend off merciless flies, midges (sandflies) and mosquitoes (p250)
- your bathing suit – a must for the countless glorious beaches you'll encounter along the way
- plenty of driving music!

TOP TENS

Must-See Movies

These classic West-Aussie-focussed movies give you a great insight into the region's fascinating history and hardships. So dim the lights, tuck into some popcorn and prepare to be intrigued. For reviews, see p27.

- *Ten Canoes* (2006), directed by Rolf de Heer
- *Rabbit-Proof Fence* (2002), directed by Phillip Noyce
- *Shame* (1987), directed by Steve Jodrell
- *We of the Never Never* (1982), directed by Igor Auzins
- *Gallipoli* (1981), directed by Peter Weir
- *Dingo* (1991), directed by Rolf de Heer
- *Blackfellas* (1993), directed by James Ricketson
- *Last Train to Freo* (2006), directed by Jeremy Sims
- *Japanese Story* (2003), directed by Sue Brooks
- *Roadgames* (1981), directed by Richard Franklin

Top Reads

From historic tales of triumph over adversity to tomes examining the isolation of West Aussie life, WA's literary traditions are strong, with many of the following books achieving critical acclaim in Australia and abroad. For reviews, see p27.

- *Cloudstreet* (1991), by Tim Winton
- *The Merry-Go-Round in the Sea* (1965), by Randolph Stow
- *A Fortunate Life* (1981), by AB Facey
- *My Place* (1987), by Sally Morgan
- *Land's Edge* (1993), by Tim Winton
- *The Shark Net* (2000), by Robert Drewe
- *The Well* (1987), by Elizabeth Jolley
- *Benang* (1999), by Kim Scott
- *Wheatlands* (2000), by Dorothy Hewett & John Kinsella
- *Red Dog* (2001), by Louis de Bernières

Our Favourite Festivals & Events

Aussies love a good celebration, and the festive spirit comes easily to the people of the West! These are our top 10 favourites – other events are listed on p252 and throughout this book.

- Perth International Arts Festival, January to February (p67)
- National Aboriginal & Islander Day Observance Committee (Naidoc) Week, throughout WA, July (p252)
- Broome's Shinju Matsuri (Festival of the Pearl), September (p229)
- Kalgoorlie-Boulder Racing Round, September (p158)
- Perth Wildflower Festival, September (p253)
- Royal Perth Show, October (p253)
- Fremantle's Blessing of the Fleet, October (p84)
- Awesome Arts Festival, November (p253)
- Margaret River Wine Region Festival, November (p253)
- Fremantle Festival, November (p84)

in WA can still be quite economical for international visitors, with reasonably priced accommodation, and excellent-value food and general everyday costs.

A midrange traveller who plans to hire a car, see the sights, stay in midrange B&Bs or hotels and have a decent restaurant meal in the evening should expect to be out of pocket at least $160 per day (if travelling as part of a couple).

At the low-cost end, if you camp or stay in hostels, cook your own meals and avoid big nights out in the pub, you could probably manage on $60 per day; for a budget that realistically enables you to have a good time, set aside $80. These low-cost figures don't include long-haul trips, which can punish the budget wallet. Unless you plan to park yourself on a beach for your entire holiday, transport and fuel costs will be one of your biggest expenses (see Getting Around, p266).

TRAVEL LITERATURE

Before heading west, pick up some travel literature to help inspire your planning phase.

Robyn Davidson's *Tracks* (1980) describes the author's trek across 2700km of the outback from Alice Springs to Shark Bay in WA, equipped only with humour, determination and a handful of wild camels.

In *Penelope Bungles to Broome* (2002), affable journalist Tim Bowden drives his beloved 4WD (Penelope) across the Kimberley, Pilbara and Nullarbor, and writes about the star attractions of the West and their history as well as the challenges of travelling through the region. However, it's taken us months to get over the photo of him showering in the nude…

Tony Horwitz's entertaining *One for the Road, An Outback Adventure* (1999) is a high-speed account of his round-Oz hitchhiking trip, including pit stops in Perth and Broome.

INTERNET RESOURCES

Commonwealth Bureau of Meteorology (www.bom.gov.au/weather/wa) Up-to-the-minute information on WA weather and warnings.

Lonely Planet (www.lonelyplanet.com) Succinct summaries, links to other sites and the Thorn Tree forum.

NatureBase (www.naturebase.net) Official website of the Department of Environment & Conservation (formerly CALM), with detailed information on all national parks in the state.

Perth Now (www.news.com.au/perthnow) Online news site linked to the WA's *Sunday Times* newspaper, with local, national and international news stories and features.

RTRfm (www.rtrfm.com.au) The website of Perth's excellent independent radio station features upcoming gigs as well as a live feed of the station.

Swellnet (www.swellnet.com.au) Daily surf forecasts and webcams for WA; also try Coastalwatch (www.coastalwatch.com).

Tourism Western Australia (www.westernaustralia.com) State government–run site, with excellent sections on accommodation, restaurants, tours and attractions.

West Australian (www.thewest.com.au) Online version of the newspaper; features up-to-date local news, features and opinion.

Western Australia Government (www.wa.gov.au) Official website of the state government of WA; gateway to WA information and services.

LONELY PLANET INDEX

Litre of petrol
$1.15 upwards!

Litre of bottled water
$3.50

Middy of beer (VB)
$3-3.50

Souvenir T-shirt
$25

Street snack (meat pie)
$3.50

HOW MUCH?

Bottle of good-quality WA wine $15-20

Cup of coffee $3-5

Double room in country pub $60-80

Surfing lesson $45

Whale-watching trip $60

Itineraries

CLASSIC ROUTES

COASTAL CRUISING
One Month / Perth to Broome

Beachcombers, sun-worshippers and water-babies can cruise up Western Australia's splendid coasts to laze on white-sand beaches, swim in crystal-clear seas and snorkel over splendid coral reefs. From **Perth** (p52) take the Brand Hwy north to Cervantes for sunset at the spectacular **Pinnacles Desert** (p173). Hightail it to **Geraldton** (p185) and head offshore to the beautiful **Houtman Abrolhos Islands** (p188). Next stop **Kalbarri** (p190), for fishing and canoeing the sandstone gorges of **Kalbarri National Park** (p190). Continue to World Heritage–listed **Shark Bay** (p193) for marvellous marine life. Splash about with friendly bottlenose dolphins at **Monkey Mia** (p196) then take the **Wula Guda Nyinda walk** (p196) to learn about the indigenous Malgana people's relationship to the sea. Crunch over miniature cockleshells at **Shell Beach** (p193) before continuing to chilled-out **Coral Bay** (p203) and **Exmouth** (p204), for excursions into **Ningaloo Marine Park** (p208) to snorkel, swim with whale sharks, and watch whales on their migration south. Break up the last long haul at **Dampier** (p213) and **Port Hedland** (p218), on your way to **Broome** (p223) to enjoy the sublime sunset over **Cable Beach** (p232).

Travellers can easily do this 3200km journey in a month, but two months would do this spectacular coastline justice and allow you to spend longer at Ningaloo Marine Park, Monkey Mia and Broome.

DRIVING OVER THE TOP   One Month / Broome to Northwest Loop

Take this 4WD camping adventure in Australia's winter – the Dry season in the tropical north – so that you're finishing in spring before the Wet starts. Begin where 'Coastal Cruising' (opposite) ends, or fly into Broome, hire a 4WD and camping gear, and start 'Coastal Cruising' in spring, when it's starting to warm up in the south. Drag yourself away from cosmopolitan **Broome** (p223) after stocking up on supplies, then take to the Great Northern Hwy for the long haul to the outback town of **Fitzroy Crossing** (p239) and a cruise through magnificent **Geikie Gorge** (p238). Enjoy the wildlife – kangaroos, emus and eagles – and the empty road on the way to **Halls Creek** (p239) before camping and bushwalking the beehive domes of the Bungle Bungle Ranges at **Purnululu National Park** (p240). At **Kununurra** (p241) explore **Mirima National Park** (p242) and **Lake Argyle** (p243) and visit the crocodile park at **Wyndham** (p241). Camp your way along the unsealed **Gibb River Road** (p235), stopping off to walk gorgeous **Emma Gorge** (p237) and cruise El Questro Wilderness Park's **Chamberlain Gorge** (p237) to see indigenous art. Don't smile at the crocodiles as you walk through beautiful **Windjana Gorge** (p238), but take time to see how cute bats are in **Tunnel Creek** (p238). Stay overnight at dusty **Derby** (p235) before really escaping to camp on the remote **Dampier Peninsula** (p234). Here, Aboriginal communities with indigenous hosts can show you the best crabbing spots and take you fishing and swimming. Dream about doing it all again on the beaches back in **Broome** (p223).

You could complete this 2000km trip in three weeks, but more comfortably over a month, and with so many wonderful stops en route, why rush? Why not consider working on a pearling boat in Broome or outback station, or volunteering at a national park?

TAILORED TRIPS

SOMETHING WILD

If you like to walk on the wild side – if you're partial to jagged coastal cliffs and craggy windswept countryside, and you love your wildlife untamed – then WA's southwest is for you. Start with a snorkel with wild dolphins in Koombana Bay at **Bunbury** (p115). Beachcombers can marvel at the breathtakingly rugged coastline while surfers can ride some wild waves at **Yallingup** (p121) and **Margaret River** (p123). Head to **Augusta** (p126), Australia's most southwesterly point, to watch magnificent humpback whales (June to September) from windy Cape Leeuwin. Climb

60m-tall karri trees in the untamed Gloucester National Park at **Pemberton** (p131) and do the **Tree Top Walk** (p134) through the thick canopy of tingle trees in the awesome forest of the Valley of the Giants. Gape at massive sand dunes and enormous granite boulders at **William Bay National Park** (p136), west of **Denmark** (p136). You can get close to wild sea lions on the rocky outcrops, but not too close (the area is known for its freak waves). Finally, gaze at the south's most awe-inspiring scenery, north of **Albany** (p141) at the spectacular **Stirling Range National Park** (p140), where the remarkable thousand-metre-high mountain peaks dramatically strike through the clouds.

THE GRAPE ESCAPE

WA's original wine-making region, the historic **Swan Valley** (p87), just a short drive from Perth, should be your first port of call – Houghton's, founded back in 1836, is your go-to winery here. The region that really put WA's wines firmly on the world stage, however, is the stunning **Margaret River region** (p123), a couple of hours or so south of Perth. The famous four from the early days (not so way back in the late '60s and early '70s), Cullen Wines,

Cape Mentelle, Moss Wood and Vasse Felix, are all worth a visit. Continue your tasting tour with a couple of the 'newer' wineries – Leeuwin Estate and Voyager Estate. Still thirsty? Boot not full yet? Well if the Margaret River is just too popular for you, head to the Great Southern region, centred around sleepy **Mt Barker** (p140). Big names here include Plantagenet and Goundrey, and in the Frankland River area try Ferngrove and Frankland Estate. Further south a string of eminent winemakers call **Denmark** (p136) home, including West Cape Howe and Howard Park.

For detailed information on our favourite regions and vineyards, see p47.

Snapshot

Western Australia (WA) is booming as if a new gold rush has hit. With a fast-growing state economy that's constantly ahead of the national average, low unemployment and a very optimistic fiscal outlook, WA's confidence is tangible. This self-assuredness was upgraded to extreme buoyancy in September 2006 when one of the local Australian Rules football teams, the West Coast Eagles, won the national competition – for there is nothing the locals love better than one-upping the eastern states.

However, there's more to this sentiment than just winning a game of footy. WA has, since its inception, felt undervalued and underfinanced by the eastern states, and in turn by the federal government, which it sees as always happy to reap the rewards of WA's vast mining riches, but continually slow to recompense with federal infrastructure projects. Any hint of erosion of state powers reawakens the debate of WA seceding from Australia, a long-held, sometimes acted on, but ultimately unfulfilled desire (see p25).

While WA's economic outlook is generally rosy, the big western state has its fair share of droughts, bushfires, floods and cyclones that play havoc with its pastoral and farming communities. Water conservation is a huge issue in WA and in the lead-up to the 2005 state elections, it became a focal point. The Opposition Liberal-National coalition leader, Colin Barnett, came up with a bizarre proposal to build the world's longest canal to deliver water to Perth from the Kimberley to solve the problem. The Labor Premier, Geoff Gallop, proposed a $350 million desalination plant. Common sense won through and so did the Labor Party. However, less than one year after being re-elected, Gallop resigned in order to fight his battle with depression. Alan Carpenter was sworn in as his successor on 25 January 2006.

WA's current boom is being driven by an audacious mining sector; however, this is not without its controversies. The fate of the state's old-growth forests and natural wilderness areas (such as Ningaloo Reef) has been widely debated, with the interests of mines, resorts and other business development constantly at odds with conservationists (see p36). One thing they can all agree on is how unwelcome the state's newest guest, the cane toad, is. This pest's entry into WA has constantly been in the news, with the formation of local vigilante groups such as the 'Kimberley Toad Busters', with its slogan, 'If everyone was a toadbuster, the toads would be busted.'

One development replacing cane toads and football as water-cooler conversation was the successful native claim title over the metropolitan area of Perth by the local Noongar Aboriginal people in September 2006. While this landmark decision has given other claimants across Australia renewed hope, back in Perth the talk was about the challenge to the decision at both federal and state levels. While there might be a gold rush on, it appears that closure for the long-standing issue of native title will have to wait.

FAST FACTS

Population: about 2.04 million people, 25.6 million sheep & lambs

Foreign-born Western Australians: around 33%

GSP (Gross State Product) growth: approx 2.7% (2004–05)

Inflation: 3% (2006)

Percentage of Australian exports: 25%

Unemployment rate: 3.6%

Average gross weekly income: $811.70

Western Australia's coastline: 12,500km long

Number of wildflower species: 12,000

WA has approximately one-third of Australia's landmass and one-tenth of the population

History   Michael Cathcart

FIRST ARRIVALS

People first arrived on the northern shores of Australia at least 40,000 years ago. As they began building shelters, cooking food and telling each other tales, they left behind signs of their activities. They left layers of carbon – the residue of their ancient fires – deep in the soil. Piles of shells and fish-bones mark the places where these people hunted and ate. And on rock walls across Western Australia (WA) they left paintings and etchings – some thousands of years old – which tell their stories of the Dreaming, that spiritual dimension where the earth and its people were created, and the law was laid down.

Contrary to popular belief, these Aboriginal people, especially those who lived in the north, were not entirely isolated from the rest of the world. Until 6000 years ago, they were able to travel and trade across a bridge of land that connected Australia to New Guinea. Even after white occupation, the Aborigines of the northern coasts regularly hosted Macassan fishermen from Sulawesi, with whom they traded and socialised.

So when European sailors first stumbled on the coast of 'Terra Australis', the entire continent was occupied by hundreds of Aboriginal groups, living in their own territories and maintaining their own distinctive languages and traditions. The fertile Swan River Valley around Perth, for example, is the customary homeland of about a dozen groups of Noongar people, each speaking a distinctive dialect.

The prehistory of Australia is filled with tantalizing mysteries. In the Kimberley, scholars and amateur sleuths are fascinated by the so-called Bradshaw paintings. These enigmatic and mystical stick-figures are thousands of years old. Because they look nothing like the artwork of any other Aboriginal group, the identity of the culture who created them is the subject of fierce debate.

Meanwhile there are historians who claim that the Aborigines' first contact with the wider world occurred when a Chinese admiral named Zheng He visited Australia in the 15th century. Others say that Portuguese navigators mapped the continent in the 16th century.

DUTCH FIND NOTHING TO TRADE

These are intriguing theories. But most authorities believe that the first man to travel any great distance to see Aboriginal Australia was a Dutchman named Willem Janszoon. In 1606, he sailed the speedy little ship *Duyfken* out of the Dutch settlement at Batavia (modern Jakarta) to scout for the Dutch East India Company, and found Cape York (the pointy bit at the top of Australia), which he thought was an extension of New Guinea.

Ten years later, another Dutch ship, the *Eendracht*, rode the mighty trade winds across the Atlantic, bound for the 'spice islands' of modern Indonesia. But the captain, Dirk Hartog, misjudged his position, and stumbled onto the island (near Gladstone) that now bears his name. Hartog inscribed the details of his visit onto a pewter plate and nailed it to a post. In 1697, the island was visited by a second Dutch explorer named De Vlamingh who swapped Hartog's plate for one of his own.

Other Dutch mariners were not so lucky. Several ships were wrecked on the uncharted western coast of the Aboriginal continent. The most infamous of these is the *Batavia*. After the ship foundered in the waters off modern Geraldton in 1629, the captain, Francis Pelsaert, sailed a boat to the Dutch East India Company's base at Batavia. While his back was turned, some

---

Michael Cathcart teaches history at the Australian Centre, University of Melbourne. He is well known as a broadcaster on ABC Radio National and presented the ABC TV series *Rewind*.

The most comprehensive history of WA is the 836-page *A New History of Western Australia* (1981), edited by CT Stannage. It has nearly 20 contributors and includes excellent coverage of the clash of white and Aboriginal cultures, colonisation, religion, sport, unionism and party politics.

demented crewmen unleashed a nightmare of debauchery, rape and murder on the men, women and children who had been on the ship. When Pelsaert returned with a rescue vessel, he executed the murderers, sparing only two youths whom he marooned on the beach of the continent they knew as New Holland. Some experts believe the legacy of these boys can be found in the sandy hair and the Dutch-sounding words of some local Aborigines. The remains of the *Batavia* and other wrecks are now displayed at the Western Australian Museum in Geraldton (p185) and in the Fremantle Shipwreck Galleries (p81), where you can also see De Vlamingh's battered old plate.

The Dutch were business men, scouring the world for commodities. Nothing they saw on the dry coasts of this so-called 'New Holland' convinced them that the land or its native people offered any promise of profit. When another Dutchman named Abel Tasman charted the western and southern coasts of Australia in 1644, he was mapping, not a commercial opportunity, but a maritime hazard.

MEANWHILE, OVER EAST

Today, the dominant version of Australian history is written as though Sydney is the well-spring of Australia's identity. But when you live in Western Australia, history looks very different. In Sydney, white history traditionally begins with Captain James Cook's epic voyage of 1770, in which he mapped the east coast. But Cook creates little excitement in Albany, Perth or Geraldton – places he never saw.

Cook's voyage revealed that the eastern coastline was fertile, and he was particularly taken with the diversity of plant life at the place he called 'Botany Bay'. Acting on Cook's discovery, the British government decided to establish a convict colony there. The result was the settlement of Sydney in 1788 – out of which grew the great sheep industry of Australia.

By the early 19th century, it was clear that the Dutch had no inclination to settle Western Australia. Meanwhile, the British were growing alarmed by the activities of the French in the region. So on Christmas Day 1826, the British army warned them off by establishing a lonely military outpost at Albany, on the strategically important southwestern tip of the country.

PERTH

The challenge to Aboriginal supremacy in the west began in 1829, when a boatload of free immigrants arrived with all their possessions in the territory of the Noongar people. These trespassers were led by Captain James Stirling – a swashbuckling and entrepreneurial naval officer – who had investigated the coastal region two years earlier. Stirling had convinced British authorities to appoint him governor of the new settlement, and promptly declared all the surrounding Aboriginal lands to be the property of King George IV. Such was the foundation of Perth.

Stirling's glowing reports had fired the ambitions of English adventurers and investors, and by the end of the year, 25 ships had reached the colony's port at Fremantle. Unlike their predecessors in Sydney, these settlers were determined to build their fortunes without calling on government assistance and without the shame of using convict labour.

As a cluster of shops, houses and hotels rose on the banks of the Swan River, settlers established sheep and cattle runs in the surrounding country. This led to conflict with the Aborigines, following a pattern which was tragically common throughout the Australian colonies. The Aborigines speared sheep and cattle – sometimes for food, sometimes as an act of defiance. In the reprisals which resulted, people on both sides were killed, and by 1832 it was clear the Aborigines were organising a violent resistance. Governor

Strange Objects (1990) by Gary Crew and *The Devil's Own* (1990) by Deborah Lisson, two fiction books for teens, interweave the history of the *Batavia* shipwreck with contemporary characters and plotlines. Entertaining (and sometimes challenging) books for the kids.

Robert Hughes' bestseller *The Fatal Shore* (1987) offers a colourful and exhaustive historical account of convict transportation from Britain to Australia, and features a section on WA in this era.

Stirling declared that he would retaliate with such 'acts of decisive severity as will appal them as people for a time and reduce their tribe to weakness'.

FRONTIER CONFLICT

In October 1834 Stirling showed he was a man of his word. He led a punitive expedition against the Noongar, who were under the leadership of the warrior Calyute. In the Battle of Pinjarra, the Governor's forces shot, according to one report, around 25 Aborigines and suffered one fatality themselves. This display of official terror had the desired effect. The Noongar ended their resistance and the violence of the frontier moved further out. (The pugnacious historian Keith Windschuttle rejects the idea that the frontier was violent, and argues that the Pinjarra incident was no more than a forceful police action.) You can learn more about conflict on the frontier at the Round House (p81) in Fremantle and at the Rottnest Museum (p92) on Rottnest Island.

'In 1850 – just as the practice of sending British convicts to eastern Australia ended – shiploads of male convicts started to arrive in Fremantle harbour'

THE CONVICTS

Aboriginal resistance was not the only threat to the survival of this most isolated outpost of the British Empire. The arid countryside, the loneliness and the cost of transport also took their toll. When tough men of capital could make a fortune in the east, there were few good reasons to struggle against the frustrations of the west, and most of the early settlers left. Two decades on, there were just 5000 Europeans holding out on the western edge of the continent. Some of the capitalists who had stayed began to rethink their aversion to using cheap prison labour.

So in 1850 – just as the practice of sending British convicts to eastern Australia ended – shiploads of male convicts started to arrive in Fremantle harbour. They hacked roads out of the countryside and erected public buildings, including the prison (p81), Government House (p66), the Perth Town Hall (p66), the lunatic asylum, which now houses the Fremantle Arts Centre (p81), and the governor's summer residence – now the Quokka Arms. Most of the 10,000 men transported to the west over the next 18 years, however, worked on remote cattle and sheep runs, far from the main settlement.

EXPLORATION & GOLD

Meanwhile, several explorers undertook journeys into the remote Aboriginal territories, drawn in by dreams of mighty rivers and rolling plains of grass 'further out'. Mostly their thirsty ordeals ended in disappointment. But the pastoralists did expand through much of the southwestern corner of WA, while others took up runs on the rivers of the northwest and in the Kimberley.

Perhaps the most staggering journey of exploration was undertaken by an Aboriginal man called Wylie and the explorer Edward Eyre, who travelled from South Australia, across the vast, dry Nullarbor Plain, to Albany.

By the 1880s, the entire European population of this sleepy western third of Australia was not much more than 40,000 people. In the absence of democracy, a network of city merchants and large squatters exercised political and economic control over the colony.

The great agent of change was gold. The first discoveries were made in the 1880s in the Kimberley and Pilbara, followed by huge finds in the 1890s at Coolgardie and Kalgoorlie, in hot, dry country 600km inland from Perth. So many people were lured by the promise of gold that the population of the colony doubled and redoubled in a single decade. But the easy gold was soon exhausted, and most independent prospectors gave way to mining companies who had the capital to sink deep shafts. Soon, the miners were working, not for nuggets of gold, but for wages. Toiling in hot, dangerous conditions, these men banded together to form trade unions which remained a potent force in the life of Western Australia throughout the following century.

THE GREAT ENGINEER

The year 1890 also saw the introduction of representative government – this was a full generation after democracy had arrived in the east. The first elected premier was a tough, capable bushman named John Forrest, who borrowed courageously in order to finance vast public works to encourage immigrants and private investors. He was blessed with the services of a brilliant civil engineer named CY O'Connor. O'Connor oversaw the improvement of the Fremantle harbour, and built and ran the state's rail system. But O'Connor's greatest feat was the construction of a system of steam-powered pumping stations along a mighty pipeline to drive water uphill, from Mundaring Weir near Perth to the thirsty goldfields around distant Kalgoorlie.

By the time John Forrest opened the pipeline, O'Connor was dead. His political enemies had defamed him in the press and in parliament, falsely accusing him of incompetence and corruption. On 10 March 1902, O'Connor rode into the surf near Fremantle and shot himself. Today, the site of his anguish is commemorated by a haunting statue of him on horseback, which rises out of the waves at South Beach.

Ironically, just as the water began to flow, the mining industry went into decline. But the 'Golden Pipeline' continues to supply water to the mining city of Kalgoorlie where gold is once again being mined, on a Herculean scale unimaginable a century ago. Today, there is a pipeline museum at Mundaring Weir. You can also follow the National Trust's Heritage Trail along the pipeline to Kalgoorlie, where you can visit the astonishing Super Pit and the Goldfields Museum.

ABORIGINES

At the turn of the century, the lives of many Aborigines became more wretched. The colony's 1893 Education Act empowered the parents of white schoolchildren to bar any Aboriginal child from attending their school, and it was not long before Aborigines were completely excluded from state-run classrooms. The following decade, the government embarked on a policy of removing so-called 'half-caste' children from their parents, placing them with white families or in government institutions. The objective of the policy was explicit. Full-blood Aborigines were to be segregated in the belief that they were doomed to extinction, while half-caste children were expected to marry whites, thereby breeding the Aborigines out of existence. These policies inflicted great suffering and sadness on the many Aborigines who were recognised in the 1990s as 'the stolen generations'.

'Half-caste children were expected to marry whites, thereby breeding the Aborigines out of existence'

WARS & DEPRESSION

On 1 January 1901, Western Australia and the other colonies federated to form the nation of Australia. This was not a declaration of independence. This new Australia was a dominion within the British Empire. It was as citizens of the Empire that thousands of Australian men volunteered to fight in the Australian Imperial Force when WWI broke out in 1914. They fought in Turkey, Sinai and in Europe – notably on the Somme. Over 200,000 of them were killed or wounded over the terrible four years of the war. Today, in cities and towns across the state, you will see war memorials that commemorate their service.

Though mining, for the time being, had ceased to be an economic force, farmers were developing the lucrative Western Australian wheat belt, which they cultivated with the horse-drawn stump-jump plough, one of the icons of Australian frontier farming. At the same time, a growing demand for wool, beef and the expansion of dairying added to the state's economic growth.

Nevertheless, many people were struggling to earn a living – especially those ex-soldiers who were unable to shake off the horrors they had endured in the trenches. In 1929, the lives of these 'battlers' grew even more miserable when the cold winds of the Great Depression blew through the towns and farms of the state. So alienated did West Australians feel from the centres of power and politics in the east that, in 1933, two-thirds of them voted to secede from the rest of Australia. Although the decision was never enacted, it expressed a profound sense of isolation from the east which is still a major factor in the culture and attitudes of the state today.

In 1939, Australians were once again fighting a war alongside the British, this time against Hitler in WWII. But the military situation changed radically in December 1941 when the Japanese bombed the American Fleet at Hawaii's Pearl Harbor. The Japanese swept through Southeast Asia and, within weeks, were threatening Australia. Over the next two years they actually bombed several towns in the north of the state including Broome, which was almost abandoned.

It was not the British, but the Americans, who came to Australia's aid. As thousands of Australian soldiers were taken prisoner and suffered in the torturous Japanese prisoner-of-war camps, Western Australians opened their arms to US servicemen. Fremantle was transformed into an Allied naval base for operations in the Indian Ocean, while a US submarine-refuelling base was established at Exmouth. In New Guinea and the Pacific, Americans and Australians fought together until the tide of war eventually turned against the enemy.

Largely set in Western Australia, *Gallipoli* (1981, directed by Peter Weir, screenplay by David Williamson) is an iconic Australian movie exploring naivety, social pressure to enlist and, ultimately, the utter futility of this campaign.

POSTWAR PROSPERITY

When the war ended, the story of modern Western Australia began to unfold. Under the banner of 'Postwar Reconstruction', the federal government set about transforming Australia with a policy of assisted immigration, designed to populate Australia more densely as a defence against the 'hordes' of Asia. Many members of this new workforce found jobs in the mines, where men and machines turned over thousands of tonnes of earth in search of the precious lode. On city stock exchanges, the names of such Western Australian mines as Tom Price, Mt Newman and Goldsworthy became symbols of development, modernisation and wealth. Now, rather than being a wasteland that history had forgotten, the West was becoming synonymous with ambition, and a new spirit of capitalist pioneering. As union membership flourished, labour and capital entered into a pact to turn the country to profit. In the Kimberley, the government built the gigantic Ord River Irrigation Scheme, which boasted that it could bring fertility to the desert – and which convinced many Western Australians that engineering and not the environment contained the secret of life.

There was so much country, it hardly seemed to matter that salt was starting to poison country in the wheat belt or that mines scoured the land. In 1952, the British exploded their first nuclear bomb on the state's Monte Bello Islands. And when opponents of the test alleged that nuclear clouds were drifting over Australia, the government scoffed. The land was big – and anyway, we needed a strong, nuclear-armed ally to protect us in the Cold War world.

This spirit of reckless capitalism reached its climax in the 1980s when the state became known as 'West Australia Inc' – a reference to the state in operation as a giant corporation in which government, business and unions had lost sight of any value other than speculation and profit. The embodiment of this brash spirit was an English migrant named Alan Bond, who became so rich that he could buy anything he pleased. In 1983, he funded a sleek new racing yacht called *Australia II* in its challenge for the millionaire's yachting prize, the America's Cup. Equipped with a secret – and now legendary – winged keel, the boat became the first non-American yacht to win the race. It seemed as everyone in Australia was cheering on the day Bond held aloft the shining silver trophy.

But in the 1990s, legal authorities began to investigate the dealings of Alan Bond, and of many other players in West Australia Inc. Bond found himself in court and spent four years in jail after pleading guilty to Australia's biggest corporate fraud.

For more information about native title claims in the west, and throughout Australia, see the National Native Title Tribunal website (www .nntt.gov.au).

TODAY

Today the population of the entire state is just two million people – about half of whom have come from overseas. Fewer than 70,000 of these are Aborigines. In 1993, the federal government recognised that Aborigines with an ongoing association with their traditional lands were the rightful owners, unless those lands had been sold to someone else. Since then, substantial areas of the state have passed into Aboriginal ownership. But Aborigines remain a disadvantaged minority, plagued by alcoholism, violence and poor health. At the same time, a young Aboriginal adult living in WA is 52 times more likely to spend time in jail than a non-Aborigine. Throughout the state, men and women of good will continue to work for 'reconciliation' between the two groups, but the advances take time and are often frustrated by the impatience of white powerbrokers with the process.

For detailed information on current indigenous issues see 'Living Black' on SBS's website (www.sbs .com.au/livingblack).

WESTERN AUSTRALIA IN BLACK & WHITE

Like indigenous Australians in the rest of the country, the 70,000 or so Aborigines who live in Western Australia (WA) are the state's most disadvantaged group. Many live in deplorable conditions, outbreaks of preventable diseases are common and infant mortality rates are higher than in many developing countries.

The issue of racial relations in WA is a problematic one, and racial intolerance is still evident in many parts of the state. Especially (but not exclusively) in the remote northwest, a form of unofficial apartheid appears to exist, and travellers are bound to be confronted by it.

Another political issue in WA is the mandatory sentencing law. Introduced by the Court government in 1996, it is considered to discriminate against Aboriginal people (young Aborigines are 52 times more likely to experience jail time than a non-Aborigine). The law provides that third-time property offenders receive a mandatory 12-month jail sentence. Given the extreme disadvantage indigenous Australian children suffer, many consider that it is difficult for them to avoid participation in criminal acts. Human rights groups, including the United Nations, have protested against the law.

However, it is not all bad news for WA's Aborigines. Indigenous-owned businesses are becoming more prominent throughout the state, especially in the field of tourism (see p197), and many people of indigenous descent now take leadership roles on bodies such as shire councils and tourist boards.

We have provided information about indigenous businesses and tours wherever possible throughout this book. To explore Aboriginal WA further, grab a copy of Lonely Planet's *Aboriginal Australia & the Torres Strait Islands*.

Though the population of the state is small, it continues to grow and diversify. In many ways, Western Australia has been a state-in-waiting; its development has started and stalled several times in its short European history. But the dynamism and friendliness of the place – and the scale of the landscape – are seductive. If sometimes the place seems too unmindful of its heritage, perhaps that's because it is still dreaming of its future.

The Culture

REGIONAL IDENTITY

If Australians are shaped by their isolation from the rest of the world, Western Australians are removed an additional step from the majority of Australians living along the eastern coastline, more than 3000km away. This isolation has moulded Western Australians into a hardy, self-sufficient and innovative people, staunchly independent and parochial to the point that the notion of seceding from the rest of Australia occasionally surfaces. First mooted soon after Federation in the early 20th century, secession is still advocated by many who complain that the west's rich mineral resources contribute far more to the federal coffers than is returned in funding projects and services.

Western Australians feel the distance and differences from the east coast keenly, and wear their distinctiveness from the east with pride – especially on the sporting field, where defeating teams from the east coast is savoured. With Western Australia's (WA's) economy buzzing, most locals will tell visitors that this is the best place in Australia (if not the world!) to live and that the eastern capitals such as Melbourne and Sydney have no redeeming features – but often they appear to be protesting just a little too much.

Perhaps some of this desire to have a distinct identity stems from one-third of WA residents being born overseas; this steady stream of immigrants (Brits, Irish, New Zealanders, continental Europeans, South Africans and Asians) brings differing cultures to the melting pot. However, because of the high proportion of 'Western' immigrants (from the UK and New Zealand), the melting pot is still decidedly Western in flavour. In addition, with three-quarters of the WA population located in the Perth region, the melting-pot metaphor runs out of steam once you get to the regional areas. Indeed in many towns the indigenous population lives almost a completely separate existence to everyone else.

The Australian landscape has shaped a national character that is used to hardship, and in this Western Australians are no different to their eastern brethren. Living with adversity has also helped mould the anti-authoritarian, rebellious nature that comes from the country's convict past: Australians prefer to support the underdog over someone who has become too successful, too popular or 'too big for his boots'. Australians also prefer to be modest and not 'crow' about success. While 'getting ahead' (owning your house, a couple of cars and a boat) is popular in WA, boasting is not really part of the Australian character. It's a society where egalitarian values – you're no better than your neighbour and he's no better than you – are esteemed above all.

In the same vein, Australians often use humour as a social levelling tool. For those not familiar with its unique character, a first encounter with Australian humour can be a confusing experience.

Australian children are infused with the essential characteristics of the local humour – self-deprecation, sarcasm, irony and the occasional obscenity. One of the worst social faux pas in Australia is to take yourself too seriously, and youngsters learn how to 'take a joke' along with how to walk and talk.

Social interaction, particularly 'down the pub', is often a mix of jokes, amusing anecdotes and personal teasing. Visitors can be shocked to hear best mates trading insults ('taking the piss') or labelling each other a '**** bastard', until they realise it's meant in the nicest possible way. Swear words are often used as close terms of affection, and if you're being teased – welcome to the group.

Make sure you're always in on the joke with Lonely Planet's *Australian Phrasebook*, which has 256 pages of rhyming slang, Aussie expressions, national songs, Aboriginal languages and other cultural titbits.

Aussies love a nickname, and Western Australians are the lucky recipients of the title 'sandgropers', named after a relative of the grasshopper who loves to burrow in sandy soils.

LIFESTYLE

Almost three quarters of Western Australians live in Perth, where they thrive on a diet of mostly sunny weather, a high standard of living, pristine beaches, lush parks, good cafés and restaurants, and a laidback atmosphere that makes it seem more like a large country town than a city. Accordingly, most locals you'll meet will be relaxed and friendly – as you would be if you were as blessed with the Aussie version of the good life as they are.

Life's a beach for many Perthites, who strip off the business suit at the end of the day and head for the closest stretch of coastline they can find, often with a fishing rod or a surfboard. Holidays generally see most families headed straight for their favourite beach, often with a caravan in tow.

The Great Australian Dream has long been to own a house on a quarter-acre block, and the majority of folks still rate home ownership very highly on their 'to do' list. Inside the average Western Australian middle-class suburban home, you'll probably find a married heterosexual couple, though it is becoming increasingly likely they will be de facto, or in their second marriage.

Our 'dad and mum' couple will have an average of 1.4 children; however, the birth rate has been falling over the last few years, as more couples put off having children, preferring to focus on higher education and financial security before parenthood.

POPULATION

Australia's population passed the 20 million mark in December 2003 and it's estimated that the population is now just over 20.7 million. Although WA is the largest state in the country it's also the most sparsely populated, being home to less than 10% of the population – an estimated 2.04 million in 2006.

Australia has been strongly influenced by immigration, and its ethnic mix is among the most diverse in the world. Some 33% of the population in WA is foreign-born, with the majority coming from the UK (11%), New Zealand (2%), Italy (1%), Malaysia (1%) and South Africa (1%). Around 3% of the state's population identify as being of Aboriginal origin.

Despite the extraordinarily low population density, population policy is fiercely debated in Australia. Opponents of increased immigration argue the dry Australian landscape can't sustain more people (among other arguments); others say population growth is an economic imperative, particularly considering Australia's declining birth rates.

SPORT

Sport is an obsession for many in the west, and there's no sport that arouses more passion and pride than Australian Rules Football (or Aussie Rules). Though the national competition developed from the Victorian league, it has featured successful teams from other states for several years, including WA's beloved West Coast Eagles (which has won the premiership three times, the latest in 2006) and the Fremantle Dockers. You can catch a match from March to August (with the finals in September) at Subiaco Oval and at Fremantle – just remember to choose a side when you arrive (you will be asked who you go for)! If the Eagles and Dockers are playing elsewhere, there's the local Western Australian Rules competition for teams in and around Perth.

For more on Aussie Rules, see the websites of the Australian Football League (www.afl.com.au), the West Coast Eagles (www.westcoast eagles.com.au) or the Fremantle Dockers (www.fremantlefc.com.au).

In summer, sports fans' focus quickly shifts and the hordes head for the **WACA** (Western Australian Cricket Association ground; ☎ 08-9265 7222; Nelson Cres, East Perth) to catch the drama of one-day and Test match cricket (the five-day international version of the game). A Test match is played in Perth most seasons, and there are regular interstate matches where the Western Warriors battle against other states for the national championship (formerly known as the Sheffield Shield but now named after whoever buys the commercial rights).

ARTS
Cinema

Given that Australia only makes a couple of dozen feature films a year, it's no surprise that WA does not have a large film industry. However there are some excellent films (available from libraries and video outlets throughout the state) that showcase the landscapes and explore local issues, culture and history. Remote, stunning locations and common themes of struggle and hardship characterise many of these movies.

One of the latest films with a Western Australian setting is the psychological drama *Last Train To Freo* (2006), the first film by well-known actor and theatre director Jeremy Sims, about a couple of ex-cons catching the last train to Fremantle, joined by a young female law student who is unaware that the guards are on strike.

Ten Canoes (2006), directed by Rolf de Heer, takes a humorous and poetic look at the lives of a couple of Aboriginal tribes in the Northern Territory. It won a special jury prize at the Cannes Film Festival as well best film at the Aussie version of the Oscars, the Australian Film Institute (AFI) awards. Another de Heer film worth viewing is *Dingo* (1991), which follows a dingo trapper (and mad-keen jazz enthusiast) on an unlikely journey from outback WA to the jazz clubs of Paris.

The powerful *Rabbit-Proof Fence* (2002), directed by Phillip Noyce, is based in 1931 WA, a time when mixed-race Aboriginal children were routinely taken from their parents and sent to training camps to become domestic help for white families.

Japanese Story (2003), directed by Sue Brooks, was a hit with Australian critics and crowds, with the stunning Pilbara landscape sharing centre stage with highly regarded actress Toni Colette, playing a gritty Perth geologist whose trip to the Pilbara mines takes some unexpected turns.

The raw and powerful *Shame* (1987), directed by Steve Jodrell, is set in an isolated WA community where Deborah Lee-Furness (wife of actor Hugh Jackman) shines as a tough, motorbike-riding lawyer who rumbles into town and is horrified by the town's reaction to a gang rape.

Though filmed in the Northern Territory, *We of the Never Never* (1982) was based on a real-life story and novel set on a station in the Kimberley. It's an excellent depiction of the hardships women faced in the Australian outback in the early 20th century.

Largely set in WA and starring a very young Mel Gibson, Peter Weir's heart-rending film about the ill-fated battle of WWI, *Gallipoli* (1981), carries a timeless message about the futility of war.

Blackfellas (1993), based on Archie Weller's novel *The Day of the Dog*, traces a young Noongar man's struggle to come to terms with his culture while surviving in a white man's world.

Literature

Encompassing the unpolished, rough humour of early writers from the northwest and goldfields to sophisticated works from a string of modern writers, WA's literary tradition is remarkably rich.

The most prolific of WA's writers was Katharine Susannah Prichard, who wrote extensively on local themes, often infusing her work with communist idealism (she was a lifelong party member). Her two renowned works are *Working Bullocks* (1926), set in the karri forests of the southwest and exploring the relationship between man and the environment, and the

WA has given the film world a couple of big names: Hollywood leading man Heath Ledger, star of *Brokeback Mountain* and *A Knight's Tale*; and Frances O'Connor, who features in *AI* and *The Importance of Being Earnest*.

With *Ten Canoes*, Australia's most intriguing film maker, Rolf de Heer, managed to make the first successful film about Aborigines that doesn't have a white fella's point of reference. And it's funny and poignant, with a wonderful narration by David Gulpilil.

prize-winning *Coonardoo* (1929), examining the taboo subject of black-white sexual relationships.

Born in 1935 and raised in Geraldton, Randolph Stow has used WA as the setting for some of his best-loved novels. Award-winning *To the Islands* (1958) is set in the far northwest and follows the path of a disillusioned white man and his Aboriginal companion on a journey of self-discovery. The semi-autobiographical *The Merry-Go-Round in the Sea* (1965) is a rites-of-passage tale of a child growing up in a small coastal town in WA.

One of Australia's most celebrated contemporary writers is Tim Winton, born in Perth in 1960. Many of his books celebrate the beauty of the WA landscape, particularly his nostalgic *Land's Edge* (1993), where he affectionately reminisces about childhood summers on the coast, and celebrates his powerful connection with the sea, inspiring us to discover the wild west for ourselves.

Winton's award-winning *Cloudstreet* (1991), an epic family saga based in postwar Perth, received rave reviews from local and international audiences –it's considered by many to be his best work. However it was *Dirt Music* (2001) that gained Winton more international exposure by being short-listed for the UK's Booker Prize. That novel explores the search for love and meaning against the backdrop of remote fishing villages, Broome and islands off the north coast. Winton's latest work, *The Turning* (2006), is a collection of short stories.

Another of WA's great modern writers is English-born Elizabeth Jolley, who has won numerous awards for her unusual short stories and novels. *The Well* (1987), which explores the relationship between an eccentric middle-aged woman and the young girl who comes to live with her, won the 1986 Miles Franklin Award (Australia's top literary award) and was made into a film in 1997. Jolley's most recent works include *An Innocent Gentleman* (2001) and *Learning to Dance* (2006).

In 1981 the Fremantle Arts Centre published *A Fortunate Life,* a moving autobiography by 'Aussie battler' AB Facey (see boxed text, p173), which follows his many trials and tribulations from Gallipoli to the Depression to life on the land in rural WA.

Western Australian journalist-turned-author Robert Drewe successfully interweaves intimate stories of life, love and relationships with important historical events. *The Drowner* (1997) combines a powerful love story with tales of drought in parched Australia and the CY O'Connor pipeline to the Kalgoorlie goldfields.

Also by Drewe, *The Shark Net* (2000) is a widely acclaimed memoir of a childhood spent in Perth in the 1950s and '60s, full of insights, joys and tragedies, including the murder of a close boyhood friend by serial killer Eric Edgar Cooke, the last person hanged at Fremantle Prison (p81).

Once dominated by writers of British and Irish descent, WA's literary scene has evolved to better reflect the state's multicultural makeup. Indigenous writers tend to focus on the theme of identity in often intensely personal autobiographies. Jack Davis' *The First-Born and other Poems* (1970) was a watershed in Aboriginal literature.

Sally Morgan's successful and groundbreaking autobiography *My Place* (1987) charts the author's discovery and exploration of her Aboriginality and her search for her true identity.

An outstanding talent is the Aboriginal writer Archie Weller. His *The Day of the Dog* (1981), tracing the fall of the traditional male role in Aboriginal society, garnered great reviews and was highly commended in the 1980 Vogel literary award. It was also made into the movie *Blackfellas* in 1993 (see Cinema, p27).

Nobody has captured the spirit of WA and its people as well as Tim Winton. With *Dirt Music* (2001), Winton even provides a soundtrack, available on CD.

Robert Drewe's latest work, *Grace* (2005), sees an inner-city Sydney film reviewer flee to the Kimberley and work in a wildlife park in 'Port Mangrove' while attempting to get his life back together.

Finally, Kim Scott's excellent *Benang* (1999), which won the Miles Franklin Award in 2000, is a confronting but rewarding read about the assimilation policies of the 20th century and the devastating effect they had on Aboriginal Australia.

Dance & Theatre

WA has a wonderfully vibrant dance scene. The **Western Australian Ballet** (www.waballet.com.au) has a permanent home at His Majesty's Theatre (p77) and the **Western Australia Academy of Performing Arts** (www.waapa.ecu.edu.au) offers degrees for those wishing to pursue the rigours of life as a dancer. Students will certainly need plenty of stamina if they want to join Perth's **Skadada** (www.skadada.com), who bill themselves as an 'electronic circus company' and gained critical acclaim for their Electronic Big Top show (which was staged in 1999).

The Western Australia Academy of Performing Arts (www.waapa.ecu .edu.au) stages performances all year round, ranging from full stage productions to free recitals. See the website for details.

Theatre is also strong in WA – no surprise given the number of excellent writers the state has nurtured. The **Perth Theatre Company** (www.perththeatre.com .au) has a strong commitment to Western Australian and Australian writers, while the **Black Swan Theatre Company** (www.bstc.com.au) is the state's flagship theatre company. The latter hosts a mix of theatre classics and innovative local productions, such as 2006's *Red Dog*, based on the legend of Red Dog (see the boxed text, p213).

ABORIGINAL ART

Art is a fundamental part of Aboriginal life and the Dreaming, serving as a connection between past and present, between people and the land. While art is a means for people to express themselves, their identity, culture and beliefs, just as importantly it's a political and economic enterprise.

Artists of all ages are experimenting with styles that reflect their experiences, circumstances and influences. These days they're just as likely to use acrylics and printmaking as they would have stringy bark or pandanus leaf. Get an introduction to Aboriginal art at Perth's Art Gallery of Western Australia (p63), home to one of the world's best indigenous collections, and Holmes à Court Gallery (p64), WA's best private collection. (The former curator of the Holmes à Court Gallery, Belinda Carrigan, owns Gecko Gallery in Broome.)

While paintings from Western Australia's (WA's) central Australian communities is among the most readily identifiable contemporary art, there's an enormous range of work being created. And while regional styles are distinct, each community within a region has an identifiable style, just as they have their own language and laws. *A Guide to Aboriginal Art and the Aboriginal Owned Art Centres* describes the work created by different communities, and its online database (www .aboriginalart.org) lets you search for different styles, artists, techniques and communities.

Some standout artists from WA include Noongar artist Julie Dowling, the first indigenous graduate of Curtin University's Fine Arts program, whose work regularly features on the walls of the best public and private collections; Peter Newry from the Kimberley, whose indomitable land maps marked out in natural pigments reflect the landscape of his country; and Pintupi woman Ningura Napurrula from Kiwikurra in the Western Desert, whose strong, stunningly simple works hang in the new Musée du Quai Branly in Paris.

Indigenous art is created for the tourist market as much as it is the fine-art market, so whether you're buying art as a souvenir or investment, it's important to buy ethically. Only buy from galleries dealing with Aboriginal communities, from art centres at communities, or direct from individual artists; don't buy art from a bloke who approaches you in the car park with a painting under his jacket. These kinds of dodgy dealings devalue the work and the artist's reputation and have a negative economic impact on the artist and community. Get hold of *Purchasing Australian Aboriginal Art, A Consumer Guide* (www.ankaaa.org.au). But above all, buy what you like, buy something you have a connection to.

Music

WA has a vibrant pop music scene, and while most of the state's bands stick to the popular pub-rock genre that Aussies love, the most imaginative of WA's artists is The Sleepy Jackson, fronted by blue-eyeliner-wearing oddball Luke Steele. The Sleepy Jackson's second album *Personality (One Was A Bird One Was A Spider)* showcases Steele's Brian Wilson–sized vision and highly-tuned pop sensibilities.

Ex-bandmates of Steele's formed the group End of Fashion, which has had success in Australia and New Zealand with its self-titled album of formulaic Aussie indie-pop. To keep it in the family, Luke Steele's sister Katy Steele has her own band, Little Birdy, which released its second album, the catchy, inventive *Hollywood* in late 2006. Another Perth band bothering the charts across Australia is Eskimo Joe, a pop-rock band whose third album *Black Fingernails, Red Wine* saw them expand their sound considerably.

More earthy are the Waifs, a folk/country/pop trio, who actually formed in Broome but are Perth-based. In 2003 their career went through the roof, with a double platinum album (*Up All Night*), a few awards and a tour with Bob Dylan. A friend of theirs (well, Perth *is* like a big country town!) is one John Butler, former busker and guitarist/singer-songwriter who fronts the imaginatively titled John Butler Trio, whose roots-rock is incredibly popular in Australia.

The Sleepy Jackson's *Personality (One Was A Bird One Was A Spider)* is a much more focused album than the first, *Lovers*. On this opus, Luke Steele channels Phil Spector's Wall of Sound, with dreamy George Harrison-esque guitars floating through, topped with Steele's own unique voice and spiritual themes.

Environment Tim Flannery

The first naturalists to investigate Australia were astonished by what they found. Here the swans were black – to Europeans this was a metaphor for the impossible – while mammals such as the platypus and echidna were discovered to lay eggs. It really was an upside-down world, where many of the larger animals hopped, where each year the trees shed their bark rather than their leaves, and where the 'pears' were made of wood (a woody pear is a relative of the waratah).

It's worthwhile understanding the basics about how nature operates in Australia. This is important because there's nowhere like Australia, and once you have an insight into its origins and natural rhythms, you will appreciate the place so much more.

THE LAND

There are two big factors that go a long way towards explaining nature in Australia: its soils and its climate. Both are unique. Australian soils are the more subtle and difficult to notice of the two, but they have been fundamental in shaping life here. On the other continents, in recent geological times processes such as volcanism, mountain building and glacial activity have been busy creating new soil. Just think of the glacial-derived soils of North America, north Asia and Europe. They feed the world today, and are made by glaciers grinding up rock of differing chemical composition over the last two million years. The rich soils of India and parts of South America were made by rivers eroding mountains, while Java in Indonesia owes its extraordinary richness to volcanoes.

All of these soil-forming processes have been almost absent from Australia in more recent times. Only volcanoes have made a contribution, and they cover less than 2% of the continent's land area. In fact, for the last 90 million years, beginning deep in the age of dinosaurs, Australia has been geologically comatose. It was too flat, warm and dry to attract glaciers, its crust too ancient and thick to be punctured by volcanoes or folded into mountains. Look at Uluru and Kata Tjuta (the Olgas). They are the stumps of mountains that 350 million years ago were the height of the Andes. Yet for hundreds of millions of years they've been nothing but nubbins.

Under such conditions no new soil is created and the old soil is leached of all its goodness, and is blown and washed away. The leaching is done by rain. Even if just 30cm of it falls each year, that adds up to a column of water 30 million kilometres high passing through the soil over 100 million years, and that can do a great deal of leaching. Almost all of Australia's mountain ranges are more than 90 million years old, so you will see a lot of sand here, and a lot of country where the rocky 'bones' of the land are sticking up through the soil. It is an old, infertile landscape, and life in Australia has been adapting to these conditions for aeons.

Australia's misfortune in respect to soils is echoed in its climate. In most parts of the world outside the wet tropics, life responds to the rhythm of the seasons – summer to winter, or wet to dry. Most of Australia experiences seasons – sometimes very severe ones – yet life does not respond solely to them. This can clearly be seen by the fact that although there's plenty of snow and cold country in Australia, there are almost no trees that shed their leaves in winter, nor do any Australian animals hibernate. Instead there is a far more potent climatic force that Australian life must obey: El Niño.

Tim Flannery is a naturalist, explorer and award-winning writer. He lives in Adelaide where he is director of the South Australian Museum and a professor at the University of Adelaide.

Tim Flannery's *The Future Eaters* is a 'big picture' overview of evolution in Australasia, covering the last 120 million years of history, with thoughts on how the environment has shaped Australasia's human cultures.

B Beale and P Fray's *The Vanishing Continent* gives an excellent overview of soil erosion across Australia. Fine colour photographs make the issue more graphic.

OLDEST, BIGGEST, LONGEST... *Susie Ashworth*

- Western Australia covers 2.5 million sq km – 32.9% of the entire country.
- Its coastline stretches for 12,500km – 34% of the entire coastline of Australia.
- Mt Meharry (1245m), in the Pilbara, is the highest point.
- The Gascoyne (760km) is the longest river.
- The world's oldest rocks (4.1 billion years old) can be found at Mt Narryer, inland from Shark Bay.
- Mt Augustus is the largest rock in the world, twice the size and three times as old as Uluru in the Northern Territory.
- Marble Bar is reputedly the hottest town in Australia, with summer averages of 41°C.
- At 474m above sea level, Tom Price is the highest town in WA.
- Wagin is home to the 'biggest ram in the southern hemisphere', a 15m-tall fibreglass monstrosity.
- The 1833km-long Rabbit Proof Fence is the longest fence in the world.
- WA is home to Australia's 'second largest country', Hutt River Province Principality (p192), run by Prince Leonard and Princess Shirley.

The cycle of flood and drought that El Niño brings to Australia is profound. The rivers – even the mighty Murray River, the nation's largest, which runs through the southeast – can be miles wide one year, while you can literally step over its flow the next. This is the power of El Niño, and its effect, when combined with Australia's poor soils, manifests itself compellingly. As you might expect from this, relatively few of Australia's birds are seasonal breeders, and few migrate. Instead, they breed when the rain comes, and a large percentage are nomads, following the rain across the breadth of the continent.

WILDLIFE

Australia's plants and animals are just about the closest things to alien life you are likely to encounter on Earth. That's because Australia has been isolated from the other continents for a very long time – at least 45 million years. The other habitable continents have been able to exchange various species at different times because they've been linked by land bridges. Just 15,000 years ago it was possible to walk from the southern tip of Africa right through Asia and the Americas to Tierra del Fuego. Not Australia, however. Its birds, mammals, reptiles and plants have taken their own separate and very different evolutionary journey, and the result today is the world's most distinct – and one of its most diverse – natural realms.

Animals

Australia is, of course, famous as the home of the kangaroo and other marsupials. Unless you visit a wildlife park, such creatures are not easy to see as most are nocturnal, although you are likely to see a kangaroo in rural areas in the daytime. Their lifestyles, however, are exquisitely attuned to Australia's harsh conditions. Have you ever wondered why kangaroos, alone among the world's larger mammals, hop? It turns out that hopping is the most efficient way of getting about at medium speeds. This is because the energy of the bounce is stored in the tendons of the legs – much like in a pogo stick – while the intestines bounce up and down like a piston, emptying and filling the lungs without needing to activate the chest muscles. When you travel long distances to find meagre feed, such efficiency is a must.

Marsupials are so efficient that they need to eat a fifth less food than equivalent-sized placental mammals (everything from bats to rats, whales and ourselves). But some marsupials have taken energy efficiency much further. If you visit a wildlife park or zoo you might notice that far-away look in a koala's eyes. It seems as if nobody is home – and this is near the truth. Several years ago biologists announced that koalas are the only living creatures that have brains that don't fit their skulls. Instead they have a shrivelled walnut of a brain that rattles around in a fluid-filled cranium. Other researchers have contested this finding, however, pointing out that the brains of the koalas examined for the study may have shrunk because these organs are so soft. Whether soft-brained or empty-headed, there is no doubt that the koala is not the Einstein of the animal world, and we now believe that it has sacrificed its brain to energy efficiency. Brains cost a lot to run – our brains typically weigh 2% of our bodyweight, but use 20% of the energy we consume. Koalas eat gum leaves, which are so toxic that they use 20% of their energy just detoxifying this food. This leaves little energy for the brain, and living in the tree tops where there are so few predators means that they can get by with few wits at all.

Despite anything an Australian tells you about koalas (aka 'dropbears'), there is no risk of one falling onto your head (deliberately or not) as you walk beneath their trees.

The peculiar constraints of the Australian environment have not made everything dumb. The koala's nearest relative, the wombat (of which there are three species), has a large brain for a marsupial. These creatures live in complex burrows and can weigh up to 35kg, making them the largest herbivorous burrowers on Earth. Because their burrows are effectively air-conditioned, they have the neat trick of turning down their metabolic activity when they are in residence. One physiologist who studied their thyroid hormones found that biological activity ceased to such an extent in sleeping wombats that, from a hormonal point of view, they appeared to be dead! Wombats can remain underground for a week at a time, and can get by on just a third of the food needed by an equivalent-sized sheep. One day perhaps, efficiency-minded farmers will keep wombats instead of sheep. At the moment, however, that isn't possible, for the largest of the wombat species, the northern hairy-nose, is one of the world's rarest creatures, with only around 100 surviving in a remote nature reserve in central Queensland.

One of the more common marsupials you might catch a glimpse of in the national parks around Australia's major cities is the species of antechinus, or marsupial mouse. These nocturnal, rat-sized creatures lead an extraordinary life. The males live for just 11 months, the first 10 of which consist of a concentrated burst of eating and growing. And like teenagers, the day comes when their minds turn to sex, which then becomes an obsession. As they embark on their quest for females they forget to eat and sleep. Instead they gather in logs and woo passing females by serenading them with squeaks. By the end of August – just two weeks after they reach 'puberty' – every single male is dead, exhausted by sex and burdened with swollen testes. This extraordinary life history may also have evolved in response to Australia's trying environmental conditions. It seems likely that if the males survived mating, they would compete with the females as they tried to find enough food to feed their growing young. Basically, antechinus dads are disposable. They do better for antechinus posterity if they go down in a testosterone-fuelled blaze of glory.

Pizzey and Knight's *Field Guide to the Birds of Australia* is an indispensable guide for birdwatchers and anyone else even peripherally interested in Australia's feathered tribes. Knight's illustrations are both beautiful and helpful in identification.

If you are very lucky, you might see a honey possum. This tiny marsupial is an enigma. Somehow it gets all of its dietary requirements from nectar and pollen, and in the southwest there are always enough flowers around for it to survive. No-one, though, knows why the males need sperm larger even than those of the blue whale, or why their testes are so massive. Were humans as well endowed, men would be walking around with the equivalent of a 4kg bag of potatoes between their legs!

TOP TEN WESTERN AUSTRALIA WILDFLOWER SPOTS

- ✔ Kings Park (p62), Perth
- ▣ Fitzgerald River National Park (p147), between Albany and Esperance on the south coast
- ▣ Porongurup National Park (p138), north of Albany
- ▣ Stirling Range National Park (p140), also north of Albany
- ✔ Mullewa (p177), in the central Midlands
- ▣ Dryanda Woodland (p172), southern Wheatbelt
- ✔ Kalbarri National Park (p190), on the Batavia Coast
- ▣ The Wheatbelt (p170)
- ▣ Wongan Hills (p176), in the central Midlands
- ✔ Morawa (p176), also in the central Midlands

So challenging are the conditions in Australia that its birds have developed some extraordinary habits. The kookaburras, magpies and blue wrens you are likely to see – to name just a few – have developed a breeding system called 'helpers at the nest'. The helpers are the young adult birds of previous breedings, which stay with their parents to help bring up the new chicks. Just why they should do this was a mystery until it was realised that conditions in Australia can be so harsh that more than two adult birds are needed to feed the nestlings. This pattern of breeding is very rare in places like Asia, Europe and North America, but it is common in a wide array of Australian birds.

Plants

Australia's plants can be irresistibly fascinating. If you happen to be in the Perth area in spring it's well worth taking a wildflower tour. The best flowers grow on the arid and monotonous sand plains, and the blaze of colour produced by the kangaroo paws, banksias and similar native plants can be dizzying. The sheer variety of flowers is amazing, with 4000 species crowded into the southwestern corner of the continent. This diversity of prolific flowering plants has long puzzled botanists. Again, Australia's poor soils seem to be the cause. The sand plain is about the poorest soil in Australia – almost pure quartz. This prevents any one fast-growing species from dominating. Instead, thousands of specialist plant species have learned to find a narrow niche, and so coexist. Some live at the foot of the metre-high sand dunes, some on top, some on an east-facing slope, some on the west and so on. Their flowers need to be striking in order to attract pollinators, for nutrients are so lacking in this sandy location that insects like bees are rare.

If you do get to walk the wildflower regions of the southwest, keep your eyes open for the sundews. Australia is the centre of diversity for these beautiful, carnivorous plants. They've given up on the soil supplying their nutritional needs and have turned instead to trapping insects with sweet globs of moisture on their leaves, and digesting them to obtain nitrogen and phosphorus.

The Wildflower Society of Western Australia's excellent website (http://members.ozemail.com.au/~wildflowers) has an extensive list of recommended wildflower guides, suggested routes for wildflower regions, and details of shows and exhibitions.

ENVIRONMENTAL ISSUES

The European colonisation of Australia, commencing in 1788, heralded a period of catastrophic environmental upheaval, with the result that Australians today are struggling with some of the most severe environmental problems to be found anywhere. It may seem strange that a population of just 20 million, living in a continent the size of the USA minus Alaska, could inflict such damage on its environment, but Australia's long isolation, its fragile soils and difficult climate have made it particularly vulnerable to human-induced change.

Damage to Australia's environment has been inflicted in several ways, the most important being the introduction of pest species, destruction of forests, overstocking rangelands, inappropriate agriculture and interference with water flows. Beginning with the escape of domestic cats into the Australian bush shortly after 1788, a plethora of vermin, from foxes to wild camels and cane toads, have run wild in Australia, causing extinctions in the native fauna. One out of every 10 native mammals living in Australia prior to European colonisation is now extinct, and many more are highly endangered. Extinctions have also affected native plants, birds and amphibians.

The destruction of forests has also had a profound effect. Most of Australia's rainforests have suffered clearing, while conservationists fight with loggers over the fate of the last unprotected stands of 'old growth'. Many Australian rangelands have been chronically overstocked for more than a century, the result being extreme vulnerability of both soils and rural economies to Australia's drought and flood cycle, as well as extinction of many native species. The development of agriculture has involved land clearance and the provision of irrigation, and here again the effect has been profound. Clearing of the diverse and spectacular plant communities of the Western Australian Wheatbelt began just a century ago, yet today up to one-third of that country is degraded by salination of the soils. Between 70kg and 120kg of salt lies below every square metre of the region, and clearing of native vegetation has allowed water to penetrate deep into the soil, dissolving the salt crystals and carrying brine towards the surface.

In terms of financial value, just 1.5% of Australia's land surface provides over 95% of agricultural yield, and much of this land lies in the irrigated regions of the Murray–Darling Basin. This is Australia's agricultural heartland, yet it too is under severe threat from salting of soils and rivers. Irrigation water penetrates into the sediments laid down in an ancient sea, carrying salt into the catchments and fields. If nothing is done, the lower Murray River will

The Climate Project is a programme that trains ordinary citizens (in the US, Australia and the UK so far) to become Climate Change Messengers who present the information delivered by Al Gore in the documentary, *An Inconvenient Truth*. For more, go to www .theclimateproject.org.

In *The Weather Makers*, Tim Flannery argues passionately for the urgent need to address - NOW - the implications of a global climate change that is damaging all life on earth and endangering our very survival. It's an accessible read.

TICKET TO NATURE Susie Ashworth

A visit to some of Western Australia's national parks is a must, with most of the state's big-ticket natural attractions protected in these areas.

Most parks are managed by the **Department of Environment & Conservation** (DEC; ☎ 6364 6500; www.dec.wa.gov.au; The Atrium, Level 4, 168 St Georges Tce, Perth), which has offices throughout the state. Camping is allowed in designated areas of some parks (around $12.50 per night for two people). DEC produces informative brochures on the major national parks and nature reserves in the state, as well as reams of other literature and maps. To be assured of a camp site during peak periods, park rangers recommend turning up early in the morning, when camp sites are being vacated, to secure a spot. This book will identify where camping is possible in the beautiful wilderness of WA.

Nature lovers can save some dosh with a DEC park pass. One of the most convenient pass options is the Holiday Park Pass ($35), which gives unlimited entry for four weeks. If you need more time, the Annual All Parks Pass ($75) gives access for a year, while the Annual Local Park Pass ($20) gives 12 months' entry to one park or a group of local parks. Passes are available from DEC offices (except Crawley), the shop at www.naturebase.net, visitors centres around the state and at park entrances. Unfortunately, these passes do not cover entry to the Tree Top Walk or Monkey Mia. The unlucky folk who only have time for one or two parks should opt for the daily vehicle fee – $10 per car per day ($5 for motorcycles and $4 for bus passengers).

WILDERNESS BATTLEGROUND Susie Ashworth

The 280km-long Ningaloo Reef is arguably Western Australia's most precious natural attraction: a stunning marine park that serves as a spawning ground, nursery and sanctuary for hundreds of species and a remote slice of wilderness for visitors to explore. In recent years it's been a battleground between developers planning to install a $200 million resort on the reef and conservationists desperate to protect it. Local author Tim Winton became the figurehead of the conservationists' campaign, and thousands of nature lovers rallied to the cause. In July 2003 the government finally rejected the resort, stating it would not accept any development that threatened the fragile coast. To find out more about continuing campaigns, see www.save-ningaloo.org.

But Ningaloo is just the latest in a long line of battles between conservationists and business interests clashing over the future of Western Australia's remaining wilderness. In the 1970s, environmentalists took on the Albany whaling industry (see p146). Since the 1980s the fight has been over the logging of spectacular old-growth jarri, karri and wandoo forests in the southwest. In the late '90s, West Australians took to the streets to rally for their beloved forests. The Labor Party was swept into state office on a strong environmental platform in 2001, promising to end the logging of old-growth and to introduce ecologically sustainable forest management. In the 2005 state election the high pressure topic was water conservation, echoing growing concern across the country, which continues at the time of writing.

Contact the **Department of Environment & Conservation** (DEC; www.dec.wa.gov.au) for an update on new protected areas and the management of 25 million hectares of National Park and marine reserves; or the **Wilderness Society Western Australia** (www.wilderness.org.au/regions/wa) for another perspective and current campaigns.

become too salty to drink in a decade or two, threatening the water supply of Adelaide, a city of over a million people.

Despite the enormity of the biological crisis engulfing Australia, governments and the community have been slow to respond. It was in the 1980s that coordinated action began to take place, but not until the '90s that major steps were taken. The establishment of **Landcare** (www.landcareaustralia.com.au), an organisation enabling people to effectively address local environmental issues, and the expenditure of $2.5 billion through the National Heritage Trust Fund have been important national initiatives. Yet so difficult are some of the issues the nation faces that, as yet, little has been achieved in terms of halting the destructive processes. Individuals are also banding together to help. Groups such as the **Australian Bush Heritage Fund** (www.bushheritage.asn.au) and the **Australian Wildlife Conservancy** (AWC; www.australianwildlife.org) allow people to donate funds and time to the conservation of native species. Some such groups have been spectacularly successful; the AWC, for example, already manages many endangered species over its 1.3-million-acre holdings.

So severe are Australia's problems that it will take a revolution before they can be overcome, for sustainable practices need to be implemented in every arena of life – from farms to suburbs and city centres. Renewable energy, sustainable agriculture and water use lie at the heart of these changes, and Australians are only now developing the road-map to sustainability that they so desperately need if they are to have a long-term future on the continent.

Western Australia Outdoors

If you love exploring the great outdoors you've come to the right place. Western Australia's (WA's) extensive coast and immense interior make it a perfect playground for outdoor enthusiasts, with countless tracks to follow, mountains to climb, waves to surf and reefs to explore.

BUSHWALKING

WA is blessed with some stunning bushwalking terrain, from the cool fertile forests of the southwest and the seemingly endless walking trail of the **Bibbulmun Track** (see the boxed text, p38) to the national parks of the north in the rugged, tropical Kimberley.

Get in touch with like-minded souls through the numerous bushwalking clubs around the state; for a list of clubs and some useful links, contact **Bushwalking Australia** (www.bushwalkingaustralia.org).

These Perth suppliers can provide bushwalking equipment and advice:
Mountain Designs (☎ 9322 4774; www.mountaindesigns.com.au; 862 Hay St, Perth)
Paddy Pallin (☎ 9321 2666; www.paddypallin.com.au; 884 Hay St, Perth)

For national park news and updates, and detailed descriptions of national park trails, see the newly minted Department of Environment and Conservation website (DEC; www.naturebase .net), or pick up brochures from local DEC offices.

Perth & Surrounds

What better way to start than with WA's first national park, the **John Forrest National Park** (p98), where there's plenty of hiking as well as camping and picnicking facilities. There's an easy 15km walk that takes in waterfalls and has excellent views. For a tougher walk, head to the rugged **Walyunga National Park** (p98), where there's a medium-to-hard 18km walk (and some easier variations) that fords the Avon River and has excellent wildlife-viewing. If you're heading north, the **Yanchep National Park** (p103) offers an excellent array of walks from short, easy strolls to challenging full-day walks such as the Yaberoo Budjara walk trail, which follows an Aboriginal walking trail.

Down South

Serious walkers gravitate to the rugged craggy beauty of the **Stirling Range National Park** (p140) north of Albany, one of the state's prime bushwalking

---

RESPONSIBLE BUSHWALKING

Please consider the following when hiking to help preserve the ecology and beauty of Western Australia.

- Do not urinate or defecate within 100m (320ft) of any water sources. Doing so pollutes precious water supplies and can lead to the transmission of serious diseases.
- Use biodegradable detergents and wash at least 50m (160ft) from any water sources.
- Avoid cutting wood for fires in popular bushwalking areas as this can cause rapid deforestation.
- Hillsides and mountain slopes are prone to erosion; it's important to stick to existing tracks.
- Bushwalking in much of the state's bushland is restricted because of the risk of spreading dieback, a nasty fungal disease that attacks the roots of plants and causes them to rot. Its spread can be prevented by observing 'no go' road signs and by cleaning soil from your boots before and after each hike.

areas. The popular Bluff Knoll climb (6km, three to four hours) will take your breath away – and so will the park's 1500 different species of wildflowers. Experienced hikers love the challenging 15.5km Stirling Ridge walk, WA's only alpine walk. Time your trip in late spring or early summer (September to November) to capture the park in all its flowering glory and be prepared for wind-chill and rain (and sometimes snow!) in winter.

Also north of Albany is the smaller **Porongurup National Park** (p138), with its signature granite rocks and pocket of dense karri forest. It offers a range of trails for bushwalkers, from the easy 10-minute Tree in the Rock stroll to the medium-grade Hayward and Nancy Peaks (three hours) and challenging three-hour Marmabup Rock hike. Wildflowers and a flurry of bird activity make springtime the peak season for Porongurup, but the park can be visited at any time of year.

Lonely Planet's Walking in Australia guide gives plenty of detail on a number of walks in WA, mainly in the southwest and on the south coast.

WA has long stretches of spectacular coastline punctuated by interesting walks. Guaranteed to be a highlight of your trip are stunning walks through **Walpole-Nornalup** (p134), **Fitzgerald River** (p147) and **Cape Le Grand** (p151) national parks.

For travellers with stamina and some time on their hands, the **Cape-to-Cape Track** (p117) follows the coastline 135km from Cape Naturaliste to Cape Leeuwin, takes five to seven days, and has four wild camp sites en route.

Up North

Summer's no picnic in the sweltering, remote national parks of the north, and high season for many is late autumn, winter and early spring (April to October). Terrain in these arid regions can be treacherous, so always do your homework, be prepared with water and supplies, and check in with the ranger's office before setting out.

Kalbarri National Park (p190) draws hikers with a seductive mix of scenic gorges, thick bushland and rugged coastal cliffs. The popular six-hour loop takes advantage of the dramatic seascapes and features a series of lookouts, including the Nature's Window, a favourite with photographers.

Rugged, sometimes hazardous treks can be taken into the dramatic gorges of the **Karijini National Park** (p215) and are popular with experienced bushwalkers – especially the walk to Mt Bruce summit (9km, five hours).

Visitors to the Kimberley's **Purnululu National Park** (p240) come to see one of Australia's most amazing sights – the striped beehive-shaped domes of

---

THE BIBB TRACK

If you've got eight spare weeks up your sleeve, consider trekking the entire Bibbulmun Track, a long-distance walking trail that winds its way south from Kalamunda, about 20km east of Perth, through virtually unbroken natural environment to Walpole and along the coast to Albany – a total of 963km.

Bushwalkers trek through magnificent southwest landscapes, including jarrah and marri forests, wandoo flats carpeted with wildflowers, rugged granite outcrops, coastal heath country and spectacular cliffs, headlands and beaches.

Camp sites are spaced at regular intervals, most with a three-sided shelter that sleeps eight to 15 people, plus a water tank and pit toilets. The best time for walking is from late winter to spring (August to October).

Thousands of walkers use the Bibbulmun each year, though most are only on the track for two or three days. For more information, contact the Department of Environment and Conservation's **Bibb Track Office** (☎ 9334 0265; www.calm.wa.gov.au/tourism/bibbulmun_splash.html).

There is also plenty of information about the track on the Department of Education & Conservation's **NatureBase** (www.naturebase.net) website.

PLAYING FAVOURITES

Here are our five favourite national parks and why we love them so:

- Fitzgerald River National Park (p147) – wildflowers and whales
- Karijini National Park (p215) – gorgeous gorges galore!
- Ningaloo Marine Park (p208) – superlative snorkelling and surfing
- Shoalwater Islands Marine Park (p94) – wild dolphin wonderland
- Windjana Gorge National Park (p238) – cruising through crocodile country

the World Heritage–listed Bungle Bungles. Walks include the easy Cathedral Gorge walk, and the more difficult overnight trek to Piccaninny Gorge. The park is only open from April to December.

CAMPING

WA is an outstanding place to go camping. Considering that most people go camping to 'get away from it all', this enormous state provides that in spades, especially in the national parks, where sleeping in a swag under the stars is almost obligatory. The weather is a major concern for campers; it can be uncomfortable in the north during summer due to the heat and flash flooding, and pretty miserable and cold in the south during winter. See When to Go (p11), and note that school holidays are not a good time for solitude in WA.

CYCLING

Cyclists are made very welcome in WA. There are excellent day, weekend or even multiweek cycling routes. Perth has an ever-growing network of bike tracks, and you'll find the southwest region of WA good for cycle touring. While you'll find thousands of kilometres of good, virtually traffic-free roads in country areas, the distances between towns makes it difficult to plan – even if the riding is virtually flat!

For practical advice on cycling around WA, see p266. For bike hire in Perth, see p65.

Perth (p52) is a relatively bike-friendly city, with a good recreational bike-path system, including routes that follow the Swan River all the way to Fremantle, and extensive paths through Kings Park overlooking the city. For cycling maps, brochures and guides to particular routes, contact the **Department of Planning and Infrastructure** (☎ 9216 8000; www.dpi.wa.gov.au/cycling; 441 Murray St, Perth).

Cyclists rule on virtually car-free Rottnest Island (p91). It's a liberating place to ride, with long stretches of empty roads circumnavigating the island, allowing you to stop off at each beach for a swim! You can hire bikes on the island; see p94.

Mountain bikers have been exploring the **Munda Biddi Mountain Bike Trail** (www.mundabiddi.org.au), which means 'path through the forest' in the Noongar Aboriginal language. When completed, it will be the mountain-biking equivalent of the Bibbulmun Track (opposite), taking off-road cyclists some 900km from Mundaring on Perth's outskirts through the beautiful, scenic southwest to Albany on the south coast. The first stage (to Collie, 332km) had been completed at the time of research, with camps situated en route a day's easy ride apart, with water, bike storage and bike repair facilities. You can pick up the excellent map pack ($31) and more information from **Department of Environment and Conservation** (DEC; ☎ 9334 0333).

TOP FIVE INDIGENOUS CULTURAL TOURS

■ Wula Guda Nyinda, Monkey Mia (p196) – learn to love bush tucker, to let the bush talk to you, and how to identify the size of an animal by his poo, with Darren 'Capes' Capewell.

■ Kodja Place Indigenous Tours, Kojonup (p172) – Noongar elder Jack Cox teaches you traditional practices and tells wonderful Dreaming stories over billy tea.

■ Mamabulanjin Tours, Broome (p227) – learn traditional fishing, hunting and survival techniques as you walk the mangroves of Roebuck Bay.

■ Yamatji Cultural Trails, Geraldton (p185) – compare the traditional past with contemporary issues around the camp fire, in a swag, under the stars.

■ Yanchep National Park, Yanchep (p103) – let the Noongar people give you a dance lesson or two and get to give the didgeridoo a go.

DIVING & SNORKELLING

With plenty of fascinating dives on offer throughout the state, including stunning marine parks and shipwrecks, WA is the perfect place to don a wetsuit and take the plunge. Local tourist offices can often help out with brochures and booklets on top regional diving or snorkelling spots.

Close to Perth, divers can explore shipwrecks and marine life off the beaches of **Rottnest Island** (p92); or head south to explore the submerged reefs and historic shipwrecks of the West Coast Dive Park within **Shoalwater Islands Marine Park** (p94), near Rockingham. You can take a dive course in Geographe Bay with companies based in **Dunsborough** (p120) or **Busselton** (p117), with its excellent dives under the jetty, on Four Mile Reef (a 40km limestone ledge about 6.5km off the coast) and the scuttled HMAS *Swan*.

Other wrecks popular with divers are the HMAS *Perth* (at 36m) which was deliberately sunk in 2001 in King George Sound near **Albany** (p141); and the *Sanko Harvest*, near **Esperance** (p148). Both wrecks are teeming with the marine life which has made the artificial reefs home.

Divers seeking warmer water should head north. A staggering amount of marine life can be found just 100m offshore within the **Ningaloo Marine Park** (p208), making this pristine piece of coastline fantastic for diving and snorkelling. On the **Turquoise Bay Drift Snorkel** (p208), you drift over the coral, get out down the beach, and do it again! If that whets your appetite, take in one of the most spectacular underwater experiences in the world – diving or snorkelling alongside the world's largest fish, the whale shark. Tours are available from **Exmouth** (p204) and **Coral Bay** (p203).

FISHING

With more than 6000km of coastline, WA is a fishing enthusiast's paradise. From sailfish in the north to trout in the south there are all types of fishing on offer. Fishing is the state's largest recreational activity and you'll find locals dropping a line just about anywhere there's water – and catching their dinner nearly every time.

Ocean lovers can find a place to fish just about anywhere along the coast at any time of year. Close to Perth, recreational fishers dangle a hook at **Rottnest Island** (p91), with King Wrasse and Western Australian dhufish (previously called the jewfish) both plentiful around the island.

South of Perth, popular fishing hot spots include **Mandurah** (p95), with options for deep-sea fishing, catching tailor from the long golden stretches of beach or nabbing Mandurah's famed blue manna crabs and king prawns in the estuaries. You can scoot down to **Augusta** (p126) to chase salmon in

For local tips, events, news and rides, contact the Bicycle Transportation Alliance (www.multiline.com.au/~bta; 2 Delhi St, West Perth).

The magazine and website *Western Angler* (www.westernangler.com.au) are great resources for the serious WA fishing enthusiast.

the Blackwood River or whiting in the bay; or drop a line into the fish-rich waters underneath the famous jetty at **Busselton** (p117).

Sunny **Geraldton** (p185) is an excellent place to fish, with Sunset Beach and Drummond Cove popular spots, or you can take one of the excellent fishing charters out to the nearby **Houtman Abrolhos Islands** (p188). There's great fishing all along the coast from here and as you move up into the hotter, steamier northwest, the fishing charter operators start to multiply, with a good chance to hook a monster fish at **Exmouth** (p204), the **Dampier Archipelago** (p213) and the game-fishing nirvana of **Broome** (p223). The northern Kimberley is also a popular spot for catching the tough-fighting and tasty barramundi.

You'll need a recreational fishing licence if you intend catching marron (freshwater crayfish) or rock lobsters, if you use a fishing net, or if you're freshwater angling in the southwest. They cost $22 to $38 or there's an annual licence covering all fishing activities for $75. Buy one from the **Department of Fisheries** (☎ 9482 7333; www.fish.wa.gov.au; SGIO Building, 168-170 St George's Tce, Perth), from its regional offices or online. Note that there are strict bag and size limits – see the website for specific details.

SURFING & WINDSURFING

If you're here to surf, WA is simply brilliant. Beginners, intermediates, wannabe pros and adventure surfers will find excellent conditions to suit their skill levels along WA's coast. WA gets huge swells (often over 3m), so it's critical to align where you surf with your ability. Look out for strong currents, huge sharks and territorial local surfers who are often far scarier than a hungry white pointer.

The state's traditional surfing home is the southwest, particularly the beaches from **Yallingup** to **Margaret River** (see the boxed text, p121), and this stretch is perfect for a surf trip, with heaps of different breaks to explore.

Back up around **Perth** (p52) the surf is a lot smaller, but there's often good conditions at bodyboard-infested **Trigg** (p64) and **Scarborough** (p64). Don't despair if waves are small, simply head off to **Rottnest Island** (p91) where the surf is usually much bigger and better – check out Strickland Bay.

Heading north there are countless reef breaks waiting to be discovered on a surfing safari (hint: take a 4WD), with the best-known spots being the left-hand point breaks of Jake's Point near **Kalbarri** (p190), Gnaraloo Station, 150km north of **Carnarvon** (p197), as well as Surfers Beach at **Exmouth** (p204). Buy the locals a beer and they might share the location of some lesser-known world-class spots. We're not brave enough to do it in print – we have family living here.

Windsurfers and kite-surfers have plenty of choice spots to try out in WA as well, with excellent flat-water and wave-sailing. Kite-surfers in particular will appreciate the long, empty beaches and offshore reefs away from crowds.

After trying out Perth's city beaches, the next place to head is **Lancelin** (p104), which is home to a large population of surfers, especially in summer. Both flat-water and wave sailing are excellent here. Further up the coast, **Geraldton** (p185) is another surfing hot spot – especially at the renowned Coronation Beach. The Shark Bay area has excellent flat-water sailing and the remote Gnaraloo Station, 150km north of **Carnarvon** (p197) is a world-renowned wave-sailing spot.

WILDLIFE-WATCHING

For most visitors to WA there's no better wildlife-watching than seeing the southern right and humpback whales make their way along the whole coast. In June the gentle giants are often spotted off the southern coast near Cape

Leeuwin on their annual pilgrimage from Antarctica to the warm tropical waters of the northwest coast. They can then be seen again on their slow southern migration down the coast in spring and early summer. Whale-watching tours leave from **Perth** (p65), **Rockingham** (p94) and **Cape Leeuwin** (p126), and generally cost around $60/45 per adult/child for a three-hour cruise.

Southern right and humpback whales are also spotted off the Great Australian Bight, and regularly make themselves at home in the bays and coves of St George Sound in **Albany** (p141) from July to October. In whale-watching season, they are often also spotted from the cliff tops of the south coast, from **Fitzgerald River National Park** (p147), **Bremer Bay** (p148), **Cape Arid National Park** (p151) and **Torndirrup National Park** (p146).

Dolphins can be seen up close year-round at several places in the west, including the Dolphin Discovery Centre at **Bunbury** (p115), on an interactive dolphin tour from **Rockingham** (p94), or at the beach resort of **Monkey Mia** (p196), famous for its friendly colony of bottlenose dolphins as well as for checking out 10% of the world's dugong population munching on seagrass.

For excellent regional-specific advice, including events and a series of bird-watching guides, see the website of Birds Australia Western Australia Inc (http://birdswa.iinet.net.au).

WA is also a bird-watcher's delight, with an enormous variety of species and two of the four official Birds Australia observatories. The **Eyre Bird Observatory** (p167), surrounded by mallee scrub and spectacular sand dunes, is a remote getaway off the Nullarbor for serious nature lovers. The **Broome Bird Observatory** (p234), in the middle of a mudflats region, attracts a staggering 800,000 birds each year. **Yalgorup National Park** (p97), south of Mandurah, is another important habitat for a wide variety of water birds, and is a magnet for local bird-watchers.

Food & Drink

Western Australia (WA) has fantastic fresh produce, enviable wines and an eclectic mix of culinary influences that often merge to create a wonderful dining experience – especially when mixed with sunshine and a sea view! Visitors will be surprised by the wide range of food available in restaurants, markets, delis and cafés – especially in Perth, Fremantle and Broome, as well as southern towns such as Margaret River and Albany. However, the further you get away from the tourist trail the less willing chefs are to deviate from the classic Aussie pub menu of steak and seafood simply presented. One thing that doesn't change, however, is the critically acclaimed wines of WA, where both big- and small-name vineyards produce world-class vintages.

The mix of European, Asian and indigenous ingredients and cooking methods is often termed 'Modern Australian' (Mod Oz). While in other countries this 'fusion' style of cuisine earns the term 'con-fusion' when poorly executed, in Australia this arguably works well. While there are no definitive dishes in the Mod-Oz style, an example of this might entail a French-trained Aussie chef cooking a kangaroo fillet using Asian-inspired ingredients.

STAPLES & SPECIALITIES

With a wonderful, wild coastline, it's no surprise that most of WA's best food comes from the sea. Fresh WA seafood is harnessed from some of the purest waters you'll find anywhere, and usually cooked with great respect for the ingredients' freshness.

Along the endless coastline, cateries serve fish such as red emperor, coral trout, dhufish, pink snapper, King George whiting, threadfin salmon and the esteemed barramundi from the tropical north. Visitors can tuck into superb rock lobsters from Geraldton, dine on sardines caught near Fremantle, or munch on mussels and Exmouth Gulf prawns. Unique to the southwest are delicious marron, prehistoric-looking freshwater crayfish that feature on menus throughout the forest region.

Thanks to a large migrant population, travellers are also treated to a huge choice of cuisines – anything from Thai, Indian and Japanese to Chinese, Italian and Turkish. In the supermarkets of Perth the expat community can find everything they need to recreate their favourite dishes.

While nationalistic citizens around the world gaze at their coat of arms and get a tear in their eye, many Australians salivate. Yes folks, both the kangaroo and the emu make appearances on Australia's coat of arms and menus.

DRINKS
Non-Alcoholic Drinks

Australians drink a lot of fizzy soft drinks as well as having an odd obsession with flavoured milk (chocolate, coffee and strawberry are favourites), which often replaces breakfast! A good cup of tea these days means a tea bag in a cup of hot water, but Aussies still love a good 'cuppa'.

TRAVEL YOUR TASTEBUDS

Yes, indeed, you can eat Australia's cute coat-of-arms animals, the kangaroo and the emu. Kangaroo is by far the most popular menu item of the two and its deep, purple-red meat is sweet and strongly flavoured (akin to game) and is generally served rare. In the north, you might encounter crocodile on the menu, a white meat similar to fish with a texture closer to chicken. On some bush-tucker walks you might be offered the witchetty grub, which looks like a giant maggot and tastes nutty, but with a squishy texture. It tastes better if you eat it with your eyes shut.

Perth and Fremantle are coffee-crazed (see the boxed text, p71), and addicts will be pleased with the offerings in Margaret River, Albany and Broome, but might be struggling to find a good espresso elsewhere, where a barista is often thought to be a South American freedom-fighter.

These days cafés in urban WA make a decent coffee, but there is still that little naming-convention problem: a short black is an espresso, a flat white is like a cappuccino without the foam and a 'long macchiato' is a coffee-making crime.

Alcoholic Drinks

Foster's, Carlton Draught, Tooheys, XXXX and Victoria Bitter (VB) are all well-known Australian beers. The Swan Brewery, the west's biggest producer of beer, has two major brands: Swan and Emu.

Far more interesting are WA's excellent boutique breweries. Matilda Bay produces a range of beers with plenty of character and distinct styles. Redback (a smooth wheat beer), Beez Neez (a honey-wheat beer), and Matilda Bay Bohemian Pilzner (strong-flavoured bitter) are all worth trying, as are the Reserve Beer range.

Fremantle's Little Creatures Pale Ale is a favourite tipple and its other boutique brews (the light Rogers' beer, the refreshing Pilsner and the brilliantly clear Bright Ale) are all popular in Perth and Fremantle. Visit the Little Creatures brewery, bar and restaurant in Fremantle (p85).

There are several other boutique breweries in pubs in Perth and Fremantle and yes, Guinness-lovers, your 'must-have' brew is occasionally found on draught in Irish pubs.

Australian beer is served ice-cold and has a higher alcohol content than British or American beers. Standard beer is around 5% alcohol, although most breweries now produce light beers (around 2% to 3% alcohol) and 'mid-strength' beers (around 3.5%). The flavour of these beers has improved enormously over the past few years – so there's no excuse for getting caught over the alcohol limit when driving.

Saving the best 'til last, some of the country's finest wines can be found in WA. See the Wineries chapter, p47.

CELEBRATIONS

West Aussies love a good party and with such great weather, where better to indulge in food and wine than the great outdoors? Celebrations often take the form of barbecues (barbies), whether it's to watch a footy match (with the TV outside), celebrate a birthday or just as an excuse to get together. At these ritualistic get-togethers, the man of the house traditionally cooks, wearing an apron that bears an amusing slogan regarding the grill-master's drinking, cooking or sexual abilities. As Christmas falls in the middle of summer, even the traditional baked Christmas dinner is shunned in favour of a barbecue, with copious amounts of fresh seafood and steaks sizzling away. Generally held in the mid-afternoon, it allows time for a late-afternoon siesta followed by sneaking a few leftovers. If a barbie's not on, another popular celebration venue for groups is the local Indian, Chinese or Thai restaurant where you can BYO (bring your own alcohol) and order up a storm.

In Australia BYO (Bring Your Own) is a tradition in which a restaurant allows you to bring your own alcohol. If the restaurant also sells alcohol, the BYO bit is usually limited to bottled wine only (no beer, no casks). A corkage charge is almost always added to your bill.

As WA's wine-growing regions have developed, so has the accompanying food industry. Down in the gourmet centre of Margaret River, foodies flock to the Margaret River Wine Region Festival in November, while Fremantle celebrates the sardine in January. Elsewhere in the state, most wine regions throw harvest festivals, which combine wine-tasting with samples of the region's best local produce. For more details on these festivals, see p252.

WHERE TO EAT & DRINK

Perth has the kind of dining scene that you would expect for a cosmopolitan city, with the range of options encompassing small, cheap Asian eateries, fine-dining restaurants and everything in-between. In small towns, however, the choice narrows considerably. Usually you'll end up eating at a pub, with its ubiquitous 'counter meals', so called because they used to be eaten at the bar counter (and sometimes still are). The food is simple: seafood or meat with chips, often with a self-service salad bar. If you can't decide between seafood or meat, try the quintessential Aussie pub meal, surf 'n' turf (seafood and steak in the same dish).

What you will notice when you're in larger towns is the BYO option at cafés and restaurants. This can make restaurant dining more economical as you're not paying the restaurant's mark-up on wines.

See p248 for information on opening hours.

Quick Eats

The insidious big-name fast-food outlets have infiltrated towns and highways all over the state. Other quick eats come from milk bars (a kind of delicatessen/general store), which serve home-made hamburgers (with bacon, egg, pineapple and beetroot if you so desire). Most towns close to the sea have at least one busy fish and chip shop and it's an Aussie tradition to take your battered fish and chips down to the beach, to enjoy the sea breezes and be stalked by menacing seagulls.

Another Aussie tradition is the ubiquitous meat pie – predominately steak and gravy in a pastry case. While the demand for more interesting choices has led to the introduction of gourmet pies, such as spinach and feta pies squeezed in among the beef options, don't go asking for these at a roadhouse in the outback – real men just have a meat pie with sauce!

VEGETARIANS & VEGANS

Vegetarians not straying from the beaten tourist track will fare quite well. Cafés seem to always have vegetarian options, and the best restaurants may even have complete vegetarian menus. If you are venturing to less-populated country areas, your food choices are as slim as a supermodel. Vegans will find the going much tougher, but there are usually dishes that are vegan-adaptable at restaurants.

EATING WITH KIDS

Dining with children in Australia is easy. Besides the obvious fast-food joints, children are very welcome at WA's omnipresent Chinese, Thai and Italian restaurants. Kids' items are usually available at cafés, and you'll often see families dining early in bistros and clubs – where there's either a separate kids' menu or kid-sized portions of dishes such as pasta or fish and chips.

Seafood and steak on the one plate (usually called surf 'n' turf) is an Aussie tradition. While chefs dare not get too creative with the dish, they get creative with its name – here are our favourites: reef & beef, ocean & earth, paddock & pond, prawns with horns.

ORDERING, BILLS & TIPPING

Overseas visitors are often baffled at Aussie cafés and pubs where there are waiters but no table service. In some cafés and pubs you go to the counter and order, and pick up your food and drinks yourself. The more sophisticated version of this is where they give you a number or an electronic device and they either bellow out your number or the device rings like a cell phone when your food is ready. Another variation is where you order and are given a number to display on your table so the waiter can bring the food over. And then there are cafés with good old-fashioned table service.

Whichever way you order and receive your bill, the total at the bottom is all you are expected to pay. It should include GST (as should menu prices) and there is no 'optional' service charge added. Waiters are paid reasonably well, so they don't rely on tips to survive. Often, though, especially in urban WA, people tip a few coins in a café, while the tip for excellent restaurant service can be as high as 15% in the better establishments. The pesky incidence of add-ons (for bread, water, surcharges on weekends etc) is unfortunately rising.

HABITS & CUSTOMS

Australian table manners are fairly standard – avoid talking with your mouth full, wait until everyone has been served before you eat, and don't use your fingers to pick up food unless it can't be tackled another way.

If you're invited to dinner at someone's house, take a gift. You may offer to bring something for the meal (sometimes a course such as dessert or a salad), but if the host refuses, take a bottle of wine.

'Shouting' is a revered Aussie custom where people in a bar or pub take turns to buy drinks for their group. It's unclear whether getting drunk is the aim or a consequence of this tradition – but don't leave before it's your turn to shout! At a toast, everyone should touch glasses.

A smoking ban for all indoor areas of pubs, bars and clubs came into effect from July 2006, which is why you'll see addicts puffing away outside these establishments. Never light up in someone's house unless you ask first – and don't take offence when you're pointed outside!

In WA the opening dish of a three-course meal is called the entrée, the second course (the North American entrée) is called the main course and the sweet bit at the end is called dessert, sweets, afters or pud.

MENU DECODER

Australians love to shorten everything, including people's names, so expect many words to be abbreviated. Some food- and beverage-related words you might hear:

barbie – a barbecue, where men do the cooking and bond over beers while the womenfolk sip wine and pretend to be impressed by the manful meat-wrangling

Chiko Roll – a large, spring roll–like pastry for sale in takeaway shops

Esky – an insulated ice chest to keep necessary supplies, such as beer

sanger/sando – a sandwich

slab – a case of beer

snags – sausages

Tim Tam – a chocolate biscuit that lies close to the heart of most Australians

Vegemite – salty, dark-brown yeast extract that's best served spread on toast; iconic and adored by the Aussie masses, it's generally greeted with a shake of the head by visitors

Wineries Campbell Mattinson & Terry Carter

While it's perhaps odd that we chiefly owe the current worldwide popularity of Western Australia's (WA's) wines to a 1965 academic publication entitled *The Climate & Soils of Southern WA in Relation to Vine Growing*, once you taste the results that led from this study, you'll certainly be toasting its author, Dr John Gladstone. The wineries that sprung up following his report laid the foundations for the region's formidable reputation.

Australian wine has exploded in both quality and quantity since that time and WA, particularly in terms of quality, has been a leading force in that change. Today WA is recognised as a world-class producer of a wide variety of table wines – red and white, both decadently expensive and delightfully affordable. Arguably like no other region in the world, the words 'Produced in Western Australia' signify, at the very least, a fantastically drinkable drop.

It's not that wine is new to WA, however. The most famous of the long-standing WA wine producers, Houghton, was founded way back in 1836, just outside Perth in the Swan Valley (p87). Its White Burgundy (now White Classic), first produced in 1937, is one of Australia's best-known wines – but even with that heritage, the Swan Valley as a wine-growing region has taken a back seat to the Margaret River's sublime grape-growing conditions, and Houghton today grows huge volumes of grapes in the southwest. For just as government geologist and keen wine enthusiast Dr John Gladstone foretold, just about anywhere south of Perth – especially those areas with the cooling influence of a nearby coastline – has the potential to be a very fine area for the production of wine. Cheers, Doctor!

Campbell Mattinson is a journalist of over 20 years and an award-winning writer. In 2005 Campbell picked up the prestigious NSW Wine Press Club Wine Communicator Award, and he was a finalist at the World Food Media Awards in both 2003 and 2005.

MARGARET RIVER

If you're looking for WA's best wines, look no further than the coastal area of Margaret River, 250km southwest of Perth. Before the good Doctor pinpointed the area as having the right soils and the right climate to produce first-class wines, Margaret River was a struggling, isolated town a lengthy journey from one of the world's most isolated capital cities.

Dr Gladstone got it right – as did the pioneering wine families who took up his advice. Although a great number of other terrific wineries are very well established, these four founding wineries are the cornerstone of Margaret River and form the basis of the region's reputation among the great wine regions of the world:

For information and tasting notes about Western Australian wines, and to shop online for reds and whites, visit www.mrwines.com.

Cape Mentelle (☎ 9757 0888; www.capementelle.com.au; Walcliffe Rd, Margaret River) Makes consistently excellent Cabernet Sauvignon and a wonderful example of the current 'it' wine, Sauvignon Blanc/Sémillon.
Cullen Wines (☎ 9755 5277; www.cullenwines.com.au; Caves Rd, Cowaramup) Still in the family, it produces a superb Chardonnay and an excellent Cabernet Merlot.
Moss Wood (☎ 9755 6266; www.mosswood.com.au; Metricup Rd, Willyabrup) Makes a heady Sémillon, a notable Cabernet Sauvignon and a surprising Pinot Noir.
Vasse Felix (☎ 9756 5000; www.vassefelix.com.au; cnr Caves & Harmans Rds, South Cowaramup) Good all-round winery and a must-see on any Margaret River winery tour.

The Margaret River region is flanked by a roaring surf coast and is generally blessed with long and often very dry summers, qualities that seem to infiltrate the wines, which are ripe, rich and stylish – they almost seem suntanned – and are often of stunning quality. Besides the initial four, the list of notable wineries in Margaret River is so long and impressive that it's impossible to include them all, but standouts include the following:

Devil's Lair (☎ 9757 7573; www.devils-lair.com; Rocky Rd, Witchcliffe) Small, cosy, stylish cellar door with top-of-the-line Chardonnay and Cabernet. Check out its Fifth Leg series as well.

Howard Park (☎ 9756 5200; www.howardparkwines.com.au; Miamup Rd, Cowaramup) Brilliant Cabernet and Shiraz, and a wide range of styles and prices. It also makes the MadFish range of wines.

Leeuwin Estate (☎ 9759 0000; www.leeuwinestate.com.au; Stevens Rd, Margaret River) A brilliant estate, with excellent wines, a stylish cellar door, highly regarded restaurant and an annual sell-out concert series (see p252). Oh, and they make one of the best Chardonnays in Australia – the Art Series Chardonnay.

Pierro (☎ 9755 6220; www.pierro.com.au; Caves Rd, Willyabrup) Powerful Chardonnay and Sauvignon Blanc to die for, in a quaint, leafy setting.

Voyager Estate (☎ 9757 6354; www.voyagerestate.com.au; Stevens Rd, Margaret River) A true gem, with great wines across the board and an elegant cellar door and restaurant.

Xanadu Estate (☎ 9757 2581; www.xanaduwines.com; Terry Rd, Margaret River) Broad range (including the popular Secession label), decent cellar door and restaurant.

It almost sounds cruel to label the following wineries as 'second-tier', but when you've got such a stellar line-up, that's generally how they are regarded. Still, all the following offer excellent wines in distinctive surroundings, and even then a good deal more wineries from Margaret River could be listed.

Brookland Valley (☎ 9755 6042; www.brooklandvalley.com.au; Caves Rd, Willyabrup) Getting better all the time; the Chardonnay and Merlot are fantastic.

Happs (☎ 9755 3300; www.happs.com.au; Commonage Rd, Dunsborough) Extensive, impressive range of wines and pottery.

Juniper Estate (☎ 9755 9000; www.juniperestate.com.au; Harman's Rd, South Cowaramup) Emerging star. Check out the Estate Shiraz and Semillon.

Moss Brothers (☎ 9755 6270; www.mossbrothers.com.au; Caves Rd, Willyabrup) Often neglected but wrongly so. Great Shiraz!

Willespie (☎ 9755 6248; www.willespie.com.au; Harman's Mill Rd, Willyabrup) Unusual Verdelho and an excellent shiraz.

Margaret River also produces a great deal of wine using a combination of the Sémillon and Sauvignon Blanc grapes. These very popular fruity wines are not Margaret River's very best but they are often the most affordable – and are highly regarded. Cape Mentelle, Cullen Wines and **Lenton Brae** (☎ 9755 6255; Caves Rd, Willyabrup) all make particularly exotic examples.

SWAN VALLEY

While the strength of WA wine production is clearly in the cooler southern wine regions, the Swan Valley still has something to offer, not least because it makes a pleasant day trip from Perth, with the closest of the wineries, **Waters Edge Winery** (☎ 9277 2989; www.watersedgewinery.com.au; 77 Great Eastern Hwy, South Guildford), barely a 25-minute drive northeast of the city centre. The Swan Valley is WA's oldest wine region and while in quality terms it's generally not seen as a major contributor to Australia's growing wine reputation, it's good wine-tourism country, with fine food, full-flavoured wine, and hot dry weather perfect for outdoor wining and dining. Wine quality in the Swan Valley has lifted in recent years, especially in the production of fruity white wines made from Chardonnay, Chenin Blanc, Verdelho, as well as red wines made from Shiraz. The Swan Valley can also be visited by boat – up the Swan River, stopping at the Sandalford Winery – which adds to its charm.

The Swan Valley's most distinguished wine is in fact one of Australia's most famously affordable wines. Houghton White Classic (formerly White Burgundy) is a blend of a number of different white-wine grapes, drinks like a mix of tropical, zesty fruits, and even cellars well over five or more years –

Watershed Premium Wines (☎ 9758 8633; www.watershedwines.com.au; cnr Bussell Hwy & Darch Rd, Margaret River) is a relative newcomer in the Margaret River area, but its wines are already starting to attract attention.

While 2004, 2005 and 2006 were great years in WA for both quantity and quality of grapes, this means that there is currently an oversupply of wine – and while that's bad news for producers, it's good news for consumers.

a perfect memento of your trip. It's a good introduction to the rest of the range at **Houghton** (☎ 9274 9540; www.houghton-wines.com.au; Dale Rd, Middle Swan), from the very cheap to the very expensive; it's the area's best winery. Not that the area's short of wineries – at last count there were more than 30 of them. The following is a selection of the best:

Jane Brook Estate (☎ 9274 1432; www.janebrook.com.au; Toodyay Rd, Middle Swan) Clean, pure wines and outdoor dining facilities.

Lamont Wines (☎ 9296 4485; www.lamonts.com.au; Bisdee Rd, Millendon) Owned and run by the famous WA food-and-wine family, both of which are on impressive show here.

Sandalford (☎ 9374 9300; www.sandalford.com; West Swan Rd, Caversham) An old favourite with a large range and extensive facilities for visitors, including tours of the winery.

PEEL & GEOGRAPHE REGIONS

This area stretches south of Perth, in the direction (but short) of Margaret River, from Rockingham to Donnybrook. The Peel region starts about 70km south of Perth – which often means that it's hot and dry and rugged. Like the Swan Valley, wine in this region is not generally considered of great significance – though a few wineries entirely buck that trend. **Peel Estate** (☎ 9524 1221; www.peelwine.com.au; Fletcher Rd, Baldivis) is the most obvious of them. Established in 1974 by Will Nairn, it has for much of that time produced one of Australia's best Shiraz wines, along with excellent Cabernet, a big Zinfandel, Chardonnay and Verdelho. It's a beautiful cellar door made predominantly of local Tuart-tree wood, with views through to the working winery. While not in the same class as Peel Estate, the **Millbrook Winery** (☎ 9525 5796; www.millbrookwinery.com.au; Old Chestnut Lane, Jarrahdale), a short drive west, is also worth the trip, with a large new cellar door and a 'drink now' range, the Barking Owl.

Further south, in the slightly cooler Geographe region, you'll find a large selection of wineries of varying quality, though the standouts are clear: **Capel Vale** (☎ 9702 1012; www.capelvale.com; Mallokup Rd, Capel) has a 30-year history of winemaking excellence, particularly with Chardonnay, Shiraz and more recently Merlot. It's all been made easier to enjoy with the recent re-building of the cellar door complex. Its only serious rival in the region is **Killerby Vineyards** (☎ 1800 655 722; www.killerby.com.au; Minninup Rd, Stratham) just south of Bunbury, which founded the region in 1973 and is highly regarded for its Chardonnay and Shiraz. **Willow Bridge Estate** (☎ 9728 0055; Gardincourt Dr, Dardanup) also produces a large number of well-priced wines, its whites being of particular note.

GREAT SOUTHERN

The Great Southern region will never challenge Margaret River's preeminence among wine-touring regions – Margaret River is so spectacularly beautiful – but from a purely wine-quality point of view, it's arguable that one day it will give Margaret River a run for its money. While not as developed in terms of wine tourism, it's still a fantastic wine region to tour. Shiraz, cabernet sauvignon, riesling and sauvignon blanc do especially well here.

The region stretches from the southeast town of Frankland, further southeast to Albany, and then west again to Denmark. Mt Barker, smack-bang in the middle of the region, is 350km southeast of Perth.

The thing that excites people about Great Southern's wines is that although they're full of flavour and power, they tend not to blow your head off – they have a sense of elegance to them. This combination of elegance and power is a much-desired and rare trait in a wine, and across all the above-mentioned varieties Great Southern seems capable of attaining it.

There are great wineries to explore here. In Frankland, the following produce terrific dry white and red wines:

Alkoomi (☎ 9855 2229; www.alkoomi.com.au; Wingeballup Rd) Still a family-run business, it produces a great Cabernet Sauvignon and Riesling.
Ferngrove (☎ 9855 2378; www.ferngrove.com.au; Ferngrove Rd) Produces an honest Chardonnay, an excellent Shiraz and a brilliant Cabernet Sauvignon/Shiraz blend, 'The Stirlings'.
Frankland Estate (☎ 9855 1544; www.franklandestate.com.au; Frankland Rd) One of the key wineries that can justly revitalise Riesling – fantastic stuff.

You'll find a greater concentration of wineries southwest of Frankland at Mt Barker and among the nearby Porongurup range – it's a region of increasing significance. Riesling and shiraz are consistently great performers here, with lean, long-flavoured cabernet sauvignon heading steadily the same way. Wineries to look for:
Forest Hill (☎ 9848 2199; www.foresthillwines.com.au; Muir Hwy, Mt Barker) Try their Cabernet Sauvignon.
Goundrey Wines (☎ 9851 1777; www.goundrey.com; Muir Hwy, Mt Barker) Go for their excellent value Offspring range.
Plantagenet Wines (☎ 9851 3111; www.plantagenetwines.com; Albany Hwy, Mt Barker) The area's best winery – try its Chardonnays, Rieslings and reds.

Further south, at Albany and more especially at Denmark, you'll find some of the most esteemed wine names in Australia: **Howard Park** (☎ 9848 2345; www.howardparkwines.com.au; Scotsdale Rd, Denmark), also at Margaret River (p47), put this region on the map and nears legendary status for its superb Cabernet Sauvignon, Riesling and Chardonnay. **West Cape Howe** (☎ 9848 2959; www.westcapehowewines.com.au; South Coast Hwy, Denmark) is a winery offering straightforward wines that are excellent value. A winery in the region notable for its Pinot Noir is **Wignall's Wines** (☎ 9841 2848; www.wignallswines.com.au; Chester Pass Rd, Albany).

PEMBERTON & MANJIMUP

If you travel east of Margaret River in the direction of the Great Southern wine region, about halfway between the two you'll hit the Pemberton–Manjimup area (280km due south of Perth) – which just goes to prove how ideal the deep south lands of WA are to vineyards. Pemberton is a beautiful, undulating area home to vast numbers of the area's famous karri trees, and with its cool-ish climate produces cooler wine styles – Pinot Noir, Merlot and Chardonnay in particular. Excellent producers in Pemberton:
Salitage Wines (☎ 9776 1771; www.salitage.com.au; Vasse Hwy) A large, stylish winery with all the bells and whistles – and the wines to back it up. Try one of the winery tours.
Smithbrook Wines (☎ 9772 3557; www.smithbrook.com.au; Smith Brook Rd) Probably the best wines in this area, though tasting is by appointment only. Excellent Merlot.

UNCORKED

If you've gone to remove the cork on a wine in Western Australia only to realise that it has a screw-cap, don't feel short-changed – many excellent Aussie wines now have screw-caps to reduce the number of wines that suffer from 'cork taint'. There's no consensus amongst wine makers on the subject, but you won't find too many who disagree that screw-caps cheapen the appearance of a bottle. A new closure named Vino-lok, which has the appearance of a cork-stopped bottle but uses a glass stopper, will hit the market soon, but as it currently costs the same as cork, those who have already gone to screw-caps probably won't change. But what is changing is the closure for bottles of bubbly. The 'pop', followed by an errant cork flying across the room, could be a thing of the past – many respected sparkling wine producers are replacing the cork with the humble crown seal – the same seal used for a bottle of beer. Can a sizzle possibly match a pop?

OTHER AREAS

Visiting a winery isn't always about finding the most fabulous wine on the planet, so here are a couple of others worth keeping in mind:

Paul Conti Wines (☎ 9409 9160; www.paulcontiwines.com.au; 529 Wanneroo Rd, Woodvale), due north of Perth (a 30-minute drive), is quite geographically distinct from its Swan Valley colleagues. Established in 1948, it's now producing good, flavoursome Chardonnay and Shiraz.

Western Range Wines (☎ 9571 8800; www.westernrangewines.com.au; Chittering Rd, Lower Chittering) comprises a number of tiny-sized wineries, which, banded together, create something a whole lot more noticeable. It's an hour's drive northeast of Perth in the Chittering Valley (quintessential hot, dry, north-of-Perth countryside) and the wines are very good. There are many other wineries nearby too.

The Wine Industry Association of Western Australia (www.winewa.asn.au) runs wine courses for consumers and the industry – check the website for details.

Perth

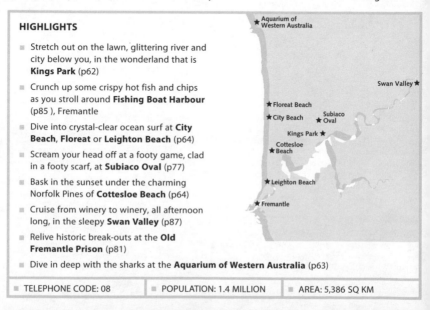

Perth

Planted by a river and almost permanently housed under a great blue sky, the city of Perth takes natural beauty to extremes. Bounded by pristine parkland, the streets are curiously squeaky-clean. The sleepy Swan River – black swans bobbing atop – winds its way past the city and out to the Indian Ocean. Grassland and bike tracks straddle the city for miles. Yet this is not how Perth defines itself.

Its heart is down the beach, tossing around under clear ocean surf and stretching out on the sand. The city's famous royal-blue and chalk-white beaches trace this outermost point of Australia for some 40km, and you can have one to yourself on any given day – for a city this size, Perth is sparsely populated.

When many a traveller came to visit in the 1990s, the city was dismissed as 'dullsville'. The streets were dead, there was nowhere to party. Locals were just too lackadaisical, at home, in their boardshorts and desert boots, tinkering with the barbecue.

Today it has all changed. Another mining boom has made young property owners rich, and they're feeling damn good. They're out eating, socialising, spending money, flexing their muscles in the sun. A successful native title claim – although under appeal at the time of research – has at least acknowledged indigenous ties to the land. This is a huge feat for the Noongar people. And amidst all this, the city's fabulous beaches remain unchanged.

HIGHLIGHTS

- Stretch out on the lawn, glittering river and city below you, in the wonderland that is **Kings Park** (p62)
- Crunch up some crispy hot fish and chips as you stroll around **Fishing Boat Harbour** (p85), Fremantle
- Dive into crystal-clear ocean surf at **City Beach**, **Floreat** or **Leighton Beach** (p64)
- Scream your head off at a footy game, clad in a footy scarf, at **Subiaco Oval** (p77)
- Bask in the sunset under the charming Norfolk Pines of **Cottesloe Beach** (p64)
- Cruise from winery to winery, all afternoon long, in the sleepy **Swan Valley** (p87)
- Relive historic break-outs at the **Old Fremantle Prison** (p81)
- Dive in deep with the sharks at the **Aquarium of Western Australia** (p63)

★ Aquarium of Western Australia

Swan Valley ★

★ Floreat Beach

★ City Beach
Subiaco ★ Oval

Kings Park ★

Cottesloe ★ Beach

★ Leighton Beach

★ Fremantle

| ■ TELEPHONE CODE: 08 | ■ POPULATION: 1.4 MILLION | ■ AREA: 5,386 SQ KM |

HISTORY

The site that is now the city of Perth had been occupied by groups of the Aboriginal Noongar tribe for thousands of years before the first Europeans settled there. The tribe's ancestors can be traced back some 40,000 years (evidenced by discoveries of stone implements near the Swan Bridge).

In December 1696 three ships in the fleet commanded by Willem de Vlamingh anchored off what is now known as Rottnest Island. On 5 January 1697 a well-armed party landed near present-day Cottesloe Beach, then marched eastward to a river near Freshwater Bay. They tried to contact some of the Noongar to inquire about survivors of the *Ridderschap van Hollant*, lost in 1694, but they were unsuccessful. So they sailed north, but not before de Vlamingh had bestowed the name 'Swan' on the river.

Perth was founded in 1829 as the Swan River Colony, but it grew very slowly until 1850, when convicts were brought in to alleviate a labour shortage. Many of Perth's fine buildings were built using convict labour.

Even then, Perth's development lagged behind that of the cities in the eastern colonies. That is, until the discovery of gold in the mid-1880s increased the population fourfold over the following decade and initiated a building boom.

The mineral wealth of Western Australia (WA) has continued to drive Perth's growth. In the 1980s and 1990s, though, the city's clean-cut, nouveau-riche image was tainted by a series of financial and political scandals. Today Perth is back on track, thanks to another mining boom, and so the frontier-town image is again thriving.

Largely excluded from this race to riches is the Noongar people. In 2006, however, the Perth Federal Court recognised the Noongar people's connection to the land. Though this decision was quickly appealed by the state government, it was a huge step forward for indigenous rights, and proof that Perth still harbours the pioneering spirit that built it.

ORIENTATION

The city of Perth lies along a sweep of the Swan River. The river borders the city centre to the south and east, and links Perth to its port, Fremantle.

The train line runs along the north of the city centre. Immediately north of the train line

is Northbridge, a big entertainment enclave with hostels. To the west, Perth rises to Kings Park, which overlooks the city and the Swan River. The suburbs extend west to Cottesloe and Scarborough on the Indian Ocean.

The city is 10km to 13km from the airport; for more information on the airport shuttle, bus and taxi, see p78.

Maps
Perth Map Centre (Map pp58-9; ☎ 9322 5733; www .mapworld.com.au; 900 Hay St; ☽ 9am-5.30pm Mon-Thu, 9am-6pm Fri, 10am-4pm Sat) Full range of maps and travel guides.

INFORMATION
Bookshops
All Foreign Languages Bookshop (Map pp58-9; ☎ 9321 9275; 101 William St; ☽ 9am-5.30pm) Travel books, foreign-language guides, phrasebooks, Lonely Planet guidebooks.
Boffins Bookshop (Map pp58-9; ☎ 9321 5755; 806 Hay St; ☽ 9am-5.30pm) Boffins' technical and specialist range includes travel. There's a well-mannered station of boffins upstairs.
Dymocks (Map pp58-9; ☎ 9321 3969; 705-707 Hay St Mall; ☽ 9am-5.30pm) WA travel section and maps, plus a decent range of contemporary literary fiction.
Oxford St Books (Map pp56-7; ☎ 9443 9844; 131 Oxford St, Leederville; ☽ 10.30am-10.30pm) Knowledgeable staff, great range of fiction and a travel section.
Planet Books (Map pp58-9; ☎ 9328 7464; 636-638 Beaufort St; ☽ 10am-10pm Sun-Thu, 10am-12am Fri & Sat) A big polished concrete shell decked out with leather lounges and a brazen chandelier. Stacked with books.

Emergency
Ambulance, fire, police (☎ 000)
Lifeline (☎ 13 11 14) Crisis counselling.
Police station (Map pp58-9; ☎ 131 444; Beaufort St)
RACWA roadside assistance (☎ 13 11 11)
Sexual Assault Resource Centre's crisis line (☎ 9340 1828; ☽ 24hr)

Internet Access
Travel Forever (Map pp58-9; ☎ 6267 0700; www .travelforever.com.au; 123-125 William St; per hr $3; ☽ 9am-6pm Mon-Sat, 10am-5pm Sun)
Traveller's Club (Map pp58-9; ☎ 9322 1406; www .travellersclub.com.au; 137A William St; per hr up to $2.50; ☽ 9am-7pm Mon-Thu, 9am-6pm Fri, 9am-5pm Sat & Sun)

(Continued on page 62)

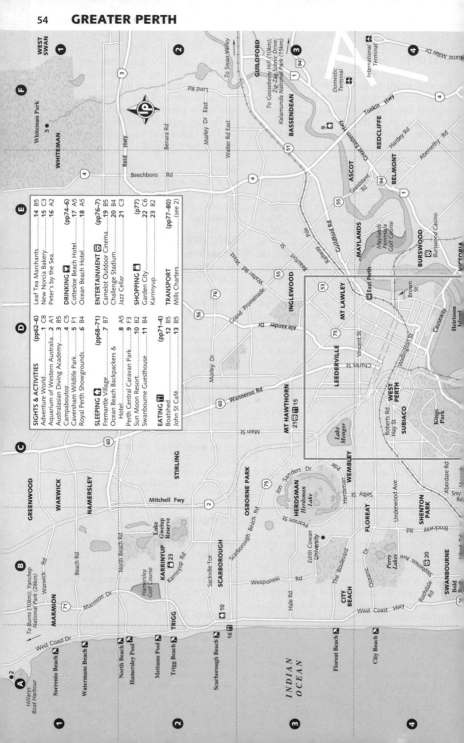

0 — 5 km
0 — 3 miles

To Perth
International
Tourist Park
(3km)

KEWDALE

Welshpool Rd

Kewdale Rd

Orrong Rd

QUEENS
PARK

Wharf St

CANNINGTON

To Tumbulgum
Farm (12km)

Yale Rd

30

GOSNELLS
Golf Club

Nicholson Rd

Warton Rd

To Albany (400km)

EAST
VICTORIA
PARK

Albany Hwy

BENTLEY

Leach Hwy

Manning Rd

Hill View Tce

Willeri Dr

CANNING VALE

Bannister Rd

Ranford Rd

SOUTH
PERTH

COMO

Coode St

Point Rd

labouchere Rd

villa

(Under Construction)

Kwinana Fwy

MANNING

Canning River

Curtin
University

Kent St

Karel Ave

Bull Creek Station
(Under Construction)

Bull Creek Dr

BULL
CREEK

13

JANDAKOT

Jandakot
Airport

Melville Glades
Golf Club

Matilda Bay

See Perth Map (pp56–7)

APPLECROSS

Reynolds Rd

Kwinana Fwy

1 2

Kwinana Fwy

SWAN RIVER

Lucky
Bay

Alfred
Cove

Risely St

Wireless
Hill Park 22

7 1

KARDINYA

Murdoch
University

MURDOCH

Farrington Rd

NORTH
LAKE

North
Lake

BIBRA
LAKE

Bibra
Lake

Forrest Rd

Yangebup
Lake

Murdoch Dr

Broadway

French
Consulate

Princess Rd

Edith Cowan
University

DALKEITH

The Ave

Jutland
Pde

Point Walter

Point Resolution

North Lake Rd

14

1

Lake
Claremont

Carrington St

NEDLANDS 3

Freshwater
Bay

Mosman
Bay

PEPPERMINT
GROVE

19

Loch St

MOSMAN
PARK

Wellington St

North St

Eric St

COTTESLOE

13

8

14

Marine Pde

BICTON

Preston Point

Preston Point Rd

Wichmann Rd

Canning Hwy

EAST
FREMANTLE

Marmion St

Leach Hwy

South St

Stock Rd

Royal Fremantle
Golf Club

Rockingham Rd

SPEARWOOD

COOGEE

Spearwood Ave

Phoenix Rd

Forrest Rd

Forrest Rd

Swanbourne
Beach

18

13

8

17

Cottesloe
Beach

NORTH
FREMANTLE

Leighton Beach

INDIAN OCEAN

See Fremantle Map (pp82–3)

FREMANTLE

SOUTH
FREMANTLE

Cockburn Rd

7

To Rockingham (20km)

To Rottnest
Island (17km)

5

6

7

8

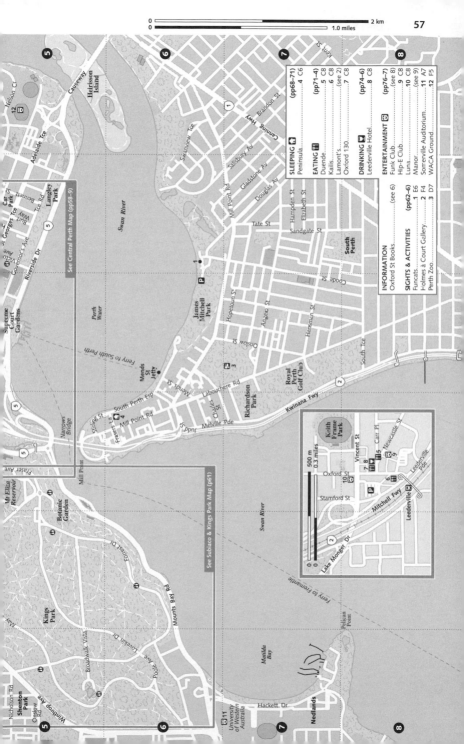

0   800 m
0   0.5 miles

INFORMATION
King Edward Memorial Hospital
For Women..........................1 A2
Kings Park Visitors Centre........2 D4

SIGHTS & ACTIVITIES (pp62–6)
Surf Sail Australia...................3 C1
Yoga Company.......................4 A2
Yoga Space...........................5 D2

SLEEPING (pp68–71)
Outram.................................6 D2

EATING (pp71–4)
Boucla..................................7 A3
Café Café..............................8 A1

Chez Jean-Claude
Patisserie...........................9 A3
Chutney Mary's....................10 A2
Ecco....................................11 A1
Food...................................12 A2
Fraser's Restaurant................13 D4
Rialto's................................14 A2
Station St Markets.................15 A1
Subiaco Hotel.......................16 A2

ENTERTAINMENT (pp76–7)
Ace Subiaco.........................17 A1
Moonlight Cinema..................18 A5
Regal Theatre.......................19 A1
Subiaco Arts Centre...............20 A2
Subiaco Oval........................21 B1

SHOPPING (p77)
Indigenart............................22 C2

(Continued from page 53)

Internet Resources

www.heatseeker.com.au Gig guide and ticketing.
www.perth.citysearch.com.au Entertainment and restaurants.
www.scoop.com.au Entertainment.

Media

Free guides to Perth include *What's On* and *Your Guide to Perth & Fremantle*, available at hostels, hotels and tourist offices.

Express Long-running street rag and a good source of live music information. Available in cafés and record stores.
Go West Backpacker magazine with information on activities throughout WA, and seasonal work.
West Australian Local newspaper with cinema times.

Medical Services

King Edward Memorial Hospital for Women (Map p61; ☎ 9340 2222; 347 Bagot Rd, Subiaco)
Lifecare Dental (Map pp58-9; ☎ 9221 2777; Forrest Chase; 🕒 8am-8pm)
Royal Perth Hospital (Map pp58-9; ☎ 9224 2244; Victoria Sq) In CBD.
Travel Medicine Centre (Map pp58-9; ☎ 9321 7888; 5 Mill St; 🕒 8am-5pm Mon-Fri)

Money

Accessing Aussie dollars is straightforward; ATMs are plentiful. There are currency-exchange facilities at the airport and city banks, and branches of major banks in the CBD.

Amex (Map pp58-9; ☎ 1300 132 639; 109 St Georges Tce) Within the Westpac building.
Travelex (Map pp58-9; ☎ 9321 7811; 760 Hay St; 🕒 9am-5pm Mon-Fri, 9am-1pm Sat) The branch at the international airport is open Sundays.

Post

Main Post Office (GPO; Map pp58-9; ☎ 9237 5460, 13 13 18; 3 Forrest Pl; 🕒 8am-5.30pm Mon-Fri, 9am-12.30pm Sat)

Tourist Information

i-City Information Kiosk (Map pp58-9; Murray St Mall; 🕒 9.30am-4.30pm Mon-Thu & Sat, 9.30am-8pm Fri, 12pm-4.30pm Sun) Volunteers answer your questions and run walking tours.
Travel Forever (Map pp58-9; ☎ 6267 0700; www .travelforever.com.au; 123-125 William St) Books tours and runs the Job Centre (p260).
Traveller's Club (Map pp58-9; ☎ 9322 1406; www .trsaust.co.au; 137A William St) Excellent resource centre. Books tours, has a bulletin board, and runs the Travel Recruitment Centre (p260).

Western Australian Visitors Centre (Map pp58-9; ☎ 1300 361 351; www.westernaustralia.net; cnr Forrest Pl & Wellington St; 🕒 8.30am-5.30pm Mon-Thu, 8.30am-6pm Fri, 9.30am-4.30pm Sat, noon-4.30pm Sun) A good resource for a trip anywhere in WA.

SIGHTS

Sightseeing is best married with the outdoors: view buildings and landmarks from the Swan River or the heights of Kings Park, or take an even more leisurely pace in the Swan Valley (with a full belly; p88). Many of Perth's sights are in the CBD; the Cultural Centre, which includes the Art Gallery of WA, the State Museum and the Perth Institute of Contemporary Arts, is in Northbridge.

Kings Park

Kings Park (Map p61) cuts a swathe from the Swan River back up to the inner suburbs, affording the best views of the city and the Swan, day or night. Its 4-sq-km, bush-filled expanse is carefully tended by a team of khaki-clad gardeners and boffins, year-round; walking and running tracks wind through the land; and picnic spots, lookouts, wildflowers and playgrounds abound. In short, it's the city's pride and joy.

The architect-designed **Lotterywest Federation Walkway** (tree-top walk; admission free; 🕒 9am-5pm) is a broad 222m-long, glass-and-steel structure that winds over stands of eucalypts. It's a highlight. The walkway starts near the Lord Forrest Statue, on the roundabout on Fraser Ave. If your legs are feeling weary – or if you've a penchant for riding buses disguised as trams – the tourist tram tours the park. Pick-up is behind the visitors centre. Just tell the driver if you don't want the full tour, which continues to the city.

Another highlight is the 170,000-sq-m **Botanic Garden**, with over 2000 plant species from WA. In spring you can enjoy an impressive display of the state's famed wildflowers. Free **guided walks** (☎ 9480 3659; 🕒 10am & 2pm) of Kings Park and the Botanic Garden are available year-round.

Kings Park Visitors Centre (🕒 9.30am-4pm) is opposite the war memorial on Fraser Ave. Nearby you'll find a kiosk, café, gift shop and Frasers restaurant.

To get here take bus 37 (39 on weekends), heading west along St Georges Tce (S-stand), to the visitors centre. Alternatively, catch the red Central Transit (CAT) bus to the entrance

See p72 for self-catering options.

BEST PICNIC SPOTS

- Fraser Ave, Kings Park (opposite), just past the Bali Memorial, for the city's best views
- Hyde Park (p64), North Perth, Vincent St side – idyllic and low-key
- City Beach (p64), near the kiosk, for a beachside picnic without the sand
- Esplanade Reserve (p83), Fremantle, for restful pines and lawn by the harbour

of Kings Park (stop 26, or Ord St before Havelock, a short walk to the entrance of Kings Park). You can also walk up (steep) Mount St from the city or climb Jacob's Ladder from Mounts Bay Rd, near the Adelphi Hotel, a climb demanding enough to provide a sense of achievement at the top.

Art Gallery of Western Australia

Founded in 1895, the **Art Gallery of Western Australia** (Map pp58-9; ☎ 9492 6600; www.artgallery .wa.gov.au; Perth Cultural Centre, Northbridge; admission free, except some special exhibitions; ☾ 10am-5pm, tours 11am & 1pm Tue-Thu, 12.30pm & 2pm Fri, 1pm Sat, 11pm & 1pm Sun), founded in 1895, houses the state's pre-eminent art collection. The indigenous artworks are the highlight of the gallery, with Western Desert works from Fitzroy Crossing, Balgo Hills and Warburton –including works by Jimmy Pike, Rover Thomas, Shane Pickett and Christopher Pease – given pride of place.

There are also important post-WWII works by artists such as Arthur Boyd, Albert Tucker and Sidney Nolan; other Australian historical works; landscape watercolours of the region, including Fremantle and Rottnest; and contemporary pieces by artists such as Ricky Swallow. The coffee shop and gallery store are worthwhile.

Perth Institute of Contemporary Arts

Cutting-edge contemporary art – installations, performance, sculpture and video works – lives at **Perth Institute of Contemporary Arts** (Map pp58-9; ☎ 9227 6144; www.pica.org.au; Perth Cultural Centre, Northbridge; admission free; ☾ 11am-6pm Tue-Sun), commonly referred to by its acronym, PICA (pee-kah). This gallery has long promoted new and experimental art, and exhibits graduate works annually.

Western Australian Museum

The **museum** (Map pp58-9; ☎ 9212 3700; www.museum .wa.gov.au; Perth Cultural Centre, Northbridge; admission free; ☾ 9.30am-5pm, tours 11am & 2pm) includes an excellent 'land and people' display that examines the history of the indigenous people and the more recent past; a gallery of dinosaur casts; a good collection of meteorites; and mammal, butterfly and bird galleries. In the courtyard, set in its own preservative bath, is 'Megamouth', a curious-looking species of shark with a soft, rounded head. Only about five of these benign creatures have ever been captured; this one beached itself near Mandurah, south of Perth.

The museum complex also includes Perth's original **gaol**, built in 1856 and used until 1888 – once a favourite spot for hangings. There is a shady **café** (☾ lunch) on the ground floor of the gaol building, as well as the **children's discovery centre**, which runs popular programmes in school holidays on themes such as biodiversity.

Aquarium of Western Australia

Few will fail to be impressed by this **aquarium** (AQWA; Map pp54-5; ☎ 9447 7500; www.aqwa.com.au; Hillarys Boat Harbour, Hillarys; adult/child $24/$13; ☾ 10am-4pm). Here you can wander through a 98m underwater tunnel as gargantuan turtles, stingrays, fish and sharks stealthily glide over the top of you. A series of mini marine worlds show off the state's underwater treasures: intriguing sea dragons, seahorses, moon jellies (which billow, iridescent, through a giant cylinder), venomous fish, sea snakes, and even the odd grumpy-looking octopus. Watch stingrays and seals play in the underwater viewing area.

The daring can snorkel or dive with the sharks in the giant aquarium with the help of the inhouse divemaster. Book in advance ($105, with your own gear; 1pm and 3pm). Or you can simply dip your hands into the touch pool and get to know guys like the port Jackson shark, sea stars, sea cucumbers and the Western stingaree.

To get here on weekdays, take the Joondalup train to Warwick Interchange and then transfer to bus 423. On the weekend, catch the train to Greenwood station, then hop on bus 456 to Hillarys Boat Harbour. AQWA is by the water, behind Hillarys shopping complex.

Parks & Gardens

Kings Park (p62) may be the city's premier green patch, but there are a number of other enjoyable parks and gardens, each with its own character and purpose. **Hyde Park** (Map pp58–9) is one of Perth's most exquisite parks, a top spot for a picnic or lazy book-reading session on the lawn. A flat path traces the small lake, and the grounds are dotted with palms, firs and Moreton Bay figs – there's plenty of shade. It's walking distance from Northbridge.

Stirling Gardens (Map pp58-9; cnr St Georges Tce & Barrack St) comprise lovingly tended, pristine gardens and lawn that make a great spot for lunch. The nearby **Supreme Court Gardens** (Map pp58–9), which look out onto the river, are larger and offer little shade but are still a popular lunch stop.

Lake Monger (Map pp56–7), in Wembley, is where local birdlife meet: in spring black swans and their ducklings plod about the grounds, nonplussed. A number of bird species reside here. The flat 3.5km path that circles that lake is also the local jogging track, and there's plenty of grass for cricket, football and picnics. It's walking distance from Leederville train station.

Other Sights

Close your eyes and think of England as you listen to the ringing of the **Swan Bell Tower** (Map pp58-9; ☎ 9218 8183; adult/child $6/4; ☽ 10am-4pm, ringing noon-1pm Mon, Tue, Thu, Sat & Sun). Just north of Barrack St Jetty, the tower contains the royal bells of St Martin's-in-the-Fields, dating from the 14th century. These were given to WA by the British government in 1988, and are the only set known to have left England. Clamber to the top for 360-degree views of Perth by the river.

The **Perth Mint** (Map pp58-9; ☎ 9421 7277; cnr Hill & Hay Sts; adult/child $9.90/4.40; ☽ 9am-4pm Mon-Fri, 9am-1pm Sat & Sun, gold pours hourly weekdays & 10am, 11am & noon Sat & Sun) sounds staid but is oddly compelling. Dating from 1899, the mint shows off a variety of coins, and you can stroke a 12.54kg gold bar worth about $200,000, mint your own coins and watch gold pours (as part of a tour).

Located by the idyllic river in East Perth, the small but active **Holmes à Court Gallery** (Map pp56-7; ☎ 9218 4540; 11 Brown St; www.holmesacourt gallery.com.au; admission free; ☽ noon-5pm Thu-Sun) hosts a changing display of works from one of Australia's finest private art collections as well as touring exhibitions. The gallery was started by the late millionaire industrialist Robert Holmes à Court in the 1970s, and today the collection comprises more than 3000 artworks. About one-third of these are indigenous, with the best canvas and bark paintings by indigenous artists in private hands; the remainder includes some of Australia's leading contemporary artworks. Access the gallery from the river end of Brown St, where there is parking.

ACTIVITIES
Beach Swimming & Surfing

Run by the Surf Life Saving Club of WA, the website www.mybeach.com.au has a profile of all the city beaches, including weather forecasts and information about amenities and beach patrolling. Note that many city beaches are rough with strong undertow and rips – swim between the flags.

Popular swimming beaches include **Cottesloe Beach** (Map pp54–5), with cafés, pine trees and fantastic sunsets; **City Beach** (Map pp54–5), with a lawn area and amenities; **Floreat Beach** (Map pp54–5), less crowded but sometimes windy; **Leighton Beach** (Map pp82–3; North Fremantle); and **Trigg Beach** (Map pp54–5), also a surf beach that is dangerous when rough and prone to rips. **Swanbourne Beach** (Map pp54–5) is the nude (gay) beach.

Port Beach (Map pp82–3; North Fremantle), City Beach and Leighton are also surf beaches. And **Scarborough Beach** (Map pp54–5) is a popular young surfers' spot, though good surf can be found in pockets all the way up and down the coast, depending on the weather (ask a local).

To the north lies a string of excellent swimming beaches: **North Beach** (Map pp54–5), **Watermans Beach** (Map pp54–5), **Hamersley Pool** (Map pp54–5) and **Mettams Pool** (Map pp54–5). Up here there are plenty of picnic areas and barbecues – Mettams is almost like a turquoise paddle pool – and a paved bike path snakes through the scrub, following the shoreline. **Sorrento Beach** (Map pp54–5), south of Hillarys Boat Harbour, is patrolled because the onshore winds make the surf rough. **Burns Beach**, much further north, is yet another well-set-up swimming beach.

There are a couple of surf schools, including **surfschool.com** (☎ 6267 0700; per lesson $45) and **Adrift Learn to Surf Tours** (☎ 1800 094 480; www

---

BEACHES BY PUBLIC TRANSPORT

No wheels? No problem. The following beaches are all very accessible by public transport:

City Beach Bus 81 or 84 from Wellington St, Perth. Thirty minutes one-way; buses leave every half-hour week-days. On weekends, route 85 takes over.

Cottesloe Cottesloe train station. About 20 minutes from Perth; trains leave every 15 minutes. Check that your train stops at Cottesloe – some express trains don't.

Floreat Bus 84 from Wellington St; less than 30 minutes one-way. Buses leave hourly. On weekends, route 85 takes over.

Port & Leighton North Fremantle train station. Less than 30 minutes from city; trains leave every 15 minutes. Some express trains don't stop at North Fremantle.

Scarborough Bus 400 from Wellington St bus station. Forty minutes, one-way; buses leave every 15 to 20 minutes.

Swanbourne Swanbourne train station. Just under 20 minutes; trains leave every 15 minutes.

.adriftsurfing.com; one-day surf tour $95). Both operate in Lancelin.

Water Sports

Here you'll enjoy some of the cleanest city beaches in the world and some of the best surf in the country. It all makes for great wind-surfing, kite-boarding, surfing (see opposite) and bodyboarding. Check wind speeds at the website www.seabreeze.com.au.

When the afternoon sea breeze blusters in, windsurfers take to the Swan River, Leighton and beaches north of Perth. You can hire windsurfers at **Surf Sail Australia** (Map p61; ☎ 1800 686 089; www.surfsailaustralia.com.au; 260-262 Railway Pde, West Leederville).

Because Rottnest is a coral reef with tropi-cal fish so close to Perth, it's a top spot for scuba diving and snorkelling. There are many companies, including the **Australasian Diving Academy** (Map pp54-5; ☎ 9389 5018; www.ausdiving .com.au; 3/142 Stirling Hwy, Nedlands; 4-day open-water dive course plus Rottnest dive $525; without Rottnest dive $375), which hires out equipment and teaches you how to dive.

It'll take you five minutes to learn how to sail one of the catamarans for hire on the South Perth foreshore – try **Funcats** (Map pp56-7; ☎ 0408 926 003; Coode St jetty, South Perth; per hr 2 people $30).

If the wind has kicked up and you just need to stroke through some cool water, Perth has some excellent 50m pools, includ-ing **Beatty Park** (Map pp58-9; ☎ 9273 6080; 220 Vin-cent St, Leederville; adult/child $4/$2.80) and **Challenge Stadium** (Map pp54-5; ☎ 9441 8259; Stephenson Ave, Mt Claremont; adult/child $4.50/$3.40), favoured by the super-sporty. To get here, take westbound bus 28 from Wellington St, Perth (about 20 minutes; hourly).

Cycling

Cycling is an excellent way to explore Perth, though some drivers are still learning to share the roads. Kings Park has some good bike tracks. There are also cycling routes along the Swan River, running all the way to Fremantle, and along the coast. For cycling route maps, see www.dpi.wa.gov.au/cycling. Or if you want to pick up your own hard copies, pop in to the **Bicycle Transportation Alliance** (Map pp58-9; ☎ 9420 7210; 2 Delhi St, West Perth; per map $3.95). Bike shops also sell these. To hire bikes, try the **Cycle Centre** (Map pp58-9; ☎ 9325 1176; 282 Hay St; mountain bikes per day/afternoon $25/$15; ☺ 9.30am-5.30pm Mon-Fri, 9am-1pm Sat, 1-4pm Sun).

Whale-Watching

The whale-watching season runs from Sep-tember to December. The three-hour trip with **Mills Charters** (Map pp54-5; ☎ 9246 5334; www .millscharters.com.au; Hillarys Boat Harbour; adult/child $65/$50) is very informative. The search is for the humpback whale, as it returns to Antarctic waters after wintering in the waters of north-west Australia. Mills has a new hydrophone, which is like a microphone that's dropped into the water, so that you can listen to the whales singing.

Also recommended:

Boat Torque (Rottnest Express; Map pp58-9; ☎ 9421 5888; tours $53) Leaves Barrack St Jetty at 11am Wed, Sat and Sun.

Oceanic Cruises (Map pp58-9; ☎ 9325 1191; www .oceaniccruises.com.au; adult/child $53/$27; ☺ Wed & Fri-Sun). Leaves Perth at 12pm.

Yoga

The following outfits run yoga sessions:

Yoga Company (Map p61; ☎ 9388 6683; 136 Rokeby Rd; www.theyogacompany.com.au; per session $16) Hatha.

Yoga Space (Map p61; ☎ 9243 5114; www.yogaspace
.com.au; Shop 6, Seasons Arcade, 1251 Hay St; per session
$14) Ashtanga.

WALKING TOUR

This tour traces some old remnants of Perth.
It also spans the new, and takes you to the best
views of the city atop Kings Park. Start in the
Cultural Centre, out the front of the **Art Gallery of Western Australia (1**, p63). Head over the
walkbridge towards the train station. At the
newsagency, head right down the last set of
escalators (don't cross the second walkbridge).
Take your first left, across Wellington St and
into the square. The **post office (2)** looms to
your right. Bear southeast up Murray St Mall,
then right down Barrack St. At the corner of
Hay and Barrack you'll find the beautifully
restored **Town Hall (3)**, the only convict-built
town hall in the country (1867–70).

Continue southeast up Hay St, then turn
left up Irwin St. At the corner of Irwin and
Murray is the **Fire Safety & Education Museum
(4)**, Perth's fire headquarters between 1900
and 1979. Further along the street a fig arches
lazily over the road, and you'll pass the red-
brick buildings of **Royal Perth Hospital (5)**. Waiting down the end of the street is **St Mary's
Cathedral (6**; 1863), sited on its own square.
Wander around Victoria Ave to **Perth Concert
Hall (7**; p77) – a fine auditorium and grand
structure built in the early 1970s – nestled to
the right of the Duxton.

Continue along St Georges Tce, with
Government House (8; ☽ 12-2pm) to your left,

a Gothic-looking fantasy built between 1859
and 1864, followed by the impressive **Council
House (9)**, designed by Howlett and Bailey in
the early 1960s. Past Council House, head
southwest through Stirling Gardens and down
to the creamy-yellow **courthouse (10)**, adjacent
to the Supreme Court. The courthouse is one
of Perth's oldest buildings (1837).

Wind south of the Supreme Court and
make for the river. Within moments the **Swan
Bell Tower (11**; p64) will be in view: a modern
copper-and-glass structure that contains St
Martin's-in-the-Fields, royal bells dating to
the 14th century. Double back up Barrack
St, northwest along the Esplanade, and up
Howard St. Back on St Georges Tce, bear left:
the **Palace Hotel (12)**, now homes to Bankwest, is
to your right. Continue to King St, but before
you turn, note the **Old Perth Boys School (13)**, a
modest structure today dwarfed by gleaming
office towers. On the corner of King and Hay,
you'll find **His Majesty's Theatre (14**; p77), where
you can look around in the lobby.

If you don't wish to make the climb to
Kings Park, head up to **King St café (15**, p71)
for some cake. Otherwise, back on St Georges
Tce, you'll see **Cloisters (16**; 1858) to your right,

WALK FACTS

Start Art Gallery of Western Australia
Finish Kings Park
Distance 4.5km
Duration Two hours to Kings Park

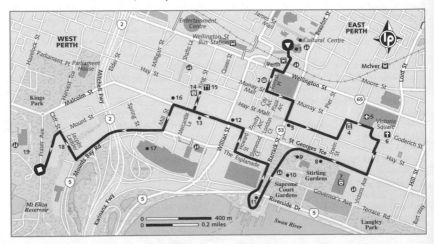

originally a school and notable for its brick-work. Roll down Mill St (not signed), straight for the **Perth Convention Exhibition Centre (17)**, one of Perth's vaunted landmarks. Stick to the north side of the road as it winds under the underpass, and keep an eye out for **Jacob's Ladder (18)**, up a path by the Adelphi Hotel. Once you're at the end of Cliff St, head northwest, following Fraser Ave in to **Kings Park (19**; p62), along to the architect-designed Bali Memorial and, further, various lookouts. Perhaps have a snooze on the lawn.

To return to the city, go back to the round-about on Cliff St, and head down Mount St and across the overpass to St Georges Tce. Or hop on the free red CAT bus at Havelock St.

PERTH FOR CHILDREN

There's plenty of free kids' entertainment: **Cottesloe Beach** (Map pp54–5) has long been a family favourite and, just south, **Leighton** (Map pp54–5) beach is fairly sheltered and shallow. **Kings Park** (p62) has numerous playgrounds, walking tracks and gardens. And there's always the bike tracks (p65) that stretch along the river and the coast, long enough to tire out any young kelpie.

The **Royal Perth Show** (Map pp54–5), held September to October, is an ever-popular family outing, all sideshow rides, showbags and proudly displayed poultry. And many of Perth's big attractions – the **Aquarium of Western Australia** (p63), the **Western Australian Museum** (p63) and the **Art Gallery of Western Australia** (p63) – cater well for young audiences.

Perth Zoo (Map p61; ☎ 9474 3551; www.perthzoo .wa.gov.au; 20 Labouchere Rd, South Perth; adult/child/family $17/8.50/45; ☼ 9am-5pm), across the river from the city centre in South Perth, is a consistent attraction. The zoo has a number of interesting collections, including a nocturnal house, an Australian wildlife park, a numbat display and a reptile 'encounter' room. Enjoy the sunshine by taking the ferry across the river from Barrack St jetty to the Mends St jetty, from which the zoo is walking distance. Otherwise catch bus 30 or 31 (to front of zoo) or 34 (to north of zoo) from Wellington St bus station or the Esplanade Busport.

Scitech (Map pp58-9; ☎ 9481 6295; City West Centre, cnr Sutherland St & Railway Pde, West Perth; adult/child $14/9; ☼ 9.30am-4pm Mon-Fri, 10am-5pm Sat & Sun) is another option – especially if it's raining. It has over 160 hands-on, large-scale science and technology exhibits.

Adventure World (Map pp54-5; ☎ 9417 9666; 179 Progress Dr, Bibra Lake; adult/child $39/32; ☼ 10am-5pm Thu-Mon Sep-Apr), packed with kids and teen-agers, has all the palm-sweat-inducing rides such as 'Bounty's Revenge', a giant boat that swings around in an arc, as well as pools and waterslides. Open daily school holidays and through December, it's 18km south of Perth.

Slip on a gingham shirt and drive down to **Tumbulgum Farm** (☎ 9525 5888; www.tumbulgum farm.com.au; 1475 South Western Hwy, Mundijong; admission free; farm shows adult/child $15/8; ☼ 9.30am-5pm), 6km south of Armadale on South West Hwy. Tumbulgum is a big display farm where you can feed animals, milk cows, and catch some sheep-mustering and whip-cracking. Wander around the grounds for free.

TOURS

Organised tours of Perth abound. Tour bro-chures can be found in hotel lobbies and visi-tors centres. For day tours to Rottnest Island, see p92; for Shoalwater Islands Marine Park, see p94; for Fremantle, see p83; for state-wide tours, see p258; for surf tours, see p64.

Recommended tours:

Big Sky Tours (☎ 9443 8473; www.bigskytours.com .au) Backpacker-happy tours that wind up with beer in Northbridge.

Boat Torque (☎ 9421 5888; www.boattorque.com.au) To Fremantle and Rottnest.

Captain Cook Cruises (☎ 9325 3341; www.captain cookcruises.com.au) Goes to the Swan Valley and Fremantle.

City Explorer Tram (☎ 9322 2006; www.perthtram .au; adult/child $24/10) This hop-on, hop-off tram, which is actually a bus, takes you around some of Perth's main attrac-tions – the city, Kings Park and Barrack St jetty. It departs from 565 Hay St (near Barrack St) at least five times daily.

Oceanic Cruises (☎ 9325 1191; www.oceaniccruises .com.au; adult/child $119/75) Operates lunch cruises to the Swan Valley.

Out & About Wine Tours (☎ 9377 3376; www .outandabouttours.com.au) Follows a similar theme to Swan Valley tours, but has a stronger focus on wine. Runs a twilight tour.

Swan Valley Tours (☎ 9299 6249; www.svtours .au) Food-driven tours that cruise up the Swan.

FESTIVALS & EVENTS

New Year's Day sees Perth's biggest day at the races, the **Perth Cup** (www.perthracing.org.au) come to town, with the party people heading to 'Tentland' for DJs and daiquiris.

Artists like Laurie Anderson, Antony Gormley (who once exhibited on a dry salt lake near Kalgoorlie) and Philip Glass (who once took to the desert, with his piano) perform at the annual **UWA Perth International Arts Festival** (www.perthfestival.com.au) alongside the top local talent. Held for several weeks in January and February, the program spans theatre, classical music, jazz, contemporary art, dance – the whole gamut. It's worth scheduling your trip around the festival, particularly if you're nocturnal.

Perth Pride (www.pridewa.asn.au), a gay and lesbian event, is in October, as is the annual Pride March. **Artrage** (www.artrage.com.au), October to November, is a cutting-edge contemporary arts festival.

SLEEPING

Perth is very spread out: choose your location carefully. Northbridge is overpopulated with hostels, and is best for those unperturbed by noise. But the CBD and Northbridge are close to all forms of public transport, and hopping out to inner-city suburbs such as Leederville and Mt Lawley is simple. If you care most for the beach, consider Cottesloe, Swanbourne or Scarborough, as public transport to the beaches from the city can be time-consuming. South Perth is a good choice for families, due to its proximity to child-friendly attractions and the wide-open spaces.

Note that many midrange and top-end hotels fiddle with their rates daily.

City Centre
BUDGET
our pick **Perth City YHA** (Map pp58-9; ☎ 9287 3333; www.yha.com.au; 300 Wellington St; 4-bed dm $24, 6- & 7-bed dm $21, s $50, d without bathroom $62, d with bathroom $75, non-YHA members add $5; 🖳 🖳) This is the YHA experience at its best. Sure, it's a little predictable, and has that boarding-school feel in the halls (there are 240 beds), but the floorboards gleam – and charmingly creak – and the brightly painted rooms still smell new. In a well-preserved 1940s art deco building, Perth City YHA is in a quieter part of town. Perhaps the best bit is the bathrooms: half the rooms have brand-spanking-new ensuites. Family and twin rooms also available.

Royal Hotel (Map pp58-9; ☎ 9481 1000; wentpert@fc-hotels.com.au; cnr Wellington & William Sts; s $70, without bathroom $54-60, d $87-98, without bathroom $65-70; 🕱) A creaking, character-filled historic building, Royal Hotel is well-placed for early morning trips out of town (the busport's metres away).

Family rooms are light but noisy, with kitchenettes and cane bedheads. Cute but modest single rooms have atticlike roofs.

MIDRANGE
City Waters Lodge (Map pp58-9; ☎ 9221 2794; www.citywaters.com.au; 118 Terrace Rd; s/d/f from $82/90/135; 🕱) City Waters is an old-school motel: rooms face the carpark, railings are rickety, and there's a friendly lass at reception. Rooms are light-filled, if simple, and the waterfront location is top-notch – nothing comes between you and the river. Top floor rooms are best; river views exist but are difficult to secure.

Riverview on Mount Street (Map pp58-9; ☎ 9321 8963; www.riverview.au.com; 42 Mount St; d from $95; 🕱 🖳) There's a lot of brash new money up here on Mount St, but character-filled Riverview stands out as the best personality on the block. Its refurbished 1960s bachelor pads sit neatly atop the modern foyer and relaxed, minimalist café. Rooms are sunny and simple, even if beds are a few years old. Rooms at the back, which have garden rather than river views, are quieter.

Miss Maud (Map pp58-9; ☎ 9325 3900; www.missmaud.com.au; cnr Murray & Pier Sts; d from $139; 🖳) Anyone with a love of Scandinavia, kitsch or *The Sound of Music* will find a few of their favourite things in the alpine murals and dainty rooms. The Scandinavian rooms are best, as they're bigger and well maintained. The smorgasbords (from $40 per person) are enough to feed a goat herd.

TOP END
Melbourne (Map pp58-9; ☎ 9320 3333; www.melbournehotel.com.au; cnr Hay & Milligan Sts; d from $150; 🕱) Classic country charm wafts through this modern-day heritage-listed hotel. Built in the gold-rush era, its façade – particularly the deep corrugated-iron balcony that wraps around the building – recalls the mining-town pub perched on the edges of the red-dust desert. Inside you'll find a stylish and serious dining room, and a polished bar and café buzzing with office workers. Rooms are unpretentious and comfortable, though 1st-floor rooms facing Murray St can be noisy.

Seasons (Map pp58-9; ☎ 1800 999 004; www.seasonsofperth.com.au; 37 Pier St; d $160; 🖳 🖳) Standing proudly in the eastern pocket of the CBD, Seasons is a large hotel with newly refurbished rooms that are big and fresh-feeling (think white linen and duck-egg-blue covers). But not all rooms have been refurbished just yet, so be sure to ask. Views start from the 8th floor, and some rooms have a better wi-fi signal than others.

Medina (Map pp58-9; ☎ 9267 0000; www.medina .com.au; 138 Barrack St; studio/d $161/195; ✖ ⬚) When the Medina's rooms were designed, the owner conducted extensive research, staying in his own rooms, handpicking the furnishings, generally pretending to be a sharp-eyed traveller. It's all come together nicely – these apartment-sized hotel rooms are minimalist yet welcoming. All one-bedrooms have balconies, and rooms on Barrack St tend to have more natural light (not always easy to obtain in Perth).

Mont Clare Apartments (Map pp58-9; ☎ 9224 4300; www.montclareapartments.com; 190 Hay St, East Perth; 1-/2-bedroom apt from $170/190; ✖) Friendly and unfussy, Mont Clare's apartments are spacious and, notably, private. Even reception's cordoned off discretely – they leave you to do your own thing. It's all a bit chalk-white and plain, but in summer the pool makes this a cool and restful spot. Fully self-contained. Discounts for stays longer than six nights.

Saville Park Suites (Map pp58-9; ☎ 9267 4888; www .savillesuites.com; 201 Hay St, Perth; 1-/2-bedroom apt from $185/210; ✖ ⬚) There are 152 apartments here; this is no modest building block. And it could easily feel like a massive, faceless apartment factory, but somehow it doesn't. Instead, this Tuscan-orange structure close to the Swan River is relaxed and friendly. Privacy is preserved, anonymity eschewed. Apartments are roomy, with laundries, dishwashers and good-sized benches – plenty of room to chop up some local rock lobster here.

Rydges Perth (Map pp58-9; ☎ 1800 857 922, 9263 1800; www.rydges.com/perth; cnr King & Hay Sts; d from $195; ✖) The floor-to-ceiling portholelike windows here are the real highlight; get into your robe and watch the world from up high. The rooms, happily enough, are massive and stylish: comfortable new beds, white- and matt-coloured linens, attention to detail. It's all fun retro with a flash of 1970s California. The light-filled CBD restaurant-bar busies itself with free-running Margaret River Chardonnay and local deep-sea catches.

Outram (Map pp58-9; ☎ 9322 4888; www.theoutram .com; 32 Outram Street, West Perth; s/d from $295/335; ✖) Blink and you'll miss it. That's how discreet the Outram is, with its understated European style – an olive-green pitched-roof building quietly nestled among the small office blocks

---

LONG-TERM ACCOMMODATION

Sharing a house with travellers is an economical option, if you're a couple particularly, and affords a break from the hostel scene. Check the bulletin boards at Traveller's Club and Travel Forever (p53) and http://au.easyroommate.com. You should be able to rent a fully furnished room for two for not much more than $200 to $300 per week, for a minimum of two weeks. Be sure to inspect before laying down cash.

---

of West Perth. Super-stylish open-plan rooms (including the bathroom, with a walk-through shower) have king-sized beds draped in white linens, flat-screen TVs, and spas big enough to hide a pony. This is more switched-on luxury for those in the know rather than out-and-out indulgence.

Northbridge & Around

Most of Perth's hostels are in Northbridge. There are so many here, in fact, that it's possible to walk around and inspect rooms before putting your money down – some are not up to snuff.

BUDGET

Britannia (Map pp58-9; ☎ 9227 6000; www.perthbritannia .com; 253 William St; dm $19-22, s $35, tw & d from $50; ⬚) If you want to launch yourself into the heart of the action, Britannia's your answer. This is a no-frills backpackers in the centre of Northbridge, with some of the area's best cheap eats just up the road. Dorms are good value, though the kitchen is, admittedly, a bit like a shearer's canteen. Staff are friendly, and there's a busy vibe about the place.

Billabong Backpackers Resort (Map pp58-9; ☎ 9328 7720; www.billabongresort.com.au; 381 Beaufort St; dm $20-23, d $65; ⬚ ⬚) Billabong is a big, relaxed hostel (about 150 beds), brought to life by Australiana murals along the walls. Well-kept dorms are very good value, though doubles aren't quite as good a deal. Beer-clutching boys and gals conglomerate around Billabong's pool all hours – even when it's too cold to swim – and get together for soccer and more beers when the sun goes down.

Coolibah Lodge (Map pp58-9; ☎ 9328 9958; www .coolibahlodge.com.au; 194 Brisbane St; dm/s $21/41, d $52-56; ✖ ⬚) Built on two big old colonial-style homes, Coolibah Lodge is comfortable and homely but nothing fancy. It's one of the oldest hostels on the block, actually, so there's a real backpackers vibe in here – no pretence. Dorms are tidy if a bit pokey, and doubles are of a good standard.

Oneworld Backpackers (Map pp58-9; ☎ 9228 8206; www.oneworldbackpackers.com.au; 162 Aberdeen St; dm/d $22/58; 🖵) Oneworld is like a hippy backpackers on an inheritance: clean, green and beautifully maintained. Polished floorboards beam brightly in all the rooms of this nicely restored old house, and the dorms are big and sunny, if a little messy sometimes. The kitchen is large and functional, with everything provided, and the hostel tends to be quiet at night.

our pick Governor Robinsons (Map pp58-9; ☎ 9328 3200; www.govrobinsons.com.au; 7 Robinson Ave; dm $22, d from $60; 🖵) In two restored colonial homes, this small and beautifully furnished hostel (chesterfields, floorboards) is more like a cosy B&B than a backpackers. The kitchen's a highlight – a bit like cooking at your rich friend's parents' place – and the gas-top stove works a treat. Dorms are fresh and clean, if a little snug. And the sparkling new Federation-style bathrooms are a real hit.

Witch's Hat (Map pp58-9; ☎ 9228 4228; www.witchshat.com; 148 Palmerston St; dm/d $23/64; 🖵 🖵) Witch's Hat is something out of a fairytale. The building itself could be mistaken for a gingerbread house, and the witch's hat (an Edwardian turret) stands proudly out the front, beckoning the curious to step inside. Dorms are light and uncommonly spacious, and there's a red-brick barbecue area out back. Kids retire at 10.30pm.

MIDRANGE
Pension of Perth (Map pp58-9; ☎ 9228 9049; www.pensionperth.com.au; 3 Throssel St; s/d from $115/145; 🖵 🖵 🖵) Pension of Perth's French turn-of-the-century style lays luxury on thick: chaise lounges, rich floral rugs, open fireplaces and gold-framed mirrors. There's even a 100-year-old French walnut bedhead. Two doubles with bay windows (and slightly small bathrooms) look out onto the park; the spa room is round the back. And it's across the road from Hyde Park, which is gorgeous.

Hotel Northbridge (Map pp58-9; ☎ 9328 5254; www.hotelnorthbridge.com.au; 210 Lake St; d with spa $120-140; 🖵 🖵) Hotel Northbridge has long been the star attraction for couples and folks from the country. It's not the hippest kid in the city, but

a recent refurbishment has dropped a spa in every single room – and kept the prices down. Considering it's in the heart of Northbridge, that's pretty good value.

South Perth
Peninsula (Map p61; ☎ 9368 6688; www.thepeninsula.net; 53 South Perth Esplanade; 1-/2-bedroom ste $135/165; 🖵 🖵) What the Peninsula lacks in amenities (no laundry, no oven) it makes up for with its riverside location, perfect for lazy ferry rides and sunset strolls along the river. It's a slightly older complex.

Cottesloe, Swanbourne & Scarborough
BUDGET
Ocean Beach Backpackers (Map pp54-5; ☎ 9384 5111; http://oceanbeachbackpackers.com; cnr Marine Pde & Eric St, Cottesloe; 6-/8-bed dm with bathroom $21, d with bathroom $63) This is not just a big, bright, surfie hostel. It's so close to the beach you're almost on the sand (no other hostel in Perth gets this close), and the dorm rooms have ocean views. However, the train line doesn't come up here from the city (the bus does), so this is best for those focused on the beach and happy to take things slow.

MIDRANGE & TOP END
Swanbourne Guesthouse (Map pp54-5; ☎ 9383 1981; www.swanbourneguesthouse.com.au; 5 Myera St, Swanbourne; d $95) Peace and solitude are the key here. Off a leafy residential street, 20 minutes' walk from Swanbourne Beach, you'll hear nothing more than the birds twittering from your sun-filled room.

Sun Moon Resort (Map pp54-5; ☎ 9245 8000; www.sunmoon.com.au; 200 West Coast Hwy, Scarborough; d $126-198, 2-bedroom ste $176-226; 🖵 🖵) Here the Bali-style resort makes an unlikely friend in Scarborough, but the two work together nicely. Wood-slatted pathways lead you under shady palms while bright-orange carp splash in the pond below. The rooms are enormous, and the terracotta-tiled floor is cool and pleasing under bare feet. Batik furnishings adorn otherwise minimalist rooms. Just across the highway from the beach.

Ocean Beach Hotel (Map pp54-5; ☎ 9384 2555; www.obh.com.au; cnr Marine Pde & Eric St, Cottesloe; d/f $180/340; 🖵) The only boutique-style hotel on Cottesloe Beach. Inside, smart, playful colours and contemporary furnishings bring this art-deco building to life. Stark white linens rest on deep-blue twill carpets, all set off by plum-coloured cushions and blond-wood chairs. Rooms are big, with a separate dining area; from the hallway, all you see are the waves. It's like one big LSD-driven shrine to the sea.

Greater Perth

Perth Central Caravan Park (Map pp54–5; ☎ 9277 1704; www.perthcentral.com.au; 34 Central Ave, Redcliffe; unpowered/powered sites for 2 $30/32, cabins for 2 $95; ⊗ ⊛) This small caravan park, 8km east of the city, is the closest to Perth. The refurbished one-bedroom chalets are functional; the two bedrooms are a little older but not pokey. Tent sites are conveniently close to amenities. It's a pleasant enough spot to stop.

Perth International Tourist Park (☎ 1800 626 677; 186 Hale Rd, Forrestfield; unpowered sites for 2 $30, powered sites for 2 $33–$35, studio rooms $56, 1-bedroom cabins $120; ⊗ ⊡ ⊛) This caravan park, 15km out of the city, is more of a holiday complex than a passing-through point. It's big, with plenty of accommodation options, including cheap backpackers rooms. These are just a simple spot to rest your head, but do have big square balconies to lounge about on. There's a huge public pool up the road.

EATING

Every day, the finest regional produce is trucked in to Perth and rolled out onto the tables of the city's best restaurants and cafés. Serious dining has been around for a while, and is now thriving in Mt Lawley, Nedlands, Subiaco and the Swan Valley. But cheap, top-value meals have long been available, too, especially in Northbridge, where you can still get a cracking cha kway teow for $7 or a belly-bloating laksa for $8. No doubt this tradition will continue.

BYO is widely accepted (but check ahead); a lot of restaurants do mark their wine list up by about $15 per bottle.

City Centre

CAFÉS

Tiger, Tiger (Map pp58–9; ☎ 9322 8055; shop 4, Murray Mews, signed off Murray St; mains $6.50–$8.50; ⊗ breakfast & lunch) Young bespectacled bloggers tap away on their laptops in this wi-fi hotspot, pondering the source of the café's name (Blake? Chinese idioms?). It's a coveted spot. And it's not just good looks and good cheer in here, with the polished concrete floor, communal table, and antique-style wooden chairs – the food's worth the twist down the laneway. Slices of

---

THE BEST COFFEE

The latte in Perth was long derided as the 'Western Milkshake': oversized, weak, milky. Probably in a tall glass with a handle. Today, the standard is greatly improved, and you can easily source a good espresso – so long as you know where to go. Here are the top spots:

- Café Café (p73) – a pilgrimage
- Soto Espresso (p73) – a relaxation form
- Tiger Tiger (left) – a secret

Many coffee shops top up short and long macchiatos with milk as a matter of course. If you just want a stain of milk, be sure to say so.

---

bread as thick as your arm attempt to clasp pieces of kangaroo, home-spun chutney and fresh greens; hot chocolates come with sesame seeds, hazelnuts and coconut. It all works.

King Street café (Map pp58–9; ☎ 9321 4476; 44 King St; mains $18.50–33; ⊗ breakfast, lunch & dinner) Officially called No 44 King St, this stalwart played a crucial role in creating a café culture when only immigrants and well-travelled types drank espresso. Great wine list and expansive menu, including desserts like apple and rhubarb parcels served with port custard.

RESTAURANTS

our pick Annalakshmi (Map pp58–9; ☎ 9221 3003; www.annalakshmi.com.au; Jetty 4, Barrack St, behind Bell Tower; pay by donation; ⊗ lunch Tue-Fri, dinner Tue-Sun) Take in the 360-degree views of the Swan River and the city – decidedly romantic. But this is no touristy cash cow: Annalakshmi is a curry house run by volunteers (formidable baby-boomers, in the main) and you pay by donation. Assorted hippies and other locals line up for spicy potato-and-pumpkin curries and fragrant dhal. Chilled coconut-milk and cardamom desserts cleanse the palate. It's all good fun.

Matsuri (Map pp58–9; ☎ 9322 7737; cnr Hay & Milligan Sts; mains $13–20.80; ⊗ lunch Mon-Fri, dinner) You'll feel a bit like a carp in a fish tank here – floor-to-ceiling glass runs the perimeter of this large Japanese restaurant. Matsuri has long been a consistent Perth favourite, and today it's as good as ever. The tempura udon with sushi set ($17.80) is enough to feed two salarymen.

Balthazar (Map pp58-9; ☎ 9421 1206; cnr Sherwood Ct & the Esplanade; mains from $26, desserts $13.50; ☺ dinner Mon-Sat, lunch Mon-Fri) There's a distinct feel of the New York bistro in this low-lit, discreet restaurant tucked away on the Esplanade. The menu's worth observing closely – it's refreshingly original, with a strong European twist. Dishes like caramelised witlof, Roquefort tempura, and fenugreek brulée with fresh strawberries grace the menu. They're serious about food and wine here but the atmosphere's not snotty.

QUICK EATS

Taka (Map pp58-9; ☎ 9324 1234; shops 5 & 6 Shafto Ln; mains $6.50; ☺ lunch & dinner Mon-Sat) This straightforward Japanese eatery whips out standards like tempura, udon and sushi (ten pieces for $6). Takeaway and sushi packs too. There's another branch on the corner of Wellington and Barrack, where lines run 20 metres long at lunchtime (but move fast).

Organica (Map pp58-9; ☎ 9321 0345; Shop 3B Shafto Ln) Down the Hay St end of Shafto Ln, Organica is an organic-produce specialist that turns out fantastic freshly squeezed orange juice, hand-made rolls and plenty of other quick, healthful bites.

Northbridge
CAFÉS

Tarts (Map pp58-9; ☎ 9328 6607; 212 Lake St; breakfast $9.90, lunch $7-14; ☺ breakfast & lunch) Massive tarts piled with berries, apples or lime curd; rich scrambled eggs tumbling off thickly sliced sourdough; mini custard tarts stacked with glazed strawberries. Tarts is good food and country style, in the city. Packed like a hamper on weekends.

RESTAURANTS

Sparrow (Map pp58-9; ☎ 9228 2238; 434A William St; lunch from $5.50; dinner from $6; ☺ lunch Fri & Sat, dinner Mon-Sat) Perfect for those on a sparrow-sized budget, this little eatery is filled with locals in search of a taste of home, whether they're craving nasi goreng, rendang curry, or a little gado gado. The 1970s decor and tiled floor will keep you feeling grounded.

Good Fortune Roast Duck House (Map pp58-9; ☎ 9228 3293; 344 William St; mains from $6; ☺ lunch & dinner Wed-Mon) This is the real thing – just like being in China. Locals charge in for family-sized feeds of barbecue pork, roast duck and noodles – the front window is crammed with options. An entire boneless duck is only about $17, and you can ask for a half-serve.

Hong Kong BBQ Chinese Restaurant (Map pp58-9; ☎ 9228 3968; 76 Francis St; noodle soup $8, rice dishes $7.50-$12; ☺ lunch & dinner Thu-Tue) This welcoming, small restaurant, with the family-run vibe, is among the best Cantonese in town. The *san choy bow*, peppered with roast duck, is superb.

Red Teapot (Map pp58-9; ☎ 9228 1981; 413 William St; mains from $7.90, noodles $8.90-$10.90; ☺ Mon-Sat lunch & dinner) This intimate restaurant is always busy with diners enjoying stylishly executed Chinese favourites like fragrant prosperous chicken and chilli salt squid.

Viet Hoa (Map pp58-9; ☎ 9328 2127; 349 William St; mains $8-16; ☺ lunch & dinner) Don't be fooled by the bare-bones ambience of this corner Vietnamese restaurant – or you'll miss out on the fresh rice-paper rolls and top-notch *pho* (beef-and-rice-noodle soup). Greenery creeping up the beams gives the place an off-beat feel. Busy even on Monday nights.

SELF-CATERING

Below we've listed the pick of the crop.

Boatshed (Map pp54-5; ☎ 9284 5176; 40 Jarrad St, Cottesloe) Enormous upmarket shed stacked with fresh produce, soft drinks and bread.

Chez Jean-Claude Patisserie (Map p61; 333 Rokeby Rd; ☺ 6am-6.30pm Mon-Fri) Line up with the locals for brioche and baguettes.

City Farm (Map pp58-9; train-station end of Brown St, East Perth; ☺ until 12pm Sat & Sun) Local organics producers sell eggs, avocados, spinach, beef, coffee and juice. About 20 stalls.

Kailis (Map pp56-7; ☺ 9443 6300; 101 Oxford St, Leederville) Big fresh seafood supplier.

Kakulas Bros (Map pp58-9; ☎ 9328 5744; 183 William St; ☺ Mon-Sat) Ramshackle provisions store overflowing with dirt-cheap legumes, nuts and olives.

New Norcia Bakery (Map pp54-5; ☺ 9443 4114; 163 Scarborough Beach Rd, Mt Hawthorn) Perth's best bread.

Station St Markets (Map p61; Subiaco Markets; ☺ Thu-Sun) Cheaper fresh produce. No meat.

Also recommended:

Welcome Inn Tea House (Map pp58-9; ☎ 9227 8886; 354 William St; ☾ dim sum) Good for no-fuss yum cha.

Riverside Chinese Restaurant (Map pp58-9; ☎ 9328 1688; 74 Francis St; mains $7-15; ☾ dim sum & dinner Wed-Mon) Authentic Chinese and cheap dim sum.

Maya Masala (Map pp58-9; ☎ 9328 5655; cnr Lake & Francis Sts; mains $13-16; ☾ lunch & dinner) Southern Indian.

Joy Garden (Map pp58-9; ☎ 9227 8638; 65 Francis St; mains $15-20; ☾ dim sum & dinner Wed-Mon) Top-rate Chinese. Banquets (for ten) $28 a head.

Inner-City Suburbs
CAFÉS

Soto Espresso (☎ 9227 7686; 507 Beaufort St, Mt Lawley; breakfast $4-10, lunch $8.50; ☾ 7am-midnight) Modern Soto opens out onto the street, welcoming its inner-city crowd – stay-at-home dads, ladies who lunch and shop, bleary-eyed students. The lime-green banquette is a great spot to watch all the comings and goings, and the rather large *croque-monsieur* (a fancy fried cheese-and-ham sandwich) will tackle any hangover. Open late.

Oxford 130 (Map pp56-7; 130 Oxford St, Leederville; sandwiches $7.50; ☾ 6am-midnight) Art and music posters are plastered over one wall. Big jars of jam and lemon butter rest on the bench-top, expectant. There's even a little home-drawn graffiti. Slices of toast are as thick as your copy of *Infinite Jest*, and the No 22 sandwich – pesto, semisundried tomatoes, avocado, cheese and spinach – comes recommended. Elbow your way into a booth, or pull up a crate out front, and let the day slip by.

RESTAURANTS

Duende (Map pp56-7; ☎ 9228 0123; 662 Newcastle St, Leederville; tapas $9-17; ☾ 6pm-late, late lunch Sun) A long list of modern-twisted tapas is served up at sleek Duende, where a late-night glass of dessert wine and *churros* (Spanish doughnuts served with hot chocolate sauce), or perhaps some duck prosciutto served with thin slices of apple, are par for the course.

Lamont's (Map pp54-5; ☎ 9202 1566; 11 Brown St, East Perth; mains $18-38; ☾ breakfast Sat & Sun, lunch Tue-Sun, dinner Wed-Sat) White tablecloths and high-backed chairs sit out on the veranda, metres from the river's edge. The surrounds are pristine, and it's quiet. Inside, fire-engine-red flourishes and canary-yellow beams signal that cutting-edge food's coming out of this kitchen. It sure is: asparagus with cauliflower

pannacotta and Sturgeon caviar, butter-grilled Pemberton marron with mesclun and salsa verde – it all changes with the seasons. Access is off Brown St, by the river.

Must Winebar (Map pp58-9; ☎ 9328 8255; 519 Beaufort St, Mt Lawley; mains $29.95-36.50; ☾ noon-late) This is probably Perth's best wine bar. It's also a restaurant, and a great one at that, with European-style dishes like beef-cheek ravioli with wild-mushroom crème or duck-leg confit with braised red cabbage. If you're just in the area, you're obliged to at least stop in here for a glass of Sauvignon Blanc.

Fraser's Restaurant (Map p61; ☎ 9481 7100; Fraser Ave, Kings Park; mains $31-39; ☾ breakfast, lunch & dinner) Atop Kings Park, overlooking the city and the glittering Swan River, Fraser's location is unrivalled. And the food itself has enjoyed a good name for years – Mod Oz standards like chargrilled rock lobster and Mt Barker chicken confit. It's a big space.

Jackson's (Map pp58-9; ☎ 9328 1177; 483 Beaufort St, Highgate; mains $32-46, 9-course tasting menu $95, with wine $140; ☾ dinner Mon-Sat) If you love fine food and wine, don't deny yourself one of Perth's top dining experiences: Neal Jackson's tasting menu. This is a serious, long-established dining room that enjoys an excellent reputation. The menu spans dishes like crispy pork belly with caramelised apple and sage, or wagyu beef steak with celeriac and Roquefort mash.

Subiaco
CAFÉS

Café Café (☎ 9388 9800; Shop 20, Subiaco Sq, 29 Station St; breakfast $7.50-$10.90, lunch $7.50-$9.90; ☾ breakfast & lunch) Locals speak longingly about Café Café as some sort of shrine to the bean – many consider its coffee the best in Perth. Metres from the Subiaco train station, this is a down-to-earth, unfussy spot where the focus is more on the Illy coffee than the food.

Boucla (☎ 9381 2841; 349 Rokeby Rd; mains $12; ☾ breakfast & lunch Mon-Sat) Boucla may be a little isolated from the thick of the Rokeby Rd action, but that's a good thing. This Middle Eastern–inspired den of sheeshes, artworks and crafts is a locals' secret. Honey-sticky sweets smile at you from the corner, and huge tarts filled with blue-vein cheese and roast vegetables spill off plates. The salads are great too.

Food (☎ 6380 2000; 151a Rokeby Rd; mains $14, shared platters $69, morning or afternoon tea $7.90; ☾ lunch Mon-

PERTH

Sat) As its name suggests, this café is straight-forward, practical, and very focused on the food. Choose your dukkah-crumbed chicken wings with mango chutney – or perhaps some veggie-and-rice-noodle fritters – at the counter, then snap up a spot on the bright-blue lounge out front.

RESTAURANTS

Ecco (☎ 9388 6710; 23 Rokeby Rd; pizzas $19; ⏱ 11am-late Tue-Fri) With black-and-white prints of home (Italy) licked along the walls, small and rustic Ecco is all about simple Italian pizza done well. Slip into a wooden table inside, or gaze at passersby out front, and get busy munching.

Chutney Mary's (☎ 9381 2099; 67 Rokeby Rd; mains $12-24; ⏱ lunch & dinner) The feisty, authentic Indian food here is much-loved. The menu's huge, and much of it's devoted to vegetarian favourites like malai kofta and dal makhani. The vibe's colourful and casual.

Subiaco Hotel (☎ 9381 3069; www.subiacohotel.com.au; 465 Hay St; mains $16-28; ⏱ breakfast, lunch & dinner) The Subiaco Hotel is an institution. Middie-clutching men perch themselves for hours in the side bar, friends banter in lounges by the central bar, and suit-clad lunchers get down to business in the dining room. The sun-speckled courtyard is wonderful in summer, and it's heaving on weekends.

Rialto's (☎ 9382 3292; 424 Hay St; mains $35; ⏱ lunch Mon-Fri, dinner Mon-Sat) Bold red leather, slick black stools, chalk-white walls and chairs: Rialto's is see-and-be-seen Euro-chic with flair. And food is a very serious business, with dishes like pan-fried rabbit served with endive, speck and Danish fetta sauce. Locals view this place as an essential experience.

Cottesloe & Scarborough
CAFÉS

Leaf Tea Merchants (Map pp54-5; ☎ 9284 3830; Shop 1, 29 Napoleon St, Cottesloe; high tea $20, mains $7.95-14.50; ⏱ lunch) Leaf Tea could be dismissed as nothing more than fancy tea in a homeware store. But look closer: these people are obsessed with high tea and all its attendant delights, such as tiffins, three-tier cake stands, delectable almond-berry teacakes and egg-and-home-made-mayonnaise finger sandwiches. A huge range of herb, fruit and berry infusions come in glass teapots.

John St Café (Map pp54-5; ☎ 9384 3390; 37 John St, Cottesloe; mains $11.40-19; ⏱ breakfast & lunch) Dwarfed by gargantuan stands of pines and tucked up a residential street, cute John St Café is the spot for your late-morning fry-up. Dig into massive eggs Benedict, or a BLT with basil pesto and cherry tomatoes. Two minutes' walk from the beach.

QUICK EATS

Peter's by the Sea (Map pp54-5; ☎ 9341 1738; 128 The Esplanade, Scarborough; burgers & kebabs $5-10; ⏱ lunch & dinner) A while back, the developers of the huge Observation City complex tried to buy out this Perth icon, but its owners refused to budge, and the complex was built around it. Similarly, locals have been refusing to buy their burgers anywhere else for decades. The bacon-and-egg burgers are well-known hangover cures.

DRINKING

Much like Los Angeles, Perth's gems are studded throughout the suburbs – the CBD has lost the locals' attention. Generally, the big mainstream drinking venues are in Northbridge; smaller, more laid-back clubs and bars are in Mt Lawley and Leederville. Some big beer gardens are strewn around the suburbs, notably in Cottesloe.

One of the first things you'll notice is that pubs are enormous. This is because of massively expensive licences; once you've got one, you have to turn out the beers at a rapid rate to make a return. Big drinking venues have become part of the culture. And although the licensing laws have recently been changed, this culture is likely to continue for a while yet.

Connections (p76) is the main gay club. Other good places, such as Luxe (opposite), the Brisbane (opposite) and Grapeskin (below), are gay-friendly rather than gay-only.

Bars
CITY CENTRE

our pick Hula Bula bar (Map pp58-9; ☎ 9225 4457; 12 Victoria Ave; ⏱ late Wed-Sun) You'll feel like you're back on Gilligan's Island here, especially with the big fake parrot perched over your shoulder. This tiny Polynesian-themed bar is decked out in bamboo, palm leaves and totems, and the ostentatious cocktails come in ceramic monkey's heads. Plus it's got the tackiest toilets in town. A rather cool but relaxed crowd jams in here weekends.

Box Deli (Map pp58-9; ☎ 9322 6744; 918 Hay St; ⏱ 9.30am-late Mon-Fri, 4pm-late Sat) This bar-cum-restaurant has a distinct club feel, with its deep bar and decks. A well-located spot for a pre-dancing drink.

NORTHBRIDGE

Grapeskin (Map pp58-9; ☎ 9227 9596; 215 William St, Northbridge; ☯ 11am-midnight Mon & Tue, 11am-1am Wed & Thu, 11am-2am Fri & Sat, 11am-10pm Sun) This slick-but-cosy wine bar, next door to the Brass Monkey, used to be a gym, but the only weights being lifted these days are glasses heavy with wines and cocktails. There's a great big bar on which you can rest your elbow and marvel at the wines and spirits lined along an entire wall – so long as the place isn't already heaving. Gay-friendly.

Universal (Map pp58-9; ☎ 9227 6771; 221 William St, Northbridge; ☯ until 2am Wed-Sat, 10pm Sun) The unpretentious Universal, for jazz and blues enthusiasts, is one of Perth's oldest bars.

INNER-CITY SUBURBS

Brisbane (Map pp58-9; ☎ 9227 2300; www.thebrisbane hotel.com.au; cnr Beaufort & Brisbane Sts, Mt Lawley; ☯ 11.30am-late Mon & Tue, 11.30am-midnight Wed-Sat, 11.30am-10pm Sun) The Brisbane's a big 'n' slick beer hall-cum-bar with a massive outdoor area. Huge palms and yukkas provide a balmy holiday feel and, inside, Andy Warhol–inspired prints subtly confirm the inner-city spirit that keeps this place thumping night after night.

Luxe (Map pp58-9; ☎ 9228 9680; 446 Beaufort St, Mt Lawley; ☯ late Wed-Sun) With retro wood panelling, big sexy lounge chairs and Twin Peaks–style red-velvet curtains, Luxe is one of the coolest spots around. Like any serious bar, it's also armed with decks and a specialist cocktail bar. The crowd here is usually very relaxed and friendly.

Must Winebar (Map pp58-9; ☎ 9328 8255; 519 Beaufort St, Mt Lawley; ☯ noon-late) Considering there's French house floating through the sound system and the perfect glass of wine in your hand (there are 40 by the glass, 500 on the wine list), it's very difficult to leave this buzzing bar in the thick of Beaufort St. It's probably the best wine bar in Perth, and the food is also excellent.

Pubs

CITY CENTRE

Belgian Beer Café (Map pp58-9; ☎ 9321 4094; 347 Murray St; ☯ 11am-midnight Mon-Sat, noon-10pm Sun) The Belgian Beer bar is a good spot to start your evening. With loads of beers like Stella

and Hoegaarden on tap, it's a bit like a big cheery beer barn.

NORTHBRIDGE

Deen (Aberdeen Hotel; Map pp58-9; ☎ 9227 9361; 84 Aberdeen St; ☯ 5pm-2am Mon, 5pm-2am Thu-Sat) The Deen's popular with travellers, especially on Monday night's backpacker night (the band kicks off at 9pm). Thursday is all about Brazilian dancing – just slug back some cheap beer and your salsa will improve in no time. Other nights see DJs, pool tables and big lines out the front.

Brass Monkey (Map pp58-9; ☎ 9227 9596; cnr James & William Sts, Northbridge; ☯ 11am-midnight Mon-Tue, 11am-1am Weds-Thu, 11am-2am Fri & Sat, 11am-10pm Sun) This is a great big heritage pub with different areas, each with its own vibe. Take your pick: sit up on a stool at the bar, lean back in the relaxed beer garden, or hunker down on a chesterfield by the fire (and sports screen). There's a restaurant upstairs, too.

INNER-CITY SUBURBS

Flying Scotsman (Map pp58-9; ☎ 9328 6200; 639 Beaufort St, Mt Lawley; ☯ 11am-midnight Sun-Thu, 11am-1am Fri & Sat) There's nothing particularly Scottish about the young, chilled-out crowd that gathers here for pints over small communal tables – if anything they're a bit Aussie-indie. The place will be either heaving or dead, depending on what else is up.

Leederville Hotel (Map pp56-7; ☎ 9286 0150; 742 Newcastle St, Leederville; ☯ noon-midnight Mon-Thu, noon-1am Fri & Sat, noon-11pm Sun) The good old Leederville has been turning out beers and Midori shakers for many generations. The something-for-everyone philosophy is etched out in the sports screens, dance floors, pool tables and, on Fridays, very-fun Funk Club, upstairs. Wednesdays are big with the younger folk.

Queens (Map pp58-9; ☎ 9328 7267; 520 Beaufort St, Mt Lawley; ☯ until midnight Mon-Sat, until 10pm Sun) This is a big federation-style pub, popular on Sundays. A nice cold beer in the sun-speckled courtyard is the standard routine.

SUBIACO

Subiaco Hotel (Map p61; ☎ 9381 3069; cnr Hay & Rokeby Rd, Subiaco; ☯ 7am-late) The Subi's a local favourite and the institution of choice for a pre-footy beer. It's also not bad for a Sunday sundowner or an afternoon of quiet beers and people-watching.

PERTH

COTTESLOE

Ocean Beach Hotel (Map pp54-5; ☎ 9384 2555; cnr Marine Pde & Eric St; ⏰ 11am-midnight Mon-Sat, 11am-10pm Sun) Keep a sharp eye out for the OBH's very own bumper sticker: 'There's nothing like a country crowd'. Backpackers and country kids drink up the beer and soak up the sun at this rambling beachside pub, especially on Sundays.

Cottesloe Beach Hotel (Map pp54-5; ☎ 9383 1100; 104 Marine Pde; ⏰ 11am-midnight Mon-Sat, 11am-10pm Sun) Grab a spot on the lawn in the massive beer garden, or watch the sun set from the balcony, where guys check out chicks all afternoon long. Sundays are big.

ENTERTAINMENT

Most of the big clubs are in Northbridge; Leederville and Mt Lawley are also nightlife spots. Theatre and classical music are found in Subiaco and the city.

To check out what is happening around town online, see p62.

Nightclubs

Geisha (Map pp58-9; ☎ 9328 9808; 135a James St, Northbridge; ⏰ 11pm-6am Fri & Sat) Geisha's a small-and-pumping DJ-driven club. The vibe's usually music-focused and chilled out.

Manor (Map pp56-7; entry $6, after midnight $8) Search for this spot down a laneway behind the Hip-E Club (through the carpark off Newcastle St), and dance to till your heart's content among the chandeliers and chesterfields. There's a small but danceable space downstairs, and another bar and lounge chairs upstairs for when you need to catch your breath. DJs play funk and retro tunes till the wee hours.

Funk Club (Map pp56-7; 742 Newcastle St, Leederville) Upstairs at the Leederville Hotel on Friday nights, the Funk Club is full of colour and fun. A happy bunch bop away for hours up here, seemingly unaware of the entirely different vibe downstairs.

Connections (Map pp58-9; ☎ 9328 1870; 81 James St, Northbridge; ⏰ Wed, Fri & Sat) This is the one real gay club, supposedly the first of its kind in Australia. Saturday nights pull a fun gay and straight crowd, though things can be hit-or-miss – you'll just have to try your luck.

Velvet Lounge (Map pp58-9; 639 Beaufort St, Mt Lawley) Out the back of the Flying Scotsman is this small, red-velvet-clad lounge with hip-hop, drum 'n' bass, house and funk. Punters pop in and out of here and the Flying Scotsman (p75) all night long.

Other clubs:

Ambar (Map pp58-9; ☎ 9325 0000; 100 Murray St) The place for international DJs.

Hip-E Club (Map pp56-7; ☎ 9227 8899; 663 Newcastle St, Leederville; ⏰ Tue-Sun) Thrust about to 'Tainted Love' all night long. Tuesday is backpackers night.

La Bog (Map pp58-9; ☎ 9228 0900; 361 Newcastle St, Northbridge; ⏰ 6pm-6am Mon-Sat, 8pm-1am Sun) Bump 'n' grind to Eddie Vedder belting out 'Better Man'. Backpackers night on Tuesday.

Metro City (Map pp58-9; ☎ 9228 0500; 146 Roe St, Northbridge) Ten theme bars in this thumping super-club.

Rise (Map pp58-9; ☎ 9328 7447; 139 James St) Serious clubbers head here for non-stop trance.

Live Music

Amplifier (Map pp58-9; ☎ 9321 7606; 385 Murray St, rear; ⏰ 8am-late Fri & Sat) Good old Amplifier's one of the best places for live (mainly indie) bands.

ourpick Bakery (Map pp58-9; ☎ 9227 0629; 233 James St) Run by Artrage, Perth's contemporary arts festival body, the Bakery draws the art crowd. Popular indie gigs are held almost every weekend.

Rosemount Hotel (Map pp58-9; ☎ 9328 7062; cnr Angove & Fitzgerald Sts, North Perth; ⏰ 11am-late Mon-Sat, 11am-10pm Sun) Local and international bands play regularly in this spacious pub, all wood and floorboards. There's a pool table round the front, and a big round bar as the central feature. It even comes with a restful beer garden.

Jazz Cellar (Map pp54-5; ☎ 9385 8111; cnr Scarborough Beach Rd & Buxton St; admission $10; ⏰ Friday night) Look for the shoe shop, behind which you'll spot a carpark. Then you'll find a red telephone booth: step through and down the stairs to find an older crowd of jazz freaks revelling in swing. Admission gets you a cup of tea or coffee – BYO alcohol (none for sale at the venue).

Hyde Park Hotel (Map pp58-9; ☎ 9328 6166; cnr Bulwer & Fitzgerald Sts, Northbridge) The Hydie's still punky and a bit sticky. Indie and rock bands play here certain nights (check the gig guides).

Big international acts play at Metro City nightclub. Occasionally musicians like Chris Isaak and Augie March play at **Kings Park** (www.mellenevents.com). The **Perth Jazz Society** (www.perthjazzsociety.com) meets every Monday night at the Hyde Park Hotel to play swing and modern jazz. The **Jazz Club of WA**, which plays traditional jazz and Dixieland, meets at the same place Tuesday night.

Cinemas

The three art-house cinemas in Perth:

Astor (Map pp58-9; ☎ 9370 1777; 659 Beaufort St, Mt Lawley) In a spearmint and gold art deco building, the Astor doesn't screen as many films as Luna and Paradiso.

Cinema Paradiso (Map pp58-9; ☎ 9227 1771; www.luna palace.com.au; Galleria complex, 164 James St, Northbridge)

Luna (Map pp56-7; ☎ 9444 4056; www.lunapalace.com .au; 155 Oxford St, Leederville) $10 Monday twin-features and a bar.

Hollywood blockbusters are screened at the following:

Ace Subiaco (Map p61; ☎ 9388 6500; 500 Hay St, cnr Alvan St)

Hoyts Cinema City (Map pp58-9; ☎ 9325 2377; 580 Hay St)

There are a number of outdoor cinemas open during summer (including Luna, above):

Camelot Outdoor Cinema (Map pp54-5; ☎ 9385 4793; Memorial Hall, 16 Lochee St, Mosman Park)

Moonlight Cinema (Map p61; ☎ 1300 551 908; www .moonlight.com.au; Kings Park Botanic Garden)

Somerville Auditorium (Map pp54 5; www.perth festival.com.au; UWA, 35 Stirling Hwy, Crawley; ✆ Dec-Mar) A quintessential Perth experience, the arthouse Somerville is on beautiful grounds surrounded by pines. Picnicking before the film is a must.

Theatre & Classical Music

Check the *West Australian* newspaper for theatre programmes. For theatre, dance and classical music:

His Majesty's Theatre (Map pp58-9; ☎ 9265 0900; 825 Hay St)

Perth Concert Hall (Map pp58-9; ☎ 9484 1133; 5 St Georges Terrace) Home to the Western Australian Symphony Orchestra (WASO).

Playhouse Theatre (Map pp58-9; ☎ 9484 1133; 3 Pier St)

Regal Theatre (Map p61; ☎ 9484 1133; 474 Hay St)

Subiaco Arts Centre (Map p61; ☎ 9382 3385; 180 Hamersley Rd, Subiaco)

Sport

The *West Australian* has details of all sports games.

During the Australian Football League (AFL) season it's hard to get locals to talk about anything but the two local teams – the Fremantle Dockers and the West Coast Eagles –

and the joy of beating 'the Vics' (any Victorian team is considered an arch-enemy).

Subiaco Oval (☎ 1300 135 915; 250 Roberts Rd, Subiaco) There's a great atmosphere during AFL games here.

Western Australian Cricket Association ground (WACA; Map pp54-5; ☎ 9265 7222; Nelson Cres, East Perth) In summer, cricket fans spend a lazy afternoon here watching a one-day or test match.

Perth Oval (Members Equity Stadium; Map pp58-9; ☎ 9492 6000; Lord St, Perth) The Perth Glory soccer team has many obsessive fans. See them in action here.

Challenge Stadium (Map pp54-5; ☎ 9441 8222; Stephenson Ave, Mt Claremont) Perth Wildcats play NBL basketball here.

SHOPPING

Perth's not known for its shopping, but there are some interesting spots around town, and it is a good place to buy indigenous art.

78 Records (Map pp58-9; ☎ 9322 6384; 914 Hay St) This place has been around since '78 – well, almost. It's as big as a warehouse and has a massive range.

Keith & Lottie (Map pp58-9; ☎ 9328 8082; 276 William St, Northbridge) An indie kid's delight, this extremely cute store has journals, badges, necklaces, t-shirts, a few homewares, coats and tops.

Indigenart (Map p61; ☎ 9388 2899; 115 Hay St, Subiaco) Reputable Indigenart carries major Kimberley, Papunya Tula and Arnhem Land artists. Works span weavings, canvases, works on paper and limited edition prints.

Form (Map pp58-9; ☎ 9226 2799; 357 Murray St) Just around the corner from King St, Form stocks vases and craft pieces by Australian artists as well as design books, broaches, jewellery and bags.

If you suddenly find you have nothing to wear, try **Periscope** (Map pp58-9; ☎ 9321 6868; 30 Kings St) or **Varga Girl** (Map pp58-9; ☎ 9321 7838; 349 Murray St). Both carry Australian designers. Varga Girl has a good range of dresses, some vintage pieces and jeans.

Elephant-size shopping malls are **Garden City** (Map pp54-5; 125 Risely St, Booragoon), south of the city centre, and the more upmarket **Karrinyup** (Map pp54-5; 200 Karrinyup Rd, Karrinyup), north.

GETTING THERE & AWAY
Air

Qantas (☎ 13 13 13; www.qantas.com.au; 55 William St) and **Virgin Blue** (☎ 13 67 89; www.virginblue.com.au)

fly between Perth and other Australian state capitals. **Jetstar** (www.jetstar.com) runs cheapies from Avalon, Melbourne.

Skywest (☎ 1300 660 088; www.skywest.com.au) flies between Perth and regional destinations such as Esperance and Broome. Qantas also flies to Broome and Kalgoorlie.

Bus

The long distance coach bookings office is located at the Perth train station.

Greyhound (☎ 13 14 99; www.greyhound.com.au) has daily services from the East Perth terminal to Darwin via Broome.

Transwa (☎ 1300 662 205; www.transwa.wa.gov.au) operates services from the bus terminal at East Perth train station to many destinations around the state.

South West Coach Lines (☎ 9324 2333) focuses on the southwestern corner of WA, doing trips from the Esplanade Busport to most towns in the region, including Bunbury, Busselton and Margaret River.

Integrity Coach Lines (☎ 1800 226 339, 9226 1339; www.integritycoachlines.com.au) runs services between Perth and Port Hedland via Meekathara and Newman.

Train

The intrastate rail network, run by **Transwa** (☎ 1300 662 205; www.transwa.wa.gov.au), is limited to the following services:

Perth–Kalgoorlie-Boulder ($71.80, once daily) Prospector, from East Perth terminal. Some trains leave 7.15am.

Perth–Northam ($13.55, twice daily) Avon Link, from East Perth railway station.

Perth–Merredin ($36.45, thrice weekly) Avon Link, from East Perth railway station.

Perth–Bunbury ($23.90, twice daily) Australind, from Perth train station.

There are connections with Transwa's more extensive bus service.

The Perth–Mandurah railway should be operating mid-2007. See www.newmetrorail .wa.gov.au for the latest.

There is only one interstate rail link: the famous Indian Pacific transcontinental train journey, run by **Great Southern Railway** (☎ 13 21 47; www.trainways.com.au), which leaves from East Perth station. To Perth from Sydney, one-way fares are about $590 (seat only), $422 (seat only, backpacker rate) or $1320 (sleeper cabin). Between Adelaide and Perth, fares are $355 (seat only), $253 (seat only, back-

packer), or $1005 (sleeper cabin). There are connections to the Ghan (to Alice Springs and Darwin) and the Overland (to Melbourne) trains.

You can buy train tickets at the Interstate and Country booking office at the Perth train station. The office is off Wellington St.

GETTING AROUND
To/From the Airport

The domestic and international terminals of Perth's airport are 10km and 13km east of Perth respectively. Taxi fares to the city are around $25/35 from the domestic/international terminal.

The **Perth Airport City Shuttle** (☎ 9277 7958; www.perthshuttle.com.au) provides transport to the city centre, hotels and hostels. It meets incoming domestic and international flights. The shuttle costs $12/15 from the domestic/international terminal. Bookings are essential (24 hours ahead if possible).

Transperth bus 37 travels to the domestic airport from Kings Park (or Esplanade Busport) via St Georges Tce ($3.20; pick-up at C-stand, St Georges Tce near William St) every 20 mins, every 30 to 60 minutes early morning, evenings and weekends.

Car & Motorcycle

Driving in the city takes a bit of practise, as some streets are one-way and many aren't signed. Perth is well-equipped with car parks – you shouldn't have problems finding one. You'll have no trouble getting fuel, but prices can fluctuate day to day.

All of the major car rental companies – **Avis** (Map pp58-9; ☎ 13 63 33; 46 Hill St), **Budget** (Map pp58-9; ☎ 13 27 27; 960 Hay St), **Hertz** (Map pp58-9; ☎ 13 30 39; 39 Milligan St) and **Thrifty** (☎ 1300 367 227, within WA 136 139; 198 Adelaide Tce) – are in Perth. Some local operators – like **Bayswater Hire Car** (☎ 9325 1000; 160 Adelaide Tce) – can be cheaper, but make sure you read the fine print. Note that some insurance policies, even with the bigger companies, don't cover you outside the metropolitan area after dark – in case you hit a roo.

Public Transport

Perth's central public transport organisation, **Transperth** (☎ 13 62 13; www.transperth.wa.gov.au), operates buses, trains and ferries. There are Transperth information offices at the Perth train station in Wellington St and at the Esplanade Busport on Mounts Bay Rd, by the new convention centre. Transperth provides timetables and advice about getting around Perth, available from the offices and its website. There is also a 'journey planner' on the website.

There's a free transit zone for all buses and trains within the city. Look for the 'FTZ' sign. On regular Transperth buses and trains, a short ride of one zone costs $2.10, two zones $3.20, three zones $4. Zone one includes the city centre and the inner suburbs, and zone two extends to Fremantle, Sorrento and Midland. If you're planning a busy day of sightseeing, the DayRider ($7.70) is good value. It gives you unlimited travel after 9am weekdays and all day on the weekend. Note that international student cards are not counted as 'concession'.

If you're in Perth for a while, it may be worth buying a SmartRider card, which covers you for bus, train and ferry. It's $10 to purchase, then you add value to your card. The technology deducts the fare as you go, so you don't have to figure out fares and zones yourself. The SmartRider works out 15% cheaper than buying single tickets (25% if you load directly from the bank). The FamilyRider lets two adults and up to five children travel for a total of $7.70 weekdays.

BUS

For travellers, the free Central Area Transit (CAT) services in the city centre are fantastic. There are computer readouts (and audio) at the stops telling you when the next bus is due.

Using the CAT, you can get to most sights in the inner city. Pick up a CAT map at the Perth train station.

The red CAT operates east–west from Outram St, West Perth, to the WACA in East Perth. It runs every five minutes from 6.50am to 6.20pm weekdays. It also operates every 25 minutes from 10am to 6.15pm weekends.

The blue CAT operates north–south from the river to Northbridge. On weekdays, services run every seven minutes, 6.50am to 6.20pm, and, on Fridays, every 15 minutes 6.20pm to 1am. On weekends, there's a bus every 15 minutes 8.30am to 1am Saturday and 10am to 6.15pm Sunday.

The yellow CAT runs from East Perth up Wellington St to West Perth every 10 minutes, 6.50am to 6.20pm weekdays, and every 30 minutes 10am to 6.15pm weekends.

The metropolitan area is also serviced by a wide network of Transperth buses. See the information office at Perth train station for timetables and advice or use the 'journey planner' on its website.

FERRY

A popular way of getting to the zoo, Transperth ferries cross the river from the Barrack St jetty in the city to the Mends St jetty in South Perth. Services run every 20 to 30 minutes 6.50am-7.24pm weekdays, and around 8.10am-9.15pm weekends.

TAXI

Perth has a decent system of metered taxi cabs, though the distances in Perth makes

---

HAPPY VANNING

If you're heading up north for, say, more than two weeks, consider the campervan. You won't be hampered by hostel check-in timetables and other hassles, leaving you to go where you want, when you want. And it can be quite economical once costs are split between two or three people. In general, if you're just planning to tour the southwest, a hire car is better value – accommodation's plentiful, and distances aren't as great.

There are a number of campervan rental companies in Perth, including the following:
Campaboutoz (Map pp54–5; ☎ 1800 210 877; www.campaboutoz.com.au; 198 Hampden Rd, Nedlands)
Wicked Campers (Map pp58–9; ☎ 1800 246 869; 49 Shenton St, Northbridge) With graffiti-style murals splashed across the vans (not all are painted).

Be rigorous and compare deals carefully. You should be able to get unlimited kilometres, roadside assistance, and pick-up and delivery within metropolitan Perth.

If you've done the sums and decided to purchase, Freo has a number of secondhand car yards, including a cluster in North Freo, near Mojo's on Stirling Hwy. There's also the **Traveller's Autobarn** (☎ 9228 9500; www.travellers-autobarn.com.au; 365 Newcastle St, Northbridge).

frequent use costly, and on busy nights you may have trouble flagging one down off the street. There are ranks throughout the city and in Fremantle. The two main companies are **Swan Taxis** (☎ 13 13 30, 9422 2240) and **Black & White** (☎ 13 10 08, 9333 3377), both of which have wheelchair taxis.

TRAIN
Transperth also operates suburban train lines to Armadale, Fremantle, Midland, Thornlie and the northern suburb of Clarkson (Joondalup) from around 5.20am to midnight weekdays. Trains run until about 2am Saturday and Sunday. The line to Mandurah via Rockingham should be operational by mid-2007.

All trains leave from Perth station on Wellington St. Your rail ticket can also be used on Transperth buses and ferries within the ticket's area of validity; the free transit zone extends to Claisebrook and City West stations. You're also free to take your bike on the train in non-peak times.

During the day, some of the Fremantle trains run through to Midland.

FREMANTLE

☎ 08 / pop 25,500

Creative, relaxed, open-minded: Fremantle's spirit is entirely distinct from Perth's. Perhaps it has something to do with the port and the city's working-class roots. Or the hippies, who first set up home here a few decades ago and, today, can still be seen casually bobbling an old bicycle down the street. Artists always make a difference, and painters, writers and musicians have been toiling away here for years.

Freo lies at the mouth of the Swan, 19km from Perth, making it more like another suburb these days than a city of its own. And there's more than the friendly atmosphere to enjoy here – Freo's home to some fantastic museums, historic buildings, galleries, pubs and cafés. At night on weekends, kids from the suburbs move in to party and cruise the main drag.

HISTORY
This area was settled thousands of years ago by the Noongar people. Several trails once joined on the south side of the Swan River, at a natural bridge almost spanning the Swan.

This was the hub of intertribal trading routes. Aboriginal groups quickly came to occupy various parts of the area, known to them as Manjaree.

Fremantle's European history began when the ship *HMS Challenger* landed here in 1829. The ship's captain, Charles Fremantle, took possession of the whole of the west coast 'in the name of King George IV'. Like Perth, the settlement made little progress until convict labour was employed. These hardworking labourers constructed most of the town's earliest buildings; some of them, such as the Round House, Fremantle Prison and Fremantle Arts Centre, are now among the oldest in WA.

As a port, Fremantle wasn't up to much until the engineer CY O'Connor created an artificial harbour in the 1890s. In 1987 the city of Fremantle was the site of the unsuccessful defence of what was, for a brief period, one of Australia's most prized possessions – the America's Cup yachting trophy. Preparations for the influx of tourists transformed Fremantle into a more modern and colourful city. In 1995 the Fremantle Dockers played their first game. And in 2006 a native claim title over the metropolitan area was successful – acknowledgment of the Noongar people's ties to the land (though the claim is now under appeal).

INFORMATION
Chart & Map Shop (☎ 9335 8665; 14 Collie St) Great range of maps and travel guides.

etech (☎ 9239 8189; 53 South Tce; per hr $6; ✓ 8am-8.30pm Mon-Thu, 8am-4pm Fri, 8.30am-3pm Sat) Quiet internet access.

Fremantle Hospital (☎ 9431 3333; Alma St)

Fremantle Post Office (☎ 13 13 18; 13 Market St)

New Edition Bookshop (☎ 9335 2383; 50 South Tce; ✓ 9am-late) Excellent bookstore. Stocks locals titles.

Travellers Centre (☎ 9335 8776; 16 Market St; internet per hr $5) Travellers' hangout with loads of travel information and internet terminals.

Visitors Centre (☎ 9431 7878; Kings Square; ✓ 9am-5pm Mon-Fri, 11am-3pm Sat, 11.30am-3pm Sun) On the northwest side of the town hall.

SIGHTS & ACTIVITIES
Western Australian Maritime Museum
Housed in a stunning, architect-designed building on the harbour, just west of the city centre, the **Western Australian Maritime Museum** (☎ 9431 8444; www.museum.wa.gov.au; Victoria Quay; mu-

seum adult/child $10/3, submarine $8/3, museum & submarine $15/5; 9.30am-5pm) is a fascinating exploration of WA's relationship with the ocean. It faces out to the sea, which has shaped so much of the state's, and Fremantle's, destiny.

You can't miss the display of **Australia II**, the famous winged-keel yacht that won the America's Cup yachting race in the 1980s (and stole it away from the Americans, ending their 132-year domination of the competition – an achievement which is the source of much Sandgroper pride). Other boats on show include an **Indonesian fishing boat**, introduced to the Kimberley and used by the indigenous people, and a **pearl lugger** used in Broome. Even a classic 1970s panel van (complete with fur lining) makes the cut – because of its status as the surfer's vehicle of choice.

Well-presented displays cover an exhausting range of topics – from how Aboriginal fish traps work to the sandalwood trade. If you're not claustrophobic, take a tour of another ocean-going machine, the submarine **HMAS Ovens**. The vessel was part of the Australian Navy's fleet from 1969 to 1997. Tours leave every half hour from 10am to 3.30pm.

Fremantle Arts Centre & History Museum

An impressive neo-Gothic building, the **Fremantle Arts Centre** (9432 9555; www.fac.org.au; cnr Ord & Finnerty Sts; 10am-5pm) was originally constructed by convict labourers as a lunatic asylum in the 1860s. Saved from demolition in the late 1960s, the building now also houses the **Fremantle History Museum** (9430 7966), which focuses on the diverse nationalities that make up the town's population.

Today the arts centre has a changing programme of interesting exhibitions; during summer, it's a hive of cultural activity, with concerts, courses and workshops. There's a café and craft shop with books, and the gorgeous elm-strewn gardens have benches.

Old Fremantle Prison

In some ways, the **Old Fremantle Prison** (9336 9200; www.fremantleprison.com.au; 1 The Terrace; day tours adult/child $16/8, night tours $20/10.50; 10am-6pm, last tour 5pm), with its foreboding 5m-high walls, dominates present-day Fremantle. Certainly tales of adventures and hardships in here have lived on in the city's imagination.

Suitably enough, the prison was built by convict labour, and it operated from 1855

right through 1991, playing host to people like bushranger Moondyne Joe, a famed escape artist (p100); Brenden Abbott, a bank robber who escaped in prison guard's uniform; and Eric Edgar Cooke, the last person to be hanged in WA.

You can only enter on a tour, which depart every half-hour – and they're highly recommended. Another good time to visit is after 7.30pm Wednesday and Friday for the night tours by torchlight.

Maritime Museum Shipwreck Galleries

Although the maritime museum commands a lot of attention, don't miss the intriguing **Shipwreck Galleries** (9431 8444; Cliff St; admission by donation; 9.30am-5pm), where you can happily poke around for hours learning about gungho seafaring adventures and misfortunes.

The museum (in a building constructed in 1852 as a commissariat store) has a display on WA's maritime history with particular emphasis on the history, recovery and restoration of the famous wreck **Batavia**, in addition to other Dutch merchant ships and some more recent wrecks.

At one end of the Batavia gallery is a huge **stone facade** intended for an entrance to Batavia Castle. It was being carried by the Batavia when it sank. The dominant feature of the gallery, however, is the reconstruction of a part of the hull from recovered timbers, which you can view from ground level as well as from a mezzanine floor above.

Round House

Out on Arthur Head, the western end of High St near the Maritime Museum, is the **Round House** (9336 6897; admission by donation; 10am-3.30pm). Built in 1831, it's the oldest public building in WA. It was originally a local prison and the site of the colony's first hanging.

Later, the building was used for holding Aborigines before they were taken away to Rottnest Island. To the Noongar people, the Round House is a sacred site because of the number of their people killed while incarcerated here.

Gold Rush Buildings

Fremantle boomed during the WA gold rush and many buildings were constructed during, or shortly before, this period. **Samson House** (cnr Ellen & Ord Sts; admission by donation of $3; 1.15-5pm

FREMANTLE

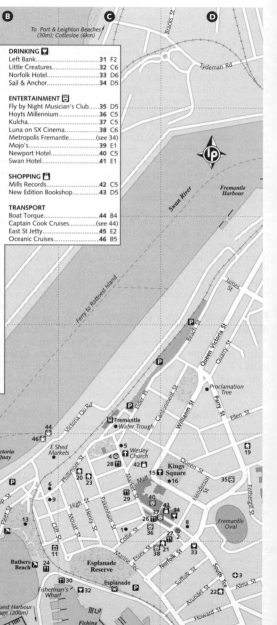

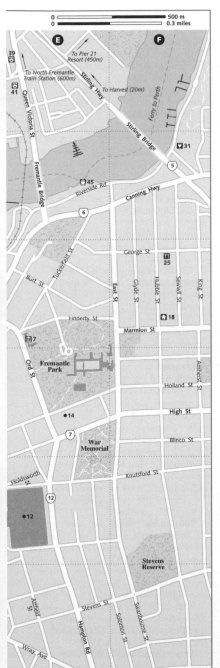

Sun) is a well-preserved 1888 colonial home in Ellen St. **St Johns Anglican Church** (1882), on the corner of Adelaide and Queen Sts, contains a large stained-glass window.

Other buildings of the boom era include Fremantle **Town Hall** (1887) in Kings Square; the 1903 former **German consulate building** (5 Mouat St); the 1907 **Fremantle Train Station**; and the Georgian-style **Customs House**, on the corner of Cliff and Phillimore Sts.

Whale-Watching

Recommended whale-watching tours:
Boat Torque (Rottnest Express; ☎ 9421 5888; tours $32; ☽ 11am & 1.15pm Wed, Sat & Sun) Leaves Fremantle (C shed).
Oceanic Cruises (☎ 9335 2666; www.oceaniccruises .com.au; adult/child $32/19; ☽ 1.15 Wed & Fri-Sun). Leaves Fremantle (B shed).

Other Attractions

Originally opened in 1897, the colourful **Fremantle Markets** (☎ 9335 2515; cnr South Terrace & Henderson St; ☽ Fri-Sun) was reopened in 1975 and today draws slow-moving crowds combing over souvenirs like plastic boomerangs and swan-shaped magnets. The fresh produce section is a good place to stock up on snacks.

The huge **Esplanade Reserve**, behind the Fishing Boat Harbour and full of Norfolk Island pines, is a good spot to relax.

FREMANTLE FOR CHILDREN

Fremantle is great for kids. You can walk everywhere, from the grass and pine expanse of the **Esplanade Reserve** and back up to the markets. Have fish and chips on **Fishing Boat Harbour**, watch buskers (ice-cream in hand) at the **markets** (above), visit the **Maritime Museum** (p80), or catch the train to the two great beaches, **Port Beach** and **Leighton Beach**. At Fishing Boat Harbour, there's also popular and flat **Bathers Beach**, which is great for a splash.

TOURS

The **Fremantle Tram** (☎ 9433 6674; www.fremantle trams.com.au), in fact a bus that looks like an old-fashioned trolley car, leaves from the Fremantle Town Hall. The historic tours of Fremantle, which go up to the war memorial (great views), leave at 9.45am but you can hop on at other stops around the city (adult/child $20/5). The 'Very Scary Ghostly Tour' (adult/child $48/32) runs 6.45pm Fridays and visits the prison, graveyards and other spooky spots.

The training ship **STS Leeuwin II** (☎ 9430 4105; www.leeuwin.com), a 55m, three-masted barquentine, is based at Berth B, Victoria Dock. You can go out for a day sail (adult/child $99/69) or do a brunch or twilight trip (adult/child $75/40).

FESTIVALS & EVENTS

Perhaps the most interesting is the annual **Blessing of the Fleet** (Esplanade Reserve), an October tradition brought to Fremantle by Mediterranean immigrants. In November is the big, 10-day **Fremantle Festival**, where the streets come alive with performances and parades. Food-lovers will enjoy the annual **Sardine Festival** (January).

SLEEPING

There's a dearth of accommodation in Freo. Generally B&Bs offer the best midrange value, but there are also some good apartments.

Budget

So long as you have your own vehicle, the three caravan parks are fairly accessible. Fremantle Village is only about 3km from the centre of Freo, and Coogee and Woodman Point only a few extra minutes' drive down Cockburn Rd. All three are pleasantly located along the shoreline.

Old Firestation Backpackers (☎ 9430 5454; www.old-firestation.net; 18 Phillimore St; 6- & 8-bed dm/4-bed dm/d $18/20/50; 🖳) The brawny firemen have long left the building, but there's still plenty of entertainment in this converted firestation: free internet, fusball, Playstation and a sunny courtyard. Not that you'd want to stay on-site all the time. You're right on the harbour here, with Port and Leighton Beaches a five-minute bike ride away. Girls have their own space, including a decent-sized kitchen. Dorms are good value, with natural light and the afternoon sea breeze fluttering in.

YHA Backpackers Inn Fremantle (☎ 9431 7065; bpinnfreo@yahoo.com.au; 11 Pakenham St; 8-/4-bed dm/s/d without bathroom/d with bathroom $18/20/35/45/60, nonmembers extra $3.50; 🖳) It's as if Freo's famously pleasant afternoon sea breeze, the Fremantle Doctor, has just floated through Backpackers Inn. New management has breathed fresh life into this YHA – the only one in the city – and rooms are bright and clean. Flicks are shown on the mini cinema screen every night, there's a huge indoor recreation area, and it's close to the action.

Pirates (☎ 9335 6635; 11 Essex St; dm/d $22/70; 🖳) This sun- and fun-filled hostel in the thick of the Freo action is a top spot to socialise. Rooms are in great shape, and the girls-only bathroom upstairs is freshly tiled and polished. The kitchen area is well-equipped, and eye-catching wall murals of the sea remind you that an ocean swim is minutes away.

Fremantle Village (Map pp54-5; ☎ 9430 4866; www.fremantlevillage.com.au; 1 Cockburn Rd, South Fremantle, near cnr Rockingham Rd; powered tent site $27, chalets for two per week $265, per extra person $20; 🔀) Fremantle Village is a functional caravan park, and the closest to Freo. It's more set up for long-termers – there's a minimum four-week stay.

Coogee (Map pp54-5; ☎ 9418 1810; http://aspenparks.com.au; Cockburn Rd, near Mayor Rd turnoff; chalets for 2 from $95, paved site for 2 $34) This bigger caravan park has a slightly more upmarket feel. It's popular with young families, and has a tennis court and café.

Woodman Point (Map pp54-5; ☎ 9434 1433; http://aspenparks.com.au; 132 Cockburn Rd, Munster; chalets for 2 from $125; powered tent site for 2 from $38; 🔀 🖳 🐾) A particularly pleasant spot, with tent sites (Coogee doesn't have these). It's usually quiet, and its location makes it feel more summer beach holiday than outer-Freo staging post.

Midrange

Norfolk Hotel (☎ 9335 5405; 47 South Terrace; d from $95, tr from $105-115, d without bathroom from $70) While eucalypts and elms stand quietly in the sun-streaked beer garden, the old limestone Norfolk harbours a secret upstairs: its rooms. Wrought-iron bedheads, crisp white linens and country-style furnishings make this a comfortable spot to rest up. Lounges come with sofas, fans and fridges, and there's a welcoming communal sitting room. There's no air-con, and it can be noisy on weekends, but it's still good value.

100 Hubble (☎ 9339 8080; www.100hubble.com; 100 Hubble St, East Fremantle; s $100, d from $150; 🖳) This must be Fremantle's most eccentric accommodation. You'll sleep in a beautifully restored 1950s train carriage, shower in an outdoor telephone booth, and relax on the sun-filled veranda, paved with gravestone off-cuts. Lovingly created by a well-known Freo artist, this environmentally conscious guesthouse is even heritage listed – for its treasured recycled objects.

Terrace Central B&B (☎ 9335 6600; info@terracecentral.com.au; 83-85 South Tce; d/3-bedroom apt $132/180, rates higher on Sat; ✜ ▣) Terrace Central may be a character-filled B&B at heart, but its larger size – there are about eight rooms here – affords you a little bit of extra space. It's also full of character: miniature boats, flying mallards, giant wooden giraffes, even mounted plates. There are two modern apartments out the back, which sleep up to eight. Doubles are roomy.

Fremantle Colonial Accommodation (☎ 9430 6568; fremantle.col@westnet.net.au; 215 High St; B&B d $145, 2-bedroom apt $150, cottages from $180; ✜ ▣) Rambling two-storey terrace or historic prison cottage? Whichever you choose, both embrace the colonial theme with gusto. White-painted wrought-iron bed frames, floral quilt covers and dusty-pink walls open out onto lacework balconies. The prison cottages, next door to the Old Fremantle Gaol, must have the best location in Freo. They're big and comfortable.

Top End

Port Mill B&B (☎ 9433 3832; www.babs.com.au/portmill; 3/17 Essex St; d from $170) This must be the lovechild of Paris and Freo – and one of the most luxurious B&Bs in town. Crafted from local Freo limestone (built in 1862 as a mill), inside it's all modern Parisian style, with gleaming taps, contemporary French furniture and wrought-iron balconies. French doors open out to the sun-filled decks, where you can tinkle your china over breakfast.

Quest Harbour Village (☎ 9430 3888; www.questhar bourvillage.com.au; Mews Rd, Challenger Harbour; 1-bedroom apt $190, 2-bedroom apt $220-280, 3-bedroom apt $280-330; ✜) Not many locals know this quiet set of apartments, nestled on the harbour. (Which is hard to believe, since they're really quite a find.) All rooms face the harbour and have balconies for maximum nautical experience. Downstairs the rooms are light and simple, if a little dated, and kitchens are fully equipped. Upstairs, there's a more contemporary feel, with solid-coloured furnishings and plenty of room.

Pier 21 Resort (☎ 9336 2555; www.pier21.com.au; 9 John St, North Fremantle; studios $190, 1-bedroom apt from $205, 2-bedroom apt from $245; ✜ ▣) Pier 21 is in an unlikely spot. Along the harbour in North Freo, few pass here by road. Once you're here, though, it all makes sense: it's quiet, and the glittering boat harbour is your backyard. Rooms are spacious and bright, and there's a tennis court, pool and spa.

EATING

Eating in Freo is more about casual Italian or fish and chips than serious fine dining. The two main spots are South Tce and Fishing Boat Harbour. People-watching from outdoor tables on South Tce is also a legitimate lifestyle choice.

South Tce & Around

Gino's (☎ 9336 1464; 1 South Tce; mains $9-24; ☯ breakfast, lunch & dinner) Old-school Gino's must be Freo's most famous café. Pot-bellied Italian men, scriptwriters, musicians and other assorted locals treat it as their second living room, and these days it's a bit of a tourist attraction. When the café was recently refurbished, the coffee machine was simply moved out the front, onto the pavement, and the locals sipped their espressos outdoors, nonplussed. There's no budging these guys.

Istanbul (☎ 9335 6068; 19b Essex St; mains $17.90-21.90; ☯ lunch & dinner) Istanbul is one down-to-earth, no-frills Turkish restaurant. It's damn good, especially for vegetarians, who'll be overloaded with salads, tabouleh, *mezze* and other delicious delights. Comes with an attention-grabbing belly dancer.

Maya (☎ 9335 2796; 77 Market St; mains $18.90-25; ☯ dinner Tue-Sun, lunch Fri) Maya's white tablecloths and wooden chairs signal classic style without the pomp. Its well-executed Indian favourites have made it a popular local spot, right through the week, for years. Special menu Friday.

SELF-CATERING

Kakulas Sister (☎ 9430 4445; 29-31 Market St) This provedore – packed with nuts, quince paste and Italian rocket seeds – is a cook's dream, and an excellent spot to stock up on energy-filled snacks. If you've been to Kakulas in Northbridge, you'll know the deal.

The Fremantle Markets (p83) is also a good spot for fruit and other picnic items.

Fishing Boat Harbour

Cicerello's (☎ 9335 1911; 44 Mews Rd; mains $11.50-20; ☯ lunch & dinner) This fish and chips factory's been around since 1903. It's also a quintessential Fremantle experience. Choose your fish and chips, then pick a spot out on the boardwalk or in the concrete-floored space inside. It's all very casual. (No-one's going to care if you're in your tracksuit, for instance.) Watch out for the seagulls – they can act like demonic robots from some b-grade sci-fi flick when they're in the mood.

Little Creatures (☎ 9430 5555; www.littlecreatures .com.au; 40 Mews Rd; mains $14-20; ⏲ lunch & dinner Mon-Fri, brunch & dinner Sat & Sun) Little Creatures is quite a gem. In a cavernous converted boat shed overlooking the harbour, this brewery can get chaotic at times (as can the service), but the home-brewed ales are well worth the wait. And the food is excellent – juicy yet crunchy prosciutto-wrapped prawns, classic chilli tomato mussels, wood-fired pizzas. You can inspect the brewery vats yourself from the deck on the second floor or almost nuzzle the boats from the boardwalk out back – you're right on the harbour. No bookings.

Mussel Bar (☎ 9433 1800; 42 Mews Rd, Fishing Boat Harbour; mains $18-29; ⏲ lunch & dinner Tue-Sun) Mussel Bar's large glass windows afford romantic views of the glittering harbour. You would say the location is the main reason to come down here, if it weren't for the food. (It's excellent.) Choose from five types of mussel dishes, including traditional chilli and Thai green curry. Mains like blue-manna-crab parpadelle are standouts.

North & East Fremantle

Harvest (☎ 9336 1831; 1 Harvest Rd, North Fremantle; mains $28-32; ⏲ dinner Tue-Sat, lunch Thu-Sun, breakfast Sat & Sun) First you'll find a green-painted cottage, complete with picket fence. Swing through the heavy, fuchsia-painted metal doors and into the dark-wood dining room lined with artworks and curios. Then settle down to comforting dishes like oxtail pie with cauliflower mash, caramelised red wine and shallot juice. Sunday breakfast is big.

George St Bistro (☎ 9339 6352; 73 George St mains $29-34; ⏲ dinner Mon, lunch & dinner Wed-Sun) George St Bistro is coveted by the locals – nestled along quiet, leafy George St, it's something of a secret. The European-German menu includes dishes like light linguine with chorizo and squid in a subtle tomato sauce. Contemporary art takes pride of place along the walls, and the banquette and small tables lend a European feel.

DRINKING

Most of the big pubs in town are lined up along South Tce.

Little Creatures (☎ 9430 5555; 40 Mews Rd, Fishing Boat Harbour; ⏲ late) In a huge old boatshed, by the harbour, this brewery's ales are a great source of WA pride. The four home-brewed ales here – Pale Ale, Little Pilsner, Roger's Amber and the Bright Ale – are fantastic. You can view the brewing vats from the second floor (it's all open), or drink up on the deck and watch the boats, out back.

Norfolk Hotel (☎ 9335 5405; 47 South Tce; ⏲ late) Slow down to the Freo pace and take your time over one of the many beers on tap here – Asahi, Coopers, Becks, James Squire. The limestone courtyard, with the sun streaking in through the elms and eucalypts, is downright soporific sometimes. There's a big sports screen tucked around the side so you don't miss anything.

Sail & Anchor (☎ 9335 8433; 64 South Tce; ⏲ 11am-midnight Mon-Thu, 11am-1am Fri & Sat, 11am-10pm Sun) Built in 1854, this Fremantle landmark has been impressively restored to recall much of its former glory. Downstairs is big and beer-focused; it's more sedate upstairs, where there's a veranda.

Left Bank (☎ 9319 1315; 15 Riverside Rd; ⏲ 7.30am-midnight Mon-Sat, noon-9pm Sun) This Edwardian riverside inn, up from the East St jetty and overlooking the water, is patronised by lively young 'uns in the downstairs café and bar.

ENTERTAINMENT

Given Freo's long been an enclave for artists, it's no wonder the city has turned out so many talented musicians – Eskimo Joe, the Waifs, the John Butler Trio.

Mojo's (☎ 9430 4010; 237 Queen Victoria St; ⏲ 7pm-late) Good old Mojo's is one of Freo's long-standing live music pubs – a real stalwart. Local and national bands (mainly Australian rock 'n' roll and indie) and DJs play at this small venue, and there's a sociable beer garden out back. Rest one elbow on the bar and turn your attention to an up-and-coming local band.

Fly by Night Musician's Club (☎ 9430 5976; Queen St, opposite carpark below gaol) Variety is the key at Fly by Night, in this huge, shedlike venue that's been around for about 20 years. All kinds perform – The Kill Devil Hills, Renee Geyer, Jeff Lang.

Kulcha (☎ 9336 4544; www.kulcha.com.au; 1st fl, 13 South Tce) World culture's the focus here, with Afghani paintings, Hungarian and Romanian music and African drumming workshops. Book ahead.

Other live music venues include the enormous **Metropolis Fremantle** (☎ 9336 1880; 58 South

Tce; 9pm-4am Fri, 9pm-5am Sat), where international bands and DJs perform. On the weekends, energetic miniskirts and chesty young things jump around for hours. Local bands play at the **Newport Hotel** (☎ 9335 2428; 2 South Tce; noon-midnight Mon-Thu, noon-1am Fri & Sat, noon-10pm Sun), and the **Swan Hotel** (☎ 9335 2725; 201 Queen Victoria St, North Fremantle) has DJs and bands in the basement.

Retro **Luna on SX** (☎ 9430 5999; www.lunapalace .com.au; Essex St) is the arthouse cinema; blockbusters screen at **Hoyts Millennium** (☎ 9430 6988; hoyts.com.au; Collie St).

SHOPPING

Fashion stores run along Market St, towards the train station.

Kakulas Sister (☎ 9430 4445; 29-31 Market St) Treat yourself to an essential snack-preparing item, or browse the nuts, seeds, lentils and oils, in this amazing provedore.

New Edition (☎ 9335 2383; 50 South Tce; 9am-late) This excellent, well-stocked bookstore carries fiction as well as a range of local titles.

Mills Records (☎ 9335 1945; 22 Adelaide St) Your spot for music and tickets.

Fremantle Arts Centre (☎ 9432 9555; www.fac.org .au; cnr Ord & Finnerty Sts; 10am-5pm) This is an inspiring place to browse local arts and crafts.

GETTING THERE & AROUND

A very pleasant way to get here is by ferry from Perth's Barrack St jetty to the East St jetty, but allow plenty of time. **Oceanic Cruises** (☎ 9325 1191; www.oceaniccruises.com.au) has boats leaving fives times daily (adult/child $17/11) from jetty five. **Captain Cook Cruises** (☎ 9325 3341; www.captaincookcruises.com.au) also does the trip (adult/child $36/18), leaving at 9.45am and 11am, and its cruises include wine tastings on the way back.

Transperth train (☎ 13 62 13; www.transperth.wa.gov .au) is the most convenient way to get to Freo. One-way trips take 30 minutes from the city, and you can enjoy ocean views as you enter North Fremantle. Trains run about every 15 minutes (adult $3.20) during the day, 30 minutes evenings.

There are also countless buses between Perth city and Fremantle. These include buses 103, 106, 111 158 and 107. Some travel via the Canning Hwy; others go via Mounts Bay Rd and Stirling Hwy. The journey planner, on Transperth's website, is a useful planning tool.

The **Fremantle Airport Shuttle** (☎ 9335 1614; www.fremantleairportshuttle.com.au; from $25 per person) departs Fremantle for the airport about 12 times daily about every half-hour to hour. Arrange pick-up from your accommodation.

There is a plethora of one-way streets and parking meters in Freo. It's easy enough to travel by foot or on the free CAT bus service, which takes in all the major sites on a continuous route every 10 minutes from 7.30am to 6pm on weekdays and 10am to 6.30pm on the weekend.

GUILDFORD & THE SWAN VALLEY

The National Trust–classified town of Guildford was one of the first colonial settlements in Perth. Sited on the Swan River, it was established in 1829 as an inland port. These days trains stop at Guildford, but to explore the Swan Valley you'll need a tour (p67) or a car. For National Park hikes in the Swan Valley region, see p98.

INFORMATION

Swan Valley & Eastern Region visitors centre (☎ 9379 9400; cnr Swan & Meadow Sts, Guildford; 9am-4pm) Well-stocked with information and maps.

SIGHTS & ACTIVITIES

Woodbridge House (Ford St, Guildford; 1-4pm Thu-Tue) is an 1885 colonial mansion overlooking the river. The **Old Courthouse, Gaol & Museum** (Meadow St, Guildford; adult/child $2/free; 9-3pm Wed, noon-4.30pm Sat, 2-4pm Sun) is right by the visitors centre. Call the visitors centre to double-check opening hours ahead of your visit. The 1841 **Rose & Crown Hotel** (☎ 9279 8444; 105 Swan St) claims to be WA's oldest pub. Have a beer in the cellar bar (formerly a convict-built well) and, while you're there, check out the sealed-off tunnel which used to connect the hotel with the river.

In West Swan is the 26-sq-km **Whiteman Park** (☎ 9209 6000; www.whitemanpark.com; enter from Lord St or Beechboro Rd; 8.30am-6pm), Perth's biggest reserve. It's more recreation area than unbridled forest, with craft displays, old railway buildings and engines (including a vintage steam train) and tram rides. But there are plenty of outdoor activities, with picnic and barbecue spots at Mussel Pool, over 30km of walkways, and bike paths.

The park also hosts the well-maintained **Caversham Wildlife Park & Zoo** (☎ 9248 1984; www.cavershamwildlifepark.com.au; adult/child $15/6; 🕑 8.30am-4.30pm), which has creatures such as cassowaries, echidnas, kangaroos, potoroos, quokkas and native birds. To get here take bus 60 from the Esplanade Busport in Perth to Morley, change to the Ellenbrook-bound bus 336, and get off at Whiteman Park. (This takes at least 1½ hours, one-way.)

Rambling along the Swan River from Guildford to Upper Swan is Perth's very own bucolic restaurant scene: the **Swan Valley**. Only 18km northeast of the CBD, the region was once overshadowed by Margaret River's wine-producing success – few wineries in the Swan Valley managed to produce top-shelf wines (it's too hot). So the Swan Valley found a new life by focusing on food.

Margaret River Chocolate Company (☎ 9250 1588; 5123 West Swan Rd; 🕑 10am-5pm), with its good-quality chocolates, jams and preserves, is often mobbed by families and tour groups. Bring your picnic basket to **Houghton Wines** (☎ 9274 9540; Dale Rd, Middle Swan; 🕑 10am-5pm), a spectacular historic property with rolling hills, huge jacaranda trees, and cellar door sales. **Gomboc Gallery** (☎ 9274 3996; 50 James Rd, Middle Swan; 🕑 10am-5pm Wed-Sun) has a good sculpture park.

EATING & DRINKING

Lamont's (☎ 9296 4485; 85 Bisdee Rd; www.lamonts.com .au; tapas $6.50-13.50; 🕑 lunch, tapas Sat & Sun) Now that Lamont's fine-dining efforts are focused in East Perth, it's just lazy tapas and snacks up here under the open sky. Try some Manjimup crinkle-cut fries or plump, top-quality kalamata olives.

Sittella (☎ 9296 0237; www.sitella.com.au; 100 Barrett St, off Great Northern Hwy; mains $24.50-$30; 🕑 cellar door & lunch Tue-Sun) Sitella's one of the best places to eat in the Valley – Perthites sneak out of the office to lunch up here regularly. Take your time over mains like crispy roasted duckling on kumara puree with mandarin confit, and soak up the view of the vines.

Riverbank (☎ 9377 1805; www.riverbankestate.com .au; 126 Hamersley Rd; mains $25-29; 🕑 lunch daily, breakfast Sun) A pleasant, open restaurant that looks out onto the vines, Riverbank's menu is one of the best. How about Harvey beef fillet wrapped in prosciutto on berlotti beans with mushroom butter? Or twice-cooked crispy-duck-and-eggplant curry with sticky rice and fiery tomato chutney? You could follow this with, say, some dark-chocolate pots and cinnamon Spanish doughnuts. Picnic platters for two ($40) are available Sunday.

Sandalford (☎ 9374 9301; 3210 West Swan Rd; mains $32; 🕑 lunch) Sandalford is one of two big-time, long-term operators out here (the other is Houghton's). And this winery's menu and environs are testimony to its experience. It's so nice out here, actually, that it's a popular wedding function spot. Mains include dishes like Serrano ham with poached pears and quince paste, or mussels and marron with chilli broth and fennel-and-pea risotto. The cellar door is worth a stop.

Also recommended:

Mash (☎ 9296 5588; 10250 West Swan Rd; mains $16-$22; 🕑 lunch Mon-Thu, lunch & dinner Fri-Sun) Right by Duckstein, this brewery has a younger crowd and attitude.

Duckstein (☎ 9296 0620; 9270 West Swan Rd, Henley Brook; mains $19.50-26.50; 🕑 lunch & dinner Wed-Sat, lunch Sun) This brewery turns out well-executed German classics like the grilled bratwurst and Hefeweizen (wheat beer).

Black Swan café (☎ 9296 6090; 8600 West Swan Rd; mains $22; 🕑 cellar door & lunch Mon-Sun, dinner Wed-Sat, breakfast Sun)

Around Perth

While Western Australia (WA) is huge, you don't really have to travel too far from the capital to treat yourself to a little slice of peaceful beach or bush. In around 45 minutes – about the same time it'll take you to master the kayak – you'll be frolicking with wild dolphins at Shoalwater Marine Park, crunching through John Forrest National Park or clambering up the crest of the Darling Range, with views of city and sea spread out below.

Travel a little further out to destinations like Mandurah or Dwellingup, and you'll be scooping brilliant-blue crabs out of the estuary or snaking your way down the handsome Murray, canoe paddle in hand.

For pioneering heritage, head to the Avon Valley and historic towns such as Toodyay and York, classified by the National Trust. North of Perth, Lancelin is a world-renowned windsurfing wonderland and the Yanchep National Park is great for wildlife and walking trails.

If that's all too much trouble, just jump on the ferry to Rottnest Island. In 25 minutes you'll have set foot on a turquoise and white-sand playground. Wobble your bicycle around the island and choose your own bright-blue bay. And you won't *have* to lie on the beach all day: there's some of the best diving, snorkelling, surfing and fishing out here too.

Wherever you decide to go, you will probably arrive at the same conclusion: no wonder the locals spend every waking moment outdoors.

AROUND PERTH

HIGHLIGHTS

- Play with scores of charismatic wild dolphins in **Shoalwater Marine Park** (p94), near Rockingham, September to May
- Snorkel along the trail of underwater plaques through coral reef at **Little Salmon Bay** (p92), Rottnest Island
- Crack the legs of the freshly cooked blue-manna crab you caught yourself in the **Mandurah Estuary** (p95)
- Fling yourself into the handsome old Murray River, one eye peeled for the perfect picnic spot, at **Dwellingup** (p96)
- Picnic in seclusion at **Walyunga National Park** (p98), alongside the impressive Avon River
- Hike around enormous, bird-filled wetlands at **Yalgorup National Park** (p97)
- Enjoying jazz on the atmospheric streets of heritage-listed **York** (p101) in October

AROUND PERTH

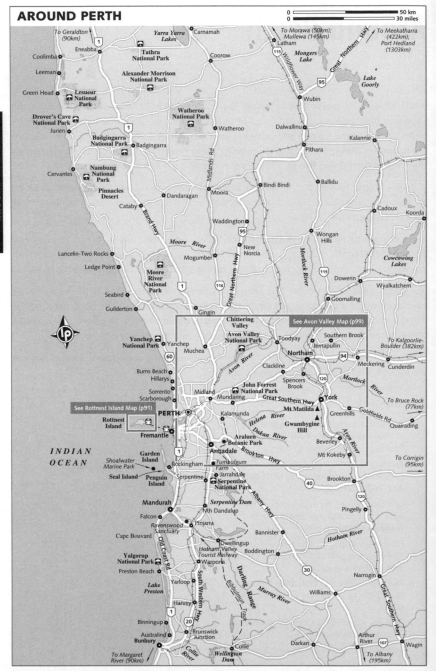

ROTTNEST ISLAND

☎ 08 / pop 475

When it comes to **Rottnest Island** (www.rottnest
.wa.gov.au), opinions swing one of two ways:
some see the island as a carefree, clear-water
paradise; others insist it's overrated. It's the
former, of course – those who think it's overrated must have gone in bad weather. (It's
unpleasant when the wind really kicks up.)

Rotto, as it's known to the locals, is ringed
by secluded tropical beaches and bays, about
19km from Fremantle. Swimming, snorkelling, fishing, surfing and diving are the island's raison d'être. And cycling round the
11km-long, 4.5km-wide island is a real highlight; just ride around and pick your own bit
of beach to spend the day.

Rotto is also the site of annual school leavers' and end-of-uni-exams parties, a time
when the island is overrun by young people
partying night and day. Check the calendar.

Car-free Rottnest generates its own power
and water, so it's very important to use it
sparingly.

History

There are signs of Aboriginal occupation on
Rottnest dating from 7000 years ago, when
a hill on a coastal plain became the island
after being cut off by rising seas. It was, however, uninhabited when Europeans arrived.
Dutch explorer Willem de Vlamingh claimed

AROUND PERTH

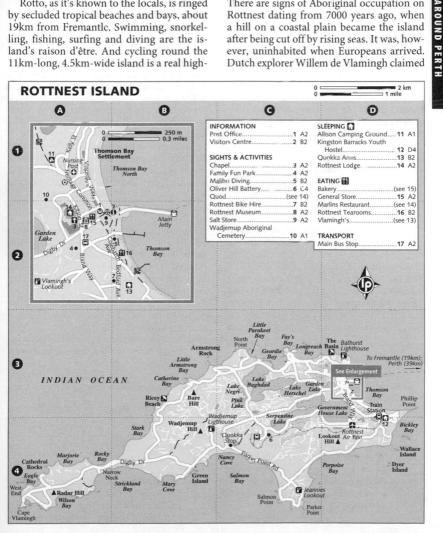

ROTTNEST ISLAND

INFORMATION
Post Office.................................1 A2
Visitors Centre..........................2 B2

SIGHTS & ACTIVITIES
Chapel.......................................3 A2
Family Fun Park.......................4 A2
Malibu Diving..........................5 A2
Oliver Hill Battery....................6 C4
Quod.....................................(see 14)
Rottnest Bike Hire...................7 B2
Rottnest Museum.....................8 A2
Salt Store..................................9 A2
Wadjemup Aboriginal
    Cemetery..........................10 A1

SLEEPING 🛏
Allison Camping Ground.....11 A1
Kingston Barracks Youth
    Hostel..............................12 D4
Quokka Arms.........................13 B2
Rottnest Lodge.......................14 A2

EATING 🍴
Bakery..................................(see 15)
General Store..........................15 A2
Marlins Restaurant.............(see 14)
Rottnest Tearooms..................16 B2
Vlamingh's...........................(see 13)

TRANSPORT
Main Bus Stop.........................17 A2

discovery of the island in 1696 and named it Rotte-nest (rat's nest) because of the numerous king-sized 'rats' (which were actually quokkas) he saw there. The Noongar tribe knew it as Wadjemup.

The Rottnest settlement was originally established in 1838 as a prison for Aborigines from the mainland. Although there were no new prisoners after 1903, the existing prisoners had to serve out their sentences until 1920. The island is a sacred site to the Noongar because hundreds of their people died there. For more, see opposite.

Information

At the settlement, behind the main jetty, there's a shopping area with ATMs, a general store and a bottle shop.

Post office (☽ 9am-1pm & 1.30-4pm Mon-Fri) Inside the gift shop.

Ranger (☎ 9372 9788, after hours 0419 951 635)

Visitors centre (☎ 9372 9752; ☽ 7.30am-5pm Sat-Thu, 7.30am-7pm Fri) At the end of the main jetty.

Sights

To learn about the island's history (including its dark past of shipwrecks and Aboriginal incarceration), visit the **Rottnest Museum** (Kitson St; admission by gold coin donation; ☽ 10.45am-3.30pm), in the old hay-store building.

The photographic exhibition at the 19th-century **salt store** (Colebatch Ave) deals with a different chapter of local history: when the island's salt lakes provided all of WA's salt. You can also wander around the **convict-built buildings** such as the octagonal **Quod** (1864), where the prison cells are now hotel rooms and part of the Rottnest Lodge hotel. Not far away from Thomson Bay is **Vlamingh's Lookout**

QUOKKAS

The quokka was known to the Aborigines as the *quak-a*, which was heard by Europeans as 'quokka'. Quokkas were once found throughout the southwest but are now confined to forest on the mainland and a population of 8000 to 12,000 on Rottnest Island. You will see several during your visit. Don't be surprised if one comes up to you looking for a titbit – many are almost tame. But don't feed them, as this can make them sick, and hot chips don't make for a very well-rounded diet.

(unsigned) on Lookout Hill. Go up past the old cemetery for panoramic views of the island. Also of interest is the **Oliver Hill Battery**, 3.2km from the settlement. This gun battery was built in the 1930s and played a major role in the defence of the WA coastline and Fremantle harbour.

Activities

The family-friendly **Basin** is the most popular beach, though there are many smaller secluded beaches such as **Little Parakeet Bay**. Hire bikes from **Rottnest Bike Hire** (multigear/single-gear bike per day $24/17, bond $25; ☽ 8.30am-4pm).

Surfers like the breaks at Strickland, Salmon and Stark Bays. Try **snorkelling** at the Basin, Little Parakeet Bay, Longreach Bay, Geordie Bay and Little Salmon Bay (where there's a snorkel trail of underwater plaques); **fishing** at Little Salmon Bay and Ricey Beach. Much depends on the weather, though, so check www.seabreeze.com.au and make sure you don't pick a windy spot.

Some of Rottnest Island's shipwrecks are accessible to snorkellers, but getting to them requires a boat. Marker plaques around the island tell the sad tales of how and when the ships sank. The gift shop sells the knowledgeable *Snorkellers' Guide to Rottnest Island*, which covers 20 bays.

Snorkelling and diving equipment, surfboards and bodyboards can be hired from **Malibu Diving** (☎ 9292 5111; www.rottnestdiving.com.au; Thomson Bay), which also runs daily snorkelling trips and open-water, four-day scuba diving courses (beginners $395).

Rottnest is ideal for **bird-watching** because of the varied habitats: coast, lakes, swamps, heath, woodlands and settlements. Coastal birds include cormorants; bar-tailed godwits; whimbrels; fairy, bridled and crested terns; oyster-catchers; and majestic ospreys. For more, get *The Birdlife of Rottnest Island* by Denis Saunders and Perry de Rebeira from the gift shop.

The **Family Fun Park** (☎ 9292 5156; putt-putt adult/child $8/5, trampolines per 10min $2.50; ☽ 9am-4pm) is the spot for putt-putt (mini-golf) and trampolines.

Tours

From the Salt Store you can join a volunteer guide on one of the **free daily walks** (11am, 1pm and 2pm) that take in the settlement's historic buildings, the **Wadjemup Aboriginal cemetery**, the sea wall and boat sheds, the **chapel** and the Quod, or the lighthouse or quokkas.

Hour-long **Indigenous Heritage Tours** (adult/child $11/5; ☺1.15pm) explain the Noongar's connection with Rottnest and include the Quod, where many died, the cemetery, and stories from the Dreamtime. These excellent tours leave outside the visitors centre, also the place to buy tickets.

A two-hour **bus tour** (adult/child $24.50/12.20) leaves from the visitors centre at 11am, 1.30pm and 1.45pm. There's also the **Oliver Hill Train & Guns tour** (adult/child $16.60/8.30; ☺1.30pm), which takes you by train to the 9.2-inch-diameter gun and tunnel on Oliver Hill (departs from the train station), and one-hour **Wadjemup Lighthouse tours** (adult/child $15/6; ☺10.45am & 11.45am), which depart from the bus station.

From November to March, **Capricorn Kayak** (☎6267 8059; www.capricornseakayaking.com.au; half-day tours $99) runs sea-kayaking tours around the Rottnest coastline.

Enjoy the reef and wrecks from above the water in the semi-submersible boat, the **Underwater Explorer** (www.underwaterexplorer.com.au; adult/child $20/13). Forty-five-minute tours leave from the main jetty four times daily September to May; contact the visitors centre for times. Underwater Explorer also runs **snorkelling cruises** (90min cruises adult $28; ☺from 12.30pm Nov-Apr).

Sleeping

Rottnest Island is wildly popular in summer and school holidays, when ferries and accommodation are booked out months in advance.

Allison camping ground (☎9432 9111; Thomson Bay; camp sites per person $8.50) Camping is restricted to this leafy camping ground, which has barbecues. It's known as Tentland by the surfers and students who colonise this patch of Rotto. Be vigilant about your belongings.

Kingston Barracks Youth Hostel (☎9432 9111; dm $24; 🖳) If you stay in these old army barracks, you might find yourself fighting with school groups for a spot in front of the potbelly stove. Check in at the accommodation office at the main jetty before you make the 1.8km walk, bike or bus trip to Kingston.

Rottnest Island Authority Cottages (☎9432 9111; 4-bedroom oceanfront villas Sun-Thu/Fri-Sat $170/200, 4-bedroom oceanfront cottages Sun-Thu/Fri-Sat from $210/260) There are more than 250 villas and cottages – some that have magnificent beachfront positions – for rent around the island. Linen

provided. Note that there are off-season discounts; accommodation was refurbished late 2006.

Rottnest Lodge (☎9292 5161; www.rottnestlodge .com.au; Kitson St; d/f from $170/240; 🏊) It's claimed there are ghosts in this comfortable complex, which is based around the former Quod and boys reformatory school. If that worries you, ask for one of the cheery rooms with a view in the new section fronting onto a salt lake.

Quokka Arms (☎9292 5011; quokkaarms@rottnest island.com; 1 Bedford Ave; s/d $180/200) This beachfront building (1864) was once the gubernatorial summer holiday pad, but these days it's Rotto's most popular watering hole. The rooms are clean but nothing fancy; some have water views.

Eating

There's no exceptional dining to be had on the island; in general, self-catering is your best option. The general store is like a small supermarket.

Rottnest Bakery (☎9292 5023; Thomson Bay shopping mall) Next to the general store, this is the place to pick up your pie.

Rottnest Tearooms (☎9292 5171; Thomson Bay; mains $17.50-30) Grab an oceanfront table on the veranda and keep the kids happy with a burger (if that fails, try the playground). Water views.

Vlamingh's (☎9292 5011; Quokka Arms, 1 Bedford Ave; mains $17.50-30) After a sunset drink at the pub, wander a few metres over to this beachside restaurant, serving dishes like mushroom, pumpkin and fennel risotto.

Marlins Restaurant (☎9292 5161; Rottnest Lodge, Kitson St; mains $23.30-32) Marlins is the other higher-end option on the island, focused on seafood-inflected risotto and pastas. The surrounds may be a bit dated, but it's intimate and relaxing nonetheless.

Getting There & Away

Besides points of departure, all the ferry services are basically the same. Return trips adult/child start at $51/21 from Fremantle (25 minutes) and $66/28 from Perth (1½ hours). There's an extra evening service on Friday. Check the websites for exact departure times, as these change seasonally.

Boat Torque (Rottnest Express; www.rottnestexpress .com.au; Fremantle ☎9335 6406; Northport ☺9430 5844; Perth ☺9421 5888) departs Fremantle (C Shed, Victoria Quay) about five times daily; and

Northport terminal, Fremantle, about four times daily. There's a thrice-daily service from Perth. Secure parking is available at Northport, and you can arrange bike hire.

Oceanic Cruises (☎ 9325 1191 Perth, 9335 2666 Fremantle; www.oceaniccruises.com.au) departs Perth about three times daily. From Fremantle, there's a service from the East St jetty once in the morning and from the B Shed about four times daily.

Rottnest Fast Ferries (☎ 9246 1039; www.hillarysfast ferries.com.au) runs trips from Hillarys Boat Harbour to Rotto three times daily from September to June.

Rottnest Air-Taxi (☎ 1800 500 006; www.rottnest .de) has a same-day return fare from Jandakot airport in Perth starting at $240. Extended return is $300. This price is for a four-seat plane (three passengers), so it can be a good deal.

Getting Around
Bicycles are the time-honoured way of getting around the island. Rottnest is just big enough (and with enough hills) to make a day's ride good exercise. Hire a bike from one of the ferry companies or Rottnest Bike Hire (p92). Helmets (compulsory) and locks (bicycles are often stolen) are provided.

There are two bus services. A free shuttle runs between the main accommodation areas and the airport, departing from the accommodation office roughly every 20 minutes, with the last bus at about 7pm. The Bayseeker (day pass adult/child $7.50/3.80) is a jump-on, jump-off service that does a loop around the island. From Geordie Bay to the bus stop, it's free.

SOUTH OF PERTH

Getting There & Away
The new train lines from Perth to Rockingham and Mandurah should be running by mid-2007. In the meantime, get to Rockingham bus station on bus 866 ($5.70) from the Esplanade busport. Buses 920 and 126 run to Rockingham from Fremantle train station. Then from the Rockingham bus station you can catch buses 112 or 113 to the visitors centre and cafés.

For Mandurah, catch the Transperth express bus 867 ($8.20, 65 minutes) from the Esplanade Busport in Perth. You'll arrive at Mandurah bus station, from which the 164, 165 or 169 bus will take you into town.

Be aware that most of the above-mentioned bus routes will have changed once the train line is operational.

Transwa (☎ 1300 662 205) operates a number of bus services that pass through Mandurah and stop at all the towns between Mandurah and Bunbury.

From Armadale, 29km south of Perth, the South Western Hwy skirts the Darling Range then heads south to Bunbury via Pinjarra. Transwa runs services that stop at all towns along the South Western Hwy in this section. The *Australind* train travels to Pinjarra ($12.90, 1¼ hours) from East Perth bus station.

ROCKINGHAM
☎ 08 / pop 81,000
The quiet seaside town of Rockingham, some 47km south of Perth, was founded in 1872 as a port, although over time this function was taken over by Fremantle. Today, a number of British migrants call Rockingham home.

Rockingham itself doesn't have much to offer travellers. The nearby Shoalwater Islands Marine Park, by contrast, is one of the greatest highlights of the region. Here you can play with dolphins, sea lions and fairy penguins in the wild in a pristine, beautifully preserved environment.

The **visitors centre** (☎ 9592 3464; 43 Kent St; ⏰ 9am-5pm Mon-Fri, 9am-4pm Sat & Sun) has plenty of information.

Sights & Activities
Shoalwater Islands Marine Park includes Penguin and Seal Islands. **Penguin Island**, home to about 1200 fairy (little) penguins and less than 700m offshore, is a well-run eco-tourism destination: no food is sold on the island, toilets are composting, and the island is closed for bird breeding much of the year. Apart from bird-watching (pied cormorants, pelicans, crested and bridled terns, oystercatchers), you can swim and snorkel in the crystal-clear waters. **Seal Island**, a conservation area for the Australian sea lions, is off-limits to the public (sea lions are viewed nearby from the water). Pack your own lunch and water. The naval base of Garden Island can be reached only by private boat.

Rockingham Wild Encounters (☎ 9591 1333; www .rockinghamwildencounters.com.au) organises a lot of the marine park activities. You can join a **dolphin swim tour** ($185 from Wellington St coach stand, Perth, or Val St jetty, Rockingham; ⏰ tours Sep-May, 7am from Perth, 7.30am from Rockingham) – there are some 180 bottlenose dolphins out here. Travellers rave about these tours. The dolphins aren't fed and don't perform tricks; they play with small groups of swimmers for the fun of it. Perth hotel pickup is available for an extra $20. Alternatively, there are two-hour **dolphin-watch tours** (adult/child $75/38 from Wellington St coach stand, Perth, $55/28 from Val St jetty, Rockingham; tours Sep-May, 7.45am from Perth, 8.45am from Rockingham), where you cruise around with the dolphins. If you're lucky you'll see some pale-skinned baby dolphins.

Combine all three on the **dolphin, penguin and sea lion day tour** (adult/child $111.50/65.50 from Wellington St coach stand, Perth, $91.50/55.50 from Val St jetty, Rockingham; tours Sep-May, 7.45am from Perth, 8.45am from Rockingham). These tours include dolphin-spotting, a cruise to Seal Island to observe sea lions lolling about on the sand, and Penguin Island, where you can observe the fairy penguins in the wild and see them feeding at the discovery centre. You're then free to walk around the island, about 97% of which is a bird sanctuary.

There's also the **penguin and seal island cruise** (adult/child $31.50/22.50 from Mersey Point, Rockingham; hourly, 10am-4pm), which takes in both islands over 45 minutes. Or you can simply hop over to Penguin Island on the **ferry** (adult/child $15.50/12.50; hourly 9am-3pm). The ferry ticket includes entry to the penguin discovery centre. Tours depart from Mersey Point jetty, also the spot to buy tickets. To get to Mersey Point from Rockingham bus station, catch bus 113. **Sea kayaks** (single kayak per day $80) and sea-kayaking tours are available too.

Capricorn Seakayaking (6267 8059; http://capricorn seakayaking.com.au; $139 from Perth and Fremantle) runs sea-kayaking tours around Penguin and Seal Islands, November to March.

Sleeping & Eating

Beachside Apartment Hotel (1800 888 873; beachside@iinet.net.au; Rockingham Beach Rd; 1-bedroom apt $160, 2-bedroom apt with ocean view $190, 2-bedroom apt $180;) Right on the esplanade, these apartments are spacious, sunny and secure. There are discounts for stays longer than seven nights. Reception is located at 58 Kent St.

Peel Manor House (9524 2838; www.peelmanor house.com.au; Fletcher Rd, off Stakehill Rd, Baldivis; d $180) This large English-style manor (built some ten years ago) has about 16 double rooms. Sited on enormous grounds with a quiet garden out

back, it feels like a restful country retreat, if a little contrived. Tastefully furnished rooms are almost as big as Buckingham Palace. No kids.

Thai by the Sea (9591 1989; 224 Safety Beach Rd; mains $14.90-21.50; dinner) Not far from Mersey Point, this is a friendly and popular spot.

Betty Blue (9528 4228; 3-4 The Boardwalk; mains $15-24; breakfast, lunch & dinner) The salty-sea-air vibe here is casual, the menu focused on seafood.

Anna's (9528 4228; 8 The Boardwalk; mains $36; dinner Wed-Sun) Anna's is the local fine-dining experience, and it has an excellent reputation. European-style dishes include braised rabbit pie with wild mushroom and potato mash.

MANDURAH

08 / pop 70,200

Sited on the calm Mandurah Estuary 75km from Perth, Mandurah was originally a beach resort, dormitory suburb and retirement haven, often the butt of gibes from Perth residents who felt the city was beneath them. These days, Mandurah has really come into its own, and is a quietly bustling, developed spot that's relaxed and decidedly unaffected. It's one of the best places in the region for fishing, crabbing, prawning (March to April) and dolphin-spotting. Life down here is lived out on the water.

The **visitors centre** (9550 3999; 75 Mandurah Tce; 9am-4.30pm Mon-Fri, 9.30am-4pm Sat & Sun), on the estuary boardwalk, is well-informed.

Sights & Activities

Take a dolphin-spotting cruise through the estuary, Peel Inlet and Murray River with **Mandurah Ferry Cruises** (9535 3324; www.mandurah ferrycruises.com; Estuary Boardwalk; adult/child $15/8; hourly 10.30am-3.30pm summer, 10:30am-2:30pm rest of year). You can also do a half-day trip, adult/child $52/24 with lunch on board. These depart at 10am; bookings recommended.

You don't need your own boat to go **crabbing** and **fishing**. Simply bring your own gear down and head to the accessible estuary for blue manna crabs and fish; you can also fish on the beach (ask local fishermen where's good on the day). **Tuckey's Tackle** (9535 1228; 152 Mandurah Tce) sells fishing and crabbing gear (scoop net, bucket, measurer). Crabbing and fishing gear is relatively cheap and simple ($15 to $30 for a flick fishing rod, less than $20 for crabbing gear), which is why no-one bothers to hire it out.

AROUND PERTH

There's a designated, boat-free **swimming** area on the far side of the estuary, just north of Mandurah Bridge. Here dolphins have been known to swim up to unwitting kids for a frolic.

The regional **Mandurah Performing Arts Centre** (☎ 9550 3900; www.manpac.com.au; Ormsby Tce) is next to the **Reading Cinema** (☎ 9535 2800; 7 James Service Pl) on the boardwalk.

The only historic building open to the public is **Hall's Cottage** (Leighton Pl, Halls Head; ☷ 1-4pm Sun), built in the 1830s.

Sleeping

Mandurah becomes congested with holiday-makers during summer and school holidays; you may need to plan ahead.

Yalgorup Eco Park (☎ 9582 1320; www.ecopark .com.au; 8 Henry Rd, Melros Beach; powered/unpowered sites $45/40, 2-person chalets $160; ☷) Yalgorup Eco Park is a high-end caravan park on Melros Beach, great for fishing. Environmentally friendly practices include the use of grey water and chemical-free cleaning products, but otherwise that's about as far as 'eco' stretches. There's a range of accommodation from campsites to couples' cabins to family-friendly villas. From Mandurah, take the Old Coast Rd south and follow the signs.

Atrium Hotel (☎ 9535 6633; www.atriumhotel.com .au; 65 Ormsby Tce; d from $119; ☷ ☷) The Atrium was once Mandurah's premier hotel. These days it's looking dated and faded, but it's still functional good value if you can get a good rate. There are two swimming pools, including an indoor number in the atrium.

Quest Mandurah (☎ 9535 9599; www.questmandurah .com.au; 20 Apollo Pl; 2-person studio $138, 2-bedroom apt $202, 2-bedroom apt waterfront $228, 3-bedroom apt with courtyard $228; ☷ ☷) With light-blue weath-erboards and white-painted gutters, the self-contained apartment complex backs directly on to the estuary. Rooms are clean, spacious and bright, and the three-bedroom apartments 51 and 52, with courtyards and estuary views, must be pick of the bunch.

Eating & Drinking

Miami Bakehouse (☎ 9534 2705; Shop 6, Falcon Grove Shopping Centre, Old Coast Rd, Miami; pies $4-4.90; ☷ until 8pm) This celebrity of a bakery has about as many awards as the state's top show pony, including ribbons from the Perth Royal Show. Connoisseurs will not regret the 10km hike to get here – the pies are incredible.

> **BONZER BACKROADS – PLEASURES OF THE POOLE**
>
> Head south of Dwellingup on 2WD-friendly River Rd for 10km until you reach **Lane Poole Reserve**, on the banks of the Mur-ray River. It's a wonderful place to stop for a barbecue, picnic, bushwalk or (in summer, when the waters are calmer) swim. The best spots for swimming are Island Pool and near the Baden-Powell water spout.

Cicerello's (☎ 9535 9777; 73 Mandurah Tce; mains $10.50-26.40; ☷ lunch & dinner) If you don't have fish and chips on the waterfront, it's just not the quintessential beach holiday. Cicerello's is big and laid-back; choose your calamari, battered fish, fish burger or chilli mussels and take it all in slow over the estuary.

Brighton Hotel (☎ 9534 8864; 10-12 Mandurah Tce; mains $16.50-28.50; ☷ lunch & dinner) The locals treat this big curvaceous number as their local wa-tering hole. Watch the sun set over the estuary with a glass of wine.

SOUTH WESTERN HIGHWAY
Jarrahdale & Serpentine National Park
☎ 08 / pop 440

Established in 1871, Jarrahdale is an old mill town. It's very small and sleepy, and that's part of its charm. The town's old post office, built in 1880, serves as a **visitors centre** (☷ 10am-4pm Sat & Sun). Walk trail maps are available here.

The area of forest running between Serpen-tine and Jarrahdale, 50km south of Perth, in-cludes Serpentine National Park. At the base of the park are **Serpentine Falls** (car $9; ☷ 8.30am-5pm), which can be accessed from Falls Rd, south of the Jarrahdale turn-off on South Western Hwy. There are walking tracks and picnic areas near the Serpentine Dam, off Kingsbury Dr.

Picturesque **Millbrook Winery** (☎ 9525 5796; Old Chestnut Lane, signed off Jarrahdale Rd; mains $19-39; ☷ lunch Wed-Sun) is an excellent lunch choice. The expansive two-storey facility overlooks a small lake and surrounds. It's tranquil, and the food – like beef fillet with a sweet onion compote, garlic roast chats and Millbrook winery jus – is jolly good. Book ahead.

Dwellingup
☎ 08 / pop 550

Dwellingup is a small, forest-covered town-ship with character. Primarily it's a base for hiking, cycling, swimming, and canoeing on the Murray – the surrounding area is filled with adventure. It's 97km south of Perth.

The **Bibbulmun Track** (www.bibbulmuntrack.org.au) passes through this timber town on its journey southwards, and the **Munda Biddi** (www.munda biddi.org.au) bike trail passes through here to Collie (and will eventually reach Albany). The **Hotham Valley Tourist Railway** terminates here from Pinjarra. See the **visitors centre** (☎ 9538 1108; Marrinup St; ☑ 9am-4.30pm Mon-Fri, 10am-3pm Sat & Sun) for more information.

Don't waste any time getting out to the beautiful Murray. **Dwellingup Adventures** (☎ 9538 1127; www.dwellingupadventures.com.au; 1-person kayaks & 2-person canoes $28 per day; ☑ 8.30am-5pm) is the place to hire bikes, kayaks and canoes. Or join a paddling tour (half-day, one-person kayak, $50); white-water rafting tours are available June to October and start at $98.

The **Forest Heritage Centre** (☎ 9538 1395; Acacia St; adult/family $5/10; ☑ 10am-5pm) is an interesting architect-designed rammed-earth building in the shape of three gum leaves. There's a woodwork gallery and three trails leading off from the centre.

Millhouse Café & Chocolate Company (☎ 9538 1122; McLarty St; mains $9-18; ☑ lunch Thu, lunch & dinner Fri-Sun) is a good spot to reboot yourself with a glass of wine and café-style treat such as the Millhouse chicken-and-mushroom pie.

Pinjarra & Around

☎ 08 / pop 6640

Pinjarra, 86km south of Perth, was once the site of a bloody incident in 1834 (whether it was a massacre or battle is a matter of debate between historians – and Noongars and the local council). Settlers here launched a reprisal on members of the Bindjareb Noongar tribe for raids and the killing of a servant. Many Noongars were killed, though accurate figures are difficult to find.

These days, it's a quiet town sited on the banks of the Murray River. The **visitors centre** (☎ 9531 1438; cnr George & Henry Sts; ☑ 9.30am-4pm Mon-Sat, 10am-4pm Sun) is in the historic building Edenvale, with **tearooms** (☎ 9531 2223; cnr George & Henry Sts; coffee or tea & scone $4.50; ☑ lunch) out the back. Behind the historic mud-brick post office is a lovely grassed picnic area and **suspension bridge** over the river. Fat geese and ducks quack below. St John's Church, built 1861 to 1862 from mud bricks, is over beside the original 1860 schoolhouse.

Northwest of Pinjarra on Pinjarra Rd is the popular **Peel Zoo** (☎ 9531 4322; info@peelzoo.com; Ravenswood Sanctuary, Sanctuary Dr, off Pinjarra Rd; adult/ child $13/5), overrun by a bunch of local ducks, kangaroos, wombats, reptiles and parrots.

From May to October, the **Hotham Valley Tourist Railway** (☎ 9221 4444; www.hothamvalley railway.com.au; adult/child $34/18; ☑ Wed-Sun) runs steam trains from Pinjarra to Dwellingup through blooming wildflowers and jarrah forests. Trains leave Pinjarra at 11am.

About 4km south of Pinjarra is the **Old Blythewood Homestead** (South Western Hwy, south of Pinjarra; adults $4; ☑ 10am-4pm Sat & Sun), an 1859 colonial farm.

Yalgorup National Park

About 112km south of Perth, this **national park** (car $9) is famous for its coastal lakes lined by **thrombolites** – rocklike structures built by micro-organisms. Thrombolites existed in the oceans 600 million years ago. To view the thrombolites, go to the Lake Clifton viewing platform, on Mt John Rd off Old Coast Rd.

If you enjoy wetlands, Yalgorup is an excellent place to hike and camp. The two main hikes down here are the **Lake Pollard** trail (6km) and the **Heathlands** walk trail (4.5km), also signed as the **Lake Preston** trail. The Lake Pollard trail begins about 8km down Preston Beach North Rd (not Preston Beach Rd, as marked on some maps). The pleasant Martins Tank Lake campground is just to the right of the trail's entrance. The trail takes in tuart, jarrah and bull banksia to the lake, which is also known for its black swans (October to March).

The Heathlands trail to Lake Preston starts at the information bay on Preston Beach Rd (before the turn-off to Preston Beach North Rd) and explores the tuart woodland. Further along Preston Beach Rd is Preston Beach.

Enter Yalgorup from Preston Beach Rd off Old Coast Rd.

THE DARLING RANGE

The Darling Range – commonly known as the Perth Hills – boasts great picnicking, barbecues and bushwalks. Forest winds across hills for miles up here, and the distinct landscape provides a sense of escapism. Kalamunda is the bigger township with a secluded vibe; Mundaring's feature is its weir.

Getting There & Away

Transperth buses 296, 299 and 799 ($4, one hour) travel from Perth's Esplanade Busport to Kalamunda bus station. (Buses 282 and 283 also run but take slightly longer.) To Mundaring, catch a Transperth train to Midland train station and then bus 318, 320 or 330 to Mundaring ($5.70, 70 minutes).

MUNDARING

☎ 08 / pop 35,500

Mundaring's a laid-back spot with a small artistic community 35km east of Perth. It's also a stop-off before going down to **Mundaring Weir**, a dam built some 100 years ago to supply water to the goldfields more than 500km to the east. The reservoir has an attractive setting with walking tracks.

The **visitors centre** (☎ 9295 0202; 7225 Great Eastern Hwy; www.mundaringtourism.com.au; ☼ 10am-4pm Mon-Fri, call to check Sat & Sun times) is in the Old School. Across the road is the **Mundaring Arts Centre** (☎ 9295 3991; 7190 Great Eastern Hwy; ☼ 10am-5pm Mon-Fri, 10am-4pm Sat & Sun), which exhibits and sells the work of local artists.

The **Perth Hills National Parks Centre** (☎ 9295 2244; www.naturebase.net/nearertonature; Mundaring Weir Rd), run by DEC, hosts a series of kids programs like 'frog forage' and 'meet the marsupials'. Book ahead. The centre is also a well-set-up campground, with showers, and the Bibbulmun Track passes through here.

Freshwater **Lake Leschenaultia** (admission per car $6; ☼ 8.30am-dusk) is a picturesque lake complete with pontoon. Robert Coover's *Quenby and Ola, Swede and Carl* echoes out here. North of the Great Eastern Hwy, near Chidlow.

The 16-sq-km **John Forrest National Park** (admission per car $9), near Mundaring, was the state's first national park. With protected areas of jarrah and marri trees, native fauna, waterfalls and a pool, it's long been a favourite.

From November to April, kick back in a deck chair and watch a movie at the open-air **Kookaburra Cinema** (☎ 9295 6190; Allen Rd), just off the road to Mundaring Weir.

Sleeping & Eating

Djaril Mari YHA Hostel (☎ 9295 1809; Mundaring Weir Rd; dm $23, linen $4, self-contained cottage per person $21) This hostel is in a quiet bush setting close to the weir, about 8km south of town. Choose from dorms or a self-contained cottage that sleeps 12 (you'll need a minimum of six people to stay here).

Mundaring Weir Hotel (☎ 9295 1106; Mundaring Weir Rd; d Sun-Thu $100, Fri $115, Sat $125; ☒) This rambling place has seen better days, but is still popular with Perth escapees. The separate units overlook a pool.

Loose Box (☎ 9295 1787; www.loosebox.com; 6825 Great Eastern Hwy; fixed-price menu $135; ☼ dinner Wed-Sat, lunch Sun) A French fine-dining restaurant with provincial décor, Loose Box has enjoyed a good reputation for many years. The impressive menu shows off regional produce like Manjimup truffles.

KALAMUNDA

☎ 08 / pop 50,000

Kalamunda is a quiet township on the crest of the Darling Range. The area had its beginnings as a timber settlement, but it's since become a haven for those keen to enjoy the seclusion of the hills – and still be close to the city. (It's a 30-minute drive.)

From **Zig-Zag Dr**, just north of Kalamunda off Lascelles Pde, there are fantastic views over Perth to the coast. Even if you're just passing through, the trip up here is worth it.

At **Kalamunda National Park** you can walk and picnic in beautiful surroundings. There are also a number of wineries (like Hainault Vineyard and Darlington Estate) nearby.

South of Kalamunda, just off Brookton Hwy, is **Araluen Botanic Park** (☎ 9496 1171; www.araluenbotanicpark.com; adult/child $8/4; ☼ 9am-6pm). It's quite a gem. Originally constructed in the 1920s by the Young Australia League (YAL) as a bush retreat, the park was neglected for years and became overgrown. Recently, excavations have revealed elaborate garden terraces, waterfalls and an ornamental pool. July to October, the famous tulips are in bloom. Get here via Croydon Rd, Roleystone.

Stirk's Cottage (admission free; ☼ 1.30pm-4.30pm Sun), built of mud brick and shingle in 1881, is on Kalamunda Rd.

At **Le Paris-Brest Café Patisserie** (☎ 9293 2752; 22 Haynes St; mains $16.90-23.90; ☼ breakfast & lunch Tue-Sun) in Kalamunda, all you have to do is find a spot underneath the replica Eiffel Tower and await your French-style pastry.

WALYUNGA NATIONAL PARK

The Avon River cuts a narrow gorge through the Darling Range at **Walyunga National Park** (car/motorcycle $9/3; ☼ 8am-5pm) in Upper Swan. Walyunga is a great place for hiking and picnicking, the river much like a handsome carpet python winding through the range. This 18-sq-km park is off the Great Northern Hwy, 40km northeast of Perth.

The bushwalks include a 5.2km return walk to Syd's Rapids as well as a 1.2km Aboriginal Heritage Trail. The best trail is the 10.6km Echidna Loop, which has tremendous views over the Swan and Avon Valleys. The park has one of the largest known camp sites of the Noongar people; the camp site was still in use in the late 1800s. The area may well have been occupied by Aborigines for more than 6000 years.

AVON VALLEY

The lush green Avon Valley – with its atmospheric homesteads with big verandas, rickety wooden wagons and moss-covered rocks – was 'discovered' by European settlers in early 1830 after food shortages forced Governor Stirling to dispatch Ensign Dale to search the Darling Range for arable land. What he found was the upper reaches of the Swan River, but he presumed it was a separate river, which

is why its name changes from the Swan to the Avon as it crosses the Great Northern Hwy. The valley was very soon settled, just a year after Perth was founded, and many historic stone buildings still stand proudly in the towns and countryside in the area. The picturesque Avon River is popular for picnics.

Getting There & Away

The best way to explore the valley is by car as this gives you the flexibility to make stops along the way.

Transwa (☎ 1300 6622 05) runs buses twice a day to York ($13, one hour) and Northan ($17, 90 minutes), and a train once a day to Toodyay ($14, 75 minutes) from East Perth.

TOODYAY
☎ 08 / pop 674

Tiny historic Toodyay, only 85km northeast of Perth, is a popular weekend destination for city folk who like to while away an hour or so browsing the bric-a-brac shops and having a beer on the veranda of an old pub. As you'd expect of a town classified by the National

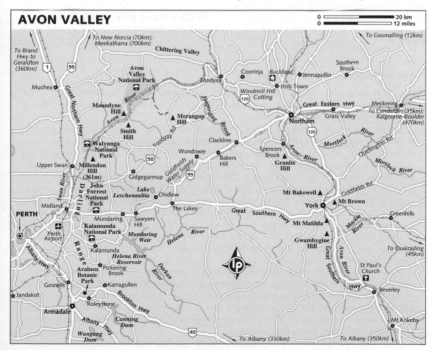

AVON VALLEY

..st, it has scores of atmospheric heritage buildings and charm oozes from its old stone bricks. Originally known by the name Newcastle, Toodyay (pronounced '2J'), came from the Aboriginal word *duidgee* (place of plenty), and was adopted around 1910.

A **gourmet food festival** is on in August and a lively **jazz festival** is held here during the last weekend of October.

There is also a **visitors centre** (☎ 9574 2435; visitorscentre@toodyay.wa.gov.au; 7 Piesse St; ☒ 9am-5pm Mon-Sat, 10am-5pm Sun).

Sights & Activities

Next to the visitors centre is the restored stone 1870 **Connor's Mill** (adult/child $2.50/2). Grab a copy of *Historic Toodyay: Stirling Self Guided Tour* to get the most out of your visit.

The **Old Newcastle Gaol Museum** (☎ 9574 5053; www.toodyay.com; 17 Clinton St; adult/child $2/1; ☒ 10am-3pm Mon-Fri, 10am-4pm Sat & Sun), built in the 1860s, has a Moondyne Gallery, telling the story of bushranger Joseph Bolitho Johns (aka Moondyne Joe; see the boxed text, below), while historic **St Stephen's Church** (1862) is also worth a look. But the best way to spend your time in Toodyay is just wandering the streets. **Coorinja** (☎ 9574 2280; Toodyay Rd; ☒ 10am-5pm Mon-Sat), 6km west of town, is the oldest inland **winery** in WA, having started in the 1870s.

It now specialises in fortified wines so buy a bottle of port.

Sleeping & Eating

Toodyay Caravan Park (☎ 9574 2612; Avon Banks, Railway Rd; camp/caravan sites $17/21; ☒) If you're staying overnight – most people don't – this caravan park has shady sites on the banks of the Avon.

Victoria Hotel (☎ 9574 2206; 116 Stirling Tce; s/d $55/90) This hotel has renovated rooms. Also does counter meals ($11 to $26).

Cino's on the Terrace (☎ 9574 4888; 102 Stirling Tce; meals $7-16; ☒ 9am-9pm) Cino's brings a bit of big city sophistication to this country town with delicious breakfasts, a global menu that stretches from Thai to Turkish, great coffee and scrumptious cakes.

Cola Café & Museum (☎ 9574 4407; 128 Stirling Tce; snacks $5-14) Coca-Cola memorabilia runs amok here. Order a cola spider (remember, those? Coke with a scoop of ice-cream for those who missed out!) and a big burger and play 'guess the 1950s tune'.

If you're after a counter meal, you won't go hungry at the **Victoria Hotel**.

AVON VALLEY NATIONAL PARK

Featuring granite outcrops, forests and wonderful fauna, this **national park** (car/motorcycle

---

THE MYTHOLOGY OF MOONDYNE JOE

It's perhaps odd that while the state of Victoria's most famous outlaw, Ned Kelly, is known for his gun battles with the law, Western Australia's most illustrious bushranger, Moondyne Joe, is famous for escaping. Over and over again.

Joseph Bolitho Johns (1828–1900), sent to Western Australia for larceny, arrived in Fremantle in 1853 and was granted an immediate ticket of leave for good behaviour. This good behaviour lasted until 1861 when he was arrested on a charge of horse stealing, but Johns escaped that night from Toodyay jail on the horse he rode in on, sitting snugly on the magistrate's new saddle. He was recaptured and sentenced to three years imprisonment. Between November 1865 and March 1867 he made four attempts to escape, three of them successful. When eventually captured he was placed in a special reinforced cell with triple-barred windows in Fremantle. He didn't need to escape from this, because in 1867 he managed to escape from the prison yard while breaking rocks. He served more time in Fremantle prison when recaptured and was conditionally pardoned in 1873. After release he worked in the Vasse district and kept his nose relatively clean, but suffered from poor mental health later in life until his death in 1900. You can see his grave at Fremantle cemetery.

While Moondyne Joe was a criminal, these days it pays to be in the 'Moondyne Joe' business. Three books, including the latest, a prize-winning juvenile fiction novel called *The Legend of Moondyne Joe* (by Mark Greenwood), have been written about him; a Moondyne festival is held in Toodyay on the first Sunday of May; a cave in Margaret River is named after him; not to mention a pub, caravan park and who knows what else. Let's hope he doesn't escape his final resting place and start asking for royalties...

$10/5) is accessed from Toodyay and Morangup Roads. The Avon River flows through the centre of the park in winter and spring, but is usually dry at other times.

The Avon Valley National Park is the northern limit of the jarrah forests, and the jarrah and marri are mixed with wandoo woodland. Bird species that make use of the forests included rainbow bee-eaters, honeyeaters, kingfishers and rufous treecreepers. Animals and reptiles live in the understorey: honey possums and western pygmy-possums hide among the dead leaves, and skinks and geckos are everywhere.

There are **camp sites** (☎ 9574 2540; $14) with basic facilities (eg pit toilets and barbecues).

NORTHAM

☎ 08 / pop 6227

Northam, the major town of the Avon Valley, is a busy commercial centre on the railway line to Kalgoorlie-Boulder. The line from Perth once ended here and miners had to make the rest of the weary trek to the goldfields by road.

Northam is a likable country town with some fine heritage buildings but there's little here to interest travellers.

The **visitors centre** (☎ 9622 2100; www.northam .com.au; 2 Grey St; ☒ 9am-5pm Mon-Fri, 9am-4pm Sat & Sun) is in a corrugated-iron building on the banks of the Avon River where you can book transport and get lots of regional information. Pick up the *Experience the Avon Valley* brochure with lots of info and maps.

Sights & Activities

Morby Cottage (☎ 9622 2100; adult/child $2/1; ☒ 10.30am-4pm Sun), built in 1836 as the home of John Morrell (founder of Northam), has been restored and now houses various Morrell family heirlooms and other early Northam memorabilia. The **Old Railway Station Museum** (☎ adult/child $2/50¢; ☒ 10am-4pm Sun), housed in a National Trust–registered building (1836), has a large collection of railway memorabilia.

Annual events in Northam include the **Vintage on Avon** vintage sports car rally (March), and the **Avon River Festival and Descent** (August), a gruelling 133km white-water rafting event for powerboats, kayaks and canoes, which starts from the visitors centre.

The skies above Northam, and other areas in the Avon Valley, are popular with flying, paragliding, skydiving and hang-gliding enthusiasts. **Windward Adventures** (☎ 9621 2000; www .windwardballooning.com; weekday/weekend flight $225/275) offers champagne balloon flights at sunrise, breakfast and sunset.

Sleeping & Eating

Avon Bridge Hotel (☎ 9622 1023; www.avonbridgehotel .com.au; 322 Fitzgerald St; s/d $65/88; ☒) While most travellers don't stay overnight, if you get the urge this stylish hotel has comfortable rooms with all mod cons. The gourmet restaurant, bar and café (meals $11 to $32) are *the* spots of the moment, popular with locals and visitors alike.

O'Hara's Restaurant (meals $15-31) A casual, popular eatery.

Rivers Edge Café (☎ 9622 8500; 1 Grey St; meals $10-17) The verandas of this big corrugated iron building on the river (home to the visitors centre) are a wonderful place to soak up the sun and river views over a slice of scrumptious cake and good coffee.

Drinking

Shamrock Hotel (☎ 9622 1092, 112 Fitzgerald St) A good spot for a beer.

YORK

☎ 08 / pop 3200

Charming York is the most atmospheric spot in the Avon Valley and is a wonderful place to while away a couple of hours on a Sunday, when it's at its liveliest. A stroll down the main street, Avon Terrace, with its restored old buildings, is a real step back in time – so much so that the whole town has been classified by the National Trust.

Only 97km from Perth, York is the oldest inland town in WA, first settled in 1831, just two years after the Swan River Colony. The settlers here saw similarities in the Avon Valley and their native Yorkshire, so Governor Stirling bestowed the name York on the region's first town.

Convicts were brought to the region in 1851 and contributed to the development of the district; the ticket-of-leave hiring depot was not closed until 1872, four years after transportation of convicts to WA ceased. During the gold rush, York prospered as a commercial centre, servicing miners who were heading to Southern Cross.

These days, York is a festival town – catch the **antique and collectables fair** at Easter, plus York's vibrant **jazz festival** in October.

AROUND PERTH

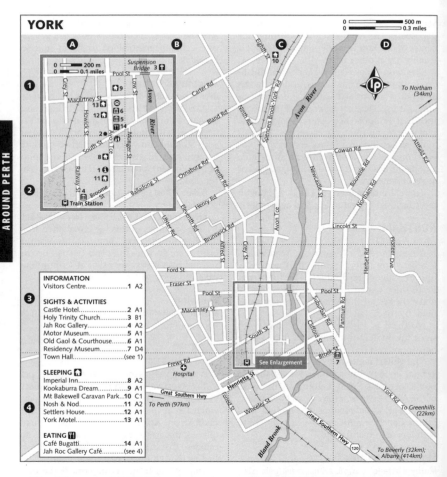

INFORMATION
Visitors Centre......................1 A2

SIGHTS & ACTIVITIES
Castle Hotel.........................2 A1
Holy Trinity Church............3 B1
Jah Roc Gallery...................4 A2
Motor Museum.....................5 A1
Old Gaol & Courthouse........6 A1
Residency Museum.............7 D4
Town Hall.......................(see 1)

SLEEPING
Imperial Inn..........................8 A2
Kookaburra Dream...............9 A1
Mt Bakewell Caravan Park..10 C1
Nosh & Nod........................11 A2
Settlers House....................12 A1
York Motel.........................13 A1

EATING
Café Bugatti.......................14 A1
Jah Roc Gallery Café...........(see 4)

The **visitors centre** (☎ 9641 1301; www.yorktourist bureau.com.au; Avon Tce; ✆ 9am-5pm), in the old town hall has lots of info on the town, including a free visitors guide and map.

Sights & Activities
There are delightful 19th-century buildings on Avon Tce, in the centre of town, such as the **town hall**, **Castle Hotel**, **police station**, **Old Gaol & Courthouse** and **Settlers House**.

Built in 1858, the interesting **Residency Museum** (☎ 9641 1751; Brook St; adult/child $3.50/1.50; ✆ 1-3pm Tue, Wed & Thu, 11.30am-3.30pm Sat & Sun) houses some intriguing historic exhibits, ranging from an antique egg rack and a butter churn, to beautiful old black-and-white photos of York.

The **Holy Trinity Church** (Pool St), by the Avon River, was completed in 1854 and features stained-glass windows designed by WA artist Robert Juniper, and a rare pipe organ. The **suspension bridge** across the Avon was built in 1906.

York's characterful **Motor Museum** (☎ 9641 1288; 116 Avon Terrace; adult/child $7/3.50; ✆ 9.30am-3pm) is a must for vintage-car enthusiasts.

The wonderful **Jah Roc Gallery** (☎ 9641 2522; 7-13 Broome St; ✆ 10am-5pm), housed in a converted flour mill, exhibits and sells stunning jarrah furniture, art and craft by local artisans.

York has earned a reputation as the state's **skydiving** centre; the drop zone is about 3km from town. Contact Perth-based **Skydive Express** (☎ 1800 355 833; www.skydive.com.au) for more info.

Sleeping & Eating

Mt Bakewell Caravan Park (☎ 9641 1421; Eighth Rd; unpowered/powered sites $19/21) You can pitch your tent in a bush setting here.

Kookaburra Dream (☎ 9641 2936; 152 Avon Tce; dm/s/f $22/29/85; 🖥) If you decide to stay the night, this is the best budget option. It's an excellent centrally-located backpackers in a restored old building dating to 1890. Travellers loved the laid-back vibe, barbecue facilities and big continental breakfasts. You can also get good discounts on skydiving and hot air ballooning.

Imperial Inn (☎ 9641 1010; 83 Avon Tce; hotel d $45, motel d $90) In a beautiful stone building on the main street, the Imperial offers quaint basic rooms in the old hotel and standard motel units out the back.

York Motel (☎ 9641 1010; 10 William St; d $90; 🔀) The friendly, accommodating owner of this modern, comfortable motel with well-equipped renovated rooms will help you get a room elsewhere if her popular motel is full.

Settlers House (☎ 9641 1096; 125 Avon Tce; d from $130; 🔀) Originally a staging post and guesthouse for goldfields travellers and once home to WA's first provincial newspaper, staying in this historic building is like a step back in time. The characterful bar is also popular.

Nosh & Nod (☎ 9641 1629; www.noshnod.com.au; 75 Avon Tce; d $95-125, mains $12-28) Has a delightfully cluttered and eclectically decorated restaurant specialising in comfort food (from hearty portions of lasagne to traditional bangers and mash), and comfy self-contained rooms with spas out the back.

Jah Roc Gallery Café (☎ 9641 2522; 7-13 Broome St; snacks $4-12 🕑 lunch) Pleasantly set in a leafy courtyard, Jah Roc is a lovely spot for a leisurely coffee and scrummy cake.

Café Bugatti (☎ 9641 1583; 104 Avon Tce; mains $12-24; 🕑 lunch Wed-Mon, dinner Fri & Sat) is equally as popular with locals as it is tourists who head here for big portions of delicious Italian food and a great kids' menu.

NORTH COAST

The coast road north of Perth leads to some popular spots, each with a unique drawcard. Within an hour's drive of the city centre, Perth's outer suburbs give way to the bushland oasis of Yanchep National Park, with plenty of wonderful wildlife and walking trails.

The coastline ranges from tranquil bays at Guilderton, which are good for swimming and fishing, to windswept beaches at Lancelin, with excellent conditions for windsurfing and kite-surfing, attracting water-lovers from around the world.

YANCHEP & AROUND
☎ 08

Yanchep, 50km north of Perth, is best known for its national park of bushy woodlands and wetlands that are home to hundreds of species of fauna and flora. The town is generally referred to as 'Yanchep Two Rocks' because of the closeness of neighbouring town, Two Rocks. There are also plenty of activities outside the park, including surfing and fishing on its beautiful beaches.

Yanchep National Park (☎ 9561 1004; www.nature base.net; per car $10; 🕑 visitors centre 9.15am-4.30pm) has the rare claim of having an inn within its boundaries, but it's the easy walking trails through natural bushland that are the main attraction. The free map you get upon entry details the shorter walks (around 2km, one hour) but for longer walks, you will need to purchase trail guides from the visitors centre. The park features splendid underground caves (which can be viewed on daily tours), an abundance of wildlife, including cuddly koalas, kangaroos, emus and cockatoos, and the lovely wetlands area of Wagardu Lake. Local Noongar guides run excellent Aboriginal tours on indigenous history, lifestyle and culture, including didgeridoo and dance performances. You can buy wonderful artefacts and art from the gift shop also.

Yanchep Inn (☎ 9561 1001; Yanchep National Park; hotel s/d $28/60, motel d $90; 🔀) has basic rooms with shared facilities. The attached motel rooms are more comfortable with en suite, air-con and TV. The restaurant serves counter meals ($9 to $27), or you can focus on drinking in the views and a beverage from the veranda.

Rooms are fashionably boho-chic at the lovely **Mariska B&B** (☎ 0412 040 035; www.mariska .com.au; 14 Oldham Way, Yanchep; per person Sun-Thu $35, Fri & Sat $40), and open out to a wide, encircling balcony slung with hammocks. You can prepare your own breakfast in the modern kitchen, or have it made for you.

Yanchep Sun City (Two Rocks) is a marina with a supermarket and a few takeaways. You can't miss it: it's just beyond the giant carved bust of King Neptune.

AROUND PERTH

GUILDERTON

☎ 08 / pop 150

Some 43km north of Yanchep, Guilderton is a popular family holiday spot. Children paddle safely in the mouth of the Moore River while adults enjoy the excellent fishing, surfing and sunbathing. A number of shipwrecks off the coast lend weight to the staid brown-brick lighthouse that oversees the coast. It's said that the *Vergulde Draeck*, part of the Dutch East India Company fleet, ran aground nearby in 1656 carrying a treasure of guilders. And that's how the settlement was named, though older generations still know it as Moore River.

The **Guilderton Caravan Park** (☎ 9577 1021; 2 Dewar St; 2-person unpowered/powered site $16/19.50, 4-person chalet $80-104) is the holidaymakers' hub in this laid-back town. Cabins are self-contained, but you'll need your own linen. The park has a general store selling essentials, as well as takeaway-style food.

The **Moore River Roadhouse** (☎ 9577 1023; Mullins St; meals $5-18) fries up burgers and fish and chips – perfect for a post-swim pig out. Basic ingredients are also available for self-caterers.

LANCELIN

☎ 08 / pop 800

What do you do when the beach is windy? Harness yourself to a really big kite and strap yourself to a surfboard, of course! Afternoon offshore winds and shallows protected by an outlying reef make for perfect kite-surfing and windsurfing conditions at Lancelin. The town (130km north of Perth) plays host to action-seekers from around the world in summer for its consistently windy conditions. In January it's a veritable festival of wind-worshippers during the **Lancelin Ocean Classic** race, which starts at Ledge Point.

Head to the beach and watch the wind- and kite-surfers whoop it up. **Werner's Hot Spot** (☎ 9655 1553) offers windsurfing ($20) and kite-surfing ($70) lessons. Werner also hires out gear from his Kombi parked at the beach from October to March (phone at other times and he'll meet you). There are gentle waves at the main beach for traditional surfing.

The mountainous soft, white dunes out the back of town are a playground for sandboarders. You can hire a board from **Have a Chat General Store** (☎ 9655 1054; 104 Gingin Rd) and from **Offshore** (☎ 9655 2828; Hopkins Rd). It'll cost you $10 for two hours, plus 10 minutes of arduous climbing for a few seconds of thrills.

The dunes are also home to the 32-seat American school bus on enormous monster-truck wheels that takes delighted travellers on a wild ride through the sand; contact **Desert Storm Adventures** (☎ 9655 2550; www.desertstorm .com.au; adult/child $35/25). More dune action can be had by hiring an **off-road motorbike** (☎ 0417 919 550; 2-/4-wheel bike per hour $65/70).

Sleeping & Eating

There are two supermarkets and takeaways along Gingin St.

Lancelin Lodge YHA (☎ 9655 2020; www.lancelin lodge.com.au; 10 Hopkins St; dm $23, d/f from $60/80; 🖳 🛋) This award-winning hostel is well equipped and welcoming, with wide verandas and lots of communal spaces to spread about. Catering mainly to windsurfers, the excellent facilities include a big kitchen, barbecue, wood-fire pizza oven, decent-sized swimming pool, ping-pong table, volleyball court and free use of pushbikes and boogie boards!

Windsurfer Beach Chalets (☎ 9655 1454; kateand kim@bigpond.com.au; 1 Hopkins St; d $110, extra person $15) A great choice for groups of friends and families (each chalet sleeps six), these self-contained two-bedroom units look a lot better from the outside (a very stylish contemporary design) than they do inside, but this is the closest accommodation to the windsurfing beach. They're functional and well-equipped and have a sun terrace that backs onto a grassy area. There's also a communal barbecue area.

Lancelin Caravan Park (☎ 9655 1056; Hopkins St; unpowered/powered site per person $10/12; on-site vans $35) Sailborders love camping out at this neat park – not for the facilities and amenities, which are rudimentary, but more for the location. This place is about as close to the beach as you can get.

Offshore Café (☎ 9655 2828; Hopkins Rd; meals $5-16; 🕑 lunch) Decent burgers and sandwiches.

Endeavour Tavern (☎ 9655 1052; 58 Gingin Rd) A classic beachfront Aussie pub with a beer garden overlooking the ocean, and pool table, darts and a TAB. The casual eatery serves decent seafood, and the specialty is crayfish with chips and salad for $35.

Getting There & Away

Catch-a-bus (☎ 9655 2020) is the only bus service to Lancelin; it's a private shuttle service run by the YHA Lancelin Lodge. It offers drop-offs and pick-ups between Perth and Lancelin ($25) on demand.

Fremantle Markets (p83)

PETER B. BENNETTS

Cottesloe Beach (p64)

ROSS BARNETT

The skyline of Perth (p52) at sunset

ROSS BARNETT

PETER PTSCHELINZEW

Penguin Island (p94), Shoalwater Islands Marine Park

Rottnest Island (p91)

RICHARD I'ANSON

Coastal limestone outcrops, Shoalwater Islands
Marine Park (p94)

WAYNE WALTON

JOHN HAY

Blackwood River (p162), Bridgetown

CHRIS MELLOR

Gloucester Tree (p131), near Pemberton

Leeuwin Estate winery (p122)

OLIVER STREWE

Tree Top Walk (p134), Valley of the Giants

Coastline near Albany (p141)

Ancient Empire boardwalk (p134), Walpole-Nornalup National Park

Exchange Hotel (p159) and shops, Kalgoorlie-Boulder

Sculpture at sunset, Lake Ballard (p161)

Gold mine near Kalgoorlie-Boulder (p154)

WAYNE WALTON

Nature's window (p190), Kalbarri National Park

CLAVER CARROLL

Dolphin, Monkey Mia (p196)

Pinnacles Desert (p173), Nambung National Park

HO

PETER PTSCHELINZEW

Turquoise Bay (p208), Ningaloo Marine Park

Karijini National Park (p215)

ROSS BARNETT

Eagle Rock Falls (p217), near Newman, the Pilbara

PETER PTSCHELINZEW

CHRISTOPHER GROENHOUT

Gantheaume Point (p233), near Broome

MICHA

Rock art, the Kimberley (p222)

Geikie Gorge National Park (p238)

RICHAR

The Southwest

The green and lush southwestern corner of Western Australia (WA) makes a fantastic contrast to the stark, sunburnt country of much of the state.

Forests of magnificent tall trees around Pemberton beckon bushwalkers while, below the shady canopy, rivers and creeks run fast after rain and offer great canoeing. Popular coastal towns like Busselton and Dunsborough, within easy reach of Perth, are crazily busy in holiday periods, when families with dolphin-mad kids enjoy the sheltered beaches, serious surfers tackle the ocean breaks and equally serious walkers hike the Cape-to-Cape track. Accommodation options range from cliff-top chic to beachside shack, while national parks offer greater solitude in quiet bush camp sites, and luxury spa retreats beckon the frazzled.

For the less energetic, networks of scenic drives wend their way along the coast and through the cave-riddled and forested landscape. In the renowned Margaret River region, side roads make regular detours to the cellar doors and restaurants of fabulous wineries where local produce – from crayfish and trout to cheeses and chocolates – is second to none. Distances between the myriad attractions are short, a rare event in most of WA, so drive time is mercifully limited; it's a great area to explore for a few days. This sort of country can get under your skin though, so be warned: however much time you spend here, it won't feel like nearly enough.

THE SOUTHWEST

HIGHLIGHTS

- Sample the premium wine, fabulous food and amazing architecture of the wineries of the **Margaret River** (p123) region
- Explore labyrinthine limestone caverns along Caves Drive between the capes, especially stunning **Lake Cave**, and the beautiful **Jewel** and **Ngilgi Caves** (p123)
- Front-up to the impressive coastline at Augusta's **Cape Leeuwin lighthouse** (p126), at the confluence of the great Indian and Southern Oceans
- Camp on the coast, drive the 4WD tracks, and fish the wild waters of remote **D'Entrecasteaux National Park** (p132)
- Wend your towards the creative community of **Balingup** (p117) and nearby towns
- Canoe from the forest to the sea, along the Blackwood River, starting at **Nannup** (p128)
- Get all your blues out in the gorgeous little town of **Bridgetown** (p126)
- Climb the **Gloucester Tree** (p131) at Pemberton

★ Ngilgi Cave
★ Balingup
★ Margaret River   Nannup ★   Bridgetown ★
★ Lake Cave
★ Jewel Cave
★ Augusta
Pemberton ★
D'Entrecasteaux ★
National Park

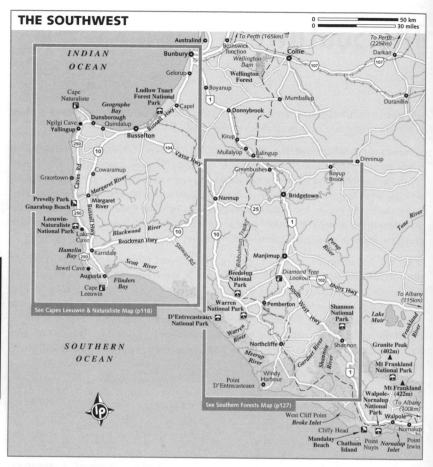

Getting There & Away

Transwa (☎ 1300 662 205; www.transwa.gov.wa.au) and **South West Coach Lines** (☎ in Perth 9324 2333, in Bunbury 9791 1955, in Busselton 9754 1666) run daily bus services from Perth to the following towns: Bunbury ($25, three hours); Busselton ($29, four hours); Dunsborough ($31, 4½ hours); Margaret River ($33, 5½ hours); and Augusta ($40, six hours).

Transwa runs a service to Pemberton ($42, eight hours) several times a week. South West Coach Lines also run regular services to Bridgetown ($31, 4½ hours), Manjimup ($35, five hours) and Balingup ($31, 5½ hours).

Goldrush Tours Golden Triangle Tour (☎ 1800 620 441; www.goldrushtours.com.au) offers a hop-on, hop-off bus pass ($475) between Perth, Margaret River and the southwest coast and forests, Albany and Esperance on the south coast, and up to Kalgoorlie.

Transwa's *Australind* train service travels from Perth to Bunbury ($23.90, 2½ hours) twice daily.

BUNBURY REGION

Close to Perth, Bunbury and its surrounds are popular with locals looking to escape the city. Its beach-dotted coastline beckons, while inland the rural townships offer peace and quiet. Gateway to the great tall forests of the southwest, and to the national parks and wineries between Capes Naturaliste and Leeuwin, the region is gearing up to service the growing numbers of visitors heading southwards.

BUNBURY

☎ 08 / pop 56,180

Bunbury, 184km south of Perth, has started to remake its image as industrial port into that of seaside holiday destination.

The town lies at the western end of Leschenault Inlet, which Nicolas Baudin, commander of *Le Géographe,* named after his botanist Leschenault de la Tour in 1803. In 1836 James Stirling sailed south from the Swan River Colony, met Henry William Bunbury, commander, at Port Leschenault and renamed the port in his honour; a classic case of colonial one-upmanship, replacing French place names with English ones.

The city is centred on a rectangle formed by Wittenoom, Clifton, Blair and Stirling Sts. Bunbury's main street is Victoria St, which bisects the town centre. Recent development around Boat Harbour, north of the centre, has seen silos converted into urban apartments and waterside restaurants. Koombana Beach, to the east, is popular for swimming and dolphin encounters, and Ocean Dr, to the west, hugs the coast with a stunning walk and cycle track running beside. The train station is 3km from town, and South West Coach Lines terminal is beside the **visitors centre** (☎ 9721 7922; Carmody Pl; ❧ 9am-5pm Mon-Sat, 9.30am-4.30pm Sun), located in the historic train station (1904). Check your email at the Old Station Coffee Lounge next door.

Sights & Activities

Bunbury's **Dolphin Discovery Centre** (☎ 9791 3088; www.dolphindiscovery.com.au; Koombana Beach; adult/child $4/2; ❧ 8am-5pm) was set up in 1989 and wild dolphins started to interact with the public in early 1990. Three pods of about 100 bottlenose dolphins regularly feed in the inner harbour, most frequently between November and April. While you're not allowed to touch them, you can wade waist-deep alongside, which you can't do at Monkey Mia. During these months, the centre also runs a **Dolphin Swim Tour** (3hr tour $125) by boat that allows you to swim with dolphins in open water; no children under eight permitted. **Dolphin cruises** (1½ hr tour adult/child $41/26) depart most days at 11am and 3pm. A dolphin-watching sea-kayak tour is offered by **Dekked Out** (☎ 9796 1000; dekkedout@iprimus.com.au; per person $50).

Several early buildings, some laced with wrought iron, still stand in the city, including **King Cottage** (☎ 9721 7546; 77 Forrest Ave; ❧ 2-4pm), which now houses a museum; the 1842 **St Mark's Church** (cnr Charterhouse & Flynn Rds) and **Bunbury Regional Art Galleries** (☎ 9721 8226; 64 Wittenoom St; admission free; ❧ 10am-4pm) in a restored 1897 pink-painted convent.

There are good **walking tracks** around the city; pick up the *Walk-it Bunbury* brochure from the visitors centre. The **Mangrove Boardwalk** (enter off Koombana Dr) allows you to explore the most southerly mangroves in WA, rich with more than 70 species of birds. Helpful panels provide information about this ancient ecosystem, thought to be about 2500 years old. In contrast, a stretch of tall **Tuart Forest** runs along the southern end of Ocean Drive.

The **Big Swamp** is a wetland bang in the middle of encroaching suburbia; there are good walking tracks, and seats to hang out and bird-watch. Kids can feed kangaroos and parrots at the **Big Swamp Wildlife Park** (☎ 9721 8380; Prince Philip Dr; adult/child $5.50/3.50; ❧ 10am-5pm), set in bushland and with good picnicking spots.

Sleeping

Dolphin Retreat YHA (☎ 9792 4690; dolphinretreatbunbury yha@iinet.net.au; 14 Wellington St; dm/s/d $19/29/48; ❑) Just around the corner from the beach, this small hostel is well-located with hammocks and a barbecue on the back veranda.

Glade Caravan Park (☎ 1800 113 800, 9721 3800; Timperley Rd; unpowered/powered sites $20/25, cabins $55-80 ⚘) Functional rather than fantastic, this spotless van park is five minutes drive from the centre of town.

Wander Inn Backpackers (☎ 9721 3242; www.bunbury backpackers.com.au; 16 Clifton St; dm/s/d $23/36/56; ❑) Down a quiet side street, in between the beach and the main strip, this friendly hostel has good adventure tours and cruises. Look for the cheerful blue-and-yellow house.

Koombana Bay Holiday Resort (☎ 9791 3900; www .bestonparks.com.au; cnr Koombana Dr & Lyons St; unpowered/powered sites $28/32, cabins from $85; ⚘) The great location of this caravan park – just over a towel's throw from Koombana Beach, and close to the dolphin centre – is reflected in its higher than usual price. There are also ample distractions for kids – such as tennis and basketball courts and a games room – and great cabins.

Rose Hotel (☎ 9721 4533; www.rosehotel.com.au; cnr Victoria & Wellington Sts; hotel s/d with shared bathroom $58/78, motel s/d $92/99) From the chandeliers

THE SOUTHWEST

hanging in the halls to the bloke wearing the armour in the lobby, the 1865 Rose Hotel oozes character. Go for the old-style hotel rooms – they're charming, even though you'll share a bathroom.

Lighthouse Beach Resort (☎ 9721 1311; www.light housebeach.com.au; Carey St; r $90-140, apt $130 🚗 🔕) Located in a fabulous setting above (funnily enough) Lighthouse Beach, the two-room self-contained apartment in this hotel is terrific value. Renovations of the property were on-going when we visited.

Clifton (☎ 9721 4300; www.theclifton.com.au; 2 Molloy St; ste $240; 🚗 🔕) For luxurious accommodation with lots of heritage trimmings, go for the top-of-the-range rooms in the Clifton's historic Grittleton Lodge (1885), with sleigh beds, a spa and a grand piano for ivory-tinkling.

Eating & Drinking

For good coffee, breakfast or light lunch try **Benesse** (Victoria St), **Caf-fez** (20 Prinsep St) or **Cafe 140** (140 Victoria St).

Fitzgerald's (Victoria St; ⏰ 6pm-late Thu-Sun) With a big beer garden and an easy, laid-back vibe, Fitzie's is popular for the Sunday session.

Fill up on traditional Irish Stew or Guinness Pie ($12.50).

Rose Hotel (☎ 9721 4533; cnr Victoria & Wellington Sts; mains $13; ⏰ lunch & dinner) The delightfully old-fashioned dining room serves tasty and filling old-fashioned classics (remember your grandma's corned silverside of beef?), and counter meals are served at the bar.

Mojo's (☎ 9792 5900; Victoria St; mains $20-30; ⏰ breakfast, lunch & dinner) Still buzzing, this modern café's sunny outdoor tables are the place to watch the world and agonise over what you'll order from the local produce–focused menu.

Walkabout Café (☎ 9791 6922; Victoria St; mains $22; ⏰ lunch & dinner) Themed around bush Australiana; you can eat kangaroo sausages and mash here and there's a good value $12.50 lunch menu.

Check out the recent foodie options at Boat Harbour, where **VAT Two** (☎ 9791 8833; 2 Jetty Rd; mains $26-32; ⏰ lunch & dinner), the Bunbury sibling of Margaret River's see-and-be-seen VAT 107, overlooks the marina. In the next block, sure to eat fish and chips on the deck at **Aristos Waterfront** (☎ 9791 6477; fish & chips $10; ⏰ lunch & dinner), while upstairs **Barbados** (☎ 9791 6555;

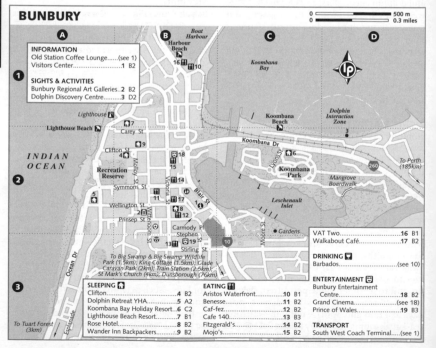

BUNBURY

INFORMATION		
Old Station Coffee Lounge	(see 1)	
Visitors Center	1	B2

SIGHTS & ACTIVITIES		
Bunbury Regional Art Galleries	2	B2
Dolphin Discovery Centre	3	D2

SLEEPING		
Clifton	4	B2
Dolphin Retreat YHA	5	A2
Koombana Bay Holiday Resort	6	C2
Lighthouse Beach Resort	7	B1
Rose Hotel	8	B2
Wander Inn Backpackers	9	B2

EATING		
Aristos Waterfront	10	B1
Benesse	11	B2
Caf-fez	12	B2
Cafe 140	13	B2
Fitzgerald's	14	B2
Mojo's	15	B2

VAT Two	16	B1
Walkabout Café	17	B2

DRINKING		
Barbados	(see 10)	

ENTERTAINMENT		
Bunbury Entertainment Centre	18	B2
Grand Cinema	(see 18)	
Prince of Wales	19	B3

TRANSPORT		
South West Coach Terminal	(see 1)	

0 — 500 m
0 — 0.3 miles

(⏳ 11am-midnight) is the place to go for a sunset drink and an evening jive.

Entertainment

The **Prince of Wales** (☎ 9721 2016; 41 Stephen St) has long been the place to see live music. For the newest movie releases, try the **Grand Cinema** (☎ 9791 4455; cnr Victoria & Clifton Sts). **Bunbury Entertainment Centre** (☎ 9791 1133; www.bunburyentertainment.com; Blair St) attracts local and overseas acts, and is the region's main cultural centre.

Getting Around

Bunbury City Transit (☎ 9791 1955; Bicentennial Sq, Carmody Pl) covers the region around the city north to Australind and south to Gelorup. There's a free bus to and from the visitors centre that connects with the trains.

BALINGUP

☎ 08 / pop 803

About 65km south of Bunbury is the lovely arts-and-crafts village of Balingup. The **visitors centre** (☎ 9764 1818; www.balinguptourism.com.au; South West Hwy; ⏳ 10am-4pm) is on the main street.

Balingup's most famous attraction is the **Old Cheese Factory** (☎ 9764 1018; Nannup Rd; ⏳ 9.30am-4pm), which sells more knick-knacks than you could poke a fridge magnet at, as well as other crafty things and foodstuffs. Its casual café serves lunches (fancy a ploughman's?) and morning and afternoon teas. The **Tinderbox** (☎ 9764 1034; www.cheekyherbs.com; South West Hwy) herbal remedies shop is also worth a poke around; its locally made products – from massage oils to head-lice treatment – are sold around the country. See website for opening hours.

In the post office building, the **Hikers Hideaway** (☎ 9764 1049; hotbunks@wn.com.au; 26 Brockman St; $28 pp; 🖳) has just 10 beds in three rooms; book if you can, if it's busy you'll have to share a room. Popular with hikers walking the Bibbulmun Track, it's cheerful and informal.

Woodlands (☎ 9764 1272; Russell Rd; cottage $100), on the Mullalyup side of the village, is a self-contained cottage in a peaceful, pretty setting overlooking a valley.

Almost opposite the Old Cheese Factory and up a steep hill – the highest point in the southwest – you'll find **Balingup Heights** (☎ 9764 1283; www.bluewren.com.au; Lot 6 Nannup Rd; cottages from $140), where secluded, self-contained cottages are scattered around a quirky stone farmhouse in a truly magnificent setting.

Coffees and home-style lunches are available at a couple of cafés in town; try the Mushroom Café & Bakery on the main street.

NATURALISTE TO LEEUWIN

The gorgeous capes region is defined by the holiday resorts of Busselton and Dunsborough to the northeast; in the northwest corner is Cape Naturaliste and the surf of Yallingup; the southwest corner has Cape Leeuwin, several interesting caves, and remote Augusta at the confluence of the Indian and Southern Oceans; the regional centre is the laid-back town of Margaret River.

Known for its picturesque wineries (see p121), great surfing beaches (see p113) and labyrinthine caves, the region draws many visitors, but you really do need wheels here, as transport between the smaller centres is virtually nonexistent. The coast has real variety – cliff faces, long beaches pounded by rolling surf, and calm, sheltered bays – and arts-and-crafts places are everywhere There are accommodation options for all travellers; it's *very* busy during summer and at holiday times when prices may rise 30% higher than those given here; winter (roughly June to August) is quieter, prices level off and opening hours can be erratic.

You can walk the stunning 135km **Cape-to-Cape Track** (www.capetocapetrack.com.au) between Cape Naturaliste and Cape Leeuwin, passing though heath land, forest and sand dunes. Most Cape-to-Cape walkers take about seven days, although many choose to complete small sections. Individual walk-section brochures ($2) are available from the local visitor centres.

BUSSELTON

☎ 08 / pop 24,000

On the shores of Geographe Bay, 230km south of Perth, Busselton is a popular holiday resort with a slightly old-fashioned air. Local place names come from the early 1800s, when a French sailor named Vasse was lost at sea in Geographe Bay; Vasse (the river and district), Geographe (the bay) and Naturaliste (the cape). Busselton itself is named after the Bussell family, who were early settlers in the area. The main street, Queen St, leads down to the beach.

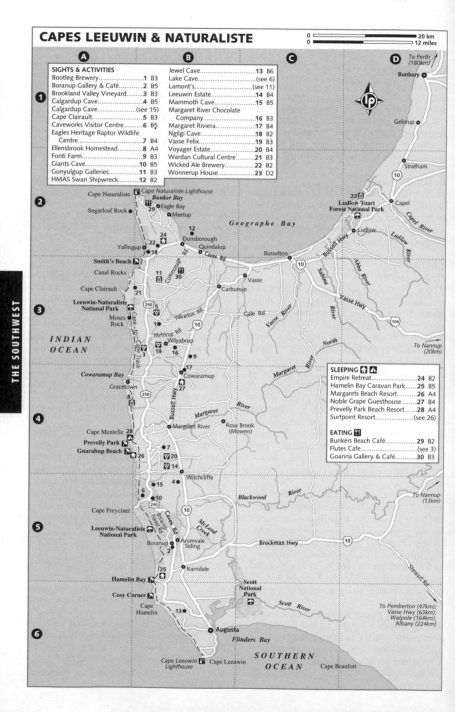

CAPES LEEUWIN & NATURALISTE

0 ——————— 20 km
0 ——————— 12 miles

SIGHTS & ACTIVITIES
Bootleg Brewery...........................1 B3
Boranup Gallery & Café...............2 B5
Brookland Valley Vineyard...........3 B3
Calgardup Cave............................4 B5
Calgardup Cave....................(see 15)
Cape Clairault..............................5 B3
Caveworks Visitor Centre.............6 B5
Eagles Heritage Raptor Wildlife
  Centre.......................................7 B4
Ellensbrook Homestead...............8 A4
Fonti Farm...................................9 B3
Giants Cave................................10 B5
Gunyulgup Galleries...................11 B3
HMAS Swan Shipwreck..............12 B2

Jewel Cave................................13 B6
Lake Cave............................(see 6)
Lamont's...............................(see 11)
Leeuwin Estate.........................14 B4
Mammoth Cave.........................15 B5
Margaret River Chocolate
  Company................................16 B3
Margaret Riviera.......................17 B4
Ngilgi Cave...............................18 B2
Vasse Felix................................19 B3
Voyager Estate.........................20 B4
Wardan Cultural Centre.............21 B3
Wicked Ale Brewery..................22 B2
Wonnerup House......................23 D2

SLEEPING
Empire Retreat...........................24 B2
Hamelin Bay Caravan Park........25 B5
Margarets Beach Resort.............26 A4
Noble Grape Guesthouse...........27 B4
Prevelly Park Beach Resort........28 A4
Surfpoint Resort...................(see 26)

EATING
Bunkers Beach Café...................29 B2
Flutes Cafe............................(see 3)
Goanna Gallery & Café..............30 B3

Still family-friendly, Busselton has plenty of diversionary activities for lively kids; think playgrounds on the foreshore, sheltered beaches, waterslides, animal farms, even a classic drive-in cinema. During school holidays the population increases fourfold, accommodation is fully booked and pricey, and the beaches and restaurants are crowded.

Busselton's **visitors centre** (☎ 9752 1288; www .geographebay.com; Causeway Rd & Peel Tce; ☼ 9am-5pm Mon-Fri, 9am-4pm Sat, 10am-2pm Sun) has a huge range of tourist information. The South West Coach Lines depot is in Albert St.

Sights & Activities

The town boasts the longest timber jetty in the southern hemisphere at 2km. Constructed in 1865, a mammoth planned renovation programme will likely close the jetty for many months in 2007; check at www.busseltonjetty .com.au. At the shore end is a free, friendly **museum**; at the ocean end is the **underwater observatory** (adult/child $20/11.50; ☼ 10.30am-3.30pm).

The former **courthouse** displays historical information on a panel by the entrance; now an arts centre, it's open to the public during exhibitions. The **Old Butter Factory Museum** (Peel Tce; adult/child $4/1; ☼ 10am-2pm Wed-Mon) shows the history of Busselton.

Diving is popular, especially on Four Mile Reef (a 40km limestone ledge about 6.5km off the coast) and on the scuttled navy vessel HMAS *Swan* off Dunsborough. The **Dive Shed** (☎ 9754 1615; www.diveshed.com.au; 21a Queen St) can take you out.

Between Busselton and Bunbury the 20-sq-km **Ludlow Tuart Forest National Park** is the world's only tall stand of tuart, a specialised eucalypt that grows nowhere but on WA's coastal limestone. In a gorgeous setting in the forest, **Wonnerup House** (☎ 9752 2039; adult/child $5/3; ☼ 10am-4pm Weds-Sun), a whitewashed colonial homestead built in 1859, has been lovingly restored by the National Trust.

Sleeping

Busselton is packed in the holidays and pretty much deserted off-season. On the Bussell Hwy, heading towards Dunsborough, caravan parks and motels line the road; better to head for town and the places in walking distance of good beaches and good food.

Kookaburra Caravan Park (☎ 9752 1516; kookpark@compwest.net.au; tents $24, cabins $50-65) In a great location on the waterfront and a short walk from town, this is a good option for campers.

Paradise Motor Inn (☎ 9752 1200; www.paradisemotor inn.aussie.com.au; 6 Pries Ave; lodge/motel d $30/70) It's not flash, but it's the best of the few places in town that offer budget accommodation. The 'lodge' has basic share-facility rooms.

Observatory Guesthouse (☎ 1800 180 343; www .observatory-guesthouse.com; 7 Brown St; s/d $77/88) A five-minute walk from the jetty, this friendly B&B guesthouse has bright, cheerful rooms and a communal sea-facing balcony.

Blue Bay Apartments (☎ 9751 1796; www.bluebay apartments.com; cnr Brown & Adelaide St; from $90) Only a couple of years old, and just a stone's throw from the beach, these self-contained apartments are bright and cheery, each with private courtyard and barbecue.

Prospect Villa (☎ 0417 099 307; 1 Pries Ave; d $90, self-contained cottage $120; ☒) Based in Busselton's oldest house, built around 1844, this B&B is full of character and quirky country furnishings. It was on the verge of changing hands when we visited, so fingers crossed for its future.

Newton House (☎ 9755 4485; newton@compwest.net .au; 737 Bussell Hwy; s/d $120/150) Built around 1851, this early settler residence, west of town, has a lovely four-room guesthouse amid green lawns and gardens of herbs and lavender. Its restaurant (mains $35; open lunch and dinner Tuesday to Saturday) offers some of the best food in the region, including fabulous home-made preserves and chutneys; book for dinner.

Eating

Star Sushi & Noodle (☎ 9751 4888; 44 Queen St; noodle soups $10; ☼ lunch & dinner) Filling and good-value Asian food is cooked to order here, to take away only.

Esplanade Hotel (☎ 9752 1078; 167 Marine Tce; mains $15; ☼ lunch & dinner) Classic pub grub is served at this almost-waterfront Busselton institution; evening meals are often themed (steak night, Mexican night and so on).

Equinox Cafe (☎ 9752 4641; www.theequinox.com .au; Jetty foreshore; lunch $15; ☼ breakfast, lunch & dinner) Lower-key and somewhat more relaxed than its goosy neighbour, this is a fine waterfront hangout.

Goose (☎ 9754 7700; www.thegoose.com.au; Jetty foreshore; mains $25; ☼ breakfast, lunch & dinner Tue-Sat) At the end of the jetty, this stylish restaurant offers an eclectic and interesting menu; tapas ($9) is served all day.

THE SOUTHWEST

Vasse (☎ 9754 8560; 44 Queen St; mains $20; ☺ lunch & dinner) Join the locals and sit outside eating good café fare and drinking beer, wine or coffee; evenings have more of a busy bar than café atmosphere.

DUNSBOROUGH

☎ 08 / pop 3300

Dunsborough, west of Busselton, is a pleasant coastal town fast developing into an increasingly chichi destination too expensive for the local family holidays that used to be its mainstay. It's also popular with school leavers, thousands of whom descend to party for a couple of weeks in late November to early December. The cheerful staff at the **visitors centre** (☎ 9755 3299; www.geographebay.com; Naturaliste Tce; ☺ 9am-5pm) has a wealth of regional information.

Sights & Activities

Northwest of Dunsborough, Cape Naturaliste Rd leads to the excellent beaches of **Meelup**, **Eagle Bay** and **Bunker Bay** (take a coffee break and absorb the stunning view at Bunkers Beach Café on the way), some fine coastal walks and lookouts, and the **Cape Naturaliste lighthouse** (☎ 9755 3955; adult/child $9/4.50; ☺ 9.30am-4pm), built in 1903.

Whale-watching for humpbacks and southern rights is a regular pastime between September and December. **Naturaliste Charters** (☎ 9755 2276; www.whales-australia.com) offers two-hour whale-watching tours by boat (adult/child $60/33). The southernmost nesting colony of the red-tailed tropicbird is at scenic **Sugarloaf Rock** (see the boxed text below).

There has been excellent **diving** in Geographe Bay since the decommissioned Navy destroyer HMAS *Swan* was purpose-scuttled in 1997 for use as a dive wreck. Marine life has colonised the ship, which lies at a depth of 30m, 2.5km offshore. **Cape Dive** (☎ 9756 8778; www.capedive.com; 222 Naturaliste Tce; two-tank dive from $175) offers dives and dive courses.

Sleeping

Dunsborough Beachouse (☎ 9755 3107; www.dunsboroughbeachouse.com.au; 205 Geographe Bay Rd; dm/s/d $25/36/56; ☐) On the Quindalup beachfront, this friendly hostel has the best beach location in town; it's an easy 2km cycle from the centre.

Dunsborough Beach Lodge (☎ 9756 7144; www.dunsboroughbeachlodge.com.au; 13 Dunn Bay Rd; dm/d $25/60) Close to the beach; some rooms at this centrally located lodge have balconies.

Dunsborough Inn (☎ 9756 7277; www.dunsboroughinn.com; 50 Dunn Bay Rd; dm/d $25/50, unit $90-139; ☐) The budget rooms are fine here, but while it's central the surroundings aren't exactly the most scenic. Ask for a room away from the road.

Dunsborough Rail Carriages & Farm Cottages (☎ 9755 3865; Commonage Rd; rail carriages $90-100, cottages $125-160) Refurbished rail carriages are dotted about this lovely bush block near Quindalup. The self-contained timber cottages may not be as fun as the carriages, but they're spacious for families.

There are many, many options for self-contained rentals in town depending on season; the visitors centre has current listings.

Eating

Goanna Gallery & Café (☎ 9759 1477; cnr Commonage & Hayes Rd; mains $16; ☺ 9am-4pm Wed-Sun) Several kilometres out of town, this fabulous café has a stunning bush setting, plenty of quirky outdoor seating, and a kids' sand pit. The simple winter lunch of homemade soup, bread and cheese is a knockout.

THE BIRD HAS FLOWN – TOO FAR SOUTH

Birders will enjoy the sight of the red-tailed tropicbird (*Phaethon rubricauda*) soaring happily in the sea breezes above Sugarloaf Rock, south of Cape Naturaliste. The section of beaches between Capes Naturaliste and Leeuwin is anything but the tropics; nevertheless, this stretch of coast is home to the most southerly breeding colony of red-tailed tropicbirds in Australia, reliably seen here between September and May.

The tropicbird is distinguished by its two long, red tail streamers – almost twice its body length. It has a bill like a tern's and, from a distance, could easily be mistaken for a Caspian tern. You'll have fun watching through binoculars as the inhabitants of this small colony soar, glide, dive then swim with their disproportionately long tail feathers cocked up. They are ungainly on land and have to descend almost to the spot where they wish to nest.

SURFING THE SOUTHWEST

Known colloquially to surfers as 'Yal's' and 'Margaret's' (when viewed from far-off Perth), the beaches between Capes Naturaliste and Leeuwin offer powerful reef breaks, mainly left-handers (the direction you take after catching a wave). The surf at Margaret's has been described by surfing supremo Nat Young as 'epic', and by world surfing champ Mark Richards as 'one of the world's finest'.

The better locations include Rocky Point (short left-hander), the Farm and Bone Yards (right-hander), Three Bears (Papa, Mama and Baby, of course), Yallingup (breaks left and right), Injidup Car Park and Injidup Point (right-hand tube on a heavy swell; left-hander), Guillotine/Gallows (right hander), South Point (popular break), Left-Handers (the name says it all) and Margaret River (with Southside or 'Suicides').

Pick up a surfing map ($4.95) from the Dunsborough visitor centre on the way through, and check out www.yallingupsurfschool.com if you need some help with your technique.

Cape Wine Bar (☎ 9756 7650; 239 Naturaliste Tce; mains from $20; ☺ dinner Mon-Thu, tasting plates at the bar Fri & Sat, tapas Sun) Buzzing most nights, the wine bar has a well-deserved reputation for fresh seasonal food.

Artezen (☎ 9755 3325; 234 Naturaliste Tce; mains from $20; ☺ 7am-5pm Sun-Thu, 7am-9pm Fri & Sat) This super-cool café serves everything from great breakfasts to interesting Asian-influenced dishes like squid salad with soba.

Within a five minute walk of the town centre you'll also find En Joia (wood-fired pizza, paper tablecloths and crayons for the kids); Inji Bar at the Dunsborough Hotel (good counter food and sports TV); Bambooe (cheap and cheerful, serving a mean bowl of laksa); Evviva Café (fresh juices and salads); Assisi (classic Italian dishes); and Yallingup Coffee Roasting Company (great coffee, no food).

YALLINGUP
☎ 08 / pop 810

Yallingup, surrounded by scenic coastline and fine beaches, is a surfing mecca (see the boxed text, above); if you prefer dry land, a series of beautiful **walking trails** track the coast between here and Smith's Beach.

The leafy **Caves Caravan Park** (☎ 9755 2196; www.cavescaravanpark.com; cnr Caves & Yallingup Beach Rds; unpowered/powered sites $16/22, cabins/chalets $65/100), one of the best around, has tastefully decorated cabins and detached private bathrooms for every site.

You'll sleep to the sound of the surf at **Yallingup Beach Caravan Park** (☎ 9755 2164; www .yallingupbeach.com.au; Valley Rd; camp sites/vans/cabins $20/50/100), with the beach just across the road from the rolling lawns.

Built in the 1930s, the splendid **Seashells Caves House Yallingup** (☎ 9750 1500; www.seashells .com.au; Yallingup Beach Rd; r $175-395) has recently undergone a major shift upmarket. Impeccably renovated – think high ceilings, polished wood, comfortable leather sofas – the rooms are gorgeous.

Everything about the intimate **Empire Retreat** (☎ 9755 2065; www.empireretreat.com; Caves Rd; ste $220-380, villas $450-490) is incredibly stylish, from the Indonesian-inspired design to the attention to detail and service. A lovely day spa is attached.

CAVES ROAD AREA

Take a day or two to drive up and down Caves Rd, and get enjoyably lost pottering along the side roads. You'll find a swag of visitor attractions, from horse-riding to wineries to pottery to woodwork to caves to animal parks. All the visitor centres in the area supply free, detailed maps of the local attractions.

Sights
WINERIES

Vineyards abound. Among those renowned for their food as much as their wine are **Lamont's** (☎ 9755 2434; margaretriver@lamonts.com.au; Gunyulgup Valley Dr; mains $35 ☺ lunch daily, dinner Sat only) where, after a delicious lunch or weekend brunch on the balcony overlooking the lake, you can wander next door to the **Gunyulgup Galleries** (☎ 9755 2177; www.gunyulgupgallereis.com .au; ☺ 10am-5pm) showcasing exquisite contemporary WA art.

Flutes Cafe (☎ 9755 6250; www.brooklandvalley .com.au; Caves Rd; mains $30; ☺ lunch noon-4pm), at the Brookland Valley Vineyard, has glass walls and a balcony overlooking a dam and rolling grounds; the platter of locally-made game terrine and salamis is good.

Cape Clairault (☎ 9755 6225; www.clairaultwines .com.au; Henry Rd, Wilyabrup; mains $26-32; ☯ lunch noon-3.30pm) is a contemporary building of timber and corrugated iron amid vineyards and eucalypts, with an eclectic, appealing menu.

The first of the commercial wineries, **Vasse Felix** (☎ 9755 5242; www.vassefelix.com.au; Harman's South Rd; mains $30; ☯ lunch to 3pm) is considered by many to have the finest restaurant in the area; it's certainly one of the most scenic. Make time also to enjoy the artworks on display from the Holmes à Court collection.

The white-washed Dutch-style buildings of **Voyager Estate** (☎ 9757 6354; www.voyagerestate.com .au; Gnarawary Rd; mains $30, Devonshire tea $8.50; ☯ lunch to 3pm) belie the winery's beautiful grand interior; its restaurant has an always-impressive seasonal menu.

Leeuwin Estate (☎ 9757 6253; Stevens Rd; mains $32; ☯ lunch) is a place for long lunches, overlooking lawns that roll gently down to the bush to form a natural amphitheatre – the site of the annual alfresco concerts. Behind-the-scenes wine tours and tastings take place at 11am, 1pm and 3pm ($9).

CAVES
Caveworks visitor centre (☎ 9757 7411; www.margaret river.com; Caves Rd; ☯ 9am-5pm), about 25km from Margaret River, has excellent screen displays about caves and cave conservation, an authentic model cave and a 'cave crawl' experience. There are displays on fossils found in the area.

Single cave tickets (adult/child $16.50/8.50) include entry to Caveworks. Three-cave passes ($42.50/8.50) can be used over several days and include entry to Caveworks and Lake, Jewel and Mammoth Caves. There are guided tours of **Lake Cave** (☯ 9.30am-4.30pm), while tours of **Jewel Cave** (☯ 9.30am-4pm), 8km north of Augusta, leave on the hour. You can enter **Mammoth Cave** (☯ 9am-4pm) yourself, and it has partial wheelchair access.

Managed by **DEC** (☎ in Busselton 9752 5555), **Calgardup Cave** (adult/child $10/5; ☯ 9am-4.15pm) is a self-guided cave, with an underground lake. **Giants Cave** (adult/child $10/5; ☯ 9.30-3.30 school & public holidays only) is also self-guided, with some steep ladders and scrambles. Helmets and torches are provided at both.

Between Dunsborough and Yallingup is the mystical **Ngilgi Cave** (☎ 9755 1288; ngilgi@ geographebay.com; adult/child $15.50/6.50; ☯ 9.30am-

4.30pm, last entry 3.30pm); a series of well-marked bush walks also start here.

There's detailed information on the region's caves at www.showcaves.com.

OTHER SIGHTS & ACTIVITIES
Near Dunsborough is **Wicked Ale Brewery** (☎ 9755 2848; www.wickedalebrewery.com.au; ☯ 10am-5pm), a small-scale and eccentric brewery in a great bush setting. There's also a chance to try the award-winning beers of **Bootleg Brewery** (☎ 9755 6300; Wilyabrup; ☯ 10am-4.30pm), which bills itself as 'a beer oasis in a desert of wine'.

Canal Rocks, a series of rocky outcrops forming a natural canal, are just outside Yallingup. A little further south on Caves Rd is **Wardan Cultural Centre** (☎ 9756 6566; www.wardan.com.au; adult/child $12/6; ☯ 10am-4pm Sep-Mar, closed Tue & Sat Apr-Aug, closed Jul), where you can get a window onto the lives of the local Wardandi Aboriginal people.

Boranup Gallery & Café (☎ 9757 7585; www.boranup gallery.com; ☯ 10am-4pm) has a beautiful selection of local arts and crafts; the attached café is a good spot to refuel.

West of Margaret River, off Caves Rd, the coastline provides spectacular surfing and walks.

On the Bussell Hwy at Cowaramup is **Fonti Farm** (☎ 9755 7588; ☯ 9.30am-5pm), whose cheeses and yogurt are distributed throughout WA – there's a viewing window into the factory kitchen, and a tiny historical display. Chocoholics should head for the **Margaret River Chocolate Company** (☎ 9755 6555; www.chocolatefactory.com .au; Harman's Mill Rd; ☯ 9am-5pm), where the chocolatier works wonders and you can even buy chocolate lip balm and bath salts! Gourmet food store **Margaret Riviera** (☎ 9755 9333; www .margaretriviera.com.au; Bottrill St, Cowaramup) stocks local produce including olive oils, preserves and cheeses.

A beautiful National Trust property 8km northwest of Margaret River, the 1857 **Ellensbrook Homestead** (adult/child $4/2; ☯ house open Sat, Sun & public holidays 10am-4pm, grounds open daily), was the first home of pioneer settlers Alfred and Ellen Bussell, led by local Noongar people to this sheltered but isolated site, with its supply of fresh water. Between 1899 and 1917, Edith Bussell, who farmed the property alone for many years, established an Aboriginal mission here. There's decent wheelchair access into the homestead grounds.

Eagles Heritage Raptor Wildlife Centre (☎ 9757 2960; www.eaglesheritage.com.au; adult/child $10/4.50;

THE CAVES OF THE CAPE

The limestone cliffs that make their jagged way along the coastline between the capes give an inkling of what lies beneath. Limestone helps the formation of caves, as water seeps through the porous substance, dissolving calcium carbonate which is later deposited to create stalactites and other formations. There are perhaps as many as 350 limestone caves dotted throughout the Leeuwin-Naturaliste Ridge between the capes. The most spectacular is Jewel Cave, while Lake Cave is undoubtedly the prettiest.

The limestone formations are reflected in the still waters of an underground stream in **Lake Cave**. Creative lighting effects enhance the forms of the stalactites and stalagmites. The vegetated entrance to this cave is spectacular and includes a karri tree with a girth of 7m. Lake Cave is the deepest of all the caves open to the public. There are more than 300 steps down (a 72m drop) to the entrance.

Caldargup Cave is an attractive illustration of the role of the caves in the local ecosystems – a stream transports nutrients to the creatures living in the cave, while tree roots hang overhead.

The caves of the region have also revealed a lot about the prehistoric fauna of the southwest. **Mammoth Cave** boasts a fossilised jawbone of *Zygomaturus trilobus,* a giant wombatlike creature, as well as other fossil remains. Fossil remains of a Tasmanian tiger *(thylacine),* believed to be 25,000 years old, have been discovered in **Jewel Cave**. The cave was discovered in 1957 and has an impressive 5.9m straw stalactite, so far the longest seen in a 'commercial' cave.

Near Yallingup is the mystical **Ngilgi Cave**, which was discovered, or rather stumbled upon, in 1899. Formations include the white 'Mother of Pearl Shawl' and the equally beautiful 'Arab's Tent' and 'Oriental Shawl'.

10am-5pm), 5km south of Margaret River on Boodjidup Rd, rehabilitates many birds of prey each year. There are free-flight displays at 11am and 1.30pm.

Sleeping

Prevelly Park Beach Resort (☎ 9757 2374; camp sites per person \$11-17, vans \$50-70, cottages \$70-120) A good budget option on the hill above the beach, though you'll want your own transport to get to the water.

Surfpoint Resort (☎ 9757 1777, 1800 071 777; www .surfpoint.com.au; Gnarabup Beach; dm/d/unit \$24/79/165; 🖳 🖳) This light and airy place offers the beach on a budget, and you can hire boogie and surf boards or take a lesson from an expert.

Margarets Beach Resort (☎ 9757 1227; www.assured .net.au; Gnarabup Beach; studio \$200, apt \$250-390; 🐾 🖳) A 64-unit stylish modern complex, but when we last visited the small shopping mall and art gallery was looking forlorn and almost empty of tenants; a temporary state of affairs, hopefully.

MARGARET RIVER

☎ 08 / pop 5600

The ample attractions of Margaret River – fantastic surf, undulating bushland, some of Australia's best wineries – make it one of

WA's most popular destinations. The town is close to the incredible surf of Margaret River Mouth, Gnarabup, Suicides and Redgate, and to the swimming beaches at Prevelly and Gracetown.

Margaret River gets very, *very* busy at Easter and Christmas (when you should book weeks, if not months, ahead), during the annual food and wine bash in November (www .mrwinefest.org.au), during surf competitions in March and November, and at the time of the renowned Leeuwin Estate open-air concerts in February.

Information

Cybercorner Cafe (2/72 Willmott Ave; per hr \$6) Internet.

Visitors centre (☎ 9757 2911; www.margaretriver .com; cnr Bussell Hwy & Tunbridge St; 9am-5pm) This sleek centre has wads of information, plus an on-site wine centre.

Sights & Activities

Need we mention that **wine tasting** is the most popular activity in the area? See p121 for a description of many of the spectacular wineries in the region. Also read our special section (p47) and drop by the **Margaret River Regional Wine Centre** (☎ 9755 5501; www.mrwines.com; 9 Bussell Hwy, Cowaramup; 10am-7pm Mon-Sat, noon-6pm Sun).

THE SOUTHWEST

If you're limited for time and overwhelmed by choice, the knowledgeable staff can plan a vineyard itinerary for you and can ship wine almost anywhere in the world.

Another popular activity around here is exploring the many **caves** of the region. See p122 for more information.

Tours

Still highly recommended is the search for forest secrets with **Bushtucker River Tours** (☎ 9757 1084; www.bushtuckertours.com; adult/child $60/30). The four-hour trip combines walking and canoeing up the Margaret River, and features aspects of Aboriginal culture along with uses of flora and tasting of bush tucker. They also offer a low-key and informative winery tour,

as does **Wine for Dudes** (☎ 9758 8699; www.winefordudes.com); both are $60.

Dirty Detours (☎ 0417 998 816; www.dirtydetours.com) does guided mountain-bike rides through the magnificent Boranup Forest ($55).

Margaret River Tours (☎ 0419 917 166; www.margaretrivertours.com), one of the longest-standing local operators, runs combined winery and sightseeing tours (half/full day $60/95) or can arrange charters. For something totally indulgent you can take a chauffeured Rolls Royce around the vineyards for a progressive lunch with the **Margaret River Lady** (☎ 9757 1212; half/full day $330/530).

There's a huge number of tour companies operating in Margaret River; see the visitors centre for all options.

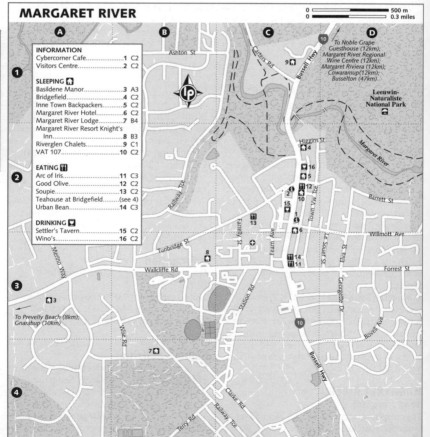

MARGARET RIVER

0   500 m
0   0.3 miles

INFORMATION
Cybercorner Cafe.....................1 C2
Visitors Centre.........................2 C2

SLEEPING
Basildene Manor......................3 A3
Bridgefield...............................4 C2
Inne Town Backpackers.........5 C2
Margaret River Hotel..............6 C2
Margaret River Lodge............7 B4
Margaret River Resort Knight's
Inn.......................................8 B3
Riverglen Chalets....................9 C1
VAT 107.................................10 C2

EATING
Arc of Iris..............................11 C3
Good Olive............................12 C2
Soupie...................................13 C2
Teahouse at Bridgefield.......(see 4)
Urban Bean...........................14 C3

DRINKING
Settler's Tavern.....................15 C2
Wino's...................................16 C2

To Noble Grape
Guesthouse (12km);
Margaret River Regional
Wine Centre (12km);
Margaret Riviera (12km);
Cowaramup(12km);
Busselton (47km)

Leeuwin-
Naturaliste
National Park

Ashton St
Carters Rd
Bussell Hwy
Higgins St
Margaret River
Barrett St
Willmott Ave
Forrest St
Railway Tce
Tunbridge St
S Farrell St
Fearn Ave
Town View Tce
Le Souef St
Fly Rd
Georgette Dr
Bovell Ave
Wallcliffe Rd
Menno Way
Station Rd
Bussell Hwy
Wise Rd
Clarke Rd
Railway Tce
Terry Rd

To Prevelly Beach (8km);
Gnarabup (10km)

THE SOUTHWEST

Sleeping

Book well in advance, especially around Easter and Christmas, and, except for budget accommodation, expect to pay at least $30 a night more than in other country towns; low season rates are given here. The best camping option is at nearby Prevelly Beach; see p123.

BUDGET

Inne Town Backpackers (☎ 1800 244 115; www.inne town.com; 93 Bussell Hwy; dm/s/d $23/50/60; ☐) In a converted house between the river and town, this smallish hostel is in a great location. Check the noticeboards here for work opportunities in town.

Margaret River Lodge (☎ 9757 9532; www.mrlodge .com.au; 220 Railway Tce; dm/s/d/f $25/55/63/73; ☐ ☒) About 1.5km southwest of the town centre, this YHA hostel is clean and modern with a pool and volleyball court in great sizable gardens.

MIDRANGE

Margaret River Hotel (☎ 9757 2655; www.margaret riverhotel.com.au; 139 Bussell Hwy; s/d/f $95/125/160) You won't pay seasonal price surges in this central, 1936 heritage building. The rooms have been beautifully restored with loads of jarrah detail, though the cheaper rooms are tiny.

Bridgefield (☎ 9757 3007; www.bridgefield.com.au; 73 Bussell Hwy; s/d $100/120) A 19th-century coach house, this lovely higgledy-piggledy B&B is all wood panels, high ceilings, tiled floors and ancient clawfoot baths.

Noble Grape Guesthouse (☎ 9755 5538; www .noblegrape.com.au; Lot 18 Bussell Hwy, Cowaramup; s/d $110/130) There are flowers everywhere – in the beautiful gardens, decorating the rooms and linen – in this modern B&B built in colonial style on the highway in Cowaramup.

Riverglen Chalets (☎ 9757 2101; www.riverglen chalets.com.au; Carters Rd; chalets $130-250; ☒) Just north of town, these good-value timber chalets are spacious and fully self-contained, with verandas looking out onto bushland; there's full disabled access to a couple of them.

TOP END

VAT 107 (☎ 9758 8877; www.vat107.com.au; 107 Bussell Hwy; r $150-180; ☒) In a purple building in town, the four big rooms are comfortable, contemporary and ooze urban style.

Margaret River Resort Knight's Inn (☎ 9757 0000, www.margaret-river-resort.com.au; 40 Wallcliffe Rd; motel/hotel/villas $160/180/330; ☒ ☒) Ignore the dinky exterior: the jarrah-dense hotel rooms here are big and gorgeous, and the motel rooms luxurious. There's a Thai restaurant attached.

Basildene Manor (☎ 9757 3140; www.basildene.com .au; Wallcliffe Rd; d $249-389; ☒ ☒) Basildene – a historic 1912 home converted to a luxury B&B hotel set among landscaped gardens with views to karri forest – is simply magnificent.

Eating

Soupie (Community Resource Centre, 33 Tunbridge St; soup & bread $3; ☺ 5-7pm Mon-Wed) In contrast to the high-profile and high-priced local food industry, this long-standing voluntary community service welcomes any helpers with a free lunch from 1pm. Profits go to green groups.

Urban Bean (☎ 9757 3480; 157 Bussell Hwy; lunch $7-10; ☺ 7.30am-4pm) A funky little place serving bleary-eyed locals their first daily brew, selling loose-leaf tea and coffee, and making good quiche-y things for lunch.

Teahouse at Bridgefield (☎ 9757 3007; 73 Bussell Hwy; lunch $10-15; ☺ breakfast & lunch) Good country cooking here, with hearty pea and ham soup to warm the cockles in winter, and great morning and afternoon teas served on the sheltered veranda.

Good Olive (☎ 9758 7877; www.tgo.com; 97 Bussell Hwy; mains $15; ☺ breakfast & lunch) An informal café serving local produce; try the platter of olives and cheeses.

Arc of Iris (☎ 9757 3112; 151 Bussell Hwy; mains $25; ☺ dinner) An old favourite, it's eclectic, lively and a throwback to the hippy generation.

VAT 107 (☎ 9758 8877; 107 Bussell Hwy; entrée/mains $20/35 ☺ breakfast, lunch & dinner) Retaining its trendy reputation, the food here remains inventive and excellent – like Jerusalem artichoke and black cabbage risotto with seared scallops – and a simple coffee on the veranda makes for great people-watching.

Drinking

Settler's Tavern (☎ 9757 2398; 114 Bussell Hwy; ☺ 11am-late) There's live music regularly at Settler's, so settle in for the evening with good pub grub and a choice of 13 beers and 18 wines by the glass.

Wino's (☎ 9758 7155; 85 Bussell Hwy; ☺ 3pm-late) Leather lounges, bentwood chairs and plenty of local wines to sample (choose a taste, a glass or a bottle) make this modern wine bar a great place to drink at.

THE SOUTHWEST

AUGUSTA

☎ 08 / pop 1700

Augusta is 5km north of Cape Leeuwin, where the Indian Ocean meets the Southern Ocean and the magnificent Blackwood River rolls into the sea. The cape, which took its name from a Dutch ship that passed here in 1622, is the most southwesterly point in Australia and on a wild day you fear being blown off the edge of the earth. The **visitors centre** (☎ 9758 0166; www.margaretriver.com; cnr Blackwood Ave & Ellis St; ⌚ 9am-5pm) has a range of information.

Sights & Activities

Whale-watching happens at Cape Leeuwin between June and September. **Naturaliste Charters** (☎ 9755 2276; www.whales-australia.com) offers two-hour whale-watching tours by boat (adult/child $60/33). **Sea Dragon** (☎ 9758 4003; stephenhughes@wn.com.au) and **Miss Flinders** (☎ 0439 424 455; www.missflinders.com) operate daily Blackwood River 'eco-cruises' (adult/child $25/10), usually leaving mid-morning.

The **Cape Leeuwin lighthouse** (adult/child $10/6; ⌚ 8.45am-5pm), opened in 1896, has magnificent views of the coastline. Entry fee includes a tour of the lighthouse; only ten people at a time can enter, so be prepared to wait a while in holiday season and enjoy a coffee and the view at the attached café.

The **Augusta Historical Museum** (Blackwood Ave; adult/child $3/1.50; ⌚ 10am-noon & 2-4pm Sep-Apr, 10am-noon May-Aug) has interesting local exhibits.

Sleeping & Eating

Hamelin Bay Caravan Park (☎ 9758 5540; hamelinbay@bordernet.com.au; low/high season tents $18/20, powered sites $20/25, cabins $90/110) Right on the beach a few kilometres north of Augusta, this secluded gem of a place gets very busy at holiday times.

Baywatch Manor Resort (☎ 9758 1290; www.baywatchmanor.com.au; 88 Blackwood Ave; dm/s $23/45, d with/without bathroom $70/55; 🖳) While there's no sign of David Hasselhoff, standards are being maintained here with lots of clean, modern rooms with great facilities that are fully equipped for travellers with disabilities. Ask about the self-contained holiday cottages around town.

Riverside Cottages (☎ 9758 1545; www.riverside cottagesaugusta.com.au; Molloy St; cottages $60-95) A tad tatty but clean and great value, various-sized self-contained cottages sit on the river bank. Cottage number eight is perfect for two, with a small balcony overlooking the water.

Georgiana Molloy Motel (☎ 9758 1255; www.augustaaccommodation.com.au; 84 Blackwood Ave; r $99-$115) Good sized, clean, well-equipped self-contained units are stand-out value here, each with a small garden area.

Augusta Bakery & Cafe (☎ 9758 1664; 121 Blackwood Ave; snacks/meals $5-16; ⌚ breakfast & lunch) Has a café-with-a-view, where local venison sausages replace the usual bangers and mash.

Colourpatch Café (☎ 9758 1295; 38 Albany Tce; takeaway/dine-in $10/25; ⌚ lunch & dinner) Watch the Blackwood River meet the waters of Flinders Bay at the self-styled 'last eating house before the Antarctic'. It sells fantastic fish, fresh from the ocean.

SOUTHERN FORESTS

The tall forests of WA's southwest are world famous, and rightly so. They are simply magnificent, with towering gums – karri, jarrah, marri – sheltering cool undergrowth. Between the forests, small towns bear witness to the region's history of logging and mining; most, like Pemberton, have redefined themselves as small-scale tourist centres from where you can bushwalk, take wine tours, canoe trips and trout- and marron-fishing expeditions. Backdrop to the townships, verdant farmland and meandering rivers such as the Blackwood make their way through the landscape.

The area of 'tall trees' lies between the Vasse Hwy and the South West Hwy, and includes the timber towns of Bridgetown, Manjimup, Nannup, Pemberton and Northcliffe. The drives between towns are spectacular.

Getting There & Away

Transwa (☎ 1300 662 205; www.transwa.wa.gov.au) runs a daily service from Perth (the East Perth terminus) to Pemberton ($42, eight hours) via Bunbury, Balingup and Bridgetown.

Goldrush Tours Golden Triangle Tour (☎ 1800 620 441; www.goldrushtours.com.au) travels through the region, stopping in Pemberton as part of its hop-on hop-off bus route between Perth and Kalgoorlie.

BRIDGETOWN

☎ 08 / pop 5930

In an idyllic setting of karri forests, farmland and the Blackwood River, Bridgetown is one of the loveliest little towns in the southwest. Despite being overrun with visitors on the

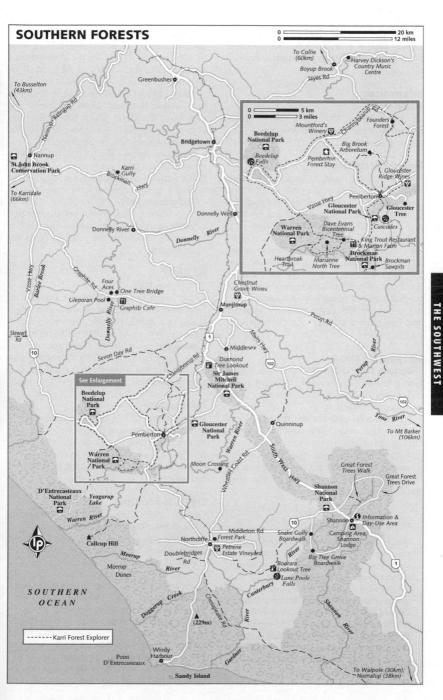

SOUTHERN FORESTS

0 — 20 km
0 — 12 miles

THE SOUTHWEST

second weekend of November during its annual **Blues at Bridgetown Festival** (www.blues atbridgetown.com) it retains a fantastic community feel.

Information

Visitors centre (☎ 9761 1740; www.bridgetown.com .au; 54 Hampton St; ☺ 9am-5pm, Sun 10am-3pm) Has a collection of apple-harvesting and cider memorabilia, and a curious jigsaw collection.

Sights & Activities

Bridgetown's old buildings include **Bridgedale House** (☎ 9761 1740; Hampton St; admission $3; ☺ 10am-2pm Fri-Sun), which was built of mud and clay by the area's first settler in 1862 and has been restored by the National Trust.

Between Balingup and Bridgetown, drop into the historic mining and timber township of **Greenbushes**. Some splendid, decaying buildings from the boom-days line the road, and heritage memorabilia is dotted through town. A series of walks loop around town and out to join the Bibbulmun track; the Balingup and Bridgetown visitors' centres keep walk trail brochures.

Sleeping & Eating

Bridgetown Valley Lodge (☎ 9761 4144; cnr Phillips & Spencer Sts; tw/d $55/60) In an old building, originally used by railway workers, this place offers basic accommodation.

Bridgetown Riverside Chalets (☎ 9761 1040; www .bridgetownchalets.com.au; 1338 Brockman Hwy; chalets $90) On a spectacular property on the road to Nannup, these four spacious stand-alone chalets (complete with pot-bellied stoves and washing machines) have wide views and friendly cows wandering around.

ELVIS SIGHTED IN WA

Follow the Brockman Hwy east of Bridgetown for 31km and you'll come across the small town of **Boyup Brook**, the centre of country music in WA. Local country-music fan and Elvis-obsessive Harvey Dickson has created **Harvey Dickson's Country Music Centre** (☎ 9765 1125; www.geocities.com/harvey dickson) here, complete with a life-size Elvis, an Elvis room and three 13.5m-tall guitar-playing men. It hosts regular rodeos as well as the **WA Country Music Festival** in February.

Nelsons of Bridgetown (☎ 9761 1645; www.nelsonsof bridgetown.com.au; 38 Hampton St; r $95-175) The central location is great, but go for the new, spacious rooms built to the side of this old Federation-style hotel.

Cidery (☎ 9761 2204; 43 Gifford Rd; ☺ lunch Wed-Mon) Sample the local drops (alcoholic and nonalcoholic ciders), which taste deliciously of pink lady apples. The outdoor tables by the river are a lovely spot for light lunches.

Riverwood House (☎ 9761 1862; Southwest Hwy; ☺ lunch Thu-Sun) Just over the bridge, this 1880 house with its balcony overlooking the river is a top spot for coffee or light lunch.

Bridgetown Hotel (☎ 97611034; Hampton St; ☺ lunch & dinner) The mix of restaurant, bar, veranda, gorgeous beer garden and regular live bands make this the place to hang out of an evening.

NANNUP

☎ 08 / pop 1200

In the heart of the southwest's forests and farmland, Nannup, 50km west of Bridgetown, is a quiet, historical town in a picturesque setting. It's home to the legendary **Nannup tiger**, similar to the (probably extinct) Tasmanian tiger, it's a striped wolflike animal, sighted so rarely that it has become almost mythical.

Information

Visitors centre (☎ 9756 1211; www.nannupwa.com; Brockman St; ☺ 9am-5pm) Check out the tiger press clippings at this centre, housed in the 1922 police station; this is also the place to book a site in the caravan park (unpowered/powered sites $17/19, cabins $55) on the river bank next door.

Sights & Activities

Garden-lovers should head to **Blythe Gardens** (admission by donation), opposite the tourist office. Once the pub's cow paddock, since 1958 the gardens have been lovingly transformed by the Blythe family into a wonderful mix of native and exotic plants. You can walk, cycle, swim and camp in pretty **St John Brook Conservation Park**, 8km west of Nannup; pick up a brochure from the visitors centre.

The **Blackwood River** begins in the salt-lake systems to the east and flows for more than 400km through forests, farmland and towns before emptying into the ocean east of Augusta. It's a good river to **canoe**, and the best time to paddle is in late winter and early spring, when the water levels are up. **Blackwood River Canoeing** (☎ 9756 1209; blackwoodrivercanoeing@ wn.com.au) runs guided canoeing trips (from $25) including equipment and basic stroke instruction, and can help you arrange longer self-guided expeditions.

Sleeping & Eating

Accommodation in Nannup tends towards B&Bs (from $100 and constantly changing; check with the visitors centre) and longer-term self-contained cottages.

Black Cockatoo (☎ 9756 1035; 27 Grange Rd; d $20) In town, this quirky guesthouse is full of eclectic objects (think wood sculptures and fabrics) and surrounded by a vibrant garden that en-croaches on the verandas.

Maranup Ford (☎ 9761 1200; www.maranupford.com .au; powered sites/cabins $16/60) Out of town, this is a working farm. Part of the 'Land for Wild-life' network, it supports sustainable farming practices and has a small camping area close to the river; canoes are available. It's 30km from Nannup, off the Bridgetown road.

Koala Thai (☎ 9756 0075; 10 Warren Rd; Thai mains $13; ☺ breakfast & lunch daily, dinner Fri-Sun) Unlikely as it may seem, this pretty café transforms itself into a Thai restaurant for eat-in or takeaway dinner at the weekend.

Hamish's Café (☎ 9756 1287; 1 Warren Rd; mains $22-33; ☺ breakfast & lunch daily, dinner Mon & Thu-Sat) When you can start the day with a brunch of poached eggs and kippers, and end it with carpetbag steak, you know you're not eating in your average country restaurant. Highly recommended.

MANJIMUP

08 / pop 4350

Surrounded by spectacular forest, the former timber town of Manjimup, the heart of WA's timber industry, is reinventing itself through a promising **wine industry** and a unique (for mainland Australia) **trufflerie** (yup, that's what truffle-growing places are called).

Information

Visitors centre (☎ 9771 1381; www.southernforests .com.au; Giblett St, ☺ 9am-5pm) The enthusiastic folk here can assist with information.

Sights & Activities

There's a particularly lovely drive between Manjimup and Nannup via **Graphite Rd**. Nine kilometres south of Manjimup is the **Diamond**

Tree Lookout. You're allowed to climb this 51m karri (not for the faint-hearted or vertigo sufferers); there's a nature trail nearby. Some 22km from town, the remains of **One Tree Bridge**, constructed from a single karri log carefully felled to span the width of the river but rendered unuseable by the 1966 floods, can be seen in a clearing in the forest. In the same location is the gorgeous **Glenoran Pool**, a sizable swimming hole in the forest. A little further down the road, the **Four Aces** are four superb karri trees – believed to be more than 300 years old – in a straight line; stand directly in front and all the trees disappear into one, makes a good photo opportunity! There's a short loop walk through the surrounding karri glade, or a 1½-hour loop bushwalking trail from the Four Aces to One Tree Bridge. The **Timber & Heritage Park** (☺ 9am-5pm), in the centre of town, is a good place to stop, picnic and potter after you've done a stock up on groceries in town.

Sleeping & Eating

Perup, 50km east of Manjimup, is the centre of a 400-sq-km forest, whose inhabitants include rare mammals such as the numbat, tammar wallaby and southern brown bandicoot. While drop-in visitors aren't encouraged, you can book through **DEC** (☎ 9771 7988) in Manjimup to stay at the ecology centre there.

Graphiti Café (☎ 9772 1283; Graphite Rd; mains $12; ☺ lunch Wed-Sun, breakfast Sun) On the Manjimup side of One Tree Bridge is this fantastic café, surrounded by karri forests. It makes a mean coffee and has a small menu of interesting food with creative veggie options such as pizza with pine nuts and blue cheese.

PEMBERTON

☎ 08 / pop 950

Deep in the karri forests, and at the centre of yet another promising wine industry, is the delightful town of Pemberton. A few days here is time well spent.

Information

DEC (☎ 9776 1207; Kennedy St; ☺ 8am-4.30pm) Has detailed information on the many local parks, and also stocks the useful Pemberton Bushwalks brochure ($3.95).
Pemberton Telecentre (Brockman St) Internet access.
Visitors centre (☎ 9776 1133; www.pembertontourist .com.au; Brockman St; ☺ 9am-5pm) Includes a pioneer museum and karri-forest discovery centre; it's also the place for Transwa bookings.

THE SOUTHWEST

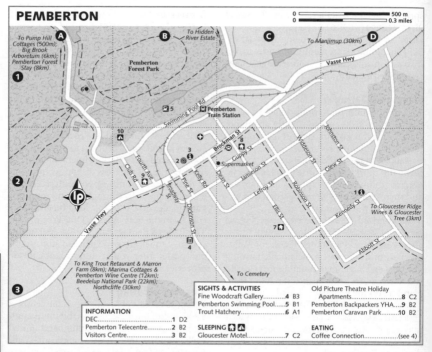

Sights & Activities

The national park forests around Pemberton are simply stunning. Aim to spend at least a day, or preferably two, driving the well-marked **Karri Forest Explorer** tracks, walking the trails, and picnicking in the green depths (see opposite).

The red wines of Pemberton's burgeoning wine industry attract favourable comparison to those from Burgundy; check at the visitors centre for wineries open to visitors. The **Pemberton Wine Centre** (☎ 9776 1211; www.marima .com.au; 🕙 9am-5pm), in Warren National Park, offers tastings of most local wines, and can

---

PURCHASE A PARK PASS

Most of the national parks around Pemberton charge a $10 entry fee per vehicle. If you plan to visit more than three parks in the state, take advantage of the all-park passes. A four-week pass costs $35; an annual pass is $75. Any Department of Environment & Conservation (DEC) office, and most visitors centres, sell them.

---

pack a mixed box to your taste (its attached café makes a mean local cheese platter).

In town, amid lush gardens, the **Fine Woodcraft Gallery** (☎ 9776 1399; Dickinson St; 🕙 9am-5pm) sells beautiful wooden objects, and art and craftworks – from alpaca felt hats to fine prints – made by highly skilled artisans.

The scenic **Pemberton Tramway** (☎ 9776 1322; www.pemtram.com.au) was built between 1929 and 1933. Trams leave Pemberton train station for Warren River (adult/child $18/9) at 10.45am and 2pm. The route travels through lush karri and marri forests with occasional photo stops; a commentary is also provided and it's fun, if noisy. A steam train makes the old sawmill trip to Eastbrook (adult/child $23.50/11.50) during school holidays.

The natural and pretty **Pemberton Swimming Pool**, surrounded by karri trees, is ideal on a hot day. A nearby **trout hatchery** supplies fish for the state's rivers.

Tours

The **Pemberton Hiking Company** (☎ 9776 1559; www.perbertonwa.com) runs well-regarded (and environmentally sound) walks through forest, clear rivers and sand dunes; half-day tours start at $40 per person. It also plans longer hikes, canoeing or tubing trips, night hikes, and trips for special-needs travellers.

Pemberton Discovery Tours (☎ 9776 0484; www .pembertondiscoverytours.com.au) operates half-day 4WD tours to the Warren and D'Entrecasteaux National Parks and other parks around Pemberton (adult/child $75/50). If you have your own 4WD you're welcome to tag along.

Wandering Vintage (☎ 9776 1757; www.wandering vintage.com.au) wanders though forest and wineries every afternoon; the half-day tour is $65. If a boat is more your style, try **Donnelly River Cruises** (☎ 0427 771018; www.donnellyrivercruises.com.au) for a half-day tour (adult/child $55/35) that takes in a visual feast from the karri forests to the cliffs of the Southern Ocean.

Sleeping
BUDGET
Pemberton Backpackers YHA (☎ 9776 1105; pemberton backpackers@wn.com.au; 7 Brockman St; dm/s/d/cottage $19/35/51/70; 🖳) This friendly backpackers, right in the centre of town, has a self-contained cottage that can sleep up to eight people over the road; the cottage is popular, so book ahead if you can.

Pemberton Forest Stay (☎ 9776 1153; Stirling Rd, Pimlea; dm/s/cabins $21/30/65) This forest getaway, a former timber workers' village, with good cabins and a forest backdrop, is at Pimlea, 9km from Pemberton; you need your own wheels to get here.

Pemberton Caravan Park (☎ 9776 1300; fax 9776 1800; Pump Hill Rd; camp sites $22, cabins $60-80) Set in a shady clearing beside a creek, this pretty camp site has good-value cabins and is a walk away from Pemberton's natural swimming pool.

MIDRANGE
Gloucester Motel (☎ 9776 1266; Ellis St; s/d $75/85) Best choice of the motels in town – it's off the main road and the verandas aren't quite on the car park. Sadie's restaurant on-site is popular and there's a decent choice on the bar menu (try 'Ian's Butt Kickin Chilli') for around $15.

Pump Hill Farm Cottages (☎ 9776 1379; www.pump hill.com.au; Pump Hill Rd; cottages $105-245) Families will love this bush property, where kids (add $12 to the cottage rate per day for each one) are taken on a daily hay ride to feed the animals, including donkeys, cows, goats and nosy ducks. Child-free folk will enjoy the ambience of the lovely, private, well-equipped cottages too.

Old Picture Theatre Holiday Apartments (☎ 9776 1513; www.oldpicturetheatre.com.au; cnr Ellis & Guppy Sts, d $110; 🐾) The town's old cinema has been revamped into lovely self-contained, spacious apartments with lots of jarrah detail and black-and-white movie photos; fantastic value.

TOP END
Marima Cottages (☎ 9776 1211; www.marima.com.au; Old Vasse Rd; cottages $150-180) Right in the middle of Warren National Park, these country-style rammed-earth-and-cedar cottages with pot-belly stoves are a true getaway.

IF YOU GO DOWN TO THE WOODS TODAY

The **Karri Forest Explorer** drive wends its way along 86km of scenic roads, punctuated by glorious walks, magnificent individual trees, pretty bush camp sites and picnic areas, and lots of interpretive signage.

Its popular attractions include the **Gloucester Tree**, named after the Duke of Gloucester, who visited in 1946. It's a splendid fire-lookout tree, laddered with a spiral metal stairway; if you're feeling fit, make the scary 60m climb to the top. This is not for the faint-hearted! The **Dave Evans Bicentennial Tree**, tallest of the 'climbing trees' at 68m, is in Warren National Park, 11km south of Pemberton. Its tree-house cage weighs two tonnes and can sway up to 1.5m in either direction in strong winds; you have been warned. The Bicentennial Tree one-way loop leads via **Maiden Bush** to the **Heartbreak Trail**. It passes through 400-year-old karri stands, and nearby Drafty's Camp and Warren Campsite are delightful for overnighting or picnics.

The enchanting **Beedelup National Park**, 15km west of town on the Vasse Hwy, shouldn't be missed. There's a short, scenic walk that crosses Beedelup Brook near **Beedelup Falls**; the bridge was built from a karri log. There are numerous bird species to be found in and around the tall trees; at ground level the busy red-winged fairy wren is commonly seen in the undergrowth. North of town, **Big Brook Arboretum** features 'big' trees from all over the world.

The track loops on and off the main roads, so you can drive short sections at a time.

BONZER BACKROADS: D'ENTRECASTEAUX NATIONAL PARK

This quiet gem of a national park, named for French Admiral Bruny d'Entrecasteaux, who led an exploratory expedition here in 1792, stretches for 130kms along the coast 60km south of Pemberton. It's a complete contrast to the tall forests, with its wild stretches of heath, sand dunes, cliffs and beaches.

The park roads around **Windy Harbour** – a collection of ramshackle holiday shacks with names like 'Wywurk', and where you can camp as long as you have all your own provisions – are sealed, and a wild and (you guessed it) windy coastal walk stretches about 3km from Windy Harbour to Point d'Entrecasteaux.

A series of decent 4WD tracks lead in from the Pemberton-Northcliffe Rd to bush and beach camp sites; locals regularly go in to fish. On the way, the tiny timber town of **Northcliffe** has forest walks and a friendly cluster of library-cum-information-cum-museum buildings on the junction.

Eating

It's a rare menu around Pemberton that doesn't feature the local specialities, trout and marron.

Coffee Connection (☎ 9776 1159; Dickinson St; mains $8-10; ☺ breakfast & lunch) Attached to the Fine Woodcraft Gallery, this garden café makes good coffee and maybe the cheapest breakfasts in town.

King Trout Restaurant & Marron Farm (☎ 9776 1352; cnr Northcliffe Rd & Old Vasse Rd; ☺ 9.30am-5pm) The menu at this café showcases trout and marron prepared in more ways than seems possible, and is part of a great combination of food and fishing activities. A daily farm tour (adult/child $5/3; 11am) may whet your appetite to hire a rod and hook your own lunch; it can be cleaned and cooked on site for a small fee. A King Trout Platter ($55 for two) can to your accommodation.

Gloucester Ridge Wines (☎ 9776 1035; www .gloucester-ridge.com.au; Burma Rd; mains $25; ☺ lunch) Possibly the leader in local lunches, this restaurant produces some of the best food in the region, and an afternoon cuppa on the sunny veranda is a welcome break from hiking the forest trails.

SHANNON NATIONAL PARK

The 535-sq-km Shannon National Park is on the South West Hwy, 53km south of Man-jimup. The Shannon was once the site of WA's biggest timber mill (it closed in 1968), and exotic plants, including deciduous trees from the northern hemisphere, are some of the few reminders of the old settlement.

The 48km **Great Forest Trees Drive** takes in pretty country – tune in to 100FM for a commentary or buy the *Great Forest Trees Drive* ($14.45) from DEC. It's a one-way loop, split in two by the highway; start at the park dayuse area on the north of the highway. From here you can also take an easy 3.5km walk to the Shannon Dam (checking out the quokka observation deck on the way), and a steeper even 5.5km circuit to Mokare's Rock, where there is a boardwalk and great views; further along, the 8km-return **Great Forest Trees Walk**, crosses the Shannon River. Off the southern part of the drive, boardwalks give access to stands of giant karri at **Snake Gully** and **Big Tree Grove**. In the park's southwest, a 6km return walking track (only for the hardy) links Boorara Tree with a lookout point over Lane Poole Falls.

There is one fine and sizable camping area in the spot where the original timber milling town used to be, and the self-contained bunkhouse Shannon Lodge is available for groups of up to eight people. For information and bookings contact the **DEC** (☎ 9776 1207) in Pemberton.

South Coast

Standing on the cliffs of the wild South Coast as the winds come in off the southern ocean and the waves pound below is a truly elemental experience. And on calm days, when the sea is varied shades of aqua and the glorious white sand beaches lie pristine and welcoming it's different again; either way you're about as close to nature as you can get.

Stunning coastal national parks in the region include Fitzgerald River and Cape Le Grand while, inland, the Porongurups and Stirling Ranges offer great bushwalking and climbing. If you're seeking solitude, even busy holiday periods here in 'The Great Southern' are relaxed; for many it's just that bit too far from Perth, and the region rewards its visitors with time away from the crowds.

Marine visitors come this way, too. The winter months bring migrating whales, some simply passing by while others calve and stay with their babies in the shallows of sheltered bays. And you know you're at the end of the continent when watching seals and sea lions on the off-shore islands of the Recherche Archipelago. When you need a change from the great outdoors, Albany – the earliest European settlement in the state – has a wealth of colonial history, and pretty rural towns like Denmark and quiet coastal Esperance invite you to sit back with a glass of fine local wine and watch the world go by.

HIGHLIGHTS

- Walk among and above the giant tingle trees in Walpole's Valley of the Giants' **Tree Top Walk** (p134)

- Whale-watch between July and October in Albany's **King George Sound** (p143)

- Fish for smaller fry in the region's sheltered bays, like those of quiet **Stokes National Park** (p151)

- Hike among the tall trees and granite out-crops of The Pass and Devil's Slide trails in the **Porongurup National Park** (p138)

- Tread lightly by bush camping at St Mary Inlet, in glorious **Fitzgerald River National Park** (p147)

- Wander through wildflowers along the walking tracks of **Point Ann** (p147) in Fitzgerald River National Park

- Relive the small-town life in some of beloved Australian writer Tim Winton's novels along the coastline of **Albany** (p141)

- Swim, surf and soak in the sun at the squeaky-clean beaches in **Cape Le Grand National Park** (p151)

SOUTH COAST

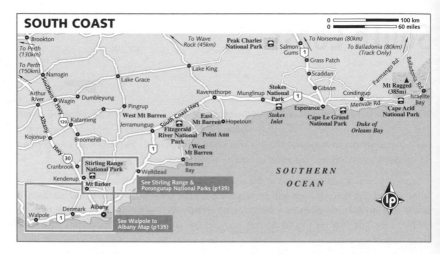

SOUTH COAST

See Stirling Range & Porongurup National Parks (p139)

See Walpole to Albany Map (p135)

Getting There & Away

SkyWest Airlines (☎ 1300 660 088; www.skywest.com.au) flies daily from Perth to both Albany and Esperance.

Transwa (☎ 1300 662 205; www.transwa.wa.gov.au) runs bus services between Perth and Denmark ($57 one way, eight hours), Albany ($48, six hours) and Esperance ($72, 10 hours); some services go via Walpole. You can also travel by train to Bunbury, then by coach from Bunbury to Albany.

Transwa also runs a service several times a week between Kalgoorlie-Boulder to Esperance ($46, five hours).

Goldrush Tours Golden Triangle Tour (☎ 1800 620 441; www.goldrushtours.com.au) offers a hop-on hop-off bus pass ($475) between Perth, Margaret River and the southwest coast and forests, Albany and Esperance on the south coast, and up to Kalgoorlie.

To make the most of this region, especially its national parks, your own wheels really are the best option.

WALPOLE & NORNALUP

☎ 08 / pop 450 & 50

The peaceful twin inlets of Walpole and Nornalup are close to majestic forests of giant tingle trees, including the famous Tree Top Walk. The heavily forested Walpole-Nornalup National Park, covering 180 sq km around Nornalup Inlet and the town of Walpole, contains beaches, rugged coastline, inlets, the Nuyts Wilderness area and the magnificent Valley of the Giants (when you're under the tall forest

canopy you'll understand the name). The South West Hwy almost meets the coast at the two inlets, then becomes the South Coast Hwy.

The helpful Walpole **visitors centre** (☎ 9840 1111; www.southernforests.com.au; South Coast Hwy; ☒ 9am-5pm Mon-Sat, 9am-4pm Sun) is in Pioneer Cottage. Contact the **Department of Environment & Conservation** (DEC; ☎ 9840 1027; South Coast Hwy) for national park and bushwalking information.

Sights & Activities

The **Tree Top Walk** (☎ 9840 8263; adult/child $6/2.50; ☒ 9am-4.15pm, 8am-5.15pm Christmas school holidays) has become Walpole's main drawcard, and it is not hard to see why. A 600m-long ramp rises from the floor of the valley, allowing visitors access high into the canopy of the giant tingle trees; you really are walking 'through' the tree tops. At its highest point, the ramp is 40m above the ground and the views below and above are simply stunning. It's on a gentle incline so it's easy to walk, and is even accessible by assisted wheelchair.

The ramp is an engineering feat in itself, though vertigo sufferers might have a few problems; it's designed to sway gently in the breeze to mimic life in the tree tops. At ground level, the **Ancient Empire** boardwalk meanders around and through the base of veteran red tingles, some of which are 16m in circumference, including one that soars to 46m.

This is part of the **Valley of the Giants** (Walpole-Nornalup) national park: inland giants are the red, yellow and Rates tingle trees, and closer to the coast is the red flowering gum.

Pleasant, shady paths lead through the forests, which are frequented by bushwalkers.

There are numerous good walking tracks around, including a section of the **Bibbulmun Track**, which passes through Walpole to Coalmine Beach (two hours). There are a number of scenic drives, including the **Knoll Drive**, 3km east of Walpole; the **Valley of the Giants Rd**; and through pastoral country to **Mt Frankland**, 29km north of Walpole. Here you can climb to the summit for panoramic views or walk around the trail at its base. Opposite Knoll Drive, Hilltop Rd leads to a **giant tingle tree**; this road continues to the **Circular Pool** on the Frankland River, a popular canoeing spot.

A trip to Walpole should include the popular **WOW Wilderness Cruise** (☎ 9840 1036; www.wow wilderness.com.au), through the inlets and river systems. This magnificent landscape and its ecology are brought to life with anecdotes about Aboriginal settlement, salmon fishers and shipwrecked pirates. A 2½-hour trip (adult/child $35/15) leaves daily at 10am.

The Frankland River, lined with karri and tingle trees, is peaceful and great for **canoeing**. Hire canoes from **Nornalup Riverside Chalets** (☎ 9840 1107; South Coast Hwy, Nornalup) for $20 per hour or $45/60 per half/full day.

Parrot Jungle Bird & Reptile Park (☎ 9840 8335; Bow Bridge; 🕙 9.30am-4.30pm), off the South Coast Hwy at Bow Bridge, is an aviary with a host of native birds, including Major Mitchell and black cockatoos, as well as exotics such as Amazon rainforest macaws. The scaly reptilian residents are handled daily at 2pm.

> ### BONZER BACKROADS – THE ROAD TO MANDALAY
>
> About 13km west of Walpole, at Crystal Springs, is an 8km gravel road to **Mandalay Beach**. Here, the *Mandalay*, a Norwegian barque, was wrecked on the beach in 1911. As the sand gradually erodes with storms, the wreck eerily appears every 10 years or so, in shallow water that is walkable at low tide (check out the photos at Walpole visitors centre). The beach is glorious, often deserted, and accessed by an impressive boardwalk across sand dunes and cliffs; it's now part of D'Entrecasteaux National Park.

Midway between Nornalup and Peaceful Bay, check out **Conspicuous Cliffs**. It's a great spot for **whale-watching** from July to November, with a boardwalk, hilltop lookout and steep-ish 800m walk to the beach.

Sleeping & Eating

For camping sites in Walpole-Nornalup National Park, including bush sites at Crystal Springs and huts at Fernhook Falls or Mt Frankland, use the honesty registration and fee boxes on site. Most accommodation is designed for self-caterers.

Coalmine Beach (☎ 9840 1026; www.coalminebeach .com.au; Knoll Dr, Walpole; unpowered/powered sites per person from $13/16, cabins from $65) You couldn't get a better location than this, under shady trees above the beach. In quiet periods you might be

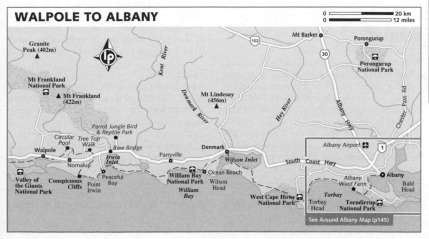

WALPOLE TO ALBANY

See Around Albany Map (p145)

lucky to hit a free fish night, where the owners cook up the day's catch.

Walpole Lodge (☎ 9840 1244; www.walpolelodge .com.au; cnr Pier St & Park Ave; dm/s/d $20/35/65; 🖳) This popular place is open plan and informal, with great info boards around the walls and casual, cheery owners.

Tingle All Over YHA (☎ 9840 1041; tingleallover2000@ yahoo.com.au; Nockolds St; dm/s/d $22/38/50) Exercise your brain with the giant chess set in the garden at this clean, basic option near the highway.

Rest Point Holiday Village (☎ 9840 1032; www .restpoint.com.au; Rest Point; camp sites $22, cabins from $65) On wide lawns with direct waterfrontage, this is a light and bright camping area.

Nornalup Riverside Chalets (☎ /fax 9840 1107; Riverside Dr, Nornalup; chalets $80-125) Stay a night in sleepy Nornalup in these comfortable, colourful self-contained chalets, just a rod's throw from the fish in the Frankland River. One chalet is adapted for disabled access.

Riverside Retreat (☎ 9840 1255; www.riversideretreat .com.au; chalets $99) Set off the road on the banks of the Frankland River, these quiet, private and well-equipped chalets are great value, with pot-bellied stoves for cosy winter warmth.

In Walpole, stop by for a casual coffee at Top Deck Café, or a filling counter meal at the Walpole Hotel Motel, both on the main road. Better still, head to **Thurlby Herb Farm** (☎ 9840 1249; www .thurlbyherb.com.au; Gardiner Rd), 14km north of town, which serves up delicious light lunches and cakes – accompanied by fresh-picked herbal teas – in a pretty café overlooking the garden. It also distils its own essential oils, and makes herb-based products including soap. The gift shop has an eclectic collection of goodies.

DENMARK
☎ 08 / pop 4000

There are many good reasons why Denmark, 55km west of Albany, attracts folk looking to opt out from city life – gorgeous coastline, rolling hills, magnificent forests and a vibrant artistic community. There are some fine beaches in the area, especially Ocean Beach, a surfer's delight, and, in the 17-sq-km **William Bay National Park**, the sheltered **Greens Pool** and **Elephant Rocks** with a backdrop of coastal dunes, granite boulders and heath land. The area also has some notable wineries, including Howard Park and West Cape Howe Wines.

Denmark was established to supply timber for the goldfields. Known by Noongar people as Koorabup (place of the black swan), there's

evidence of early Aboriginal settlement in the 3000-year-old fish traps found in Wilson Inlet.

Information
Denmark Environment Centre (☎ 9848 1644; Strickland St) Has an extensive library and bookshop.
Telecentre (🕒 10am-4pm Mon-Fri) Next door to the visitors centre, this place has internet access.
Visitors centre (☎ 9848 2055; www.denmark.com.au; Strickland St; 🕒 9am-5pm)

Sights & Activities
Surfers and anglers usually waste no time in heading to rugged **Ocean Beach**. If you're keen to try surfing, accredited local instructor Mike Neunuebel gives **surf lessons** (☎ 9848 2057) from $40. For a gentler experience **Denmark Dingy Hire** (☎ 0429 421 786; 🕒 Sep-May) can set you up with boats for the river.

Walk the **Mokare Heritage Trail** (3km along the Denmark River) or the **Wilson Inlet Trail** (6km starting at the river mouth). Put everything into perspective at **Mt Shadforth Lookout**, with its coastal view. **Mt Shadforth Rd**, which begins in the centre of town and finishes up on the South Coast Hwy west of town makes a great scenic drive, as does the longer pastoral loop of **Scotsdale Rd**. Potter along these, taking your pick of attractions including alpaca farms, wineries, cheese farms and galleries.

If you need some sweetening, swing by **Bartholomews Meadery** (☎ 9840 9349; South Coast Hwy; 🕒 9am-4.30pm), about 16km west of Denmark. The house mead (honey wine) is internationally award-winning, the honey ice cream is delicious, and the showroom takes a holistic approach to bees and beeswax for health. Check out the lovingly made mudbrick buildings (including the loo).

Tours
Visit West Cape Howe National Park ($75) or take short local tours ($25) with **Little River Discovery Tours** (☎ 9848 2604), operated by long-term resident naturalists who also run 4WD day tours to the Valley of the Giants ($81).

Denmark Bike Adventures (☎ 9848 3300; blue .wren@bigpond.com; per person from $30) offers drop-off/ ride back walking and cycling tours along the coast, wineries and forests; a great way to see the country at your own pace. Alternatively, cruise the islets of Wilson Inlet with **MV Jasmin B** (☎ 9840 8183; jasmine.b@bordernet.com.au); 2½ hour cruises run twice daily on most days.

Festivals & Events

Three times a year (December, January and Easter) Denmark hosts a colourful **market day** on the parkland by the river, with an unusual range of high-quality craft stalls, music and food. An annual **Festival of Voice** (www.dfov.org .au) – performances and workshops – takes place in June.

Sleeping

Riverbend Caravan Park (☎ 9848 1107; rivabend@ omninet.net.au; East River Rd; unpowered sites $14-20, /powered sites $17-23, cabins from $80) About 2km from town, on a quiet stretch of river, this lovely shaded site has excellent, well-equipped cabins with private verandas and a veggie garden.

Rivermouth Caravan Park (☎ 9848 1262; Inlet Dr; unpowered/powered $16/18.50, cabins $50-70; P) Ideally located for nautical pursuits, this park has sites along the Wilson Inlet beside the boat ramp.

Blue Wren Travellers' Rest YHA (☎ 9848 3300; http://bluewren.batcave.net; 17 Price St; dm/tw/d $19/48/55) Chooks live under this little timber house and the goofy house dog is spoilt by everyone. Great info panels cover the walls, and it's small enough to have a homey feel.

Ocean Beach Caravan Park (☎ 9848 1106; Ocean Beach; unpowered/powered sites $19/22; cabins $55-85) Playgrounds and space for the kids are great at this big park, popular with surfers. The cheaper cabins are *very* basic.

Denmark Waterfront (☎ 9848 1147; www.denmark waterfront.com.au; 63 Inlet Dr; lodge $75, motel $85-110, cottages from $130) With great views of the water through the gum trees, there's a range of accommodation here. The four quiet lodge rooms – tucked off the road, with a communal kitchen and great views from the balconies – are good value.

Gum Grove Chalets (☎ 9848 1378; Ocean Beach Rd; chalets from $80) These self-contained bush chalets, about 3km south of Denmark, are tatty but clean. It's good value for families or groups of friends; most sleep up to six people.

Willowleigh B&B (☎ 9848 1089; kenannrn@wn.com .au; Kearsley Rd; r $100) Enjoy the two acres of gorgeous gardens from your conservatory or veranda at this B&B on the edge of town.

Karri Mia Resort (☎ 9848 2233; www.karrimia.com .au; Mt Shadforth Rd; bungalows from $180; ⊠) With magnificent views, this property boasts tastefully furnished, self-contained bungalows.

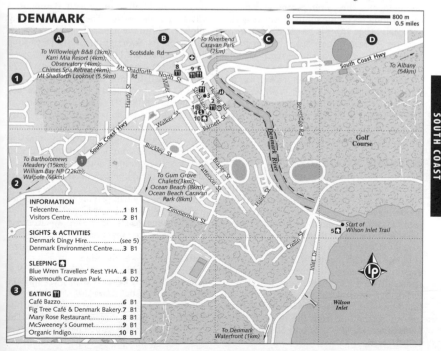

Chimes Spa Retreat (☎ 9848 2255; www.chimes.com
.au; Mt Shadforth Rd; r $230-355; ☒) Architect-designed
and decorated with Indonesian furniture; take
a look at the beautiful breakfast room. A day
spa (book ahead for pampering) completes the
five-star offering. Prices depend on the view,
the size of your bed and the number of bubbles
in your bath. No children under 14.

Eating

McSweeney's Gourmet (☎ 9848 2362; Strickland St; sandwiches from $6; ☒ breakfast & lunch) Stop here for the
best coffee in town and beautiful gourmet
sandwiches.

Fig Tree Café (☎ 9848 2051; 27 Strickland St; lunches $12;
☒ breakfast & dinner) Unhurried best describes the
style at this coffee shop, popular with locals for
long weekend breakfasts in the courtyard.

Café Bazzo (☎ 9848 3799; Holling Rd; lunches $15;
☒ breakfast & lunch, dinner Fri & Sat) A funky café with
African drums, artwork on the walls and a garden courtyard; sometimes there's live music.

Mary Rose Restaurant (☎ 9848 1951; 11 North St; light
lunch $15; ☒ breakfast & lunch Tue-Sun) After a wander
through the Old Butter Factory craft gallery,
take time for lunch – bruschetta with roast
pumpkin, blue cheese and pecans, perhaps? –
or afternoon tea on the sunny outdoors deck.

Organic Indigo (☎ 9848 2999; Strickland St; veggie
mains $16; ☒ dinner Thu-Sun) Spicy Indian food,
organic and served with love; there are lots
of veggie choices.

Observatory (☎ 9848 2600; Mt Shadforth Rd, Karri
Mia; mains $20-29; ☒ lunch & dinner) With views to
the edge of the world this eatery is a treat.
Light lunches ($13) or at least coffee and cake
are a must; check out the occasional Sunday
afternoon live music sessions.

MOUNTAIN NATIONAL PARKS

Northeast of Denmark and almost due north of
Albany are the spectacular, mountainous Stirling Range and Porongurup National Parks. A
good time to visit these is late spring and early
summer, when it is beginning to warm up and
the wildflowers are at their best. From June to
August it is cold and wet and hail is not uncommon, though the chill winter landscape of
swirling mist has its own magic. Occasionally
snow falls on the top of the ranges.

Further information on these parks can
be obtained from **DEC** (☎ 9842 4500; 120 Albany
Hwy) in Albany, or from the rangers at the
Porongurups (☎ 9853 1095) and **Stirling Ranges**
(☎ 9827 9230).

Porongurup National Park

The 24-sq-km Porongurup National Park is
12km long and has 1100-million-year-old granite outcrops, panoramic views, beautiful scenery, large karri trees and excellent bushwalks.

Karris grow in the deep-red soil (known
as karri loam) of the range's upper slopes;
nurtured by run-off from the granite, this
is 100km east of their usual range. The rich
forest also supports 65 species of orchid in
spring and, in September and October, there
are wildflowers among the trees.

Bushwalks range from the 100m **Tree-in-the-
Rock** stroll (an amazing thing, and just what it
sounds like) to the harder **Hayward and Nancy
Peaks** (four hours). The **Devil's Slide** (two hours)
is a walk of contrasts that takes you through a
pass of karri forest and onto the stumpy vegetation of the granite. Even the smell is different up
here, with views across the plains below. These
walks start from the main day-use area, and the
Castle and **Balancing Rocks** (two hours, popular
with fit families!) are 2km further southeast. A
6km **scenic drive** along the northern edge of the
park starts near the ranger's residence.

The few accommodation and eating options in the small community of Porongurup
village are all terrific. There is no camping
allowed within the national park but you can
camp on its doorstep at pretty **Porongurup
Range Tourist Park** (☎ 9853 1057; www.porongurup
rangetouristpark.com.au; unpowered/powered sites $15/20,
cabins $65; ☒). It's one of the few places that
doesn't take credit cards. The **Porongurup Shop
& Tearooms** (☎ 9853 1110; www.porongurupinn.com.au;
d/apt $25/60, cottages $80) is a gem, run by long-
term residents Di and Scott. The place has
grown higgledy-piggledy over the years to
include several rooms with shared facilities
and a self-contained cottage out the back,
along with great home-cooked food (lunches
$13) with veggies from the organic garden.
Kids will have a ball playing with the guinea
pigs and getting to know some locals.

Porongurup Chalets (☎ 9853 1255; www.porongurup
.com; chalets per night/week from $70/350) has several
comfortable A-frame chalets in this forest
setting – great weekly value.

One of the oldest country retreats in WA,
Karribank Country Retreat (☎ 9853 1022; www.karri
bank.com.au; r $90, chalets from $100; cottages from $164)
offers beautifully decorated rooms in the historic house, and its surrounding cottages. The
lovely property and garden has great views of
the Porongurups plus a delightful restaurant.

STIRLING RANGE & PORONGURUP NATIONAL PARKS

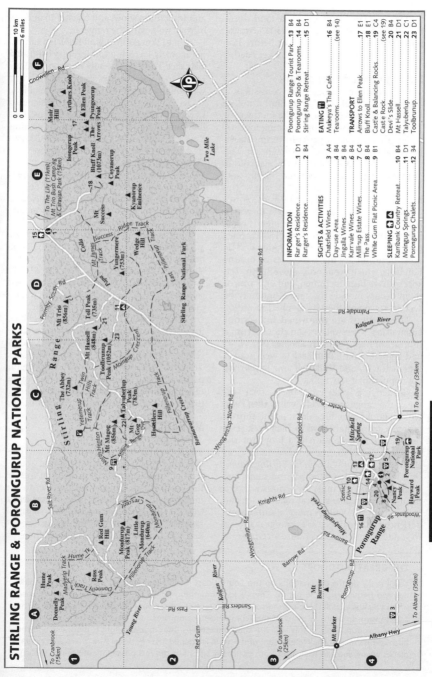

INFORMATION
Ranger's Residence..................	1 D1
Ranger's Residence..................	2 B4

SIGHTS & ACTIVITIES
Chatsfield Wines........................	3 A4
Day-use Area.............................	4 B4
Jingalla Wines............................	5 B4
Karrvale Wines..........................	6 B4
Millinup Estate Wines................	7 C4
The ?ass....................................	8 B4
White Gum Flat Picnic Area......	9 B1

SLEEPING
Karribank Country Retreat.........	10 B4
Moingup Springs........................	11 D1
Porongurup Chalets...................	12 34

Porongurup Range Tourist Park..13 B4	
Porongurup Shop & Tearooms....14 B4	
Stiring Range Retreat................	15 D1

EATING
Maleeya's Thai Café..................	16 B4
Tearooms................................	(see 14)

TRANSPORT
Arrows to Ellen Peak................	17 E1
Bluff Knoll................................	18 E1
Castle & Balancing Rocks..........	19 C4
Caste Rock...............................	(see 19)
Devil's Slide..............................	20 B4
Mt Hassell................................	21 D1
Talyuberlup...............................	22 C1
Toolbrunup...............................	23 D1

SOUTH COAST

If you're a fan of authentic Thai food, don't miss **Maleeya's Thai Café** (☎ 9853 1123; 1376 Porongurup Rd; mains $20; ⏱ Thu-Sun). It's just before Porongurup township on the Mt Barker road.

Stirling Range National Park

This 1156-sq-km national park consists of a single chain of peaks (including Bluff Knoll, at 1073m, which is the highest in the southwest), 10km wide and 65km long. Running most of its length are isolated peaks towering above broad valleys covered in shrubs and heath. The range is widely noted for its spectacular colour changes through blues, reds and purples and was named, in 1835, after Captain James Stirling, first governor of the Swan River Colony.

Due to the altitude and climate there are many localised plants in the Stirlings. It is estimated that there are more than 1500 species of native plants, 60 of which are endemic. The most beautiful are the Darwinias or mountain bells, which occur only above 300m. Ten species have been identified, and only one of them occurs outside the range; one may be seen in season on the Mt Talyuberlup walk.

The Stirlings are renowned for serious **bushwalking**. Keen walkers can choose from a number of high points: **Toolbrunup** (for views and a good climb), **Bluff Knoll** (a well-graded tourist track), and **Mt Hassell** and **Talyuberlup** are popular half-day walks.

Challenging walks cross the eastern sector of the range from **Bluff Knoll to Ellen Peak**, which should take three days, or the shorter traverse from the **Arrows to Ellen Peak** (two days). The latter option is a loop but the former, from Bluff Knoll, will require a car shuttle. *Mountain Walks in the Stirling Range*, by AT Morphet, has detailed mud-maps and track info, and is a must for serious walkers; it's usually available at local roadhouses and visitors centres. Walkers must be suitably experienced and equipped as the range is subject to sudden drops in temperature, driving rain and sometimes snow; and register in and out of your walk with the rangers.

About 12km north of Bluff Knoll is a surprising anomaly – a replica 16th-century **Dutch windmill** called The Lily. The only working windmill in Australia, it operates as a flour mill and was built by an enterprising Dutchman, Pleun Hitzert. Replica Dutch cottages of the same era sit comfortably next to it, making the bush look like something out of a Rembrandt etching. You can stay and eat at **Lily** (☎ 9827 9205; www.thelily.com.au; Chester Pass Rd, Borden; cottage from $119; ⏱ closed Mon), where lunch in the restaurant – the relocated and precisely reconstructed 1924 Gnowangerup railway station – is a delight, and may be your only chance to eat real Dutch apple cake ($6.50) in rural WA. You can also tour the windmill (adult/child $5/2).

You can camp in the National Park at **Moingup Springs** on Chester Pass Rd, near the Toolbrunup Peak turn-off. Another good option is **Mt Trio Bush Camping & Caravan Park** (☎ 9827 9270; www.mounttrio.com.au; Salt River Rd; unpowered/powered per person $10/12), a big block of bush on a farm property close to the walking tracks of the western half of the park. There are decent facilities, including wheelchair access to the showers.

The well-run **Stirling Range Retreat** (☎ 9827 9229; www.stirlingrange.com.au; Chester Pass Rd; camp/caravan sites $9/22, dm/d $19/45, cabins $79-115) is on the park's northern boundary. It has a wide range of accommodation, from a backpackers lodge to self-contained, rammed-earth cabins.

MT BARKER

☎ 08 / pop 1730

You'll pass through the town of Mt Barker – 55km northeast of Denmark, 64km southwest of the Stirling Range and 20km west of the Porongurup Range – on the way to the mountain national parks. The **visitors centre** (☎ 9851 1163; www.mountbarkertourismwa.com.au; 622 Albany Hwy; ⏱ 9am-5pm Mon-Fri, 9am-3pm Sat, 10am-3pm Sun) is in the restored train station. There's a

---

THE GREAT OUTDOORS

You'll really do the destinations on the South Coast justice (and yourself a favour) by camping out and getting closer to nature. There's just something about the smell of the morning bush when you wake, with the birdsong so close. No tent or campervan? No worries. Make use of the on-site vans or cabins in many of the (commercial) camp sites.

Our favourite spots in this area are the Porongurups (that morning light is glorious), and the bush camp site at St Mary Inlet, near Point Ann, in Fitzgerald River National Park (there aren't many places where you can walk 10m from your tent and have the real possibility of seeing whales).

panoramic view of the area from the **Mt Barker Lookout**, 5km south of town.

The town was settled in the 1830s and the convict-built 1868 police station and gaol have been preserved as a **museum** (Albany Hwy; adult/child $5/free; 10am-4pm Sat, Sun & school holidays).

All 77 species of banksia have found a home at the **Banksia Farm** (9851 1770; www.banksiafarm .com.au; Pearce Rd; adult/child $5.50/2; 9.30am-4.30pm). You can wander around alone or take a guided 'touch, taste and observe' tour at 10.30am and 2.30pm.

Southwest of Mt Barker, on the Egerton-Warburton estate, is the gorgeous **St Werburgh's Chapel**, built between 1872 and 1873. The wrought-iron chancel screen and altar rail were shaped on the property.

ALBANY

 08 / pop 28,600

Hugging the calm waters of King George Sound, Albany is the oldest European settlement in the state. The commercial centre of the Great Southern region, it was established in 1826, three years before Perth. The area was previously occupied by Aborigines and there is evidence of their presence, especially around Oyster Harbour.

Albany's raison d'être is its sheltered harbour, which made it a thriving whaling port. Whales are still a part of the Albany experience, but these days as seen through a camera lens rather than at the business end of a harpoon. Later the city became a coaling station for British ships bound for the east coast; during WWI it was the mustering point for transport ships of the 1st Australian Imperial Force heading for Egypt and the Gallipoli campaign.

The coastline around Albany features some of Australia's most rugged and spectacular scenery. Many pristine beaches mean you don't have to compete for sand space – try (misnamed) Misery Beach, or Ledge Bay and Nanarup Beach. The **Bibbulmun Track** ends (or starts) here, just outside the visitors centre. Walkers' log books are kept in the visitors centre; the exhausted and/or exuberant comments make great reading.

Orientation & Information

The main drag, York St, leads down from Albany Hwy to the harbour foreshore. Middleton Rd, starting from the northern end of York St, is the most direct route to Middleton Beach.

The informative **visitors centre** (1800 644 088, 9841 1088; www.amazingalbany.com; Proudlove Pde;

 9am-5pm) is in the old train station. For national parks information, visit **DEC** (9842 4500; 120 Albany Hwy). You can check your email at several places around town.

Sights

Albany has some fine colonial buildings. Take a stroll down **Stirling Tce** – noted for its Victorian shop fronts, the **Old Post Office** and **Courthouse** – and up York Street, where you'll see the lovely **St John's Anglican Church** and the **Town Hall**. A guided walking-tour brochure of colonial buildings is available from the visitors centre.

One of the most impressive buildings was turned into the **Albany Residency Museum** (9841 4844; www.museum.wa.gov.au; Residency Rd; admission by donation; 10am-5pm). Built in the 1850s as the home of the resident magistrate, the museum's displays tell seafaring stories, and explain local flora and fauna and Aboriginal artefacts. The 'Sea & Touch' display is a great hands-on experience for children and adults; it focuses on the marine and animal world (think sea urchins, possum fur and bones) and has a fascinating lighthouse optic display. Next to the museum is a full-scale replica of the brig **Amity** (adult/child $3/1; 9am-5pm), the ship that carried Albany's founding party from Sydney in 1826.

Opposite the museum, the 1851 **Old Gaol** (9841 1401; Lower Stirling Tce; adult/child $4/2.50; 10am-4.15pm) was constructed as a hiring depot for ticket-of-leave convicts. Most were in private employment by 1855 so it was closed until 1872, when it was extended and reopened as a civil gaol. These days it's a folk museum. Nearby is the 1832 wattle-and-daub **Patrick Taylor Cottage**.

The National Trust–owned **Old Farm at Strawberry Hill** (9841 3735; 170 Middleton Rd; adult/child $5/3; 10am-5pm) is one of the oldest farms in WA, established in 1827 as the town's government farm. The homestead features antiques and artefacts that belonged to the original owner, and lovely gardens and tearooms.

The **Vancouver Arts Centre** (9841 9260; Vancouver St; admission free; 10am-4pm), in an 1887 building formerly used as a hospital, is the centre of the area's arts community. It has regular touring exhibitions and cultural events.

On Middleton Rd you can't miss one of Albany's icons, the kitsch **Dog Rock**, which looks like a dog's head (the locals have even painted on a dog collar to reinforce the point).

As Albany was a strategic port, its vulnerability to attack loomed as a potential threat to

SOUTH COAST

Australia's security. The **Princess Royal Fortress** (Mt Adelaide; adult/child $4/2; ⏰ 9am-5pm) was built on Mt Adelaide in 1893. The restored buildings, gun emplacements and views make a rewarding visit. Particularly poignant are the photos of the troop transports on their way to Gallipoli.

There are more fine views over the coast and inland from the twin peaks, **Mt Clarence** and **Mt Melville**, which overlook the town. On top of Mt Clarence is the **Desert Mounted Corps Memorial**, originally erected in Port Said as a memorial to the events of WWI. It was brought here when the Suez crisis in 1956 made colonial reminders less than popular in Egypt. To climb Mt Clarence follow the track accessible from the end of Grey St East; turn left, take the first turn

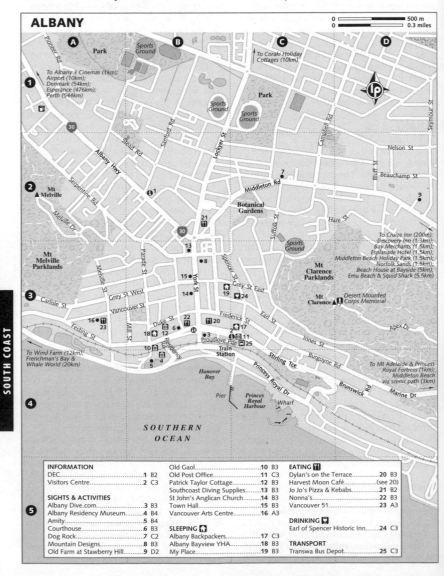

INFORMATION		
DEC	1	B2
Visitors Centre	2	C3
SIGHTS & ACTIVITIES		
Albany Dive.com	3	B3
Albany Residency Museum	4	B4
Amity	5	B4
Courthouse	6	B3
Dog Rock	7	C2
Mountain Designs	8	B3
Old Farm at Stawberry Hill	9	D2
Old Gaol	10	B3
Old Post Office	11	C3
Patrick Taylor Cottage	12	B3
Southcoast Diving Supplies	13	B3
St John's Anglican Church	14	B3
Town Hall	15	B3
Vancouver Arts Centre	16	A3
SLEEPING 🏠		
Albany Backpackers	17	B3
Albany Bayview YHA	18	B3
My Place	19	B3
EATING 🍴		
Dylan's on the Terrace	20	B3
Harvest Moon Café	(see 20)	
Jo Jo's Pizza & Kebabs	21	B2
Nonna's	22	B3
Vancouver 51	23	A3
DRINKING 🍷		
Earl of Spencer Historic Inn	24	C3
TRANSPORT		
Transwa Bus Depot	25	C3

on the right and follow the path by the water tanks. The walk is tough but the views make it worthwhile; take a picnic and enjoy a well-earned rest at the top. By car, take Apex Dr.

Activities

After whaling ended in 1978, whales slowly began returning to the waters of Albany. They're now here to the extent that it can sometimes be hard *not* to see **southern right** and **humpback whales** near the bays and coves of King George Sound from July to mid-October. **Silver Star Cruises** (☎ 0428 936 711; www.whales.com .au) and **Albany Whale Tours & Sail-A-Way** (☎ 0409 107 180) both run regular whale-watching trips (adult/child around $55/40) in season.

Other underwater fans enjoy **diving** on the artificial reef created by the scuttling of HMAS *Perth* (visit www.hmasperth.com.au for live webcam images of the wreck) in King George Sound in 2001. Dive with **Albany Dive .com** (☎ 9842 6886; www.albanydive.com; cnr York & Proud-love Sts) or **Southcoast Diving Supplies** (☎ 9841 7176; www.divealbany.com.au; 84b Serpentine Rd). Two-tank dives cost around $130.

A **scenic path** runs from Middleton Beach to the Pilot Station (from where you can follow Princess Royal Dr back into town). The walk takes about an hour, and is part of a project to link Oyster Harbour, Middleton Bay, Albany and Frenchman Bay by 35km of walking tracks.

Local anglers reckon you can throw a line anywhere in Albany and catch something. **Beach fishing** at Middleton and Emu Beaches is popular. **Spinners Charters** (☎ 9841 7151; www .spinnerscharters.com.au) runs deep-sea fishing trips. **Emu Point Boat Hire** (☎ 9842 9798, 0408 931 544) provides paddle boats, 'surfcats', canoes and motorised dinghies.

Tours

Take a four-hour cruise up the Kalgan River in the glass-bottomed **Kalgan Queen** (☎ 9844 3166; www.albanyaustralia.com) and learn about the history and wildlife of the area. Trips (adult/child $45/20) leave from Emu Point. For something a little faster, **Albany Down Under** (☎ 9842 2468; www.harleytours.ws; from $35) offers motorbike tours on a Harley Davidson.

Several local operators run day tours to the Southern Forests and wineries; check with the visitors centre.

Sleeping
BUDGET

Albany Backpackers (☎ 9842 5255; www.albanyback packers.com.au; cnr Stirling Tce & Spencer St; dm/s/d $23/40/56; 💻) Bright, cheery and with a reputation for partying, this hostel knows how to keep its guests happy with extras like coffee and cake each afternoon, complimentary bike hire and (limited) free internet access.

Albany Bayview YHA (☎ 9842 3388; albanyyha@ westnet.com.au; 49 Duke St; dm/s/d $23/40/52; 💻) In a quiet street 400m from the centre, this rambling backpackers has a lazy feel and is less frenzied than the hostel in town.

Discovery Inn (☎ 9842 5535; www.discoveryinn.net .au; 9 Middleton Rd, Middleton Beach; dm/s/d $25/45/65 💻) A ceramic bulldog guards the hallway in this great-value 1920s guesthouse close to the beach. With friendly owners, a pretty covered courtyard and great furnishings, you won't get better value than this.

Middleton Beach Holiday Park (☎ 1800 644 674; www.holidayalbany.com.au; Middleton Beach; tent/caravan sites $25/27, cabins $99-105, chalets $150-160; 💻 🐾) This beachfront caravan park is sheltered by high sand dunes (a good thing when a gale is raging). Book early – it's popular.

GO SOUTH FOR ADVENTURE

The south coast is a popular destination for adventure-sports enthusiasts, who come here for paragliding, rock climbing, abseiling or challenging bushwalking.

The Great Southern is the hub of Western Australia's climbing scene, with West Cape Howe, Torndirrup, Porongurup and Stirling Range National Parks. West Cape Howe (p146) is remote climbing territory where a group of three should be the minimum. The area has multipitch climbs on granite sea cliffs. Torndirrup National Park (p146) includes the granite climbing areas of the Gap, Natural Bridge and Amphitheatre. Bluff Knoll in the Stirling Range (p140) is the closest that WA gets to offering a real mountaineering experience and has been the scene of many 'epics'. Climbs can be up to 350m long, involving a dozen or more pitches and as many hours to complete.

Contact **Mountain Designs** (☎ 9841 1413; 222 York St; albany@mountaindesigns.com) in Albany; it's the focus for current information on all things outdoorsy.

Emu Beach Holiday Park (Map p145; ☎ 1800 984 411, 9844 1147; www.emubeach.com; Emu Point; tent/caravan sites $25/30, chalets $110-140, villas $140-160) Families love the Emu Beach area and this holiday park, close to the beach, has good facilities, including free barbecues and a kids' playground.

Cruize Inn (☎ 9842 9599; www.cruizeinn.com; 122 Middleton Rd; s/d $42/52) Lovely bright blues and Indonesian fabrics and furnishings decorate this good value self-catering place.

Norfolk Sands (☎ 9841 3585; www.norfolksands.com .au; 18 Adelaide Cres, Middleton Beach; s/d $55/80) Just a few minutes' walk from Middleton Beach, this is simple accommodation with a touch of class. The share-facility rooms are tastefully decorated with Asian-style furnishings and breakfast is served at the fantastic Bay Merchants café next door.

MIDRANGE

My Place (☎ 9842 3242; myplace@iinet.net.au; 47-61 Grey St East; r $85-120) These large self-contained rooms are not the most stylish in the world but they're clean, central and excellent value.

Coraki Holiday Cottages (☎ 9844 7068; www.coraki cottages.com.au; Lower King Rd; cottages from $115) On the edge of Oyster Bay, between the King and Kalgan Rivers, these bright, private cottages with bush surrounds are great value.

TOP END

Esplanade Hotel (☎ 9842 1711; www.albanyesplanade .com.au; cnr Adelaide Cres & Flinders Pde; d $182-255; ☲) The *grande dame* of Albany accommodation, while it's not exactly full of character, it's certainly comfortable.

Beach House at Bayside (Map p145; ☎ 9844 8844; www .thebeachhouseatbayside.com.au; Barry Crt; r from $207) This B&B is midway between Middleton Beach and Emu Point, and offers touches including port and chocs each evening.

Eating & Drinking

Jo Jo's Pizza & Kebab (☎ 9842 6000; 362 Middleton Rd; mains $5-10; ☒ lunch & dinner) This is a great place for late-night souvlaki or falafel, and is still the locals' most popular pizza joint.

Bay Merchants (☎ 9841 7821; 18 Adelaide Cres, Middleton Beach; mains $10-14, ☒ breakfast & lunch) Just a sandy-footed stroll from the beach, this café-cum-*providore* makes the best coffee in town and to-die-for gourmet sandwiches.

Dylan's on the Terrace (☎ 9841 8720; 82 Stirling Tce; mains $12-20; ☒ breakfast, lunch & dinner) With its 1950s ambience and menu of hamburgers,

pancakes and the like, Dylan's is always family friendly.

Squid Shack (☎ 0417 170 857; Emu Beach; fish & chips $12; ☒ lunch & dinner) This local institution serves fish straight from the ocean, from what is literally a shack on the beach. Take a bottle of wine and plan a sunset picnic.

Harvest Moon Café (☎ 9841 8833; 86 Stirling Tce; mains $13; ☒ lunch) In an informal bookish café setting, you'll find great vegetarian food and fresh juices.

Vancouver 51 (☎ 9841 2475; 65 Vancouver St; lunches $13; ☒ lunch Tue-Sun, dinner Fri & Sat) This great little café is perched above the coast, with balcony views and creative fusion food; Szechuan duck and spicy plums, yum. Go for the $28 two-course dinner if you can.

Nonna's (☎ 9841 4626; 135 Lower York St; lunch special $15; ☒ lunch & dinner) Classic Italian food served at reasonable prices and in a cosy setting.

Earl of Spencer Historic Inn (☎ 9841 1322; cnr Earl & Spencer Sts; mains $20; ☒ lunch & dinner) On a cold night you can't beat the warming qualities of the Earl's famous pie and pint or hearty lamb shanks. It's popular for a quiet drink or, on the weekends, for live music.

Entertainment

The *Albany Advertiser*, published on Tuesday and Thursday has information on events in and around town. The **Town Hall Theatre** has regular shows.

For the latest snog-and-shoot blockbusters, try **Albany 3 Cinemas** (☎ 9842 2210; 451 Albany Hwy), on the northern edge of town.

Getting Around

Love's (☎ 9841 1211) runs local bus services (adult/child $1.90/0.80) around town on weekdays and Saturday morning. The visitors centre has routes and timetables.

You can rent a car locally from **Rainbow Coast Car Rentals** (☎ 9841 7130) and both **Avis** (☎ 9842 2833) and **Budget** (☎ 9841 7799) have agencies out at the airport.

AROUND ALBANY

South of Albany, off Frenchman Bay Rd, is a stunning stretch of coastline that includes The Gap and Natural Bridge, rugged natural rock formations surrounded by pounding seas. Also here are the Blowholes, especially interesting in heavy seas when spray is blown with great force through the surrounding rock; the rock-climbing areas of **Peak Head** and

AROUND ALBANY

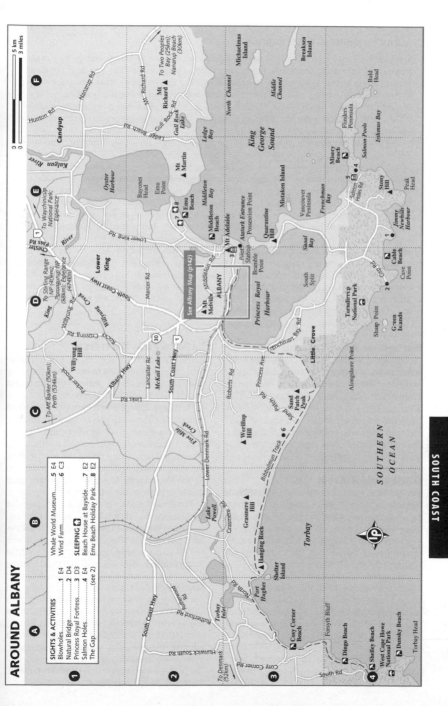

SIGHTS & ACTIVITIES
Blowholes..........................1	E4
Natural Bridge....................2	D4
Princess Royal Fortress.........3	D3
Salmon Holes.....................4	E4
The Gap........................(see 2)	
Whale World Museum............5	E4
Wind Farm.........................6	C3

SLEEPING
Beach House at Bayside.........7	E2
Emu Beach Holiday Park.........8	E2

See Albany Map (p142)

SOUTH COAST

ALBANY'S WHALING BATTLEGROUND

Talk to some Western Australians about their childhood holidays in Albany and, as well as care-free days of fishing and swimming, they're also likely to recall an almighty stench in the air and sharks circling in bloody corners of Frenchman Bay. The local whales – whose blubber created the vile smell while being melted down in pressure cookers, and whose blood spilled into water around the Cheynes Beach Whaling Station – also appear to remember this scene far too well. It took them well over a decade to return in full strength to the waters around Albany after the last whale was hunted on 20 November 1978.

The whaling industry was gruesome in a most public way – whales were hunted, harpooned and dragged back to shore to be cut up and boiled, while their teeth were salvaged to make artistic carvings called scrimshaw – which is perhaps why the environmental movement managed to make its closure one of their earlier successes. It became harder for the industry to make the smell, the blood and the sight of harpooned carcasses being towed into the harbour anything but unattractive. One of Tim Winton's earlier novels (*Shallows,*1984), set in Albany, where Winton lived for some time as an adolescent, describes how whaling became an emotional battleground for environmentalists and the many local employees of the industry, like the situation in timber towns throughout the Southwest in recent years. This pressure from protesters, as well as dwindling whale numbers and a drop in world whale-oil prices, sounded the death knell for the industry.

But Albany has cleverly managed to turn this now-unacceptable industry into a quaint tourist attraction, with the fascinating Whale World Museum (below), where you can buy scrimshaw carvings and walk on the flensing deck, and maritime festivals, which celebrate its rough-and-ready history on the seas. The whales who play in the surrounding waters are all the happier for it – as are the town's tourism-boosted coffers.

West Cape Howe National Park; steep, rocky coves such as **Jimmy Newhills Harbour** and **Salmon Holes**, popular with surfers but considered quite scary; and **Frenchman Bay** with a fine swimming beach and a shady barbecue area. This is a dangerous coastline so beware of freakish, large waves – many locals and tourists have lost their lives after being swept off the rocks. Detour to Albany's **Wind Farm**, where a walking track wends surreally among the turbines.

Whale World Museum

The interesting and worthwhile **Whale World Museum** (☎ 9844 4021; www.whaleworld.org; Frenchman Bay; adult/child/family $18/9/45; ✆ 9am-5pm), 21km from Albany, is based in Frenchman's Bay at Cheynes Beach Whaling Station, which ceased operations in November 1978. There's the rusting *Cheynes IV* whale chaser, as well as station equipment (such as whale-oil tanks – a whale weighing 40 tonnes would provide seven tonnes of oil), to inspect outside. The museum screens several 3-D gore-spattered and other films about whaling operations, and displays harpoons, whaleboat models and scrimshaw (etchings on whalebone). There are also free guided tours on the hour, and there's a superb collection of paintings of marine mammals by noted US artist Richard Ellis.

National Parks & Reserves

There are a number of excellent natural areas near Albany. From west to east along the coast you can explore several different habitats and a wide variety of coastal scenery.

West Cape Howe National Park, 30km west of Albany, is a 35-sq-km playground for naturalists, bushwalkers, rock climbers and anglers. Inland, there are areas of coastal heath, lakes, swamp and karri forest. With the exception of the road to Shelley Beach, access is restricted to 4WDs, mostly travelling through sand dunes to explore the wild coast.

Torndirrup National Park includes two popular attractions: the often windswept and elemental **Natural Bridge** and **The Gap**. Nearby the **Blowholes** put on a show when the surf's up, worth the 80-step stairway up and down. Beautiful **Misery Beach** (a contradiction in terms) is often deserted and is an easy drive in/walk down. At **Stony Hill**, a short heritage trail leads around the site of an observatory station from both World Wars. Keen walkers can tackle the hard 10km-return **bushwalk** (more than five hours) over Isthmus Hill to Bald Head, at the eastern edge of the park. The views are spectacular. Whales are frequently seen from the cliffs, and the park's varied vegetation provides habitats for many native animals and reptiles.

Some 20km east of Albany, **Two Peoples Bay** is a 46-sq-km nature reserve with a good swimming beach and scenic coastline. Little of the reserve is easily accessible; it's a significant conservation area, home to two once-thought-to-be-extinct animals: the noisy scrub bird and Australia's rarest marsupial mammal, the pointy-nosed Gilbert's potoroo. Keen naturalists should seek access permits from **DEC** (☎ 9842 4500) in Albany.

ALBANY TO ESPERANCE

The coast between Albany and Esperance is relatively isolated and unpopulated. It boasts beautiful beaches around Bremer Bay and Hopetoun, and the impressive Fitzgerald River National Park.

From Albany, the South Coast Hwy runs northeast along the coast before turning inland to skirt the Fitzgerald River National Park and finishing in Esperance, 476km later. Along the way, you'll pass through **Jerramungup**, 182km northeast of Albany, and the small town of **Ravensthorpe**, 187km west of Esperance and once the centre of the Phillips River goldfield (later, copper was also mined here). These days the area is dependent on farming, although new nickel mines in the vicinity are expected to have an ongoing economic effect. West of Ravensthorpe is the **WA standard time meridian**, indicated by a boulder with a plaque on it.

Fitzgerald River National Park

This 3300-sq-km park is designated a Unesco 'Biosphere', the intention of which is to discover and demonstrate how people and nature can live together sustainably. It is simply stunning, with a beautiful (and sometimes dangerous) coastline, sand plains, the rugged Barrens mountain range and heath country, and deep river valleys. It's accessible by good 2WD gravel roads, except after heavy rain.

Wildflowers are most abundant in spring, but flowers – especially the hardy proteas – bloom throughout the year. The park is botanically significant, containing about 1700 (20%) of WA's described species, including half the orchid species in WA (more than 80 varieties, 70 of which are endemic). It is the home of the spectacularly showy royal hakea and endemic Quaalup bell. Many **animals** are present, too. There are 19 native mammal species, including honey possums, dibblers (small endangered marsupials) and tammar wallabies; 200 species of birds, including the endangered ground parrot and western bristlebird; 41 reptile and 12 frog species. **Southern right** and **humpback whales** can be seen offshore from July to September.

There is some very good **bushwalking** here. Shorter walks are accessible at **East Mt Barren** (three hours), **West Mt Barren** (two hours) and **Point Ann** (one hour). Spend time at Point Ann if you can; the headland walking track takes you past the ruins of the 1164km-long, **number two rabbit-proof fence** (built between 1904 and 1960), while boardwalks take you out over the gorgeous bay, where whales are often seen, close by the pretty bush camp site at nearby St Mary Inlet.

The wilderness route from **Fitzgerald Beach** to **West Beach** is for serious walkers – there is no trail and no water (plan for water drops on access roads), but camping is permitted. You'll need to register with the ranger on Quiss Rd, **Jerramungup** (☎ 9835 5043); **Murray Rd** (☎ 9837 1022), just north of Bremer Bay; or at **East Mt Barren** (☎ 9838 3060).

Although the park is one of the areas in southern WA least affected by dieback fungus, precautions are in place to ensure it remains so; respect the 'no entry – dieback' signs, and clean your shoes before each walk.

The three main 2WD entry points to the park are from the South Coast Hwy (Quiss

---

NOISY SCRUB BIRD SOUNDS SUCCESSFUL

This little, near-flightless bird certainly lives up to its name: it has a powerful, ear-piercing call. The noisy scrub bird (*Atrichornus clamosus*) almost joined the thylacine in extinction. It was sighted in jarrah forest at the foot of the Darling Scarp, near Perth, in 1842, and the last recorded specimen was collected near Torbay in 1889. The bird was then thought extinct until rediscovered in 1961 at Two Peoples Bay, east of Albany.

In 1983 several breeding pairs were moved to similar habitats in Mt Manypeaks Nature Reserve (now part of Waychinicup National Park) to regenerate populations where the bird had died out. In 1987 another colony was established at the Walpole-Nornalup National Park. It is believed that there are now well over 100 breeding pairs.

Rd & Pabelup Dr), Hopetoun (Hamersley Dr), and Bremer Bay (along Swamp & Murray Rds). This last is the prettiest route, winding through acres of flowering shrubs. It's also likely to be impassable after rain, so check locally before you set out.

There are 2WD **camp sites** at St Mary Inlet (near Point Ann) and Four Mile Beach, while camping at Hamersley Inlet, Whale Bone Beach, Quoin Head and Fitzgerald Inlet is by 4WD only.

Bremer Bay

☎ 08 / pop 350

This fishing and holiday hamlet, 180km northeast of Albany and 61km from the South Coast Hwy, sits at the western end of the Great Australian Bight. From July to November it can be a good spot to observe **southern right whales**, which enter bays in the area to give birth.

If you're staying overnight **Bremer Bay Beaches Resort & Tourist Park** (☎ 98374290; www .bremerbayaccommodation.com; Wellstead Rd; camp sites/ vans/cabins $25/55/70; 🖳) has camping grounds that are green and shady with a well-equipped campers' kitchen, and the cabins – while ordinary – are a good size. It's also the local visitor centre.

A somewhat basic and eccentric place to stay (you may or may not encounter anyone else, including staff), on the outskirts of Fitzgerald River National Park, is the historic 1858 **Quaalup Homestead** (☎ 9837 4124; www.whales andwildflowers.com.au; Gairdner Rd; camp sites/cabins/cottages $15/60/110). It's 45km from Bremer Bay, and there's limited power supply.

Hopetoun

☎ 08 / pop 350

There are fine beaches and bays around Hopetoun, the eastern gateway to the Fitzgerald River National Park. It's been booming more from the proximity of a new nickel mine than from tourism, and accommodation can be hard to find. You'll find visitor information brochures in Taste of the Toun Café (Veal St).

To the west of town is the landlocked **Culham Inlet** (great for fishing – especially for black bream) and east of town is the scenic **Southern Ocean East Drive** – in 2006 in the process of being sealed – which features camping beaches at Mason Bay and Starvation Bay. The old railway track between Ravensthorpe and Hopetoun is now a **heritage walking track**.

The world's longest fence – the 1833km-long **number one rabbit-proof fence** – enters the sea in the south at Starvation Bay, east of Hopetoun; it starts at Eighty Mile Beach on the Indian Ocean, north of Port Hedland. The fence was built during the height of the rabbit plague between 1901 and 1907. However, the story goes that the bunnies beat the fence-builders to the west side so it wasn't as effective a barrier as hoped.

You'll find plenty of time for contemplation at the **Hopetoun Motel & Chalet Village** (☎ 9838 3219; cnr Veal & Canning Sts; s/d $85/95, chalets $150), a quiet little rammed-earth complex set in bushland. Eat at the Port Hotel or Taste of the Toun. In the old post office, **Deck** (🕙 Sep-May) is a welcome addition to the Hopetoun summer scene, making it hard to resist a daily ice cream. Opening hours are erratic in the winter.

ESPERANCE

☎ 08 / pop 13,000

The pretty coastal town of Esperance is the place to be for sun, sea and sand. You'll have to drive to reach some of the picture-perfect beaches, such as Lucky Bay (widely reputed to be the most beautiful beach in Australia) in Cape Le Grand, but town beaches like Twilight and Blue Haven have squeaky-clean white sand and clear, azure water. No need to fight for solitude here, as Esperance's isolation guarantees it. It is a popular resort due to its even climate, stunning coastal scenery, blue waters, good fishing and dazzling beaches. The seas offshore are studded with the many islands of the Archipelago of the Recherche, home to a variety of wildlife.

History

On the coast 200km south of Norseman, Esperance was named in 1792 when the *Recherche* and *L'Espérance* sailed through the archipelago and into the bay to shelter from a storm. Although the first settlers came in 1863, it was during the gold rush in the 1890s that the town really became established as a port. When the gold fever subsided, Esperance went into a state of suspended animation until after WWII.

In the 1950s it was discovered that adding missing trace elements to the soil around Esperance restored fertility; the town has since rapidly become an agricultural centre.

Information

Computer Alley (☎ 9072 1293; 69c Dempster St; 🕙 9am-5pm Mon-Fri, 9am-4pm Sat) Internet.

Visitors centre (☎ 9071 2330; www.visitesperance
.com; Dempster St; ☯ 9am-5pm) In the museum village;
can book tours and transport.

Sights & Activities

When you hit Esperance, a must is the 36km
Great Ocean Drive. It includes spectacular vistas
from **Observatory Point** and the lookout on **Wire-**

less Hill; popular swimming spots at **Blue Haven
Beach** and **Twilight Cove**; surfing wherever the
swell's up along the coast; and the **Pink Lake**,
stained by salt-tolerant algae. You'll also pass
the **wind farm**. There's a walking track among
the turbines that is quite surreal when it's
windy; and it often is here, with the farm supplying about 23% of Esperance's electricity.

About 100 small islands are in the **Archipelago
of the Recherche**; you'll see many of them from
the waterfront. Colonies of seals, penguins and
a variety of water birds live on the islands. **Woody
Island** (p150) is a wildlife sanctuary, which you
can visit on cruises and even stay at.

The **Museum Village** (James St; ☯ 10am-4pm Mon-Fri,
10am-1pm Sat) consists of various restored heritage buildings, including a gallery, smithy's
forge, café and craft shop. Among its local
history collection the **Esperance Museum** (Museum Village; adult/child $4/1; ☯ 1.30-4.30pm) contains
a Skylab display – when the USA's Skylab
crashed to earth in 1979, it made its fiery re-
entry at Balladonia, east of Esperance. The **Can-
nery Arts Centre** (☎ 9071 3599; Norseman Rd; ☯ 1-4pm)

has occasional exhibitions, artists' studios and a shop selling creative local artwork.

Kids will enjoy **Telegraph Farm** (☎ 9076 5044; South Coast Hwy; adult/child $10/5; ✆ 10am-5pm, closed Tue, Wed & Jun-Aug), 21km west of town. This commercial protea farm has a host of animals, including water buffalo, camels and birds. Also fun for kids is **Ralph Bower Adventureland Park**, near the Taylor St Jetty, where kids can ride about on a miniature train or climb all over the playground. The **Esperance Aquarium** (☎ 9071 7222; 53 The Esplanade; adult/child $$9/7; ✆ 10am-5pm, closed Wed May-Sep) has a small marine discovery trail and a touchpool.

Lake Warden wetland's **Kepwari Trail**, off Fisheries Rd, has a boardwalk across the lake, interpretive displays and good bird-watching.

Tours

The tour to Woody Island is highly recommended – you'll likely see seals and sea lions lolling about on rocks, sea eagles hunting prey, Cape Barren geese, common dolphins and a host of other wildlife, including whales in season. **Mackenzie's Island Cruises** (☎ 9071 5757; www.woodyisland.com.au; 71 The Esplanade) has a power catamaran that regularly tours Esperance Bay and Woody Island (adult/child half day $65/24). Mackenzies also operates a daily ferry to the island from December 26 to January 26, leaving Esperance at 7.30am and returning at noon (adult/child return $39/16).

Esperance Diving & Fishing (☎ 9071 5111; www.esperancedivingandfishing.com.au; 72 The Esplanade) can take you diving off the wreck of the *Sanko Harvest* (two-tank dive including all gear plus lunch $195) or charter fishing throughout the Archipelago.

Eco-Discovery Tours (☎ 0407 737 261; www.esperancetours.com.au) runs 4WD day tours to the coastal national parks of Cape Le Grand and Cape Arid ($138 per person, minimum four). Its associated company, **Kepa Kurl Eco Cultural Discovery Tours** (☎ 9072 1688; www.kepakurl.com.au; Museum Village), shows the country from an Aboriginal perspective (half/full day $76/145 per person, minimum two).

Sleeping

BUDGET

Woody Island (☎ 9071 5757; www.woodyisland.com.au; tent sites $12, on-site tents $25-45, huts $66-97; ✆ late Sep-end Apr) It's not every day you get to stay in an A-class nature reserve. Choose between leafy camp sites or timber bush cabins; a few have private decks and their own lighting. Power is mostly solar, and rainwater only supplies the island – both are highly valued.

Esperance Guesthouse (☎ 9071 3396; 23 Daphne St; dm/d $20/45; 🖳) Still popular, this casual, comfortable place supplies homemade bread and brewed coffee (gasp!) for breakfast.

Blue Waters Lodge YHA (☎ 9071 1040; yhaesperance@hotmail.com; 299 Goldfields Rd; dm/s/d $20/30/50; 🖳) On the beachfront about 1.5km from the centre, this is a rambling place with views over the water, a green back yard and wood fires in winter.

Crokers Park Holiday Resort (☎ 9071 5100; www.acclaimparks.com.au; 817 Harbour Rd; powered sites $22, cabins $53-72; 🐾) Of the several very ordinary camp sites in town, this stands apart for its clean, shady and decent-sized grounds and its pretty pool area. It's worth the five-minute drive from town and the water.

Goldie's Place (☎ 9071 2879; www.goldiesplaceesperance.com; 51 Goldfields Rd; d $70) A standout in comfort and value, Goldie's is a sizable, spotless and well-equipped two-bedroom unit with cheery young owners living upstairs and their friendly dog living in the garden.

MIDRANGE

Esperance B&B by the Sea (☎ 9071 5640; www.esperancebb.com; Stewart St; s/d $75/110) The views from the deck overlooking Blue Haven Beach are breathtaking, especially at sunset. This big, new beach house with a private guest wing is just a stroll from the ocean and a five-minute drive from Dempster St.

Old Hospital Motel (☎ 9071 3587; 1a William St; r from $90) Named after the 1896 old hospital building on site, the pleasant motel-style rooms – coolly tiled – are well equipped; the spacious two-room units upstairs are particularly good value.

Jetty Resort (☎ 9071 3333; www.thejettyresort.com.au; 1 The Esplanade; d $105-189, ste $249; 🖳 🐾) You can't miss this blindingly white balconied building as you drive along the Esplanade. More expensive rooms come with beach views, balconies or spas. There's a pool with a barbecue, comfy seats and a giant chess set in its garden, and a great kids' playground.

TOP END

Island View Esperance (☎ 9072 0044; www.esperanceapartments.com.au; 14-16 The Esplanade; apt $140-$270) It's easy-living in these architect-designed and tastefully furnished units, with floor-to-ceiling windows overlooking the beach across the road. The kitchens have all mod cons, and there's a spacious living area.

Eating & Drinking

Onshore Traders (☎ 9071 2575; 105 Dempster St; mains $7-13; ⦿ breakfast & lunch, closed Sun) A homewares store and *providore*-cum-café in a breezy modern space, this place has lunch specials, salads and Turkish breads, as well as decent coffee.

    Taylor Street Tearooms (☎ 9071 4317; Taylor St Jetty; mains $12-24; ⦿ breakfast, lunch & dinner) This rather attractive, sprawling café by the jetty serves good, reliable fare; the salt-and-pepper squid is becoming an institution. Locals hang out at the tables on the grass or on the covered terrace, and it's very much a child-friendly zone.

    Ocean Blues (☎ 9071 7107; 19 The Esplanade; mains $20; ⦿ breakfast, lunch & dinner, closed Mon) Wander in sandy-footed and order some simple fare (try the classic steak sandwich), or shelter from the sea breeze over an afternoon coffee and cake. Early dinner is served until 8.30pm.

    For what's been described as the best coffee in town, look for the **Coffee Cat**, a mobile red-and-black van often parked opposite the Jetty Resort.

Entertainment

The Pier Hotel (☎ 9071 1777; The Esplanade) has a throbbing nightclub on Friday and Saturday; if you're over 25 you might feel out of place. Touring bands play regularly at **Esperance Motor Hotel** (☎ 9071 1555; Andrew St).

    Fenwick 3 Cinemas (☎ 9072 1355; 105 Dempster St) shows the latest blockbusters.

Getting Around

There are plenty of **taxis** (☎ 9071 1782) in Esperance. For car rentals try **Avis** (☎ 9071 3998) or **Budget** (☎ 9071 2775). **Hollywood Car Hire** (☎ 9071 3144) is the local car rental mob.

CAPE LE GRAND & CAPE ARID

There are four national parks in the Esperance region; **DEC** (☎ 9071 3733) in Esperance has information on each.

    The closest and most popular is **Cape Le Grand**, which extends 60km east of Esperance and boasts spectacular coastal scenery, beautiful white-sand beaches and excellent walking tracks. There are fine views across the park from **Frenchman Peak**, at the western end of the park, good fishing and swimming at **Lucky Bay** and **Hellfire Bay**, and a sheltered

bush campsite at **Le Grand Beach**. Make the effort to climb Frenchman Peak (a steep 3km return walk, only for the fit) as the views from the top and through the 'eye' (the huge open cave at the top) are superb, especially during the late afternoon. **Rossiter Bay** is where explorers Edward John Eyre and the Aborigine Wylie, during their epic overland crossing in 1841, fortuitously met Captain Rossiter of the French whaler *Mississippi*. The pair spent two weeks resting on this same ship. The roads to all these places are sealed. A 15km one-way **coastal walking track** links Rossiter Bay and Le Grand Beach; you can do shorter stretches between beaches. Be sure to stop on the way to or from the park at the wonderful **Hellfire Gallery**, 20km out of Esperance, for great coffee, cake, artworks and the lavender garden; it's open Thursday to Monday.

    Further east, at the start of the Great Australian Bight and on the fringes of the Nullarbor Plain, is **Cape Arid National Park**. If the sand at Cape Le Grand is like sugar, at Cape Arid it's the texture of flour, so smooth that it squeaks when you walk on it. The park is rugged and isolated, with good bushwalking, great beaches and camp sites. Whales (in season), seals and Cape Barren geese are seen regularly here. Most of the park is accessible by 4WD only, although the Poison Creek and Thomas River sites are accessible in normal vehicles. For the hardy, there is a tough walk to the top of Tower Peak, adjacent to Mt Ragged (3km return, three hours) where the world's most primitive species of ant was found thriving in 1930.

    Other national parks in the area include pretty **Stokes National Park**, 90km west of Esperance, with an inlet, long beaches and rocky headlands backed by sand dunes, low hills and bush campground. It's popular for fishing and is 2WD accessible. **Peak Charles National Park**, 130km to the north, is a granite wilderness area with no visitor facilities.

    The **Orleans Bay Caravan Park** (☎ 9075 0033; orleansbay@bigpond.com; unpowered/powered sites $18/20, cabins $40, chalets $70), at Duke of Orleans Bay between Cape Le Grand and Cape Arid National Park, is a shady, child-friendly place to stay, 2kms from stunning Wharton Beach with its surfing, swimming, fishing and 4WD beach tracks.

    For those heading east across the Nullarbor, the **Balladonia Track** and **Parmango Rd**, north of Capes Le Grand and Arid, offer alternative routes to the Eyre Hwy (see p166).

SOUTH COAST

The Southern Outback

Welcome to iconic outback Australia, where the searing red sandscapes of summer give way to clear, cold winter days and an inland horizon that reaches forever. Along the coast, wild dune country fronts up to the lonely waters of the Great Australian Bight where, fringing it, the relentless Nullarbor Plain leads on (and on and on) to South Australia.

This is remarkable wilderness country, more so because of its long history of human settlement by the Aboriginal people, whose lands stretch in great swaths through the centre. More recently, European settlers pushed through, slowly at first, and then in seething masses as news of the discovery of gold in the late 19th century filtered out.

The gold rush became a gold boom, creating population enough for permanent settlement to be viable. This led to the creation of a pipeline some 600km in length to ensure the constant supply of water that the extraction of gold – and its miners – required. The regional centre, the handsome city of Kalgoorlie-Boulder, is testament to the wealth that gold brought, with its wide streets and substantial Victorian buildings; it retains the Wild West feel of a city on the edge. Settlement of more remote goldfields was more difficult with the constant threat of drought, and tedious hardship for the shanty-dwelling miners, searching for that elusive nugget. The ghost towns of these less-fortunate mining endeavours scatter the landscape, bearing eerie witness to the victory of the land over its early colonists.

HIGHLIGHTS

- Roam **Kalgoorlie-Boulder** (p154) with its eclectic architecture, raucous pubs and enormous mining operations

- Walk the shimmering hard-salt surface of **Lake Ballard** (p161) to view sculptor Antony Gormley's 51 haunting figures, based on the residents of nearby Menzies

- Explore the eerie ghost town of **Gwalia** (p161) and others in the goldfields

- Learn how gold fortunes were made and lost in a tiny glint of decades, along the **Golden Quest Discovery Trail** (p160)

- Drive the **Eyre Hwy** (p164), Australia's greatest sealed-road endurance test, across the Nullarbor Plain from Perth to Adelaide

- Bird-watch, and walk in the footsteps of explorer Edward John Eyre, at the renowned **Eyre Bird Observatory** (p167)

- Walk along the lonely **Great Australian Bight** (p167)

- Climb the shifting sand dunes engulfing the old telegraph station at **Eucla** (p168)

★ Gwalia

★ Lake Ballard

★ Kalgoorlie-Boulder

Eucla ★

Eyre Hwy

★ Eyre Bird Observatory

Great Australian Bight

THE SOUTHERN OUTBACK

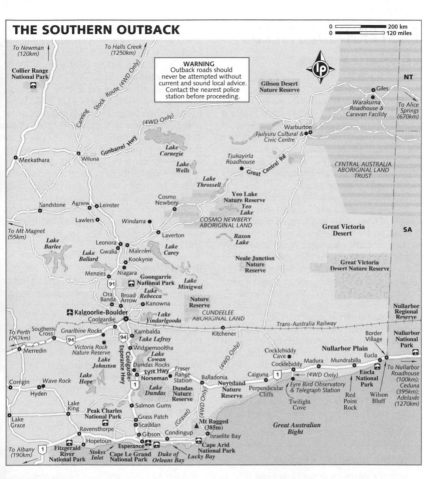

Getting There & Away

Travelling to Kalgoorlie-Boulder is easy; pretty much everywhere else, you'll need a car.

AIR

SkyWest Airlines (☎ 1300 660 088; www.skywest.com.au) and **Qantas** (☎ 13 13 13; www.qantas.com.au) fly between Kalgoorlie-Boulder and Perth at least twice daily. There are also regular SkyWest flights from Perth to Laverton, Leinster, Leonora and Wiluna.

BUS

Perth-Goldfields Express (☎ 1800 620 440; www.goldrushtours.com.au) does the Perth–Kalgoorlie trip (adult one-way $70) most days, going on to Leonora and Laverton once or twice weekly.

The same company offers the **Goldrush Tours Golden Triangle Tour**, a hop-on, hop-off bus pass ($475) that covers transport between Perth, Margaret River and the southwest coast and forests, Albany and Esperance on the south coast, and to Kalgoorlie.

TRAIN

Transwa (☎ 1300 662 205; www.transwa.wa.gov.au) runs the *Prospector* train service from Perth to Kalgoorlie-Boulder daily (one-way adult/child $72/35, seven hours). It's wise to book, as this service is popular.

The *Indian Pacific*, run by **Great Southern Railway** (☎ 13 21 47; www.trainways.com.au), also goes through Kalgoorlie-Boulder four times a week (twice to Perth and twice from Perth).

EASTERN GOLDFIELDS

KALGOORLIE-BOULDER

☎ 08 / pop 28,900

Kalgoorlie-Boulder ('Kal' to the locals) is one of Australia's great outback success stories. A long, dry and dusty 600km from Perth, it remains a prosperous and productive gold town in its own right, as well as service centre for the burgeoning mining industry's remoter outposts. Its wide streets and well-preserved Victorian buildings are testament to its early wealth and colourful history.

In 1893 Paddy Hannan, a prospector, set out from Coolgardie for another gold strike with a couple of Irish mates and stopped at the site of Kalgoorlie. He found enough gold lying on the surface to spark another rush. As in so many places, the surface gold soon dried up, but at Kalgoorlie the miners went deeper and more gold was found, leading the area into a long boom period. After WWI, however, increasing production costs and static gold prices led to Kalgoorlie's slow but steady decline.

In 1934 there were bitter race riots in twin towns Kalgoorlie and Boulder. On 29 and 30 January that year, mobs of disgruntled Australians roamed the streets, upset at the preference supposedly being given by shift bosses to workers of southern-European descent, and angrily setting fire to foreign-owned businesses and shooting at anyone deemed to be a foreigner.

Large mining conglomerates have been at the forefront of new open-cut mining operations in the Golden Mile east of Kal. It's probably the wealthiest gold-mining locale for its size in the world.

Kalgoorlie-Boulder represents Australia's raw edge, and has the feel of a US 'Wild West' frontier town. Several brothels and pubs attest to the city's function, the same since the 1890s, as a prosperous mining centre. At one stage there were 93 pubs, and the amount of alcohol consumed here is twice the state average.

Come September, the town is packed with visitors from all over WA and further afield for the annual Kalgoorlie-Boulder Racing Round. Everybody gets frocked up and very drunk to watch horses race around the red, red dirt in Kalgoorlie-Boulder, Broad Arrow and other towns.

Orientation

Although Kalgoorlie sprung up close to Paddy Hannan's original find, the mining emphasis soon shifted a few kilometres away to the Golden Mile, and the satellite town of Boulder developed to service this area. In 1989 the two towns formally merged.

The town centre in Kalgoorlie is a grid of broad, tree-lined streets. Hannan St, the main street flanked by imposing public buildings, is wide enough to turn a camel train – a necessity in turn-of-the-19th-century goldfield towns. You'll find most of the town's hotels, restaurants and offices on or close to Hannan St.

WHERE WATER IS LIKE GOLD

With the discovery of gold it became clear to the Western Australia (WA) government that the large-scale extraction of the metal, the state's most important industry, was unlikely to continue in the Kalgoorlie goldfields without a reliable water supply. Stop-gap measures, such as huge condensation plants that produced distilled water from salt lakes, or bores that pumped brackish water from beneath the earth, provided temporary relief.

In 1898, however, the engineer CY O'Connor proposed a stunning solution: he would build a reservoir near Perth and construct a 556km pipeline to Kalgoorlie. This was well before the era of long oil pipelines, and his idea was opposed violently in parliament and regarded by some to be impossible, especially as the water had to go uphill all the way (Kalgoorlie is 400m higher than Perth). Nevertheless, the project was approved and the pipeline laid at breakneck speed.

In 1903 water started to pour into Kalgoorlie's newly constructed reservoir – a modified version of the same system still operates today. For O'Connor, however, there was no happy ending: long delays and continual criticism by those of lesser vision resulted in his suicide in 1902, less than a year before his scheme proved operational.

Today you can follow the path of the water on the National Trust's interpretive Golden Pipeline Heritage Trail, which runs along the Great Eastern Hwy between Perth and Kalgoorlie; pick up a brochure from any visitors centre or check out www.goldenpipeline.com.au.

KALGOORLIE

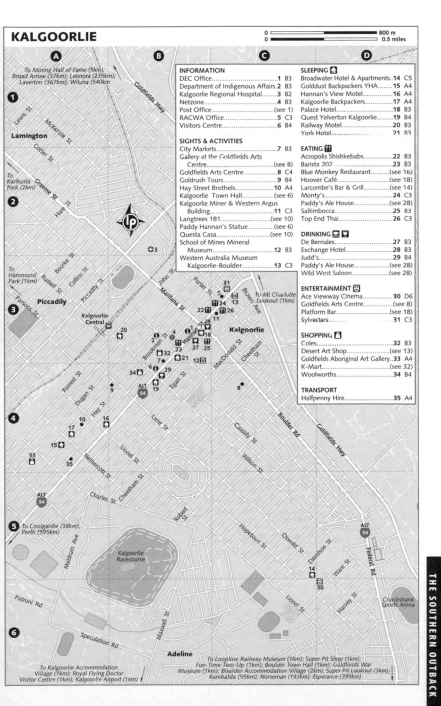

0 — 800 m
0 — 0.5 miles

INFORMATION
DEC Office...................................**1** B3
Department of Indigenous Affairs.**2** B3
Kalgoorlie Regional Hospital......**3** B2
Netzone.......................................**4** B3
Post Office..............................(see 1)
RACWA Office............................**5** C3
Visitors Centre...........................**6** B4

SIGHTS & ACTIVITIES
City Markets...............................**7** B3
Gallery at the Goldfields Arts
  Centre...................................(see 8)
Goldfields Arts Centre................**8** C4
Goldrush Tours...........................**9** B4
Hay Street Brothels...................**10** A4
Kalgoorlie Town Hall.............(see 6)
Kalgoorlie Miner & Western Argus
  Building.................................**11** C3
Langtrees 181.........................(see 10)
Paddy Hannan's Statue...........(see 6)
Questa Casa............................(see 10)
School of Mines Mineral
  Museum...............................**12** B3
Western Australia Museum
  Kalgoorlie-Boulder................**13** C3

SLEEPING
Broadwater Hotel & Apartments..**14** C5
Golddust Backpackers YHA........**15** A4
Hannan's View Motel................**16** A4
Kalgoorlie Backpackers.............**17** A4
Palace Hotel..............................**18** B3
Quest Yelverton Kalgoorlie........**19** B4
Railway Motel............................**20** B3
York Hotel..................................**21** B3

EATING
Acropolis Shishkebabs...............**22** B3
Barista 202................................**23** B3
Blue Monkey Restaurant........(see 16)
Hoover Café............................(see 18)
Larcombe's Bar & Grill...........(see 14)
Monty's....................................**24** C3
Paddy's Ale House..................(see 28)
Saltimbocca..............................**25** B3
Top End Thai.............................**26** C3

DRINKING
De Bernales..............................**27** B3
Exchange Hotel.........................**28** B3
Judd's.......................................**29** B4
Paddy's Ale House..................(see 28)
Wild West Saloon....................(see 28)

ENTERTAINMENT
Ace Viewway Cinema...............**30** D6
Goldfields Arts Centre............(see 8)
Platform Bar...........................(see 18)
Sylvesters..................................**31** C3

SHOPPING
Coles...**32** B3
Desert Art Shop.....................(see 13)
Goldfields Aboriginal Art Gallery.**33** A4
K-Mart....................................(see 32)
Woolworths................................**34** B4

TRANSPORT
Halfpenny Hire..........................**35** A4

Information

Department of Environment & Conservation (DEC; ☎ 9021 2677; post office bldg, 204 Hannan St)
Kalgoorlie Regional Hospital (☎ 9080 5888; Piccadilly St)
Netzone (☎ 9022 8342; St Barbara's Sq) Fast internet access in a central location.
Post office (204 Hannan St)
Royal Automobile Club of Western Australia Office (RACWA; ☎ 131 703; cnr Hannan & Porter Sts)
Visitors centre (☎ 9021 1966; www.kalgoorlie.com; cnr Hannan & Wilson Sts; ☺ 8.30am-5pm, 9am-5pm Sat & Sun) Stop by the town hall building to pick up a good, free town map, pick the brains of the knowledgeable staff, and browse the excellent bookshop.

Sights & Activities

MINING HALL OF FAME

If you want to understand what makes this town tick, don't miss the excellent **Mining Hall of Fame** (☎ 9026 2700; www.mininghall.com; Eastern Bypass Rd; adult/child plus underground $24/14, adult/child surface only $17/9; ☺ 9am-4.30pm). Located on Hannan's North Heritage Mining Reserve, the site of Paddy Hannan's original lease and a working mine until 1952, it explores the mining industry from the underground up. You can go 36m below the surface in a mine shaft (and see why claustrophobics don't make good miners), pan for gold and be mesmerised by a gold pour, while kids of all ages will be kept well-occupied in the interactive Exploration Zone. A Garden of Remembrance, dedicated to the immigrant Chinese who worked the goldfields, is due to open here in 2007.

If you're into mining history, allow yourself a half-day here. There are underground tours at 10am, 12.15pm and 2.45pm (you need to wear fully enclosed shoes).

WESTERN AUSTRALIA MUSEUM KALGOORLIE-BOULDER

The impressive Ivanhoe mine headframe at the northern end of Hannan St marks the entrance to this excellent **museum** (☎ 9021 8533; www.museum.wa.gov.au; 17 Hannan St; admission by donation; ☺ 10am-4.30pm). Check out the wide range of exhibits, including an underground gold vault and historic photographs, or join the free tours at 11am and 2pm. A lift takes you to a viewing point on the headframe, where you can look out over the city and mines and down into delightfully untidy backyards. The tiny British Arms Hotel (the narrowest hotel in Australia) is part of the museum.

LOOPLINE RAILWAY MUSEUM

The Loopline railway was once the most important urban transport for Kalgoorlie and Boulder, with Boulder's Golden Mile station (1897) once the busiest in Western Australia (WA). While the railway closed – hopefully only temporarily – in 2004, its story is told in the **railway museum** (☎ 9093 3055; www.loopline.com.au; cnr Burt & Hamilton Sts; adult/child $2/1; ☺ 9am-1pm), operating out of the old train station.

OTHER SIGHTS

Along Hannan St you'll find the imposing **town hall** and the equally impressive **post office**. There's an art gallery upstairs in the decorative town hall, while outside is a drinking fountain in the form of a **statue** of Paddy Hannan holding a water bag.

Northwest of Hannan St in Hay St is one of Kalgoorlie-Boulder's most notorious and popular attractions, the **Hay Street brothels**, now quietly acknowledged in the tourist brochures. Brothel tours have become de rigueur for many visitors to Kal, at **Langtrees 181** (☎ 9026 2181; www.langtrees.com; 181 Hay St; admission $25; ☺ 1pm, 3pm and 6pm) and at Australia's oldest operating brothel, **Questa Casa** (☎ 9021 4897; 133 Hay St; admission $18; ☺ 2pm).

See how the flying doctors look after the outback with the hourly tours at the **Royal Flying Doctor Service Visitor Centre** (☎ 9093 7595; Kalgoorlie-Boulder Airport; admission by donation; ☺ 10am-3pm Mon-Fri); be generous with your donation if you can, they do a fabulous job.

The **School of Mines Mineral Museum** (☎ 9088 6001; cnr Egan & Cassidy Sts; ☺ 8.30am-noon Mon-Fri; closed school holidays) has a geology display including replicas of big nuggets discovered in the area.

The **Goldfields War Museum** (☎ 9093 1083; 106 Burt St; admission free; ☺ 10am-4pm Mon-Fri, 9am-1pm Sat-Sun) has a collection of local war memorabilia and military vehicles.

At the **Gallery at the Goldfields Arts Centre** (☎ 9088 6905; Cheetham St; ☺ 10am-3pm Mon-Fri, noon-3pm Sun) you'll find monthly exhibitions by local, state and national artists.

The view from the **Super Pit Lookout** (www.superpit.com.au; Outram St; ☺ 6am-7pm), just off the Goldfields Hwy in Boulder, is awesome, with the big trucks at the bottom of the huge hole looking like kids' toys. Good information is given in the on-site signs, and the **Super Pit Shop** (☎ 9093 3488; 2 Burt St; ☺ 9am-5pm Mon-Fri) sells souvenirs and offers more detailed information. The lookout is closed for an hour or so during the daily pit blast; the time is posted around town.

The **Goatcher Theatre Curtain** in the 1907 **Boulder town hall** (☎ 9021 9600; cnr Burt & Lane Sts, Boulder) has recently been restored. The Neapolitan scene was painted in 1908 by Englishman Philip W Goatcher, one of the great theatrical scene artists of the Victorian era. The *trompe l'oeil* curtain creates an extraordinary illusion of 3-D space, and is dropped from 10am to 3pm Wednesday, and on the third Sunday of each month (Boulder's market day) from 9.30am to 12.30pm.

Hammond Park (☽ 9021 1209; Lyall St; ☽ 9am-5pm), in the west of Kalgoorlie-Boulder, is a small fauna reserve with a miniature Bavarian castle, a 1903 rotunda and open-air movie screenings during summer.

The **Mt Charlotte Lookout** and the town's **reservoir** are a few hundred metres from the northeastern end of Hannan St, off the Goldfields Hwy. The view over the town is good, but there's little to see of the reservoir, which is covered to limit evaporation. This reservoir is the culmination of the genius of engineer CY O'Connor (see the boxed text, p154) – the water in it took 10 days to get here from Perth's Mundaring Weir.

If you've had enough of holes in the ground, you can do your bit towards revegetating the bush in **Karlkurla Park**, northwest of town, by scattering a packet of native silky pear seeds (available at the visitors centre) while you enjoy the 4km of walking tracks.

Tours

Goldrush Tours (☎ 9021 2954; www.goldrushtours.com.au; cnr Lane & Hay Sts) runs all sorts of tours, including half-day jaunts around Kalgoorlie-Boulder (adult/child $25/5), as well as longer outback explorations.

You can see Kalgoorlie-Boulder and the Golden Mile mining operations from the air with **Goldfields Air Services** (☎ 9093 2116; www.goldfieldsairservices.com), based at the airport. Prices start from $50 per person, with a minimum of two people.

ARCHITECTURE, KALGOORLIE-BOULDER STYLE

As a young town, Kalgoorlie quickly reached fabled heights of prosperity. Its magnificent, enormous public buildings, erected at the turn of the 19th century, are evidence of its fabulous wealth. For a town better known for its love of beer, skimpies and horse racing, it boasts a fine collection of architectural styles. Nowhere is this better demonstrated than along Hannan St. You can expect to see curious blends of Victorian gold-boom, Edwardian, Moorish and Art-Nouveau styles, which have melded to produce a bizarre mix of ornate façades, colonnaded footpaths, recessed verandas, stuccoed walls and general overstatement.

The façade of the **York Hotel** (259 Hannan St) is one of Hannan St's most elaborate, with arches, bay windows, stucco and brick decoration, a pair of silver cupolas and a huge French-style square dome. The interior features a beautiful carved staircase. The hotel was built in 1900 and played host to many stage shows that came through Kalgoorlie.

The **Palace Hotel** (cnr Hannan & Maritana Sts) was designed to be the town's most luxurious hotel; all of its furnishings were brought in from Melbourne. The Palace was built from locally quarried stone and was the first hotel to have electric lighting. Former US president Herbert Hoover was a regular visitor during his mining youth.

The much-photographed **Exchange Hotel** (135 Hannan St), which stands just opposite the Palace Hotel, is one of Kalgoorlie-Boulder's most attractive pubs; its façade features a vast array of decorative elements, two-storey verandas, a corner tower and a corrugated, galvanised-iron roof.

The single-storey **City Markets** (272-280 Hannan St) has a triple-arched gateway topped by twin turrets. In the early 1900s the central covered courtyard was the home of greengrocers, butchers and fruiterers.

The old **Kalgoorlie Miner & Western Argus building** (125-127 Hannan St), built in 1900, was the first three-storey building in town. The upper storeys feature elaborate classical details. Kalgoorlie's first newspaper, the *Western Argus,* was published for the first time in 1894, only 17 months after gold was first discovered. The first edition of the *Kalgoorlie Miner* (still published) appeared in September 1895.

Festivals & Events

The highlight of the social calendar is the annual **Kalgoorlie-Boulder Racing Round** in early September, when locals and a huge influx of visitors dress up to the nines to watch horses race on the red dirt.

On the third Sunday of each month, Boulder's Burt St is busy with the pleasantly low-key and community-centred **Boulder Market Day**, where morning tea with homemade scones, jam and cream in the town hall is an absolute must.

Sleeping
BUDGET

Kalgoorlie Backpackers (☎ 0412 110 001; 166 Hay St; dm/s/d $20/35/50; ✺ ☐ ☎) Partly located in a former brothel, this well-run hostel with a comfy TV lounge was part-occupied by long-stay contractors when we last visited and, like the YHA, is a good place to find out about work opportunities. It's opposite Kalgoorlie-Boulder's red-light action.

Golddust Backpackers YHA (☎ 9091 3737; golddust@westnet.com.au; 192 Hay St; dm/s/d $24/35/55; ✺ ☐ ☎) Also close to the Hay St strip, this hostel has clean, basic rooms, good communal areas including a games room, and noticeboards giving information about available work in town.

Kalgoorlie Accommodation Village (☎ 9039 4800; www.resortparks.com.au/kalgoorlie.asp; 286 Burt St; unpowered/powered sites $25/26, chalets $89, units $95; ✺ ☐ ☎) This complex has great A-frame cabins, grassy sites, a kids' playground and pool, and is fully equipped for disabled travellers.

Boulder Accommodation Village (☎ 9093 1266; www.resortparks.com.au/boulder.asp; 201 Lane St; unpowered/powered sites $25/26, chalets $89, units $95; ✺ ☐ ☎) The sister complex to Kalgoorlie Accommodation Village, and home to the same excellent facilities.

MIDRANGE

York Hotel (☎ /fax 9021 2337; 259 Hannan St; s/d $45/75) One of Kalgoorlie's most unique heritage buildings, this is a fascinating rabbit warren of high-ceilinged rooms and wooden staircases. It's good-value accommodation, with breakfast included.

Palace Hotel (☎ 9021 2788; www.palacehotel.com.au; cnr Hannan & Maritana Sts; s/d $55/85, balcony s/d $90/120, apt $105; ✺) Climb the magnificent old staircase to reach the accommodation wing, a rabbit warren of various styles of rooms.

Hannan's View Motel (☎ 9091 3333; www.hannansview.com.au; 430 Hannan St; r $105; ✺) If you're in town for a while, this is a good central option with self-contained units, free in-house movies, and access to the town's Olympic pool and gym, a five-minute drive away.

TOP END

Railway Motel (☎ 9088 0000; www.railwaymotel.com.au; 51 Forrest St; apt $120; s/d $130/142; ✺ ☎) This complex, opposite the train station and built on the site of the old hotel of the same name, is a cut above the average with bright, spruced-up rooms and comfy reclining chairs. Its two-bedroom apartments dotted around town are *very* good value.

Broadwater Hotel & Apartments (☎ 9080 0800; www.broadwaters.com.au; 21 Davidson St; r from $160; ✺ ☐ ☎) This stylish complex, in a residential area between Kalgoorlie and Boulder, boasts chichi rooms with big bathrooms and garden views.

Quest Yelverton Kalgoorlie (☎ 9022 8181; www.kalgoorlie.property.questwa.com.au; 210 Egan St; r $165; ✺ ☎) Close enough to Hannan St to walk but far enough away to get a quiet night, the Yelverton's stylish, fully self-contained and serviced apartments have all you need – even a lap pool.

Eating

Barista 202 (☎ 9022 2228; 202 Hannan St; breakfast rolls $4; ☺ breakfast & lunch Mon-Sat, breakfast Sun) This buzzing café with great artwork on the walls is a welcome addition to the Kal scene. It serves Italian sandwiches and baked yummies to accompany good coffee.

Acropolis Shishkebabs (86 Hannan St; mains $8; ☺ dinner) Racing-round regulars swear by these moreish kebabs as partying fuel.

Hoover Café (☎ 9021 2788; cnr Hannan & Maritana Sts; mains $10; ☺ lunch) Attached to the Palace Hotel, this café serves great-value home-cooked lunches – a mean homemade soup and sandwich is only $10 – and morning and afternoon teas, with fresh-baked scones, until 6pm.

Top End Thai (☎ 9091 4027; 71 Hannan St; mains $15-19; ☺ dinner Mon-Sat) The service is guaranteed to be eccentric and the food tongue-tingling good at this stalwart of the Kal dining scene.

Paddy's Ale House (☎ 9021 2833; Exchange Hotel, 135 Hannan St; mains $15-28) With a wide range of tap beers, Paddy's serves up classic counter meals like bangers and mash to the hordes; $17 buffet dinners are great value.

Monty's (☎ 9022 8288; cnr Hannan & Porter Sts; mains $15-30; ◷ 24hr) The servings of standard café fare here are ginormous and, even better, they're available round the clock.

Larcombe's Bar & Grill (☎ 9080 0800; Broadwater Hotel & Apartments, 21 Davidson St; mains $18-28; ◷ breakfast, lunch & dinner) It's worth the drive from the centre of town to sip a decent coffee or wine on the veranda, and eat at this award-winning restaurant.

Blue Monkey (☎ 9091 3311; 418 Hannan St; mains $23-33; ◷ breakfast & dinner Mon-Sat, breakfast & lunch Sun) Start the day in the courtyard with a cooked breakfast ($15) and creamy coffee, and end it with a good glass of wine and Mod-Oz meal.

Saltimbocca (☎ 9022 8028; 90 Egan St; mains $25; ◷ dinner Mon-Sat) With starched white tablecloths, original artworks and a classic Italian menu, this bistro-style place is an appealing upmarket option.

Drinking

Even at the height of drought, there's never a shortage of watering holes in Kal, where some 30 pubs await your custom. Don't be surprised if the female bar staff appear somewhat skimpily clad in underwear, suspenders and high heels – 'skimpies' are the norm here, and you'll need to pick your venue if you prefer your bar staff fully clothed.

Wild West Saloon (☎ 9021 2833; Exchange Hotel, 135 Hannan St) For an anthropological experience, the front bar at the Exchange Hotel provides a window into some locals' lives at all hours of the day, with skimpies, TV sports and mine workers chain-drinking.

Paddy's Ale House (☎ 9021 2833; Exchange Hotel, 135 Hannan St) At the back of the Exchange, this Irish-style pub is for punters discerning about the brand of amber fluid they're imbibing; big-screen sports-channel TVs abound.

Judd's (☎ 9021 3046; Kalgoorlie Hotel, 319 Hannan St) With hot-pink walls and windows that open onto the street, this bar is great for catching live bands or a lively night with mates.

De Bernales (☎ 9021 4534; 193 Hannan St) For as long as we can remember, De Bernales has been the place for a quietish drink amid the Hannan St hoopla.

Entertainment

You can catch a flick in air-conditioned comfort at the **Ace Viewway Cinema** (☎ 9021 2199; Oswald St) or watch them under the stars at **Hammond Park** (p156) during summer.

Visiting artists perform regularly at the **Goldfields Arts Centre** (☎ 9088 6900; Cheetham St).

The gambling game two-up, beloved in the bush, is usually played somewhere in town each week; check at the visitors centre or see if **Fun-Time Two-Up** (☎ 9093 3467; Sheffield's Bar & Grill, cnr Burt & Lionel Sts, Boulder) is happening.

Platform Bar (☎ 9021 2788; Palace Hotel, cnr Hannan & Maritana Sts) This is where big nights out in Kalgoorlie inevitably end, boogie-ing at this late-night bar.

Sylvesters (☎ 9021 1036; 52 Hannan St) Kal's long-suffering nightclub is at the top end of Hannan St; the building was up for lease when we last visited, so the club may or may not survive the change of owner.

Shopping

The **Goldfields Aboriginal Art Gallery** (☎ 9021 1710; 222 Dugan St) sells paintings and crafts, as does the **Desert Art Shop** (☎ 9091 5505; 9 Hannan St) next to the museum, where artists may be working when you drop by.

Kalgoorlie-Boulder is a good place to buy gold nuggets fashioned into relatively inexpensive jewellery – shop along Hannan St.

Coles, K-Mart and Woolworths supermarkets, all on Hannan St, are the places to stock up for those outback trips.

Getting There & Away

See p153 for information about bus and train services to Kalgoorlie-Boulder.

Getting Around

Between Kalgoorlie and Boulder, there's a regular bus service from 7am to 6pm Monday to Friday and Saturday morning with **Trans-Goldfields** (☎ 9021 2655; adult/child $1.90/80¢). Pick it up from the local bus stops on Hannan St.

If you want to explore further afield, you'll have to drive, hitch or take a tour as public transport is limited. You can rent cars from many companies, including **Hertz** (☎ 9093 2211), **Budget** (☎ 9093 2300) and **Avis** (☎ 9021 1722), all located at the airport, and **Halfpenny Hire** (☎ 9021 1804; Hannan St).

COOLGARDIE

☎ 08 / pop 1500

Today you wouldn't pick that the quiet, dusty town of Coolgardie was once the third-biggest town in WA. These days it's a pause in the long journey to or from the Nullarbor Plain, or a daytrip from Kal, 39km to the east.

THE SOUTHERN OUTBACK

A reef of gold was discovered here in 1892 by the prospector Arthur Bayley and his mate Bill Ford, and called 'Bayley's Reward'. By the end of the 19th century, the population of Coolgardie had boomed to 15,000. There were two stock exchanges, six newspapers, more than 20 hotels and three breweries. You only have to glance at the huge town hall, courthouse and post-office building to appreciate the size that Coolgardie once was, or potter around the side streets and read the many heritage plaques outside houses and other public buildings. The gold then petered out and the town withered away quickly. During the boom of the 1990s, when world gold prices went up and mines were reopened, the population grew to around 2000, but has since declined.

The **visitors centre** (☎ 9026 6090; Warden's Court, Bayley St; ☿ 9am-noon & 12.30-4pm Mon-Fri, 10am-3pm Sat & Sun) sells a decent selection of local history books. The **Goldfields Museum** (adult/child $3.50/2), in the same building and with the same hours, has a sizable display of goldfields memorabilia, along with information about former US president Herbert Hoover's days on the WA goldfields in Gwalia.

Warden Finnerty's Residence (☎ 9026 6028; 2 McKenzie St; adult/child $3.50/2; ☿ 11am-4pm Thu-Tue) was built for Coolgardie's first mining warden and magistrate, John Michael Finnerty, and the house has been beautifully restored by the National Trust.

One kilometre west of Coolgardie is the **town cemetery**, which includes the graves of explorer Ernest Giles (1835–97) and several Afghan camel drivers. Due to the unsanitary conditions and violence on the goldfields, it's said that 'one half of the population buried the other half'. The old **pioneer cemetery** (Forrest St) was used from 1892 to 1894.

At the **Camel Farm** (☎ 9026 6159; Great Eastern Hwy; adult/child $4.50/2; ☿ 10am-4pm school & public holidays, or by appointment), 3km west of town, you can take short camel rides (from $5.50) or organise longer treks.

About 30km south of Coolgardie, on Rock Rd, is **Gnarlbine Rocks**, an important watering point for the early prospectors. **Victoria Rock Nature Reserve**, with primitive camping, is a further 18km south.

It's best to use your own wheels to get to and around Coolgardie, but you can hook up with the daily **Perth-Goldfields Express** (☎ 1800 620 440; www.goldrushtours.com.au) on its way between

GOLDEN TRAIL

If you're feeling a little adventurous, consider the **Golden Quest Discovery Trail** (www.goldenquesttrail.com). The 965km trail starts its exploration of the region's gold industry in Coolgardie, heads northwards through gold-mining ghost towns towards Leonora and Laverton, then turns south and finishes at Kalgoorlie-Boulder, passing 25 interpretive sites along the way. These reveal some fascinating characters and events and, while in good weather the route is accessible to all vehicles, more than half of the road is unsealed so you should ask about road conditions and safe travel tips before you set off. You can buy the accompanying CD-ROM and book ($40) from most visitors centres in the area.

Perth and Kalgoorlie-Boulder, or get a ride with **Goldfields Transport** (☎ 9021 2655), which runs a school bus between Kal and Coolgardie (adult/child $5.70/2.20).

NORTH OF KALGOORLIE-BOULDER

The road north is surfaced from Kalgoorlie-Boulder to the three 'Ls' – the mining towns of Leonora (237km north), Laverton (367km northeast) and Leinster (372km north). Off the main road, however, traffic is virtually nonexistent and rain can quickly close unsealed roads. There are several towns of interest along the way – including Kanowna, Broad Arrow, Ora Banda, Menzies and Kookynie. Beyond Leinster, remote Wiluna (540km north of Kal) is a true outback town.

Perth-Goldfields Express (☎ 1800 620 440; www.goldrushtours.com.au) has a weekly bus service from Perth to Leonora and Laverton via Kalgoorlie (see p153), and in the reverse direction.

Kanowna, Broad Arrow & Ora Banda
☎ 08

Kanowna is the most easily accessible of the goldfields ghost towns, 18km from Kalgoorlie-Boulder. In 1905 it had a population of 12,000, 16 hotels, two breweries, many churches and an hourly train service to Kalgoorlie. Today the population is zero, and apart from the train station platform and the odd pile of rubble, nothing remains except a grid of dusty streets and some information signs. A couple of kilometres south of the township site is the

THE SOUTHERN OUTBACK

interesting and isolated old cemetery, which includes two early headstones of a Japanese prostitute and miner killed in a local scandal. It was relocated away from town when the original graveyard was found to be sitting atop a rich vein of gold!

Kanowna is now the starting point for the annual fund-raising **Balzano barrow race**, during which teams dress up and push a miner's barrow to Kalgoorlie Boulder, in the tradition of James Balzano, who arrived at Kanowna in 1896 carrying all his worldly possessions on a primitive wheelbarrow made out of saplings and packing-case wood. The race is held in September or October and is organised by the local rotary club (www.hannansrotary.com).

Broad Arrow, 38km north of Kal, was featured in *The Nickel Queen*, the first full-length feature film made in WA. It is a shadow of its former self – at the beginning of the 20th century it had a population of 2400; now there's just one pub and a couple of derelict looking houses.

Ora Banda, 28km west of the Goldfields Hwy beyond Broad Arrow, has shrunk from a population of 2000 to less than 50. After a notorious pub-bombing in 2000, much of the original 1911 **Ora Banda Historic Inn** (☎ 9024 2444) has been rebuilt, local memorabilia adorns the walls, and an original three-way open fireplace keeps the pub cosy in winter. It's open for business, resplendent with a new beer garden and serving lunch and dinner daily; accommodation was being (re)constructed during 2006.

Lake Ballard, Menzies & Kookynie
☎ 08

Travellers continue to pass through Menzies, around 132km north of Kalgoorlie-Boulder, on the way to see British artist Antony Gormley's haunting **sculptures on Lake Ballard**, an isolated salt lake on a dirt road 51km north of town. The strange silhouettes of 51 carbonised steel figures (created from body scans of Menzies' residents) appear through the shifting mirage of the glittering salt and are quite beautiful. Check road conditions at the Caltex service station in Menzies, take plenty of drinking water and allow yourself a couple of hours to wander through this fantastic installation, created for the 2003 Perth International Arts Festival.

Menzies is another typical tiny goldfields town. At its height it had 10,000 people in

1905, and many early buildings remain, including the **train station** with its 120m platform (1898) and the imposing **town hall** (1896). **Menzies Hotel** (☎ 9024 2043; 22 Shenton St; s/d $48/65, donga $60) has *extremely* dilapidated old-style hotel rooms as well as very basic dongas.

A better accommodation option is the **Grand Hotel** (☎ 9031 3010; s/d $58/93) at the gold ghost town of **Kookynie**. Midway between Menzies and Leonora, on a good dirt road about 25km east of and parallel to the highway, this magnificent old country pub is full of local character. Quiet **Niagara Dam**, 10km from Kookynie, built with cement hauled by a 400-strong camel train, is now a top bush camping spot, with walk trails, wildlife gathering around the water, and good interpretive signs.

Leonora & Gwalia
☎ 08 / pop 1500

The mining and pastoral service centre of **Leonora** is 237km north of Kalgoorlie-Boulder and serves as the railhead for the nickel from Windarra and Leinster. Climb **Iank (Smoodgers) Hill** for a good view of the town, and check out the old public buildings on the main street near the **visitors centre** (☎ 9037 6044; www.leonora .wa.gov.au; Tower St; ☽ 9am-5pm). It's beside the Telecentre if you want to check email.

If you need to stay the night, try the **Leonora Caravan Park** (☎ 9037 6568; Rochester St; unpowered/ powered sites $10/20, on-site vans $32), or the **Central Hotel** (☎ 9037 6042; Tower St; budget/motel r $45/93), where the motel rooms are self-contained and counter meals are served in the lounge bar.

Just 4km southwest of town, **Gwalia Historic Site** was occupied in 1896 and deserted pretty much overnight in 1963, after the pit closed.

IN THE PRESIDENT'S BEDROOM

A rather unique B&B experience is offered at Gwalia's **Hoover House** (☎ 9037 7122; www.gwalia.org.au; r from $100). The three exquisitely restored bedrooms – with private use of the house verandas and gardens after the museum gates are closed at 4pm – are gorgeous. Herbert Hoover's room was probably the one overlooking the awesome open pit and – in the foreground – the croquet lawn; an optional rustic summer sunset bath, in the great outdoors with glass of wine to hand, adds just that little extra.

THE SOUTHERN OUTBACK

With houses and household goods intact, it's an eerie, fascinating ghost town. On the hillside above the wander-through townsite, the **museum** (☎ 9037 7122; adult/child $5/2; ☼ 10am-4pm) has more weird and wonderful *stuff* in it than we've ever seen, and **Hoover House** – the beautifully restored 1898 mine manager's house, named for the first Gwalia mine manager who later became 31st President of the United States – is stunning.

Wiluna
☎ 08 / pop 300

Some 300km north of Leonora, the remote town of Wiluna, formerly a gold-mining town, is now an administrative centre with a mainly Aboriginal population. The **shire office** (☎ 9981 7010; www.wiluna.wa.gov.au; Scotia St), in the restored old hospital building, provides essential visitor info for those heading off on the Canning Stock Route (below), and is the setting for the unexpectedly fabulous **Tjukurba Art Gallery**. If you've found the experience of being in Wiluna somewhat uneasy and confronting, this great exhibition of local Aboriginal art shows a different perspective of the lives of community members; it's as good as (and sells for lower prices than) most indigenous art galleries in Australia.

Most travellers come to Wiluna in a 4WD en route to or from the Canning Stock Route or Gunbarrel Hwy, and overnight at the **Wiluna Club Hotel** (☎ 9981 7012; unpowered/powered sites $15/23, hotel r $55, motel r $88), which has all the splendid contradictions of a classic outback pub. Souvenir stubby-holders in the bar are emblazoned with bare-breasted women while, in an old-fashioned dining-room with hanging lamps and lace tablecloths, a grandmotherly woman serves enormous platters of standards like roast lamb ($22). It's not a flash experience but it's authentic and, as the poem at the bar says, '…there's nowhere else you can go'.

Canning Stock Route & Gunbarrel Highway

Wiluna is the start or finish point of two of Australia's greatest 4WD adventures – the Canning Stock Route and the Gunbarrel Hwy. *Canning Stock Route – A Traveller's Guide* by R&E Gard (2004) is the drivers' bible for the Canning, and HEMA maps' detailed *Great Desert Tracks – North West Sheet* is a must for both.

The **Canning Stock Route** runs about 1800km southwest from Halls Creek to Wiluna, crossing the Great Sandy and Gibson Deserts. As the track has not been maintained for more than 30 years it's a route to be taken seriously and, if you're starting from Wiluna, pick up comprehensive road and safety information from the shire offices.

Taking the old **Gunbarrel Highway** (to the north of the Great Central Rd) from Wiluna to Warakuna near the Northern Territory (NT) border is a long, rough trip through lots of sand dunes. Like the Canning, it's suggested that for safety you drive this in convoy with other vehicles and you need to take all supplies – including fuel and water for the duration – with you. Let the police posts at either end of both tracks know your movements.

Laverton
☎ 08 / pop 1100

From Leonora you turn northeast to Laverton, a mining service town some 360km north of Kalgoorlie-Boulder, where the surfaced road ends. The cheery **visitors centre** (☎ 9031 1750; lavertontourist@westnet.com.au; Laver Pl) is combined with the library and internet access at the Telecentre. Laverton marks the start of the **Great Central Road** to Yulara (a tourist development near Uluru) via Warburton. Expect to overnight and/or stock up on supplies of fuel and water here, and *definitely* check at the visitors centre for current road conditions.

If you're looking for somewhere to camp, the **Laverton Caravan Park** (☎ 9031 1072; unpowered/powered sites $10/20; chalets $80) is the only option. **Desert Inn Hotel** (☎ 9031 1188; r $80) has rooms attached to the town's only pub, where you can also get a counter meal, and **Laverton Motel** (☎ 9031 1130; apt $110), a series of tatty (but self-contained, clean-enough, and big) recycled miners' units, is great value for families or small groups.

Great Central Road (Outback Way)

For those interested in a genuine outback experience, the unsealed Great Central Rd (officially renamed, in 2005, 'Outback Way' but as yet rarely known as such) provides rich scenery of red sand, spinifex, mulga and desert oaks. From Laverton it's a mere 1132km to Yulara and 1710km to Alice Springs.

The road, while sandy and corrugated in places, is suitable for all vehicles, though it can

PERMITS, PLEASE

The Great Central Rd traverses various pockets of Aboriginal land, and you need a permit to travel along it. If you're crossing the Northern Territory border, allow three weeks for the paperwork; contact the **Aboriginal Lands Trust** (☎ 08-9235 8000; Cloisters Sq) in Perth or the **Central Land Council** (☎ 08-8951 6320) in Alice Springs. If you're only travelling on the Western Australia (WA) side, you can get a permit online and instantly at the website of WA's **Department of Indigenous Affairs** (DIA; www .dia.wa.gov.au and link to 'entry permits'). In Kalgoorlie the **DIA office** (☎ 9021 5666; cnr Brookman & Cassidy Sts) can help with any last-minute queries.

be closed for days after rain. Diesel is available at roughly 300km intervals on the WA side, as is Opal fuel which, at the Warburton and Warakuna roadhouses, can be used instead of unleaded petrol. (Opal is unsniffable, and its provision is one of the measures in place to counteract petrol-sniffing problems in local communities.)

Coming from Laverton, the three WA roadhouses – all of which provide food, fuel and limited mechanical services – are **Tjukayirla** (☎ 9037 1108; tjukayirla@bigpond.com) at 315km, **Warburton** (☎ 8956 7656) at 567km and **Warakuna** (☎ 8956 7344) at 798km. All have a range of accommodation, from camping (around $10 per person), to budget rooms (around $40) and self-contained units (around $100); you should book ahead, as rooms are limited.

At Warburton take time to visit the **Tjulyuru Cultural & Civic Centre** (☎ 8956 7966; www.tjulyuru .com; ☷ 8am-5pm Mon-Fri), near the roadhouse; the art gallery contains an extensive collection of Warburton Aboriginal paintings. At **Giles**, 231km northeast of Warburton and 105km west of the NT border, there is a meteorological station which runs a tour daily at 8am.

Note that Warakuna, Warburton and Giles run on Northern Territory time, which is 1½ hours ahead of WA time.

SOUTH OF KALGOORLIE-BOULDER
Norseman
☎ 08 / pop 1600

To most people, Norseman is simply the crossroads town where you turn east for the journey across the Nullarbor, south to Esperance or north to Kalgoorlie and Perth. Named not for a Scandinavian but for the prospector's horse that went lame in 1894 on a nugget of gold in its hoof, the town still has active gold mines.

The **visitors centre** (☎ 9039 1071; www.norseman .info; 68 Roberts St; ☷ 9am-5pm) has good public showers and is a mine of information about the Nullarbor trek; if you've just done the big trip, staff can issue you with your very own certificate to show the folks back home. A Telecentre is close by.

MESSAGE STICK *Virginia Jealous*

I'd hoped to catch up with a friend of friend, a policeman in Kalgoorlie. But he was working out bush, about 1000km away, more than half of it along a red dirt road. That's OK, I was going out bush that way too, we'd meet up in a few days.

Then it started to rain. Not just any old rain, but the first rain of the year. It was July. I sat in a motel, waiting for the rain to stop. It didn't. I drove to the edge of the dirt and looked at the waterlogged road. Then a bloke came and put out the 'road closed' sign. So I turned around.

I was (of course) out of mobile phone range. He had a satellite phone, its number unknown to me. Even if I had known it, many of the phone boxes were out of order in the occasional small town or roadhouse I passed. He rang our mutual friend, who phoned and emailed me. I was still out of range and away from internet. Some days later, back in town, I read and heard his messages. They said:

"Good call not to go on. Road still closed. People ignoring 'road closed' signs. Vehicles slipping and rolling over. People injured. We're out there fetching them and slipping all over the place too. Why DO they do it?!"

I don't know the answer to that. But I thought if I got the chance to tell the policeman's story, I would. And, next time, maybe get a sat phone.

THE SOUTHERN OUTBACK

The **Historical & Geological Collection** (☎ 9039 1593; Battery Rd; adult/child $2/1; ☺ 10am-1pm Mon, Wed, Thu & Fri or by request), in the quaint old School of Mines building, has items from the gold-rush days.

There's an excellent view of the town and surrounding salt lakes from the well-signposted **Beacon Hill Mararoa Lookout**, over the more than 4.2 million tonnes of mountainous tailings. Be sure to take a break and do this; there are excellent interpretive signs at the lookout about this extraordinary landscape, and a short loop walk track on the hillside to stretch those car-weary legs.

SLEEPING & EATING

Gateway Caravan Park (☎ /fax 9039 1500; 23 Prinsep St; unpowered/powered sites $18.50/23, on-site vans $49, cabins $69-89; ☒) Good cabins and a bushy atmosphere make this a reliable option.

Lodge 101 (☎ 9039 1541; 101 Prinsep St; dm/s/d $25/35/55) After the relentless road, this colourful house – with friendly owners, clean and comfortable rooms and knick-knacks galore – is a cheery place to rest your cramped bones.

Great Western Motel (☎ 9039 1633; Prinsep St; s/d $90/140; ☒ ☒) If you're looking for cool respite, try these motel rooms with rammed-earth walls and a leafy setting. There's a restaurant on-site.

There's not exactly a huge choice of eating options here, but you could try the reliable **Tin Camel Café** (Prinsep St), beside the tin camels on the roundabout, of course, or the 24-hour café at the BP service station, where the food ain't exotic but it's available round the clock and eaten in a 1950s-style area with red vinyl booths.

EYRE HIGHWAY (THE NULLARBOR)

It's a little more than 2700km between Perth and Adelaide – not much less than the distance from London to Moscow – across the vast and legendary **Nullarbor Plain**, and the long and sometimes lonely Eyre Hwy that crosses its southern edge. Nullarbor is bad Latin for 'no trees', but it's not entirely barren; the road is flanked by vegetation most of the way, as this coastal fringe receives regular rain, especially in winter.

The road across the Nullarbor takes its name from Edward John Eyre, the explorer who made the first east-west crossing in 1841. It was a superhuman effort that took five months of hardship and resulted in the death of Eyre's companion, John Baxter. In 1877 a telegraph line was laid across the Nullarbor, hugging the coast and roughly delineating the route the first road would take.

Later that century, miners on their way to the goldfields followed the same telegraph line across the empty plain. In 1896 the first bicycle crossing was made and in 1912 the first car was driven across, but in the next 12 years only three more cars managed to traverse the southwest of the continent.

In 1941 WWII inspired the building of a transcontinental highway, just as it had the Alice Springs to Darwin route. It was a rough-and-ready track when completed, and in the 1950s only a few vehicles a day made the crossing. In the 1960s the traffic flow increased to more than 30 vehicles a day and in 1969 the WA government surfaced the road as far as the South Australia (SA) border. Finally, in 1976, the last stretch from the SA border was surfaced and now the Nullarbor crossing is a much easier drive, but still a long one.

The surfaced road runs close to the coast on the SA side. The Nullarbor region ends dramatically on the coast of the Great Australian Bight, at cliffs that drop steeply into the ocean. It's easy to see why this was a seafarer's nightmare, for a ship driven onto the coast would quickly be pounded to pieces against the cliffs, and climbing them would be a near impossibility.

From Norseman, where the Eyre Hwy begins, it's about 730km to the WA–SA border, near Eucla, and almost 500km further to Ceduna (the name from an Aboriginal word meaning 'a place to sit down and rest') in SA. From Ceduna, it's still about 800km to Adelaide via Port Augusta.

North of the Eyre Hwy, the **Trans-Australia Railway** runs across the Nullarbor Plain. One stretch of the railway runs dead straight for 478km – the longest piece of straight railway line in the world.

One of the most comprehensive publications to cover the journey is the free *The Nullarbor: Australia's Great Road Journey*, available from visitors centres throughout WA and SA.

UNDER THE NULLARBOR

Beneath the uninhabited and barren landscape of the Nullarbor Plain lies a wealth of interest. The Nullarbor is an ancient limestone sea bed, up to 300m thick in places. About 20 million years ago, shells and marine organisms began to settle and some three million years ago the bed was gently raised, forming a huge plateau 700km long and up to 300km wide.

Within this raised plateau is Australia's largest network of caves, formed over the millennia as rain seeped through cracks in the surface limestone. The caves vary in size from shallow depressions to elaborate, deep caves with immense chambers. About 50 of the caves begin via passages in large sinkholes or dolines; others can be accessed only through narrow, vertical blowholes; many surface unexpectedly beside the 4WD tracks off the highway.

Perhaps best-known is **Cocklebiddy Cave**, 12km north of the Eyre Hwy, which has one of the longest underwater passages known in the world; in 1984 a team of French explorers set a record here for the deepest cave-dive in the world. The **Mullamullang Cave** east of Cocklebiddy is the most extensive cave network known in Australia and contains superb mineral formations known as the **Salt Cellars**. West of Eucla are the Weebubbie, Pannikin Plains and Abrakurrie Caves, which are completely off-limits because they are so unstable. The **Abrakurrie Cave** contains the largest chamber of the Nullarbor caves, 180m long and 45m wide and with a 40m-high ceiling. More caves exist on the South Australia (SA) side of the border.

As these caves are both unstable and unstaffed, they are not generally publicly accessible. You should *never* enter any of them without an experienced guide and proper safety gear. Many lives have been lost and the vertical access to a number of the caves requires highly specialised equipment; you have been warned.

Those keen to venture underground need permits; contact the Esperance office of the **Department of Environment & Conservation** (DEC; ☎ 9071 3733) or the SA **Department for the Environment and Heritage** (☎ 08-8625 3144) in Ceduna for more information.

CROSSING THE NULLARBOR
Bicycle

The Nullarbor Plain is a real challenge to cyclists. They are attracted by the barrenness and distance, certainly not by the interesting scenery. As you drive across you'll often see cyclists, at all times of the year, lifting their water bottles to their parched mouths or sheltering from the sun.

Excellent equipment is needed and adequate water supplies must be carried. Cyclists should also know where all the water tanks are located. Adequate protection (hats, lotions etc) from the sun should be used even in cloudy weather. The prevailing wind for most of the journey is west to east, the most preferable direction to be pedalling.

Bus & Train

Scheduled bus services no longer make the trip across the Nullarbor – cheap flights have made it uneconomical. If you want to make the trip by road but don't have a vehicle, your best option is probably to hang around and introduce yourself to travellers at the Norseman caravan park; the usual caveats about accepting (or giving) lifts to strangers apply.

The *Indian Pacific*, run by **Great Southern Railway** (☎ 13 21 47; www.trainways.com.au), provides one of the world's great train journeys (see p265).

Car

While the Nullarbor is no longer a torture trail where cars get shaken to bits by potholes and corrugations, or where you're going to die of thirst waiting for help to turn up if you break down, it's still wise to prepare well.

The distance between fuel stops is about 200km, so your vehicle needs to be in good shape with good tyres. The cost of fuel varies greatly: it's cheaper in towns and ridiculously

PEDAL POWER

Spare a thought for the first cyclist to cross the Nullarbor. Arthur Richardson set off from Coolgardie on 24 November 1896 with a small kit and water bag. Thirty-one days later he arrived in Adelaide having followed the telegraph line, on the way encountering hot winds, '100° in the shade' and 40km of sand hills west of Madura station.

expensive in tiny places in the outback, where you have no choice but to fill up. Mundrabilla and Eucla are generally the cheapest options (by far) for fuel on the WA side of the Nullarbor.

Carry more than enough drinking water – at least 4L per person – just in case you do have to sit it out by the road on a hot summer day. There are limited freshwater facilities between Norseman and Ceduna, and be aware that places listed as water stops may not in fact have any available.

There are no banking facilities between Norseman and Ceduna, but all roadhouses have Eftpos and take major credit cards, most have internet booths, and all have landline phones. Most mobile phones will be out of range for the duration.

Take it easy on the Nullarbor – plenty of people try to set speed records and plenty more have messed up their cars when they've run into kangaroos at night. There are many rest areas – make use of them!

Check out www.nullarbornet.com.au for more information.

Walking

The occasional fit and adventurous – and possibly stark-raving mad – soul (or should that be sole?) makes their way by foot across the Nullarbor. Needless to say this is not for the unprepared or fainthearted. Food drops must be organised well in advance, most solitary walkers push a trolley so that enough water can be carted, and speedy road-trains and vehicles are a real challenge. If you pass a walker, don't honk and give them a heart attack but stop and offer food or water if you can; they're sure to have a good story to tell in return.

NORSEMAN TO COCKLEBIDDY

Midway between Norseman and Balladonia there are simple, good-value overnight options available just off the highway in the bush at **Fraser Range Station** (☎ 9039 3210; www.fraserrangestation.com.au; unpowered/powered sites $15/25, budget s/d $40/50, renovated r from $75). Choose from camping to budget rooms to beautifully renovated rooms in the thick-walled old stone cottages of the former shearers' quarters; there are shared bathrooms and a well-equipped campers kitchen.

From Norseman, the first roadhouse you reach is **Balladonia**, 191km to the east. The small cultural heritage museum here displays themes such as Afghan camel drivers, Aboriginal settlement and the crash landing of the US National Aeronautics & Space Administration (NASA) Skylab in the 1970s; the museum was closed when we last visited, but should reopen in 2007. The **Balladonia Hotel Motel** (☎ 9039 3453; www.users.bigpond.com/balladonia; unpowered/powered sites $13/17, dm $17, s/d from $85/99; 🞨 🖳) offers a decent plate of daily specials for $12.50.

Balladonia to Cocklebiddy, some 210km, is a lonely section. The first 160km to **Caiguna** includes one of the world's longest stretches of straight road – 145km, the so-called Ninety Mile Straight. If you can't face any more road, stay the night here at the **John Eyre Motel** (☎ 9039 3459; unpowered/powered sites $12/18, s/d with shared bathroom $58/73, s/d $83/99; 🞨).

There's a decent playground for kids and shaded picnic tables at **Cocklebiddy.** The **Cocklebiddy Wedgetail Inn** (☎ 9039 3462; unpowered/powered sites $13/19, standard s/d $82/99; 🞨) has fuel, a licensed restaurant and snack bar; some budget rooms are also planned. Cocklebiddy runs on Central Western time – 45 minutes ahead of Perth time, and 45 minutes behind Adelaide time.

BONZER BACKROADS – BRUMBIES, BUSH & BULL DUST

For those travelling east across the Nullarbor, two back roads, which meet about 80km south of the Eyre Hwy, lead from east of Esperance to Balladonia. The **Balladonia Track** via Mt Ragged (299km total from Esperance) is a *really* rough 4WD route north of Cape Arid; heavy rain can close this road, so check before setting out, and be well prepared. The **Parmango Rd** (262km total from Esperance) starts at Condingup. It's bumpy but passable to 2WDs when dry (watch out for bull dust in the potholes), but becomes instantly impassable except to 4WDs after rain; check its condition with the Department of Environment & Conservation (DEC) before heading out. It's a good bush road, with the possibility of brumbies and camels alongside the track and the old Balbinia Homestead 20km off the track. Enjoy the (interactive, if you choose) underwear artwork on the gates! There's no fuel or water on either of these roads, and **DEC** (☎ 9071 3733) in Esperance has a good set of informal notes – practicalities and history – on each.

Twilight Cove, 30km south of Cocklebiddy, is the dramatic point at which the limestone escarpment cliffs of the Nullarbor meet the sea; the cove attracts whales in season and is a good spot to bush camp and fish. It's accessed by a *very* rough 4WD track, and you need to know what you're doing to drive there; ask directions at the Cocklebiddy roadhouse.

Eyre Bird Observatory

South of Cocklebiddy is the unexpected treat of **Eyre Bird Observatory** (☎ 9039 3450; www.eyrebirds .org). The observatory, on the coast some 50km from Cocklebiddy and established by Birds Australia in 1977, is staffed by volunteers and housed in the sprawling old Eyre telegraph station – a magnificent 1897 limestone building with an extraordinary history – in Nuytsland Nature Reserve. Surrounded by mallee scrubland, it looks out on to spectacular roving sand dunes which – in a lesson learned from the former Eucla telegraph station, engulfed by sand many years ago – are being stabilised by innovative use of kelp from the beach, and the hand-broadcast of seeds collected from surrounding vegetation. The waters of the **Great Australian Bight** are just a walk away through the dunes.

This is the perfect place to enjoy a wide range of desert plants and animals, and the stories of people – like the great explorer Edward John Eyre – who've passed through them; a night here is great value (see below). There are several walking tracks, bird baths where some of the 240 locally identified species can be seen, and regular beach bird-counts. There's also a dusty museum of telegraph memorabilia, an interactive display of the Morse code the telegraphists used, and

an active weather station where three daily readings are taken for the Australian meteorological office.

Accommodation is $85 per person per night and includes all meals; seniors and members of Birds Australia and YHA get a discount. Meals are eaten family-style on the wide verandas in summer or around an open wood fire in the eclectic library-cum-living room in winter. The bathroom is shared, water conservation is a high priority (so BYO linen if you can), and the power is mostly solar. There's no camping here, in order to protect these resources as well as the fragile sand dune environment.

Day visitors are welcome ($10 per vehicle), but the last 10km are soft sand and are 4WD-accessible only. If you are in a 2WD and are overnighting, the wardens will pick you up from the observatory car park, 14km off the Eyre Hwy; bookings are essential.

Eyre runs on 'Eyre time' – one hour ahead of Perth, 30 minutes behind Adelaide.

COCKLEBIDDY TO EUCLA

The journey between Cocklebiddy and Eucla is around 270km.

Some 83km east of Cocklebiddy is **Madura**, close to the hills (yes, hills!) of the Hampton Tablelands. At one time, horses were bred here for the Indian army. You get good views over the plains from the road. The ruins of the **Old Madura Homestead**, several kilometres west of the new homestead by a dirt track, have some old machinery and other equipment. If you need a cool night's sleep, the standard rooms at the **Madura Pass Oasis Inn** (☎ 9039 3464; unpowered/powered sites $12/20, budget s/d $63/73, standard s/d $84/105; ✷ ☎) are air-conditioned, the

---

THE LESSON OF THE HEADLESS TRAVELLER

'There's a mysterious grave a good half-day's walk from the Telegraph Station. Four rusted 1877 pole-bases create, with old telegraph wire, a fenced off rectangle; a rough unmarked cross is wired together at one end. The body had no head. No head, no words, no story.'

Helen Gee, temporary warden of the Eyre Bird Observatory and co-founder of the Tasmanian Wilderness Society (a woman, then, who knows about the bush), pauses.

'I love the notion of the headless traveller. There's an analogy I want to take with me from Eyre; that this place, and others as remote, are places we can travel 'without our head'. We can leave mental baggage behind, and start to look at the world afresh. I've learnt from scratch a whole lot of new things. About birds, about weather recording, about whales and sand dunes. Here there's only the scarp, the mallee, the sand track to the great dunes, the waves rolling in, the ribbed sky lighting up at sunset. It's easier here to see things for what they are. I guess one of the lessons I've learned is to leave my head behind, and do it frequently!'

camp site is shady and the pool is welcome in summer.

Mundrabilla is on the lower coastal plain. At the roadhouse the ordinary **Mundrabilla Motor Hotel** (☎ 9039 3465; Eyre Hwy; s/d $69/85; ☒) is the accommodation option; fill up with cheap(ish) fuel here if you're heading west. Heading east, it's about 65km to Eucla.

EUCLA & BEYOND

Just before the SA border is **Eucla**, which has picturesque ruins of an old **telegraph repeater and weather station**, first opened in 1877 and closed in 1927. The telegraph line now runs along the railway line, far to the north. The lonely telegraph station, 4km from the Eucla roadhouse, has been mostly engulfed by the sand dunes. The dunes around Eucla in the 33-sq-km **Eucla National Park** are a truly spectacular sight, as is the high limestone **Wilson Bluff**; get directions for this track from the Border Village. The mallee scrub and heath of the park is typical of the coastal vegetation in this region.

At Eucla, many people have their photo taken with the **international sign** pinpointing distances to many parts of the world; it's near the playground's ferroconcrete sperm whale, a species seldom seen in these parts. Another popular photo stop is at the **Travellers Cross**, atop the escarpment which overlooks the ruins of old Eucla, and the **Eyre Memorial** stone.

Eucla is the border township. **Eucla Motor Hotel** (☎ 9039 3468; unpowered/powered sites $6/18, budget s/d $30/50, s/d with bathroom $82/98; ☒ ☒) is a great spot, with good facilities, wonderful views to the ocean and a great beer garden full of hardy flowers. Eucla runs on Central Western time – 45 minutes ahead of Perth time, and 45 minutes behind Adelaide time.

Border Village (☎ 9039 3474; unpowered/powered sites $12/18, budget $27, r $89; ☒ ☐ ☒) is 13km from Eucla and just across the SA border; you may need to stay here if Eucla is full. Remember to set your watch forward 1½ hours when you get to the border.

From Border Village, it's a spectacular 200km coastal drive to the **Nullarbor Roadhouse**, and about 300km further to **Ceduna**, passing the Yalata Aboriginal Reserve, Nundroo and Penong along the way.

The Wheatbelt & the Midlands

Picture dazzling displays of wildflowers, from purple mulla mullas to red Sturt's desert peas, and abundant native wildlife, from emu families crossing a dirt road to magnificent wedge-tailed eagles circling slowly overhead. There are some of the rewards for undertaking travel through the vast regions of the Wheatbelt and the Midlands, stretching some 300km or so south of the Great Eastern Hwy up to the base of the Pilbara in the north.

You can explore tiny pastoral towns with their windmills, wheat silos, wide streets and classic Aussie pubs. You'll be privy to architectural anomalies such as Hawes' wonderful buildings, Spanish-flavoured New Norcia, Cue's goldfields architecture and eerie ghost towns.

Off the beaten track you'll discover spectacular rock formations such as Walga Rock, or the much-photographed perfect granite Wave Rock. However, you don't have to travel far to experience extraordinary sights – the remarkable Pinnacles Desert is a short drive from Perth.

There are even more rewards if you visit during spring, when the region is awash with wildflowers, including appearances by fascinating flora such as the distinctive wreath flower.

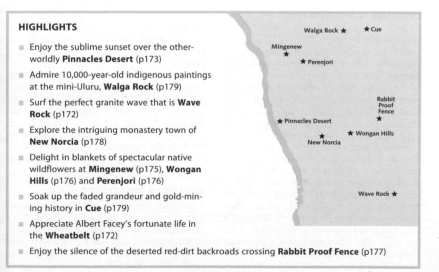

HIGHLIGHTS

- Enjoy the sublime sunset over the other-worldly **Pinnacles Desert** (p173)
- Admire 10,000-year-old indigenous paintings at the mini-Uluru, **Walga Rock** (p179)
- Surf the perfect granite wave that is **Wave Rock** (p172)
- Explore the intriguing monastery town of **New Norcia** (p178)
- Delight in blankets of spectacular native wildflowers at **Mingenew** (p175), **Wongan Hills** (p176) and **Perenjori** (p176)
- Soak up the faded grandeur and gold-mining history in **Cue** (p179)
- Appreciate Albert Facey's fortunate life in the **Wheatbelt** (p172)
- Enjoy the silence of the deserted red-dirt backroads crossing **Rabbit Proof Fence** (p177)

Walga Rock ★   ★ Cue
Mingenew ★
    ★ Perenjori
Rabbit Proof Fence ★
★ Pinnacles Desert
★ Wongan Hills
★ New Norcia
Wave Rock ★

THE WHEATBELT

CENTRAL WHEATBELT

The Great Eastern Hwy (State Hwy 94; also known as the Golden Way) starts in Perth and passes through the towns of the Avon Valley before reaching the many agricultural towns on the way to Kalgoorlie-Boulder. For much of its length it runs alongside the Golden Pipeline, the pipes that carried water from Mundaring Reservoir near Perth to Kalgoorlie-Boulder (see p154). If you've got the time, you can use the National Trust's *Golden Pipeline Heritage Trail* guidebook ($34.95) to make the trip from Mundaring to Kalgoorlie-Boulder more interesting.

GETTING THERE & AWAY

With your own wheels you can move at your own pace through the central Wheatbelt towns on your way to the goldfields. The **Perth-Goldfields Express** (☎ 1800 620 440; www.gold rushtours.com.au; Perth-Kalgoorlie adult/concession $70/43) is a bus service calling in 10 times per week en route to/from Kalgoorlie. Leaving Perth at 7.45am on Monday, Tuesday, Thursday and Friday, it stops at Cunderdin (two hours), Kellerberrin (2¼ hours), Merredin (three hours) and Southern Cross (five hours), arriving in Kalgoorlie at 3pm. On Sunday it leaves Perth at 2pm, arriving Kalgoorlie 9.15pm.

Cunderdin to Southern Cross

☎ 08

Sleepy **Cunderdin** (population 1255), 156km from Perth, is a fine spot to stretch your legs. The visitors centre is handily situated in the **museum** (☎ 9635 1291; 100 Forrest St; entry by donation; ☼ 10am-4pm), a restored steam water pumping station on the old goldfields pipeline, with exhibits on farming, gold mining and the 1968 Meckering earthquake, plus an original bush school and a Tiger Moth biplane.

If you're looking to rest your head, do it with your tongue firmly in your cheek at Cunderdin's **Ettamogah Pub** (☎ 9635 1777; cunderdinpub@westnet.com.au; 75 Main St; s/d $70/80; ☒). This wonky waterhole is a replica of an Albury-Wodonga hotel named after the pub that starred in Aussie cartoonist Ken Maynard's long-running comic for *Australasian Post* magazine. The Ettamogah does great-value counter meals and tasty steak sandwiches (mains $9 to $20).

It's worth stopping at **Kellerberrin** (population 1151), 203km from Perth, to take in the latest exhibition at the cutting-edge, contemporary **International Artspace Kellerberrin Australia** (IASKA; ☎ 9228 2444; 88-90 Massingham St; admission free; ☼ 1-5pm Thu, Fri & Sun, 10am-5pm Sat). The **visitors centre** (☎ 9045 4006; www.kellerberrin.wa.gov.au; 110 Massingham St; ☼ 9am-4.30pm) has info on other attractions.

Merredin (population 3428), 260km east of Perth, is a good place to refuel. If you want a driving break, the **visitors centre** (☎ 9041 1666; www .wheatbelttourism.com; Barrack St; ☼ 10am-4pm Mon-Fri, 10am-2pm Sat & Sun) has info on wildflower and town tours, and can tell you where to see ancient granite rock formations dating back 2,500 million years. Architectural enthusiasts will appreciate the characterful exterior of the 1928 heritage-listed **Cummins Theatre** (Bates St).

If you've done enough kilometres for one day, try Merredin's **Commercial Hotel** (☎ 9041 1052; commercialhotel@westnet.com.au; 62 Barrack St; s/d with shared bathroom $30/40) for basic rooms, or the agreeable **Merredin Caravan Park** (☎ /fax 9041 1535; 2 Oats St; unpowered/powered site $18/22).

Southern Cross (population 1200), 370km east of Perth, is the last Wheatbelt town and the first goldfields town, making a fine living from both products. Named after the stars that prospectors Tom Riseley and Mick Toomey used to guide them to discover gold here in 1888, Southern Cross was the state's first gold-rush town. Its spacious streets also inherited their names from stars and constellations. The **visitors centre** (☎ 9049 1001; www.southern-cross .info; Shire of Yilgarn, Antares St; ☼ 8.30am-4.30pm Mon-Fri) can organise bush tours and make transport bookings.

If the history of the place has you intrigued, you can discover the golden age at the mud-brick **Yilgarn History Museum** (Antares St; adult/child $2.50/50c; ☼ 9.30am-noon & 1.30-4pm Mon-Sat, 1.30-4pm Sun), the state's first miner's registry office and courthouse (1892). The **Southern Cross Palace Hotel** (☎ 9049 1555; Antares St; s/d $65/75) is a classic Aussie pub with ample verandas, affable locals and agreeable counter meals.

SOUTHERN WHEATBELT

Spectacular Wave Rock and stunning ancient granite rock formations are the highlight of this farming region, stretching from Dryandra in the west to Wave Rock in the east, and from Beverley in the north to Kojonup in the south. While Wave Rock is 200km south of

THE WHEATBELT & THE MIDLANDS

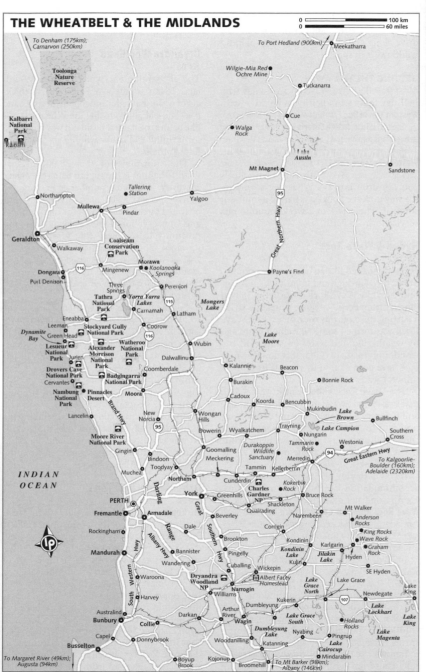

0 ——————— 100 km
0 ——————— 60 miles

To Denham (175km);
Carnarvon (250km)

To Port Hedland (900km) Meekatharra

Toolonga
Nature
Reserve

Wilgie-Mia Red
Ochre Mine

Tuckanarra

Kalbarri
National
Park

Cue

Walga
Rock

Lake
Austin

Mt Magnet

Sandstone

Tallering
Station

Yalgoo

95

Northampton

Great Northern Hwy

Mullewa
Pindar

Geraldton

Walkaway

Coalseam
Conservation
Park

Morawa

Payne's Find

Dongara
Port Denison

116

Mingenew

Koolanooka
Springs

Three
Springs

Perenjori

Mongers
Lake

Tathra
National
Park

Yarra Yarra
Lakes

115

Carnamah

Latham

Eneabba

Leeman

Stockyard Gully
National Park

Coorow

Dynamite
Bay

Green Head

116

Lake
Moore

Lesueur
National
Park

Watheroo
National
Park

Wubin

Jurien

Alexander
Morrison
National
Park

Dalwallinu

Kalannie

Beacon

Drovers Cave
National Park

Coomberdale

Cervantes

Badgingarra
National Park

Burakin

Bonnie Rock

Nambung
National
Park

Pinnacles
Desert

Moora

Cadoux

Koorda

Bencubbin

Mukinbudin

Lake
Brown

Bullfinch

Lancelin

Brand Hwy

New
Norcia

Wongan
Hills

Lake Campion

Southern
Cross

Moore River
National Park

95

Bowen

Wyalkatchem

Trayning

Nungarin

Westonia

Gingin

Goomalling

Durakoppin
Wildlife
Sanctuary

Tammarin
Rock

94

Great Eastern Hwy

Bindoon

Meckering

Merredin

To Kalgoorlie-
Boulder (160km);
Adelaide (2320km)

INDIAN
OCEAN

Muchea

Toodyay

Tammin

Kellerberrin

Darling

Northam

Cunderdin

Kokerbin
Rock

PERTH

York

Greenhills

Charles
Gardner
NP

Shackleton

Bruce Rock

Fremantle

Armadale

Beverley

Quairading

Narembeen

Mt Walker

Rockingham

Range

Dale

Brookton

Corrigin

Anderson
Rocks

King Rocks
Wave Rock

Mandurah

Albany Hwy

Bannister

Pingelly

Kondinin
Lake

Karlgarin

Graham
Rock

Wandering

Cuballing

Wickepin

Kulin

Jilakin
Lake

Hyden

SE Hyden

Waroona

Dryandra
Woodland
NP

Albert Facey
Homestead

Lake
Grace
North

Lake Grace

Newdegate

Lake
King

Harvey

Narrogin

Williams

Kukerin

107

Lake
Lockhart

Lake
King

Australind

Western Hwy

South

Arthur
River

Dumbleyung

Lake Grace
South

Holland
Rocks

Bunbury

Collie

Darkan

Wagin

Dumbleyung
Lake

Nyabing

Pingrup

Lake
Magenta

Capel

Donnybrook

Woodanilling

Katanning

Lake
Cairocup

Mindarabin

Busselton

To Margaret River (49km);
Augusta (94km)

Boyup
Brook

Kojonup

Broomehill

To Mt Barker (98km);
Albany (146km)

the Great Eastern Hwy and a similar distance east from the Great Southern Hwy, it's an easy drive along sealed roads lined with splendid wildflowers in spring.

GETTING THERE & AWAY

Most travellers visit Wave Rock on a day trip. Full-day tours from Perth can be done with **Western Travel Bug** (☎ 9204 4600; www.travelbug.com .au; tours $135) or **Active Safaris** (☎ 9450 7776; www .activesafaris.com.au; tours adult/concession $115/95) or as part of a five-day day southwest loop with **Western Xposure** (☎ 9371 3695; www.westernxposure .com.au; 5-day loop $649). With your own wheels you can drop into the Wheatbelt towns on the way to Wave Rock or as part of a southern sojourn. There is also a weekly public bus service to/from Perth.

Hyden & Wave Rock
☎ 08

Perfectly shaped like an ocean wave about to break, the 15m-high and 110m-long multicoloured granite Wave Rock is worth the 350km journey from Perth – we dare you not to strike a surfing pose on this rock of a wave! Wave Rock was formed some 60 million years ago by weathering and water erosion, and the wonderful streaks of colour that flow down its face have been caused by run-off from local mineral-water springs.

The Wave Rock **visitors centre** (☎ 9880 5182; Wave Rock; ☒ 9am-5pm), at the Wildflower Shoppe and Country Kitchen, has plenty of information and souvenirs, and can organise Aboriginal cultural tours. Remember to buy your ticket ($6 per car) from the machine at the start of the short walk to the rock.

If you're staying overnight, phone ahead – accommodation can fill with tour groups. Camp amid the gum trees near the rock at **Wave Rock Resort & Caravan Park** (☎ 9880 5022; waverock@waverock.com.au; unpowered/powered site $22/25, cabin $85; ☒). BYO linen for the cabins, or pay an extra $12 if you're without.

In Hyden, 4km east, **Wave Rock Motel** (☎ 9880 5052; hotelmotel@waverock.com.au; 2 Lynch St; d $117; ☒ ☒) has well-equipped rooms, a comfy lounge with fireplace, and an indoor bush bistro. The Hyden **visitors centre** (☎ 9880 5182; 20 Marshall St; ☒ 9am-5pm) has information on local wildflower specialities, including stunning spring orchids.

Transwa (☎ 1300 662 205; www.transwa.wa.gov.au) runs a bus from Perth to Hyden every Tuesday

($42, five hours), with the return service to Perth each Thursday.

Dryandra Woodland
☎ 08

The enchanting eucalypt Dryandra Woodland, 164km southeast of Perth, with its thickets of white-barked wandoo, powderbark and rock she-oak, hint at what the Wheatbelt was like before the natural bushland was bulldozed for farming and native wildlife eradicated by feral animals.

The showpiece of this 28,000-hectare wildlife habitat is the superb **Barna Mia Animal Sanctuary**, home to a number of endangered native species. After-dark torchlight tours, operated by the Department for Environment and Conservation (DEC), provide a rare opportunity to see these cute furry creatures up close. Book through **DEC** (☎ weekdays 9881 9200, weekends 9884 5231; narrogin@dec.wa.gov.au; tours adult/child/family $13/7/35) by 4pm for post-sunset tours on Monday, Wednesday, Friday and Saturday.

For the full escapist experience, stay at the 1920s forestry settlement of **Lions Dryandra Village** (☎ 9884 5231; www.dryandravillage.org.au), 8km from the animal enclosure, in rustic woodcutters' cabins. Midweek you'll pay $25/10 per adult/child; on weekends and holidays there's a minimum charge ($50/75 for a cabin sleeping two/four, and $100 for a cabin sleeping eight to 12 people). Enjoy several wonderful bushwalking and cycling tracks, including the 5km **Ochre Trail**, focused on local indigenous Noongar culture. The woodland is 22km northwest of Narrogin, signposted from the Southern and Albany Hwys.

Other Wheatbelt Towns
☎ 08

Wickepin (population 679), 210km from Perth, is home to the atmospheric **Albert Facey Homestead** (☎ 9888 1005; Wogolin Rd; adult/ child $2.50/1; ☒ 10am-4pm Mar-Nov; Fri, Sat & Sun Dec-Feb, at other times see newsagent opposite) in the centre of town. Even if you haven't read Albert Facey's extraordinary autobiography, *A Fortunate Life* (see opposite) a visit still provides a sobering insight into the struggles of outback life during the Great Depression. Facey fans will appreciate the 86km self-drive **Albert Facey Heritage Trail**, taking in significant sites featured in the book. Pick up a brochure from the friendly staff across the road from the homestead at

A FORTUNATE LIFE

The story of Albert (AB) Facey (1894–1982) is a remarkable and heart-rending one. Before Facey had turned two his father died and soon after his mother abandoned him, leaving his grandmother to raise him until he was eight – at which time he went off to work.

Facey mainly worked in outback Western Australia (WA) as a farm labourer; his tough childhood saw him cheated by employers and one time so badly whipped that he was presumed to be on his deathbed. Later he fought in a boxing troupe before signing up to fight in WWI, where he landed at Gallipoli (where two of his brothers were killed).

Facey was badly injured in WWI, struggled through the Great Depression and lost a son in WWII, however his optimism rarely wavered. While Facey didn't teach himself to write until his return from Gallipoli, after this he kept copious notes about his experiences. Facey only stopped writing after the death of Evelyn, his wife of nearly 60 years. Facey was aged 85 when his manuscript was accepted for publication by the Fremantle Arts Centre Press in 1979.

The autobiography, *A Fortunate Life*, was released in 1981 and Facey passed away nine months later, just long enough for him to see how deeply affecting the book was to anyone who read it. Apart from its emotional resonance, it's an important historical document, as Facey experienced many of the significant events that helped shape Australia's cultural identity. While he saw his life as a fortunate one, Australia is more fortunate that Albert so simply yet powerfully documented his life and the events that helped shaped a nation.

the **Telecentre** (☎ 9888 1500; Wogolin Rd; ✆ 9am-5pm Mon-Fri), which doubles as a visitors centre.

Kojonup (population 2119), 39km southwest of Katanning, was established in 1837 as a military outpost to protect travellers taking the mail run from the Swan Settlement (Perth) to Albany. Still a popular pie-stop on the Perth–Albany drive, Kojonup has a cutting-edge museum, the interactive **Kodja Place Interpretive Centre** (☎ 9831 0500; www.kodjaplace.net .au, www.kojonupvisitors.com; Albany Hwy; adult/child $6/3; ✆ 9am-5pm). You can sit around a Noongar campfire, ride an old school bus and drive a farm ute. Noongar guide Jack Cox also offers excellent indigenous cultural tours ($5).

CENTRAL MIDLANDS

There are four main routes north through the central Midlands, with three (roughly) parallel routes running to Geraldton: the Brand Hwy hugs the coast, and two inland roads branch off from (Hwy 116) or intersect (Hwy 115) the Great Northern Hwy. The fourth option is to follow the Great Northern Hwy north through the outback.

BRAND HIGHWAY

This coastal road (National Hwy 1) is the most popular route, with a number of side roads leading off to features such as the Pinnacles Desert and small fishing villages.

From Cervantes, a sealed road follows the coast before rejoining the Brand Hwy and running through to Dongara-Port Denison. This stretch is marked by a few small towns and verdant national parks.

NATIONAL PARKS

Those with 4WD vehicles and a love of nature should explore the following parks and reserves – particularly during the spring wildflower explosion. Contact **DEC** (☎ 9652 1911; Bashford St, Jurien) for more information.

Alexander Morrison National Park (8.5 sq km) Extensive strands of low woodland and mallee.

Badgingarra National Park (130 sq km) Walking trails, wildflowers.

Drovers Cave National Park (27 sq km) Limestone caves.

Lesueur National Park (270 sq km) Significant for the rich diversity of plants.

Tathra National Park (43 sq km) Walking trails through typical bushland.

Watheroo National Park (445 sq km) Heathland and woodland, Jingenia Caves.

Cervantes & Pinnacles Desert
☎ 08

Nambung National Park (bus passenger/car $4/9), 17km from Cervantes, is home to the spectacular, otherworldly Pinnacles Desert, where thousands of limestone pillars are scattered in a moon-like landscape across a golden desert floor. The lime-rich desert sand originated

THE WHEATBELT &
THE MIDLANDS

from seashells, which compacted with rain and subsequently eroded, forming individual pillars, some towering up to 5m. A good gravel loop-road runs through the formations so you can stop to walk among them.

The cruisy crayfishing town of **Cervantes** (population 750), 245km north of Perth, makes a wise overnight stop to enjoy the Pinnacles at sunset when the light is sublime and the crowds thin. Crayfishing season is from mid-November to June, when the fresh sweet crustaceans provide a compelling reason to visit.

About 20km south of Cervantes at Thirsty Point, **Hangover Bay's** white-sand beach is good for a dip, and you can cook on the gas barbecues here and further north at Kangaroo Point.

Get information on accommodation, wildflowers and Pinnacles tours at Cervantes' **visitors centre** (☎ 9652 7700; www.turquoisecoast.org .au; Cadiz St ☹ 10am-5pm). There's a general store, liquor shop and takeaway here too.

TOURS
Australian Excursions (☎ 9455 3162, 1800 048 000; www.supporttours.com.au; tours adult/concession $162/144) Offers full-day tours to the Pinnacles, taking in wildflowers and sand-boarding.
Turquoise Coast Enviro Tours (☎ 9652 7047; 59 Seville St; 3hr Pinnacles tour $40) These guided tours (incorporating a 2½-hour walk) leave Cervantes at 8am and 2½ hours before sunset.

SLEEPING & EATING
Pinnacles Caravan Park (☎ 9652 7060; cervpinncpark@ westnet.com.au; 35 Aragon St; unpowered/powered site $22/25, on-site van/cabin $70/60) This shady park is in a prime tent-pitching position next to the beach. Excellent facilities and a supermarket are a plus.
Cervantes Lodge & Pinnacles Beach Backpackers (☎ 9652 7377, 1800 245 232; www.cervanteslodge.com.au; 91 Seville St; dm $23, d with shared bathroom $75, d with views $95) Travellers love the communal kitchen and beach proximity, and the cleanliness of the place makes up for its lack of charm.
Cervantes Holiday Homes (☎ 9652 7115; rose knowles@bigpond.com.au; cnr Malaga Ct & Valencia Rd; cottage d from $75; ☒) These spotless, spacious self-contained cottages come with fully equipped kitchens, comfy lounge and TV, and are great value.
Ronsard Bay Tavern (☎ 9652 7009; 1 Cadiz St; mains $12-26; ☹ 11am-2pm & 6-8.30pm) Locals love this place for its fireplace, big screen TV, dart boards, pool tables and jukebox. Not to men-

tion its delicious counter meals – try the seafood basket.

GETTING THERE & AWAY
Greyhound (☎ 13 14 99) has services from Cervantes to Perth ($39, four hours, daily) and Geraldton ($20, 2½ hours, daily). Buses continue north to Jurien (20 minutes) and Leeman (35 minutes).

Jurien Bay
☎ 08 / pop 1500
Swimming and sailboarding the pristine waters off a white sandy beach, fishing for delicious snapper and dhufish, and feasting on fresh crayfish are just some of the attractions that keep travellers returning to Jurien Bay, 266km north of Perth.

You can snorkel with sea lions and watch humpback whales migrate south (September to December) with **Jurien Bay Charters** (☎ 9652 1109; www.juriencharters.com; Jurien Marina; 2½hr sea-lion tour adult/child $80/40).

Pitch your tent or camp your van at the very edge of the beach at the **Jurien Bay Tourist Park** (☎ 9652 1595; www.jurienbaytouristpark.com.au; Roberts St; unpowered/powered site $23/25; on-site van $70; 1-/2-bedroom chalet $110/140) then cook your own freshly-caught fish in its campers kitchens.

The popular local watering hole, **Jurien Bay Hotel Motel** (☎ 9652 1022; jurienhotel@wn.com.au; 5 White St; s/d $80/95; ☒ ☒), has comfy, spotlessly clean motel rooms out back, with the added bonus of fresh crayfish on the menu in season at its Sea Change Restaurant (mains $17 to $28) and decent counter meals (meals $7 to $22) in the bar.

At **Lesueur's** (☎ 9652 2113; 36 Bashford St; meals $4-9; ☹ 8.30am-5pm) you can order a gourmet sandwich and real espresso (yeah!) from the corrugated-iron counter. For dinner, opt for pasta or seafood at the pseudo-rustic **Sandpiper Tavern** (☎ 9652 1229; cnr Roberts & Sandpiper Sts; mains $12-24; ☹ 11am-2.30pm & 6-8.30pm). There are several snazzy Asian and seafood takeaways on Bashford St, while self-caterers can check out the supermarket at the Jurien Bay Shopping Centre, along with an ATM, newsagency and post office.

Green Head & Leeman
☎ 08
Get away from it all at the laid-back fishing villages of Green Head (population 300) and Leeman (population 680), where there's little to

do besides swim and fish in secluded bays. Both are pretty but Leeman's picturesque old wooden jetties at Pioneer Park give it the edge.

Sea Lion Charters (☎ 9953 1012; sealioncharters@ hotmail.com; 24 Bryant St, Green Head; half-day tours adult/child $75/30) offers tours to interact with friendly sea lions living offshore on Fisherman's Islands.

Travellers who stay here have trouble leaving the lovely beachside **Green Head Caravan Park** (☎ 9953 1131; 9 Green Head Rd, Green Head; unpowered/ powered site $18/21, on-site van from $47). The hospitable owners treat guests like family with regular barbecues and discounts for longer stays.

Leafy **Leeman Caravan Park** (☎ 9953 1080; 29 Thomas St, Leeman; unpowered/powered site $19/20, on-site van from $68, cabin from $58) offers lots of shade and space just 100m from the beach.

Green Head has a general store and pub with an ATM, while Leeman is slightly more sophisticated with seafood takeaways and a surf shop. With its fresh burgers and rolls, Leeman's **Snack Shack** (☎ 9953 1110; Spencer St; $3-9; ☻ 8.30am-3pm) lives up to the promise of its signage: 'A great little place to feed ya face!'.

MIDLANDS ROAD (HIGHWAY 116)

This is the route to take if you prefer wildflowers, wheat silos and wide-veranda pubs over white-sand beaches and cobalt sea bays. It's possible to weave in and out to experience a bit of both.

GETTING THERE & AWAY

Transwa (☎ 1300 662 205; www.transwa.wa.gov.au) has a Perth–Geraldton service that runs four times weekly via Moora ($25, three hours) and Mingenew ($46, 5½ hours).

Moora

☎ 08 / pop 2574

Like most Wheatbelt towns, tall gum trees line Moora's wide streets, the railway runs through the centre of town, and buildings are festooned with wonderful murals depicting rural life. The largest town between Geraldton and Perth, Moora is central to the area's vast sheep and wheat industry. The spring wildflower season here is spectacularly colourful.

Campers will enjoy the grassy sites and great facilities (including barbecues and free washing machines and dryers) at shady **Moora Caravan Park** (☎ 0409 511 400, 9651 1401; Dandaragan St; unpowered/powered site $16/21). The good-value rooms at **Moora Motel** (☎ 9651 1247; 44 Roberts St; s/d $80/90; ☒) are spotless and have toaster and kettle.

Moora's **Pioneer Bakery & Restaurant** (☎ 9651 1277; 50 Padbury St; meals $5-20; ☻ 7.30am-5pm Mon-Fri, 7.30am-2pm Sat) has lots of old-fashioned charm, bakes fresh bread daily (a rarity in these towns!) and serves real coffee.

You can dine in or take away at the **Gourmet Café** (☎ 9651 1043; 97 Gardiner St; meals $7-22; ☻ 6am-9pm), which does tasty toasted sandwiches, big burgers, steaks and salads.

Drovers Inn (☎ 9651 1108; cnr Dandaragan & Padbury Sts; mains $15-26; ☻ 5-9pm Wed-Sun) is a classic Aussie pub with lots of atmosphere and a characterful restaurant serving the usual counter meals.

Access the internet at the **Telecentre** (☎ 9653 1053; Padbury St; per hr $8; ☻ 8.30am-4pm Mon-Fri). There's a supermarket, newsagency and ATMs on Dandaragan and Padbury Sts.

Mingenew

☎ 08 / pop 525

For most travellers Mingenew, 383km north of Perth, is an overnight stop on the inland route north or a base for wildflower wanders the speciality here being orchids and everlastings. The **visitors centre** (☎ 9928 1081; Mingenew post office; ☻ 9am-5pm Jul Sep) has wildflower info and maps.

The **Coalseam Conservation Park**, 34km northeast of town, is named after the seams of coal that can still be seen in the riverbed of the Irwin River, and is the site of the first coal deposit discovery in Western Australia (WA) in 1846. Admire the splendid wildflowers, such as the pink schoenia, and check out the ancient fossil shells embedded in the cliffs.

The **Commercial Hotel** (☎ 9928 1002; mingenew hotel@bigpond.com; Midlands Rd; hotel s/d with shared bathroom $60/70, motel d $98) does home-style counter meals for lunch and dinner (mains $18 to 28) and has comfy rooms with shared bathrooms upstairs and basic but clean motel units next door. Breakfast is included in the rates.

A real bush setting awaits under the big gum trees of the **Mingenew Springs Caravan Park** (☎ 9928 1019; Lee Steere St; unpowered/powered site $12/17).

There's a well-stocked supermarket, bakery and fuel stop on Midlands Rd.

WONGAN HILLS TO MULLEWA (HIGHWAY 115)

An alternative route north through the Wheatbelt towns takes you from Wongan Hills, crossing the Great Northern Hwy at Wubin, and continuing inland roughly parallel to the

Midlands Rd (Hwy 116), to Mullewa. Expect wildflowers in season, wheat silos, and wide-street towns with classic corner pubs.

GETTING THERE & AWAY

Transwa (☎ 1300 662 205; www.transwa.wa.gov.au) leaves from Geraldton to Mullewa ($13, one hour), Morawa ($25, 2½ hours) and Wubin ($38, four hours).

Wongan Hills

☎ 08 / pop 1462

Fields of yellow-flowered canola and barley provide a welcome break from the wheatfields and bushland. Bushwalkers enjoy Wongan Hills for its well-organised walking trails and wonderful spring wildflowers, including the unique crimson verticordias.

The friendly volunteers at the **visitors centre** (☎ 9671 1973; Railway Station, Wongan Rd; 9am-5pm Mar-Dec) can point you toward the wildflowers and provide maps and organise guides for the popular Mt Matilda and Speaker's Chair walking trails through **Wongan Hills Nature Reserve**, the **Fowler Gully Reserve** for remnants of natural woodlands, and the **Rogers Nature Reserve** for spectacular verticordias and other wildflowers.

Sleep under shady gum trees at the **Wongan Hills Caravan Park** (☎ 9671 1009; Wongan Rd; unpowered/powered site $15/20, cabin $60, chalet $90).

The historic art deco **Wongan Hills Hotel** (☎ 9671 1022; www.wonganhillshotel.com.au; 5 Fenton Pl; hotel s/d $45/65, motel d $75) offers older-style pub rooms and modern motel-style accommodation. While takeaway is available from an international menu ($12 to $24), eating in the original art deco dining room makes for a refreshing change.

There's an excellent, well-stocked supermarket and a bakery on Fenton Place.

Perenjori

☎ 08 / pop 573

Perenjori, 350km from Perth between Wubin and Mullewa, is named after the indigenous word for waterhole, *perangary*. It's a popular stop on the 'wildflower way' and the country bursts with colour year-round, from the yellow of wattle in autumn through to the pink of everlastings in spring. The **visitors centre** (☎ 9973 1105; Fowler St; 9am-4pm Mon-Fri), also home to the **pioneer museum** (adult/child $2/50c), has handy self-drive tour brochures, *The Way of the Wildflowers* and *Monsignor Hawes Herit-*

age Trail, and can provide access to the beautiful **St Joseph's Church,** designed by the prolific John Hawes (see the boxed text, p188).

If you're heading to the Great Northern Hwy, stop at **Mongers Lake Lookout** for views across the blinding-white salt lake, signposted from the red-dirt Perenjori–Wanarra Roads. Not far away, **Camel Soak**, 500m off Rabbit Proof Fence Rd (see the boxed text, opposite), was sunk to provide water for the camel teams used to construct the fence. There is abundant birdlife here – you will spot pink and grey galahs, red-tailed black cockatoos, white corellas and emus.

The red-dirt, eucalyptus-shaded **Perenjori Caravan Park** (☎ 9973 1193; Crossing Rd; unpowered/powered site $3/13, van $23, cabin $50) offers decent facilities, including a campers kitchen.

The friendly, family-owned **Perenjori Hotel** (☎ 9973 1020; Fowler St; hotel s/d with shared bathroom $40/60, motel s/d $60/70) has basic pub rooms with shared bathrooms and motel rooms with private ones; both include breakfast. Prop yourself at the bar to tuck into hearty counter meals ($12 to $22) with the locals.

Perenjori Newsagency and Café (Fowler St) also does takeaway food.

Morawa

☎ 08 / pop 880

The highlight of Morawa – a town that survives on wheat, wool and wildflowers – is the splendid Hawes-designed **Church of the Holy Cross** and its one-room stone hermitage where Monsignor Hawes lived for many years.

The **visitors centre** (☎ 9971 1421; 34 Winfield St; 8.30am-4.30pm May-Oct) can supply travellers with information about wildflower drives and sites.

Call ahead if you intend staying in town as accommodation quickly fills with contract workers. **Morawa Caravan Park** (☎ 9971 1204; White Ave; unpowered/powered site $15/20) has tidy sites.

Guests enjoy staying at the **Marian Convent B&B** (☎ 9971 1555; morawanuts@wn.com.au; Davis St; dm $20, s/d $50/80). Opposite Hawes' church, it has basic twin rooms, a backpacker dorm, a big communal kitchen and a cosy dining room.

Morawa Motor Hotel (☎ 9971 1060; cnr Solomon Tce & Manning St; motel s/d $75/95;) has basic motel rooms (hotel rooms were being renovated at time of research) and serves hearty counter meals for lunch and dinner ($12 to $24).

There's a supermarket, bakery and coffee shop on Winfield Street.

THE WASCALLY WABBIT-PROOF FENCE

In keeping with the rich tradition of being completely clueless to the delicate balance of Australia's natural habitat, in 1859, farmer Thomas Austin imported 24 rabbits to the state of Victoria from England. They were to provide him with 'a touch of home…a spot of hunting…[and] could do little harm'. Good thinking Tom. Fast-forward to 1894 and the offspring of Tom's randy rabbits had eaten crops and pastures across Australia's eastern states, before reaching the Western Australia (WA) border.

To combat the spread of the wascally wabbits into WA, construction of a 1833km-long Rabbit Proof Fence began in 1901, taking seven years to complete. As construction of the fence advanced, so did the rapacious rabbits. Two more adjoining fences were built: Fence 2 in 1905 and Fence 3 in 1908. However, biological warfare proved more effective than 3256km of fence with the introduction of myxomatosis in 1950, 1080 poison in 1956 and the calicivirus in 1996.

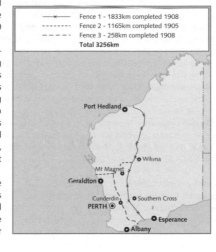

Today the fence is maintained by the Department of Agriculture, and used as a baiting corridor for wild dogs, to contain feral goats and to halt emu migrations. Every 10 years or so, dependent on seasonal conditions (eg drought), emus migrate en masse in search of food. At these times, the hapless birds are said to be in plague proportions, and threaten to damage crops and farm-fences, with up to 70,000 emus pressed up against the fence line.

Unfortunately the fence will be of little help in stopping the latest threat to WA's fauna and flora: the cane toad, introduced into Queensland in 1935 to control the native cane beetle and now slowly jumping their way across the country…

Mullewa

☎ 08 / pop 1057

People make pilgrimages to Mullewa in spring for the town's famous wreath flower, the star of the annual Wildflower Show (late August). Mullewa's other main attraction is the splendid Romanesque **Our Lady of Mt Carmel Church** (Doney St), designed and built by John Hawes (see the boxed text, p188), and the adjoining **Priest House** (☾ 10am-noon Jul-Oct), now a museum honouring Hawes. Typical of Wheatbelt towns, murals depict Mullewa's history on buildings around town. The helpful **visitors centre** (☎ 9961 1500; cnr Jose St & Maitland Rd; ☾ 9am-4.30pm Mon-Fri Feb-Dec) has information on self-drive tours to view wildflowers and Hawes buildings.

The struggle between pioneer pastoralists and the ancestors of Mullewa's sizable Aboriginal community is recognised at the heritage site of **Butterabby Graves**, 16km south of Mullewa. It's the location of two bloody 1864 conflicts between pastoralists and five Aboriginal men who killed them over territorial disputes, and the site of the public execution of the indigenous men.

If the barbed wire doesn't bother you, **Mullewa Caravan Park** (☎ 9961 1161; 7 Lovers Lane; unpowered/powered site $10/15) has tidy sites; head down the block to the centre of town to pay at the **Ampol Garage/Deli** (☎ 9961 1180). The well-stocked deli also has an ATM.

Railway Motel Hotel (☎ 9961 1050; Gray St; s/d $66/88) has rooms in an old pub, and decent counter meals ($12 to $24).

GREAT NORTHERN HIGHWAY

Outback travel doesn't get any more real than Hwy 95 (Great Northern Hwy), the inland route from Perth to Port Hedland. Not long after leaving monastic New Norcia, the bushland and wheatfields give way

---

BENEDICTINE BUSINESS

In this rural area of Western Australia (WA), where the largest structures are the corner pubs in tiny towns, your first sight of New Norcia comes as quite a shock. In Australia's only monastic town, the Byzantine-influenced St Ildephonsus and Gothic Revival style of St Gertrude's, both former colleges, are as striking as they are incongruous set in this landscape.

Just as absurd must have been the sight of two Spanish Benedictine monks, Dom Joseph Serra and Dom Rosendo Salvado, who arrived here in 1846 to start a mission for the local Aborigines, the Noongar people. Dom Rosendo Salvado envisaged a self-sustaining village where Aborigines were encouraged to settle as land-holders, as a way of becoming 'civilised'. Salvado was a rare figure in these times, being sympathetic to indigenous culture and learning the local language.

It was under its second abbot, Dom Fulgentius Torres, who took over at the turn of the 19th century, that New Norcia changed dramatically. Torres designed and supervised the building of both St Gertrude's Ladies College in 1908 and St Ildephonsus College for boys in 1913. Today the National Trust has registered 27 of the 65 buildings in the town.

Despite the architectural splendour, New Norcia will always be associated with what has become known as the 'stolen generation' (see p21), based on the 1997 report *Bringing Them Home*. While the number of indigenous children (particularly those of mixed Aboriginal and European descent) forcibly taken from their parents is still disputed by some, the fact remains that many of these children grew up in missions such as New Norcia.

The closure of the last school in 1991 removed the community's main source of income. To survive financially, New Norcia had to publicly exploit the very thing that kept it independent from the outside world: its very fine foodstuffs. Day after day visitors line up in the shop, arms laden with local goodies such as fabulous breads, cakes and olive oils.

---

to endless stretches of semiarid desert and the small mining towns of Mt Magnet, Cue and Meekatharra. While you'll see plenty of wildlife, many hours can slip by before you see another vehicle, usually in the form of a road-train.

GETTING THERE & AWAY

Integrity Coach Lines (☎ 1800 226 339; www.integrity coachlines.com.au) has a weekly service along the Great Northern Hwy that leaves Perth each Thursday. It passes through New Norcia ($20, two hours), Mt Magnet ($80, seven hours), Cue ($90, eight hours) and Meekatharra ($105, 10 hours).

Transwa (☎ 1300 662 205; www.transwa.wa.gov.au) coaches leave Perth on Tuesday, Thursday, Friday and Sunday, arriving in New Norcia two hours later, and return to Perth on Tuesday and Thursday ($20).

New Norcia

☎ 08 / pop 51
The splendid monastery settlement of New Norcia, 132km from Perth, consists of a cluster of ornate Spanish-style buildings set incongruously in the Australian bush. Established in 1846 by Spanish Benedictine monks as an Aboriginal mission, today the working

monastery holds prayers and retreats alongside a multi-million dollar business producing boutique breads and gourmet goodies (see the boxed text, above).

New Norcia Museum & Art Gallery (☎ 9654 8056; www.newnorcia.com; Great Northern Hwy; combined museum, tour & tastings ticket adult/child $23/12; ⏲ 9.30am-5pm Aug-Oct, 10am-4.30pm Nov-Jul) traces the intriguing history of the monastery and houses impressive art, including works by Charles Blackman and Pro Hart, and one of the country's largest collections of post-Renaissance religious art. The **Museum Gift Shop** sells kitsch souvenirs (dig those monk figurines!), Abbey Wines, cold-pressed olive oils, honeys, preserves, *pan chocolatti*, *biscotti*, nutcakes, and over 20 different types of breads baked in the monks' 100-year-old wood-fired oven.

Guided **town tours** (tickets from museum; adult/child $12.50/5.50; ⏲ 9am, 11am & 1.30pm) enable you to get a look inside the monk's private chapel within the monastery, the abbey chapel, and the frescoed college chapels; the 9am tour generally lasts one hour, and the 11am and 1.30pm tours are two hours. **Meet a Monk** (adult/child $12.50/5.50; ⏲ 10.30am Mon-Fri, 4.30pm Sat) gives you the chance to find out what it's like to be a monk. Choral concerts and organ recitals are also held.

The grand **New Norcia Hotel** (☎ 9654 8034; hotel@newnorcia.com; Great Northern Hwy; s/d with shared bathroom & breakfast $70/85) has sweeping stair-cases, high ceilings and atmospheric public spaces. The understated rooms open onto an enormous veranda. An international menu ($18 to $25) is available at the bar or in the elegant dining room.

You can also stay at the **Monastery Guest-house** (☎ 9654 8002; guesthouse@newnorcia.wa.edu.au; full board $75) within the walls of the southern cloister, in gender-segregated rooms.

Mt Magnet

☎ 08 / pop 1180

After gold was discovered at Mt Magnet in 1891, locals claim 'they dug it up like pota-toes'. Mt Magnet, 567km from Perth, is the state's oldest operating gold-mining settle-ment, and its wide streets and once-grand hotels are remnants of its heyday.

The friendly volunteers at the **visitors centre** (☎ 9963 4177; Hepburn St; ⏰ Jul-Oct) can provide in-formation on a 1.4km heritage walk, self-drive tours, and where to see spectacular carpets of spring wildflowers.

Marvel at the enormous open-cut mines from **Warramboo Hill Lookout**. The **Granites**, a stunning 15m-high red rocky escarpment, 7km north of town (signposted), is home to Walga Rock (also known as Walganna) and its 10,000-year-old Aboriginal paintings. It's a very popular picnic and sunset-watching spot. The area is sacred to the local Barimaia peo-ple; the paintings have been damaged before and the site is undergoing restoration.

The **Mt Magnet Caravan Park** (☎ 9963 4198; Hep-burn St; unpowered/powered site $12/17) can provide a patch of dirt to park for the night.

Miners and backpackers exchange stories in the communal kitchen and barbecue areas at the good-value **Outback Gold** (☎ 9963 4433; 12 Scott Close; dongas $35, s/d with shared bathroom $55/66, self-contained units s/d $77/88; ▨ ▣).

The **Commercial Club Hotel** (☎ 9963 4021; Hepburn St; hotel s/d $49/70, motel s/d $77/99; ▨) has comfort-able motel rooms and hearty counter meals ($12 to $22).

There's a supermarket, a café and a few shops on Hepburn St.

Cue

☎ 08 / pop 350

If you've been underwhelmed by the Wheat-belt towns, you'll think you've struck gold when you get to Cue, 'the Queen of the Murchison', 80km north of Mt Magnet and 650km northeast of Perth. Cue boasts fine examples of classic goldfields architecture, a legacy of the 1892 gold rush – the grand Gentleman's Club (1895) and Government Buildings (1896), the spooky Masonic Lodge (1899), and the atmospheric Austin St shops with their iron awnings. Unfortunately many remain abandoned, giving Cue a cinematic ghostliness that's intriguing.

In the grand Gentlemen's Club building, the **visitors centre** (☎ 9963 1041; Cue Shire Council of-fices, Austin St; ⏰ 9am-4pm Mon-Fri) has *Cue Heritage Trail* booklets, info on wildflowers (July to October) and amateur gold-prospecting, and will happily evaluate your gold nuggets!

Visit during **QFest** (www.qfest.com), a four-day family festival in mid-October celebrating the town's diversity through indigenous culture, music, dance, comedy, circus and enormous fire-sculptures.

The crumbling ruins of ghost towns **Day Dawn**, 5km southwest, and **Big Bell**, 30km west, are atmospheric.

Dusty **Cue Caravan Park** (☎ 9963 1107; Austin St; unpowered/powered site $15/18) has basic facilities.

The **Murchison Club Hotel** (☎ 9963 1020; Austin St; hotel s/d with shared bathroom $60/85, motel s/d $88/110; ▨) has budget rooms upstairs and does hearty counter meals (mains $16 to $28).

The classic **Queen of the Murchison Hotel** (☎ 9963 1625; Austin St; s/d $77/110; ▨ ▣) received a multi-million dollar facelift a few years ago, and while its rooms are cosy and clean, the teddy bears and dolls scattered about the hotel are somewhat disconcerting.

BONZER BACKROADS – FROM CUE TO A VIEW

From Cue, with a 4WD you can take the red-sand road to the massive red granite monolith of **Walga Rock**, also known as Walganna, 48km west of Cue. This mini-Uluru is a significant Abo-riginal art site – *walga* means 'ochre painting' in the local Warragi language – with an impressive 'gallery' of 10,000-year-old desert-style paintings of animals, hands and, mysteriously, a sailing ship. Along the way you'll see plenty of eagles, emus, kangaroos and wild goats.

Historic **Bells Emporium** (Austin St) still operates as a supermarket and liquor store.

Meekatharra

☎ 08 / pop 1529

Meekatharra, 764km north of Perth and 541km northeast of Geraldton, has a large indigenous population, the Ngoonooru Wadjari and Yugunga-Nya peoples, and while its name means 'place of little water', this town supports some of the area's largest cattle and sheep stations, and significant mining ventures.

While there are few sights in Meekatharra, it makes a good stopover on the long haul north. Call ahead as accommodation can fill quickly with workers.

The shire office **visitors centre** (☎ 9981 1002; www.meekashire.wa.gov.au; Main St; ⏲ 9am-4.30pm Mon-Fri) has little tourist info but can advise on road conditions. Internet access is at the **Telecentre** (☎ 9980 1811; 55 Main St; ⏲ 9am-5pm Mon-Fri).

The future of the state's first **School of the Air** (☎ 9981 1032; Meekatharra District High School, High St; ⏲ 8-10.30am) was undecided at the time of writing after two fires in late 2006; however, you can visit the **Royal Flying Doctor Base** (☎ 9981 1107; Main St; ⏲ 9am-2pm).

You can watch a flick with local families under the stars at the corrugated-iron **Meekatharra Picture Gardens** (☎ 9981 1002; Main St; ⏲ 7.30pm Fri & Sat).

The rather dusty **Meekatharra Caravan Park** (☎ 9981 1253; Main St; powered sites tent/van $17/19, cabins $70) requires tent-campers to pay for a powered site.

The **Commercial Hotel** (☎ 9981 1020; 77 Main St; hotel s/d with shared bathroom $35/45, motel s/d $75/90) has great-value and well-maintained motel rooms, and does delicious counter meals ($10 to $22) – the burgers and steaks are memorable.

Get fuel and stock up on water and food at the supermarket on Main St.

Central West Coast

The sunny Central West Coast extends north from the seaside fishing towns of Dongara-Port Denison on the Batavia Coast through splendid Shark Bay to the fertile Carnarvon and arid Gascoyne region. It's an enormous area incorporating scenery as varied as rugged coastline, rolling green country, craggy bushland and tropical plantations.

The windswept Batavia Coast and fishing town of Geraldton is beloved by windsurfers and anglers, while sun-worshippers are happier heading to the beaches of Monkey Mia or Kalbarri, which has the added attraction of a stunning national park surrounding it (think deep river gorges and steep sea cliffs, awash with wonderful wildflowers in spring).

Shark Bay's World Heritage listing recognises its unique natural conditions – pristine turquoise waters, submerged sea-grass meadows and prolific marine life and wildlife. And it really is a special place. Famous for Monkey Mia's visiting dolphins and its large dugong population, and, more significantly for geologists, its ancient stromatolites, the area also has a rich Aboriginal history and culture that's equally as precious. It's now even more accessible to travellers through wonderful indigenous tourism initiatives, and bush walks like *Wula Guda Nyinda* – it means 'you come this way'. So, what are you waiting for?

HIGHLIGHTS

- Canoe the golden gorges of the Murchison River at **Kalbarri National Park** (p190)
- Crunch over millions of metres-deep miniature cockle shells at **Shell Beach** (p193)
- Learn to love bush tucker and animal tracking on a **Wula Guda Nyinda walk** (p196) around Monkey Mia
- Spot dolphins, dugongs, turtles and rays on a **Monkey Mia cruise** (p196)
- Shudder at tales of shipwrecks at Geraldton's **Western Australian Museum** (p63)
- Sense the pioneering spirit at windswept **Central Greenough Historic Settlement** (p185), Greenough
- Tick off architectural miracles on **Hawes' Holy Heritage Trail** (p188), Geraldton
- Untangle cultural complexities at Denham's cutting-edge **Shark Bay World Heritage Discovery Centre** (p194)

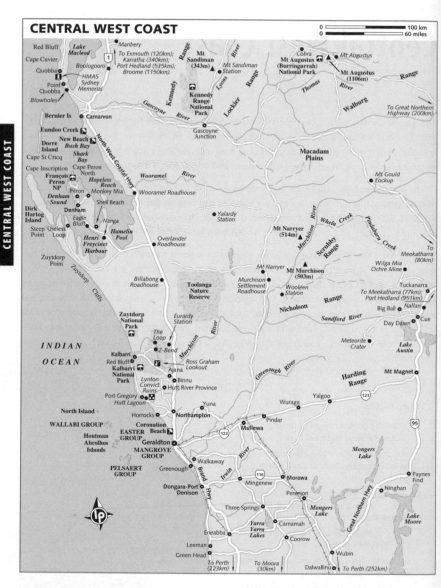

CENTRAL WEST COAST

CENTRAL WEST COAST (side tab)

BATAVIA COAST

The coastline from Dongara-Port Denison to Kalbarri has a rich history. Reminders of early European contact with Australia are prominent features, from the shipwrecks littering the coast, with the calamitous story of the *Batavia* recounted at Geraldton's riveting museum, to the slice of 19th century pioneering life preserved in charming Greenough.

DONGARA-PORT DENISON

☎ 08 / pop 3000

The tranquil seaside towns of Dongara and Port Denison, 359km from Perth, are treasured for their pristine beaches and laid-back atmosphere. Dongara's main street, Moreton Tce, is shaded by century-old fig trees, which set this old town apart from its sibling. There are superlative beaches for swimming, surfing, fishing and strolling, such as South Beach, Seaspray Beach and Surf Beach.

Information

Moreton Tce has several banks with ATMs

Telecentre (☎ 9927 2111; 11 Moreton Tce; ☺ 9am-4pm Mon-Fri) Internet.

Visitors centre (☎ 9927 1404; www.irwin.wa.gov .au/tourism; 9 Waldeck St; ☺ 9am-5pm Mon-Fri, 10am-2pm Sat & Sun) In Dongara's old post office.

Sights & Activities

Pick up the *Walk Dongara-Denison* brochure from the visitors centre and choose from 12 historic or nature-based rambles. Wildlife lovers should amble the **Irwin River Nature Trail** for black swans, pelicans and cormorants.

Wonderful historic buildings include restored **Russ Cottage** (Point Leander Dr; adult/child $2.50/50¢; ☺ 10am-noon Sun), built in the late 1860s, with a kitchen floor made from compacted anthills, and the sandstone **Royal Steam Flour Mill** (Brand Hwy). Its steam engines ground wheat from surrounding farms between 1894 and 1935. In the old police station, the cells of the **Irwin District Museum** (☎ 9927 1404; admission $2.50; ☺ 10am-4pm Mon-Fri) hold interesting historical displays.

Denison Beach Marina brims with boats that haul crayfish, the towns' livelihood. Join the free 2pm tours of the bustling **Live Lobster Logistics Centre** in season (November to January) and enjoy the gorgeous views from the **Fisherman's Lookout Obelisk** at Port Denison.

Sleeping

Dongara Denison Tourist Park (☎ 9927 1210; www .dongaratouristpark.com.au; 8 George St, Port Denison; unpowered/powered sites $20/27, on-site vans $65, chalets $150) Backing on to beautiful South Beach, this verdant park in natural bushland has a good campers kitchen, free barbecues and a lush pergola dining area. The swish fully equipped chalets are ideal for families.

Midcoast Dongara Backpackers (☎ 9927 1581; dongarabackpack@westnet.com.au; 32 Waldeck St, Dongara; dm/s/d $20/30/50; train s/d/carriage $20/50/90) The highlight of this friendly, relaxed hostel, with pleasant gardens, is the opportunity to stay in an atmospheric 1906 train carriage (which sleeps

eight) – it's very cool! And a great deal cooler if a group of friends rent the whole thing.

Dongara Denison Beach Holiday Park (☎ 9927 1131; www.ddbeachholidaypark.com; 250 Ocean Drive, Port Denison; unpowered/powered sites $30/35, on-site vans $80, chalets $135) Waterfront chalets have splendid sea views of the beach just a few steps away, but equally as impressive are the van sites with ensuites with power/TV sockets, private bathrooms and storage! Discounts midweek.

Lazy Lobster (☎ 9927 2177; lazylobster@bigpond.com .au; 45 Hampton St, Port Denison; d units $80, chalets $90; ☒) A home away from home, these comfy units and chalets are fully self-contained although their suburban street location is rather uninspiring.

Port Denison Holiday Units (☎ 9927 2544; 14 Carnarvon St, Port Denison; d $90; ☒) These spotless spacious units are just a block from the beach; ask for a room at the back with marina views.

our pick Priory Lodge (☎ 9927 1090; priory@dodo .com.au; 11 St Dominics Rd, Dongara; d/f $70/90; ☒ ☒) The Priory Lodge started life as a hotel in 1881, before being bought by the Dominican sisters in 1890 to serve as a nunnery and, from 1928, a ladies college. It boasts charming period furniture, polished floorboards, wonderful old black-and-white photos and wide verandas. Add to that a swimming pool, leafy grounds, and a charming restaurant. The atmospheric bar hosts regular live music, traditional roast dinners are served on Sundays, and Friday and Saturday are pizza nights. Did we mention the outback-style wood-fire pizza oven?

Eating

Coffee Tree Book Café (☎ 9927 1400; 8 Moreton Tce, Dongara; light meals $6-16; ☺ 8am-5pm) Enjoy delicious sandwiches, salads and cakes as you browse a book under the shade of a Moreton Bay fig tree at this delightful secondhand bookshop-cum-café.

Dongara Hotel Motel (☎ 9927 1023; 12 Moreton Tce, Dongara; mains $11-24; ☺ 11am-2pm & 6-9pm) The lacklustre dining room at Dongara's oldest pub (1867) serves up hearty portions of counter meal standards, from steak and chips to seafood baskets, and crayfish in season.

Toko's (☎ 9927 1497; 38 Moreton Tce, Dongara; mains $16-25; ☺ Wed-Sun) This rustic corner BYO restaurant does great global standards for lunch and dinner, from Asian snacks (samosas, tempuras etc) to Italian pastas, plus seasonal seafood. Try the local farmed marron with honey, chilli and ginger sauce ($14.50).

Southerleys (☎ 9927 2207; Point Leander Dr, Port Denison; mains $17-28; ⊙ noon-2pm & 6pm-late) Soak up the rays on the sun terrace while you enjoy fresh seafood at this casual seafront bistro. Licensed and BYO.

There's a supermarket and takeaways on Moreton Tce and a good bakery on Waldeck St in Dongara, while a coffee shop, bakery, liquor shop and general store make up the **Port Store** (52 Point Leander Dr) in Port Denison.

Getting There & Around

Dongara-Port Denison is accessible via the Brand Hwy (National Hwy 1) or the Indian Ocean Drive from Cervantes, or via the Midlands Rd (State Hwy 116).

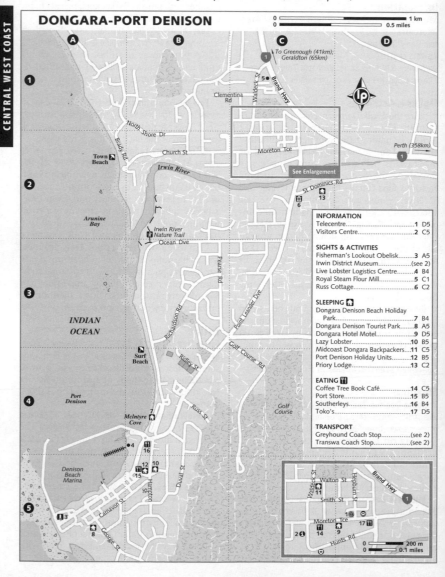

DONGARA-PORT DENISON

INFORMATION
Telecentre	1 D5
Visitors Centre	2 C5

SIGHTS & ACTIVITIES
Fisherman's Lookout Obelisk	3 A5
Irwin District Museum	(see 2)
Live Lobster Logistics Centre	4 B4
Royal Steam Flour Mill	5 C1
Russ Cottage	6 C2

SLEEPING
Dongara Denison Beach Holiday Park	7 B4
Dongara Denison Tourist Park	8 A5
Dongara Hotel Motel	9 D5
Lazy Lobster	10 B5
Midcoast Dongara Backpackers	11 C5
Port Denison Holiday Units	12 B5
Priory Lodge	13 C2

EATING
Coffee Tree Book Café	14 C5
Port Store	15 B5
Southerleys	16 B4
Toko's	17 D5

TRANSPORT
Greyhound Coach Stop	(see 2)
Transwa Coach Stop	(see 2)

CENTRAL WEST COAST

Daily **Greyhound** (☎ 13 20 30) buses to Broome ($293, 15 hours) and Perth ($44, six hours) stop at the visitors centre. **Transwa** (☎ 1300 6622 05; www.transwa.wa.gov.au) goes to Perth ($44, six hours) from the visitors centre.

GREENOUGH
☎ 08 / pop 100

Historic, windswept Greenough was once an active administrative centre in its 1860s heyday. Its traditional stone buildings have been preserved at the charming **Central Greenough Historic Settlement** (☎ 9926 1084; Brand Hwy; adult/child/family $5/2.50/12; ☺ 9am-4pm), which also serves as a visitors centre. Buy the *Greenough Walkaway Heritage Trail* booklet ($4) to get the most out of your meander around the atmospheric hamlet. Allow an hour to explore the renovated old schoolhouse, jail, courthouse, police station, churches and cottages. Don't miss the wonderful exhibition in the community hall using video, photos and historic documents to share fascinating stories about everyday life in Greenough. The visitors centre has a stylish café serving light meals and delicious cakes, selling local products from beeswax candles to handmade soaps, and housing a slick interpretative display.

The **Pioneer Museum** (☎ 9926 1058; Phillips Rd; adult/child $5/2; ☺ 10am-4pm) recreates a day in the life of an 1880s homestead with kitsch displays featuring mannequins representing the Maley family, the original owners.

Hampton Arms Inn (☎ 9926 1057; hamptonarms@ westnet.com.au; Company Rd; s/d $65/85) is a classic Aussie inn (1863) with delightfully old-fashioned rooms, a cluttered bookshop crammed with rare and out-of-print books, a quaint restaurant (mains $21 to $32), and one of those old bars you don't want to leave.

Transwa (☎ 1300 6622 05; www.transwa.wa.gov.au) services on the Kalbarri-Geraldton route stop at Greenough on the Brand Hwy daily.

GERALDTON
☎ 08 / pop 19,054

Capital of the Midwest, Geraldton has a unique ambiance that we attribute to its odd combination of architecture – classic 19th century pubs, a European-influenced cathedral, faded 1950s rural vernacular, and sleek contemporary design. Ultimately, though, it still feels like a seaside holiday town, especially when you spot the candy-striped light-house, set your eyes on the catch of the day, wander the windswept beaches – a paradise for wind- and kite-surfers – and breathe in that salty sea air.

Information

There are several banks with ATMs along the main street, Marine Tce.

Book Tree (176 Marine Tce; ☺ 9.30am-4.30pm Mon-Fri) Scour the floor-to-ceiling shelves of preloved books for some road-reading.

Cup of Life Book Café (☎ 9965 5088; Marine Tce Mall; ☺ 9am-5pm Mon-Fri, 9am-3pm Sat, 10am-2pm Sun) Good selection of books, kids' playpen, café and internet terminals.

Geraldton Regional Hospital (☎ 9956 2222; Shenton St; ☺ 24hr) Emergency facilities.

Visitors centre (☎ 9921 3999; www.geraldtontourist .com.au; Bill Sewell Complex, Chapman Rd; ☺ 9am-5pm Mon-Fri, 10am-4pm Sat & Sun) There's lots of great info here and the helpful staff will book accommodation, tours and transport. Make sure you pick up some self drive tours and a *Walk-It Geraldton-Greenough* brochure with 24 walks you can do!

Sights & Activities

The slick regional **Western Australian Museum** (☎ 9921 5080; www.museum.wa.gov.au; 1 Museum Pl; admission by donation; ☺ 10am-4pm) is unmissable. Its Midwest Gallery has engaging displays on the area's indigenous, pioneer, natural, social and economic history, while the wonderful Shipwreck Gallery documents the tragic story of the *Batavia*. The museum shop has an excellent range of books on Australian history and society, Aboriginal culture and history, Aussie literature, fantastic kids books and quality souvenirs.

The elaborate **Cathedral of St Francis Xavier** (Cathedral Ave) is the finest example of the architectural achievements of the multiskilled Monsignor Hawes (see the boxed text, p188). Construction began in 1916, but the plans were so grandiose for what was essentially a country-town church, that it wasn't completed until 1938. Its most striking features include imposing twin towers with arched openings, a central dome, Romanesque columns and boldly striped walls.

Geraldton Regional Art Gallery (☎ 9964 7170; 24 Chapman Rd; admission free; ☺ 10am-4pm Tue-Sat, 1-4pm Sun) has an excellent permanent collection, including paintings by Norman Lindsay and Elizabeth Durack, provocative contemporary work and engaging changing exhibitions.

CENTRAL WEST COAST

Yamatji Cultural Trails (☎ 9956 1126; www.yamaji culturaltrail.com.au) will open your eyes to the customs, traditional practices, history and contemporary issues affecting the Mid West indigenous Yamatji people through tours to significant sites around Geraldton. You get to sleep under the stars and hear Dreamtime stories on the 2½-day tour.

If you want to take a bit of Yamatji culture home with you, check out the **Marra Indigenous Art & Design shop** (☎ 9965 3440; www.marra.com.au; Bill Sewell Complex, Chapman Rd; ☼ 10am-4pm Mon-Fri, 9am-1pm Sat), which sells vibrant paintings, woven bowls, wooden artefacts, didgeridoos, beaded necklaces and CDs.

Old Geraldton Gaol Craft Centre (☎ 9921 1614; Bill Sewell Complex, Chapman Rd; admission free; ☼ 10am-4pm) has local crafts for sale, but more compelling are the gloomy cells that housed prisoners from 1858 to 1986, and the historic documents detailing their grim circumstances.

At **Fisherman's Wharf** (☎ 9921 3999; Geraldton Harbour; tours adult/child $5/2.50; ☼ 9.30am Mon-Fri Nov-Jun) you can do a tour following the lobsters' journey from fishing boat to restaurant table and buy fresh seafood from the market.

The striking monument on the hill overlooking Geraldton is the **HMAS Sydney Memorial** (sign-posted from George St), commemorating the 1941 loss of the ship and its 645 men after a skirmish with a German ship. Up close you'll see the dome is made up of flying birds and the bizarre figure is that of a woman looking out to sea.

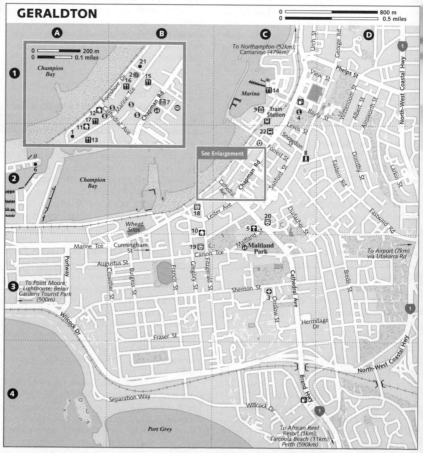

GERALDTON

Sleeping

BUDGET

Batavia Backpackers (☎ 9964 3001; Bill Sewell Complex, Chapman Rd; dm/s/d $18/22/38; 🖳) While it can't compete with Foreshore, its location in a beautiful building behind the visitors centre makes it a convenient choice if you're arriving by bus, although its reception hours are limited: 8.30am to 11.30am, and 3pm to 7pm.

Foreshore Backpackers (☎ 9921 3275; 172 Marine Tce; dm/s/d/t $22/30/50/50; 🖳) The charm of this elegant old building with its high ceilings and wooden floors, and the manager's thoughtful touches, such as a lovely old water jug or flowers on the sideboard, are appealing. But then there's the central location, great sea views, budget tours, a barbecue area, hammocks, big kitchen, and a games room with pool tables and a groovy first-class bar from a Virgin plane!

Belair Gardens Tourist Park (☎ 9921 1997; www .belairbig4geraldton.com.au; Willcock Dr; unpowered/powered sites $19/23, cabins $55; 🖳) By the lighthouse and across from Point Moore beach, this shady park has great facilities, including campers kitchen, barbecue area and tennis court.

MIDRANGE & TOP END

African Reef Resort (☎ 9964 5566; www.africanreef.com .au; 5 Broadhead Ave; s/d from $95/115; 🅿 🖳) If you have a car, this beautiful Tarcoola Beach location just a five minutes drive into town won't bother you at all. Especially when you see the sweeping coastal vistas! The self-contained ones are the best bet – ask for ocean views.

Batavia Motor Inne (☎ 1800 014 628, 9921 3500; 54 Fitzgerald St; d $98, self-contained r $110; 🅿 🖳) A typical Aussie motel, the Batavia has spacious, clean, comfortable rooms with tea and coffee facilities and TV, and self-contained rooms with kitchens.

Ocean Centre Hotel (☎ 9921 7777; www.oceancentre hotel.com.au; cnr Foreshore Dr & Cathedral Ave; standard/ deluxe/deluxe with view $110/120/150; 🅿 🖳) The spacious rooms, sunset views from the balcony, convenient central location, and high-speed in-room internet (although it costs), go some way in making up for the curt service.

Eating

Geraldton has myriad takeaways, coffee lounges, bakeries, supermarkets, and of course, a great fish market!

Go Health Lunch Bar (☎ 9965 5200; 122 Marine Tce; light meals $5-13; 🕑) Fresh juices and smoothies, excellent espresso and healthy sandwiches and light meals are served over the cool corrugated iron counter of this friendly café.

Bellavista (☎ 9964 2681; cnr Marine Tce & Cathedral Ave; meals $7-19 🕑 10am-9pm Tue-Sat) Former Melbournian John Todaro brings some badly needed city style and authentic Italian – filling focaccias, delicious risottos, and handmade pasta (try the prawn linguini) – to Geraldton. Todaro has a passion for local art, environment and politics; check out the changing exhibitions on the walls.

Tanti's (☎ 9964 2311; 174 Marine Tce; mains $8-20; 🕑 lunch Wed-Fri, dinner Mon-Sat) This casual BYO restaurant is packed every night with regulars who keep returning for its tasty Thai favourites. Takeaway also available.

Topolinis Caffe (☎ 9964 5866; 158 Marine Tce; mains $11-30; 🕑 8.30am-late) The home-style Italian at this relaxed licensed eatery keeps the locals happy. The $26 dinner and movie deal and half-price pasta on Monday are popular.

CENTRAL WEST COAST

HAWES' HOLY HERITAGE TRAIL

The architect and priest Monsignor John Hawes is a distinctive and enigmatic figure in the region's history. Born in Surrey, England in 1876, Hawes showed a love of architecture at an early age, later studying it and becoming intrigued by the Arts and Crafts Movement, which eschewed the complexities of Victorian style for a more organic simplicity – ideas which later served Hawes well.

On the cusp of a successful career in 1901, Hawes converted to the Anglican faith, became ordained in 1903, and was called to the Bahamas where he utilised his architectural skills in rebuilding storm-damaged churches. Another dramatic conversion to Catholicism saw Hawes ordained as a Catholic priest a couple of years later. While studying in Rome, Hawes met the Bishop of Geraldton and arrived in Australia in 1915 to work as the Murchison goldfields pastor. Working tirelessly for the next 24 years as a parish priest at Mullewa and Greenough, he also designed 24 buildings – 16 of which were realised.

His notable buildings include the **Church of Our Lady of Mt Carmel** and **Priest House** in Mullewa (p177), the **Church of the Holy Cross** in Morawa (p176), the **Church of St Joseph** in Perenjori (p176), and the imposing **Cathedral of St Francis Xavier** in Geraldton (p185). Working on these was often a struggle for Hawes as skilled labour and materials were hard to come by, so in many instances the tenacious man did much of the building himself.

Hawes was never completely at home in Australia and harboured a yearning to return to the Bahamas. Under the pretext of taking a sabbatical in Europe, Hawes left Australia in 1939 and headed for the Bahamas where he lived on the remote island of Cat. Hawes lived as a virtual recluse until he was moved to a hospital in Miami where he died in 1956. His body was taken back to his final construction – the tomb he had built on Cat Island.

The *Monsignor Hawes Heritage Trail* pamphlet ($5) is available from the visitors centre in Geraldton.

Freemasons Hotel (☎ 9964 3467; cnr Marine Tce & Durlacher St; meals $12-32; ☺ 11am-midnight Mon-Sat, 11am-10pm Sun) This classic old Aussie pub has a modern brasserie with seafood, steak and Asian dishes. Only opt for the sizzling stone slabs if you're prepared to cook your own food but eat it the chef's way – we weren't allowed to add extra oil to our burning food when we asked!

Conversations by Indigo (☎ 9965 0800; Bayly St, Batavia Coast Marina; mains $14-32; ☺ 10am-late Mon-Sat, 8am-late Sun) In a stunning contemporary building overlooking the new marina, this is Geraldton's best restaurant with an inventive global menu and a great selection of WA wines. The Indigo Oysters in chilli, coriander and lime-spiked vodka are sublime.

Entertainment

Freemasons is a favourite drinking spot with regular live music and occasional DJs and dance nights.

Nitey (☎ 9921 1400; 60 Fitzgerald St; ☺ Thu-Sat) A popular red-walled club that sees locals lining up until late to boogie away. Get here before 3am, as there's no entry between then and 5am closing.

Geraldton 4 Cinemas (☎ 9965 0568; cnr Marine Tce & Fitzgerald St; adult/child $12/8) Head here for the latest flicks.

Queens Park Theatre (☎ 9956 6662; cnr Cathedral Ave & Maitland St) Stages theatre, comedy, concerts and films.

Getting There & Around

SkyWest (☎ 1300 66 00 88) has flights to and from Perth daily, as well as regular flights to Carnarvon, Denham (for Monkey Mia), Exmouth and Karratha.

Greyhound (☎ 13 20 30) buses run from the Bill Sewell Complex to Perth daily ($54, 6¾ hours), as well as Broome ($284, 22 hours) and all points in between. **Transwa** (☎ 1300 6622 05; www.transwa.wa.gov.au) also goes daily to Perth ($50, six hours) and three times weekly to Kalbarri ($22, 2½ hours).

Geraldton Bus Service (☎ 9923 1100) operates eight routes to local suburbs (all-day ticket $2.50). **Bike Force** (☎ 9921 3279; 54 Marine Tce) hires bikes for $15/70 per day/week.

HOUTMAN ABROLHOS ISLANDS

Better known as 'the Abrolhos', this archipelago of 122 coral islands is about 60km off the coast of Geraldton. While they're home to sea lion colonies, a host of sea birds, golden orb spiders, carpet pythons and the Tammar wallaby, much of the beauty of the Abrolhos lies beneath the water. Here *Acropora* corals abound and, thanks to the warm Leeuwin Current, a rare and spectacular mix of tropical and temperate fish species thrives.

The beautiful but treacherous reefs surrounding the islands have claimed many ships over the years, including the ill-fated *Batavia* (see the boxed text, below).

As the islands are protected and there are no tourist facilities, you can't stay overnight. Only licensed crayfishing families are permitted to shack up on the islands in season (March to June). But you can go on bush walks and picnics, fly over, dive, snorkel, surf or fish the Abrolhos. A number of boats and light planes leave from Geraldton.

Flights are not only faster and more fun, they generally work out cheaper, at around $200 per person. Try **Geraldton Air Charters** (☎ 9923 3434; www.geraldtonaircharter.com.au) or **Shine Aviation Services** (☎ 9923 3600; www.abrolhos.com .au). **Abrolhos Odyssey Charters** (☎ 0428 382 505; www.abrolhoscharters.com.au) runs popular fishing, diving and snorkelling trips.

Get the excellent *Houtman Abrolhos Islands Visitors Guide* from Geraldton's visitors centre.

NORTHAMPTON

☎ 08 / pop 780

This charming National Trust–classified town was established to exploit lead and copper deposits discovered in 1848. Its historic stone architecture is splendid – grand buildings with big verandas and quaint stores with corrugated tin awnings. It's worth calling in if you're around during the annual **Airing of the Quilts** in October, when Northampton's heritage buildings are draped with beautiful patchwork bed covers.

Pick up a free *Heritage Walk* pamphlet from the **visitors centre** (☎ 9934 1488; www.north amptonwa.com.au; ⏱ 9am-3pm Mon-Fri, 9am-noon Sat) in the old police station on Hampton Rd (the highway). Check out **Chiverton House** (☎ 0428 866 596; Hampton Rd; admission $2; ⏱ 10am-noon & 2-4pm Fri-Mon), an early mining cottage dating to 1896, which has been converted into a fascinating pioneer museum.

The stately **Old Convent** (☎ 9934 1692; 61 Hampton Rd; dm/s/d $17/22/48) is a wonderful stone building designed by Monsignor Hawes (see the boxed text, opposite), converted to backpacker accommodation. Next door, the striking **St Mary's Church** (Hawes again) is a dignified structure made from weathered stone.

The town's pubs serve hearty counter meals. The **Miners Arms** (☎ 9934 1281; Hampton Rd; r $80) is the most comfortable. If you are

---

SHIPWRECKS AND SURVIVORS

Early in the morning on 4 June 1629, the Dutch East India Company's ship, the *Batavia*, ran aground on an Abrolhos Islands reef off the coast of Terra Australis Incognita, as Australia was known to them. The ship was taking the fastest route to Batavia (Jakarta) in Java – heading due east once around the Cape of Good Hope and then along the Western Australian coast to Indonesia. Quite often these ships were caught in storms or misjudged the depth of the reefs close to the Australian coast earning this stretch of coastline the name Shipwreck Coast.

The captain of the *Batavia*, Francis Pelsaert, sailed a boat to the Dutch East India Company's base at Batavia to get help and supplies. While his back was turned, a gruesome mutiny took place and on the captain's return, he executed all those involved apart from two young men who were left ashore, becoming perhaps the first white men on Australian soil.

Another notable wreck was the *Zuytdorp*, which ran aground beneath the towering cliffs about 65km north of Kalbarri in 1712. Wine bottles, other relics and the remains of fires have been found on the cliff top, and the discovery of the extremely rare Ellis van Creveld syndrome (rife in Holland at the time the ship ran aground) in Aboriginal children suggests that *Zuytdorp* survivors lasted long enough to introduce the gene to Australia.

For more on the Dutch connection to Australia, see the History chapter. The remains of the *Batavia* and other wrecks can be seen at the Western Australian Museum in Geraldton (p185) and in the Fremantle Shipwreck Galleries (p81).

Batavia Coast Dive Academy (☎ 9921 4229; www.bataviacoastdive.com) offers tours diving to a more recent shipwreck, the *South Tomi*, sunk off the Geraldton coast in 2004.

camping or caravanning, try **Northampton Caravan Park** (☎ 9934 1202; Hampton Rd; unpowered/powered sites $17/22).

Greyhound (☎ 13 20 30) stops at the Miners Arms Hotel daily (Perth to Northampton $77, eight hours).

NORTHAMPTON TO KALBARRI

From Northampton take the scenic coastal road if you're heading to Kalbarri. Otherwise, continue north along Hwy 1.

About 4km off the highway you reach the turn-off for the tiny coastal town of **Horrocks** (19km west), with a sheltered beach and good fishing. The pleasant **caravan park** (☎ 9934 3039; unpowered/powered sites d $17/21) backs onto the beach.

The atmospheric convict settlement of **Lynton** – with its stone homestead, flourmill and stables – is worth a brief visit.

The **Pink Lake** is an algae-filled blue lake with pale pink tones, caused by a naturally occurring beta-carotene; it's farmed for use as a Vitamin A supplement and colouring agent. **Port Gregory** (47km from Northampton) is a relaxed village with a beautiful beach and wooden jetty that's perfect for fishing holidays and family retreats. Pitch a tent or camp your van at the laid-back **caravan park** (☎ 9935 1052; unpowered/powered sites d $20/22, on-site vans $50, cabins shared/ensuite $65/85).

Hutt River Province (see p192) is accessible from Ogilvie Rd; look for the blue signs.

KALBARRI

☎ 08 / pop 2000

Picturesque Kalbarri is a perennially popular seaside spot that changes personality overnight with the coming of the school holidays. One day the locals will be wandering down to the empty windswept beaches with surfboards or fishing rods in hand, the next they'll find themselves confronted with a sea of lurid fluorescent plastic and a flood of Perth families on bike and foot, in garish sun-protection gear with boogie boards under their arms.

At the mouth of the Murchison River, Kalbarri's proximity to the dramatic coastline and the surrounding national park means plenty of beach and bush leisure opportunities.

Information

There are ATMs at the shopping centres on Grey and Porter streets.
Kalbarri Café (☎ 9937 1045) For internet.

Visitors centre (☎ 1800 639 468, 9937 1104; www .kalbarriwa.com; Grey St; ☷ 9am-5pm) Has lots of info on the national park and activities around town and can book accommodation and tours.

Sights & Activities
KALBARRI NATIONAL PARK

This ruggedly beautiful **national park** (per car $9) with its magnificent river red gums and Tumblagooda sandstone contains over 1000 sq km of gorgeous bushland, stunning river gorges and magnificent coastal cliffs. There's myriad wildlife, including 200 species of birds, and spectacular wildflowers, including banksias, grevilleas and kangaroos paw, between July and November.

To get to the river gorges from Kalbarri, head 11km east along Ajana Kalbarri Rd to the turn-off, and follow the 20km stretch of dirt to the gorges. A number of lookouts provide superb gorge vistas: at **The Loop** (400m from the car park), there's a natural rock arch, **nature's window**, framing the view upstream (and an 8km walk for the more adventurous); from **Z-Bend** (500m from car park) the gorge plunges 150m to the river below; at **Hawk's Head** there are great views from the picnic grounds; and from **Ross Graham** you can access the river.

The park extends south of Kalbarri to a string of rugged coastal cliff faces, including **Red Bluff**, **Rainbow Valley**, **Pot Alley**, **Eagle Gorge** and **Natural Bridge**. A walking/cycling path from town goes as far as Red Bluff (5.5km) passing **Jakes**, an excellent surf break. From the cliff tops you may spot humpback whales (August to November) and dolphins (year-round).

OTHER SIGHTS & ACTIVITIES

Pelican Feeding (☎ 9937 1104; Grey St waterfront near boat hire; free; ☷ 8.45am), Kalbarri's most popular attraction, proves that sometimes the simplest things in life are the sweetest.

Rainbow Jungle (☎ 9937 1248; Red Bluff Rd; adult/child $11.50/4.50; ☷ 9am-5pm Mon-Sat, 10am-5pm Sun) is a beautiful bird habitat and breeding centre set in luxuriant tropical gardens about 4km south of Kalbarri. It has Australia's largest free flight aviary providing a chance to see astonishingly colourful parrots, lorikeets and cockatoos, including endangered species, in action.

At **Kalbarri Wildflower Centre** (☎ 9937 1229; off Ajana Kalbarri Rd; adult/child $4/free; ☷ 9am-5pm) you can amble along a wonderful nature and wildflower trail (1.8km) that winds its way through native plants and flowers labelled for identification.

Kalbarri Boat Hire (☎ 9937 1245; www.kalbarri boathire.com; per hr $10-50), on the foreshore, hires out kayaks, canoes, surf cats, paddle bikes/ boats, barracuda bikes and powerboats to explore the Murchison River.

Other activities include **fishing**, **surfing**, **sandboarding**, **abseiling**, **charters**, **horse-riding** and **camel rides**; see the visitors centre for more details.

Tours

The visitors centre has full details and takes bookings.

Kalbarri Adventure Tours (☎ 9937 1677; www .kalbarritours.com.au; adult/child $65/50) Runs popular daily trips combining 8km of active hiking and 6km scenic canoeing in the national park.

Kalbarri Air Charter (☎ 9937 1130; Grey St; 20min flights adult/child from $45/30) Offers scenic flights over the Murchison River gorges and coastal cliffs.

Kalbarri Boat Hire (☎ 9937 1245; www.kalbarriboat hire.com; adult/child $60/40) Does four-hour breakfast and lunch canoe safaris on the Murchison River.

Kalbarri Safari Tours (☎ 9937 1011; www.kalbarri safaritours.com.au; per hr $59-75) Operates 'ocean and outback' quad bike, canoe and 4WD safaris.

Kalbarri Scenic Tours (☎ 9937 1161; www.kalbarri coachtours.com.au; adult/child/concession $45/22/40) Runs daily national park, heritage and Hutt River Province coach tours.

CENTRAL WEST COAST

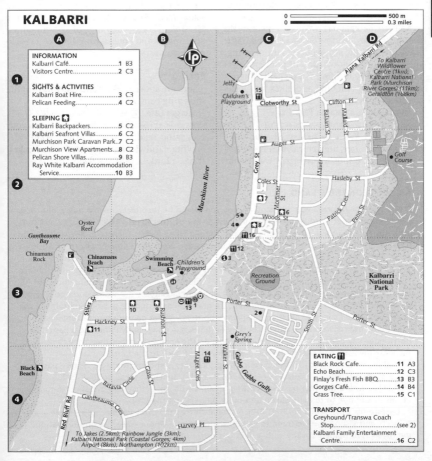

KALBARRI

0 — 500 m
0 — 0.3 miles

INFORMATION
Kalbarri Café..................1 B3
Visitors Centre................2 C3

SIGHTS & ACTIVITIES
Kalbarri Boat Hire............3 C3
Pelican Feeding...............4 C2

SLEEPING
Kalbarri Backpackers...........5 C2
Kalbarri Seafront Villas.......6 C2
Murchison Park Caravan Park..7 C2
Murchison View Apartments....8 C2
Pelican Shore Villas...........9 B3
Ray White Kalbarri Accommodation
Service....................10 B3

EATING
Black Rock Cafe...............11 A3
Echo Beach...................12 C3
Finlay's Fresh Fish BBQ........13 B3
Gorges Café..................14 B4
Grass Tree...................15 C1

TRANSPORT
Greyhound/Transwa Coach
Stop......................(see 2)
Kalbarri Family Entertainment
Centre....................16 C2

To Kalbarri Wildflower Centre (1km); Kalbarri National Park (Murchison River Gorges) (11km); Geraldton (168km)

To Jakes (2.5km); Rainbow Jungle (3km); Kalbarri National Park (Coastal Gorges; 4km); Airport (8km); Northampton (102km)

Kalbarri Wilderness Cruises (☎ 9937 1104; cruises $30) Runs popular cruises down the Murchison River to The Loop and Z-Bend.

Sleeping

Kalbarri has lots of accommodation, but it's often full during school holidays – avoid this period if you can; otherwise, book well ahead. The visitors centre has a long list of places they can book on your behalf.

BUDGET

Murchison View Apartments (☎ 9937 1096; cnr Grey & Ruston Sts; 2-bedroom units from $145; 🖭 🖾) These spacious fully self-contained apartments (with DVD/CD players, fridge/freezer, stove etc) opposite the waterfront have balconies, perfect for kicking back after a day down at the beach.

Kalbarri Backpackers (☎ 9937 1430; www.yha .com.au; cnr Woods & Mortimer Sts; dm $20-22, s/d $28/56; 🖭 🖾) While the atmosphere is uninspiring, the facilities are good (decent pool and bar-becue) and the location is excellent. There's a range of tours on offer and bikes for guests to hire ($10 per day).

Murchison Park Caravan Park (☎ 9937 1005; cnr Woods & Grey Sts; unpowered/powered sites $20/24, air-con cabins $75; 🖾) With its grassy, shaded sites and great facilities, this central, family-owned caravan park opposite Kalbarri's waterfront is the best place to pitch your tent or park your van.

MIDRANGE & TOP END

Kalbarri Seafront Villas (☎ 9937 1025; www.kalbarri seafrontvillas.com.au; 108 Grey St; 1-/2-bedroom units from $155/175; 🖭 🖾) These spacious, clean units overlooking the waterfront come with televi-sion, DVD players and microwaves.

Pelican Shore Villas (☎ 9937 1708; pelicanshores@ westnet.com.au; cnr Grey & Kaiber Sts; 2-/3-bedroom front villa from $185/205; 🖭) These stylish contemporary designed units are the best in town, with all mod cons (including DVD, microwave, pri-vate laundry), floor-to-ceiling windows and big balconies overlooking the sea.

Ray White Kalbarri Accommodation Service (☎ 1800 777 776; www.kalbarriaccommodation.com.au; Kalbarri Arcade, 44 Grey St; accommodation per week from $290-1200) Has a wide range of self-contained apartments and houses, from fibro cottages to contemporary designer apartments.

Eating

There are supermarkets and takeaways at the shopping centres.

Gorges Café (☎ 9937 1200; Marina Complex, Grey St; meals $5-14; ⏱ 8am-4pm Wed-Mon) Catch up on your magazine reading at this bright BYO café, serving sandwiches, light meals, and cakes. It has a funky, laid-back feel to it.

PRINCE LEONARD'S LAND

If you thought Australia was an island nation, you would be incorrect. Down a dusty, dirt road, 75km northwest of Northampton, lies the **Principality of Hutt River** (☎ 9936 6035; www.huttriver .net), Australia's 'second largest country'. It was formed when farmer Leonard Casley, appalled by new government quotas on wheat production, seceded from the Commonwealth of Australia on 21 April 1970.

While the Western Australian (WA) government tried to overturn the secession, HRH Prince Leonard had done his constitutional homework – more than 30 years later the Prince and his Princess Shirley remain the monarchs of the only principality in the world declared without bloodshed. With four sons, three daughters, 24 grandchildren and 22 great-grandchildren, the family tree would suggest that the principality's borders will not be compromised anytime soon. Asked if he ever envisioned a palace coup by his heirs, the now elderly Prince, who has retained his wonderfully deadpan sense of humour, replied, 'They consider it, but then they think about the work involved and change their minds before I get back to the farm'.

And the work involved in running your own principality is endless. There are visitors' passports to be stamped, naturalisation services to conduct (the principality has around 13,000 citizens worldwide with a five-year passport costing $300), and a post office and gift shop to run – all of this in addition to running sheep and other interests on the property.

Despite his busy schedule, HRH Prince Leonard takes time out for the little people – loyal subjects and visitors are welcome to call on the residence. Phone ahead to ensure that one of the royals is at home – royalty with a delicious sense of the absurdity of it all!

Black Rock Cafe (☎ 9937 1062; 80 Grey St; meals $10-28; ✆ 7am-late) This casual licensed eatery, with sunny outdoor seating overlooking the sea, keeps the crowds coming back with great gourmet breakfasts and lunches and a creative global fusion menu in the evening.

Grass Tree (☎ 9937 2288; 94-96 Grey St; mains $10-$30; ✆ 9am-late Thu-Tue) While this licensed café-restaurant opposite the waterfront serves delicious breakfasts and light lunches, dinner is what it does best – expect innovative Asian-inspired global fusion using the freshest local produce.

Finlay's Fresh Fish BBQ (Magee Cres; mains $12-20; ✆ 5.30-8.30pm Tue-Sun) In a former fish factory, this big tin shed of a BYO eatery prides itself on offering 'no service, no corkage, no glasses, no frills' – just big servings of abuse (don't fear if the cook yells at you, it's part of the fun of the place) alongside huge portions of home-style barbecued seafood and steaks. You can also sing for your supper and they'll feed you in return. Seriously.

our pick **Echo Beach** (☎ 9937 1033; Upstairs, Porter St; mains $17-34; ✆ 8am-late) This stylish restaurant with a cool jazz soundtrack makes a refreshing change from the usual uninspiring country eateries. Its Mod-Oz cuisine is delicious and wine list eclectic. Try the outback tasting plate (barbecue kangaroo skewers, tempura crocodile, smoked rabbit, Murchison goat cutlets and bush tomato relish!) followed by Carnarvon tiger prawns and Kalbarri dhufish.

Getting There & Around

Buses stop/depart from the visitors centre. **Greyhound** (☎ 13 20 30) buses head to Perth ($108, 11 hours), Exmouth ($163, 10½ hours) and Broome ($294, 24½ hours), while **Transwa** (☎ 1300 6622 05; www.transwa.wa.gov.au) services Perth several days a week ($63, 7 hours).

Kalbarri Auto Centre (☎ 9937 1290) rents 4WDs and sedans from $40 a day and picks up and delivers to your door, while **Kalbarri Family Entertainment Centre** (☎ 9937 1105; 30 Porter St) rents bikes from $15 per day.

SHARK BAY

World Heritage–listed Shark Bay incorporates two stunning peninsulas running parallel to the mainland and surrounded by a rich marine park. It's an outstanding example of an ongoing geological process (the shaping of its seabed by seagrass); a unique natural phenomena (its hypersaline marine waters); a fantastic example of a major stage in earth's evolutionary history (the Stromatolites of Hamelin Pool; see p194); and it has important habitats where threatened animal species survive (Shark Bay's peninsulas and islands; see p195). What makes a visit to Shark Bay so satisfying is that you can experience all of these extraordinary features.

Shark Bay also has a rich history and culture. Originally inhabited by the Malgana, Nhanda and Inggarda peoples who depended on both the sea and bush for their subsistence, Shark Bay offers opportunities for visitors to take indigenous cultural tours to learn about the land from their perspective. The local people were probably the first indigenous Australians to encounter Europeans – Shark Bay was the site of the first recorded landing by a European on Australian soil. In 1616, Dutch explorer Dirk Hartog anchored at the island that now bears his name, just off Denham, Shark Bay's main town.

OVERLANDER ROADHOUSE TO DENHAM

Leaving the highway just after the Overlander Roadhouse, the first turn-off (about 27km along) takes you to **Hamelin Pool**, a marine reserve containing the world's best-known colony of **stromatolites**. These brown rocklike formations are made up of modest microbes almost identical to organisms that existed 1900 million years ago and evolved into more complex life. They're extremely fragile, so there's a boardwalk (with information panels) that allows no-impact viewing; visit at low tide.

The nearby 1884 **Postmasters Residence & Telegraph Office** (☎ 9942 5905; ✆ 9am-4pm) served as a telephone exchange until 1977. This unassuming little outpost was also unwittingly responsible for transmitting messages from NASA's own Gemini space-mission craft in 1964 after communications between the tracking station and Carnarvon's dish went down. It now serves delicious Devonshire teas (tea, scones and jam) and has displays on the stromatolites.

The miniature cockleshells that cover the extraordinary **Shell Beach**, 50km from Hamelin, are 10m deep in places. These shells are peculiar to Shark Bay and cement together after rain, making sturdy white bricks – look out for them in Denham.

SEAGRASS AND STROMATOLITES

Below the surface of the crystal-clear waters of sensational Shark Bay sits the world's largest seagrass meadow. Differing from seaweed, which doesn't flower or have roots, seagrass meadows create their own ecosystem, providing a nursery for small fish, prawns and a gigantic grazing ground for 10% of the world's dugong population. Seagrass also restricts swell and tidal movements, increasing sedimentation, which in turn has contributed to the heavily salty and protected environment required for the development of rare marine features, such as stromatolites.

These single-celled 'rock layers' are the oldest form of life on earth and are often called 'living fossils'. Discovered by scientists in 1956, the stromatolites colony at Hamelin Pool is the first living example found in the world and is relatively young, estimated to be 3000 years old. The hypersalinity and stillness of the water here is rare, meaning that competitors and predators for the microbes that create stromatolites can't survive.

At the next turn-off, **Nanga Bay Resort** (☎ 9948 3992; nangabay@wn.com.au; unpowered/powered sites $15/23, dm $20, d cabins $63, d motel $125; ⊠ ⚲), catering mainly to families and grey nomads, is a ranch-like place with a range of sleeps, from motel units to fisherman's huts. Facilities include tennis courts, a shop, and rustic bar and restaurant. You'll need your own wheels.

From **Eagle Bluff**, there are spectacular clifftop views, wonderful birdlife (yes, eagles), and sharks swimming in the clear waters below.

DENHAM

☎ 08 / pop 1140

Australia's most westerly town, laid-back Denham, with its crystal-clear water and charming beachfront, makes a decent base for visiting the marine park, nearby François Peron National Park, and Monkey Mia, 26km away. Originally established as a pearling town, Denham's streets were once paved with pearl shell. All you'll see is bitumen these days, but some shell-brick buildings still stand.

Almost all visitor facilities are on the main thoroughfare, Knight Tce. The accredited visitors centre is the privately run **Denham & Monkey Mia visitors centre** (☎ 9948 1773; sharkbayvisitor@bigpond.com.au; 29 Knight Tce; ⏰ 8am-5pm; ⌨), which can book accommodation and tours, and organise car rental. **DEC** (☎ 9948 1208; Knight Tce; ⏰ 8am-5pm Mon-Fri) has plenty of information on the World Heritage area and national park. There's a post office on Knight Tce and an ATM at Heritage Resort.

Sights & Activities

In a striking contemporary building, this slick cutting-edge **Shark Bay World Heritage Discovery Centre** (☎ 9948 1590; www.sharkbayinterpretivecentre .com.au; 53 Knight Tce; adult/concession $10/8; ⏰ 9am-6pm) – one of Western Australia's best – has compelling exhibitions on Shark Bay's natural environment, its indigenous people and the many explorers who've ventured here.

On the way into town, **Ocean Park** (☎ 9948 1765; www.oceanpark.com.au; Shark Bay Rd; adult/child $10/5; ⏰ 10am-4pm) is a locally run aquaculture farm featuring an artificial lagoon stocked with sharks, turtles, stingrays and fish.

Tours

Mac Attack (☎ 0419 925 692; www.sportfish.com.au; adult/child $150/100) Runs full-day fishing safaris, along with whale-watching and sightseeing trips

Majestic Tours (☎ 9948 1627; www.ozpal.com /majestic; per person $60-135) Has full-day 4WD tours, including François Peron National Park and Shell Beach.

Power Dive (☎ 9948 1905; www.divefun.com.au; per person $70) Offers snorkelling and diving safaris in François Peron National Park.

Shark Bay Coaches & Tours (☎ 9948 1081; www.sb coaches.com; per person $70) Full-day tours to key sights.

Sleeping & Eating

Denham has accommodation for all budgets and long-stay/off-season discounts. There is a supermarket, a bakery, café and takeaways on Knight Tce.

Bay Lodge (☎ 1800 812 780, 9948 1278; baylodge@wn .com.au; 95 Knight Tce; dm $20-22; ⌨ ⚲) Every room at this YHA hostel has its own ensuite, kitchen, living and dining facilities with TV/DVD. The owners will also spoil you, taking you on complimentary 4WD fishing, swimming and wildlife-spotting tours, and holding bush barbecue nights. They also provide a daily shuttle bus to Monkey Mia.

Seaside Tourist Village (☎ 1300 133 733, 9948 1242; www.sharkbayfun.com; Knight Tce; unpowered/powered sites

$22/26, d cabins $60, 1-/2-bedroom chalets $99/115; ⚄)
Seaside Tourist Village is a great big beachside
park with good facilities, including barbecues,
and self-contained chalets with verandas overlooking the sea.

Denham Villas (☎ 9948 1264; www.denhamvillas
.com; 4 Durlacher St; villas $95-150; ⚄) These spa-
cious fully self-contained villas (with proper
kitchen and laundry) are excellent value and
ideal for families.

Oceanside Village (☎ 1800 680 600, 9948 3003; www
.oceanside.com.au; 117 Knight Tce; chalets $120-160; ⚄)
Lego-land may come to mind when you see
these identical little white-and-blue houses,
but they're actually rather swish – some even
have spas. The best are on stilts on the hillside
with great views of the sea.

Shark Bay Hotel (☎ 9948 1203; 43 Knight Tce; mains
$12-26) While this typical Aussie pub bistro is
nothing flash, it's a great spot to eat a hearty
counter meal, get to know some locals and
play a few rounds of pool.

our pick **Old Pearler Restaurant** (☎ 9948 1373;
Knight Tce; meals $12-39) Built from seashell bricks,
this splendid stone building houses one of
Western Australia's most atmospheric old
restaurants. Its cosy interior, with fireplace,
rustic wooden furniture, and candlesticks on
the walls, is the perfect place to feast on hearty
Australian favourites like steak Dianne and
crayfish mornay.

Getting There & Away

Skywest (☎ 1300 660 088) has flights from Geraldton and Carnarvon, linking to Perth, Exmouth and Karratha.

Daily shuttle buses ($30, 1½ hours) from
Denham and Monkey Mia connect with the
north- and south-bound **Greyhound** (☎ 13 20
30) services at the Overlander Roadhouse on
the main highway (Denham to Carnarvon
($79, 5½ hours).

Bay Lodge (☎ 9948 1278) runs a daily shuttle
bus to Monkey Mia (return for nonguests $16)
that leaves from the Shell service station on
Knight Tce at 7.45am, returning from Monkey Mia at 4.30pm; bookings essential.

FRANÇOIS PERON NATIONAL PARK

Renowned for its dramatic golden cliffs, pristine white-sand beaches, salt lakes, and rare
marsupial species, this **national park** (per bus
passenger/car $4/9), 4km from Denham on the
Monkey Mia Rd, will reward those with 4WD
vehicles and an adventurous spirit. There's a
visitors centre at the old Peron Homestead,
6km from the main road, where a former
artesian bore has been converted to a soothing
35°C **hot tub**, a novel spot for a sunset soak.
There are **camp sites** ($9) with limited facilities
at Big Lagoon, Gregories, Bottle Bay and Her-
ald Bight. If you don't have your own wheels,
take a tour to the park (see opposite).

CENTRAL WEST COAST

RETURN TO EDEN

When French naturalist François Péron visited the shores of Shark Bay in 1801 and 1803, he
recorded the presence of over 20 species of land mammals living in the harsh climate of the
region. Just some 200 years later, less than one third of the mammals remained. With the environment degraded by decades of poor farming practices and infested with feral foxes, cats, goats
and rabbits, the future of the natural species of mammals found in this area appeared in doubt.
Today, however, the area is the subject of Australia's largest and most ambitious ecosystem
regeneration programme: Project Eden.

Established in 1995, the Department of Environment and Conservation (DEC) project is attempting to eradicate feral animals, re-establish populations of endemic species, and develop
techniques that can be applied to other degraded arid zones in Australia. The key has been the
isolation of the peninsula from mainland Australia with a 3.4km fence at the isthmus as well as
baiting, preventing feral species from repopulating. The eradication of foxes from the area has
been successful and the feral cat population has been significantly reduced.

A breeding centre in François Peron National Park has collected breeding pairs of rare marsupials
from the offshore Dorre and Bernier islands, and zoos and rehabilitation centres across Australia.
The reintroduction of three locally extinct species has been successful: woylies, bilbies and mallee
fowls are now surviving in the area. However feral cat predation has halted the reintroduction of
rufous-hare wallabies and banded-hare wallabies. Still, as one prominent local Aborigine put it to
us, 'the country is beginning to heal itself'. With a little help from its friends of course.

To learn more, visit www.sharkbay.org.

MONKEY MIA
☎ 08

World-famous for the wild dolphins that turn up in the shallow water for feeding each day, the beach resort of **Monkey Mia** (entrance adult/child/family $6/2/12), 26km northeast of Denham, now tops many travellers' list of things to do. It's now so popular that the morning feeding session (around 7.45am) is a bit of a circus and it's hard to get close to the action; hang around after everyone leaves until the second feeding for a more satisfying experience.

Interaction with the dolphins is carefully managed to minimise impact so observe the rules of behaviour outlined in the entry brochure; don't touch the dolphins as they can contract viruses from humans, and always follow the ranger's instructions. There's a swimming area next to the interaction zone. If a dolphin joins you, let them swim around you while you stay still but never chase or approach them as it may stress them, particularly if they're with calves.

The **DEC Dolphin Information Centre** (☎ 9948 1366; ☽ 7.30am-4pm) has lots of info, shows videos and hosts presentations. There are great books for sale in the shop and you can also buy tour tickets here.

You can also volunteer to work full-time with the dolphins for up to two weeks; you'll need to arrange this well in advance of your trip as it's understandably popular. Contact Volunteer Coordinator Alison True (☎ 9948 1366; alison.true@dec.wa.gov.au).

Tours

Take an eight-minute boat ride from Monkey Mia jetty across to the floating **Blue Lagoon Pearl Farm** (☎ 9948 1325; www.bluelagoon.com.au; 1hr tours adult/child $20/10; ☽ 11am) to learn how the beautiful black pearls are cultured.

Wildsights (☎ 1800 241 481, 9948 1481; www.monkey miawildsights.com.au; 1-2½ hr tours $39-64; ☽ 9am, 10.30am & 1pm) runs wonderful wildlife-spotting cruises on the *Shotover* catamaran. You'll get to see dugongs, dolphins, loggerhead turtles, sea snakes and perhaps even tiger sharks. The **Aristocat II** (☎ 9948 1446) offers similar trips at similar prices.

Local Aboriginal guide Darren 'Capes' Capewell leads the excellent **Wula Guda Nyinda Aboriginal Cultural Tours** (☎ 0429 708 847, 9948 1320; www.monkeymia.com.au; adult/child day tour $25/10; night tour $25/10; ☽ 9am, 4.30pm, 8.30pm). You'll learn 'how to let the bush talk to you' (see opposite),

some local Malgana language, how to identify bush tucker and native medicine, and how to read animal tracks and tell the size of an animal from their droppings. The evening 'Dreaming' walks are magical.

Sleeping & Eating

Monkey Mia is a resort and not a town, so eating and sleeping options are limited to the Monkey Mia Dolphin Resort. Self-catering is a good option.

Monkey Mia Dolphin Resort (☎ 1800 653 611, 9948 1320; www.monkeymia.com.au; tent sites $11, van sites back/beach $27/32, garden units $205, beachfront villas $275) This leafy resort offers a range of accommodation from great-value tent and van sites to top-end villas within splashing distance of the beach. The facilities are good and the beach is a short stroll away.

Dolphin Lodge (dm $24-28, d shared ensuite $62, park homes $109) The Resort's newest beachfront accommodation is suffering an identity crisis with more expensive seafront motel rooms (beachside dolphin units) sharing walls with backpacker dorms. (We know who has the better deal!) There's an excellent communal kitchen, lots of outdoor seating, internet kiosks and a laundry.

Bough Shed Restaurant (☎ 9948 1171; meals $6-34; ☽ 7am-8pm) While there are no surprises on the menu at this waterfront eatery, with the ubiquitous salt and pepper prawns ($18) and seafood platters ($110), we will hand it to them for inventing a creative new name for surf 'n' turf: 'pond and paddock', a huge Kimberley rib steak with Pemberton marron.

Monkey Bar (☎ 9948 1320; meals $7-18; ☽ 8am-late) This casual bar at the Dolphin Lodge serves good-sized counter meals and snacks, and it's a popular spot for a round of pool and a few drinks.

Getting There & Away

The only public transport to Monkey Mia from Denham is the Bay Lodge shuttle (see p195). It means you'll have to spend a full day here, but that's no hardship if you do a tour or two or simply bring a towel and book.

THE GASCOYNE

Despite taking its name from the 760km Gascoyne River – which, together with the Lyons River, has a catchment area of nearly 70,000 sq

---

MALGANA COUNTRY *Terry Carter*

You could see Darren 'Capes' Capewell as a one-man Aboriginal Embassy in Monkey Mia. Except this is his country, his local area – Malgana country. A fit, handsome, thirty-something ex-Aussie Rules player of considerable note, Capes has run his own cultural walks, Wula Guda Nyinda (you come this way) here since late 2004.

While other visitors wait for the dolphins to turn up for breakfast, we take Capes' morning walk, Buna (daytime) Dreaming. Before heading off, Capes entertains some young travellers with his didgeridoo playing. Soon he has a young Japanese girl amusingly acting out the movements of the animals that he's sounding out on the didgeridoo. And our walk turns out to be no less engaging.

'Today you mob are Malgana people', says Capes as he proceeds to take us on a fascinating and information-overload-inducing walk covering Malgana language, 'respect for country', bush tucker, bush medicine, bush survival, tracking and local history. I take an instant liking to the tiny edible berries that grow on what locals call the 'Charlie tree', named after a tribe member who used to enjoy taking naps under them. The berries are sweet and juicy and it's amazing that what appears to be scrubby bushland to us is actually a bush tucker supermarket. Capes spots some rather innocuous clouds on the horizon and instantly proclaims it's going to rain tomorrow. We think he's eaten too many berries.

When we arrived at Monkey Mia we'd been on the road for a month but had only met a few Aborigines working in tourism. Capes explains to us why it's taken so long for Aborigines to start running their own tour companies: 'Thinking in terms of product doesn't come too easy to our mob – while talking about our culture comes easy', he says. He had strong support from the **Western Australian Indigenous Tour Operators Committee** (WAITOC; www.waitoc.com) through training, networking and mentoring when setting up his business.

Research has shown that 80% of overseas visitors are seeking an Aboriginal cultural experience, but only 20% are getting it. Clearly the industry needs quite a few more 'Capes' to set up shop.

The next morning it's raining, just as Capes predicted. 'Well, what did you expect?', says Capes. 'This is my country!'

---

km – this is mostly sunburnt country because the river seldom flows above ground west of the Kennedy Range. Verdant Carnarvon is the region's hub, with a rugged coastline stretching north. To the east is the ancient, arid Kennedy Range and massive Mt Augustus.

CARNARVON

☎ 08 / pop 6900

At the mouth of the Gascoyne River, fertile Carnarvon, with its fruit and vegetable plantations and thriving fishing industry, makes a good stopover between Denham and Exmouth. This lush centre of the dry Gascoyne has a variety of decent accommodation and well-stocked supermarkets.

Information

There's a post office on Camel Lane and a couple of ATMs on Robinson St.

Visitors centre (☎ 9941 1146; www.carnarvon.org.au; Civic Centre, 11 Robinson St; ☿ 9am-5pm Mon-Fri, 9am-noon Sat) Has lots of information on the town and region,

and can provide walking trail and self-driving maps. It also sells unique local products, such as the tasty dried 'Mango Leather'.

Wise Owl Book Exchange (Babbage Island Rd) Has a good selection of secondhand books.

Sights & Activities

On the outskirts of town, the **OTC Dish** (Mahoney Ave) was established by NASA in 1966 as a tracking station for the Gemini and Apollo space missions, and tracked Halley's Comet in 1986. It was closed in 1987 although there are plans to open it for tours in the future.

Carnarvon's luxuriant plantations provide nearly 70% of the state's tropical fruits and vegetables. While some, such as the banana producers, offer **plantation tours** (see visitors centre for details) you can get a taste of everyone's delicious produce at the **Gascoyne Growers Market** (Gascoyne Civic Centre Carpark; ☿ 8am-noon Sat May-Nov).

You can ride a restored **steam train** (adult/child $7/5) from the end of the town footbridge to the **Historic Precinct**, and another along **One Mile Jetty**, where locals fish for mulloway; you can also walk along the jetty ($4/3).

The multicultural **Carnarvon Pioneer Cemetery** (Crowther St) is worth a wander; it's the final resting place of pioneers from as far away as Afghanistan and China.

Tours

Carnarvon Fishing Charters (☎ 0417 923 723, 0407 995 432; day trips per person $150) offers fishing trips and whale-watching including bait, ice and fishing gear.

Stockman Safaris (☎ 9941 2421; stockman safaris@wn.com.au; town tours adult/child $30/17, blowholes, Quobba & salt mine tours $55/39, Kennedy Range tours $120/90) runs a variety of tours that take in the town, local and regional sites.

Sleeping

Coral Coast Tourist Park (☎ 9941 1438; coralcoastpk @westnet.com.au; 108 Robinson St; unpowered/powered sites d $20/22 🐕 🖳) This pleasant shady park, with well-manicured grounds, has a tropical pool and a new campers kitchen.

our pick **Fish & Whistle** (☎ 9941 1704; 35 Robinson St; dm/s $22/35; 🐕 🖳 🖳) This big, breezy backpackers is a hit with travellers for its enormous communal spaces, excellent kitchen, BBQ area and big verandas, not to mention no bunks and private rooms! To top it off, the friendly owners treat guests like family, help them find seasonal work, drive them to work everyday, and take them fishing on their days off. And there's comfy flashpacker sleeps out back. Little wonder travellers don't want to leave!

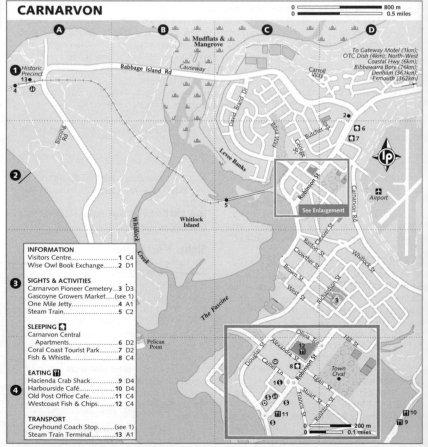

Carnarvon Central Apartments (☎ 9941 1317; www.carnarvonholidays.com; 120 Robinson St; 1-/2-bedroom apt $95/115) These modern apartments are spotlessly clean and fully self-contained – ideal for self-caterers.

Gateway Motel (☎ 9941 1532; 309 Robinson St; d $98) The motel rooms here may be basic but the management is accommodating. Arrive late after a long drive and they just might wrap up some leftovers from the Chinese buffet ($18) for you!

Eating

There's a supermarket, a couple of takeaways and cafés on Knight Tce.

Old Post Office Cafe (☎ 9941 1800; 10 Robinson St; pizzas $15-21; ☒ 5.30pm-10.30pm Tue-Sat) Locals and travellers alike enjoy tucking into the authentic pizzas and delicious pastas on the raised front veranda of this stylish yet casual eatery. And you can't help liking the music, which is easily the hippest in town. Licensed and BYO.

Harbourside Café (☎ 9941 4111; Small Boat Harbour; mains $15-30; ☒ 9am-8pm) This place has a recipe that works – the freshest seafood, served in good-sized portions, in imaginative ways, at reasonable prices, on a casual sunny waterfront terrace. How can they go wrong? Local favourites include the Shark Bay prawn omelette ($16) for brunch; tandoori scallops ($15); Cajun calamari ($18), and Moroccan snapper ($27).

Hacienda Crab Shack (9941 4078; Small Boat Harbour; price varies, by weight; ☒ 7am-4pm) Come here for fresh sweet steamed crabs and other delicious straight-from-the-sea-food.

Westcoast Fish & Chips (☎ 9941 1879; Carnarvon Blvd Shopping Centre, Robinson St) Get your scrummy seafood takeaway here. While the seafood baskets ($12) are big, we loved our prawn burgers ($7).

Getting There & Around

Skywest (☎ 1300 660 088) flies to Perth daily, and has less frequent flights to Denham and Exmouth, with links to Geraldton and Karratha.

Daily **Greyhound** (☎ 13 20 30) buses that go to Perth ($139, 13 hours) and Broome ($218, 21 hours), via Port Hedland ($139, 14 hours), stop at the visitors centre.

KENNEDY RANGE

This spectacular mountain plateau, just south of the Tropic of Capricorn some 170km east of Carnarvon, runs north from Gascoyne Junction for 195km and in places is 25km wide. A huge mesa pushed up from a seabed millions of years ago; the range has fossilised seashells in its cliffs. The southern and eastern sides of the plateau have eroded to create dramatic 100m-high cliffs and canyons and are covered with red sand dunes and spinifex. The discovery of ancient artefacts here attests to the presence of Balardung and Warriyangga peoples some 20,000 years ago.

An expedition led by Francis Gregory explored the park in 1858, resulting in its naming after the then-governor of WA, and while it was examined for minerals, the mining potential was fortunately deemed to be too low.

Some 295 species of plant have been recorded in the park with 40% of these being annual wildflowers. Cliff-top eyries provide perfect vantage points for the magnificent flora and fauna, such as the wedge-tailed eagle. There are several good walks you can do; pick up the walking trail guide from visitors centres before leaving.

While the eastern escarpment can be reached in a conventional vehicle in good weather, bad weather can quickly close the road to all vehicles; 4WD vehicles are recommended. Neither fuel nor water is available

CENTRAL WEST COAST

BONZER BACKROADS – BLOWHOLES AND BEACH SHACKS

About 20km north of Carnarvon along the main highway is the Blowhole Rd turn-off. This sealed road leads 49km to the frenzied **blowholes** and swaths of desolate, windswept coastline. Keep a sharp eye on the ocean: as the sign says, 'king waves kill'. Just 1km further north is secluded **Point Quobba**, where locals have beach shacks and come for the fishing and swimming. You can often spot turtles, whales (in season) and sea eagles. There are rocky camp sites ($5), but no facilities.

Around 10km further north (mostly unsealed) find **Quobba Station** (☎ 08-9941 2036; www .quobba.com.au; 2-person unpowered/powered sites $16/18, fishing shack/chalet d from $40/80), an oceanfront property with plenty of rustic accommodation and a mini store.

in the park so travel with adequate supplies. Overnight camping is permitted in the main visitor area at the base of the eastern escarpment of the Kennedy Range.

MT AUGUSTUS NATIONAL PARK

Mt Augustus (1106m), or Burringurrah as the local Wadjari people know it, is protected in this national park 476km from Carnarvon. Over twice the size of Uluru (Ayers Rock) and three times as old (the granite underneath the layered rocks is estimated to be 1700 million years old), it's the biggest 'rock' in the world. It looks less dramatic because of its partial vegetation cover.

There are Aboriginal engravings at three main sites: **Ooramboo** has engravings of animal tracks on a rock face; at **Mundee** the engravings are in a series of overhangs; and **Beedoboondu**, the starting point for a climb to the summit, has engravings of animal tracks and hunters.

From the car park near Beedoboondu, a strenuous excursion to the rock's top can take at least six hours and is 12km return. There is a shorter walk of 6km (2½ hours return) from Ooramboo that also has elevated views.

The best way to get to Mt Augustus is with your own wheels (4WD recommended) from the west coast via Gascoyne Junction, 175km east of Carnarvon. Take plenty of supplies and fuel, although there is a general store and pub at the Junction. There is accommodation at the base of the rock at **Mt Augustus Outback Tourist Resort** (☎ 9943 0527; camp/caravan sites $18/22, motel d $80), which has basic facilities and a licensed restaurant.

Coral Coast & the Pilbara

The tranquil blue Coral Coast is named after the colourful coral beds that make up marvellous Ningaloo Reef, and the marine park is devoted to preserving this delicate reef and the abundance of marine life that call it home. If snorkelling and diving these gorgeous waters isn't enough for you, the Coral Coast is one of the few places in the world where you can swim with the world's biggest fish, the (harmless) whale shark. When you're not doing that, watch whales, manta rays, turtles and rare dugongs. If that's all too much for you there are great waves to surf, calm waters to swim, beautiful beaches to laze about on and delicious fresh seafood to enjoy.

The rugged, red-dirt Pilbara – a vast region of arid land with a parched skin and a big heart of iron ore – couldn't be in greater contrast. It's the dusky dirt within the rich earth that has massive machines tearing into the ranges, remarkably long trains rolling through the desert, and tidy lush green towns like Tom Price and Newman developing incongruously in the middle of nowhere.

What these amazingly different regions do have in common are two of Western Australia's (WA's) most spectacular national parks: Ningaloo Marine Park and Karijini National Park, and lots of wide open space to drive through to get between them!

HIGHLIGHTS

- Watch the massive humpback whales migrate south at **North West Cape** (p208)
- Swim with the 'gentle giant' whale sharks in **Ningaloo Marine Park** (p208)
- Snorkel over splendid coral and marine life at sublime **Turquoise Bay** (p208), Ningaloo Marine Park
- Track turtles and becoming a certified 'turtle scout' at the **Jurabi Turtle Centre** (p206)
- Cool off in an idyllic water hole at **Millstream-Chichester National Park** (p214)
- Gape at the spectacular four gorges at Oxers Lookout in **Karijini National Park** (p215)
- Spot rare black-footed rock wallabies on a cruise along stunning **Yardie Creek** (p209)
- Tour the colossal open-cut **Mt Whaleback iron-ore mine** (p217) at Newman

★ Jurabi Turtle Centre
★★ North West Cape
★ Yardie Creek
★ Ningaloo Marine Park
★ Millstream-Chichester National Park
★ Karijini National Park
★ Newman

CORAL COAST & THE PILBARA

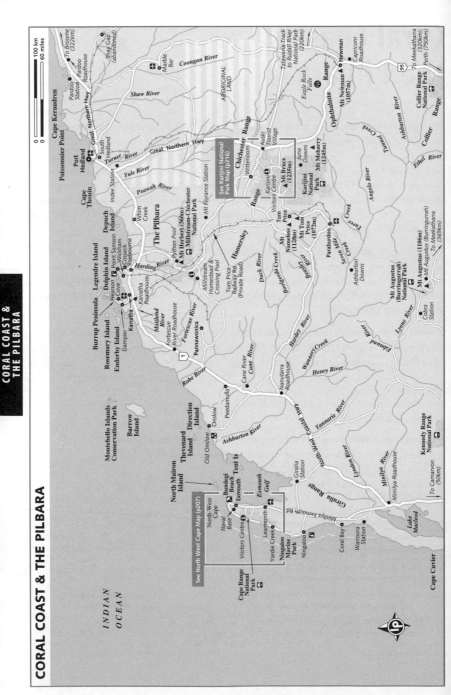

CORAL COAST

The Coral Coast extends from Coral Bay to Onslow and is the hub for sojourns out to the spectacular Ningaloo Marine Park – arguably WA's greatest and most precious natural attraction. Sublime beaches and dramatic gorges run alongside the reef on the North West Cape, preserved by Cape Range National Park.

CORAL BAY

☎ 08 / pop 120

Coral Bay is a tiny beachcomber community nestled on a beautiful bay, at the southern tip of Ningaloo Marine Park. The town consists of one street, down which you amble to the white-sand beach to swim and snorkel on the reef offshore. It's a super base for outer-reef activities too, such as swimming with whale sharks, scuba diving, whale-watching and fishing.

Coral Bay's Main Beach is designated for swimming; it's enclosed by a protective reef and there's good snorkelling within 50m of the shore. You can hire snorkelling gear, bodyboards and glass-bottom canoes ($8 to $20 per hour) on the beach.

Just 20 minutes walk north of Main Beach is Point Maud, where manta rays swim, and around the point is Bateman Bay, a breeding ground for reef sharks from October to March. While you can safely watch the sharks swimming in the shallow waters (at some times, as many as 200 'play' here), do not swim here.

Coral Bay has no shire services; private owners supply its electricity and water (not all taps provide desalinated water for drinking), but there are plans to establish Coral Bay as a town and develop tourism here in order to sustain the increasing number of visitors.

Coral Bay's main shopping centre on Robinson St has an ATM, newsagent and internet access in the 'visitors centres' (which the tour-operator booking offices like to call themselves).

Tours

Popular tours from Coral Bay include snorkelling, diving, swimming with whale sharks, whale-watching, spotting marine life (dolphins, dugongs, turtles and manta rays), and coral-viewing from glass-bottom boats. Most tour prices include equipment and refreshments. Tour operators have offices in the shopping centre.

Coral Bay Adventures (☎ 9942 5955; www.coralbay adventures.com.au) Sixteen years in the business, this excellent company offers half-day and full-day trips to do wildlife-watching ($175), swim with whale sharks ($330), whale-watching ($100) and coral-viewing ($30).

Coral Bay Charter (☎ 9942 5932) Offers similar tours to Coral Bay Adventures: whale-watching ($88), snorkelling with manta rays ($110), nature-spotting ($125) and coral-viewing, from glass-bottom boats ($29) and with snorkelling ($39).

Coral Breeze (☎ 9948 5190; www.coralbaytours.com .au) Takes travellers cruising on the reef on a small catamaran for snorkelling, swimming, wildlife-spotting and sunset cruises (adult/child from $75/37).

Coral Coast Tours (☎ 9948 5190) Does full- and half-day 4WD outback wildlife safaris (half-day wildlife safari adult/child from $120/72) and tours around Cape Range to Exmouth via the 4WD coastal track (full-day Cape drive $170/114).

Ningaloo Experience (☎ 9942 5824; www.ningaloo experience.com) This company offered the only official eco-certified tour at the time of research, and its wildlife-watching/snorkelling tours get consistently good feedback (adult/child from $135/95).

Ningaloo Reef Dive (☎ 9942 5824; www.ningalooreef dive.com) Specialises in diving and snorkelling. Offers snorkelling with whale sharks ($350), reef dives ($145) and PADI diver training courses (from $380).

Sub-Sea Explorer (☎ 9942 5955) Operates popular, daily one-hour coral-viewing tours from glass-bottom boats (adult/child $30/15).

Sleeping & Eating

Avoid school holidays if you can, and if you can't, book well ahead.

Ningaloo Club (☎ 9948 5100; www.ningalooclub.com; dm $22-25, d/tr with shared bathroom $70/90; ✴ 🖳 🖴) This excellent hostel wins awards for being the cleanest in WA! It boasts a central pool, well-equipped kitchen, and a big lounge area with bar and pool table. It also sells Greyhound tickets, books discounted tours, and Easyrider Backpackers Tour buses (p206) stop here.

Bayview Coral Bay Resort (☎ 9385 7411; www .coralbaywa.com; unpowered/powered sites $25/28; cabin d from $80, chalet $105-230, Coral Bay Lodge units $140-150, villas $170-210, White House $345; 🖴) Bayview Coral Bay Resort offers an absolutely enormous range of quality accommodation, including lovely grassy sites for pitching the tent or parking the van, along with spacious, comfortable self-contained villas, units, chalets and cabins, motel-style rooms at Coral Bay Lodge. There is also the White House, which is a huge four-bedroom place with all mod

CORAL COAST & THE PILBARA

cons including DVD player, fully equipped kitchen and laundry. The resort facilities are far-ranging, too: swimming pool, barbecues, tennis courts, kids' playground – you name it, it's got it!

Ningaloo Reef Resort (☎ 9942 5934; www.coral bay.org; motel d $155; beach units d $165; ❌ ☒) Another laid-back resort with several levels of accommodation, plus pub, bottle shop and restaurant.

Shades Restaurant (☎ 9942 5863; meals $8-30) Shades, at the Ningaloo Reef Resort, offers everything from pastas and pizza to seafood and curries, along with takeaway.

Reef Cafe (☎ 9942 5882; meals $11-20) does filling pizzas while **Fins Cafe** (☎ 9942 5900; meals $8-28) serves breakfast, light lunches and the usual café standards (BYO).

There's a good bakery and supermarket at the shopping centre but prices are high. If you're self-catering, stock up in Carnarvon or Exmouth.

Getting There & Away

Coral Bay is 1200km north of Perth, and is accessible from north and south by a sealed road off the Manilya–Exmouth Rd.

Skywest Airlines (☎ 1300 660 088; www.skywest .com.au) flies into Exmouth's Learmonth Airport, a 75-minute drive from Coral Bay; most Coral Bay resorts can arrange a private taxi service on request. **Greyhound** (☎ 1300 473 946 863; www. greyhound.com.au) has regular bus services via Exmouth and, along with Easyrider Backpacker Tours buses, stops at the Ningaloo Club.

EXMOUTH

☎ 08 / pop 2500

Sunny Exmouth, with its delicious shrimps (it has a thriving prawn industry), is a busy tourist base for an increasing number of travellers eager to experience Ningaloo Marine Park and Cape Range National Park.

Exmouth is a former US naval communications base, and its strategic role is still evident from the towers that dominate the northern tip of the cape in order to track ocean movements. The September 11 attacks sparked fear for the towers – even ex-military buildings appropriated by tourism were closed.

Information

Department for Environment and Conservation (DEC; ☎ 9949 1676; 22 Nimitz St; ☾ 8am-5pm Mon-Fri) Supplies maps and brochures. Pick up *Parks of the*

Coral Coast: Cape Range National Park & Ningaloo Marine Park, Watching Whales, and *Experiencing Whale Sharks in Ningaloo Marine Park* for info on interacting with marine life sensitively. The visitors centre should also stock these.

D&A Hire Bookshop (☎ 9949 1425; cnr Murat Rd & Pellew St; ☾ 10am-5pm Tue-Fri, 10am-1pm Sat & Sun) Has a decent selection of secondhand books.

Exmouth Hospital (☎ 9949 1011; Lyon St)

Post office (Maidstone Cres)

Visitors centre (☎ 1800 287 328, 9949 1176; www .exmouthwa.com.au; Murat Rd; ☾ 9am-5pm Mon-Fri, 9am-noon Sat & Sun) Has lots of great stuff on the national parks and good fishing spots, and can book tours, flights, bus tickets and accommodation. Also has internet access.

What Scooters (☎ 9949 4748; 102 Murat Rd; ☾ 8.30am-7pm) Has laptop and wireless connection.

Sights & Activities

There's little to do in Exmouth apart from fish and swim and enjoy the wildlife – you'll pass kangaroos on the drive into town, emus wandering *around* town, and there's a great deal of birdlife, including gorgeous pink-breasted galahs. Exmouth is really a base for people driving into the national parks, doing tours, or heading off to surf on the cape. The swish new marina development, still under construction at the time of research, could change all that.

If you're looking for a spot to swim around Exmouth, head to **Town Beach**, a serene white-sand beach with a small snack-shack, which is really a pleasant place to spend sunset. Otherwise, the best beaches are north of Exmouth at the tip of the North West Cape; see Around Exmouth (p206).

Tours

Fun tours from Exmouth include swimming with whale sharks, whale-watching, wildlife-spotting, scuba diving, sea-kayaking, fishing, and coral-viewing from glass-bottom boats. There are many more tours than those listed here – see the visitors centre.

Capricorn Kayak Tours (☎ 1800 625 688; www .capricornseakayaking.com.au) Offers a range of coastal and camping tours by sea kayak from April to October. Tours include paddles with barbecue (adult $49), half-day Coral Coast ($68), full-day lagoon explorer ($115), and two-/five-day camps under the stars ($335/745).

Ningaloo Coral Explorer (☎ 9949 4499; www.bundegi .com.au) In addition to the usual tours, this company offers two-hour coral-viewing in glass-bottom boats ($30) with snorkelling ($50) and twilight whale-watching ($50). Trips leave from Bundegi (the bus to Bundegi is $5).

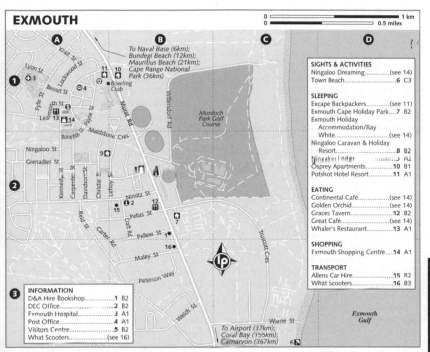

EXMOUTH

To Naval Base (6km);
Bundegi Beach (12km);
Mauritius Beach (21km);
Cape Range National
Park (36km)

Murdoch
Park Golf
Course

SIGHTS & ACTIVITIES
Ningaloo Dreaming..............(see 14)
Town Beach...........................**6** C3

SLEEPING
Excape Backpackers...........(see 11)
Exmouth Cape Holiday Park...**7** B2
Exmouth Holiday
Accommodation/Ray
White.............................(see 14)
Ningaloo Caravan & Holiday
Resort..............................**8** B2
Ningaloo Lodge.....................**9** A2
Osprey Apartments..............**10** B1
Potshot Hotel Resort...........**11** A1

EATING
Continental Café...................(see 14)
Golden Orchid.....................(see 14)
Graces Tavern......................**12** B2
Great Café...........................(see 14)
Whaler's Restaurant.............**13** A1

SHOPPING
Exmouth Shopping Centre....**14** A1

TRANSPORT
Allens Car Hire....................**15** B2
What Scooters......................**16** B3

Exmouth
Gulf

To Airport (37km);
Coral Bay (155km);
Carnarvon (367km)

INFORMATION
D&A Hire Bookshop..............**1** B2
DEC Office............................**2** B2
Exmouth Hospital..................**3** A1
Post Office............................**4** A1
Visitors Centre......................**5** B2
What Scooters......................(see 16)

CORAL COAST &
THE PILBARA

Ningaloo Dreaming (☎ 9949 4777; www.ningaloo dreaming.com; Exmouth Shopping Centre, Maidstone St) This eco-certified company offers whale-shark cruises, whale-watching, wildlife-spotting and scuba-diving courses, plus a combined whale-shark swim and dive course ($750). Cruises are from $199. There are many others offering similar tours.

Ningaloo Ecology Cruises (☎ 9949 2255; www .ecology.com.au) Operates one- to 2½-hour glass-bottom boat trips to view coral in the Ningaloo Reef, leaving from Tatabiddi on the west coast of the cape (trips from $50). The company offers free bus transfer to Tatabiddi.

Surf Ningaloo (☎ 0429 202 523, 9949 1176; www .yallingupsurfschool.com) Offers half-day surfing tours, private lessons (from $60), and sunset BYO-cheese-and-biscuit surfs.

Sleeping

Accommodation is limited; don't even think about arriving in Exmouth without a booking during high season (April to October). It's a long way to go to find a bed.

Exmouth Cape Holiday Park (☎ 1800 621 101, 9949 1101; www.aspenparks.com.au; cnr Truscott Cres & Murat Rd; unpowered/powered sites $18/26, dm $48, cabin d $65;) This great-value park has a range

of sleeps, from shady camp sites to backpacker dorms, along with terrific facilities (barbecues, campers kitchen and swimming pool), plus it's just a short stroll to the beach.

Potshot Hotel Resort (☎ 9949 1200; www.potshot resort.com; Murat Rd; Excape dm/d $24/59 d; Potshot motel d $89, studio d $139; Osprey d from $159) This bustling resort, with several bars, two eateries, a tropical swimming pool, and decent bottle shop, offers a range of clean and comfortable sleeps, from simple motel rooms to swish apartments. Travellers love the Potshot's Excape Backpackers – all rooms and dorms have bathrooms, there's a great communal kitchen and barbecue area, a good internet café, and it's within arms reach of the pub! Osprey Apartments, across the road, are stylish, spacious, self-contained units, some with a swish mezzanine bedroom, with cane furniture and spa baths. Discounted weekly rates are available.

Ningaloo Lodge (☎ 1800 880 949, 9949 4949; www .ningaloolodge.com.au; Lefroy St; d $95;) These basic rooms with fridge and TV – and communal kitchen, barbecue and pool – are the best budget motel deal in town.

Exmouth Holiday Accommodation/Ray White
(☎ 9949 1144; www.exmouthholidays.com.au; Exmouth Shopping Centre; holiday houses per week $700-1400; ❄) If you're planning a longer getaway, Ray White Real Estate has a wide range of weekly rentals, from fibro shacks to enormous two-storey homes with verandas all around.

Eating & Drinking

Continental Café (Exmouth Shopping Centre; snacks $3-10; ☽ 8am-5pm Mon-Sat, 8.30am-3pm Sun) This cosy coffee shop serves 'gourmet coffee', along with lots of light lunch and snack food, sandwiches, wraps, pies, muffins and cakes.

Golden Orchid (☎ 9949 1740; Exmouth Shopping Centre; meals $8-17; ☽ 11.30am-2pm Mon-Fri, 5-10pm daily) If you're craving Asian food, head here for tasty Chinese and Thai dishes. The $8 lunch specials are excellent value. BYO.

Great Café (☎ 9949 1244; Exmouth Shopping Centre; meals $8-19) The outdoor terrace of this casual BYO eatery gets crowded with backpackers enjoying generous serves of pasta, salads, nachos, pizza and the like.

Graces Tavern (☎ 9949 1000; Murat Rd; pizza $16-23, meals $17-32) Oddly, Graces has a 'fine dining' restaurant and a more casual bistro that share the same menu, only the bistro is cheaper. Unless you're hankering for a night out, go for one of the delicious pizzas instead.

Whaler's Restaurant (☎ 9949 2416; 5 Kennedy St; mains $18-27; ☽ noon-2pm & 6-9pm Tue-Sun) While Exmouth is pretty laid-back, people put on their 'going-out clothes' for dinner at this breezy terrace eatery. Expect an international menu – mainly Italian and seafood, with the odd Asian-influenced dish thrown in. Licensed and BYO.

Graces Tavern and Potshot Hotel are the town's main watering holes; each has pool tables, darts, a juke box and live music.

There are two supermarkets, takeaways and a bakery at **Exmouth Shopping Centre** (Maidstone Cres).

Shopping

The **Exmouth Shopping Centre** (Maidstone Cres) has banks with ATMs (there's also an ATM at the visitors centre), and decent shopping, including surf, camp and dive stores.

Getting There & Away

Exmouth's Learmonth Airport is 37km south of town and there are daily **Skywest Airlines** (☎ 1300 660 088; www.skywest.com.au) flights to Karratha and Carnarvon, with links to Denham, Geraldton and Perth.

If travelling by your own wheels (by far the best way to explore the cape and national parks), from the North West Coastal Hwy take the turn-off to Exmouth (200km) at the Minilya Roadhouse.

Red Earth Safaris (☎ 9279 9011; www.redearthsafaris .com.au) offers six- and eight-day tours ($599 to $735) from Perth to Exmouth, along with a weekly 1½-day Perth express service departing Exmouth 7am Sunday ($140). **Easyrider Backpacker Tours** (☎ 9226 0307; www.easyridertours .com.au) stops at Exmouth Tuesday, Friday and Sunday at 6.45am on its Coastal Cruiser to Perth (May to November), while its Perth express service stops here on Monday and Wednesday at 6.45am.

Buses stop at the visitors centre. **Greyhound** (☎ 1300 473 946 863; www.greyhound.com.au) has three services a week to/from Perth ($211, 20 hours). Alternatively, you can hop off the daily Greyhound Perth–Darwin bus at the Giralia turn-off and pick up the Exmouth shuttle there ($60, two hours). From Exmouth there are three weekly services to Coral Bay ($65, two hours). Travelling north from Exmouth, you have to change buses at the Giralia turn-off.

Getting Around

The **Airport Shuttle Bus** (☎ 9949 1101) meets all flights and shuttles the 37km into town ($20); reservations are required for a ride back to the airport. The **Bundegi Beach Bus** (☎ 9949 4499) operates a service to Bundegi Beach, 12km north of Exmouth. The cost is $10 return; there are departures at 12.30pm and 1.30pm, returning at 2.20pm and 4.45pm.

What Scooters (☎ 9949 4748; 102 Murat Rd) rents mopeds for $35 per day; a driving licence is required. There are several car-hire companies in town, including **Allens** (☎ 9949 2403; Nimitz St), with cars starting from $50 per day. Rent a pushbike from **Ningaloo Caravan & Holiday Resort** (☎ 9949 2377; Murat Rd) for around $12 per day.

AROUND EXMOUTH
☎ 08

The best beaches are north of Exmouth, on the tip of the North West Cape, and on the east coast in Ningaloo Marine Park. You'll need a car or scooter to reach them, as there's no public transport, except to Bundegi beach (to which you can get a shuttle bus; see Getting Around, above).

CORAL COAST &
THE PILBARA

Take Murat Rd to the communication towers and **Bundegi Beach**, 12km north of Exmouth. This curved, creamy-sand beach is backed by sand dunes, with seashells and coral washed up on its shores, crystal-clear, calm waters, and friendly pelicans. The **Bundegi Beach Shack** (☎ 9949 4499; phone for times) sells snacks and is licensed, making this a sublime spot for sunset.

Turn onto Yardie Creek Rd and take the first right, signposted 'Mildura Wreck' (a 1907 cattle ship you can see from shore), to get to the excellent **Surfers Beach**, at 17km. It's ruggedly beautiful, with creamy sand backing onto grassy dunes, and great waves for experienced surfers. Along the way there are several car parks, a couple with excellent fa-

cilities, including toilets, a beach shelter and viewing platform.

Almost across the road from Surfers Beach, **Ningaloo Lighthouse Caravan Park** (☎ 9949 1478; www.ningaloolighthouse.com; Yardie Creek Rd; unpowered/ powered sites $20/26, cabins $75, bungalows $100, lighthouse/ lookout chalets $125/170; ❄ ❄) has one of the best locations of any caravan park in WA. It's not only the closest to Surfers Beach and Ningaloo Marine Park, but its wonderful lighthouse and lookout chalets have magnificent views of the entire cape. Book well ahead; some reserve up to a year in advance for school holidays.

You'll see **Vlamingh Head Lighthouse** (☎ 0407 970 647; tours free), built in 1912, up on the hill – there are spectacular views from here and you're likely to see some emus on the way.

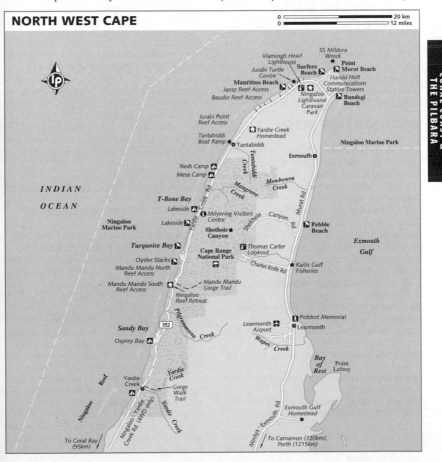

NORTH WEST CAPE

A short distance down the road is the wonderful **Jurabi Turtle Centre**. Visit at night to watch turtles nest and hatch their eggs – first get the pamphlet *Sea Turtles in Ningaloo Marine Park* from DEC, and follow the code of conduct – although it's more rewarding to volunteer to work here tracking turtles and become a certified 'turtle scout'. Contact **DEC** (☎ 9949 1676; exmouth@calm.wa.gov.au).

You're now driving down the western side of the cape and there are gorgeous beaches all along here, such as clothing-optional **Mauritius Beach**, 21km from Exmouth, and the superb white beaches and still azure waters of **Lakeside** (54km), **Turquoise Bay** (65km) and **Oyster Stacks** (69km), all super for snorkelling.

The entrance to **Cape Range National Park** (admission per vehicle $10) is at 40km. At 53km you'll find the **Milyering visitors centre** (☎ 9949 2808; Yardie Creek Rd; ☽ 9am-5pm), which serves Ningaloo Marine Park and Cape Range National Park. You can buy tickets for the Yardie Creek cruise (opposite) here and, if you have a 4WD, find out about the condition of the sandy coastal track that continues south to Coral Bay (two to three hours; can be crossed at low tide only).

NINGALOO MARINE PARK
☎ 08

The Ningaloo Marine Park boundaries protect more than 250km of waters and foreshore areas from Bundegi Reef in the northeast of the North West Cape peninsula to Amherst Point in the southwest.

The Ningaloo reef is amazingly accessible, lying only 100m offshore from some parts of the peninsula, and is home to a staggering array of **marine life**. There are sharks, manta rays, humpback whales, turtles, dugongs and more than 500 species of fish.

There's wonderful marine activity to enjoy year-round:
November to February Turtles – four known species nestle and hatch in the sands.
March and April Coral spawning – an amazing event 10 to 12 days after the full moon.
May to July Whale sharks – these big guys come for the coral spawning.
May to November Manta rays – these creatures migrate dramatically in big schools.
July to November Humpback whales – also migrating south, they have fun splashing about on the way.

What also makes Ningaloo special is its **coral** – over 220 species of hard coral have been recorded in the waters, ranging from the slow-growing bommies to delicate branching varieties. The hard corals found here are less colourful than soft corals, but have amazing formations. For eight or nine nights after the full moon in March and April there is a synchronised mass spawning, when branches of hermaphroditic coral simultaneously eject eggs and sperm into the water.

It's this coral that attracts the park's biggest drawcard, the solitary speckled **whale shark**, or *Rhiniodon typus*. Ningaloo is the only place in the world where these gentle giants arrive like clockwork each year to feed on plankton and small fish, making it a mecca for marine biologists and visitors alike. The largest fish in the world, the whale shark can weigh up to 21 tonnes, although most weigh between 13 and 15 tonnes, and reach up to 18m long.

Activities
Most people visit Ningaloo Marine Park to snorkel. Stop at **Milyering visitors centre** (☎ 9949 2808; Yardie Creek Rd; ☽ 9am-5pm) to get maps and information on the many gorgeous beaches where you can kick those flippers – especially if you haven't snorkelled before, as there are dangerous currents you need to be aware of. The shop at the visitors centre sells and rents snorkelling equipment (about $15 per day to hire).

The best snorkelling spots:
Lakeside Snorkel out with the current before returning to the original point.
Oyster Stacks Just metres offshore, the Oyster Stacks shelter many species of fish.
Turquoise Bay Everyone's favourite. Walk 300m south along the beach, swim out for about 40m and float face down – the current will carry you over coral bommies and abundant sea life. Get out at the sand bar then run back along the beach and start all over!

Tours
While there are myriad tours to spot marine life leaving from Exmouth (p204) and Coral Bay (p203), swimming with a whale shark is the most popular. Whale-shark tours cost around $350 and operate out of both Exmouth and Coral Bay. Exmouth operators have shorter travel times on the water and adhere to a 'no sighting policy' (ie you take the next trip if a whale shark isn't spotted), but many would argue that the Coral Bay operators have a higher encounter rate (although all use spotter planes) and there are

fewer other boats to battle with. The price generally includes snorkelling gear, wetsuit, refreshments/lunch and park fees. Outside the whale-shark season, tours go out searching for manta rays. You need to be a capable swimmer to get the most out of both experiences. All you need for the wildlife-spotting tours – where you search for whales, dugongs, turtles and fish – are a keen set of eyes!

Many operators also offer diving trips and courses (up to $750 for PADI Open Water Certificates with trips and medical). Good dive spots off North West Cape include the Labyrinth and Blizzard Ridge in Lighthouse Bay, the Navy Pier near Bundegi Beach (one of Australia's top dive sites) and the Muiron Islands, 10km northeast of North West Cape. The Muiron Islands are also a breeding sanctuary for green, loggerhead and hawksbill turtles.

CAPE RANGE NATIONAL PARK
☎ 08

The stunning, 510-sq km **Cape Range National Park** (admission per vehicle $10) comprises about a third of the North West Cape peninsula and is rich in wildlife – kangaroos, emus, echidnas and lizards are easily spotted on a walk or drive through the park. Spectacular deep canyons and rugged red limestone gorges dramatically cut into the range. These flow with deep blue water that mirrors the cliffs when calm. The gorges gradually soften, giving way to white sand, which leads to the crystal waters of Ningaloo Reef.

The park is accessible from the east coast from the unsealed Charles Knife Rd and Shothole Canyon Rd, which in turn are accessed from the Minilya–Exmouth Rd, although these roads won't take you through to the west coast. From the west coast the park is accessible from Yardie Creek Rd.

The excellent **Milyering visitors centre** (☎ 9949 2808; Yardie Creek Rd; ◷ 9am-5pm) has a comprehensive display of the area's natural and cultural history, and great maps and publications.

Sights & Activities
On the east coast, the scenic drive to **Charles Knife Canyon** along Charles Knife Rd, 23km south of Exmouth, dramatically follows the ridges of the range with breathtaking views below. **Shothole Canyon** is reached from Shothole Canyon Rd, 16km south of Exmouth, along a dry creek-bed of a road that gets you up close to the colourful canyon walls.

On the west coast, you can drive to the start of the walk into **Mandu Mandu Gorge** (3km return) via an access road 20km south of the Milyering visitors centre, for fantastic panoramic vistas of the gorge.

Drive to **Yardie Creek**, where the sealed Yardie Creek Rd ends, to do the easy 1.5km return walk to the creek. You can take a very pleasant one-hour **Yardie Creek Cruise** (☎ 9949 2659; adult/child $25/12) up the short, sheer gorge to see rare black-footed rock wallabies and lots of birdlife. It runs daily in season.

If it's low tide, those with 4WDs should be able to continue south to Coral Bay via a sandy track along the coast, although check road conditions first with the Milyering visitors centre.

Sleeping
There are compact **camping grounds** (sites per person $6.50) along the coast within the parks. Facilities and shade are minimal, but most have toilets. Sites are limited and allocated upon arrival (it's not possible to book in advance). Milyering visitors centre has a list of sites with photos of their beaches. Get info in advance from **DEC** (☎ 9949 1676; 22 Nimitz St, Exmouth).

Ningaloo Reef Retreat (☎ 1800 999 941, 9942 1776; www.ningalooreefretreat.com; near Mandu Mandu Gorge Rd entrance; swag per person $155, wilderness tent d $530) is another example of the new breed of 'luxury' wilderness escapes that seem to offer just a fraction more than a normal camping experience but at 10 times the price. What makes this one special is its duneside location, water views, luxe dining tent, camp kitchen and library.

Getting There & Away
If you're not on a tour, you need your own transport to explore Ningaloo Marine Park and Cape Range National Park. There is no local transport; the Ningaloo Reef Bus is no longer operating.

MINILYA ROADHOUSE TO KARRATHA
☎ 08

From Minilya you can bypass the North West Cape by continuing along the North West Coastal Hwy. About 50km north of Minilya, signs indicate where the Tropic of Capricorn crosses the highway. It's about 60km further north to the sealed road that heads west to **Giralia Station** (☎ 9942 5937; www.giralia.com; budget d $50, homestead $100) a hospitable working sheep station, with a range of accommodation.

CORAL COAST & THE PILBARA

Nanutarra Roadhouse (☎ 9943 0521; unpowered/ powered sites $19/21, d units $60; ☺ 6.30am-10pm), on the Ashburton River, has food, fuel and a bed for the night. The sealed Nanutarra–Wittenoom Rd runs east to the Pilbara's interior: the mining towns of Tom Price and Paraburdoo, the magnificent Karijini National Park, and the Great Northern Hwy.

Some 40km north on the North West Coastal Hwy is the turn-off to the coast at Onslow. Continuing north along the highway, some 78km from the Onslow junction, is the Pannawonica Rd leading east to the mining town of the same name (47km).

Another 43km north is the **Fortescue River Roadhouse** (☎ 9184 5126), with fuel for you and the car. It's around 100km further on to Karratha.

ONSLOW
☎ 08 / pop 800

After a history that's included cyclones, WWII bombing and atomic testing, these days isolated Onslow, 82km from the highway, is quiet and untroubled and enjoying its peace.

Established as a pearling port in 1883, Onslow was relocated in 1925 with many of the original buildings moved to the new site. Remains of Old Onslow include a crumbling cemetery and tramway, 48km west of Onslow.

Onslow gained the moniker Cyclone City after being severely hit at least four times up until the late 1960s. During WWII the town was a refuelling station for US submarines, and hence its target by Japanese bombs in 1942. Islands just offshore were the target of British bombs, with atomic tests in the '50s (see the boxed text, opposite).

Today Onslow survives on its salt-mining industry. Visitors come for the fishing (and they'll see the salt on its way to sea, on their way to the beach) and there's little to make them feel guilty about doing nothing else.

The **visitors centre** (☎ 9184 6644; Second Ave; ☺ 9am-4pm Mon-Sat, 10am-2pm Sun Apr-Oct, closed Nov-Mar) can point you toward the best fishing spots and give you info on local fishing, diving and snorkelling tours, and (expensive) getaways on Direction and Thevenard Islands,

---

BRAND NEW NOMADS by Terry Carter & Lara Dunston

We were heading off-road in an absolutely wild part of the Western Australian (WA) coast – somewhere near Carnarvon. Our map showed a tiny squiggle indicating a dirt track, so we took it, hoping to get another vantage point to check out the magnificently craggy coastline. It's here that we ran into Harry and Marge.

Harry and Marge are not 'grey nomads', the retirees that tour Australia indefinitely, moving from caravan park to caravan park, sipping slowly from retirement funds or frugally spending that precious pension cheque. Harry and Marge are a new breed in the Aussie tradition of caravanning.

Harry and Marge have been around the world and now they want to see this part of Australia at their own pace. They are equipped to go *anywhere* and are better prepared than a caravan park full of grey nomads combined. After six weeks on the road, they have only stayed in a van park twice. Harry despairs that travellers in the van parks keep to themselves, preferring to watch TV rather than chat with neighbours, sharing a few brews and solving the world's problems. Harry and Marge prefer the roadside stops where more like-minded travellers camp and share their 'roads-less-travelled' experiences.

To attain the self-sufficiency that allows them to camp in a location with no power, no running water, and no supermarket for weeks at a time, involved $10,000 worth of vehicle and van preparation – on top of the purchase of the 4WD and a high-tech Tvan (www.tracktrailer.com), a camper trailer that you can tow to just about anywhere a 4WD can go.

Their self-sufficiency doesn't mean that they're going without, though. To keep fridges cold, lights running, and bits and pieces of technology charged (including a laptop and cameras), they use two solar panels. To them, self-sufficiency and eco-friendliness are good companions.

However, these semi-retirees were finding it hard to slow down and relax, especially Harry, who left his job as a project manager. 'Looking for great light, clouds, and birds to photograph' was what Harry wanted to concentrate on – well, besides painting and working his way through what appeared to be about a year's worth of reading. And all the while comfortably camped in one of the most beautiful spots in WA, if not the world.

Doing nothing has never sounded so appealing.

part of the **Mackerel Islands** (☎ 9184 6444; www
.mackerelislands.com.au). The visitors centre is also
home to a small **museum** (entry by donation) with
fascinating memorabilia. Pick up the *Old Onslow Heritage Trail* pamphlet to get the most
out of your visit.

Onslow's accommodation is on its lovely
beachfront. The shady **Oceanview Caravan Park**
(☎ 9184 6053; Second Ave; unpowered/powered sites $18/25,
onsite vans $40, cabins $65; ❄) has a range of sleeps,
from camp sites to cabins. Look no further.

Nikki's (☎ 9184 6121; First Ave; mains $16-27;
❄ 6.30pm-late Tue-Sat) is Onslow's best restaurant,
with tables on big verandas overlooking the
beach, and fresh seafood on the menu.

There's a supermarket on Second Ave.

THE PILBARA

Stretching along the coast from Onslow to
Port Hedland are the transport towns that ship
mountains of iron ore overseas, while inland
are the mines, machines, and the neat company
towns that service them. Also inland are the
land's natural scars – the magnificent gorges of
Karijini and Millstream-Chichester National
Parks, home to spectacular gorges, wonderful
waterfalls and tranquil water holes.

KARRATHA
☎ 08 / pop 12,500

The commercial centre of the Pilbara,
Karratha (Good Country) was developed in
the late 1960s as a single-purpose company
town to house the overflow of workers from
Dampier (25km away), which had reached
saturation point. Today it supports a plethora

of companies and industries, including the
iron, salt, gas and fertiliser industries. People are here to work; as a result there's little
entertainment, but there are good shopping
malls in which to stock up on essentials before
you move on.

Karratha **visitors centre** (☎ 9144 4600; info@tourist
.karratha.com; Karratha Rd; ❄ 8.30am-5pm Mon-Fri, 9am-
4pm Sat & Sun, shorter hours Dec-Mar) has internet access, lots of info on the region and local sights
(including the Burrup Peninsula), and can
organise fishing charters and dives in the
beautiful Dampier Archipelago or Montebello Islands (from $150 per person). It can
also supply permits (free) to use the private
company road to Tom Price.

The visitors centre can also book you on
one of the many industrial tours, including to
Dampier Salt, Dampier Port and Northwest
Shelf Gas Venture. These free tours gener-
ally run Monday to Friday from April to
November.

The shopping centre has ATMs and a
newsagent. The 3.5km **Jaburara Heritage Trail**
($2), from the visitors centre, guides visitors
through significant traditional sites and details Karratha's history from the displace-
ment and eventual extinction of the Jaburara
people, to the development of billion-dollar
industries.

Sleeping & Eating
Call ahead if you intend to stay the night on
your way through, as hotels fill with corporate
and government guests.

Karratha Backpackers (☎ 9144 4904; 110 Wellard
Way; dm/d $22/54; ❄ ▣) This backpackers re-
cently had a much-needed overhaul under new

MUSHROOM CLOUDS OVER MONTEBELLO ISLANDS

While the Montebello Islands are today a peaceful marine conservation reserve, on 3 October 1952
the islands had the dubious distinction of hosting the first British nuclear weapon test, code-named
'Operation Hurricane'. A retired frigate, the *Plym,* anchored in Main Bay off Trimouille Island, was
the test target and was predictably vaporised in the blast. Two more tests were carried out on
Alpha and Trimouille Islands in 1956. While the British and Australian governments moved on to
bungle bigger tests at Maralinga in South Australia, the same lack of concern for the health of
local populations and servicemen working on the projects remained a constant.

These days, however, Mother Nature is starting to get things back into balance and the islands are thriving with land and marine fauna: more than 100 plant species, plenty of sea birds
and brilliant fishing. The radiation warning signs remain, along with commemorative plaques,
but the islands are considered safe to visit; the best way is to charter a boat. The area also has
some of the best surf conditions in Australia – just don't say you had a 'blast' surfing here, the
joke's been done a million times…

CORAL COAST &
THE PILBARA

KARRATHA

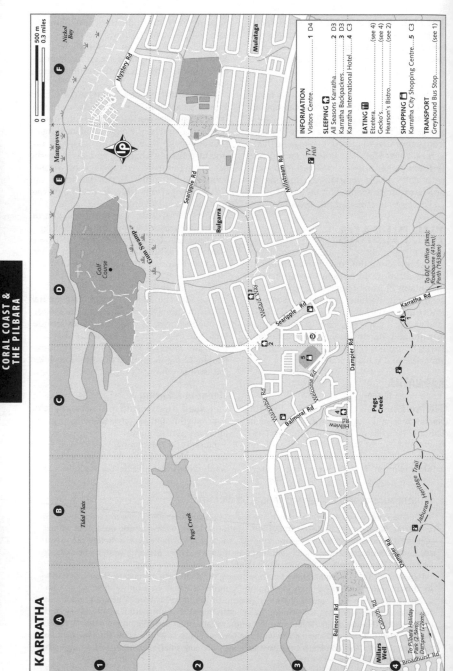

INFORMATION	
Visitors Centre....................	1 D4

SLEEPING 🏠	
All Seasons Karratha..........	2 D3
Karratha Backpackers..........	3 D3
Karratha International Hotel..	4 C3

EATING 🍴	
Etcetera............................	(see 4)
Gecko's.............................	(see 4)
Hearson's Bistro................	(see 2)

SHOPPING 🛍	
Karratha City Shopping Centre...	5 C3

TRANSPORT	
Greyhound Bus Stop............	(see 1)

500 m
0.3 miles

enthusiastic management. Clean, comfortable rooms are set around a courtyard, and there's a good communal kitchen and TV lounge.

Pilbara Holiday Park (☎ 1800 451 855, 9185 1855; www.aspenparks.com.au; Rosemary Rd; unpowered/powered sites $28/31, motel d from $120, studio d $135; ✿ 🖳 🖳) This neat, leafy park has a range of good self-contained accommodation, shady sites, a kids' playground, campers kitchen, TV room and kiosk.

All Seasons Karratha (☎ 9185 1151; www.accorhotels .com.au; Searipple Rd; d $185; ✿ 🖳) This central hotel has spacious, comfortable rooms with fridge, TV and phone, just behind the shopping centre.

Karratha International Hotel (☎ 9185 3111; Balmoral Rd; d $195; ✿ 🖳) The town's best hotel has spacious, sophisticated, self-contained rooms, but it's almost always full, so settle for a meal at one of its excellent restaurants.

The eatery at the All Seasons Karratha, **Hearson's Bistro** (Searipple Rd; mains $17-28), is one of Karratha's best and has a pleasant poolside setting. Stylish **Etcetera** (Balmoral Rd; meals $19-32) at Karratha International Hotel is the best in town, with a creative, high-quality menu, but the more casual bar and eatery, **Gecko's** (Balmoral Rd; meals $16-27), with its pastas, seafood and grills, is also fab.

There is a supermarket, takeaways and cafés in the main shopping centre.

Getting There & Around

Qantas (☎ 13 13 13; www.qantas.com.au) has direct daily flights to/from Perth, while **Skywest Airlines** (☎ 1300 660 088; www.skywest.com.au) travels via Exmouth and has links to Carnarvon, Denham and Geraldton. **Northwest Regional Airlines** (☎ 1300 136 629; www.northwestregional.com.au) has flights to/from Port Hedland and Broome three times a week.

Greyhound (☎ 1300 473 946 863; www.greyhound .com.au) has daily services to/from Perth ($232, 22 hours) and Broome ($126, 11 hours) from the visitors centre.

DAMPIER
☎ 08

Dampier, some 25km from Karratha, is the region's main port. Spread around King Bay, it overlooks the 42 pristine islands of the **Dampier Archipelago** and supports a wealth of marine life in its coral waters, but travellers generally only head here when they can't get a room in Karratha. The archipelago is popular with anglers and a number of charter-boat operators head there (inquire at the Karratha visitors centre, p211).

On the way into town, at the information bay, is the bronze memorial statue of the legendary Pilbara character, **Red Dog** (see the boxed text, below).

Dampier Mermaid (☎ 9183 1222; www.dampier mermaid.com.au; The Esplanade; d $155; ✿ 🖳 🖳) has basic but comfortable rooms, with the best having great ocean views. It's mostly occupied by contract workers, so book ahead. There's also a bar and bistro but **Barnacle Bob's** (☎ 9183 1053; The Esplanade; mains $10-19), overlooking Dampier Harbour, does good seafood.

A FASCINATING 'TAIL'

Red Dog was a kelpie-cross, born in 1971 of no fixed address, who befriended a bus driver in Dampier and often hitched rides – always sitting in the same seat behind the driver. After the driver was killed in an accident, the now well-known Red Dog set about searching for his master.

As local folklore has it, Red Dog hitched rides on rail cars, buses and private cars all over: as far north as Broome and as far south as Perth. He would wait by the roadside until a car whose engine hum he recognised came by, and jump in front of it, forcing it to stop. Before the driver had time to recover from the shock, Red Dog was in the passenger seat and wouldn't disembark until he reached his chosen destination – indicated by a bark!

However, Red Dog wasn't looking for a new home. He'd often be taken care of by local families, but soon his wandering spirit would kick in and he'd be off on another adventure. After he died in 1979 the local community erected a bronze statue in his honour at the entrance to Dampier, and while Red Dog isn't around to soil seats across Western Australia (WA), his legend just keeps getting bigger. In 2006 a play, the enigmatically titled *Red Dog*, hit the stage in Perth, and two books, Beverley Duckett's *Pilbara Wanderer* and Louis de Bernières (famous for *Captain Corelli's Mandolin*) *Red Dog*, have been written about the charismatic canine. How far away can a feature film be?

ROEBOURNE AREA

While atmospheric Roebourne and Cossack are the sites of the first European settlements to the Pilbara, seaside Point Samson is a fine spot for doing nothing but marking the time with the tides. The area gets busy during school holidays, and swelteringly hot in summer.

Roebourne
☎ 08 / pop 970

Roebourne, 40km east of Karratha, is the oldest Pilbara town still in existence (1866) and home to a large Aboriginal community. It was once a grazing and copper-mining centre and has some grand buildings.

The region's **visitors centre** (☎ 9182 1060; Queen St; ☾ 9am-4pm Mon-Fri, 9am-4pm Sat & Sun, shorter hours Nov-Apr) is housed in the Old Gaol, which is also a **museum** (admission by donation). Other historic buildings include the **Holy Trinity Church** (1894) and the **Victoria Hotel**, the last of five original pubs.

Cossack
☎ 08

Cossack's historic bluestone buildings (1870–98) and riverside location make it a quiet stopover. It lies at the mouth of the Harding River and was the district's main port from the mid- to late 19th century, but was supplanted by Point Samson and then abandoned. Attractions include the **Social History Museum** (adult/child $2/1; ☾ 9am-4pm), which celebrates the town's halcyon days. The pioneer cemetery has a tiny Japanese section dating from the days when Cossack was WA's first major pearl-fishing town. **Cossack Adventure Cruises** (☎ 9182 1060; cruise $80) offers a cruise up the mangrove-lined Harding River and out to Jarman Island.

Cossack Backpackers (☎ 9182 1190; dm $21) has clean rooms in the atmospheric old police barracks, but you'll need to bring your own food as the nearby **Cossack Café** (☎ 9182 1550; light meals $4-10) opens for lunch only.

Point Samson
☎ 08 / pop 230

Point Samson is a pleasant seaside town that supports a substantial commercial fishing industry. There's good **snorkelling** off Point Samson and Honeymoon Cove, a postcard-pretty beach featured in myriad tourist brochures (bring your own gear).

Samson Beach Caravan Park (☎ 9187 1414; Samson Rd; unpowered/powered sites $18/26) is a tiny park in lovely, leafy surrounds, conveniently close to the water and the tavern. Bookings are essential in school holidays.

Swish **Point Samson Resort** (☎ 9187 1052; www .pointsamson.com; 56 Samson Rd; motel/studio d $195/205; ☒ ☒) has comfortable rooms in tropical gardens, and one of the best restaurant's in the region, **Ta Ta's** (mains $17-32), with a creative, mainly seafood, menu in stylish surroundings. The seafood laksa is scrummy.

Moby's Kitchen (☎ 9187 1435; mains $6-11; ☾ 11am-2pm & 6-8.30pm Mon-Fri, 11am-8pm Sat & Sun) has good old-fashioned takeaway fish and chips, overlooking the sea.

MILLSTREAM-CHICHESTER NATIONAL PARK
☎ 08

The tranquil water holes of the Fortescue River are cool, lush oases in the midst of arid, spinifex-covered plateaus and basalt ranges. Around 120km south of Roebourne, this 2000-sq-km park is well worth a detour – you'll be rewarded by panoramic vistas.

The unmanned Millstream **visitors centre** (☎ 9184 5144; ☾ 8am-4pm) was once the homestead of a pastoral station and now has displays on the park's history, ecosystems and traditional owners, the Yinjibarndi people.

In the park's north, the enchanting **Python Pool** (a two-minute walk from the car park) is worth a look, and a swim if it's warm enough. It's linked to Mt Herbert by the **Chichester Range Camel Trail** (8km, three-hour round trip), from where it's a further 45-minute clamber to the peak. Further south, **Chinderwarriner Pool** and **Crossing Pool** are lovely water holes with lilies and shady palms. The **Murlunmunyjurna Trail** (7km, two hours return) features river crossings over palm-trunk bridges and interpretive plaques next to vegetation explaining the plant's uses to the Yinjibarndi people. Pick up a park map from the visitors centre.

Shady bush **camp sites** (☎ 9184 5144; per person $7) are located at Snake Creek, Crossing Pool and Deep Reach Pool; all have pit toilets and the latter two sites have gas barbecues.

TOM PRICE
☎ 08 / pop 3400

Dubbed WA's 'Top Town' due to its position 454m above sea level, Tom Price is, somewhat surprisingly, the state's highest town and makes a great base for exploring Karijini National Park.

Mt Nameless (1128m), known as Jarndunmunha by the local indigenous people, is 4km west of Tom Price. One of the highest mountains in the state, it's accessible by 4WD only and offers good views of the area, especially at sunset.

Most travellers make a detour to Tom Price on the way north from the Great Northern Hwy. Others travel some 355km east from the Nanutarra Roadhouse (off the North West Coastal Hwy) or 290km south of Karratha via the private company road (permit available from Karratha's visitors centre, p211), following the rail line used for transporting iron ore from the mine to the coast.

Many travel here out of curiosity. Tom Price was a closed town for many years, established in 1962 for mine workers and named after the vice president of US company Kaiser Steel, who supported opening the Pilbara region to mining. These days it's an 'open' town under the Ashburton shire which has developed into a leafy green neighbourhood with neat comfortable homes, manicured lawns, and wide tree-lined streets, all somewhat incongruously situated in this most unforgiving interior.

The **visitors centre** (☎ 9188 1112; www.tompricewa.com.au; Central Rd) can supply permits to travel on the company road (you have to watch a 10-minute safety video first) and books tours. The fascinating two-hour **mine tour** ($19; ☼ 10am daily in season) takes you into the massive bowels of the huge open-cut pit. While you may not always get down to the pit, on the days you don't you may be lucky to see a blast instead. The bus for the tour leaves from the visitors centre. The two-hour **Wilanah Walkabout tour** (per person $36, minimum four people) is an enlightening indigenous bush-tucker walk.

Pull up a plastic chair and watch a flick at the **open-air cinema** (Stadium Rd; adult/child $8/5) on Saturday night. The shopping mall on Central Rd has ATMs, a supermarket, cafés and takeaways.

Tom Price Tourist Park (☎ 9189 1515; Mt Nameless Rd; unpowered/powered sites $18/22, cabin d $92; ☒ ☒) has decent budget facilities but it's on the outskirts of town. **Tom Price Hotel Motel** (☎ 9189 1101; budget s/d $70/80, motel standard/deluxe d $133/144; ☒) has clean, comfy rooms, but book ahead as it fills with workers. The bistro (mains $16 to $28) does delicious burgers, seafood and steaks – the porterhouse is divine!

KARIJINI NATIONAL PARK
☎ 08

Given its breathtaking gorges, spectacular waterfalls, idyllic swimming holes, stunning wildflowers and myriad wildlife, it's no wonder that Karijini National Park, just 50-odd kilometres east of Tom Price, is the region's most popular attraction.

Most of Karijini's splendid attractions are easily accessible, located in the park's north, off the 67km-long Banyjima Dr. The quality of this unsealed road varies depending on how deep into the tourist season it is; it's not easy going for conventional vehicles and it's advisable to do it in a 4WD. Entry is the standard national park fee of $10/4 per car/bus passenger.

Make sure you get a copy of DEC's *Karijini: Visitor Information & Walk Trail Guide* from the visitors centre. It's important to choose the walks to suit your level of fitness, and take care: the trails through the park are more dangerous than they appear – particularly after rain when they get slippery, while flash flooding can occur.

Information
The state-of-the-art **visitors centre** (☎ 9189 8121; Banyjima Dr; ☼ 9am-4pm May-Oct, 10am-4pm Nov-Apr), in the northeastern corner of the park, is managed by the traditional owners of Karijini, the Banyjima. The slick interpretive displays give a thought-provoking overview of the natural and cultural history of the park, and is well worth an hour or two of your time.

Sights & Activities
Accessing Banyjima Dr via Karijini Dr from the east, you soon reach the turn-off to beautiful **Dales Gorge**, where you can camp. A short sharp descent takes you to **Fortescue Falls**, the beautiful swimming hole of **Fern Pool**, and through to **Circular Pool**, where there's a pleasant walk along the cliff top.

From Kalimina Rd a 30-minute walk takes you into the depths of **Kalimina Gorge**, where there's a small tranquil pool. Another 11km along is Joffre Falls Rd that leads to **Knox Gorge**, passing the lookout over the spectacular **Joffre Falls**.

The final turn-off is Weano Rd, which takes you to the park's signature attraction, the breathtaking **Oxers Lookout**, where there are extraordinary views of the junction of the Red, Weano, Joffre and Hancock Gorges. It's one of WA's most spectacular sights.

CORAL COAST & THE PILBARA

KARIJINI NATIONAL PARK

While it's technically possible to climb down into **Hancock Gorge** from here, locals advise against it, and guides will no longer take you. You'll notice a touching memorial to Jim Regan, a volunteer SES rescuer who died in April 2004 rescuing a couple of backpackers here. Unfortunately even the most experienced people can get themselves into trouble, particularly if there's a flash flood as there was on that day. And sadly other people can die trying to save them.

Other attractions include **Hamersley Gorge**, off Nanutarra–Wittenoom Rd in the park's northwest, and **Wittenoom Gorge** in the far north. It's reached by an 11km sealed road that takes you past old asbestos mines, small gorges and pretty pools. Avoid the road if

there's been rain, as there are several creek crossings to negotiate and flash flooding is a possibility here also.

Tours

Given Karijini's remote location and unforgiving roads, you might want to head here on a tour. Local company **Lestok Tours** (☎ 9189 2032; www.lestoktours.com.au) runs comprehensive full-day tours ($130) to Karijini from Tom Price that get consistently good feedback.

Sleeping & Eating

Within Karijini there are two basic **camping grounds** (☎ 9189 8157; per person $12), one at Dales Gorge and the other at Savannah, about 4km up Weano Rd, although at the time of research

Savannah was undergoing redevelopment to construct luxury tented accommodation.

Auski Tourist Village (☎ 9176 6988; Great Northern Hwy; s/d $45/50, motel d $120; ❄) is on the highway, 35km north of the Karijini Dr turn-off; this convenient option serves typical roadhouse fare. The Greyhound bus stops here.

Getting There & Away

Most travellers will make their way here with their own wheels, the best way to explore the region. Access to the Karijini National Park is via Karijini Dr, which leaves the Great Northern Hwy 226km south of Port Hedland and 162km northwest of Newman. Greyhound buses stop at the Auski Tourist Village, 35km north of the turn-off, on Saturday.

The unsealed Tom Price Railway Rd takes you between Tom Price and Karratha, but it's a private road and you must get a (free) permit from the visitors centres at **Tom Price** (☎ 9188 1112; Central Rd) or **Karratha** (☎ 9144 4600; Karratha Rd).

NEWMAN

☎ 08 / pop 3600

Established by mining giant BHP during the 1970s as a company town, neat and leafy Newman, 250km east of Tom Price, sits rather incongruously in this harshest of outback country. While it doesn't have a great deal of personality, it's as good a place as any to spend the night and has excellent supermarkets so you can stock up for further travels.

The swish **visitors centre** (☎ 9175 2888; www .newman-wa.org; Fortescue Ave; ❄ 9am-5pm; shorter hours Oct-Apr) comes as a complete surprise. If you've been travelling in the outback for a while you may want to spend some time here just soaking up the big city sophistication and browsing through the excellent books on indigenous culture, Australian history and travel (including Lonely Planet guides). The friendly staff can provide information, book accommodation and get you on tours to the enormous open-cut **Mt Whaleback iron-ore mine** (adult/child $10/6.50; ❄ 8.30am & 10.30am Apr-Oct) to see some colossal equipment and one seriously big hole. Book ahead for the tours.

There are a number of gorges near Newman that feature either natural pools or walking trails: **Eagle Rock Falls**, 33km north along the Great Northern Hwy, has both.

Dearlove's Caravan Park (☎ 9175 2802; Cowra Dr; unpowered/powered sites $18/24, cabin $80; ❄) is a sprawling, shady, central park with decent facilities, including a campers kitchen and gas barbecues.

WHISPER-QUIET WITTENOOM

The drive into the town of Wittenoom along the Munjina–Wittenoom Rd takes you past some spectacular views of the Hamersley Range. It's eerily quiet here – on our drive in and out of the town we passed not one vehicle. However, in its heyday of the 1950s Wittenoom was a prosperous mining town and at one stage the biggest in the region. Between 1937 and 1966 blue asbestos, or crocidolite, was mined here, first by the WA mining magnate Lang Hancock and later by a subsidiary of CSR. Blue asbestos was seen as a remarkable material – strong, heat resistant, with excellent flame-retardant and insulating properties, and a high resistance to chemicals. There was only one problem: the asbestos dust fibres were making people ill.

While this was known as early as the 1920s when asbestosis (a chronic inflammation of the lungs) was termed a medical condition, it wasn't until workers starting dying of mesothelioma – a rare lung cancer – that the mines were closed. Since 1979 the Western Australian (WA) government and its departments have tried to shut the town of Wittenoom down – in the past by bulldozing empty buildings and turning off the water supply, and most recently, cutting the power.

Local tourism offices are told not to promote Wittenoom as a tourist destination, and despite the physical beauty of the surroundings, we did feel somewhat ill at ease here. Not because of the risk of inhaling asbestos fibres (which is small in the town itself), but because its heartbreaking history hangs heavy in the air. It's up to the individual to decide whether to visit, and while the stoic last residents of the town might disagree, there is something ghoulish about visiting an area that's most notable for being the site of one of Australia's worst examples of corporate greed.

One day, the questions about the long-term future of Wittenoom will need to be answered, because simply trying to wipe it off the map doesn't adequately give closure to the many of the town's workers and former residents who are facing a long, slow death.

Seasons Hotel Newman (☎ 9177 8666; www
.seasonshotel.com.au; Newman Dr; budget s/d $46/64, motel
d/tr/f $147/162/174; ✖ ☑) is the best option in
town. It's a rather smart motel, especially
for these parts, with spotless, comfortable
rooms, a contemporary designed restaurant,
and an inviting pool that lies amongst tropical gardens.

Red Sands Tavern (☎ 9177 8866; Newman Dr; mains
$15-26) does hearty counter meals – they have
to be hearty to fill the stomachs of the local
guys! – and has pool tables and occasional
live bands.

There are several takeaway options in and
around the shopping centre.

Integrity Coach Lines (☎ 1800 226 339; www
.integritycoachlines.com.au) has services daily in each
direction linking Perth and Newman ($198,
16 hours).

MARBLE BAR
☎ 08 / pop 360

After a very long summer in 1924, when for
161 consecutive days the temperature never
dipped below 37.8°C, Marble Bar earned itself
a reputation as the hottest place in Australia.
It seems rather appropriate then that the main
attraction in Marble Bar is a natural pool,
about 5km west of town. Chinaman Pool is
just beyond the 'marble bar' in a rock-face
for which the town is named, which is actually a 'bar' of jasper that pioneers mistook
for marble.

Marble Bar attracted settlers with the
promise of gold in the late 1800s, and substantial nuggets unearthed here included Little Hero, Bobby Dazzler and General Gordon.
The town's gold-mining heritage is detailed
at the **Comet Gold Mine** (☎ 9176 1015; ☉ 9am-4pm),
about 8km south of town, with displays on
mining and gemstones.

Ironclad Hotel (☎ 9176 1066; www.geocities.com/iron
cladhotel; 15 Francis St; dm $22, donga s/d $65/80, motel s/d
$95/110) is a classic old pub that's the heart and
soul of the town with well-used pool tables, a
likable beer garden and home-cooked counter
meals (mains $11 to $24).

PORT HEDLAND
☎ 08 / pop 15,000

The industrious town of Port Hedland, with
its low-rise corrugated buildings and fibro
houses, is caked in dark red dirt. Its massive
dock handles the iron ore mined at Newman
and exports more tonnage than any other
Australian port. It's the stockpiles of ore
dominating the skyline that are the source of
that layer of dust that coats the town.

The original settlement and port are built
on a small island connected to the mainland
by a 3km causeway. About 15km south of
town, South Hedland is a sprawling modern
residential centre housing the spillover of
workers from Port Hedland.

If you're not moved by the colossal size of
the industry here, Port Hedland has excellent
supermarkets and is a good place to rest and
restock for the journey ahead.

The helpful Port Hedland **visitors centre**
(☎ 9173 1711; 13 Wedge St; ☉ 8.30am-4pm Mon-Sat,
10am-2pm Sun, shorter hours Nov-May) has internet access. There are ATMs along Wedge St and in
the **Boulevard shopping centre** (cnr Wilson & McGregor
Sts). Phone the **hospital** (☎ 9158 1666; Sutherland St)
in an emergency.

Sights & Activities

Charming **Dalgety House Museum** (☎ 9173 4300; cnr
Wedge & Anderson Sts; admission $3; ☉ 10am-3pm May-Oct,
via Town Tour only Nov-Apr), dating from 1903, is
one of the town's few remaining examples of
early-20th-century architecture. Its displays
interpret the story of Port Hedland as a gateway to the world and the role of Dalgety & Co
in the town's development.

From **Marapikurrinya Park** at the end of
Wedge St, you can watch impossibly large
tankers glide in and out of port during the
day, and see BHP's Hot Briquetted Iron plant
on Finucane Island light up like a fairy castle
at night.

The visitors centre is the departure point
for the mind-boggling **BHP Billiton iron-ore plant
tour** (adult/child $15/8; ☉ 9.30am Mon-Fri). If you're
impressed by size, don't miss this!

BONZER BACKROADS – CLIFFS AND RIDGES

Just over 100km south of Newman along the Great Northern Hwy is the access road to the 2352-
sq-km **Collier Range National Park**. At the upper reaches of the Ashburton and Gascoyne Rivers,
the ranges vary from low hills to high ridges bounded by cliffs. It's accessible by 4WD only and
you'll need to be totally self-sufficient as there are no facilities.

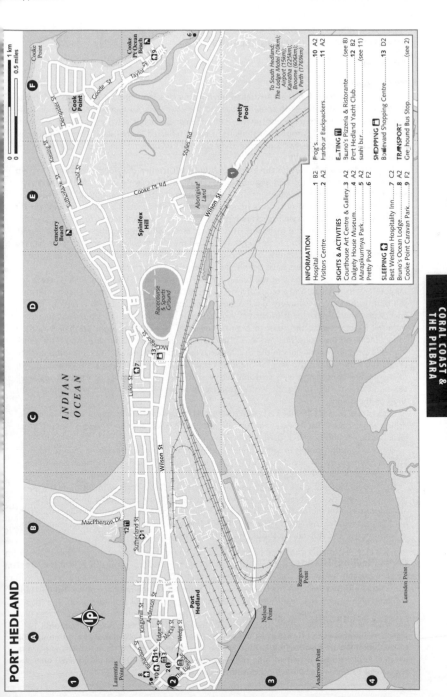

PORT HEDLAND

INFORMATION
Hospital	**1**	B2
Visitors Centre	**2**	A2

SIGHTS & ACTIVITIES
Courthouse Art Centre & Gallery	**3**	A2
Dalgety House Museum	**4**	A2
Marapikurrinya Park	**5**	A2
Pretty Pool	**6**	F2

SLEEPING 🛏
Best Western Hospitality Inn	**7**	C2
Bruno's Ocean Lodge	**8**	A2
Cooke Point Caravan Park	**9**	F2

Fog's	**10**	A2
Harbour Backpackers	**11**	A2

EATING 🍴
Bruno's Pizzeria & Ristorante	(see 8)	
Port Hedland Yacht Club	**12**	B2
sushi bar	(see 11)	

SHOPPING 🛍
Boulevard Shopping Centre	**13**	D2

TRANSPORT
Greyhound Bus Stop	(see 2)	

To South Hedland;
The Lodge Motel (10km);
Airport (15km);
Karratha (225km);
Broome (606km);
Perth (1769km)

CHRISTMAS & COCOS (KEELING) ISLANDS

Christmas Island

☎ 08 / pop 1300

While Christmas Island (CI) is an Australian territory, its closest neighbour is Jakarta, Indonesia, 360km to the north, with Perth some 2300km to the southeast. A rugged limestone mountain, CI was settled in 1888 to mine phosphate – still the main economic activity. Its people are a mix of Chinese, Malays and European-Australians, a blend reflected in the island's food, languages, customs and religions. Several Singapore-style colonial buildings remain, as do traces from the Japanese occupation in WWII.

The island is most famous for the events of August 2001, when the Norwegian container ship *Tampa*, with its cargo of rescued asylum seekers, was refused permission to land on Australian soil, despite having asylum seekers needing urgent medical attention on board. The island was subsequently excised from Australia's migration zone and designated a future holding-pen for asylum seekers. As such, asylum seekers held on CI do not have full access to legal challenges and reviews available on the mainland. This policy, along with sending these 'undocumented' arrivals to other countries for processing, was dubbed the 'Pacific Solution', and has been heavily criticised by the UN High Commissioner for Refugees (UNHCR) and many NGOs such as Amnesty International. Asylum seekers have been held on the island as recently as 2006.

In spite of this activity, 63% of the island remains protected by CI National Park. There is tall rainforest on the plateau, and a series of limestone cliffs and terraces that attract endemic nesting sea birds including the gorgeous golden bosun and rare Abbott's booby. CI is famous for the spectacular annual movement in November/December of millions of red land crabs marching from the forest down to the coast to breed. They cover everything in sight on their migration routes, including the roads. Marine life is also dramatic, with bright corals and fish on the fringing reefs attracting snorkellers in the dry season, when international yachties also drop anchor. Divers come throughout the year for the drop-off wall and cave dives, and are especially drawn to the possibility of diving with seasonal whale sharks (roughly October to April). A sea swell can bring decent surf during the wet season (roughly December to March) and there's a surf shop on the island.

CI's **visitors centre** (☎ 9164 8382; www.christmas.net.au) can coordinate accommodation, diving, fishing and car hire. Visit its excellent website for links to travel agents offering packages, other local businesses and detailed island information.

Visitor accommodation is in self-contained units, motel-style rooms or resort-style suites from $85 per night. Expect to pay about $5 to $10 for lunch and $20 for dinner in the several Chinese and European-Australian restaurants.

National Jet Systems (book through Qantas, ☎ 13 13 13) flies a circle from Perth, via the Cocos (Keeling) Islands, two or three times a week (five to seven hours depending on route). There is also a return charter flight at least once a week from Singapore and Jakarta (50 minutes), which must be booked directly with **CI Travel** (☎ 9164 7168; www.citravel.com.au). Visa requirements are as for Australia, and Australians should bring their passports.

Cocos (Keeling) Islands

☎ 08 / pop 600

Some 900km further west are the Cocos (Keeling) Islands (CKI), the necklace of low-lying islands around a blue lagoon that inspired Charles Darwin's theory of coral atoll formation. The islands were settled by John Clunies-Ross in 1826 (and briefly by a huge contingent of British forces during WWII), and his family remained in control of the islands and their Malay workers until 1978, when CKI became part of Australia's Indian Ocean territories. Now a population of about 500 Malays and 100 European-Australians live on the two settled islands. It's a very low-key place in which to walk, snorkel, dive, fish, surf and relax. Check out the two island-information websites www.cocos-tourism.cc and www.cocos-solutions.com.

Courthouse Arts Centre & Gallery (☎ 9173 1064; Edgar St; �9am-4pm Mon-Fri) has a rotation of contemporary art exhibitions (with chic champagne openings), as well as a gallery shop with Aboriginal and local art and crafts for sale.

Between November and February **flatback turtles** nest on nearby beaches. The best spot to see them is Cemetery Beach, but make sure you follow the code of conduct; the visitors centre has detailed information.

Pretty Pool, 7km east of the town centre, is a popular fishing and picnicking spot (beware of stonefish). Just to the north, Goode St is the best place to view Port Hedland's **Staircase to the Moon** (see boxed text, p227).

Sleeping & Eating

Harbour Backpackers (☎ 9173 4455; 11 Edgar St; dm/d $20/45; ☒ ☐) Travellers make themselves very at home at this rather cluttered hostel, and watching TV in the central living room is like hanging out at a friend's place. Its few rooms surround the lounge, and there's a big shady front terrace and sushi bar ($3 to $7; open 10am to 2pm Monday to Friday).

Frog's (☎ 9173 3787; 20 Richardson St, dm/s/d $22/32/46; ☒ ☐ ☒) On the foreshore, Frog's has a decent kitchen/dining area, a communal TV/video room, barbecue, laundry, and lockers in dorms. Booking ahead is a must here as reception is only open from 5pm to 10pm.

Cooke Point Caravan Park (☎ 9173 1271; www.aspenparks.com.au; cnr Athol & Taylor Sts; unpowered/powered sites $28/32, backpacker d $65, motel d $90, unit d $110; ☒ ☒) Park your van or pitch your tent on the red dirt at this tidy caravan park overlooking Pretty Pool and the ocean. Expect good amenities, including a terrific campers kitchen and an inviting pool, and a range of decent motel-style accommodation to suit all budgets.

Bruno's Ocean Lodge (☎ 9173 2635; 7 Richardson St; motel d $70; ☒) If you can't get a room elsewhere in town, these well-worn rooms do the trick. Unfortunately our bed was riddled with bedbugs when we last checked-in.

Best Western Hospitality Inn (☎ 9173 1044; Webster St; d $135, with ocean view $169; ☒ ☒) This exceptional motel does a great job of keeping the red dirt out. It's easily the most comfortable in town, with spacious, spotless rooms featuring TV, microwave, kettle and coffee plunger, and groovy tables and chairs. Make sure you make it by 8pm for last orders in the excellent restaurant. The seafood and meat dishes are memorable. Room price includes breakfast.

Port Hedland Yacht Club (☎ 9173 3398; Sutherland St, mains $10-18) This is a popular spot with local families for traditional fish and chips wrapped in butchers' paper. It's licensed and has outdoor seating on a terrace overlooking the port.

Locals swear by the generous servings of honest Italian at **Bruno's Pizzeria & Ristorante** (☎ 9173 2047; meals $11-24; ��(6pm-late). There is a supermarket and café at the **Boulevard Shopping Centre** (cnr Wilson & McGregor Sts).

Getting There & Away

Qantas (☎ 13 13 13; www.qantas.com.au) flies to Port Hedland from Perth daily, while **Northwest Regional Airlines** (☎ 1300 136 629; www.northwestregional.com.au) flies to Broome and Karratha three times a week.

Greyhound (☎ 1300 473 946 863; www.greyhound.com.au) has daily buses to/from Perth ($267, 26 hours) and Broome ($87, seven hours) from the visitors centre and the South Hedland shopping centre. There's also a slightly quicker inland service to Perth (via Newman) on Friday. **Integrity** (☎ 1800 226 339; www.integritycoachlines.com.au) has two services a week to Perth and Broome, from the same departure points.

Getting Around

The airport is 13km from town; **Hedland Taxis** (☎ 9172 1010) charges around $30. **Hedland Bus Lines** (☎ 9172 1394) runs limited weekday services between Port Hedland and Cooke Point, and on to South Hedland ($2.50).

The Kimberley

With just two opposing seasons, the Wet and the Dry, it makes sense that the Kimberley is a land of extremes – semiarid plains dotted with spinifex and outback roads that flow like rivers, spectacular ranges cut by steep stony gorges and tiny pockets of tropical rainforest and tranquil waterholes. It's these dramatic contrasts that make a trip here so compelling.

But despite the region's many attractions, from the pristine Dampier Peninsula and splendid Cape Leveque, to the magnificent gorges of Geikie, Wandjina and Tunnel Creek, to the rough and tumble of Gibb River Rd – there's still no place as engaging or as full of contradictions as Broome.

Broome has a rich, ancient indigenous history and an exotic 19th century pearling past. And then there's the present, a big outback town that plays host to amateur rodeos the same week it holds its annual cultural festival, the Shinju Matsuri, with Japanese food and dragon boat races. But the contradictions of this town are most obvious in its dramatic natural landscapes of contrasting colours – turquoise waters, white-sand beaches, red rock formations and deep blue skies.

All of these things are bewitching, and none of them disappoint.

HIGHLIGHTS

- Enjoy sublime sunsets on the sands of **Cable Beach** (p232), near Broome
- Explore **Broome's** (opposite) complex cultures, exotic history and natural beauty
- See a movie under the stars at Broome's **Sun Pictures** (p231)
- Cruise spectacular **Geikie Gorge** (p238) to view splendid indigenous rock art
- Learn about country with Aboriginal communities at **Cape Leveque** (p234)
- Wildlife-spot: emus and roos on the road, eagles overhead, bats at **Tunnel Creek** (p238), and crocs at **Windjana Gorge** (p238)
- Rough-road by 4WD along spectacular **Gibb River Rd** (p235)
- Bushwalk the **Bungle Bungles** at ancient **Purnululu National Park** (p240)

BROOME REGION

With the Timor Sea lapping the Kimberley's northern shores, Broome is closer to Indonesia than it is to most Australian states, and this isolation is pronounced by long empty stretches of road. The Kimberley and the Pilbara are separated by the westerly edge of the Great Sandy Desert, which extends from the Northern Territory to the Indian Ocean.

PORT HEDLAND TO BROOME

The highway runs inland from Port Hedland to Broome for 611km. Willie-willies whip through dusty, flat, featureless terrain while the coast to the west is lovely and unspoilt.

If you want to break the journey, there are great beaches for fishing along the way – the sharks seem to agree! The exit to **Cape Keraudren Reserve** is 154km from Port Hedland, near Pardoo Roadhouse; there are **camp sites** (per vehicle $6) but no facilities. Around 245km from Port Hedland, shady **Eighty Mile Beach Coastal Resort & Caravan Park** (☎ 9176 5941; unpowered/powered sites $25/28, cabins d $50-154) backs on to the beautiful white-sand beach; there's a shop for essentials. **Port Smith Lagoon Caravan Park** (☎ 9192 4983; unpowered/powered sites $23/25, cabin d $60-130), 477km from Port Hedland, is on a tidal lagoon.

BROOME

☎ 08 / pop 14,000

An improbable combination of colours – red from the pindan (rust-coloured dirt), the aquamarine of Roebuck Bay and the pearl white of Cable Beach's sands – make Broome's landscape memorable. The dramatic contrasts of colour and weather, from dry vibrant winters to wet torpid summers, along with the town's rich history and cultural complexity, give Broome an atmosphere and energy like no other. This vitality has enticed adventurers, entrepreneurs, artists and travellers to Broome, who have given the town a sense of the cosmopolitan – a vibrant culture, great cuisine, fine art, and unique style that you won't find elsewhere.

Initially established as a pearling centre by Japanese entrepreneurs in the 1880s, Broome quickly attracted Chinese and Malays who joined local Aboriginal divers in the dangerous side of the business. Pearl diving was in open water, and initially without a breathing apparatus; many divers were taken by sharks or got the bends. Pearling peaked in the early 1900s, when the town's 400 luggers supplied 80% of the world's mother-of-pearl (mainly used for buttons). Today, pearl farms have replaced open-sea diving and a handful of successful family-run companies continue to provide the world with exquisite Broome pearls.

KIMBERLEY TOURS

Myriad multiday tours explore the Kimberley. Itineraries, prices and dates vary; shop around and ask questions before committing. Prices usually include meals, accommodation, equipment and park fees.

Kimberley Adventure Tours (☎ 1800 083 368, 9191 2655; www.kimberleyadventures.com.au) Operates tours between Broome and Darwin taking in the Gibb River Rd and Purnululu National Park ($1395, nine days).

Kimberley Wild (☎ 9193 7778; www.kimberleywild.com) An ecotourism finalist, offering tours from Broome including day trips to Windjana/Tunnel Creek ($219), Geikie Gorge ($249) and Cape Leveque ($219), and a three-day Kimberley Indigenous Experience (from $879).

Kimberley Wilderness Adventures (☎ 1800 804 005, 9192 5741; www.kimberleywilderness.com.au) Award-winning eco-certified company (co-owned with East Kimberley Aboriginal collective). Offers multiday tours, including the popular 13-day Kimberley Complete (from $4995).

Specialist tours can make for memorable experiences:

Alligator Airways (☎ 1800 632 533; www.alligatorairways.com.au) Offers a variety of air trips from Kununurra, including full-day Lake Argyle and Bungle Bungles tour ($495).

King Leopold Air (☎ 9193 7155; www.kingleopoldair.com.au) Air tours of western Kimberley including half-day Buccaneer Explorer ($360), taking in Horizontal Falls, and full-day Prince Regent Explorer via Mitchell Falls ($640).

Willis's Walkabouts (☎ 8985 2134; www.bushwalkingholidays.com.au) Multiday bushwalking tours around Northern Kimberley. From $425 for a two-day trip and up to $5395 for a 28-day tour.

During the Dry, Broome buzzes; this is the best time to visit. During the Wet, prices drop, opening hours are shorter and locals breathe a collective sigh of relief and get on with their lives. While some like visiting during this time, keep in mind many attractions shut and roads can close – you'll need to do more planning and have a certain degree of flexibility.

Orientation

The town of Broome is situated on the west coast of the Dampier Peninsula. Within Broome, Chinatown, the commercial heart, and Old Broome, the administrative and residential centre, are in the town's east, overlooking Roebuck Bay. Hamersley St runs from Chinatown, south through Old Broome to

THE KIMBERLEY

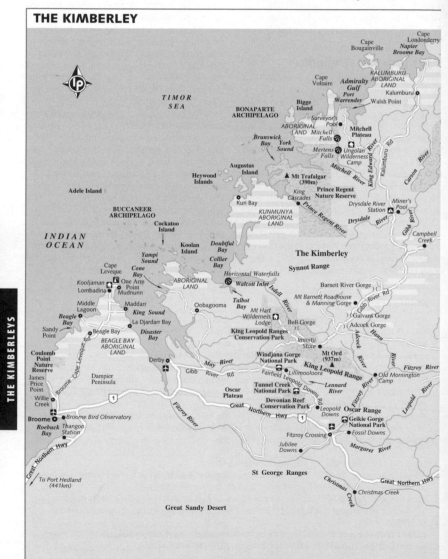

Town Beach, while Frederick St leaves China-town heading west to meet Cable Beach Rd and Cable Beach, and runs into Port Drive, which leads to Broome's deep water port in the south. The majority of Broome's accommodation, restaurants and sights are located in Chinatown, Old Broome, Town Beach and Cable Beach.

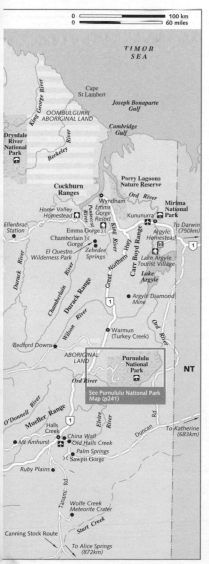

Information

BOOKSHOPS

Kimberley Bookshop (Map p228; ☎ 9192 1944; 4 Napier Tce; 9am-5pm Mon-Fri, 9am-2pm Sat) Stocks an extensive range of books on Broome, the Kimberley, Aboriginal art, fiction, non-fiction and travel guides.

Magabala Books (Map p228; ☎ 9192 1991; www .magabala.com; 2/15 Saville St; 9am-4pm Mon-Fri) Australia's only independently operated indigenous publishing house has a wonderful selection of indigenous novels, poetry, social history, biographies and children's literature.

EMERGENCY

Broome District Hospital (Map p228; ☎ 9192 9222; 28 Robinson St; 24hr)

INTERNET ACCESS

Internet access costs anything from $5 to $10 per hour.

Galactica DMZ Internet Café (Map p228; ☎ 9192 5897; 4/2 Hamersley St; per hr $5; 10am-8pm) Broome's best; 40 terminals with internet access, skype & webcams; BYO laptop for broadband access; and burn CDs/ DVDs among other services. Located next to McDonalds.

INTERNET RESOURCES

Events in the Kimberley (www.eventsinthekimberley .com.au)

Kimberley Tourism Association (www.kimberley tourism.com)

MONEY

There are ATMs on Carnarvon, Hamersley and Short Sts, and Napier Tce.

POST

Post office (Map p228; Paspaley shopping centre)

TOURIST INFORMATION

Broome Visitors Centre (Map p228; ☎ 9192 2222; www.broomevisitorcentre.com.au; Male Oval, Short St; 8.30am-5pm Mon-Fri & 8.30am-4pm Sat & Sun Apr-Nov, 9am-5pm Mon-Fri & 9am-1pm Sat & Sun Dec-Mar) Has masses of info on the Kimberley (including road conditions) and Broome (including Staircase to the Moon and tide times), and books transport, accommodation and tours.

Sights & Activities

Enchanting **Chinatown** is Broome's historical and commercial heart, but while there's scant evidence of the Chinese now (apart from a few shops, restaurants and street names), its atmosphere comes from its vernacular architecture. Corrugated-iron buildings with lattice, louvres and verandas line Carnarvon

THE KIMBERLEY

St, Short St, Dampier Tce and Napier Tce; charming **Sun Pictures** (p231) is the highlight. But while the buildings were once home to boarding houses, tailors and grocers – and in nearby Sheba Lane, brothels, opium dens and gambling joints – they now house boutiques, cafés and art galleries. To get the most out of your visit, buy *Broome Heritage Trail* ($3,

visitors centre) or *The Story of the Chinese in Broome* ($10, Kimberley Bookshop).

Pearl Luggers (Map p228; ☎ 9192 2059; www.pearl luggers.com.au; 31 Dampier Tce; admission free, 75min tours adult/child $19/9; ◷ tours 9am, 11am & 2pm, times vary weekends & in Wet) offers compelling tours covering Broome's tragic pearling past, including rare archival film, and a chance to try deli-

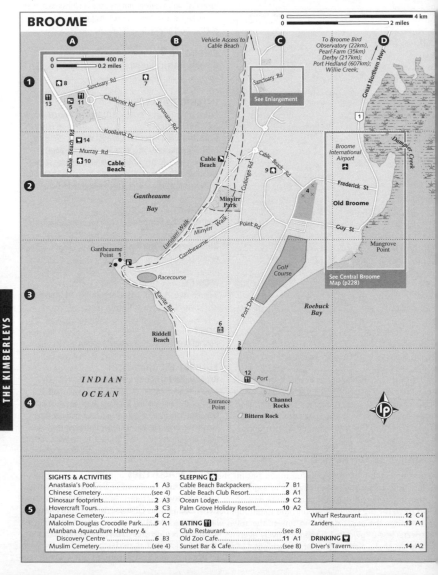

BROOME

cious pearl meat (different to oyster). Book ahead for tours. If you enjoy this don't miss **Willie Creek Pearl Farm** (right). Equally fascinating is **Broome Museum** (Map p228; ☎ 9192 2075; 67 Robinson St; adult/child/concession $5/1/3; ☺ 10am-4pm Mon-Fri & 10am-1pm Sat & Sun), with a wonderful collection of early photos documenting the town's multicultural history and exhibits on pearling and luggers, exploitation and exploration, hardship and mateship.

A number of cemeteries testify to the multicultural makeup of Broome society. There's a small pioneer cemetery (Map p228) overlooking Roebuck Bay by Town Beach, while on Frederick St, there's a **Japanese Cemetery** (Map p226) with 919 graves (mostly pearl divers), a **Chinese cemetery** (Map p226) with more than 90 graves and several monuments, and a **Muslim Cemetery** (Map p226). Unfortunately at the time of research, over 100 Japanese graves had been sadly desecrated during the Shinju Matsuri festival.

The elegant old teak **courthouse** (Map p228; Hamersley St) was built in 1889 to house staff from the Eastern Extension Australasian and China Telegraph Company which linked Broome to Java by an underwater cable – it came ashore at Cable Beach, ran across the current airport site, and finished here! Markets are held in the Courthouse gardens every Saturday.

Broome has a vibrant arts scene that provides a wonderful chance to see some spectacular indigenous painting and work by Kimberley artists. There are many engaging art galleries (see p232).

Tiny **Town Beach** (Map p228) is fine for a dip, while the **port** (Map p226) has a pleasant sandy beach from where you can swim across to the rocks, and good fishing from the jetty.

The interesting **Manbana Aquaculture Hatchery & Discovery Centre** (Map p226; ☎ 9192 3844; www.manbana.com.au; Murakami Rd; guided tours adult/child/concession $19/10/15; ☺ 10am & 1.30pm Mon-Fri) is Australia's first indigenous-owned commercial aquaculture hatchery and a discovery centre exploring the role the Kimberley waters have played in the lives of local Aboriginal people. Learn how they fished and pearled, get close to a variety of live marine species, and feed barramundi!

Activities

Activities on offer include **fishing charters, kayaking, bird-watching, Harley tours** and **skydiving.** The visitors centre has details.

Tours

Broome Sightseeing Tours (☎ 9192 5041; www.broomesightseeingtours.com; adult/child $85/65) Award-winning comprehensive four-hour guided multimedia tour.

Hovercraft Tours (☎ 9193 5025; www.broomehovercraft.com.au; 1hr tour adult/child $72/50, sunset tour $110/75) 'Fly' over tidal flats to visit historical sights and enjoy magnificent sunsets. BYO drinks on the sunset tour.

Mamabulanjin Tours (☎ 9192 2660; mabtours@wn.com.au; adult/child $66/33) Half-day indigenous guided tour of Roebuck Bay covering Aboriginal traditions, culture, storytelling, traditional fishing, hunting and survival techniques.

Red Sun Camels (☎ 9193 7423; www.redsuncamels.com.au; 40min morning ride adult/child $30/20, 1hr sunset ride $50/30) While several of Broome's camel tour companies are perhaps riding off into the sunset (see p233), you should still do the same on the sunset camel ride.

Willie Creek Pearl Farm (☎ 9193 6000; www.williecreekpearls.com.au) This place gives a fascinating insight into modern pearl farming with compelling presentations on oyster insemination and a boat ride on the azure-coloured estuary. You can visit by half-day bus tour from Broome (adult/child $65/33), or you can self-drive (4WD recommended) and join the two-hour tour at the farm ($33/15).

Willie Pearl Lugger Cruises (☎ 0428 919 781; www.williecruises.com.au; adult/child $95/50) Sail on a traditional pearl lugger to see the sunset, whales (July to September), dolphins (September to March) and other marine life. Price includes transport, barbecue and drinks.

THE KIMBERLEYS

STAIRCASE TO THE MOON

The reflections of the rising full moon hitting the rippled Roebuck Bay mud flats, exposed at low tide, create the optical illusion of a golden stairway leading to the moon, called (naturally) the Staircase to the Moon. It has quite an impact on Broome's locals and visitors alike. If you're in town for the few days around the full moon, between March and October (the visitors centre publishes the exact dates and times), the town will be abuzz with everyone eager to see the spectacle. At Town Beach there's a lively evening market with food stalls and people bring their fold-up chairs and a bottle of something!

THE KIMBERLEYS

CENTRAL BROOME

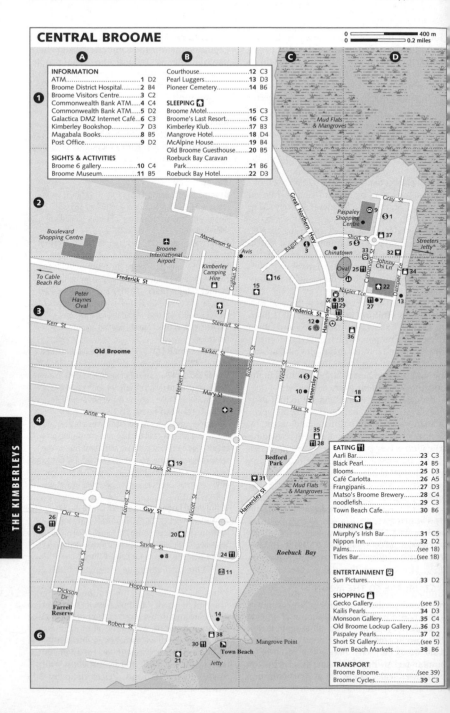

| 0 | 400 m |
| 0 | 0.2 miles |

INFORMATION
ATM.......................................1 D2
Broome District Hospital.......2 B4
Broome Visitors Centre.........3 C2
Commonwealth Bank ATM....4 C4
Commonwealth Bank ATM....5 D2
Galactica DMZ Internet Café..6 C3
Kimberley Bookshop..............7 D3
Magabala Books....................8 B5
Post Office...........................9 D2

SIGHTS & ACTIVITIES
Broome 6 gallery.................10 C4
Broome Museum..................11 B5

Courthouse..........................12 C3
Pearl Luggers......................13 D3
Pioneer Cemetery................14 B6

SLEEPING
Broome Motel......................15 C3
Broome's Last Resort...........16 C3
Kimberley Klub....................17 B3
Mangrove Hotel...................18 D4
McAlpine House...................19 B4
Old Broome Guesthouse......20 B5
Roebuck Bay Caravan
   Park..................................21 B6
Roebuck Bay Hotel..............22 D3

EATING
Aarli Bar............................23 C3
Black Pearl.........................24 B5
Blooms...............................25 D3
Café Carlotta......................26 A5
Frangipanis.........................27 D3
Matso's Broome Brewery......28 C4
noodlefish...........................29 C3
Town Beach Cafe.................30 B6

DRINKING
Murphy's Irish Bar...............31 C5
Nippon Inn.........................32 D2
Palms.............................(see 18)
Tides Bar........................(see 18)

ENTERTAINMENT
Sun Pictures.......................33 D2

SHOPPING
Gecko Gallery....................(see 5)
Kailis Pearls.......................34 D3
Monsoon Gallery................35 C4
Old Broome Lockup Gallery.....36 D3
Paspaley Pearls...................37 D2
Short St Gallery................(see 5)
Town Beach Markets...........38 B6

TRANSPORT
Broome Broome...............(see 39)
Broome Cycles....................39 C3

Festivals & Events

Dates for Broome's celebrations can vary from year to year; check with the visitors centre and book accommodation in advance.

Staircase to the Moon Three magical nights each month from March to October. See p227 for details.

Big Moon Rising (www.bamf.org.au) Broome Arts and Music Festival; held in April and May.

Broome Fringe Arts Festival June.

Western Australian Ballet's Ballet on the Beach June.

Kimberley Cup Broome's end of season horseracing carnival; July.

NAIDOC Week National recognition of Aboriginal & Torres Strait Islander culture; July.

Opera Under the Stars (www.operaunderthestars.com.au) August.

Shinju Matsuri Festival of the Pearl (www.shinjumatsuri.com) Held in September; includes Dragon Boat Races.

Worn Art A fabulous spectacle of fashion, performance, music and dance; October.

Mango Festival A celebration of the fruit in all its forms, from daiquiris to chutneys, with Great Chefs and Great Bartenders of Broome competitions. November.

Sleeping

Accommodation is plentiful but you need to book ahead or have the flexibility to take advantage of booking sites such as www.wotif.com, which have last minute deals.

BUDGET

Broome's Last Resort (Map p228; ☎ 9193 5000; www.broomeslastresort.com.au; 2 Bagot St; dm $20-25, d $65; ❄ 🖳 🕹) Has a wonderful laid-back tropical vibe thanks to wide verandas, a swimming pool shaded by palm trees, hammocks, bar, pool tables and jukebox. The friendly management throw in free breakfast, town tours, barbecues, beach trips, a daily happy hour, and pool comps where you can win a tattoo!

Roebuck Bay Caravan Park (Map p228; ☎ 9192 1366; 91 Walcott St; unpowered/powered sites d $23/28, on-site vans d $75; ❄) Right on the milky waters of Roebuck Bay's Town Beach, and short bus rides to Chinatown and Cable Beach, this shady park has good facilities, including a communal kitchen and barbecue area.

Kimberley Klub (Map p228; ☎ 1800 004 345, 9192 3233; www.kimberleyklub.com; 62 Frederick St; dm $24-26, d $80; ❄ 🖳 🕹) This big breezy place has a similar feel to Broome's Last Resort but on a grander scale. There are myriad common areas, a poolside bar, hammock spaces, a massive kitchen, big-screen TV, table tennis, beach volleyball, free beach shuttle, and themed nights including bingo and open mic nights. YHA discount.

MIDRANGE

Roebuck Bay Hotel Motel (Map p228; ☎ 9192 1221; www.roebuckbayhotel.com.au; Carnarvon St; budget/standard/superior motel d $100/120/140; ❄ 🕹) In Chinatown, this is Broome's oldest hotel, built in 1890. Comfortable rooms surround a tropical swimming pool; the best are upstairs overlooking the pool, while the budget sleeps back onto the pub's noisy band area. The backpackers (dorm rooms $16 to $19), in a separate building next to the live gig/dance space, attracts a party crowd.

Broome Motel (Map p228; ☎ 1800 683 867, 9192 7775; www.broomemotel.com.au; 51-57 Frederick St; d $115, self-contained d $145; ❄ 🕹) This central motel with spotless, comfortable rooms (with TV, fridge, and tea and coffee facilities) represents one of Broome's best motel deals, with double rooms dropping by $10 after two nights. Prices can dip as low as $85 in the off-season.

Ocean Lodge (Map p226; ☎ 1800 600 603, 9193 7700; www.oceanlodge.com.au; 1 Cable Beach Rd; d/f $140/160; ❄ 🕹) Halfway between Cable Beach and Chinatown, these spacious clean rooms are looking a little worn, but guests love the swimming pool, expansive tropical garden and barbecues where they can cook their own food. Prices drop as much as $50 in the off-season.

TOP END

Mangrove Hotel (Map p228; ☎ 1800 094 818, 9192 1303; www.mangrovehotel.com.au; Carnarvon St; d $205 ❄ 🕹) The stylish executive rooms (contemporary Asian-inspired design) have divine views over Roebuck Bay's aquamarine waters and the hotel's large swimming pools (and drop by $30 in the off-season). Rumour is the budget rooms will be renovated into flashpacker accommodation.

Old Broome Guesthouse (Map p228; ☎ 9192 6106, 0429 335 845; www.oldbroomeguesthouse.com.au; 64 Walcott St; d $240; ❄ 🕹) This tranquil property, decorated in the Broome style with Asian Zen minimalist touches, is the perfect escape for people averse to hotels. The individually styled rooms have enormous sunken baths and private courtyards; if you can bring yourself to leave them there are breezy public spaces to laze around. Prices drop by $45 off-season.

McAlpine House (Map p228; ☎ 9192 3886; www .mcalpinehouse.com; 84 Herbert St; d from $300; ✂ ☐ ☎) By the time you've been collected from the airport, handed a glass of sparkling wine, and shown to your comfortable Kimberley-style suite in Captain Kennedy's atmospheric old home (dating to 1910), you'll be feeling like a pearling master. Spend a few days lazing in a hammock, picking mangoes from the tree, swimming in the serene pool, and drinking cocktails on the big verandas at this stylish boutique guesthouse, and you'll be wishing you were. Doubles are $100 cheaper in the off-season.

Eating

Broome has the only serious dining scene between Perth and Darwin. If you're a foodie, savour it while you can. During the Wet some eateries close, keep shorter hours, or only offer takeaway. Self-caterers will welcome well-stocked supermarkets and bakeries at Paspaley and Boulevard shopping centres.

Town Beach Cafe (Map p228; ☎ 9193 5585; Robinson St; mains $6-25; ✆ 7am-8pm Mon-Sat) Order from the busy counter inside – try the tempura king prawns or beer battered fish and chips – then take your number to a terrace table overlooking the beach at this busy BYO seafood café.

Café Carlotta (Map p228; ☎ 9192 7606; Jones Pl; mains $7-28; ✆ 5.30-10pm Mon-Sat) Owners Mic and Charlotte make regular research trips to Italy, and it shows in the daily handmade pastas and authentic wood-fired pizzas. While locals swear by the sizzling garlic prawns, we're just happy to be somewhere that serves Illy coffee. BYO.

Aarli Bar (Map p228; ☎ 9192 5529; cnr Frederick & Hamersley Sts; tapas & mains $9-16, pizzas $16; ✆ 7am-late Tue-Sat Mar-Nov) Funky little Aarli Bar isn't actually a bar – it's BYO only. However there's a colourful tiled bar inside lit up with Moroccan lanterns, and it is also part–tapas bar, with large portions of modern Med-influenced tapas. What Aarli does best, though, is authentic wood-fired pizza – delicious! Bookings essential.

our pick Wharf Restaurant (Map p226; ☎ 9192 5800; Port of Pearls House, Port Drive; mains $9-20; ✆ 10am-10pm) Chilling out with a crisp glass of white and a dozen fresh oysters (half-price from 2pm to 5pm) overlooking the aquamarine seawaters of Roebuck Bay is sublime. Craig Douglas has been keeping locals and tourists sated for 10 years with his fabulous quality seafood (you

won't find bigger or better oysters elsewhere) and a great list of delicious WA wines by the glass sourced by partner Jazz. If you can resist another dozen oysters (we couldn't) then try the chilli blue swimmer crab.

Frangipanis (Map p228; ☎ 9193 6766; 5 Napier Tce; mains $10-32; ✆ 7.30am-late) Snag a table on the terrace and share the signature Tasting Plate ($18.50) of Med and mod-Oz flavours: grilled kangaroo skewers, wild olives, feta, chorizo, haloumi, duck shanks and Turkish bread. It also does delicious pastas and seafood. Conveniently, it's licensed and BYO.

Black Pearl (Map p228; ☎ 9192 1799; 4/63 Robinson St; mains $11-27; ✆ 8am-late) The Med and Mod-Oz cuisine at this stylish BYO eatery can be a bit hit and miss – as can the service. But when both are good, they're great, and when they're not, they're sloppy. Visit on a good day and score a table under the shade sails overlooking Roebuck Bay and you're sure to risk a second visit.

Matso's Broome Brewery (Map p228; ☎ 9193 5811; 60 Hamersley St, cnr Carnarvon St; mains $11-30; ✆ 7am-late) Excellent Mod-Oz meals served under the ceiling fans in an atmospheric house dating to 1900 or on verandas overlooking Roebuck Bay. Try the delicious 'Ocean and Earth' platter of game sausages, croc skewers, beer battered barramundi, and chilli soft shell crab ($45 for two); tasty tapas-style snacks (oysters, tiger prawns etc) from 3pm to 6pm; or authentic curry from Matso's Curry Hut (from 6pm Thursday to Tuesday).

Blooms (Map p228; ☎ 9193 6366; 12 Carnarvon St; mains $12-26; ✆ 7am-late) A convenient pre-/post-cinema spot with a pleasant pavement terrace, Blooms does decent light dishes (salt and pepper squid, fish cakes etc), sandwiches and pastas, and has good wines by the glass. Allow plenty of time – the service when we visited was terrible.

noodlefish (Map p228; ☎ 9192 1697; 6 Hamersley St; mains $21-28; ✆ 6-9pm Tue-Sat Apr-Oct, takeaway only Nov-Feb) Mitch opened noodlefish in 1993 and his contemporary Asian cuisine – from grilled threadfin salmon, green paw paw salad and sweet chilli, to red curry of Kimberley king prawns with fresh herbs – remains unmatched in Broome. BYO only.

Drinking

Matso's Broome Brewery (Map p228; ☎ 9193 5811; 60 Hamersley St) There's no better spot in Broome to kick back with a beer than Matso's wide veran-

FUN AT THE SUN

There's stars on the screen and in the sky at Broome's **Sun Pictures** (below), the world's oldest operating outdoor cinema. Operating almost continuously since 1916, the theatre has a fascinating history.

Originally, this double-fronted tin structure was an Asian emporium that was, in part, a Japanese playhouse for traditional theatre performances. Sold in 1913 to master pearler Ted Hunter, it was converted to a 500-seat cinema. From 1916 to 1933 silent movies were screened, to a tinkling piano accompaniment – often played by local a personality named 'Fairy' – until the projector was adapted for sound in 1933 and Sun Pictures screened its first 'talkie'.

Before a levee bank was built in 1974, the theatre suffered from tidal flooding and women were often carried out of the theatre to higher ground. The theatre also went through a period of racially segregated seating, with the well-to-do Europeans having better seats and the Malays, Koepangers, Filipinos and Aborigines having a separate entrance. While both WWII and the introduction of TV and video to the Kimberly region saw the theatre temporarily close, it was restored between 1998 and 2000.

Today reclining in the canvas deckchairs armed with a choc-top (a classic Australian ice-cream treat) and watching a film as children play, bats make a racket and the odd aircraft flies overhead (it's right on the flightpath!) is as quintessential a Broome experience as a Cable Beach sunset.

das overlooking Roebuck Bay. The wonderful award-winning beers are brewed on site – the Monsoonal Blonde is sensational – and there's live music Sundays in the courtyard from 3pm to 6pm, and occasional DJs and bands on weekend nights.

Roebuck Bay Hotel (Map p228; ☎ 9192 1221; 45 Dampier Tce) Affectionately known as the 'Roey', this is your typical Aussie pub. It boasts a blokes' sports bar with pool tables, darts and skimpies (barmaids in g-strings), a beer garden with counter meals (Cheffy's), a band venue (Pearlers Lounge), and a club/concert venue (the Oasis), with live music and dance parties with DJs.

On Friday nights locals like to down beers under the tiki torches while the sun goes down over Roebuck Bay at **Tides Bar** (Map p228; Mangrove Hotel, Carnarvon St), before moving inside to the **Palms** (Map p228; ☎ 9192 1303; Mangrove Hotel, Carnarvon St). Backpackers love the Tuesday jam nights at **Murphy's Irish Bar** (Map p228; ☎ 9192 1002; Mercure Hotel, Weld St) and Wednesday nights at the **Nippon Inn** (Map p228; ☎ 9192 1941; Dampier Tce) for its 'best beer gut' and wet T-shirt competitions.

Entertainment

Sun Pictures (Map p228; ☎ 9192 3738; www.sun pictures.com.au; 27 Carnarvon St; adult/concession/child/family $14.50/11.50/9/40) This is the world's oldest operating picture gardens (see above). Sinking back into a canvas deckchair or sprawling out on the grass under the stars will go down as one of your most memorable moviegoing experiences. Munch on popcorn, choc tops or Mexican food as you enjoy Aussie cinema, Kimberley-produced docos and mainstream family flicks. Film buffs should do the History Tour ($5), running 10.30am and 1pm, Monday to Friday.

Diver's Tavern (Map p226; ☎ 9193 6066; Cable Beach Rd; ☽ 7am-late) Hosts occasional music festivals and books excellent live bands including Aussie legends such as Paul Kelly and Tex Perkins, while the regular house bands pack the place out for the Sunday 'sesh'.

Shopping

Broome specialises in pearls and Aboriginal art and while both make treasured souvenirs, they're also great investments. You don't have to be rich – pearl earrings can cost less than $100, photographic prints from $40 upwards, while small limited-edition art prints can start at around $100. For more information on Aboriginal art see l.

Monsoon Gallery (Map p228; ☎ 9193 5379; www.mon soongallery.com.au; Hammersley St; ☽ 10am-5pm) Has an eclectic range of art by Aboriginal and other locals, along with quality prints, photography, sculpture, textiles, glass and ceramics.

Old Broome Lockup Gallery (Map p228; ☎ 9193 5633; www.lockup.groovylips.com; Carnarvon St; ☽ 10am-5pm) This was a jail for Aborigines up until the 1950s, and it now sells art by local indigenous painters, along with photography, carvings, didgeridoos and music created by resident artists.

THE KIMBERLEYS

BROOME'S BOOMING ART SCENE

Broome's lively art scene is a wonderful surprise for visitors missing city culture and for those travellers wanting to learn more about the Kimberley's indigenous culture and art.

There are quality art galleries all over Broome, with several on Short St, Chinatown, that have brought some big city sophistication to town, with regular changing exhibitions and inclusive champagne openings. Each gallery has a special area of focus and represents particular artists or work with just a few Aboriginal communities.

In a 100 year-old house (one of Broome's oldest: note the wind tunnel!), **Short St Gallery** (Map p228; ☎ 9192 2658; www.shortstgallery.com; 7 Short St, Chinatown; 10am-5pm) was Broome's first gallery and specialises in contemporary indigenous Kimberley art.

Belinda Carrigan, a renowned curator of indigenous art who directed the Holmes à Court Collection for ten years, owns **Gecko Gallery** (Map p228; ☎ 9192 8909; www.geckogallery.com.au; 9 Short St; 10am-6pm Mon-Fri, 10am-2pm Sat & Sun, closed Sun & Mon during Wet), which specialises in Central Desert and Utopia art.

Broome 6 Gallery (Map p228; ☎ 9192 6821; www.broome6.com.au; 6/20 Hammersley St; 10am-5pm) started off representing six local artists but shows other Kimberley artists and is a great supporter of the Mowanjum Community working in the Wandjina Art Tradition.

Look out for the work of Broome's greatest talent, Moroccan-Australian Krim Benterrak, a Kimberley resident of some 20 years, who captures the magical colour and light of Broome better than anyone. Serious art lovers can see his work in his home studio by appointment (☎ 9192 1490).

If you're looking for lustrous pearls, two pioneering family businesses produce the best quality pearls in the most stunning settings. Having established Broome's first underwater pearl farm on a Roebuck Bay seabed, **Kailis Pearls** (Map p228; ☎ 9192 2061; cnr Marine Terrace & Collie St; 9.30am-5pm Mon-Fri, 11am-4pm Sat & Sun) creates elegant understated designs. **Paspaley Pearls** (Map p228; ☎ 9192 2203; 2 Short St; www.paspaleypearls.com; 9.30am-5pm Mon-Fri, 9.30am-1pm Sat, 9.30am-1pm Sun May-Oct only) started Australia's first cultured pearl farm 420km north of Broome at Kuri Bay in the 1950s and has been setting splendid pearls in stylish designs ever since.

For local arts, crafts, incense, candles, hippy gear and hemp clothes, head to the **Courthouse Markets** (Map p228; Sat morning Oct-Apr, Sat & Sun morning May-Sep) or the Town Beach Markets during the Staircase to the Moon (see p227).

Getting There & Away

Broome has flights or links to all Australian capitals and towns throughout the Kimberley.

Qantas (☎ 13 13 13; www.qantas.com.au) flies daily to Broome from Perth and Darwin, while **Airnorth** (☎ 13 13 13) flies between Broome, Darwin and Kununurra. **Northwest Regional Airlines** (☎ 1300 136 629; www.northwestregional.com.au) flies to Broome, Fitzroy Crossing, Halls Creek, Karratha and Port Hedland. **Skippers Aviation** (☎ 9478 3989; www.skippers.com.au) flies between Broome and Derby.

Greyhound (☎ 13 20 30) stops at the Broome visitors centre on its daily Perth–Darwin service.

Getting Around

The **Town Bus Service** (☎ 9193 6585; www.broomebus.com; adult/child $3/1.30, hop-on-hop-off day pass adult/child $9/free) links Chinatown with Cable Beach every hour (7.10am to 6.05pm June to mid-October, 10.23am to 6.05pm mid-October to May). **Nightrider** (☎ 9192 8987; adult/child one-way $3.50/2.50, all night pass $6/3) runs every half-hour from 6.30pm until midnight. Get timetables from the visitors centre.

Broome Broome (Map p228; ☎ 9192 2210; www.broomebroome.com.au) has air-con cars from $30 a day, 4WD from $105 (plus insurance), and scooters from $35 for two days. **Broome Cycles** (Map p228; ☎ 9192 1871 Chinatown, 0409 192 289 Cable Beach; $50 deposit) rents bikes for $18/70 per day/week. For taxis phone **Broome Taxis** (☎ 9192 1133) or **Chinatown Taxis** (☎ 1800 811 772).

CABLE BEACH

Cable Beach comprises the long stretch of wonderful white-sand beach and the expanding laid-back suburb backing on to it, 4km west of Broome's Chinatown. At the northern end, near the surf club, you can hire beach umbrellas, deck chairs, surfboards, and boogie boards (all under $10). Nude sunbathing is allowed beyond the rocks further north.

Amble along three well-marked trails through **Minyirr Park**, running along Cable Beach, a spiritual place for the Rubibi people, or go with an **indigenous guide** (☎ 9194 0150). The Broome Visitors Centre has brochures with a map.

Australia's original crocodile hunter, owner of **Malcolm Douglas Crocodile Park** (☎ 9192 1489; Cable Beach Rd; adult/child/family $20/16/50, ☻ 10am-5pm Mon-Fri, 2-5pm Sat & Sun Apr-Nov, croc-feeding tours 3pm, alligator-feeding tours 11am Mon-Fri), was making classic Aussie adventure films *Across the Top* and *Follow the Sun* in the late 1960s when the late Steve Irwin was just a kid. To get the most out of your visit to Douglas' croc park, time it with a feeding tour.

Broome's coast has one of the most varied collections of **dinosaur footprints** in the world – nine different types – and a group of 10 well-preserved footprints around 135 million years old at **Gantheaume Point**, 7km south of Broome. At extremely low tides these are exposed, but they're difficult to find. You'll easily be able to identify **Anastasia's Pool**, carved into the rock by the former lighthouse keeper to ease his wife's arthritis.

Sleeping

Cable Beach Backpackers (☎ 1800 655 011, 9193 5511; www.cablebeachbackpackers.com; 12 Sanctuary Rd; dm $20-25, d $65; ☻ ⌨ ⌨) Within splashing distance of Cable Beach, this relaxed place has a lush tropical courtyard, swimming pool, big communal kitchen and bar. The friendly management picks guests up from their bus, provides shuttle buses into town, hosts free

sausage sizzles and rents surfboards, bikes and scooters.

Palm Grove Holiday Resort (☎ 1800 803 336, 9192 3336; www.palmgrove.com.au; cnr Cable Beach & Murray Rds; unpowered/powered sites $32/36, studio d $155, 2-bedroom park homes $180; ☻ ⌨) Across the road from Cable Beach, this shady caravan park has free barbecues, campers kitchen, and a gorgeous swimming pool. The well-equipped studios and 'park homes' are in the Broome style and rates drop substantially in the off-season.

Cable Beach Club Resort (☎ 1800 199 099, 9192 0400; www.cablebeachclub.com; Cable Beach Rd; d from $255; ☻ ⌨ ⌨) What makes this idyllic resort special is the unique combination of Broome architecture and Eastern Zen style. Add to that lush gardens, serene swimming pools, great eateries and friendly service. It all makes for a memorable stay.

Eating & Drinking

Sunset Bar & Cafe (☎ 9192 0470; Cable Beach Club Resort, Cable Beach Rd; mains $12-25; ☻ 6.30am-late) Arrive around five to get a prime sunset-viewing spot as sunset cocktails is a ritual for Cable Beach Club guests. The great-value global menu spans everything from crispy pizzas to tasty Asian noodles, and the popular Sunset Seafood Platter for two ($75).

Diver's Tavern (☎ 9193 6066; Cable Beach Rd; mains $12-29; ☻ 11am-10pm) This is the place to head for a few games of pool and a no-nonsense counter meal. The delicious Divers Burgers ($16) are deservedly popular although many find it hard to resist 'Half An Ass' (a half-kilo rump, gravy, chips and salad $26).

Old Zoo Cafe (☎ 9193 6200; 2 Challenor Rds; mains $17-27; ☻ 7am-late) In one of Lord McAlpine's old zoo buildings, this café is popular with locals

THE KIMBERLEYS

THE CABLE BEACH CAMEL COUP

One of Western Australia's most iconic images is a camel train silhouetted by a golden sunset at Cable Beach. But behind this idyllic scene a tale of intrigue has been playing out. Until mid-2006, four licensees were issued to lead camel trains along the beach. However, in July 2006 one operator, Red Sun Camels, was awarded all four licences for 2007, effectively putting the other three operators out of business – including the man who started the industry, Abdul Casley and his Ships of the Desert. Paying $100,000 a year for each of the five-year permits (they were formerly $500 each) and throwing in a couple of new four-wheel-drives for the council rangers for beach patrols, Red Sun Camels has a monopoly on Cable Beach camel rides. Appeals, public protests and questions about what happened behind the scenes have had Broome buzzing for months. While you could say it's just business, in a relatively small town such as Broome, where the concept of a 'fair go' still means something, the whole episode is seen as being as sour as camel's breath.

and travellers alike for its laid-back atmosphere and tropical gardens. Expect delicious breakfasts, light meals and a great selection of wines by the glass.

Zanders (☎ 9193 5090; Cable Beach Reserve, Cable Beach Rd; mains $18-27; ☺ 7am-late) Its beachside location keeps Zanders busy, especially around sunset, while its range of eating options – from takeaway at picnic tables to bistro-style eating with table service – keeps everyone happy. Unfortunately the menu – salt and pepper squid, seafood basket, surf 'n' turf – is predictable.

Club Restaurant (☎ 9192 0411; Cable Beach Club Resort, Cable Beach Rd; mains $30-34; ☺ 4pm-late) Dress up for Broome's best restaurant in an elegant dining room decorated with Lord McAlpine's antiques and Sidney Nolan paintings. The must-try dish is the tangy Pearl Meat Ceviche with rocket, green paw paw, lime and toasted coconut ($24).

AROUND BROOME
Broome Bird Observatory
On the Roebuck Bay shores, 25km from Broome, this wonderful **bird observatory** (☎ 9193 5600; Crab Creek Rd; admission & binocular hire adult/child $5/free) is a vital staging post for hundreds of migratory species, including 49 waders (nearly a quarter of the world's total species). An incredible 800,000 birds arrive each year, travelling some 12,000km to get here, on their way to or from Asia and Siberia. Join an excellent two-hour tour (from observatory/Broome $50/85); a full-day tour of the freshwater lakes ($120/155, BYO lunch); a one-hour introductory walk ($15); or do a seven-day all-inclusive course ($790 including transfers, accommodation and meals). You can camp on-site ($11 per person), or rent a room (single/double $30/$55) or fully-contained chalet (double $105). Transfers from Broome are $35. If you're driving, access is via a decent dirt road, which can be closed in the Wet.

Dampier Peninsula
Stunning scenery of aquamarine waters, white-sand beaches and red rock formations, along with the opportunity to learn about the indigenous culture and country of the Ngumbarl, Jabirrjabirr, Nyulnyul, Nimanburru and Bardi peoples, your hosts and guides, are great reasons to visit the remote Dampier Peninsula.

Access to the isolated Aboriginal communities is by 4WD only, along the rough, corrugated, red pindan 200km-long Cape Leveque Rd (turn-off 9km east of Broome). You must plan your trip in advance, obtain permits and book accommodation before leaving. Permits exist to protect privacy of the community, preserve Aboriginal heritage and culture, and the natural environment, as well as ensuring your own safety. You can obtain a free transit permit in advance online from the **Department of Indigenous Affairs** (☎ 1300 651 077; www.dia.wa.gov.au); this can take around three days to be processed. Get the *Dampier Peninsula Travellers Guide* from Broome visitors centre, which can make accommodation arrangements for you. You need to be completely self-sufficient and take fuel, food and water to last the period you'll be away. Check road conditions before leaving.

The first turn-off, Manari Rd, takes you to the **Willie Creek Pearl Farm** (see p227), while another 40km north is **Coulomb Point Nature Reserve**, which protects unique pindan vegetation and the rare bilby.

Back on Cape Leveque Rd, it's 110km to **Beagle Bay** (☎ 9192 4913; entry per person $5), notable for the extraordinarily beautiful mother-of-pearl altar at Beagle Bay church, built by Pallotine monks in 1918. There are no public facilities or accommodation, just a shop and fuel (weekdays only). Contact the office on arrival.

Tranquil, unspoilt **Middle Lagoon** (☎ 9192 4002; entry per car $8, unpowered/powered sites per person $13/16, beach shelters d $44, cabins d $125-200), 170km from Broome, is ideal for swimming, snorkelling and fishing, and is popular with Broome families. No fuel available.

Between Middle Lagoon and Cape Leveque, **Lombadina** (☎ 9192 4936; www.lombadina.com.au; entry per car $5, dm $44, unit d $165, guided walks 1hr $33, 2hr $55, boat tours from $154), about 200km from Broome, has fishing, whale-watching, mudcrabbing, and indigenous 'footprint' tours. Fuel is available Monday to Friday. Around 7km from Lombadina, gorgeous **Chile Creek** (☎ 9192 4141; www.chilecreek.com; camp sites per person $17, bush shelters per person $25) keeps it real with basic bush shelters and a rustic camp kitchen where travellers share stories.

Cape Leveque is rather spectacular, with pristine beaches and stunning red cliffs, and ecotourism award-winner **Kooljaman** (☎ 9192 4970; www.kooljaman.com.au; camp sites d $32 plus $5 for power, beach shelters/mini safari tents d $60, cabins d $140, safari tents d $240) is the most sophisticated of the communities, with accommodation ranging

THE KIMBERLEYS

from hill-top resort-style safari tents with panoramic views to thatched beach huts. Kooljaman gets busy during the in-season, but is almost deserted off-season. **Dinkas Restaurant** (mains $10-22; ☽ Apr-Oct) offers eat-in or a bush butler service!

Peninsula Transfers (☎ 9192 2660; one way adult/child $95/60; ☽ depart 8am Sun, Wed & Fri Apr-Oct) operates 4WD services from Broome to Beagle Bay, Lombadina and Cape Leveque. Other destinations and the return trip must be negotiated when booking. Tour operators to Cape Leveque from Broome include indigenous-owned **Chomley's Tours** (☎ 9192 7307; www.chomleystours.com.au; 2-day tour incl 3hr Aboriginal guided tour $310) and **Over the Top Adventure Tours** (☎ 9192 5211; www.4wdtourswa.com; one/two day Cape Leveque tour $225/410).

GIBB RIVER ROAD

The Gibb River Rd was constructed as a 'beef road' to move cattle to and from surrounding stations. Spanning some 660km from Derby to Wyndham and Kununurra, it may be more direct than the highway by several hundred kilometres, but it's a rough, corrugated 4WD-only dirt road that's often closed after rain, and is closed altogether during the Wet.

The route leads through vast empty country and dramatic terrain. The scorched earth is scarred with occasional lush gorges and awesome riverbeds, their rocky surfaces parched during the Dry and surging with water during the Wet.

If you want just a taste of back-country adventure, do the 'tourist loop' that takes you 125km along the Gibb River Rd from Derby to the Fairfield Leopold Downs Rd turn-off, then 124km past Windjana Gorge and Tunnel Creek to the Great Northern Hwy, 43km west of Fitzroy Crossing.

The neighbourhood is made up of Aboriginal communities and private cattle stations, so if you plan to leave the main roads, get permission first from owners. Apply for permits to transit or visit Aboriginal communities online from the **Department of Indigenous Affairs** (☎ 1300 651 077; www.dia.wa.gov.au); permits may take three days to be processed. Get *Travelling in Outback Western Australia* or check www.dpi .wa.gov.au/pastoral for information on driving through pastoral stations; the *Travellers Atlas of Western Australia* shows lease boundaries.

The *Gibb River & Kalumburu Roads Travellers Guide* ($4 from visitors centres) is indispensable with essential advice, sights, fuel stops and accommodation listings (often tented cabins at stations, which must be booked in advance). Make sure you're driving a high clearance 4WD, have spare tyres and tools, and stock up on several days' food and water in case you get stranded. Before leaving check **road conditions** (☎ 1800 013 314; www.mainroads.wa.gov.au; ☽ 24hr).

If you're not an experienced four-wheel-driver, opt for the hop-on, hop-off **Gibb River Road Bus** (☎ 1800 197 262; www.gibbriverbus.com.au; multistop ticket one way/return $260/390; ☽ departs Derby 6am Wed, Fri & Sun, Kununurra 6am Tue, Thu & Sat, May-Sep only). Many organised tours also travel the road (see p223).

DERBY
☎ 08 / pop 5000

Drowsy Derby, the administrative centre for west Kimberley, sits astride a peninsula jutting into King Sound, surrounded by tidal mud flats. Its mangroves attract over 200 bird species, including migratory waders. This is crocodile country so squeeze the last bit of beach out of Broome (219km south) before heading here. Derby is short on sights but makes a decent base for trips to the national parks of the ancient Devonian Reef (see p238) and the islands of the Buccaneer Archipelago; it's also the western entrance to the Gibb River Rd.

HORIZONTAL WATERFALLS

One of the most intriguing features of the Kimberley coastline is the phenomenon known as the 'Horizontal Waterfalls'. Despite the name, the falls are simply tides gushing through narrow coastal gorges in the Buccaneer Archipelago, north of Derby. What makes it such a spectacle is the huge tides – often varying up to 11m, the rate of the water flow reaches an astonishing 30 knots as it's forced in and out of the constricted sandstone gorges. The two narrow gaps, the first being 20m wide and the second 10m wide, often see the 'waterfall' reach a height of 4m. The falls are best seen by air and form part of many tour operators' itineraries (inquire at the Derby and/or Broome visitors centres).

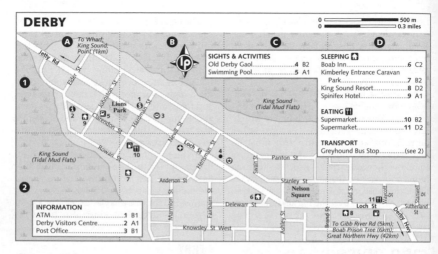

Information

The supermarket and ATMs are on Loch and Clarendon Sts.

Derby visitors centre (☎ 1800 621 426, 9191 1426; www.derbytourism.com.au; 2 Clarendon St; ☼ 8.30am-4.30pm Mon-Fri, 9am-1pm Sat & Sun Apr-Sep, 8.30am-4.30pm Mon-Fri & 9am-noon Sat Oct-Mar) Sells bus tickets, can advise on road conditions, and books local mud crabbing and fishing tours.

Post office (Loch St)

Sights & Activities

Derby's first wooden jetty was built in 1894 to serve the growing pastoral population and gold rush, while the current **wharf** opened in 1964 to export cattle (nowadays mainly lead and zinc). Locals like to fish here for north-west salmon, shark and mud crabs and it's the best place to see the colossal 11m tides. There are crocodiles, so if you want to swim head for the swimming pool on Clarendon St.

The **Old Derby Gaol** (Loch St), next to the police station, is the town's oldest building, dating to 1906, and is a grim reminder of the violence between the indigenous people and European settlers that racked the town from the late 1800s.

The **Boab Prison Tree**, 7km south of town, is Derby's most famous attraction. With a girth of 14m and a hollow trunk it's said to be over 1000 years old. Prisoners were locked up here en route to Old Derby Gaol.

Begun in 1960, the **Boab Festival** (July) entertains locals with concerts, sports (including mud footy) and street parades.

Tours

Derby's biggest drawcard is its proximity to the natural splendour of remote **King Sound** and the **Buccaneer Archipelago**, uninhabited islands that are best viewed from the air or sea. **One Tide Charters** (☎ 9193 1358; www.onetide .com; 5-day tours $2450) offer all-inclusive multiday 'sea safaris' with camping overnight at idyllic spots. **Kimberley Seaplanes** (☎ 9191 1760; www .horizontalfalls.com.au; fly-cruise-fly 5hr/overnight tours from Derby $395/$495) and **Buccaneer Sea Safaris** (☎ 9191 1991, 0419 917 797; www.buccaneerseasafaris.com; 4-day tours from Derby $1790, from Broome $2100) offer tours combining sea and sky vistas. You can do the flight only with **Bush Flight** (☎ 9193 2680; www .bushflight.com; 90min tour from Derby $255).

Sleeping & Eating

Kimberley Entrance Caravan Park (☎ 9193 1055; www.kimberleyentrancecaravanpark.com; 2 Rowan St; unpowered/powered sites $18/24) Friendly managers Ian and Julie provide great facilities in leafy surrounds.

Spinifex Hotel (☎ 9191 1233; Clarendon St; dm $25, budget s/d $45/60, motel d $85; ✶) Rooms at the Spini may be basic but most travellers will pass their time in the affable pub, which also does decent meals (mains $11 to $22).

Boab Inn (☎ 9191 1044; boabinn@bigpond.com; Loch St; s/d $110/145; ✶ ✶) The best value accommodation in town. Prices drop by $40 in the off-season. Rooms are clean and comfortable and there are excellent counter meals (mains $12 to $26) in the pub's restaurant. They even have a real espresso machine!

King Sound Resort (☎ 9193 1044; Loch St; d $150; ❄ ☒) Make this your last resort. The rooms are spacious but were infested with cockroaches when we stayed.

Point (☎ 9191 1195; mains $11-26; ☯ 10am-late) In a prime sunset-watching spot overlooking the jetty, this BYO place is Derby's best, serving delicious seafood. The barramundi and croc steaks are very popular. It also does takeaway.

Getting There & Away

Skippers Aviation (☎ 9478 3989) flies to Broome Monday to Saturday. Daily **Greyhound** (☎ 13 20 30) buses to Darwin and Perth stop at the visitors centre.

GIBB RIVER ROAD TO WYNDHAM–KUNUNURRA ROAD

Mowanjum Wandjina Art (☎ 9191 1104; ☯ 8am-3pm Mon-Fri; phone ahead), about 4km along Gibb River Rd, is an Aboriginal community renowned for its artists painting in the Wandjina style.

The 5000-acre **Birdwood Downs Station** (☎ 9191 1275; www.birdwooddowns.com; Gibb River Rd; camping s $11, savannah huts d $120; about 20km from Derby, offers outback accommodation and trail rides through the savannah (per person $50 for a 90-minute ride).

After crossing the Lennard River bridge (120km from Derby) you'll come to the Yamarra Gap in the King Leopold Range (145km). Narrow 5km-long **Lennard River Gorge**, 8km off Gibb River Rd, has a refreshing pool and waterfall.

At 184km you'll see the turn-off (and 50km rough drive) to enchanting **Mt Hart Wilderness**

Lodge (☎ 9191 4645; www.mthart.com.au; d incl 3-course dinner & breakfast per person $180).

About 26km past the Mt Hart turn-off is stunning **Bell Gorge**, 29km down a rough track, with a picturesque waterfall and camping at **Silent Grove** (adult/child $9/2).

Refuel and meet some locals at characterful **Imintji Store** (☎ 9191 7471), your last chance to get supplies. Next to Imintji Aboriginal Community is **Imintji Wilderness Camp** (☎ 1800 889 389; www.kimberleywilderness.com.au; d incl breakfast $135) with safari tents.

Mornington Wilderness Camp (☎ 9191 7406; camping adult/child $15/7, safari tents full board d $450), on the Fitzroy River, is 100km south of the 247km mark, with spacious tents and tours.

Horseshoe-shaped **Galvans Gorge** has a swimming hole less than 1km off the road at the 286km mark.

Mt Barnett Roadhouse (☎ 9191 7007; camp sites $10), at the 306km point, is owned by the Kupingarri Aboriginal Community and has fuel and a store. **Barnett River Gorge** is another good swimming spot, 5km off the 328km mark.

At 406km you reach the Kalumburu turn-off (see p238). The Gibb River Rd continues through spectacular country; at 579km there are views of the Cockburn Ranges, the Cambridge Gulf and the Pentecost and Durack Rivers. About 2km further is **Home Valley Homestead** (☎ 9161 4322; www.homevalley.com.au; camp sites per adult/child $10/5 plus $10 for power, homestead per person incl breakfast $80) with swimming, fishing and horse-riding.

At 590km is the infamous **Pentecost River** crossing. Take care: water levels are hard to predict and salt water crocs love it here.

THE BEASTLY BOAB

One of the key features of the Kimberley are its huge and austere boab trees. An anomaly of Australian fauna, the boab (*Adansonia gregorii*) is found only in the Kimberley and Victoria River area of the Northern Territory. Intriguingly, the only other places where members of the boab family are found is Madagascar and Africa.

Most visitors only see the trees in the Dry and being deciduous, they have already lost their leaves – giving them that stark appearance. One local story is that the boab formed too high an opinion of itself, displeasing the gods so much they pulled it out of the ground and thrust it back in upside-down, exposing its roots and earning it the nickname 'upside-down tree'.

However, at the beginning of the Wet, the boab produces new leaves and large white flowers. The boab produces a fruit as well, which the local Aborigines use for decoration by carving pictorial scenes onto the hard surface of the fruit. Aborigines have also used the tree widely for such things as shelter, food, medicine and water. The European settlers, of course, found a different use for the often hollow centre of the boab tree, as 'lock-ups' (prisons) for Aborigines, the best-known example being the Boab Prison Tree near Derby (opposite).

At 614km, the million-acre **El Questro Wilderness Park** (☎ 9169 1777; www.voyages.com.au; park permit $15; ☺ Apr-Nov) has a range of accommodation, including luxurious **El Questro Homestead** (d incl meals $1780; ☒); the more down-to-earth **El Questro Station Township** (camp sites per person $15, safari tents d $135, bungalows d $298; ☒), the best value; and over-rated **Emma Gorge Resort** (safari-style tent cabins d $248; ☒ ☒), at 623km. There are restaurants and bars at the Township and Emma Gorge resorts. Highlights include boat tours up the wonderful **Chamberlain Gorge** to see indigenous art, and the 40-minute bush walk along gorgeous **Emma Gorge** to a pretty pool and waterfall.

At 630km you cross King River and at 647km you finally hit bitumen: Wyndham is 48km to the northwest, and Kununurra is 52km east.

NORTHERN KIMBERLEY

KALUMBURU ROAD

While unsealed Kalumburu Rd is in better condition than the Gibb River Rd in some spots, in others its severely corrugated or covered in rocks or bull dust. During the Wet, the road becomes a river, and after the Wet, locals find parts of it have disappeared altogether; it may not open again until May or even June. Distances are given from the junction of the Gibb River and Kalumburu Rds, 419km from the Derby Hwy and 248km from the Wyndham-Kununurra Rd.

You need permits to visit the Kalumburu community; apply in advance online from the **Department of Indigenous Affairs** (☎ 1300 651 077; www.dia.wa.gov.au; free) – permits from here may take a week to be processed – and the **Kalumburu community** (☎ 9161 4300; kalumburumission@bigpond .com; 7-day permit per car $35).

After crossing the Gibb River at 3km and Plain Creek at 16km, you reach the first fuel stop at 59km, **Drysdale River Station** (☎ 9161 4326; www.drysdaleriver.com.au; camp sites $9-14, d $130), where you can get supplies, meals and, in the Dry, scenic flights to Mitchell Falls (per person $250).

The Mitchell Plateau turn-off is at 172km, from where it's 70km to the turn-off to spectacular **Mitchell Falls**, 16km downhill; you have to walk the final 3km. In the Dry, the water spills down the terraces; in the Wet, it thunders over all the escarpments and a scenic

flight from Kununurra is the only way to see the spectacle. There is accommodation at the **Ungolan Wilderness Camp** (☎ 1800 889 389; www .kimberleywilderness.com.au; safari B&B $135), at the turn-off to the falls. The *Gibb River & Kalumburu Roads Travellers Guide* lists further options on remote areas of the coast accessible by air only.

From the Mitchell Plateau turn-off, the road heads northeast, crossing **Carson River** at 247km. In another 20km you'll arrive at **Kalumburu Aboriginal Community** (☎ 9161 4333), a picturesque mission nestled among giant mango trees and coconut palms, with a shop, food and **fuel** (☺ 8am-4pm Mon-Fri). You can pitch a tent at Honeymoon Bay (☎ 9161 4366; camp sites $9).

GREAT NORTHERN HIGHWAY

DEVONIAN REEF NATIONAL PARKS

The West Kimberley's three national parks feature three stunning gorges that were once part of a western 'great barrier reef' in the Devonian era, 350 million years ago. Windjana Gorge and Tunnel Creek National Parks are accessed via Fairfield Leopold Downs Rd (linking the Great Northern Hwy with Gibb River Rd), while Geikie Gorge National Park is just northeast of Fitzroy Crossing.

The walls of beautiful **Windjana Gorge** soar 100m above the Lennard River, which surges in the Wet but is a series of pools in the Dry. Scores of freshwater crocodiles sunbake on its banks and lurk in the water. Bring plenty of water for the 7km return walk from the **camp ground** (site $9) to the end of the gorge. The ruins of **Lillimooloora** homestead (1893) are 3km from Lennard River; once a police outpost, this is where Aboriginal tracker Jandamarra shot Constable Richardson (see p240).

Tunnel Creek is a 750m-long passage, 3m to 15m wide, created by the creek cutting through a spur of the Napier Range. In the Dry, you can walk all the way to the end; be prepared to meet bats along the way and wade through cold, knee-deep water in places. Take a strong torch and change of shoes. There are Aboriginal paintings at either end. No camping.

The magnificent **Geikie Gorge** is 18km north of Fitzroy Crossing on a sealed road. The best way to enjoy the gorge and its abundance of wildlife (including bull sharks and crocs – no swimming!) is on an entertaining **DEC boat tour** (☎ 9191 5121, 9195 5500; tickets from DEC kiosk at Geikie Gorge; 1hr tour adult/child $20/5; ✆ 8am, 9.30am, 11am & 3pm Jun-Aug; fewer trips & times vary Apr-May & Sep-Oct). You can also take cultural bush walks and boat tours with an indigenous guide through **Darngku Heritage Tours** (☎ 9191 5355; 2hr walk adult/child $55/45, 3hr boat cruise $70/55).

Tours

Tour companies also go to the gorges from Broome and Derby.

Australian Adventure Travel (☎ 1800 621 625; www.safaris.net.au; 5-day tour $895) Departs from Broome to all gorges via the Gibb River Rd, then Kununurra.

Broome Day Tours (☎ 1800 801 068; 1-day tour $190) Geikie Gorge & Windjana.

Derby Bus Service(☎ 9191 1426; 1-day tour $121) Windjana & Tunnel Creek.

Kimberley Getaway Safaris (☎ 9193 7139; www .kimberleysafaris.com.au; 1 day tour $595) From Broome to all gorges.

FITZROY CROSSING

☎ 08 / pop 1100

This is a true outback town, located where the Great Northern Hwy crosses the Fitzroy River, with a large Aboriginal population hailing from the Gooniyandi, Bunuba, Walmajarri and Wangkajungka communities. Fitzroy Crossing is a good access point for Geikie and Windjana Gorges and Tunnel Creek. The **visitors centre** (☎ 9191 5355; fxinfo@sdwk. wa.gov.au; ✆ 8am-5pm Apr-Sep, 9am-4pm Mon-Fri Oct-Mar) is on the highway.

The oldest pub in the Kimberley, lively **Crossing Inn** (☎ 9191 5080; crossinginn@bigpond.com.au; Skuthorpe Rd; unpowered/powered sites d $17/21, dongas s/d $60/80, motel s/d $93/110; ✖) provides a chance to meet locals, inside its tin shed and across the road at the billabong. Basic accommodation is at the back of the pub. The tin walls feature wonderful paintings by talented local high school students.

Fitzroy River Lodge Motel Hotel & Caravan Park (☎ 9191 5141; Great Northern Hwy; unpowered/powered sites $11/25, safari tents d $135, motel d $175; ✖ ✆) has a wide range of high-quality accommodation, from comfortable motel rooms and safari tents to shady camping spots, and a friendly bar with delicious counter meals (mains $10 to $23).

Northwest Regional Airlines (☎ 1300 136 629) has daily flights to Broome and Halls Creek.

Greyhound (☎ 13 20 30) has daily buses to Perth and Darwin that stop at the visitors centre and Fitzroy River Lodge.

HALLS CREEK

☎ 08 / pop 1590

On the edge of the arid Great Sandy Desert, Halls Creek is a small predominantly Aboriginal settlement of Kidja, Jaru and Gooniyandi communities.

The **visitors centre** (☎ 9168 6262; ✆ 8am-4pm Mon-Sat, 8am-2pm Sun) is on the Great Northern Hwy and can organise tours with local companies to Wolfe Creek Meteorite Crater and Purnululu National Park.

China Wall, 5km east of town, is a quartz vein protruding 6m off the ground, the longest single fault of its type in the world.

The tranquil swimming holes of **Palm Springs** (45km from town) and **Sawpit Gorge** (52km from town) are off gravel Duncan Rd, southeast of town.

Halls Creek Caravan Park (☎ 9168 6169; lanus@ bigpond.com.au; Roberta Ave; unpowered/powered sites $19/22, dongas $24, cabins d $74; ✖) offers travellers some shady camping areas as well as a well-stocked shop.

Best Western Halls Creek Motel (☎ 9168 6001; hallscreekmotel@westnet.com.au; 194 Great Northern Hwy; dongas $50, motel d $120; ✖ ✆) has clean, well-equipped rooms, including decent budget rooms, and hearty meals at **Russian Jack's** (mains $12-28).

Kimberley Hotel (☎ 9168 6101; www.kimberleyhotel .com; Roberta Ave; budget/motel d $91/164; ✖ ✆) has comfortable rooms with all mod cons and an atmospheric bar and **restaurant** (mains $16-31) overlooking the pool.

Northwest Regional Airlines (☎ 1300 136 629) has daily flights to Fitzroy Crossing and Broome. **Greyhound** (☎ 13 20 30) has buses running between Perth and Darwin.

WOLFE CREEK METEORITE CRATER

The massive 850m-wide and 50m-deep Wolfe Creek meteorite crater – believed to have happened when a meteorite plunged into earth more than a million years ago – is the second largest in the world. According to the local Djaru people's Dreaming, the crater, Kandimalal, marks the spot where a huge rainbow snake emerged from the ground.

The crater is best appreciated from the air. **Northwest Regional Airlines** (☎ 9168 6462; www .northwestregional.com.au) offers flights ($255, 70

JANDAMARRA

As a talented young Aboriginal stockman, a Bunuba tribesman, Jandamarra, earned himself the nickname 'pigeon' for his ability to flit around like the local crested spinifex pigeon. Barely in his teens, Jandamarra was equally at home with a pair of reins, sheep shears or a gun in his hands.

Jandamarra was working with a white stockman named Richardson when the station that employed them went broke. Richardson became a policeman and enlisted Jandamarra as his tracker. At this time the relationship between the white settlers and the Bunuba people had reached a low point, with the white settlers (already struggling to survive) not taking kindly to sheep being stolen and the Bunuba, in turn, being outraged at the settlers who had invaded their land and shown little respect for their sacred sites.

The Bunuba people were rounded up by the police and the team of Richardson and Jandamarra were a redoubtable one. Having captured a fair slice of the Bunuba leaders in October 1894, Richardson took them to the Lillimooloora Police Outpost. However, one of the prisoners, Ellemarra, who'd guided Jandamarra through his tribal initiation, convinced the young man to swap allegiances. The night before departing for Derby, Jandamarra shot Richardson in his sleep and freed the prisoners. Thus began one of the few armed resistances to the white occupation.

After ambushing some white settlers, Jandamarra and his crew faced a day-long battle with police and squatters from Derby. Though heavily wounded, Jandamarra eluded the police and for three years taunted them by managing to easily evade capture. Jandamarra's ability to just slip away earned him the nickname 'magic man' among his people and it was believed that only another spirit could ever capture him.

On April 1, 1897 that spirit arrived in the form of an Aboriginal tracker named Mongo Mick, who killed Jandamarra in his Tunnel Creek hideout.

For more on Jandamarra, get a copy of the *Pigeon Heritage Trail* ($2.50) from the Derby or Broome Visitors Centres, or the fascinating *Jandamarra and the Bunuba Resistance* by Howard Pedersen and Banjo Woorunmurra.

minutes) on demand from Halls Creek. Otherwise, it's a challenging drive along a rough 4WD road. The turn-off is 16km west of Halls Creek, from where it's 137km south along the Tanami Track. You'll need plenty of food, water and fuel.

PURNULULU NATIONAL PARK & BUNGLE BUNGLE RANGE

The Purnululu National Park, 3000 sq km of ancient country, is home to the wonderful ochre and black striped 'beehive' domes of the Bungle Bungle Range.

The distinctive rounded rock towers are made of sandstone and rough conglomerates (rocks comprised of pebbles and boulders), moulded by rainfall over millions of years. Their stripes are caused by the differences in clay content and the porosity of the layers; the rock within the dark stripes is more permeable, allowing algae to flourish, while the lighter layers consist of oxidised iron compounds.

While the local Kidja people have always known about them – purnululu means 'sand-stone' in the Kidja language and Bungle Bungle is thought to be a misspelling of 'bundle bundle', a common grass – the formations were only 'discovered' during the mid 1980s, the park created in 1987, and in 2003, added to the World Heritage list.

The park has wonderful Aboriginal art galleries, gorgeous swimming holes within the gorges, and a wide array of wildlife, including over 130 bird species.

The stunning **Echidna Chasm** in the north and **Cathedral Gorge** in the south are about an hour's walk from the car parks, while the soaring **Piccaninny Gorge** is an 18km round trip that takes a full day to walk. The restricted gorges in the northern part of the park can only be seen from the air.

The park is open April to December; rangers are based here during these months. If you're driving, you'll need a high clearance 4WD, as there are five deep creek crossings. The turn-off from the highway is 53km south of Warmun, then 52km along a very rough 4WD-only track to the Three Ways junction. Allow at least 2½ hours to get to the visitors

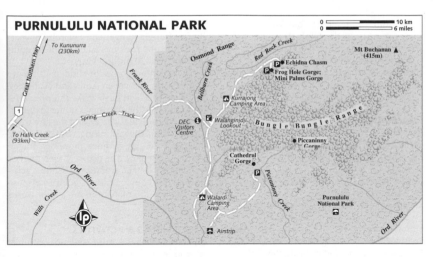

PURNULULU NATIONAL PARK

centre. **Kurrajong Camping Area** and **Walardi Camping Area** have fresh water and toilets (camp sites per person $9).

Tours

East Kimberley Tours (☎ 9168 2213; www.eastkimberley tours.com.au; 1-day tour $396, 2-day tour $796) has a wide range of tours from Kununurra, while several operators include Purnululu in multiday Kimberley tours (see p223). You can also do scenic flights from Kununurra in helicopters with **Slingair** (☎ 9169 1300; www.slingair.com.au; per person 20min tour $175, 1hr tour $450) and light planes with **Alligator Airways** (☎ 9168 1333; www.alligatorairways .com.au; 135min tour per person $230). Helicopters get you closer.

WYNDHAM

☎ 08 / pop 900

A languid outback town at the confluence of five rivers, Wyndham, 60km north of the Great Northern Hwy, was established during the Gold Rush.

Kimberley Motors (☎ 9161 1281; Great Northern Hwy; ☎ 6am-6pm) has tourist information, maps and tide charts and can book fishing and 4WD tours.

As this is crocodile country, a giant 20m concrete replica of one greets you at the entrance to town. The excellent **Wyndham Crocodile Farm** (☎ 9161 1124; Barytes Rd; adult/child $15/8; ☒ 8.30am-4pm Dry, 11am-2pm Wet) has some magnificent specimens and the guides get close to them during an entertaining tour at feeding time (11am). **Warriu Dreamtime Park**

(Koolama St) features enormous bronze statues of an Aboriginal family and some native animals. **Five Rivers Lookout** on Mt Bastion has splendid views of the King, Pentecost, Durack, Forrest and Ord Rivers entering the Cambridge Gulf; best at sunrise and sunset.

About 15km from Wyndham is **Parry Lagoons Nature Reserve**, a beautiful wetlands that teems with birds in the Wet, and the **Grotto**, a peaceful pool surrounded by lush vegetation in a small gorge.

Wyndham Caravan Park (☎ 9161 1064; Baker St, Three Mile; unpowered/powered sites per person $10/13, dongas s $45; ☒) has a wonderful boab in its shady grounds, offers fishing tours, and provides a good campers kitchen where you can cook your catch in the evening.

The rooms at **Wyndham Town Hotel** (☎ 9161 1202; O'Donnell St; s/d $88/110, meals $5-24; ☒) are basic, but you'll be spending most of your time in the atmospheric pub meeting the locals. The home-style steaks and salads are enormous.

You can do a one-day Wyndham tour from Kununurra with **Triangle Tours** (☎ 9168 1272; triangletours@bigpond.com; adult/child $165/90).

KUNUNURRA

☎ 08 / pop 6000

Kununurra is a neat, pleasant town nestled beneath the red domes of Mirima National Park, with lovely Lily Creek Lagoon lapping at its shores. Founded in 1960 as the centre for the Ord River irrigation scheme, an ambitious government incentive to harness the region's

THE KIMBERLEYS

water, tourism developed quickly thanks to the proximity of the Gibb River Rd, Lake Argyle, and Purnululu National Park.

If you're coming from the Northern Territory, note that there's a 90-minute time difference, and throw out your fruit as strict quarantine restrictions apply in WA.

Information

Boab Books (☎ 9169 2574; 114b Coolibah Dr) Has an excellent range of books on the Kimberley.

DEC office (☎ 9168 0200; Konkerberry Dr) For park permits.

District Hospital (☎ 9168 1522; 96 Coolibah Dr; ☺ 24hr) Emergency facilities.

Kununurra Telecentre (☎ 9169 1868; Coolibah Dr; ☺ 8am-5pm Mon-Fri, 9am-1pm Sat) Internet.

Visitors centre (☎ 9168 1177; www.kununurratourism .com; Coolibah Dr; ☺ 8am-5pm Mon-Fri, 9am-4pm Sat Dry, 8am-5pm Mon-Fri, 9am-1pm Sat Wet) Has tonnes of information, and can advise on road conditions and book tours.

Sights & Activities

MIRIMA NATIONAL PARK

A short stroll from town (1.5km), **Mirima National Park** (per car $9) is a stunning area of rugged sedimentary formations that look like a mini Bungle Bungle Range. The 350 million–year-old sandstone rock has taken shape by uplift over the past 20 million years.

The splendid gorges of Hidden Valley are home to spinifex-covered hills and boab trees. There are excellent bush walks and wonderful bird- and wildlife; Mirima is home to honeyeaters, finches, black kites, and the rare white quilled rock pigeon, along with wallabies, dingoes, echidnas, pythons, monitors, dragon lizards and snakes. The two easy, well-marked walking tracks take around a half-hour each – head here a couple of hours before sunset so you can see the magic the sun's light works on the rocks.

OTHER SIGHTS & ACTIVITIES

Lily Creek Lagoon is a mini-wetlands with lots of wonderful birdlife and freshwater crocs. Locals like to stroll here in the late afternoon. **Lake Kununurra**, also called Diversion Dam, has pleasant picnic spots and great fishing.

The **Waringarri Aboriginal Arts Centre** (☎ 9168 2212; 16 Speargrass Rd; ☺ 8.30am-4.30pm Mon-Fri) is an Aboriginal-owned art gallery and studio

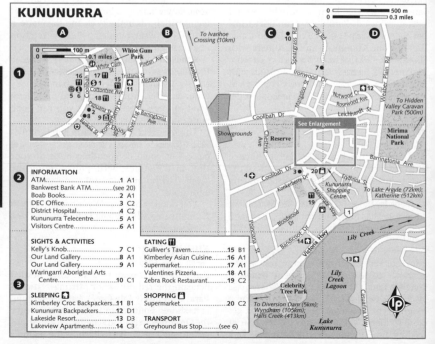

KUNUNURRA

INFORMATION	
ATM	1 A1
Bankwest Bank ATM	(see 20)
Boab Books	2 A1
DEC Office	3 C2
District Hospital	4 C2
Kununurra Telecentre	5 A1
Visitors Centre	6 A1

SIGHTS & ACTIVITIES	
Kelly's Knob	7 C1
Our Land Gallery	8 A1
Our Land Gallery	9 A1
Waringarri Aboriginal Arts Centre	10 C1

SLEEPING	
Kimberley Croc Backpackers	11 B1
Kununurra Backpackers	12 D1
Lakeside Resort	13 D3
Lakeview Apartments	14 C3

EATING	
Gulliver's Tavern	15 B1
Kimberley Asian Cuisine	16 A1
Supermarket	17 A1
Valentines Pizzeria	18 A1
Zebra Rock Restaurant	19 C2

SHOPPING	
Supermarket	20 C2

TRANSPORT	
Greyhound Bus Stop	(see 6)

To Ivanhoe Crossing (10km)

To Hidden Valley Caravan Park (500km)

See Enlargement

Mirima National Park

Showgrounds

Reserve

Kununurra Shopping Centre

To Lake Argyle (72km); Katherine (512km)

Lily Creek

Lily Creek Lagoon

Celebrity Tree Park

To Diversion Dam (5km); Wyndham (105km); Halls Creek (413km)

Lake Kununurra

White Gum Park

with local artists working in their unique abstract style using ochre pigments. **Our Land Gallery** (☎ 9168 1881; 10 Papuana St & 110 Coolibah Dr; ❧ 9am-5pm) specialises in ochre paintings from the Kimberley in the Papuana St gallery, and around the corner sells authentic Aboriginal artefacts.

Kelly's Knob is a favourite sunset viewpoint on the town's northern fringe. During the Wet, distant thunderstorms are spectacular from here, although it's sometimes struck by lightning!

Tours

A number of tour companies offer canoeing trips on the Ord River over one, two or three days. Eco-certified **Go Wild** (☎ 1300 66 33 69; www .gowild.com.au; 1-day tour per person $150) also offers abseiling tours. **Kununurra Cruises** (☎ 9168 1718; adult/child $67/25) does popular sunset 'BBQ Boat' cruises on Lily Creek Lagoon and the Ord.

Sleeping

Hidden Valley Caravan Park (☎ 9168 1790; Weaber Plains Rd; unpowered/powered sites $20/22, cabin d $95, extra adult $10; ☒) Under the looming crags of Mirima National Park, this excellent little park is a bit out of the way. The amenities are good, there's a large pool and the self-contained cabins are well priced.

Lakeside Resort (☎ 9169 1092; www.lakeside.com .au; Casuarina Way; unpowered/powered sites $18/22, self-catering studio d $125, motel d $155; ☒ ☒) At the edge of Lily Creek Lagoon, there's a good range of accommodation set within leafy gardens.

Lakeview Apartments (☎ 9168 0000; www.lakeview apartments@wn.com.au; 224 Victoria Hwy; 1-/2-/3-bedroom apt $165/195/255; ☒ ☒) These spacious, self-contained apartments across the road from Lily Creek Lagoon have all mod cons and fully-equipped kitchens.

Kununurra Backpackers (☎ 1800 641 998, 9169 1998; www.adventure.kimberley.net.au; 24 Nutwood Cres; dm $21-23, d $54; ☒ ☒) and **Kimberley Croc Backpackers** (☎ 1300 136 702, 9168 2702; www.kimberleycroc.com.au; 120 Konkerberry Dr; dm $22-24, d $55; ☒ ☒) are both excellent value with lush tropical gardens, swimming pools, barbecues, good communal facilities and Kimberley tours.

Eating

There are two well-stocked supermarkets, bakeries, and a couple of takeaways.

Valentine's Pizzeria (☎ 9169 1167; 4 Cottontree Ave; pizzas $12-20; ❧ 5-9pm) Thick with toppings, they

may not be authentic but these filling pizzas will do the trick. BYO or get it delivered to your room. Tex-Mex is also on the menu.

Kimberley Asian Cuisine (☎ 9169 3698; 75 Coolibah Dr; mains $14-21) This pan-Asian place, serving Aussie versions of Chinese and Thai, will satisfy those Asian cravings. Eat in (BYO) or takeaway.

Gulliver's Tavern (☎ 9168 1666; 196 Cottontree Ave; $14-25) Does hearty counter meals – all the usual suspects plus a smattering of Asian dishes (Thai beef salad, hokkien noodles etc) and local favourites such as the Barra Burger.

Zebra Rock Restaurant (☎ 9168 1344; Kununurra Hotel, 8 Messmate Way; $13-26) has the most sophisticated menu, albeit served in casual pub surroundings – bruschetta, tasting platters, 'Ocean and Earth', barramundi and Thai curries.

Getting There & Around

Qantas/Airlink (☎ 13 13 13) flies to Broome (three weekly) and Darwin (five weekly). **Greyhound** (☎ 13 20 30) has daily buses to Darwin and Perth that stop at the visitors centre. Destinations include Halls Creek, Fitzroy Crossing, Derby and Broome.

LAKE ARGYLE

Enormous Lake Argyle, Australia's second-largest reservoir, created by the Ord River Dam, can hold around 18 times the water of Sydney Harbour. Unfortunately, there hasn't been enough rainfall for the Lake to reach capacity since it filled to the brim in 1973 (and the spillway flowed until 1984!). However this bold 1969 initiative to harness the Ord River waters and develop the tropical north has still had amazing results: 58,000 hectares of dry clay plains have been irrigated, the riverside ecology improved, and wildlife numbers increased (especially turtles, fish and freshwater crocodiles), with some struck off endangered species lists (eg the buff-sided robin). The scenery is spectacular, with high, steep red ridges plunging into the lake's deep blue waters.

Atmospheric **Argyle Homestead** (☎ 9167 8088; adult/child $3/1; ❧ 7am-4pm Apr-Oct), home of the Durack pastoral family and currently managed by Michael Durack, was moved here when its original site was flooded. Fascinating old black-and-white photos and memorabilia are displayed and there's a small family cemetery where some of the pioneering Duracks are buried. Pick up copies of Dame Mary

Durack's *Kings in Grass Castles* and *Sons in the Saddle,* detailing the family's extraordinary achievements.

Lake Argyle Cruises (☎ 9168 7687; cruises $40-120, Kununurra transfers $15) offers several cruises, including swimming and fishing, but book ahead as they'll cancel trips if there aren't enough numbers. Award-winning **Triple J Tours** (☎ 9168 2682; admin@triplejtours.net.au; adult/child $170/100) offers the more comprehensive

'Lake Argyle-Ord River Combo Tour' visiting Argyle Homestead, cruising Lake Argyle, and returning by boat to Kununurra on the Ord River.

Lake Argyle Tourist Village (☎ 9168 7777; paradise@lakeargyle.com; Parker Rd), once a wonderful caravan park and camping grand, was closing at time of research for major redevelopment. It's due to open its luxury self-contained villas sometime in 2007.

Directory

CONTENTS

ACCOMMODATION

Western Australia (WA) offers every type of accommodation. Experiences range from the self-catering crowds in the caravan parks and camping grounds and the communal conviviality of hostels, to gourmet breakfasts in guesthouses and relaxing resorts, plus the gamut of hotel and motel lodgings. Just don't expect to find all of the above in the one town.

Listings in the Sleeping sections of this guidebook are ordered in budget order. For Perth, places that charge up to $80 per double have been categorised as budget accommodation. Midrange prices are from $80 to $150 per double, while the top-end tag is applied to places charging more than $150 per double.

PRACTICALITIES

- Leaf through the *West Australian* or the national *Australian* broadsheet from Monday to Saturday, and the *Sunday Times* on Sunday.

- Switch on the box to watch the ad-free ABC, the government-sponsored and multicultural SBS, or the commercial TV stations Seven, Nine and Ten.

- Plug your hairdryer into a three-pin adaptor (not the same as British three-pin adaptors) before plugging into the electricity supply (220-240V AC, 50Hz).

- DVDs you buy or watch will probably be Region 4 and will be based on the PAL system.

In areas other than Perth, budget is classified as doubles up to $60, midrange from $60 to $100, and top end over $100.

In most areas you'll find seasonal price variations. Over summer and at other peak times, particularly school and public holidays, prices are usually at their highest, whereas outside these times discounts and lower walk-in rates can be found. One exception is the far North, where the Wet season (November to April) is the low season and prices can drop by as much as 50%. High-season prices are quoted in this guidebook unless otherwise indicated.

B&Bs

The WA bed and breakfast (B&B) options include everything from restored miners' cottages, converted barns, rambling old houses, upmarket country manors and beachside bungalows to a simple bedroom in a family home. Tariffs are typically in the $70 to $150 (per double) bracket, but can be much higher for exclusive and/or historic houses. For online information, try www.australian bandb.com.au, www.babs.com.au or www .ozbedandbreakfast.com.

Camping & Caravan Parks

Whether you're packing a tent, driving a campervan or towing a caravan, camping in the bush is a highlight of travelling in WA. In the outback and up north you often won't even need a tent, and nights spent around a campfire under the stars are unforgettable. WA has roadside overnight stops (designated by a '24' symbol) for travellers on the road that are free and usually well positioned to break up a long drive. The handy *WA Main Roads* brochure, available at most visitors centres, covers these and details the facilities available at each stop.

Designated camp sites in national parks and state forests are often the most convenient place to stay if you want to explore a park over a few days. They cost $6.50 per adult with no or basic facilities other than a place to pitch your tent. For sites with showers (including unpowered caravan sites) the price is $7.50 per person. Note that you will also need to pay national park entrance fees – this is separate to the camping fee. If you're exploring several parks, it makes sense to pick up a one month national parks pass ($35).

Commercial caravan parks and camping grounds are found all over WA and are excellent value. Idyllically located parks can be seductive – often people end up staying months rather than days once they see that the fishing or surfing is unsurpassable! Large parks offer powered and unpowered sites. Expect to pay around $20 per site for camp sites and $25/18 for powered/unpowered caravan sites. Increasingly, caravan parks are offering more 'cabin' or 'motel' style accommodation with ensuites, and these can often be better than the town's hotel/motel accommodation – although, for most, you will need your own linen. Expect to pay upwards of $80 for these per cabin.

Before you head off be sure to get a free copy of the guide to *Caravanning, Camping and Motorhoming in WA*, available at visitors centres around the state, or visit the website www.caravanwa.com.au.

Farm & Station Stays

For a true outback experience, some of the state's farms and stations offer a rural getaway. The Gascoyne, Pilbara and Murchison areas of WA are popular spots for station stays. At some you can kick back and watch other people raise a sweat, while others require you to pull your weight. Most accommodation is very comfortable – in the main homestead (B&B-style, many providing dinner on re-

quest) or in self-contained cottages on the property. Other farms provide budget options in outbuildings or former shearers' quarters – providing you an opportunity to wear that Akubra hat without looking silly. Check out options on the websites for **WA Farms, Stations & Country Retreats** (www.farmstaywa.com) and **Australian Farmstay** (www.australiafarmstay.com.au).

Hostels

Hostels are a highly social and very economical fixture of the WA accommodation scene. The ones that are good are very, very good indeed, many with swimming pools, bars, weekly BBQs and free transport. Staff can offer help in securing seasonal work.

HOSTEL ORGANISATIONS

The **Youth Hostel Association** (YHA; ☎ 9287 3300; 300 Wellington St, Perth; www.yha.com.au; ⏰ 9am-5pm Mon-Sat) is part of the **International Youth Hostel Federation** (IYHF; www.hihostels.com), also known as Hostelling International (HI). So if you're already a member of that organisation in your own country, your membership entitles you to YHA rates in the relevant WA hostels. Visitors to Australia should purchase a HI card preferably in their country of residence, but can also buy one at major local YHA hostels at a cost of $35 for 12 months; see the HI website for further details. Australian residents can become full YHA members for $52/85 for one/two years; join online, at a state office or any youth hostel.

VIP Backpackers (☎ 07 3395 6111; www.vipbackpackers .com) has a few members in WA (several in Perth) and many more around Australia and overseas. For $39 you'll receive a 12-month membership, entitling you to discounts on accommodation and a 5% to 15% discount on other products such as air and bus transport, tours and activities. You can join online, at VIP hostels or at larger agencies dealing in backpacker travel.

INDEPENDENT HOSTELS

WA has a rapidly growing group of independent hostels of varying quality. Fierce competition for the backpacker dollar means that standards are generally kept pretty high – and there are plenty of bonus enticements, such as free internet access, courtesy buses, and discount meal and beer vouchers. If you crave peace and quiet, avoid the 'party places'; instead, stay in smaller, more intimate hostels where often the owner is also the manager. Note than in some rural areas hostels have become permanent addresses for workers looking for employment and are often booked out. Wherever possible we've omitted these from the book.

Independent backpacker establishments typically charge $19 to $26 for a dorm bed and $40 to $60 for a twin or double room (usually without bathroom), often with a small discount if you're a member of YHA or VIP.

Hotels & Motels

In the more touristy areas hotels are generally comfortable but anonymous. These places tend to have a pool, restaurant/café, room service and the expected mod-cons. We quote 'rack rates' (official advertised rates) throughout this book, but often hotels/motels offer regular discounts and special deals.

For comfortable midrange accommodation that's available all over the state, motels (or motor inns) are the places to stay. Prices vary and there's rarely a cheaper rate for singles, making them better for couples or groups of three. Most motels are reasonably modern, low-rise and have similar facilities (tea- and coffee-making, fridge, TV, air-con, bathroom) but the price will indicate the standard. You'll mostly pay between $70 and $150 for a room. In rural areas it pays to book ahead as this accommodation is often be booked out by government workers or tour groups.

Pubs

Pubs (from the term 'public house') in Australia are often called hotels – and they do often have accommodation. In country towns, pubs are invariably found in the town centre and as they were generally built during boom times, they're often the grandest buildings in town. In tourist areas some of these pubs have been restored as heritage buildings, but generally the rooms to rent remain old-fashioned, with a long, creaky amble down the hall to the bathroom. You can sometimes rent a single room at a country pub for not much more than a hostel dorm, and you'll be in the social heart of the town to boot. But if you're a light sleeper, never book a room above the bar.

Standard pubs have singles/doubles with shared facilities starting from around $30/50 – obviously more if you want a private bathroom. Some pubs have separate motel-style accommodation at the back of the hotel as well. Few have a separate reception area – just ask in the bar if there are rooms available. For women travellers, see p259.

Rental Accommodation

The ubiquitous holiday flat resembles a motel unit but has a kitchen or cooking facilities. It can come with two or more bedrooms and is often rented on a weekly basis – prices per night are higher for shorter stays. For a two-bedroom flat, expect to pay anywhere from $60 to $95 per night. The other alternative in major cities is to take out a serviced apartment. The **Tourism WA** (www.westernaustralia .com) website has a database of serviced and unserviced apartments. **Number Six** (www.number six.com.au) has a number of excellent apartments in great locations around Fremantle and Margaret River.

If you're interested in a shared flat or house for a long-term stay, delve into the classified advertisements sections of the daily newspapers; Wednesday and Saturday are usually the best days. Notice boards in universities, hostels, bookshops and cafés are also good to check out.

BOOK ACCOMMODATION ONLINE

For more accommodation reviews and recommendations by Lonely Planet authors, check out the online booking service at www.lonelyplanet.com. You'll find the true, insider lowdown on the best places to stay. Reviews are thorough and independent. Best of all, you can book online.

ACTIVITIES

With all of this brilliant sunshine and incredible landscapes and seascapes, it's little wonder that activities in WA are based around the great outdoors. WA has some remarkable bushwalking terrain and peaceful camping options, quite often located in pristine national parks. Cycling tours are popular in the south of the state, with some fun mountain-biking terrain to test your skills. WA is a fishing enthusiast's notion of heaven, with surf, stream and game fishing on the agenda – not to mention the challenge of the hard fighting (and tasty!) barramundi.

If you want to get in the water, the diving and snorkelling in WA are fantastic – in the crystal-clear waters you will encounter reefs teeming with sea life. Back up on the surface, WA is a world-renowned destination for surfers, windsurfers and kite-surfers. WA is one of the world's prime places to do some wildlife-watching – whales, dugongs, whale sharks and dolphins are just some of the visitors you'll encounter. For more details, check out the Outdoors chapter, p37.

BUSINESS HOURS

Most shops and businesses in WA are open from 8.30am to 5.30pm Monday to Friday, and from 8.30am to 5pm on Saturday. Sunday trading is from noon to 6pm in the principal tourist precincts of Perth and Fremantle, and some suburban areas such as Subiaco and Northbridge – though opening times differ from shop to shop. In the larger towns there is one late-shopping night each week with doors open until 9pm. In central Perth it's Friday; in the suburbs it's Thursday. Supermarket hours vary; you will find that delis (milk bars) and convenience stores often open until late.

Banks are normally open from 9.30am to 4pm Monday to Thursday and until 5pm on Friday. Post offices are open from 9am to 5pm Monday to Friday, but you can also buy stamps on Saturday morning at post office agencies (operated from newsagencies) and from Australia Post shops in the major cities.

Restaurants in Perth, and the larger, more tourist-oriented towns, typically open at noon for lunch and between 6pm and 7pm for dinner; most dinner bookings are made for 7.30pm or 8pm. Restaurants are typically open until at least 9pm but tend to serve food until later on Friday and Saturday. Pubs and bars often open for lunchtime tipples and continue well into the evening, particularly from Thursday to Saturday. In WA's small towns where there are only one or two options for meals, dinner service is generally finished by 8pm.

Keep in mind that nearly all attractions are closed on Christmas Day.

CHILDREN
Practicalities

Perth and most major towns have centrally located public rooms where parents can go to nurse their baby or change nappies; check with the local tourist office or city council for details. While many Australians have a relaxed attitude about breast-feeding or nappy changing in public, some don't.

Many motels and the better-equipped caravan parks have playgrounds and swimming pools, and can supply cots and baby baths – motels in the more touristy areas may also have in-house children's videos and child-minding services. Top-end hotels and many (but not all) midrange hotels are well versed in the needs of guests who have children. B&Bs, on the other hand, often market themselves as sanctuaries from all things child-related. Many cafés and restaurants lack a specialised children's menu, but many others do have kids' meals, or will provide small serves from the main menu. Some also supply high chairs.

Child concessions (and family rates) often apply for such things as accommodation, tours, admission fees, and air, bus and train transport, with some discounts as high as 50% of the adult rate. However, the definition of 'child' can vary from under 12 to under 18 years. Accommodation concessions generally apply to children under 12 years sharing the same room as adults. On the major airlines, infants travel free provided they don't occupy a seat – child fares usually apply between the ages of two and 11 years.

Medical services and facilities in Australia are of a high standard, and items such as baby food formula and disposable nappies are widely available in urban centres. Major hire-car companies will supply and fit booster seats for you at a charge.

Sights & Activities

WA is one big children's playground, with no shortage of active, interesting and educational things to do. Destinations such as Broome, Monkey Mia and Kalbarri are fantastic for children, with excellent beaches, parks and the chance to interact with the local wildlife, while Perth offers up some fascinating educational opportunities at its museums and galleries – perfect if the weather turns nasty. Every town or city has at least some parkland and many have public skateboard parks. For more ideas on how to keep kids occupied, see p67.

CLIMATE CHARTS

WA's size means there's a lot of climatic variation. See p11 for more information on the seasons.

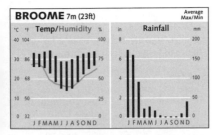

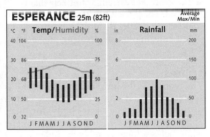

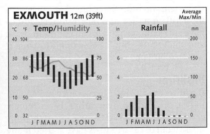

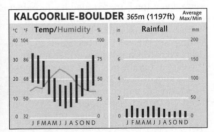

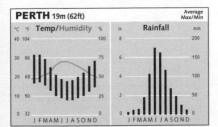

CUSTOMS

For comprehensive information on customs regulations, contact the **Australian Customs Service** (☎ 1300 363 263, 02 6275 6666; www.customs .gov.au).

When entering Australia you can bring most articles in free of duty provided that customs is satisfied they are for personal use and you'll be taking them with you when you leave. There's a duty-free quota per person of 2.25 litres of alcoholic beverages, 250 cigarettes and dutiable goods up to the value of $900 – note that perfume concentrates are included in this.

When it comes to prohibited goods, there are a few things you should be particularly conscientious about. The first is drugs, which customs authorities are adept at sniffing out. If you are carrying prescription drugs or medicines, it is advisable to have a letter or prescription from your medical practitioner describing your medication and medical condition.

The second is all food, plant material and animal products. On arrival, declare all goods of animal or plant origin (wooden spoons, straw hats, the lot). Australia takes quarantine very seriously as authorities are keen to protect Australia's unique environment and agricultural industries by preventing weeds, pests or diseases getting into the country. Luggage is screened or X-rayed – if you fail to declare quarantine items on arrival and are caught, you risk an on-the-spot fine of over $200 and an exceptionally condescending lecture, or even prosecution and imprisonment. For more information on quarantine regulations contact the **Australian Quarantine and Inspection Service** (AQIS; ☎ 1800 020 504, 02 6272 3933; www.aqis.gov.au).

DANGERS & ANNOYANCES
Animal Hazards

Australia is home to some seriously dangerous creatures and critters. On land there are poisonous snakes and spiders, while in the sea the deadly box jellyfish awaits and the theme tune from *Jaws* plays constantly as white pointer sharks cruise up and down the coast. Just so you're not safe anywhere, the saltwater crocodile spans both. However, in reality you're unlikely to see many of these creatures in the wild, much less be attacked by one – you're far more likely to suffer the consequences of downing too many beers, getting seriously sunburnt or trying not to hit that kangaroo in your headlights at dusk.

BOX JELLYFISH

There have been numerous fatal encounters between swimmers and these large jellyfish on the northern coast. Also known as the sea wasp or 'stinger', their venomous tentacles can grow up to 3m long. You can be stung anytime, but November to March is when you should stay out of the water unless you're wearing a 'stinger suit', available from sporting shops in the stinger zone.

For information on treating box jellyfish stings, see p278.

CROCODILES

Up in the northwest of WA, saltwater crocodiles can be a real danger. As well as living around the coast they are found in estuaries, creeks and rivers, sometimes a long way inland. Observe safety signs or ask locals whether an inviting waterhole or river is croc-free before plunging in – these precautions have been fatally ignored in the past, with the last fatality in 1987 and an attack in 2006.

INSECTS

For four to six months of the year you'll have to cope with those two banes of the Australian outdoors: the fly and the mosquito (or 'mozzie'). Flies are more prevalent in the outback and to counter them the humble fly net is effective, though never glamorous. Repellents such as Aerogard and Rid may also help to deter the little bastards, but don't count on it.

Mozzies are a problem in summer, especially near wetlands in tropical areas, and some species are carriers of viral infections (see p279). Try to keep your arms and legs covered after sunset and slap on that repellent.

One favourite little pest in the northern coastal areas is the biting midge (often called a sandfly). These cheeky little bloodsuckers can make a meal of you without you noticing for several hours – when you start itching. While locals can infuriatingly appear immune, it's almost a rite of passage for those heading North to be covered in bites – until you learn to cover up at dusk.

Ticks and leeches are also common. See p279 for advice on how to avoid their wrath.

SHARKS

There has been two fatal shark attacks in the last few years in WA – both at reasonably popular surfing and swimming spots. Be aware that when you are in the water you are in the shark's domain and while this isn't comfort, statistically you have a far greater chance of being struck by lightning.

SNAKES

There are many venomous snakes in the Australian bush, the most common being the brown and tiger snakes. Unless you're interfering with one, or have the misfortune to stand on one, it's extremely unlikely that you'll be bitten. The golden rule if you see a snake is to do as the Beatles do and 'let it be'.

For information on treating snake bites, see p278.

SPIDERS

The redback is the most common poisonous spider in WA. It's small and black with a distinctive red stripe on its body; for bites, apply ice and seek medical attention. The white tail is a long, thin black spider with a white tail, and has a fierce bite that can lead to local inflammation and ulceration. Hospitals have antivenin on hand for all common snake and spider bites, but it helps to know what it was that bit you.

Bushfires

Bushfires are a regular occurrence in WA and in hot, dry and windy weather, be extremely careful with any naked flame – cigarette butts thrown out of car windows have started many a fire. On a total fire ban day it's forbidden even to use a camping stove in the open.

Bushwalkers should seek local advice before setting out. When a total fire ban is in place, delay your trip until the weather improves. If you're out in the bush and you see smoke, even a long distance away, take heed – bushfires move fast and change direction with the wind. Go to the nearest open space, downhill if possible. A forested ridge, on the other hand, is the most dangerous place to be.

Crime

WA is a relatively safe place to visit but you should still take reasonable precautions. Don't leave hotel rooms or cars unlocked, and don't leave your valuables unattended or visible through a car window.

In recent years, there have been several reports of drugged drinks in Perth pubs and clubs. Authorities advise women to refuse drinks offered by strangers in bars and to drink bottled alcohol rather than that from a glass. See p259 for more precautions.

Hypothermia
More bushwalkers actually die of cold than in bushfires. Even in summer, temperatures can drop below freezing at night and the weather can change very quickly. Exposure in even moderately cool temperatures can sometimes result in hypothermia. For more information on hypothermia and how to minimise its risk, see p279.

On the Road
Australian drivers are generally a courteous bunch, but rural 'petrolheads', inner-city speedsters and drink drivers can pose risks. Potential dangers on the open road include wildlife, such as kangaroos (mainly at dusk and dawn); fatigue, caused by travelling long distances without the necessary breaks; and excessive speed. Driving on dirt roads can also be tricky for the uninitiated. For more information on these and other potential dangers, see p272).

Outback Travel
If you're keen to explore outback WA, it's important not to embark on your trip without careful planning and preparation. Travellers regularly encounter difficulties in the harsh outback conditions, and trips occasionally prove fatal. For tips and advice on travelling in the outback, see p271.

Swimming
Popular beaches are patrolled by surf lifesavers and flags mark off patrolled areas. Even so, WA's surf beaches can be dangerous places to swim if you aren't used to the often-heavy surf. Undertows (or 'rips') are the main problem. If you find yourself being carried out by a rip, just keep afloat; don't panic or try to swim against the rip, which will exhaust you. In most cases the current will stop within a couple of hundred metres of the shore and you can then swim parallel to the shore for a short way to get out of the rip and swim back to land.

On the south coast, freak 'king waves' from the Southern Ocean can sometimes break on the shore with little or no warning, dragging people out to sea. In populated areas there are warning signs; in other areas be extremely careful.

A number of people are paralysed every year by diving into waves in shallow water and hitting a sand bar; check the depth of the water before you leap.

DISCOUNT CARDS
Carrying a student card entitles you to a wide variety of discounts throughout WA. The most common card is the **International Student Identity Card** (ISIC; www.isic.org), which is issued to full-time students aged 12 years and over, and gives the bearer discounts on accommodation, transport and admission to some attractions. It's available from student unions, hostelling organisations and some travel agencies; for more information, see the website of the **International Student Travel Confederation** (ISTC; www.istc.org).

The ISTC is also the body behind the **International Youth Travel Card** (IYTC or Go25), which is issued to people who are between 12 and 26 years of age and not fulltime students, and gives equivalent benefits to the ISIC. A similar ISTC brainchild is the **International Teacher Identity Card** (ITIC), available to teaching professionals.

EMBASSIES & CONSULATES
Australian Embassies & Consulates
The website of the **Department of Foreign Affairs & Trade** (www.dfat.gov.au) provides a full listing of all Australian diplomatic missions overseas. They include:

Canada (☎ 613-236 0841; www.canada.embassy.gov.au; Suite 710, 50 O'Connor St, Ottawa, Ontario K1P 6L2) Also in Vancouver and Toronto.

France (☎ 01-40 59 33 00; www.france.embassy.gov.au; 4 Rue Jean Rey, 75724 Cedex 15, Paris)

Germany (☎ 030-880 0880; www.germany.embassy.gov .au; Wallstrasse 76-79, Berlin 10179) Also in Frankfurt.

Indonesia (☎ 021-2550 5555; www.indonesia.embassy .gov.au; Jalan HR Rasuna Said Kav C15-16, Kuningan, Jakarta Selatan 12940) Also in Medan (Sumatra) and Denpasar (Bali).

Ireland (☎ 01-664 5300; www.australianembassy.ie; 2nd fl, Fitzwilton House, Wilton Terrace, Dublin 2)

Japan (☎ 03-5232 4111; www.australia.or.jp; 2-1-14 Mita, Minato-Ku, Tokyo 108-8361) Also in Osaka, Nagoya and Fukuoka City.

Netherlands (☎ 070-310 82 00; www.netherlands .embassy.gov.au; Carnegielaan 4, The Hague 2517 KH)

New Zealand Wellington (☎ 04-473 6411; www .newzealand.embassy.gov.au; 72-78 Hobson St, Thorndon, Wellington); Auckland (☎ 09-921 8800; Level 7, Price Waterhouse Coopers Bldg, 186-194 Quay St, Auckland)

Singapore (☎ 6836 4100; www.singapore.embassy.gov
.au; 25 Napier Rd, Singapore 258507)
UK (☎ 020-7379 4334; www.uk.embassy.gov.au;
Australia House, The Strand, London WC2B 4LA) Also in
Edinburgh and Manchester.
USA (☎ 202-797 3000; www.usa.embassy.gov.au; 1601
Massachusetts Ave NW, Washington DC NW 20036-2273)
Also in Los Angeles, New York and other major cities.

Embassies & Consulates in Australia

The principal diplomatic representations to
Australia are in Canberra, but about 30 coun-
tries are represented in Perth by consular staff
or trade representatives. Look in the *Yellow
Pages* directory for a more complete listing.
Canada (Map pp58-9; ☎ 9322 7930; http://geo.inter
national.gc.ca/asia/australia/menu-en.asp; 3rd fl, 267 St
Georges Terrace, Perth 6000)
France (Map pp54-5; ☎ 6389 2230; www.ambafrance
-au.org; 10 Stirling Hwy, Nedlands 6009)
Germany (Map pp58-9; ☎ 9325 8851; www.german
embassy.org.au; 8th fl, 16 St Georges Terrace, Perth 6000)
Japan (Map pp58-9; ☎ 9321 7816; www.japan.org.au;
21st fl, Forrest Centre, 221 St Georges Terrace, Perth 6000)
Netherlands (Map p61; ☎ 9486 1579; www.nether
lands.org.au; Unit 1, 88 Thomas St, West Perth 6005)
UK (Map pp58-9; ☎ 9224 4700; www.britaus.net; Level
26, Allendale Square, 77 St Georges Terrace, Perth 6000)
USA (Map pp58-9; ☎ 9202 1224; http://perth.usconsulate
.gov; 16 St Georges Terrace, Perth 6000)

It's important to realise what your own embassy – the embassy of the country of which
you are a citizen – can and can't do to help you
if you get into trouble. Generally speaking,
it won't be much help in emergencies if the
trouble you're in is even remotely your own
fault. Remember that while in Australia you
are bound by Australian laws. Your embassy
will not be sympathetic if you end up in jail
after committing a crime locally, even if such
actions are legal in your own country.

FESTIVALS & EVENTS
January
Perth Cup (www.perthracing.org.au) New Year's Day
sees Perth's biggest day at the races, with the party people
heading to 'Tentland' for DJs and daiquiris.
Lancelin Ocean Classic In early January tiny Lancelin's
renowned blustery conditions attract thousands for its
world-famous windsurfing event, with wave, slalom and
the popular marathon event.
Fremantle Sardine Festival This one-day food
festival includes street parades and stalls on Fremantle's
Esplanade.

February
Perth International Arts Festival (www.perthfestival
.com.au) Several weeks of multiarts entertainment, including theatre, dance, music, film and visual arts.
Leeuwin Concert Series (www.leeuwinestate.com.au)
The fabulous Leeuwin Estate winery in Margaret River
hosts world-class performers from popular music, opera
and stage during its annual event in mid-February, with
other concerts running from January to April.

March
Margaret River Pro (www.margaretriverpro.com) This
World Qualifying Series (WQS) event sees the world's best
up-and-coming surfers battle it out in the epic surf at
Margaret River from late March to early April.

April
Broome Arts & Music Festival (www.bamf.org
.au) Running through to June, this festival showcases
the Kimberley's wealth of talented musicians, artists and
dancers with the Gekko Lounge performances being a
standout.

May
Ord Valley Muster (www.ordvalleymuster.com) A
two-week annual community event in the East Kimberley
featuring a grand opening concert on the banks of the Ord
River, a dam-to-dam boat race and a rodeo.

June
Port Hedland Black Rock Stakes (www.blackrock
stakes.pilbara.net.au) A hard-core annual race for charity,
where teams push 'wheelbarrows' weighted with iron ore
over a 120km course.
Broome Fringe Arts Festival Local artists highlight
'fringe arts' during this festival, which features markets, art
installations, workshops and Aboriginal art exhibitions.

July
**National Aboriginal & Islander Day Observance
Committee (Naidoc) week** Indigenous art exhibitions
and performances take place throughout WA during
Naidoc week.

August
Avon Descent (www.avondescent.com.au) In the
'world's greatest whitewater event', powerboats, kayaks
and canoes race 133km down the Avon River from
Northam.
Shinju Matsuri (Festival of the Pearl; www.shinjumatsuri
.com) Broome commemorates its early pearling years and
the town's multicultural heritage.
Broome Opera Under the Stars (www.operaunderthe
stars.com.au) World-class opera performers sing under
clear Kimberley night skies.

September

York Jazz Festival In late September jazz aficionados flock to the historic Avon Valley town of York for concerts, busking and jamming.

Kalgoorlie-Boulder Racing Round The 'round' sees lots of betting and boozing during this week of horse racing.

Perth Wildflower Festival (www.bgpa.wa.gov.au) In late September to early October, Kings Park and the Botanic Garden host displays, workshops and guided walks in this annual event celebrating WA's unique and spectacular wildflowers.

Sunshine Festival (www.sunshinefestival.com.au) Geraldton and Greenough celebrate with dragon boat races, parades and parties. Sunshine guaranteed.

October

Blessing of the Fleet Popular historic festival introduced to Fremantle by young Italian fishermen in 1948 and celebrated in mid-October.

Royal Perth Show (www.perthroyalshow.com.au) The west's biggest agriculture, food and wine show – with sideshow rides and showbags for the kids.

November

Awesome Arts Festival (www.awesomearts.com) There's plenty of activities during this contemporary arts festival for kids.

Fremantle Festival (www.fremantlefestivals.com) A week or so of performances, music, dance, comedy, visual arts, street theatre and workshops.

Broome Mango Festival Broome celebrates the mango harvest with mango-themed everything and a Great Chefs of Broome Cook-Off.

Margaret River Wine Region Festival (www.mrwine fest.org.au) This four-day festival titillates the tastebuds with the best of the southwest's wine, food, art, music and outdoor adventures.

December

Gravity Games H20 (www.gravitygamesh2o.com) Early December sees Perth's version of the Gravity Games featuring plenty of wakeboarding action on the Swan River as well as demos of skate, BMX, In-line, and FMX along with live music.

FOOD

WA serves up everything from inventive cuisine in its modern cafés and restaurants in the more popular tourist destinations to mind-numbingly monotonous menus just about everywhere else. This isn't to say that the food isn't any good once you're off the beaten tourist trail – the quality is usually very good – it's just that there is only so many ways that you can say surf 'n' turf!

When you're in the bigger cities, the best value is the modern cafés, where a good meal in casual surroundings costs under $25 and a full cooked breakfast around $15. Some inner-city pubs offer upmarket restaurant-style fare, but most pubs serve standard (often huge) bistro meals, usually in the $12 to $20 range – however this can rise to around $30 when you're in more remote areas. Bar (or counter) meals, which are eaten in the public bar, usually cost between $10 and $20. For general opening hours, consider that breakfast is normally served between 6am and 11am, lunch starts around noon until about 3pm and dinner usually starts after 6pm and last service is around 9pm to 10pm, however in country areas the cook may have shut off the deep fryer by 8pm. It's customary to tip in restaurants and upmarket cafés if the service warrants it – a gratuity of between 5% to 10% of the bill is the norm.

For more detailed information, see the Food & Drink chapter (p43).

GAY & LESBIAN TRAVELLERS

Though quite small by Sydney standards, the gay and lesbian communities of WA are active and proud, with strong communities based in Perth (particularly Northbridge) and Fremantle. In general Australians are open-minded about homosexuality, but the further into the country you go, the more likely you are to run into overt homophobia. The tide is gradually turning (at least legally), with the state government introducing anti-discrimination legislation in 2002 that equalised the legal age of consent for homosexual sex (from 21 years to 16), and gave legitimacy to de facto relationships.

The biggest event on the gay and lesbian calendar is **Perth Pride** (www.pridewa.asn.au), a monthlong arts and culture festival beginning with the Pride fair day in late September and culminating with the Pride Parade through the streets of Northbridge and an annual Pride dance party.

The best way to tune in to the queer news, views and events in Perth is through the free **OUTinPerth** (www.outinperth.com) newspaper, available in various outlets on the first day of the month. There's also the monthly lesbian magazine, **Women Out West** (www.womenoutwest.com.au), and the following helpful organisations:

Gay & Lesbian Business Directory of WA (www .qpages.com.au)

DIRECTORY

Gay & Lesbian Community Service of WA (☎ 1800 184 527, counselling line 9420 7201; www.glcs.org.au; 2 Delhi Street, West Perth, 6005)
Gay & Lesbian Tourism Australia (GALTA; www.galta .com.au)

HOLIDAYS
Public Holidays
New Year's Day 1 January
Australia Day 26 January
Labour Day First Monday in March
Easter (Good Friday to Easter Monday inclusive) March/April
Anzac Day 25 April
Foundation Day First Monday in June
Queen's Birthday Last Monday in September
Christmas Day 25 December
Boxing Day 26 December

School Holidays
The Christmas holiday season (mid-December to late January) is part of the summer school holidays, when transport and accommodation is often booked out, and there are long, restless queues at tourist attractions. There are three shorter school holiday periods during the year that alternate slightly from year to year. Generally, they fall in mid-April, mid-July, and late September to mid-October.

INSURANCE
Don't underestimate the importance of a good travel-insurance policy that covers theft, loss and medical problems – nothing will ruin your holiday plans quicker than an accident or having that brand new digital camera stolen.

Some policies specifically exclude designated 'dangerous activities' such as scuba diving, parasailing, bungee jumping, motorcycling, skiing and even bushwalking. If you plan on doing any of these things, make sure the policy you choose fully covers you for your activity of choice. Check that the policy covers ambulances and emergency medical evacuations by air.

See also p275. For information on insurance matters relating to cars that are bought or rented, see p270.

INTERNET ACCESS
You'll find internet cafés in cities, sizable towns and pretty much anywhere else that travellers congregate across WA. In addition you'll find that many backpacker hostels offer good rates and in smaller towns telecentres offer internet access. The cost ranges from under $4 an hour in the William St strip in Perth to $10 an hour in more remote locations. The average is about $6 an hour, usually with a minimum of 10 minutes' access.

If you're travelling with your own laptop, the easiest way to get online is to head to the local internet café and plug in via ethernet. Increasingly, the larger tourist centres have wi-fi hotspots that are either free or where you can purchase time via credit card.

If you want to connect to a local internet service provider (ISP) there are plenty of options, though some ISPs limit their dial-up areas to major cities or particular regions. Make sure the ISP has local dial-up numbers for the places where you intend to use it – timed long distance calls on top of internet charges will be expensive. Telstra (BigPond) uses a nationwide dial-up number at local call rates. Some major ISPs:

America Online (AOL; ☎ 1800 265 265; www.aol.com .au) Also has login numbers in all capitals and many provincial cities.
Australia On Line (☎ 1300 650 661; www.ozonline .com.au)
iPrimus (☎ 1300 850 000; www.iprimus.com.au)
OzEmail (☎ 13 28 84; www.ozemail.com.au)
Telstra BigPond (☎ 13 12 82; www.bigpond.com)

Australia uses RJ-45 telephone plugs and Telstra EXI-160 four-pin plugs, but neither are universal – electronics shops such as Tandy and Dick Smith should be able to help. If you wish to use a modem in Australia, you should check the above ISPs to see if your modem will be compatible.

For a list of useful websites, see p13.

LEGAL MATTERS
Most travellers will have no contact with the police or legal system, unless they break the rules of the road while driving. There is a significant police presence around most population centres and they have the power to stop your car and see your licence (you're

---

LEGAL AGE

Note the following for the record:

- You can drive when you're 17.
- The legal age for voting is 18.
- The age of consent for sex is 16.
- The legal drinking age is 18.

required to carry it), check your vehicle for road-worthiness and insist that you take a breath test for alcohol.

First offenders caught with small amounts of illegal drugs are likely to receive a fine rather than go to jail, but a conviction may affect your visa status. Note that if you remain in Australia after your visa expires, you will officially be an 'overstayer' and could face detention and expulsion, and be prevented from returning to Australia for up to three years.

MAPS

When you arrive in a new town, the local tourist information office will probably have a serviceable street map. For more detailed maps, try the **Royal Automobile Club of WA** (RACWA; www.rac.com.au), which has a stack of road maps available (including free downloadable route maps).

Gregory's and UBD both produce Perth street directories (around $30) that are useful for a long stay that involves plenty of city driving. *Roads & Tracks WA* is an excellent reference if you're travelling extensively through the state – especially off the beaten track.

The **WA Department of Land Information** (www .dola.wa.gov.au) produces a variety of mapping products that cover the whole state, including a range of topographical maps that are good for bushwalking.

MONEY

In this book, unless otherwise stated, all prices given in dollars refer to Australian dollars. For an idea of the money required to travel down-under, see p11.

ATMs

Australian bank branches are found throughout the state, most with 24-hour ATMs attached. Today, even in the smallest town you'll find an ATM – probably tucked away in the local pub. Most ATMs accept cards from other banks and are linked to international networks.

Cash

Australia's currency is the Australian dollar, made up of 100 cents. There are 5c, 10c, 20c, 50c, $1 and $2 coins, and $5, $10, $20, $50 and $100 notes. Although the smallest coin in circulation is 5c, prices are often still marked in single cents and then rounded to the nearest 5c when you come to pay.

There are no notable restrictions on importing or exporting travellers cheques. Cash amounts equal to or in excess of the equivalent of A$10,000 (in any currency) must be declared on arrival or departure.

Changing foreign currency or travellers cheques is usually no problem at banks throughout WA or at licensed moneychangers such as Thomas Cook or Amex in the major cities.

Credit & Debit Cards

The best way to carry your money in Australia is by plastic. Visa and MasterCard are widely accepted for everything from a hostel bed or a restaurant meal to an adventure tour, and a credit card is pretty much essential (in lieu of a large deposit) for car hire. With debit cards, any card connected to the international banking network (Cirrus, Maestro, Plus and Eurocard) will work. Charge cards such as Diners Club and Amex are not as widely accepted.

GST

The Goods and Services Tax (GST), introduced federally in 2000, is a flat 10% tax on all goods and services – accommodation, eating out, transport, electrical goods, books, furniture, clothing and so on, with the exception of basic food items (milk, bread, fruits and vegetables etc). By law the tax is included in the quoted or shelf prices, so all prices in this book are GST-inclusive. International air and sea travel to/from Australia is GST-free, as is domestic air travel when purchased outside Australia by non-residents.

If you purchase new or second-hand goods with a total minimum value of $300 from any one supplier no more than 30 days before you leave Australia, you are entitled under the Tourist Refund Scheme (TRS) to a refund of any GST paid. The scheme only applies to goods you take with you as hand luggage or wear onto the plane or ship. Also note that the refund is valid for goods bought from more than one supplier, but only if at least $300 is spent in each. For more information, contact the **Australian Customs Service** (☎ 1300 363 263; www.customs.gov.au).

DIRECTORY

Eftpos is a convenient service that many Australian businesses have embraced, even in the most remote parts of the state. It means you can use your plastic (credit or debit) to pay direct for services or purchases, and often withdraw cash as well.

Travellers Cheques

Travellers cheques are safe and generally enjoy a better exchange rate than foreign cash in Australia. Also, if they are stolen (or you lose them), they can readily be replaced. Amex, Thomas Cook and other well-known international brands are easily exchanged and are commission-free when exchanged at their bureaux, however local banks charge hefty fees (around $7) for the same service.

PHOTOGRAPHY & VIDEO

Australians are keen adopters of technology and all your requirements for digital photography and video can be met in WA. However, if you need memory cards, batteries or DV tapes, purchase them in the larger cities and towns as they're cheaper and more readily available than in the remote areas. Most photo labs have self-service machines that allow you to make your own prints and burn CDs and DVDs of your images and of course, they still stock and develop film for those keeping it old-skool.

POST
Letters

Australia's postal services are efficient and reasonably cheap. It costs 50c to send a standard letter or postcard within the country. **Australia Post** (www.auspost.com.au) has divided international destinations into two regions: Asia-Pacific and Rest of the World; airmail letters up to 50g cost $1.20/1.80, respectively. The cost of a postcard (up to 20g) is $1.10 and an aerogram to any country is 95c.

Parcels

There are four international parcel zones. You can send parcels by seamail to anywhere in the world except countries in the Asia/Pacific region (including New Zealand). A 1/1.5/2kg parcel costs $16.50/23.50/30.50. Each 500g over 2kg costs $3.50 extra.

Economy airmail rates for a 1/1.5/2kg parcel to Zone A (New Zealand) are $16/22.50/29; to Zone B (Asia/Pacific) costs $20/28.50/37; to Zone C (USA/Canada/Middle East) costs $24/34.50/45; and to Zone D (Rest of World) costs $30/43.50/57.

Sending & Receiving Mail

All post offices will hold mail for visitors, and some city GPOs (main or general post offices) have very busy poste restante sections. You need to provide some form of identification (such as a passport) to collect mail. You can also have mail sent to you at city Amex offices if you have an Amex card or travellers cheques.

See p248 for post office opening times.

SOLO TRAVELLERS

People travelling alone in WA will sometimes be left well alone, but generally you'll be greeted as a long lost relative. In fact, ending a conversation here is much harder than starting one!

Solo travellers are a common sight throughout the state and there is certainly no stigma attached to lone visitors. However, women travelling alone should exercise caution when in less-populated areas, and may find some menfolk annoyingly attentive in drinking establishments (with mining town pubs arguably the nadir); see also p259.

TELEPHONE

The two main telecommunications companies are the 51% government-owned **Telstra** (www.telstra.com.au) and the private **Optus** (www.optus.com.au). Both are also major players in the mobile (cell) market, along with **Vodafone** (www.vodafone.com.au) – other mobile operators include **AAPT** (www.aapt.com.au) and **Orange** (www.orange.net.au).

Domestic & International Calls
INFORMATION & TOLL-FREE CALLS

Numbers starting with ☎ 190 are usually recorded information services, charged at anything from 35c to $5 or more per minute (more from mobiles and payphones). To make a reverse-charge (collect) call from any public or private phone, simply dial ☎ 1800-REVERSE (738 3773) or ☎ 12 550.

Toll-free numbers (with a prefix ☎ 1800) can be called free of charge from anywhere in the country, though they may not be accessible from certain areas or from mobile phones. Calls to numbers beginning with ☎ 13 or ☎ 1300 are charged at the rate of a local call – the numbers can usually be dialled Australia-wide, but may be applicable only to a specific state or STD (no, not something you need to see a doctor about, it stands for Subscriber Trunk Dialling – a long-distance call within Australia) district. Note that telephone numbers beginning with ☎ 1800, ☎ 13 or ☎ 1300 cannot be dialled from outside Australia.

INTERNATIONAL CALLS

Most payphones allow ISD (International Subscriber Dialling) calls. The cost and international dialling code of the call will vary depending on which provider you are using.

When calling overseas you need to dial the international access code from Australia (☎ 0011 or ☎ 0018), the country code and the area code (without the initial 0). So for a London number you'd dial ☎ 0011-44-20, then the number. Also, certain operators will have you dial a special code to access their service.

If dialling WA from overseas, the country code is ☎ 61 and you need to drop the 0 (zero) in the 08 area code.

LOCAL CALLS

Calls from private phones cost 15c to 25c while local calls from public phones cost 40c; both allow for unlimited talk time. Calls to mobile phones attract higher rates and are timed. Blue phones or gold phones that you sometimes find in hotel lobbies or other businesses usually cost a minimum of 50c for a local call.

LONG-DISTANCE CALLS

Although the whole of WA shares a single area code (08), once you call outside of the immediate area or town, it is likely you are making a long-distance (STD) call. STD calls can be made from virtually any public phone and are cheaper during off-peak hours, generally between 7pm and 7am. There are a handful of main area codes for Australia:

State/Territory	Area Code
Australian Capital Territory	☎ 02
New South Wales	☎ 02
Northern Territory	☎ 08
Queensland	☎ 07
South Australia	☎ 08
Tasmania	☎ 03
Victoria	☎ 03

Mobile Phones

Local numbers with the prefixes ☎ 04xx or ☎ 04xxx belong to mobile phones. Australia's two mobile networks – digital GSM and digital CDMA – currently service more than 90% of the population but leave vast tracts of the country uncovered, including much of inland WA. Perth and the larger centres get good reception, but outside these centres it's haphazard or nonexistent, especially in the north. If you're going bush, CDMA was the service of choice (next to forking out for a satellite phone), however at the time of writing it was being replaced by Telstra's Next G service (www.nextg.com.au) that so far is not increasing the coverage of CDMA. Note that no matter which mobile service you choose (Telstra, Optus or Vodafone), coverage between outback towns in the north is currently non-existent.

Australia's digital network is compatible with GSM 900 and 1800 (used in Europe), but is generally not compatible with the USA or Japanese systems. It's easy to get connected short-term, though, as the main service providers (Telstra, Optus and Vodafone) all have prepaid mobile systems. Just buy a starter kit, which may include a phone or, if you have your own phone, a SIM card (around $15) and a prepaid charge card. The calls are a lot more expensive than with standard contracts, but there are no connection fees or line-rental charges and you can buy the recharge cards at convenience stores and newsagents. Don't forget that it's a good idea to shop around between the three carriers as their products differ.

Phonecards

A wide range of phonecards is available in WA. Phonecards can be purchased at newsagents and post offices for a fixed dollar value (usually $10, $20, $30 etc) and can be used with any public or private phone by dialling a toll-free access number and then the PIN number on the card. Call rates vary, so shop around. Some public phones also accept credit cards.

TIME

Australia is divided up into three time zones: the Western Standard Time zone (GMT/UTC plus eight hours) covers most of WA; Central Standard Time (plus 9½ hours) covers the Northern Territory, South Australia and parts of WA's Central Desert and Nullarbor regions near the border; and Eastern Standard Time (plus 10 hours) covers Tasmania, Victoria, New South Wales, the Australian Capital Territory and Queensland. So when it's noon in Perth, it's 1.30 in the afternoon in Darwin and Adelaide, and 2pm in Sydney or Melbourne.

'Daylight saving' – for which clocks are put forward an hour – operates in most states during the warmer months (October to March), and now includes WA on a trial basis for a few years.

TOURIST INFORMATION
Local Tourist Offices

For general statewide information, try the **Western Australian Visitors Centre** (☎ 1300 361 351; www.westernaustralia.com; Forrest Pl, Perth 6000), which will quickly bury you knee-deep in brochures, booklets, maps and leaflets on places all over the state.

Elsewhere, information is available from regional and local tourist offices (listed throughout the book); in many cases they are excellent, with friendly staff (often volunteers) providing invaluable local knowledge such as local road and weather conditions. However, many are woefully underfunded – so don't expect miracles.

Tourist Offices Abroad

Germany (☎ 89 2366 21 811, fax 89 2366 2199; Sonnenstrasse 9, Munich, 80331)
Japan (☎ 3 5214 0797; fax 3 5214 0799; New Otani Garden Court Bldg, Level 28F, 4-1 Kioi-cho, Chiyoda-ku, Tokyo 102-0094)
Singapore (☎ 6255 4098; fax 6255 4093; #08-02A United Square,101 Thomson Rd, Singapore, 307591)
UK (☎ 207 438 4647; fax 207 240 6690; Australia House, 6th fl, Australia Centre, The Strand, London UK, WC2B 4LG)

TOURS

If you don't feel like travelling solo or you crave a hassle-free holiday where everything is organised for you, there are dozens of tours throughout WA to suit all tastes and budgets. The hop-on hop-off bus options are a particularly popular way for travellers to get around in a fun, relaxed atmosphere. Some 'adventure' tours include serious 4WD safaris, taking travellers to places that they simply couldn't get to on their own without large amounts of expensive equipment.

The Western Australian Visitors Centre has a wide selection of brochures and suggestions for tours all over the state.

The tours listed here are only a selection of what is available (also see Tour sections in regional chapters for more extensive lists of local tours). Prices given are rates per person in twin share; there's usually an extra supplement for single accommodation. Students and YHA members often get 5% or 10% discounts. This is just a tiny taste of what's on offer:

AAT Kings Australian Tours (☎ 1300 556 100; www .aatkings.com) A long-established and professional outfit offering a wide range of fully escorted bus trips and 4WD adventures for those who prefer more luxurious accommodation than most offer. A 12-day 4WD trip from Broome covering highlights such as Geikie Gorge, the Bungle Bungles, El Questro and Windjana Gorge costs $4695.
Active Safaris (☎ 1800 222 848; www.activesafaris.com .au) Small adventure tour company running budget 4WD safaris such as a four-day Monkey Mia safari that includes the Pinnacles Desert, Geraldton and Kalbarri (from $525) and a five-day Ningaloo Reef trip from Perth to Exmouth (one way $550, return $750).
Australian Adventure Travel (☎ 1800 621 625; www.safaris.net.au) Offers numerous tours from Perth, Broome, Kununurra, Exmouth and Darwin. Includes everything from five-day trips along the Gibb River Rd (from $895) to a 12-day Kimberley discovery ($2490) featuring Windjana Gorge, Mitchell Falls, El Questro and the Bungle Bungle Range.
Dr Marion Hercock's Explorer Tours (☎ 9361 0940; www.explorertours.com.au) Intimate tours following the footsteps of early explorers. Tours tackle some serious 4WD tracks along the routes of 19th-century explorers, immersing travellers in the history of the time. A nine-day trip through the outback southeast costs $2390 and include meals, as well as guidance by experts in outback history, environment, flora and fauna.
Easyrider Backpacker Tours (☎ 9226 0307; www .easyridertours.com.au; 144 William St) Social hop-on hop-off bus service, including several different routes across WA. For example, the 'Southern Curl' tour ($249, valid for three months), departs several times a week from Perth and stops at Bunbury, Dunsborough, Margaret River, Augusta, Nannup, Pemberton, Walpole, Denmark and Albany. The 'Broometime' tour ($689, valid for six months) is perennially popular.
Planet Perth Tours (☎ 9225 6622; www.planettours .com.au) Busy budget tour operators running round trip mini-bus tours from Perth to destinations such as Broome (10 days $1490, 13 days return trip $1760) and Exmouth (5 days $660, 7 days return trip $800), with the option of returning or staying on at each destination.

TRAVELLERS WITH DISABILITIES

Disability awareness in WA is pretty high and getting higher. Legislation requires that new accommodation meets accessibility standards, and discrimination by tourism operators is illegal. Many of the state's key attractions provide access for those with limited mobility and a number of sites have also begun addressing the needs of visitors with visual or aural impairments; contact attractions in advance to confirm the facilities.

Reliable information is the key ingredient for travellers with a disability and the best source is the **National Information Communication & Awareness Network** (Nican; ☎ TTY 02 6241 1220, TTY 1800 806 769; www.nican.com.au). It's an Australia-wide directory providing information on access issues, accessible accommodation, sporting and recreational activities, transport and specialist tour operators.

People with Disabilities WA (PWDWA; ☎ 1800 193 331, 9386 6477, TTY 9386 6451; www.pwdwa.org; 37 Hampden Rd, Nedlands 6009) is another good source – its excellent website has extensive information on WA's major disability service providers.

Other useful organisations in WA include the **Association for the Blind of WA** (☎ 9311 8202; www.abwa.asn.au; 16 Sunbury Rd, Victoria Park 6100) and the **WA Deaf Society** (☎ 9441 2677, TTY 9441 2655; www.wadeaf.org.au; 46/5 Aberdeen Street, East Perth, 6004).

VISAS

All visitors to Australia need a visa – only New Zealand nationals are exempt, and even they receive a 'special category' visa on arrival. Visa application forms are available from Australian diplomatic missions overseas, travel agents or the website of the **Department of Immigration & Citizenship** (☎ 13 18 81; www.immi.gov.au).

Electronic Travel Authority (ETA)

Many visitors can get an ETA through any International Air Transport Association (IATA)-registered travel agent or overseas airline. They make the application direct when you buy a ticket and issue the ETA, which replaces the usual visa stamped in your passport – it's common practice for travel agents to charge a fee for issuing an ETA (usually US$15). This system is available to passport holders of some 32 countries, including the UK, the USA and Canada, most European and Scandinavian countries, Malaysia, Singapore, Japan and Korea. You can also make an online ETA application at www.eta.immi .gov.au, where an A$20 fee applies.

Tourist Visas

Short-term tourist visas have largely been replaced by the Electronic Travel Authority (ETA). However, if you are from a country not covered by the ETA, or you want to stay longer than three months, you'll need to apply for a visa. Standard visas (which cost A$70) allow one (in some cases multiple) entry, stays of up to three months, and are valid for use within 12 months of issue. A long-stay tourist visa (also A$70) can allow a visit of up to a year.

Visa Extensions

Visitors are allowed a maximum stay of 12 months, including extensions. Visa extensions are made through the Department of Immigration & Citizenship and it's best to apply at least two or three weeks before your visa expires. The application fee is A$205 – it's non-refundable, even if your application is rejected.

Working Holiday Maker (WHM) Visas

Young visitors (between 18 and 30 years without dependents) from Belgium, Canada, Cyprus, Denmark, Estonia, Finland, France, Germany, Hong Kong, Republic of Ireland, Italy, Japan, Republic of Korea, Malta, Netherlands, Norway, Sweden, Taiwan and the UK are eligible for a WHM visa (subclass 417), which allows you to visit for up to 12 months and gain casual employment. Tertiary educated visitors from Chile, Iran and Thailand can also apply (subclass 462). As the countries listed are updated on an ongoing basis, check the website (www.immi.gov.au) for the latest listings.

Once accepted, you can undergo training for up to 4 months and work up to six months with one employer. If you want an encore, note that for your second visa you must have completed three months seasonal work in regional Australia while on your first WHM visa – no problem given the amount of work around. The application costs $185/175 for subclasses 417/462 (generally non-refundable) and you can apply online.

WOMEN TRAVELLERS

WA is generally a safe place for women travellers, although the usual sensible precautions apply here. It's best to avoid walking alone late at night in any of the major cities and towns. Three assaults on female tourists in Broome in 2006 underscores the seriousness of this warning. If you're out on the town, keep enough money aside for a taxi home. The same applies to outback and rural towns with unlit, semi-deserted streets between you and your temporary home. Lone women should also be wary of staying in basic pub accommodation unless it appears safe and well managed.

Lone female hitchers are really tempting fate – hitching with a male companion is still silly, but safer.

WORK

A wealth of opportunities exists for travellers (both Australian and foreign) to work as volunteers or do paid seasonal work in WA all year round.

Seasonal Work

In Perth, plenty of temporary work is available in tourism and hospitality, administration, IT, nursing, childcare, factories and labouring. Outside of Perth, travellers can easily get jobs in tourism and hospitality; in agriculture and horticulture, working on enormous outback stations (properties), country farms, and at produce distribution points, doing everything from mustering sheep on motorbikes and feeding baby animals, to working as a cook or labourer and fruit picking and packing. Some places have specialised needs, such as Broome where there is lucrative work in pearling, on farms and boats.

You can line up work before you leave home or wait until you arrive. The YHA helps travellers find jobs, as do many backpacker hostels. When you hit the road, check out noticeboards at hostels, in internet cafés, supermarkets, and telecentres. The **Travel Recruitment Centre** (Map pp58-9; ☎ 9322 1406; www.trsaust .co.au; Traveller's Club, 137A William St) in Perth hooks travellers up with all manner of work, pretty much year-round, from fruit-picking and pruning to long-term jobs in the (coveted) outback. The service is free; just walk in, but be prepared to wait. The **Job Centre** (Map pp58-9; ☎ 6267 0700; www.travelforever.com.au; Travel Forever, 123-125 William St), a few doors down, offers a similar service. The following websites are also helpful:

Australian Jobsearch (www.jobsearch.gov.au) Offers a comprehensive job database.

Centrelink (www.centrelink.gov.au) The Australian Government employment service has information and advice on looking for work, training and assistance.

Grunt Labour Services (www.gruntlabour.com) A recruitment agency specialising in northern Australia, north WA, the Northern Territory and Northern Queensland.

Harvest Trail (http://jobsearch.gov.au/HarvestTrail) Specialised recruitment search for the agricultural industry, including a 'crop list' detailing what you can pick and pack when and where!

Job Shop (www.thejobshop.com.au) This WA-based recruitment agency specialising in jobs for WA as well as the Northern Territory.

West Australian (www.thewest.com.au) WA's main newspaper advertises jobs online.

Volunteering

Year-round opportunities exist for travellers to do volunteer work across WA. Overseas travellers can organise a volunteer arrangement but should first apply for a Visitor/Tourist Visa. See the **Department of Immigration** (www .immi.gov.au) website for more information.

Volunteers can work in the areas of environment and conservation; humanitarian aid; animal welfare; home help for the aged, frail, and disabled; youth and families; arts, culture and heritage; tourism; sport and recreation; and marketing and fundraising.

Information and registration for volunteering positions is available online at **Australian Volunteer Search** (www.volunteersearch.gov.au), the Australian Government volunteer recruitment service, and **Volunteering Australia** (www .govolunteer.com.au), a national organization promoting volunteering opportunities

For a wide variety of environment and conservation opportunities, see **Conservation Volunteers Australia** (www.conservationvolunteers.com .au). Meals, accommodation and transport are often provided in return for volunteering. Training opportunities are also sometimes available.

You can volunteer for similar opportunities, with the addition of community education and scientific research projects, directly through the WA state government's **Department of Environment & Conservation** (www .dec.wa.gov.au). You'll find current and future opportunities at national parks all over WA listed at www.naturebase.net/vacancies/vol unteer_programs.html. Opportunities vary enormously, from turtle tagging at Ningaloo Marine Park to feral animal control at Shark Bay. Travellers rave about their experience working with the dolphins at Monkey Mia, a program that always needs volunteer assistance (contact: alison.true@dec.wa.gov.au).

Willing Workers on Organic Farms (WWOOF; www .wwoof.com.au) place people on organic farms and provide other alternative lifestyle opportunities in return for bed and board.

You can read first hand accounts of other travellers' volunteer experiences at www .transitionsabroad.com.

Australian citizens who are unemployed may be eligible to receive Centrelink payments for volunteering. Check out their website: www.centrelink.gov.au.

Transport

CONTENTS

GETTING THERE & AWAY

For most visitors to Australia, getting here is probably going to involve a flight so long that it will allow you to watch the *Lord of the Rings* trilogy and still have time for a decent nap. It doesn't change once you hit Western Australia (WA) either – this is a huge state that requires pre-planning to get the most out of your visit.

Note that flights, tours and rail tickets can be booked online at www.lonelyplanet.com/travel_services.

ENTERING THE COUNTRY

Disembarkation in Australia is generally a very straightforward affair, with only the usual customs declarations (p249) and the fight to be first to arrive at the luggage carousel to endure.

However, recent global instability has resulted in conspicuously increased security in Australian airports, both in domestic and international terminals, and you may find that customs procedures are now a little more time-consuming.

AIR – INTERNATIONAL
Airports & Airlines

The east coast of Australia is the most common gateway for international travellers, however there are some airlines that fly direct into **Perth Airport** (code PER; ☎ 08-9478 8888; www.perthairport.com). If you do choose to fly to the east coast first, it's usually possible to book a same-day domestic flight that will wing you across the country to Perth.

AIRLINES FLYING TO & FROM AUSTRALIA

Airlines that visit Australia include the following (note all phone numbers mentioned here are for dialling from within Australia).

Air Canada (airline code AC; ☎ 1300 655 757; www.aircanada.ca) Flies to Sydney.

Air New Zealand (airline code NZ; ☎ 13 24 76; www.airnz.com.au) Flies to Adelaide, Brisbane, Cairns, Gold Coast, Perth, Melbourne, Sydney.

British Airways (airline code BA; ☎ 08-9425 5333; www.britishairways.com.au) Flies to Sydney.

Cathay Pacific (airline code CX; ☎ 13 17 47; www.cathaypacific.com) Flies to Perth, Adelaide, Melbourne, Sydney, Brisbane, Cairns.

Emirates (airline code EK; ☎ 1300 303 777; www.emirates.com) Flies to Perth, Melbourne, Sydney, Brisbane.

Garuda Indonesia (airline code GA; ☎ 08-9214 5101; www.garuda-indonesia.com) Flies to Perth, Adelaide, Melbourne, Sydney, Brisbane.

THINGS CHANGE

The information in this chapter is particularly vulnerable to change: prices for international travel are volatile, routes are introduced and cancelled, schedules change, special deals come and go, and rules and visa requirements are amended.

Airlines and governments seem to take a perverse pleasure in making price structures and regulations as complicated as possible. You should check directly with the airline or a travel agent to make sure you understand how a fare (and ticket you may buy) works. In addition, the travel industry is highly competitive and there are many lurks and perks.

The details given in this chapter should be regarded as pointers and are not a substitute for your own careful, up-to-date research.

Gulf Air (airline code GF; ☎ 08-9229 9211; www.gulf airco.com) Flies to Sydney.

Japan Airlines (airline code JL; ☎ 02-9272 1111; www .jal.com) Flies to Cairns, Brisbane, Melbourne, Sydney.

KLM (airline code KL; ☎ 1300 392 192; www.klm.com) Flies to Adelaide, Perth, Melbourne, Brisbane, Sydney.

Malaysia Airlines (airline code MH; ☎ 13 26 27, 08-9263 7043; www.malaysiaairlines.com) Flies to Perth, Adelaide, Brisbane, Cairns, Sydney.

Qantas (airline code QF; ☎ 13 13 13; www.qantas.com.au) Flies to Perth, Melbourne, Sydney, Brisbane.

Royal Brunei Airlines (airline code BI; ☎ 08-9321 8757; www.bruneiair.com) Flies to Perth, Brisbane, Darwin, Sydney.

Singapore Airlines (airline code SQ; ☎ 13 10 11, 1300 880 833; www.singaporeair.com.au) Flies to Perth, Adelaide, Brisbane, Melbourne, Sydney.

South African Airways (airline code SA; ☎ 08-9216 2200; www.flysaa.com) Flies to Perth, Sydney, Adelaide, Brisbane, Melbourne.

Thai Airways International (airline code TG; ☎ 1300 651 960; www.thaiairways.com) Flies to Perth, Brisbane, Melbourne, Sydney.

United Airlines (airline code UA; ☎ 13 17 77; www .unitedairlines.com.au) Flies to Melbourne, Sydney.

Tickets

Research the options carefully to make sure you get the best deal. The internet is the best resource for checking the latest airline prices.

Paying by credit card offers some protection if you end up dealing with a rogue fly-by-night agency in your search for the cheapest fare, as most card issuers provide refunds if you can prove you didn't get what you paid for. Alternatively, buy a ticket from a bonded agent, such as one covered by the **Air Travel Organiser's Licence** (ATOL; www.atol.org.uk) scheme in the UK. If you have doubts about the service provider, at the very least call the airline and confirm that your booking has been made.

Round-the-world tickets can be a good option for getting to Australia, and Perth is an easy inclusion on your ticket.

For online bookings, start with the following websites.

Airbrokers (www.airbrokers.com) This US company specialises in cheap tickets, especially round-the-world tickets and for the Pacific.

Cheapest Flights (www.cheapestflights.co.uk) Cheap worldwide flights from the UK.

Expedia (www.expedia.msn.com) Microsoft's travel site; mainly US-related.

Flight Centre International (www.flightcentre.com) Respected operator handling direct flights, with sites for Australia, New Zealand, the UK, the USA and Canada.

Flights.com (www.flights.com) Truly international site for flight-only tickets; cheap fares and an easy-to-search database.

TRANSPORT

CLIMATE CHANGE & TRAVEL

Climate change is a serious threat to the ecosystems that humans rely upon, and air travel is the fastest-growing contributor to the problem. Lonely Planet regards travel, overall, as a global benefit, but believes we all have a responsibility to limit our personal impact on global warming.

Flying & Climate Change

Pretty much every form of motorised travel generates CO_2 (the main cause of human-induced climate change) but planes are far and away the worst offenders, not just because of the sheer distances they allow us to travel, but because they release greenhouse gases high into the atmosphere. The statistics are frightening: two people taking a return flight between Europe and the US will contribute as much to climate change as an average household's gas and electricity consumption over a whole year.

Carbon Offset Schemes

Climatecare.org and other websites use 'carbon calculators' that allow travellers to offset the level of greenhouse gases they are responsible for with financial contributions to sustainable travel schemes that reduce global warming – including projects in India, Honduras, Kazakhstan and Uganda.

Lonely Planet, together with Rough Guides and other concerned partners in the travel industry, support the carbon offset scheme run by climatecare.org. Lonely Planet offsets all of its staff and author travel.

For more information check out our website: www.lonelyplanet.com.

Roundtheworld.com (www.roundtheworldflights.com) This excellent site allows you to build your own trips from the UK with up to six stops.
STA (www.statravel.com) Prominent in international student travel but you don't have to be a student; site linked to worldwide STA sites.
Travel Online (www.travelonline.co.nz) Good place to check worldwide flights from New Zealand.
Travelocity (www.travelocity.com) US site that allows you to search fares (in US$) to/from practically anywhere.

Asia

Most Asian countries offer fairly competitive airfare deals, with Bangkok, Singapore and Hong Kong being the best places to shop around for discount tickets.

Flights between Hong Kong and Australia are notoriously heavily booked. Flights to/from Bangkok and Singapore are often part of the longer Europe-to-Australia route so they are also sometimes full. The motto of the story is to plan your preferred itinerary well in advance.

You can get cheap short-hop flights between Perth and Denpasar in Bali, a route serviced by several airlines including Garuda Indonesia and Qantas. Some Asian agents:
STA Travel Bangkok (☎ 02 236 0262; www.statravel.co.th); Singapore (☎ 65 6737 7188; www.statravel.com.sg) Tokyo (☎ 03 5391 2922; www.statravel.co.jp)

Canada

The air routes from Canada are similar to those from mainland USA, with most Toronto and Vancouver flights stopping in one US city such as Los Angeles or Honolulu before heading on to Australia. Air Canada flies from Vancouver to Sydney via Honolulu and from Toronto to Melbourne via Honolulu.

Canadian discount air-ticket sellers (known as consolidators) and their airfares tend to be about 10% higher than those sold in the USA.
Travel Cuts (☎ 1866 246 9762; www.travelcuts.com) is Canada's national student travel agency and has offices in all major cities.

Continental Europe

From the major destinations in Europe, most flights travel via one of the Asian capitals. Some flights are also routed through London before arriving in Australia via Singapore, Bangkok, Hong Kong or Kuala Lumpur.

A good option in the Dutch travel industry is **Holland International** (☎ 070-307 6307; www.holland international.nl).

In Germany, good travel agencies include the Berlin branch of **STA Travel** (☎ 069-743 032 92; www.statravel.de).

Some agents in Paris:
Nouvelles Frontiéres (☎ 08 25 00 07 47; www .nouvelles-frontieres.fr) Also has branches outside of Paris.
OTU Voyages (☎ 01 55 82 32 32; www.otu.fr) Student/ youth oriented, with offices in many cities.

New Zealand

Air New Zealand and Qantas operate a network of flights linking Auckland, Wellington and Christchurch in New Zealand with Perth and other Australian gateway cities.

Other trans-Tasman options:
Flight Centre (☎ 0800 243 544; www.flightcentre.co.nz) Has a large central office in Auckland and many branches throughout the country.
House of Travel (www.houseoftravel.co.nz) Handles flight bookings for scores of airlines. Visit the website for the office phone numbers across both islands.
STA Travel (☎ 09-309 0458; www.statravel.co.nz) Has offices in numerous cities.

From the UK & Ireland

There are two routes from the UK: the western route via the USA and the Pacific, and the eastern route via the Middle East and Asia. Flights are usually cheaper and more frequent on the latter. Some of the best deals are with Emirates, Gulf Air, Malaysia Airlines, Japan Airlines and Thai Airways International. Unless there are special deals on offer, British Airways, Singapore Airlines and Qantas generally have higher fares but may offer a more direct route. For agents try:
Flight Centre (☎ 0870 499 0040; www.flightcentre .co.uk)
STA Travel (☎ 0870 163 0026; www.statravel.co.uk)

USA

Most of the flights between the North American mainland and Australia travel to/from the USA's west coast. San Francisco is the ticket consolidator (discounter) capital of America, although some good deals can be found in Los Angeles, New York and other big cities.
STA Travel (☎ 800 781 4040; www.statravel.com) has offices around the country, and can assist with tickets.

AIR – DOMESTIC

While the major carrier in Australia is the formerly monopolistic **Qantas** (☎ 13 13 13; www .qantas.com.au), Richard Branson's highly com-

petitive **Virgin Blue** (☎ 13 67 89; www.virginblue
.com.au) thankfully also flies all over Australia.
Routes to/from Perth include Broome, Melbourne, Adelaide, Sydney and Brisbane. In
order to compete with Virgin Blue, Qantas introduced low-cost **Jetstar** (☎ 13 15 38; www.jetstar
.com.au) in 2004, however domestic flights out
of Perth only travel to Melbourne at present.
Qantas flies direct to most Australian capital
cities as well as flying or code-sharing to several destinations in WA. See p266 for WA's
regional airlines.

Fares

Few people pay full fare on domestic travel,
as the airlines offer a wide range of discounts.
These come and go and there are regular special fares, so keep your eyes open. Regular
one-way and return domestic fares are similar
on Jetstar and Virgin Blue.

Advance-purchase deals provide the cheapest airfares. Some advance-purchase fares
offer up to 33% discount off one-way fares
and up to 50% or more off return fares. You
have to book one to four weeks ahead, and you
often have to stay away for at least one Saturday night. There are restrictions on changing
flights and you can lose up to 100% of the
ticket price if you cancel, although you can
buy health-related cancellation insurance.

LAND

The southwest of WA is isolated from the
rest of Australia, and interstate travel entails
a major sojourn. The nearest state capital
to Perth is Adelaide, 2650km away by the
shortest road route. To Melbourne it's at least
3384km, Darwin is around 4020km and Sydney 3900km. In spite of the vast distances, you
can still drive across the Nullarbor Plain from
the eastern states to Perth and then up the Indian Ocean coast and through the Kimberley
to Darwin on sealed roads – if you dare.

Border Crossings

The two most commonly used entry points
into WA from the eastern states are at Kununurra (p241), via the Victoria Hwy, near
the Northern Territory (NT) border; and Eucla
(p168), via the Eyre Hwy, close to the border
with South Australia (SA). Hardier types can
head inland for more rugged crossings into
the NT near Halls Creek; and on the Great
Central Rd to Yulara, near Giles. See Outback
Travel (p271) for more information.

Bus

Greyhound (☎ 1300 473 946 863; www.greyhound.com.au)
runs services to Darwin via Broome (A$690,
taking a day and a half). Greyhound's travel
to the eastern states (with its various passes)
uses the *Indian Pacific* (below) service to cross
from Perth to Adelaide.

See p267 for more information on Greyhound bus passes and deals.

Car, Motorcycle & Bicycle

No matter which way you look at it and where
you're coming from, driving to Perth from any
other state is a *very* long journey. But if you've
got your own wheels and companions to share
the driving and the fuel costs, it's still a cheap
way of getting to Perth…and it's certainly the
best way to see the country. Be aware that
there are strict quarantine restrictions when
crossing the border, so scoff or toss your fruit
and vegetables before you get there.

See p268 for details of road rules, driving
conditions and information on buying and
renting vehicles.

Hitching

Hitching is never entirely safe – we don't
recommend it. Hitching to or from WA across
the Nullarbor is definitely not advisable, as
waits of several days are not uncommon.

People looking for travelling companions
for the long car journeys to WA from Sydney,
Melbourne, Adelaide or Darwin frequently
leave notices on boards in hostels and backpacker accommodation.

Train

There is only one interstate rail link: the famous *Indian Pacific* transcontinental train
journey, run by **Great Southern Railway** (☎ 13
21 47; www.gsr.com.au). Along with the *Ghan* to
Alice Springs, the 4352km *Indian Pacific* run
is one of Australia's great train journeys – a
bum-numbing 65-hour trip between the Pacific Ocean on one side of the continent and
the Indian Ocean on the other.

The *Indian Pacific* travels twice weekly each
way between Sydney and Perth. From Sydney,
you cross New South Wales to Broken Hill,
then continue on to Adelaide and across the
Nullarbor Plain. From Port Augusta to Kalgoorlie-Boulder, the seemingly endless crossing
of the virtually uninhabited centre takes well
over 24 hours, including the 'long straight' on
the Nullarbor – at 478km this is the longest

TRANSPORT

straight stretch of train line in the world. You can take 'whistle-stop' tours of some towns on the way. Unlike the trans-Nullarbor road, which runs south of the Nullarbor along the coast of the Great Australian Bight, the train line crosses the actual plain. From Kalgoorlie-Boulder, it's a straight run into Perth.

CLASSES & COSTS
There are three different classes of travel on the *Indian Pacific*. The economy 'daynighter' seat is basically a recliner lounge chair, with shared shower and toilet facilities. The next class is a sleeper cabin, comprising day cabins that convert to twin sleepers, with shared shower and toilet facilities. Both these configurations are part of the 'red kangaroo' service. The 'gold kangaroo' service is basically 1st class, with single, twin or deluxe day-and-night sleeper accommodation with all meals included and served in the restaurant car. These passengers also have access to a luxurious lounge car and bar (complete with piano). For daynighter and sleeper passengers, meals are not included but can be purchased onboard.

One-way fares from Adelaide to Perth for an economy 'daynighter' seat/economy sleeper/1st-class sleeper are $395/1005/1355 ($186/609/926 for children and pensioners), while fares from Sydney are $680/1320/1790 ($322/859/1293 for children and pensioners). These fares apply from April 2007 to March 2008; see the website for prices after this date.

If you want to break the journey, you have to buy 'sector' fares, which work out to be a bit more expensive than the through fare. The 1st-class berths get booked up, especially in wildflower season (September to November), so advance bookings are a good idea.

Cars can be easily transported between Perth and Sydney or Adelaide. This makes a very good option for those not wishing to drive across the Nullarbor Plain in both directions.

GETTING AROUND

Travelling widely around WA is challenging – the distances between key towns are vast (especially in the north), requiring a minimum of an hour or two of air time but up to several days of highway cruising or red-dirt revving to traverse.

AIR
WA is so vast that unless you have unlimited time and an unlimited thirst for driving, you should consider a flight at some point. **Skywest Airlines** (☎ 1300 660 088; www.skywest.com.au) is the biggest regional airline, with a comprehensive network of flights that can replace days of dusty driving with an hour or two in the air. Connections with Perth include Albany, Broome, Carnarvon, Esperance, Exmouth, Geraldton, Kalgoorlie-Boulder, Kununurra, Monkey Mia, Port Hedland and across into Darwin in the NT.

There are several other small regional aviation companies in the state:

Airnorth (☎ 1800 627 474, 08-8920 4001; www.airnorth .com.au) Operates flights from Broome to Kununnura and Darwin.

National Jet (☎ 13 13 13; www.nationaljet.com.au) A Qantas Airways subsidiary with flights to the Australian protectorates, the Cocos (Keeling) Islands and Christmas Island, in the Indian Ocean.

Northwest Regional Airlines (☎ 08-9192 1369; www.northwestregional.com.au) Shuttles travellers between Port Hedland, Fitzroy Crossing, Broome, Halls Creek and Karratha as well as offering scenic flights.

Rottnest Air-Taxi (☎ 1800 500 006, 08-9292 5027; www.rottnest.de) Runs services to Rottnest Island as well as scenic flights.

BICYCLE
Whether you're hiring a bike to cycle around Rottnest Island, planning a day or two of riding around the Margaret River wineries, or attempting a trans-Nullarbor marathon, WA is a great place for cycling (also see p39).

Note that bicycle helmets are compulsory in WA (and all other states and territories of Australia), as are white front lights and red rear lights for riding at night.

If you're coming specifically to cycle, it makes sense to bring your own bike. Check with your airline for costs and the degree of dismantling/packing required. Within WA you can load your bike onto a bus to skip the boring bits of the country – and we've seen some cyclists in some very unlikely places in WA. Check with bus companies about how the bike needs to be secured, and book ahead to ensure that you and your bike can travel on the same vehicle.

Suffering dehydration is a very real risk in WA and can be life-threatening. It can get very hot in summer, and you should take things slowly until you're used to the heat.

Cycling in 35°C-plus temperatures is bearable if you wear a hat and plenty of sunscreen, and drink *lots* of water.

Outback travel needs to be planned thoroughly, with the availability of drinking water the main concern – those isolated water sources (bores, tanks, creeks and the like) shown on your map may be dry or undrinkable, so you can't always depend on them. Also make sure you've got the necessary spare parts and bike-repair knowledge. Check with locals (start at the visitors centres) if you're heading into remote areas, and always let someone know where you're headed before setting off.

For information on bicycle touring around WA, including suggested routes, road conditions and cycling maps, see the websites of the **Bicycle Transportation Alliance** (www.multiline.com.au/~bta) and the **Cycle Touring Association of Western Australia** (www.ctawa.asn.au).

BUS

If you don't have your own wheels, buses are the best way to see WA, having a very comprehensive route network compared with the limited railway system. All buses are modern and well equipped with air-con, toilets and videos.

Transwa

The largest operator in the mid-west and southwest is the government-operated **Transwa** (☎ 1300 662 205; www.transwa.wa.gov.au), with services that run in conjunction with limited rail services. Transwa destinations and fares (one way from Perth) are as follows: Albany ($48, six hours), Augusta ($40, eight hours), Bunbury ($25, three hours), Busselton ($29, 4½ hours), Dunsborough ($31, five hours), Esperance ($72, 10 hours), Geraldton ($50, six hours), Hyden ($42, five hours), Kalbarri ($63, 7½ hours), Margaret River ($34, 5½ hours), Pemberton ($42, 5½ hours) and York ($13, two hours). Reservations are necessary for all bus/train services.

Greyhound Australia

As well as travelling interstate, **Greyhound Australia** (☎ 1300 473 946 863; www.greyhound.com.au) has departures from Perth to Broome ($351, 31 hours), Dongara-Port Denison ($44, six hours), Exmouth ($210, 20 hours), Geraldton ($54, 6¾ hours), Kalbarri ($108, via Binnu), Monkey Mia ($149, 13 hours) and Port Hedland ($267, 26 hours). All fares listed are one way.

Students, ISIC card-holders, YHA members, VIP and Nomads card-holders get discounts of 10%. Children up to two years old get 50% off express tickets, while kids aged three to 14 get a 20% discount.

PASSES

If you're planning to travel around Australia, check out Greyhound's excellent themed bus passes. Several passes focus solely on travel in the west. The 'Pearl Diver' ($481, valid for six months) allows you to travel along the WA coastline from Perth to Broome, with notable stops such as Monkey Mia and Exmouth; the 'Western Explorer' ($736, valid for six months) covers the same ground, but also includes the Broome to Darwin route; and the 'Best of the West' ($1690, valid for one year) allows you to travel from Adelaide to Perth (via the *Indian Pacific*, p265), along the coastal highway to Broome and Darwin and return to Adelaide via the red centre.

If your trip is going to be Australia-wide, the Greyhound Aussie Kilometre Pass is purchased in kilometre blocks, starting at 2000km ($340), in 1000-kilometre blocks up to 10,000km ($1275) and onwards to 20,000km ($2450). You can get off at any point on the scheduled route and have unlimited stopovers within the life of the pass.

Also see Tours (p258) for information on companies that provide hop-on, hop-off bus services.

Other Bus Companies

Integrity Coach Lines (☎ 1800 226 339, 08-9226 1339; www.integritycoachlines.com.au) most useful routes for travellers are from Perth to Mt Magnet ($88, seven hours), Cue ($99, eight hours), Meekatharra ($115, 10 hours), Newman ($198, 16 hours) and Port Hedland ($215, 22 hours). Fares listed are one way; there are various discounts for YHA/VIP card-holders. Note that this service runs in each direction only once a week.

Perth-Goldfields Express (☎ 1800 620 440; www.goldrushtours.com.au) does the Perth–Laverton run via the Great Eastern Hwy and Kalgoorlie-Boulder. One-way fares leaving from Perth include: Merredin ($38, three hours), Kalgoorlie-Boulder ($70, 7½ hours), Leonora ($123, 10 hours) and Laverton ($138, 11 hours).

South West Coach Lines (in Perth ☎ 08-9324 2333, in Bunbury ☎ 08-9791 1955, in Busselton ☎ 08-9754 1666) services the southwest pocket of the

TRANSPORT

state and runs daily services from Perth to Bunbury ($25, three hours), Busselton ($29, four hours), Dunsborough ($31, 4½ hours), Margaret River ($33, 5½ hours) and Augusta ($40, six hours).

Backpacker Buses

While the companies offering transport options for budget travellers are pretty much organised-tour operators, they do also get you from A to B (sometimes with hop-on, hop-off services) and so can be a very cost-effective alternative to the big bus companies. The buses are usually smaller, you'll meet lots of other travellers, and the drivers often double as tour guides. See Tours (p258) for more information about backpacker buses and other tour companies.

CAR & MOTORCYCLE

There is no doubt that travelling by vehicle is the best option in WA, as it gives you the freedom to explore off the beaten track. With several people travelling together, costs are reasonable and, provided that you don't have any major mechanical problems, there are many benefits.

Motorcycles are another popular way of getting around. The climate is good for bikes for much of the year, and the many small trails from the road into the bush lead to perfect spots to spend the night. Bringing your own motorcycle into Australia will entail an expensive shipping exercise, valid registration in the country of origin and a *Carnet de Passages en Douanes*. This is an internationally recognised customs document that allows the holder to import their vehicle without paying customs duty or taxes. To get one, apply to a motoring organisation/association in your home country. You'll also need a rider's licence and a helmet. A fuel range of 350km will cover fuel stops up the centre and on Hwy 1 around the continent. The long, open roads are really made for large-capacity machines above 750cc, which Australians prefer once they outgrow their 250cc learner restrictions.

Automobile Associations

The **Royal Automobile Club of Western Australia** (RACWA; ☎ 13 17 03; www.rac.com.au; 228 Adelaide Terrace, Perth) has lots of useful advice on state-wide motoring, including road safety, local regulations and buying/selling a car (see Purchase, p270). It also offers car insurance to its mem-

bers, and membership can get you discounts on car rentals and some motel accommodation. Also useful are the road-travel specialists in bordering states:
Royal Automobile Association of South Australia (RAA; ☎ 13 11 11, 08-8202 4600; www.raa.net; 55 Hindmarsh Square, Adelaide 5000)
Automobile Association of the Northern Territory (AANT; ☎ 08-8981 3837; www.aant.com.au; 79-81 Smith St, Darwin 0800)

Driving Licence

You can generally use your own home-country's driving licence in WA for up to three months, as long as it carries your photo for identification and is in English (if it's not, you'll need a certified translation). Alternatively, it's a simple matter to arrange an International Driving Permit (IDP), which should be supported by your home licence. Just go to your home country's automobile association and it can issue one on the spot. The permits are valid for 12 months, and cost approximately $20.

Fuel

Fuel (super, diesel and unleaded) is available from service stations sporting the well-known international brand names. LPG (gas) is not always stocked at more remote roadhouses – if your car runs on gas it's safer to have dual fuel capacity. Prices vary wildly in WA and it's not always aligned with the freight costs in getting the fuel to that isolated roadhouse. The prices for unleaded fuel at the time of writing were around $1.15/L in Perth and up to $1.70/L in the more remote areas of WA. Fuel prices are a major topic of discussion in WA, with the high prices having a significant effect on tourism in the outback. For up-to-date fuel prices across WA, visit the government fuel-watch website (www.fuelwatch.wa.gov.au).

Distances between fill-ups can be long in the outback but there are only a handful of tracks where you'll require a long-range fuel tank or need to use jerry cans. However, if you are doing some back-road explorations, always calculate your fuel consumption, plan accordingly and always carry a spare jerry can or two. Keep in mind that most small-town service stations are only open from 6am to 7pm and roadhouses aren't always open 24 hours. On main roads there'll be a small town or roadhouse roughly every 150km to 200km or so.

Hire

Competition between car-rental companies in Australia is pretty fierce, so rates tend to be variable and lots of special deals come and go. The main thing to remember when assessing your options is distance – if you want to travel widely, you need weigh up the price difference between an unlimited kilometres deal and one that offers a set number of kilometres free with a fee per kilometre over that set number.

As well as the big firms, there are a vast number of local firms, or firms with outlets in a limited number of locations. These are almost always cheaper than the big operators – sometimes half the price – but cheap car hire often comes with restrictions on how far you can take the vehicle away from the rental centre.

The big firms sometimes offer one-way rentals, but there are a variety of limitations, including a substantial drop-off fee. Ask plenty of questions about this before deciding on one company over another. One-way rentals into or out of the NT or WA may be subject to a hefty fee; however, there have previously been good deals for taking a car or campervan from Broome, for example, back to Perth.

You must be at least 21 years old to hire from most firms – if you're under 25 you may only be able to hire a small car or have to pay a surcharge. It's cheaper if you rent for a week or more and there are often low-season and weekend discounts. Credit cards are the usual payment method.

Note that most car-rental companies do include insurance in the price (also see p270), but in the event of an accident the hirer is still liable for a sometimes-hefty excess. Most companies offer excess-reduction insurance on top of the rental rate.

Major companies all have offices or agents in Perth and larger centres.

Avis (☎ 13 63 33; www.avis.com.au)
Budget (☎ 1300 362 848; www.budget.com.au)
Hertz (☎ 13 30 39; www.hertz.com.au)
Thrifty (☎ 1300 367 227; www.thrifty.com.au)

If you want short-term car hire, smaller local companies are generally the cheapest and are pretty reliable. **Bayswater Car Rental** (☎ 08-9325 1000; www.bayswatercarrental.com.au) is a good-value company with an office in Perth, or you can try **Backpacker Car Rentals** (☎ 08-9430 8869; www.backpackercarrentals.com.au) for the cheapest rentals around, starting from $110 per week.

4WD & CAMPERVAN HIRE

Renting a 4WD enables you to safely tackle routes off the beaten track and get out to some of the natural wonders that most travellers miss in a conventional vehicle.

Always check the insurance conditions carefully, especially the excess, as they can be onerous. Even for a 4WD, the insurance

TRANSPORT

4WD DRIVING TIPS

We don't need to see more 4WDs on tow trucks; the victims of a dirt-road rollover, a poorly judged river crossing, or coming to grief when meeting the native fauna on the road. Here's some tips to help keep you from riding upfront in a tow truck:

■ Before heading off-road, check the road conditions at www.mainroads.wa.gov.au.

■ Recheck road conditions at each visitors centre you come across – they can change quickly.

■ Let people know where you're going, what route you're taking and how long you'll be gone.

■ Don't drive at night: it's safer to rise early (but not pre-dawn!) and finish in the mid-afternoon to avoid wildlife.

■ Avoid sudden changes in direction – 4WDs have a much higher centre of gravity than cars.

■ On sand tracks, reduce tyre pressure to 140kpa (20psi) and don't forget to reinflate your tyres once you're back on the tarmac.

■ When driving on corrugated tracks, note that while there is a 'sweet spot' speed where you feel the corrugations less, it's often too fast to negotiate a corner – and rollovers often happen because of this.

■ When crossing rivers and creeks, always walk across first to check the depth – unless you're in saltwater crocodile territory, of course!

TRANSPORT

offered by most companies does not cover damage caused when travelling 'off-road', which basically means anything that is not a maintained bitumen or dirt road.

Hertz, Budget and Avis have 4WD rentals. **Britz Rentals** (☎ 1800 331 454, 08-9478 3488; www .britz.com) hires fully equipped 4WDs fitted out as campervans, which are commonplace on northern Australian roads. Britz has offices in all the mainland capitals, as well as Perth and Broome, so one-way rentals are also possible.

Several other companies rent out campervans, including **Backpacker Campervans** (☎ 1800 670 232, 08-9478 3479; www.backpackercampervans.com) and **Wicked Campers** (☎ 1800 246 869; www.wicked campers.com.au), most notable for the lurid colour schemes of their vehicles. See the boxed text, p79, for more information.

Insurance

In Australia, third-party personal injury insurance is always included in the vehicle registration cost. This ensures that every registered vehicle carries at least minimum insurance. You'd be wise to extend that minimum to at least third-party property insurance as well – minor collisions with other vehicles can be amazingly expensive.

When it comes to hire cars, it pays to know exactly what your liability is in the event of an accident. Rather than risk paying out thousands of dollars if you do have an accident, you can take out your own comprehensive insurance on the car, or (the usual option) pay an additional daily amount to the rental

company for an 'insurance excess reduction' policy. This brings the amount of excess you must pay in the event of an accident down from between $2000 and $5000 to a few hundred dollars.

Be aware that if you're travelling on dirt roads you will not be covered by insurance unless you have a 4WD – in other words, if you have an accident you'll be liable for all the costs involved. Also, most companies' insurance won't cover the cost of damage to glass (including the windscreen) or tyres. Always read the small print.

Purchase

If you're planning a stay of several months that involves lots of driving, buying a secondhand car will be much cheaper than renting. But remember that reliability is all-important. Breaking down in the outback is very inconvenient (and potentially dangerous) – the nearest mechanic can be a very expensive tow-truck ride away!

You'll probably get any car cheaper by buying privately through the newspaper (try Saturday's *West Australian*) rather than through a car dealer. Buying through a dealer does have the advantage of some sort of guarantee, but this is not much use if you're buying a car in Sydney for a trip to Perth.

When you come to buy or sell a car, there are usually some local regulations to be complied with. In WA a car has to have a compulsory safety check and obtain a Road Worthiness Certificate (RWC) before it can

---

DRIVING THROUGH ABORIGINAL LAND

If you are planning to drive on roads in the outback that pass through Aboriginal reserves, it is essential to have the required transit permits.

Permits are issued free of charge, but you must complete an official application form. In your letter of application you should indicate your intended route, the date of your journey, the make and registration number of your vehicle, and the number and names of the people travelling with you. Transit permits for straightforward travel along an established route can be processed instantly over the internet. However, permits for extended stays or more remote roads take longer.

Permits for travel through lands in WA are issued by the **Department of Indigenous Affairs** (DIA; ☎ 08-9235 8000; www.dia.wa.gov.au; 197 St Georges Tce, Perth), and applications can be approved over the Internet (just print out the approval and take it on your trip), made in person or by mail. The DIA website has plenty of useful information, including maps, road safety and conditions, and some simple dos and don'ts.

For travel in the southern and central regions of the Northern Territory (NT), apply for permits at the **Central Land Council** (☎ 08-8951 6320; fax 8953 4345; www.clc.org.au; 33 Stuart Hwy, Alice Springs, NT 0871; ☷ 8.30am-noon & 2-4pm Mon-Fri). Simply download the permit registration from the website, and fax or post it to the Permits Officer.

OUTBACK TRAVEL

If you really want to explore outback Western Australia (WA), it's important not to embark on your trip without careful planning and preparation. While you may not necessarily need a 4WD or extensive expedition equipment to tackle most of the state's roads, you do need to be prepared for the isolation and lack of facilities you'll encounter. Vehicles should be in excellent working condition and have reasonable ground clearance. If you plan on taking a conventional vehicle on roads that are marked '4WD only' or even '4WD recommended', don't expect a warm welcome from the good Samaritan who comes to help you out if you get into difficulties. Locals and dedicated 4WD travellers are becoming increasingly frustrated with having to help out travellers either with the wrong kind of vehicle, a poorly prepared vehicle or just sheer inexperience on the part of the driver to handle outback conditions. Of course Aussies will always help out someone in genuine need, but don't expect to be put on their Christmas list.

When travelling to very remote areas, it's advisable to carry a high-frequency (HF) radio transceiver equipped to pick up the relevant Royal Flying Doctor Service bases. A satellite phone and Global Positioning System (GPS) are also handy. All this equipment comes at a cost, but it's wise to keep in the back of your mind the fact that plenty of travellers have perished in the Australian desert after breaking down.

It's essential to always carry plenty of water. In the warmer weather allow at least 5L of water per person per day, plus an extra amount for the radiator. It's best to carry water in several containers.

It's wise not to attempt the tougher routes during the hottest part of the year (October to April inclusive) – apart from the risk of heat exhaustion, simple mishaps can easily lead to tragedy at this time. Conversely, there's no point going anywhere on dirt roads in the outback if there has been recent flooding (this is particularly common in the north during the wet season). Your first stop in any outback town before heading off into the wilderness should be the visitors centre, where they can advise you about the current road conditions and upcoming weather. If the office is closed, road and weather conditions are generally posted on the notice board outside the centre. If a visitors centre advises you that a road is closed or a road is not suitable for your vehicle, heed their advice.

If you do run into trouble in the back of beyond, always stay with your car. It's easier to spot a car than a human being from the air, and you probably won't be able to carry the amount of water necessary for survival very far anyway. Police suggest that you carry two spare tyres (for added safety) and, if stranded, try to set fire to one of them (let the air out first) – the pall of smoke will be seen for miles.

Of course, before you set out, let your family, friends or your car-hire company know where you're going and when you intend to be back. Some of the favourite outback tracks in the west follow.

Canning Stock Route This historic 1800km cattle-droving trail runs southwest from Halls Creek to Wiluna and is one of the most remote 4WD routes in the world. It crosses the Great Sandy Desert and the Gibson Desert and, since the track is not maintained, it's a route to be taken very seriously. The drive should only be done in the cooler months, in a well-equipped 4WD convoy with experienced outback drivers.

Gibb River Rd This popular route between Derby and Kununurra cuts through the heart of the spectacular Kimberley, with numerous gorges being a highlight. The going is slow, but the surroundings are so beautiful you won't mind the leisurely pace needed to handle the often badly corrugated road. While we don't recommend it, conventional vehicles often do the trip in the dry season (May to November); however it's impassable in the wet season and can be risky in the early dry season due to still-swollen river crossings. For more information, see Gibb River Road (p235).

Tanami Track Turning off the Stuart Hwy just north of Alice Springs (NT), this 1100km route goes northwest across the Tanami Desert to Halls Creek in WA. The road is a graded dirt road and while conventional vehicles make the journey, it's really best suited to at least a mid-sized 4WD as it can be sandy in places. The Rabbit Flat roadhouse in the middle of the desert is only open for business from Friday to Monday, so if you don't have long-range fuel tanks, plan your trip accordingly. Get advice on road conditions in Alice Springs or Halls Creek.

be registered in the new owner's name – usually the seller will indicate whether the car already has a RWC. Stamp duty has to be paid when you buy a car; as this is based on the purchase price, it's not unknown for the buyer and the seller to agree privately to understate the price.

To avoid buying a lemon, you might consider forking out some extra money for a vehicle appraisal before purchase. The **RACWA** (☎ 08-9421 4444; www.rac.com.au) offers this kind of check in Perth and other large WA centres for around $108/140 for members/non-members; it also offers extensive advice on buying and selling cars on its website.

If you'd like to purchase your own motorcycle and are fortunate enough to have a little time on your hands, getting mobile on two wheels is quite feasible. The beginning of winter (June) is a good time to start looking. Local newspapers and the bike-related press have classified advertisement sections.

Road Conditions

This vast state is not crisscrossed by multi-lane highways; there's not enough traffic and the distances are simply too great to justify them.

On all of the main routes, roads are well surfaced and have two lanes. You don't have to get very far off the beaten track, however, to find yourself on unsealed roads, and anybody who sets out to see the state in reasonable detail will have to expect to do some dirt-road travelling. A 2WD car can cope with a limited amount of this, but if you want to do some serious exploration, then you'd better plan on having a 4WD.

Driving on unsealed roads requires special care – a car will perform differently when braking and turning on dirt. Under no circumstances should you exceed 80km/h on dirt roads; if you go faster you will not have enough time to respond to a sharp turn, stock on the road or an unmarked gate or cattle grid. So take it easy: take time to see the sights and don't try to break the land speed record!

Travelling by car within WA means sometimes having to pass road trains. These articulated trucks and their loads (consisting of two or more trailers) can be up to 53.5m long, 2.5m wide and travel at around 100km/h. Overtaking them is a tricky process; at times you will have to drive off the bitumen to get past. Exercise caution – and remember that it is much harder for the driver of the larger road train to control their vehicle than it is for you to control your car.

Road Distances

One thing you have to adjust to in WA is the vast distances. The truth is that many places of interest are a very long drive from Perth. There are rest areas where tired drivers can revive. Ask for maps from the RACWA that indicate free coffee stops and rest areas.

See the Road Distances from Perth table (opposite) for some examples of the distances from Perth to regional centres.

Road Hazards

Contact the **RACWA** (☎ 13 17 03; www.rac.com.au) for general information and advice before embarking on any long-distance car travel.

Cattle, emus and kangaroos are common hazards on country roads, and a collision is likely to kill the animal and cause serious damage to your vehicle. Kangaroos are most active around dawn and dusk, and they travel in groups. If you see one hopping across the road in front of you, slow right down – its friends are probably just behind it. It's important to keep a safe distance behind the vehicle in front, in case it hits an animal or has to slow down suddenly.

If an animal runs out in front of you, brake if you can, but don't swerve unless it is safe to do so. You're likely to survive a collision with an emu better than a collision with a tree or if you roll your vehicle.

Driver fatigue is another hazard on the long-distance drives in WA. Some outback roads can become tedious after a few hours, so on a long haul, stop and rest every two hours or so – do some exercise, change drivers or have a coffee.

It's important to note that when it rains, some roads flood. Flooding is a real problem up north because of cyclonic storms. Exercise extreme caution at wet times, especially at the frequent yellow 'Floodway' signs. If you come to a stretch of water and you're not sure of the depth or what could lie beneath it, pull up at the side of the road and walk through it (excluding known saltwater crocodile areas, such as the Pentecost River crossing on the Gibb River Rd!). Even on major highways, if it has been raining you can sometimes be driving through 30cm or more of water for hundreds of metres at a time.

ROAD DISTANCES FROM PERTH

destination	km	destination	km
Adelaide	2650km	Kalbarri	592km
Albany	409km	Kalgoorlie-Boulder	596km
Augusta	324km	Karratha	1537km
Balladonia	911km	Kununurra	3206km
Broome	2230km	Lake Argyle	3276km
Bunbury	181km	Mandurah	74km
Busselton	232km	Manjimup	307km
Carnarvon	904km	Marble Bar	1476km
Cervantes	247km	Margaret River	278km
Coral Bay	1132km	Meekatharra	763km
Cue	651km	Monkey Mia	859km
Dampier	1557km	Mount Barker	359km
Denham	834km	Newman	1186km
Derby	2383km	Norseman	724km
Dongara-Port Denison	362km	Onslow	1389km
Esperance	721km	Pemberton	335km
Eucla	1436km	Port Hedland	1638km
Exmouth	1263km	Southern Cross	369km
Fitzroy Crossing	2558km	Tom Price	1458km
Geraldton	427km	Walpole	422km
Halls Creek	2857km	Wyndham	3216km
Hyden	339km		

TRANSPORT

For statewide road-condition reports, call ☎ 1800 800 009 and follow the prompts for information about the area in which you are driving. This information is updated daily (and more frequently if necessary).

Road Rules

Driving in WA holds few surprises, other than those that hop out in front of your vehicle. Cars are driven on the left-hand side of the road (as they are in the rest of Australia). An important road rule is 'give way to the right' – if an intersection is unmarked, you must give way to vehicles entering the intersection from your right.

The speed limit in urban areas is generally 60km/h, unless signposted otherwise. The state speed limit is 110km/h, applicable to all roads in non-built-up areas, unless otherwise indicated. The police have radar speed traps and speed cameras and are very fond of using them in carefully hidden locations.

Oncoming drivers who flash their lights at you may be giving you a friendly warning of a speed camera ahead – or they may be telling you that your headlights are not on. Whatever the circumstance, it's polite to wave back if someone does this. Try not to get caught flashing your lights yourself, since it's illegal.

Seat belts are compulsory – you'll be fined if you don't use them. Children must be strapped into an approved safety seat. Talking on a hand-held mobile phone while driving is illegal.

Drink-driving is a serious problem in WA, especially in country areas. Random breath tests are used in an effort to reduce the road toll. If you're caught driving with a blood-alcohol level of more than 0.05%, be prepared for a hefty fine, a court appearance and the loss of your licence.

LOCAL TRANSPORT

Perth has an efficient, fully integrated public transport system called **Transperth** (☎ 13 62 13; www.transperth.wa.gov.au) that covers the city's public buses, trains and ferries. There are three free Central Area Transit (CAT) bus services in Perth's city centre; using the three, you can get to most sights in the inner city. Fremantle also has a free CAT bus system that takes in all the major sights on a continuous loop. See Getting Around in Perth (p78) and Fremantle (p87) for other local transport options.

Outside Perth and Fremantle, local transport is limited; however, some of the larger country towns, such as Kalgoorlie-Boulder and Albany, have limited local bus services.

Taxis are available in most of the larger towns, where locals are reliant on them as a means of beating the booze buses and police patrols.

TRAIN

The state's internal rail network, operated by **Transwa** (☎ 1300 662 205; www.transwa.wa.gov .au), is limited to services between Perth and Kalgoorlie-Boulder (the state-of-the-art high speed *Prospector,* departing East Perth; $72) the *Avon Link,* departing East Perth heading to Northam ($16) and onward to Merredin ($37); and Perth and Bunbury in the south (the *Australind,* which departs from the Perth train station on Wellington St; $24). There are connections with Transwa's more extensive bus service (see p267).

For information on the *Indian Pacific* transcontinental railway, see p265.

Health Dr David Millar

CONTENTS

Australia is a remarkably healthy country in which to travel, considering that such a large portion of it lies in the tropics. Tropical diseases such as malaria and yellow fever are unknown, diseases of insanitation such as cholera and typhoid are unheard of, and, thanks to Australia's isolation and quarantine standards, even some animal diseases such as rabies and foot-and-mouth disease have yet to be recorded.

Few travellers to Australia should experience anything worse than an upset stomach or a bad hangover – and if you do fall ill, the standard of hospitals and health care is high.

BEFORE YOU GO

Since most vaccines don't produce immunity until at least two weeks after they're given, visit a physician four to eight weeks before departure. Ask your doctor for an International Certificate of Vaccination (otherwise known as the yellow booklet), which will list all the vaccinations you've received. This is mandatory for countries that require proof of yellow-fever vaccination upon entry (sometimes required in Australia, see following), but it's a good idea to carry it wherever you travel.

Bring medications in their original, clearly labelled, containers. A signed and dated letter from your physician describing your medical conditions and medications, including generic names, is also a good idea. If carrying syringes or needles, be sure to have a physician's letter documenting their medical necessity.

INSURANCE

If your health insurance doesn't cover you for medical expenses abroad, consider getting extra insurance – check www.lonely planet.com for more information. Find out in advance if your insurance plan will make payments directly to providers or reimburse you later for overseas health expenditures. See p276 for details of health care in Australia.

REQUIRED & RECOMMENDED VACCINATIONS

Proof of yellow-fever vaccination is required only from travellers entering Australia within six days of having stayed overnight or longer in a yellow-fever infected country. For a full list of these countries visit the websites of the **World Health Organization** (www.who.int/ith) or that of the **Centers for Disease Control & Prevention** (www.cdc.gov/travel).

If you're really worried about health when travelling there are a few vaccinations you could consider for Australia. The World Health Organization recommends that all travellers should be covered for diphtheria, tetanus, measles, mumps, rubella, chickenpox and polio, as well as hepatitis B, regardless of their destination. Planning to travel is a great time to ensure that all routine vaccination cover is complete. The consequences of these diseases can be severe and while Australia has high levels of childhood vaccination coverage, outbreaks of these diseases do occur.

MEDICAL CHECKLIST

- antibiotics
- antidiarrhoeal drugs (eg loperamide)
- acetaminophen/paracetamol or aspirin
- anti-inflammatory drugs (eg ibuprofen)
- antihistamines (for hay fever and allergic reactions)
- antibacterial ointment to care for cuts and abrasions
- steroid cream or cortisone (for poison ivy and other allergic rashes)
- bandages, gauze, gauze rolls

HEALTH

HEALTH

- adhesive or paper tape
- scissors, safety pins, tweezers
- thermometer
- pocket knife
- DEET-containing insect repellent for the skin
- permethrin-containing insect spray for clothing, tents and bed nets
- sun block
- oral rehydration salts
- iodine tablets or water filter (for water purification)

INTERNET RESOURCES

There is a wealth of travel health advice on the internet. For further information, **Lonely Planet** (www.lonelyplanet.com) is a good place to start. **The World Health Organization** (www.who .int/ith/) publishes a superb book called *International Travel and Health*, which is revised annually and is available online at no cost. Another website of general interest is **MD Travel Health** (www.mdtravelhealth.com), which provides complete travel health recommendations for every country and is updated daily.

FURTHER READING

Lonely Planet's *Healthy Travel Australia, New Zealand & the Pacific* is a handy, pocket-sized guide packed with useful information including pre-trip planning, emergency first aid, immunisation and disease information and what to do if you get sick on the road. *Travel with Children* from Lonely Planet also includes advice on travel health for younger children.

IN TRANSIT

DEEP VEIN THROMBOSIS

Blood clots may form in the legs (deep vein thrombosis) during plane flights, chiefly because of prolonged immobility. The longer the flight, the greater the risk. Though most blood clots are reabsorbed uneventfully, some may break off and travel through the blood vessels to the lungs, where they could cause life-threatening complications.

The chief symptom of deep vein thrombosis is swelling or pain of the foot, ankle or calf, usually – but not always – on just one side. When a blood clot travels to the lungs, it may cause chest pain and breathing difficulties. Travellers with any of these symptoms should immediately seek medical attention.

To prevent the development of deep vein thrombosis on long flights, you should walk about the cabin, perform isometric compressions of the leg muscles (ie flex the leg muscles while sitting), drink plenty of fluids and avoid alcohol and tobacco.

JET LAG & MOTION SICKNESS

Jet lag is a common condition when crossing more than five time zones, resulting in insomnia, fatigue, malaise or nausea. To avoid jet lag try drinking plenty of (nonalcoholic) fluids and eating light meals. Upon arrival, get exposure to natural sunlight and readjust your schedule (for meals, sleep etc) as soon as possible.

Antihistamines such as dimenhydrinate and meclizine are usually the first choice for treating motion sickness. Their main side-effect is drowsiness. A herbal alternative is ginger, which works like a charm for some people.

IN AUSTRALIA

AVAILABILITY & COST OF HEALTH CARE

Health insurance is essential for all travellers. While health care in Australia is of a high standard and not overly expensive by international standards, considerable costs can build up and repatriation is extremely expensive.

Australia has an excellent health-care system. It is a mixture of privately run medical clinics and hospitals alongside a government-funded system of public hospitals. The Medicare system covers Australian residents for some health-care costs. Visitors from countries with which Australia has a reciprocal health-care agreement (New Zealand, the UK, the Netherlands, Sweden, Finland,

---

> **HANDY WEBSITES**
>
> It's usually a good idea to consult your government's travel-health website before departure, if one is available:
>
> **Australia** www.smartraveller.gov.au
> **Canada** www.travelhealth.gc.ca
> **UK** www.dh.gov.uk/policyandguidance /healthadvicefortravellers/
> **USA** www.cdc.gov/travel/

Norway, Italy, Malta and Ireland) are eligible for benefits to the extent specified under the Medicare program. If you are from one of these countries check the details before departure. In general the agreements provide for any episode of ill-health that requires prompt medical attention. For further details visit http://www.medicareaustralia.gov.au /yourhealth/going_overseas/vtta.htm.

There are excellent, specialised, public health facilities for women and children in Perth.

Over-the-counter medications are widely available at privately owned pharmacies throughout Australia. These include painkillers, antihistamines for allergies and skin-care products.

You may find that medications that are readily available over the counter in some countries are only available in Australia by prescription. These include the oral contraceptive pill, most medications for asthma and all antibiotics. If you take medication on a regular basis bring an adequate supply and ensure you have details of the generic name as brand names may differ between countries.

Health Care in Remote Areas

In Australia it is possible to get into remote locations where there may well be a significant delay in emergency services reaching you in the event of serious accident or illness – do not underestimate the vastness between most major outback towns. An increased level of self-reliance and preparation is essential; consider taking a wilderness first-aid course, such as those offered at the **Wilderness Medicine Institute** (www.wmi.net.au); take a comprehensive first-aid kit that is appropriate for the activities planned; and ensure that you have adequate means of communication. Australia has extensive mobile phone coverage but additional radio communications is important for remote areas. The Royal Flying Doctor Service provides an important backup for remote communities.

INFECTIOUS DISEASES
Bat Lyssavirus

This disease is related to rabies and some deaths have occurred after bites. The risk is greatest for animal handlers and vets. Rabies vaccine is effective, but the risk to travellers is very low.

Dengue Fever

Also known as 'breakbone fever', because of the severe muscular pains that accompany the fever, this viral disease is spread by a species of mosquito that feeds primarily during the day. Most people recover in a few days but more severe forms of the disease can occur, particularly in residents who are exposed to another strain of the virus (there are four types) in a subsequent season.

Giardiasis

Giardiasis is widespread in the waterways around Australia. Drinking untreated water from streams and lakes is not recommended. Water filters, and boiling or treating water with iodine, are effective in preventing the disease. Symptoms consist of intermittent bad-smelling diarrhoea, abdominal bloating and wind. Effective treatment is available (tinidazole or metronidazole).

Meningococcal Disease

This disease occurs worldwide and is a risk with prolonged, dormitory-style accommodation. A vaccine exists for some types of this disease, namely meningococcal A, C, Y and W. No vaccine is presently available for the viral type of meningitis.

Ross River Fever

The Ross River virus is widespread throughout Australia and is spread by mosquitoes living in marshy areas. In addition to fever the disease causes headache, joint and muscular pains and a rash, before resolving after five to seven days.

Viral Encephalitis

Also known as Murray Valley encephalitis virus, this is spread by mosquitoes and is most common in northern Australia, especially during the wet season (November to April). This potentially serious disease is normally accompanied by headache, muscle pains and light insensitivity. Residual neurological damage can occur and no specific treatment is available. However, the risk to most travellers is low.

Sexually Transmitted Diseases

STDs occur at rates similar to most other Western countries. The most common symptoms are pain while passing urine and a discharge. Infection can be present without symptoms so seek medical screening after any unprotected sex with a new partner. Throughout the country, you'll find sexual health clinics in all of the major hospitals. Always use a condom with any new sexual partner. Condoms are readily available in chemists and through vending machines in many public places including toilets.

TRAVELLER'S DIARRHOEA

Tap water is universally safe in WA. Increasing numbers of streams, rivers and lakes, however, are being contaminated by bugs that cause diarrhoea, making water purification essential. The simplest way of purifying water is to boil it thoroughly. Consider purchasing a water filter; it's very important when buying a filter to read the specifications, so that you know exactly what it removes from the water and what it doesn't. Simple filtering will not remove all dangerous organisms, so if you cannot boil water it should be treated chemically. Chlorine tablets will kill many pathogens, but not some parasites like giardia and amoebic cysts. Iodine is more effective in purifying water and is available in tablet form. Follow the directions carefully and remember that too much iodine can be harmful.

ENVIRONMENTAL HAZARDS
Bites & Stings
MARINE ANIMALS

Marine spikes, such as those found on sea urchins, stonefish, scorpion fish, catfish and stingrays, can cause severe local pain. If this occurs, immediately immerse the affected area in hot water (as hot as can be tolerated). Keep topping up with hot water until the pain subsides and medical care can be reached. The stonefish is found only in tropical Australia, from northwestern Australia around the coast to northern Queensland; antivenin is available.

Marine stings from jellyfish such as box jellyfish also occur in Australia's tropical waters, particularly during the wet season (November to April). The box jellyfish has an incredibly potent sting and has been known to cause fatalities. Warning signs exist at affected beaches, and stinger nets are in place at the more popular beaches. Never dive into water you have not first checked is safe with local beach life-saving representatives. 'Stinger suits' (full-body Lycra swimsuits) prevent stinging, as do wetsuits. If you are stung, first

aid consists of washing the skin with vinegar to prevent further discharge of remaining stinging cells, followed by rapid transfer to a hospital; antivenin is widely available.

SHARKS & CROCODILES

Despite extensive media coverage, the risk of shark attack in Australian waters is no greater than in other countries with extensive coastlines. The risk of an attack from tropical sharks on scuba divers in northern Australian waters is low. Great white sharks are now few in number in the temperate southern waters. Check with local surf life-saving groups about local risks.

The risk of crocodile attack in tropical northern Australia is real but predictable and largely preventable. Discuss the local risk with police or tourist agencies in the area before swimming in rivers and water holes.

SNAKES

Australian snakes have a fearful reputation that is justified in terms of the potency of their venom but unjustified in terms of the actual risk to travellers and locals. Snakes are usually quite timid in nature and in most instances will move away if disturbed. They are endowed with only small fangs, making it easy to prevent bites to the lower limbs (where 80% of bites occur) by wearing protective clothing (such as gaiters) around the ankles when bushwalking. The bite marks are small and preventing the spread of toxic venom can be achieved by applying pressure to the wound and immobilising the area with a splint or sling before seeking medical attention. Application of an elastic bandage (you can improvise with a T-shirt) wrapped firmly, but not tightly enough to cut off the circulation, around the entire limb – along with immobilisation – is a life-saving first-aid measure.

SPIDERS

Australia has a number of poisonous spiders although the only one to have caused a single death in the last 50 years (the Sydney funnelweb) isn't found in WA. Redback spiders are found throughout Australia. Bites cause increasing pain at the site followed by profuse sweating and generalised symptoms. First aid includes application of ice or cold packs to the bite and transfer to hospital.

White-tailed (brown recluse) spider bites may cause an ulcer that is very difficult to heal. Clean the wound thoroughly and seek medical assistance.

Heat Exhaustion & Heatstroke

Very hot weather is experienced year-round in northern Australia and during the summer months for most of the country. Conditions vary from tropical in the Northern Territory and Queensland, to hot desert in northwestern Australia and central Australia, When arriving from a temperate or cold climate, remember that it takes two weeks for acclimatisation to occur. Before the body is acclimatised an excessive amount of salt is lost in perspiration so increasing the salt in your diet is essential.

Heat exhaustion occurs when fluid intake does not keep up with fluid loss. Symptoms include dizziness, fainting, fatigue, nausea or vomiting. On observation the skin is usually pale, cool and clammy. Treatment consists of rest in a cool, shady place and fluid replacement with water or diluted sports drinks.

Heatstroke is a severe form of heat illness that occurs after fluid depletion or extreme heat challenge from heavy exercise. This is a true medical emergency: heating of the brain leads to disorientation, hallucinations and seizures. Prevention is by maintaining an adequate fluid intake to ensure the continued passage of clear and copious urine, especially during physical exertion.

A number of unprepared travellers die from dehydration each year in outback Australia. This can be prevented by following these simple rules:

- Carry sufficient water for any trip including extra in case of breakdown.
- Always let someone, such as the local police, know where you are going and when you expect to arrive.
- Carry communications equipment of some form.
- In nearly all cases it is better to stay with the vehicle rather than walking for help.

Hypothermia

Hypothermia is a significant risk especially during the winter months in southern parts of Australia. Despite the absence of high mountain ranges, strong winds produce a high chill factor that can result in hypothermia in even moderately cool temperatures. Early signs include the inability to perform fine movements (such as doing up buttons), shivering and a bad case of the 'umbles' (fumbles, mumbles, grumbles, stumbles). The key elements of treatment include changing the environment to one where heat loss is minimised, changing out of any wet clothing, adding dry clothes with wind- and water-proof layers, adding insulation and providing fuel (water and carbohydrate) to allow shivering, which builds the internal temperature. In severe hypothermia, shivering actually stops – this is a medical emergency requiring rapid evacuation in addition to the above measures.

Insect-Borne Illnesses

Various insects can be a source of irritation and, in Australia, may be the source of specific diseases (dengue fever, Ross River fever). Protection from mosquitoes, sandflies, ticks and leeches can be achieved by a combination of the following strategies:

- Wearing loose-fitting clothing with long sleeves.
- Application of 30% DEET on all exposed skin, repeated every three to four hours.
- Impregnation of clothing with permethrin (an insecticide that kills insects but is completely safe to humans).

Surf Beaches & Drowning

Australia has exceptional surf beaches, particularly on the western, southern and eastern coasts. Beaches vary enormously in the slope of the underlying bottom, resulting in varying power of the surf. Check with local surf life-saving organisations before entering the surf, and be aware of your own limitations and expertise before entering the water.

Ultraviolet (UV) Light Exposure

Australia has one of the highest rates of skin cancer in the world. Monitor exposure to direct sunlight closely. UV exposure is greatest between 10am and 4pm so avoid skin exposure during these times. Always use 30+ sunscreen, apply 30 minutes before exposure and repeat regularly to minimise sun damage.

HEALTH

Glossary

arvo – afternoon
ATM – Automatic Teller Machine; public cash dispenser operated by banks
Aussie rules – Australian Rules football

back o' Bourke – back of beyond, middle of nowhere
barbie – barbecue
battler – struggler, someone who tries hard
beaut, beauty – great, fantastic
billabong – waterhole in a riverbed formed by waters receding in *the Dry*
billy – tin container used to boil water in *the bush*
bloke – man
blowies, blowflies – large flies
bludger – lazy person, one who refuses to work
blue – argument or fight ('have a blue')
bodyboard – half-sized surfboard, also known as a boogie board
bonzer – great
boomerang – a curved, flat, wooden instrument used by Aborigines for hunting
booze bus – police van used for random breath-testing for alcohol
bottle shop – liquor shop, off-licence
Buckley's – no chance at all
bull bar – outsize front bumper on vehicle
bull dust – fine and sometimes deep dust on *outback* roads
bush, the – country, anywhere away from the city
BYO – bring your own (alcohol)

catch ya later – goodbye, see you later
chook – chicken
chuck a U-ey – to make a U-turn (turn a car around within a road)
cobber – (archaic) see *mate*
counter meal – pub meal
crack the shits – to lose one's temper
crook – ill or substandard
cut lunch – sandwiches

dag – dirty lump of wool at the back end of a sheep; also an affectionate term for a socially inept person
damper – bush loaf made from flour and water
dead set – true
DEC – Department of Environment and Conservation
didgeridoo – wind instrument made from a hollow piece of wood
digger – (archaic, from Australian and New Zealand soldiers in WWI) see *mate*
dill – idiot

dinky-di – the real thing
dob in – to inform on someone
donga – small, transportable building widely used in the *outback*
Dreamtime – complex concept that forms the basis of Aboriginal spirituality, incorporating the creation of the world and the spiritual energies operating around us
drongo – worthless or stupid person
Dry, the – dry season in northern Australia (May to October)
dunny – outdoor lavatory

eftpos – Electronic Funds Transfer at Point of Sale
Esky – large insulated box for keeping food and drinks cold

fair dinkum – honest, genuine
freshie – freshwater crocodile
furphy – rumour or false story

galah – noisy parrot, thus noisy idiot
g'day – good day; traditional Australian greeting
grog – general term for alcoholic drinks

homestead – residence of a *station* owner or manager
hoon – idiot, hooligan

icy pole – frozen lollipop, ice lolly
iffy – dodgy, questionable
indie – independent music

jackaroo – male trainee on an *outback station*
jillaroo – female trainee on an *outback station*

karri – Australian eucalyptus tree
kick the bucket – to die
knackered – broken, tired
knock – to criticise, deride
Kombi – a classic (hippies') type of van made by Volkswagen

lamington – square of sponge cake covered in chocolate icing and desiccated coconut
larrikin – hooligan, mischievous youth
lemon – faulty product, a dud
little ripper – extremely good thing
loo – toilet

marron – large freshwater crayfish
mate – general term of familiarity, whether you know the person or not
middy – 285ml glass of beer

milk bar – small shop selling milk and other basic provisions
mobile phone – cellular phone
Mod Oz – modern Australian cuisine influenced by a wide range of foreign cuisines
mozzies – mosquitoes

never-never – remote country in the *outback*
no-hoper – hopeless case
no worries! – no problems! That's OK!
Noongar – collective term used to identify Aborigines from the southwest

ocker – uncultivated or boorish Australian
offsider – assistant, partner
outback – remote part of the *bush, back o' Bourke*

pavlova – traditional Australian meringue, fruit and cream dessert; named after the Russian ballerina Anna Pavlova
Perthite – resident of Perth
perve – to gaze with lust
pindan – semi-arid country of southwestern Kimberley region
pissed – drunk
pissed off – annoyed
plonk – cheap wine
pokies – poker machines

quokka – small wallaby

ratbag – friendly term of abuse
reckon! – you bet! absolutely!
rip – a strong ocean current or undertow
road train – semitrailer truck towing several trailers
root – to have sexual intercourse
rooted – tired, broken
ropable – very bad-tempered or angry

saltie – saltwater crocodile
sandgroper – resident of Western Australia

sanger – sandwich
sealed road – bitumen road
session – lengthy period of heavy drinking
shark biscuit – inexperienced surfer
she'll be right – no problems, no worries
shoot through – to leave in a hurry
shout – to buy a round of drinks
skimpy – scantily clad female bar person
sparrow's fart – dawn
station – large farm
stolen generations – Aboriginal and Torres Strait Islander children forcibly removed from their families during the government's policy of assimilation
stroppy – bad-tempered
stubby – 375ml bottle of beer

take the piss – to deliberately tell someone an untruth, often as social sport
tinny – 375ml can of beer; also a small, aluminium fishing dinghy
too right! – absolutely!
trucky – truck driver
true blue – see *dinky-di*
tucker – food
two-pot screamer – person unable to hold their drink
two-up – traditional heads-or-tails coin gambling game

unsealed road – dirt road
ute – utility; a pick-up truck

wag – to skip school or work
walkabout – lengthy walk away from it all
Wet, the – rainy season in the north (November to April)

yabbie – small freshwater crayfish
yakka – work
yobbo – uncouth, aggressive person
yonks – a long time

The Authors

TERRY CARTER
Coordinating Author

An ex-Queenslander who misspent his youth surfing, Terry jumped at the chance to go four-wheel-driving through WA – and check out WA's secret surfing spots. Having erroneously concluded that travel writing was a glamorous occupation compared to designing books and websites, Terry has been travel writing for several years across Europe and the Middle East. Clocking over 12,000kms of research for this guide, Terry would happily do it again, but without the suicidal kangaroos next time. Terry has a Masters degree in media studies and divides his time between freelance travel writing, photography and overcoming paranoia induced by sharks being spotted off Freo.

LARA DUNSTON
Coordinating Author

It made sense that Lara's first Aussie gig for Lonely Planet would be WA. Her first flight aged four was from Sydney to Perth and her last big trip down under was with her family through the Pilbara and Kimberley. That's when Lara fell for magical Broome, its azure sea and red desert sands, the things she finds appealing about the United Arab Emirates, her home since 1998. A full time travel writer working mainly in the Middle East and Europe, Lara owes her travel addiction to her parents Warren, who died of cancer, and Tracy, who miraculously survived an accident in Perth in 2006. She now thanks them for those five years caravanning around Australia.

Our Favourite Trip

Lara and Terry's ideal trip begins with a few days in historic **Fremantle** (p80), where they make their base when in town. They'll hit the Great Northern Hwy in a 4WD for the long inland haul north to get a real sense of the outback, taking in wildflowers and wildlife on the way. They'll unwind in beautiful **Broome** (p223) with walks on the beach, visits to art galleries and ritually watching the Cable Beach sunset each day. When the road beckons again, they'll do a trip 'over the top' (see p15), before making their way back down the coast via **Shark Bay** (p193), **Monkey Mia** (p196) and **Ningaloo Marine Park** (p208). They'll finish in the south with surfing and wine-tasting in the **Margaret River** (p123).

LONELY PLANET AUTHORS

Why is our travel information the best in the world? It's simple: our authors are independent, dedicated travellers. They don't research using just the internet or phone, and they don't take freebies in exchange for positive coverage. They travel widely, to all the popular spots and off the beaten track. They personally visit thousands of hotels, restaurants, cafés, bars, galleries, palaces, museums and more – and they take pride in getting all the details right, and telling it how it is. For more, see the authors section on www.lonelyplanet.com.

REBECCA CHAU
Perth & Around Perth

Rebecca first started learning about Western Australia quite a while ago: back in the 80s, she started Year 3 in Albany. After growing up down south (where the beach really is as Tim Winton describes it), she lived in Perth for five years before travelling and living overseas. Now in Melbourne (as a commissioning editor for Lonely Planet), she makes it over to Perth's beaches and restaurants about twice a year. This research trip was so wonderful she might have to move back.

VIRGINIA JEALOUS
Southwest, South Coast & Southern Outback

Virginia has worked for Lonely Planet since 1999, at first from her home base on Christmas Island *way* off the coast of WA, in Australia's remote Indian Ocean Territories, and later during two years living and working in the Pacific Ocean. She headed back to the Australian mainland in 2006 where, after poking around the coast of the Southern Ocean for this book, she turned her sights from the seas to bask in the long red roads and wide skies of the outback. A quick 7146 road-crazed kilometres later (but who's counting?) she returned to Fremantle, vowing never to drive again until the next time.

CONTRIBUTING AUTHORS

Michael Cathcart wrote the History chapter. Michael teaches history at the Australian Centre, The University of Melbourne. He is well known as a broadcaster on ABC Radio National and presented the ABC TV series *Rewind*. He is also noted as the man who abridged Australia's best-known historian Manning Clark by turning his six-volume classic *A History of Australia* into one handy book.

Tim Flannery wrote the Environment chapter. Tim's a naturalist, explorer and writer. He is the author of a number of award-winning books, including *The Future Eaters* and *Throwim Way Leg* (an account of his adventures as a biologist working in New Guinea) and the landmark ecological history of North America, *The Eternal Frontier*. Tim lives in Adelaide where he is director of the South Australian Museum and a professor at the University of Adelaide.

Campbell Mattinson wrote the special section on Wine, which was updated for this edition by Terry Carter. Campbell Mattinson is a journalist of over 20 years and a multi-award-winning writer. In 2005 Campbell picked up the prestigious NSW Wine Press Club Wine Communicator Award, and he was a finalist at the World Food Media Awards in both 2003 and 2005. He is the author of *The Wine Hunter: The Man Who Changed Australian Wine*, and his words appear in magazines *Gourmet Traveller WINE*, *Decanter UK*, and *Australian Sommelier Magazine*.

Dr David Millar wrote the Health chapter. Dr Millar is a travel-medicine specialist, diving doctor and lecturer in wilderness medicine. He has worked in all states of Australia (except the Northern Territory) and as an expedition doctor with the Maritime Museum of Western Australia, accompanying a variety of expeditions around Australia, including the Pandora wreck in Far North Queensland and Rowley Shoals off the northwest coast. Dr Millar is currently a Medical Director with the Travel Doctor in Auckland.

Behind the Scenes

THIS BOOK

This is the 5th incarnation of Lonely Planet's Western Australia guide. The first edition was written in 1995 by one intrepid author, Jeff Williams, who covered the whole state on his own. The 4th edition was updated by a team of authors, Susie Ashworth, Simone Egger and Rebecca Turner. This guidebook was commissioned in Lonely Planet's Melbourne office, and produced by the following:

Commissioning Editor Meg Worby
Coordinating Editor Brooke Lyons
Coordinating Cartographer Sophie Richards
Coordinating Layout Designer Jim Hsu
Managing Editor Geoff Howard
Managing Cartographers Julie Sheridan, Amanda Sierp
Assisting Editors Holly Alexander, Carolyn Bain, Rowan McKinnon, Stephanie Ong
Assisting Cartographers Diana Duggan, Sally Gerdan, Emma McNicol, Andy Rojas
Cover Designer Karina Dea
Project Manager Kate McLeod

Thanks to Sally Darmody, Nicole Hansen, Trent Paton, Sarah Sloane, Celia Wood

THANKS
TERRY CARTER & LARA DUNSTON

We met so many on our travels around WA who went out of their way to share their local knowledge. We we want to say a special thanks to all the generous staff at the many WA visitors centres, most of whom are volunteers who enthusiastically give their time to share the best of their beloved towns with travellers while raising money to pay their centre's electricity bills. In particular, Lorna Day and Karen Morrissey at Mt Magnet Visitors Centre, Blaire Bailey at Tom Price Visitors Centre, Leonie at Broome Visitors Centre, Kelly Howlett at Port Hedland Visitors Centre, Sharyn Burvill at Fitzroy Crossing Visitors Centre, Karen and Deb at Exmouth Visitors Centre, and staff at the busy Kalbarri Visitors Centre. Much appreciation also to Prince Lenard of Hutt River Province for his time; and to Sharyn Burvill, Michelle Ikin, David Henry, Sue Thom, Ben Woelders, Belinda Carrigan, Harry and Marge Lakey, Alison True, Belinda Hill, Michelle, Andy and Val, Mum, Felicia and Paul. And a very special thanks to Capes for opening our ears so the bush could talk to us.

REBECCA CHAU

Thanks to Lara and Terry for their advice; Suzannah Shwer and everyone inhouse for all their hard work; Simon Cox, at Transperth; Marie Chau, for putting me up; and local eyes and ears, Panda Chau, Cam Haskell, Mark Bailey, Simon Davis and, as ever, Matt Forbes.

VIRGINIA JEALOUS

Thanks for good company, conversation, food, wine and information (not necessarily in that order) to Libby W in Dunsborough; Chris L and the Carter's Road Community near Margaret River; Lyn H in Albany; Helen G and Bob G at Eyre; almost Mason B in Kalgoorlie; and Rob W for the goldfields explorations.

THE LONELY PLANET STORY

The story begins with a classic travel adventure: Tony and Maureen Wheeler's 1972 journey across Europe and Asia to Australia. There was no useful information about the overland trail then, so Tony and Maureen published the first Lonely Planet guidebook to meet a growing need.

From a kitchen table, Lonely Planet has grown to become the largest independent travel publisher in the world, with offices in Melbourne (Australia), Oakland (USA) and London (UK). Today Lonely Planet guidebooks cover the globe. There is an ever-growing list of books and information in a variety of media. Some things haven't changed. The main aim is still to make it possible for adventurous travellers to get out there – to explore and better understand the world.

At Lonely Planet we believe travellers can make a positive contribution to the countries they visit – if they respect their host communities and spend their money wisely. Every year 5% of company profit is donated to charities around the world.

SEND US YOUR FEEDBACK

We love to hear from travellers – your comments keep us on our toes and help make our books better. Our well-travelled team reads every word on what you loved or loathed about this book. Although we cannot reply individually to postal submissions, we always guarantee that your feedback goes straight to the appropriate authors, in time for the next edition. Each person who sends us information is thanked in the next edition – and the most useful submissions are rewarded with a free book.

To send us your updates – and find out about Lonely Planet events, newsletters and travel news – visit our award-winning website: **www.lonelyplanet.com/contact**.

Note: we may edit, reproduce and incorporate your comments in Lonely Planet products such as guidebooks, websites and digital products, so let us know if you don't want your comments reproduced or your name acknowledged. For a copy of our privacy policy visit www.lonelyplanet.com/privacy.

OUR READERS

Many thanks to the travellers who used the last edition and wrote to us with helpful hints, useful advice and interesting anecdotes:

A Shakthi Allagoo, Frida Andrae **B** Elise Batchelor, John Bayley, Christine Bevans, D Bogie, Catherine Brewer **C** Lynne Coupethwaite, Simon Cox, Dianne Cresswell **D** Rene Dautel, Lauretta Davies, Annabel Davis, Mara Deacon, Matt Dechamps, Anne Dickson **E** Jens Ebert, Ken and Iyse Edwards **F** Anne Faero, Ian Fair, Rachael Feather, Alan Foster, Ken Frankcom **G** Jacqui Gardiner, Mike Garthwaite, Dom Giles, Gemma Grace, Agnes Gray, Tom Gray, Ronalie Green, Trey Guinn **H** Adrian Haas, Robin Haig, A Hall, Steve Hall, Duncan Hancox, Ian Harrison, Chris and Calvin Heal, Kerstin and Stefan Heine, Anna Helm, Colleen Hunter, Dianne Hunter, Quentin and Ann Hunter **I** Andrew Ingle **J** Anne-Isabelle and Thibaut Jahan, Alison Jarabo-Martin, A Jones, Brendan Jones **K** Chris Kaczan, Gilles Karolyi, Claire and Dave Kent, Barry Kowal **L** Jane Lamb, Kelly Lambert, Diana Lim, Martin Lundgren **M** Andrew Macklin, Jon Malcolm, Carol McGillivray, Christine Melville, Peter Milner, Josefine Missal, Sonja Mitchell, Jennifer Mundy, Anne Murith **N** Alan Newman **O** Kathy O'Leary, Leigh Oliver, John O'Neill **P** Becky Palmer, Nancy and Joseph Papa, Mike Pomfrey, Beth Primeau, Zoe Prince **R** John Rochford, Dorothy Ross **S** Gerhard Saum, Polly Seidler, Hardy Senf, Don Silliss, Ina Skafte, Christine Sly, Laurie Smith, Rod Smith, Jasmeet Soar, Miles Soppet, Gemma Sparkes, Hildegard Stahl, Simon Stockdale, Ann Stoughton, Bill Stoughton **T** Richard Taylor, Andy Thomas, Petra Thomma, John Tomich, P Turpin **U** Johnny Uitterhoeve **V** Carna Van Hove, Corinne Vandermeer, Nicholas Vass **W** Marcus Waring, Stephen Warren, Beth Weiss, Gwendolyn Wellmann, Jantien Wester, Debbie Westwell, Jennifer Willcox, Ruth and Jane Wilson, John Woodyard, Jessica Worlock **Y** Walter Yates **Z** Bernd Zolitschka

Whales

  x Albany St. Geo. Sound (141)

  xx Fitzgerald River NP (147)

   Bremer Bay - 180 Km NE Albany

      61 Km S. Coast

  xx Cape Arid NP (151) Esperance area.

  x Torndirrip NP W of Albany (146)

Index

000 Map pages
000 Photograph pages

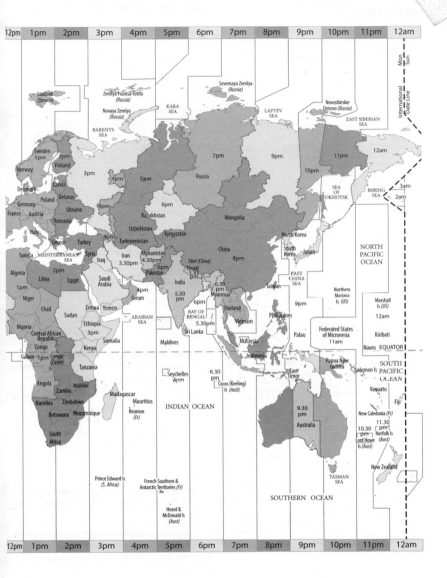

MAP LEGEND

ROUTES

Freeway	Mall/Steps
Primary	Tunnel
Secondary	Pedestrian Overpass
Tertiary	Walking Tour
Lane	Walking Trail
Under Construction	Walking Path
Unsealed Road	Track

TRANSPORT

Ferry	Rail
Bus Route	
Tram	Rail (Underground)

HYDROGRAPHY

River, Creek	Water
Intermittent River	Lake (Dry)
Swamp	Lake (Salt)
Mangrove	Mudflats
Reef	

BOUNDARIES

State	Regional, Suburb
Marine Park	Cliff

AREA FEATURES

Airport	Land
Area of Interest	Mall
Beach, Desert	Park
Building	Reservation
Campus	Rocks
Cemetery, Christian	Sports
Cemetery, Other	Urban
Forest	

POPULATION

CAPITAL (STATE)	Medium City
Large City	
Small City	Town, Village

SYMBOLS

Sights/Activities
- Beach
- Christian
- Diving, Snorkeling
- Islamic
- Monument
- Museum, Gallery
- Point of Interest
- Pool
- Ruin
- Snorkelling
- Surfing, Surf Beach
- Trail Head
- Winery, Vineyard
- Zoo, Bird Sanctuary

Eating
- Eating

Drinking
- Drinking
- Café

Entertainment
- Entertainment

Shopping
- Shopping

Sleeping
- Sleeping
- Camping

Transport
- Airport, Airfield
- Bus Station
- Cycling, Bicycle Path
- General Transport
- Parking Area
- Petrol Station
- Taxi Rank

Information
- Bank, ATM
- Embassy/Consulate
- Hospital, Medical
- Information
- Internet Facilities
- Police Station
- Post Office, GPO
- Telephone
- Toilets
- Wheelchair Access

Geographic
- Lighthouse
- Lookout
- Mountain, Volcano
- National Park
- Pass, Canyon
- Picnic Area
- River Flow
- Shelter, Hut
- Waterfall

LONELY PLANET OFFICES

Australia
Head Office
Locked Bag 1, Footscray, Victoria 3011
☎ 03 8379 8000, fax 03 8379 8111
talk2us@lonelyplanet.com.au

USA
150 Linden St, Oakland, CA 94607
☎ 510 893 8555, toll free 800 275 8555
fax 510 893 8572
info@lonelyplanet.com

UK
72-82 Rosebery Ave,
Clerkenwell, London EC1R 4RW
☎ 020 7841 9000, fax 020 7841 9001
go@lonelyplanet.co.uk

Published by Lonely Planet Publications Pty Ltd
ABN 36 005 607 983

5th Edition – May 2007

First Published – April 1995

© Lonely Planet Publications Pty Ltd 2007